# THE BATTLE OF BRUNANBURH

## A Casebook

'Sometime late in the year 937, somewhere in Britain, rival armies of uncertain size from across the wide expanses of northern Europe — from London to Dublin, from Scotland to Scandinavia — met in a place called Brunanburh.

For centuries afterward, records of the Battle of Brunanburh, as it came to be known, spread far and wide, in poem and song, in chronicles and prayers, in sagas and charters, in Anglo-Saxon, Welsh, Latin, Old Norse, Middle English, and Anglo-Norman, to say nothing of post-medieval appearances in languages around the globe. . . . The men who fought and died on that field forged a political map of the future that remains with us today, arguably making the Battle at Brunanburh one of the most significant battles in the long history not just of England, but of the whole of the British Isles . . . in one day, on one field, the fate of a nation was determined.'

— *from the Introduction*

The Battle of Brunanburh is one of the least understood battles in the history of the British Isles. For centuries, scholars have grappled with vital questions concerning the event. This book — compiled by an international team of experts — gathers, annotates and translates into English all the significant historical and literary primary sources. In addition, ten essays provide cultural contexts while laying to rest many of the most controversial questions about the conflict — including the key matter of where it took place. They also reveal the lasting significance of the battle both in terms of history and in terms of its impact across more than a thousand years of literature.

**Michael Livingston** is an Assistant Professor at The Citadel, The Military College of South Carolina, and the author of scholarly editions of *Siege of Jerusalem* (2004), *In Praise of Peace* (2005), and *The Middle English Metrical Paraphrase of the Old Testament* (2011).

EXETER MEDIEVAL TEXTS AND STUDIES
Series Editors: Vincent Gillespie and Richard Dance

Founded by M.J. Swanton
and later co-edited by Marion Glasscoe

# THE BATTLE OF BRUNANBURH

## A Casebook

*edited by*
Michael Livingston

UNIVERSITY
*of*
EXETER
PRESS

Cover image: Wood-cut illustration for *Magnus den godes saga*.
Halfdan Egedius (1877–1899). Public domain.

First published in 2011 by
University of Exeter Press
Reed Hall, Streatham Drive
Exeter EX4 4QR
UK

*www.exeterpress.co.uk*



**British Library Cataloguing in Publication Data**
A catalogue record for this book is available
from the British Library.

Hardback ISBN 978 0 85989 862 1
Paperback ISBN 978 0 85989 863 8

Typeset in 10/13 New Baskerville with Golden Cockerel Ornaments display
by Michael Livingston, with layout design by Linda K. Judy.

Printed in Great Britain by CPI Antony Rowe.

# Contents

## ILLUSTRATIONS

Cover Art. Wood-cut illustration for *Magnus den godes saga*, by Halfdan Egedius; in Snorri Sturluson, *Kongesagaer*, ed. Gustav Storm (Oslo: J.M. Stenersen, 1899; rpt. Oslo: Lie and Co., 1957), p. 502. Public domain.

MICHAEL LIVINGSTON

## PREFACE: THE SHAPE OF THE VOLUME

For lack of a better term, we have opted to term this volume a "casebook," as our intent has been to gather the sources necessary for the study of the Battle of Brunanburh between two (rather far apart) covers. Its formation has entailed a team of scholars from around the world working over several years in several different contexts and languages, all working toward this common vision. Since the book brings together so many different voices concerning the battle — both historical and contemporary — perhaps a few brief words are in order about the division of its contents and the division of labor that constructed them.

The volume proper begins with my attempt to provide a historical context not only for the Battle of Brunanburh but also for the remainder of the casebook. Following this introduction are the texts: the important medieval sources that mention the battle, presented in both their original languages and facing-page translations. These texts, as explained further below, are arranged in a tentative chronological order. Explanatory and textual notes immediately follow the collected texts, and the reader is urged to utilize these notes alongside reading of any of the included texts: headnotes present brief introductions to each item, and there are many discoveries to be found in the notes themselves. The scholars responsible for the editing and translating of the sources presented herein are also named within the source notes; where editing and translating tasks have been split between two individuals — as is the case, for example, with our Latin texts, which are typically edited by Paul Cavill and translated by Scott Thompson Smith — the material of the notes themselves should be regarded as the work of co-authorship.

The remainder of this casebook consists of nine essays that have been partitioned into two sections. The first of these groupings contains studies that are specific to the items collected within the volume. John K. Bollard and Marged Haycock lead off this linguistically arranged section with an essay providing a welcome context for the Welsh material collected here. Scott Thompson Smith then provides an in-depth overview of the wide range of Latin sources pertaining to the battle. Because of the importance (and fame) of the *Battle of Brunanburh* poem within the *Anglo-Saxon Chronicle*, this volume contains two essays focused upon it (as well as two editions and two translations of the poem itself). First, Thomas Bredehoft gives us an overarching look at both the history of the poem and the state of scholarship upon it. Second, Robert Creed provides us with the means to literally read this text: a new method of understanding Old English prosody. A. Keith Kelly follows this essay with a look at fact and fiction within *Egil's Saga*, the lone and often misunderstood Old Norse source on the battle. Completing this group of essays is Robert Rouse's overview of the shifting presence (or non-presence) of the battle in Middle English.

The second group of essays, four studies that concern broader issues of the Battle of Brunanburh, is led off by Paul Cavill's thorough examination of the evidence that place-names provide for our efforts to locate the site of the long-lost battle. His measured and logical approach to what has been a controversial topic is admirable, and it greatly solidifies the case for Bromborough as Brunanburh. Indeed, the Bromborough connection is the root for the following two essays. The first, by Stephen Harding, looks at the folklore traditions of the Wirral for evidence of the battle, and in so doing helps to localize the battle in fascinating ways. Richard Coates follows this with another Wirral-based study: a look at the socio-linguistic history of the peninsula and the ways in which this, too, might illumine what we know of the battle. The last essay in the volume, by Joanne Parker, propels us forward from these grounded considerations with a look at the afterlife of the battle in literature.

## THE NAMES

The editor's task, all too often, is to instill a well-intended sense of regularization across works that might rightly lack it, whether it is introducing consistency in the treatment of Latin abbreviations, antiquated runes, or bibliography entries. A multi-linguistic, multi-cultural volume such as this, however, by its nature introduces still more problems for the editor in search of consistency, perhaps most noticeably in regards to the spelling of names.

An obvious example, of course, is the very king of the Anglo-Saxon realm of Wessex who in the year 937 won the Battle of Brunanburh (a word with its own rather important oddities of orthography, as we shall see), who appears in Wessex sources as *Æðelstan* or *Æþelstan* and in most other sources as some approximation of Latin *Athelstanus*. While we have generally left these various spellings of the king's name in their original textual contexts, we have endeavored to be consistent (if perhaps not historically accurate) in referring to the king in commentary and translations using the single representation *Athelstan*, a common modern spelling. More troubling than this, however, is the question of how to navigate the charged waters of representing individuals whose history is largely non-English, yet who have, within the sources, Anglicized names that are commonly used within Modern English texts. The name of one of Athelstan's primary antagonists at Brunanburh, for instance, can appear under strikingly different guises to the untrained eye:

| **Gaelic** | **Latin** | **Old English** | **Old Norse** |
|---|---|---|---|
| Amhlaoibh, Awley | Anlavus | Anlaf | Óláfr |

At least some of this man's forebears had been a part of the Great Army of Danes (or Norse or Northmen or Vikings — already we are on shifting ground) that had entered the British Isles and settled there a couple generations before Brunanburh. In 937 he had recently solidified his position as king of Dublin, ruling over a people variously referred to in critical commentary as the Hiberno-Norwegians, the Norse-Gael, the Anglo-Danes, the Vikings, or (as in this volume) the Hiberno-Norse.[1] In the face of so many uncertainties, and cognizant of the political dangers inevitably bound up in such matters, I have made the admittedly difficult decision to regularize his name as *Anlaf*, which seems likely to be the most familiar to the most readers and which has the small but not-to-be-dismissed advantage of matching the name the king himself used on his coins minted at York. While this regularized spelling is, linguistically speaking, that of the Old English, it is not intended as a statement of Anglo-centricism.

[1] An overview of the histories of and the problems with some of these various labels can be found in Clare Downham's "'Hiberno-Norwegians' and 'Anglo-Danes.'"

## THE SOURCES

Given the complexities inherent in presenting texts compiled over a period of 600 years or more and written in at least five different languages from within a variety of cultures, it seems most helpful to present the accounts of the Battle of Brunanburh collected here in something close to chronological order. Such an arrangement has the advantage of allowing the reader to trace the influence of the battle as it shifts from reported event to epic battle to legend. Yet, as anyone familiar with medieval literature can confirm, determining a firm date for medieval texts is a frustrating and largely fruitless task: in most cases, the best we can manage is a range counted in decades, if not centuries. The issue is even more problematic when it comes to medieval chronicles, passages from many of which appear in this volume. For example, the various versions of the *Anglo-Saxon Chronicle* all derive from some common early stock, yet many of our surviving texts were copied centuries later, at which time their contents might have been altered. I have endeavored — with the help of the contributors, though in the final count they should remain blameless for my faults — to determine a suitable origin date for the preserved texts, but in some cases I have simply opted to date the text to its point of preservation. The fascinating *Annals of Clonmacnoise*, for instance, contains material from early in the record, perhaps even contemporaneous to the events it describes. Unfortunately, the *Annals* survives only in a translation that dates to 1627. While scholars assume that it preserves a very early and accurate tradition, the text that survives is from the seventeenth century and, therefore, appears as one of the last of our accounts, Item 52. Conversely, I have presented *Armes Prydein* as Item 1 in the volume: like the *Annals*, it survives in a later manuscript — a fourteenth-century copy in this case — but linguistic, textual, and contextual arguments strongly suggest that the poem as preserved was composed in the mid-tenth century. Despite efforts to rationalize these decisions, however, the order of texts that results is inevitably speculative, and the reader is encouraged to make his or her own determinations on the matter.

While the final selection of texts to include in the volume was also editorial, I have once again leaned heavily on the findings and opinions of the contributors. As already stated, the volume is intended to preserve the "medieval" sources for study of the battle, thus omitting most later renditions of the Battle of Brunanburh (though many are discussed in Parker's essay). Our cut-off date was the early sixteenth-century work of Boece, with only a few outliers such as the *Annals* already mentioned. Because of the repetitive nature of the chronicle tradition, we have not included text and translation for every source even within our date range: when a work did not deviate from earlier accounts, we have only included notice of its existence in the run of sources. Richard of Cirencester's *Speculum historiale*, for instance, is listed as Item 45 among our sources, but we have not included any text or translation: as the notes explain, Richard only repeats the work of earlier writers, such as John of Worcester (Item 16).[2] From beginning to end, our aim was to make available the "primary" materials for studying not only the historical event but also its shift into the realm of legend. As the tales diminish in their historicity, however, the selection of texts becomes more arbitrary. The Guy of Warwick tradition, which arguably marks the total "loss" of a historical Brunanburh, exists in many possible sources; yet I have chosen only one text, the Middle English *Stanzaic Guy of Warwick* (Item 37), to stand for all. Similarly, I have opted not to include a

[2] Other texts so treated: Items 24, 26, 27, 39, 42, and 48.

text like the Middle English *Athelston*, which, although it features a character sharing the name of the English leader at Brunanburh, has essentially nothing to do with the battle.

As with personal names in a volume with such linguistic range, there is significant possible variation in the presentation of the names of the sources we have included. Item 30, for example, can appear in various guises within English and Latin alone: *Annals of Winchester*, *Winchester Annals*, *Annales monasterii de Wintonia*, or simply *Annales de Wintonia*. In this and all other instances I have opted to regularize the majority of references to the form that will, I hope, be the most recognizable to the most readers.

## Acknowledgments

The history of this volume spans almost three decades, beginning with a colloquium on the texts relating to the Battle of Brunanburh proposed by Welsh scholar John K. Bollard to Anglo-Saxonist Robert P. Creed of the Comparative Literature Department at the University of Massachusetts-Amherst. The colloquium they jointly organized, "'The Battle of Brunanburh' Re-fought: The Historical and Literary Background," was held on 16 March 1981 and featured Bollard speaking on the Welsh poem *Armes Prydein Vawr*, Creed discussing the famed poem of the *Anglo-Saxon Chronicle*, Warren Anderson presenting an overview of the Latin texts, and Dean Ware explaining what was then known of the battle's general historical background. Plans to publish the papers were discussed, but a book did not coalesce. More than two decades later, the project came to my attention when John Bollard met with Russell A. Peck and myself.

For my own part, then, acknowledgment must be given first and foremost to John, who graciously entrusted me with executing the idea and whose support has hardly wavered even as the book grew far beyond the bounds we initially discussed for it. Even more, he kindly agreed to pick up a few key duties for the volume when some planned contributors were unable to contribute for personal reasons. In a final burst of generosity that is matched only by his capability, he compiled an extraordinary index to the volume that should be a boon to researchers.

John also joined contributors Paul Cavill and Scott Thompson Smith in reading the whole of the volume at a late stage, catching countless errors that had managed to slip through the proverbial cracks. Russell Peck and John H. Chandler kindly gave the volume a *very* thorough read-through. The blame is mine for any problems that remain, but I thank them all for preventing at least a few bits of rotting fruit from being thrown in my direction.

Our collective thanks go to Anna Henderson and the fine staff at the University of Exeter Press for taking this volume on and seeing it through to a successful conclusion.

I personally owe no small debt to Debbe Causey and Terri Johnson, Interlibrary Loan specialists of the Daniel Library at The Citadel: without their labors my own work would be poor indeed. Last, and by no means least, I must acknowledge the hidden work of my wife, Sherry, who too often had to tuck Samuel and Elanor into bed alone as I labored on one part of this volume or another.

## CONTRIBUTORS

**John K. Bollard**, a Medieval Welsh scholar, editor, and lexicographer, has published important articles on *The Mabinogi* and other early Welsh narratives. His translations of all the tales in "The Mabinogion," with full-color photographs of places in the tales, are published by Gomer Press: *The Mabinogi* (2006), *Companion Tales to The Mabinogi* (2007), and *Tales of Arthur* (2010). Translations of early Welsh Arthurian and Myrddin (Merlin) poetry appear in the *The Romance of Arthur* (Garland, 1994) and *The Romance of Merlin* (Garland, 1990). He was Managing Editor of *African American Lives* (Oxford, 2004), and the *African American National Biography* (Oxford, 2008). Currently, he is Editorial Director of the Native American Biography Project for the National Indian Education Association.

**Thomas A. Bredehoft** has written on the *Anglo-Saxon Chronicle* and on Old English meter, and his most recent book is *Authors, Audiences, and Old English Verse* (2009). His other interests include late medieval pilgrim badges and contemporary graphic narratives. His current book project is tentatively titled *The Visible Text: Text and Image from Beowulf to Maus*. He teaches at West Virginia University.

**Paul Cavill** is Lecturer in Early English at the University of Nottingham, and former Principal Research Fellow for the English Place-Name Survey. He has published widely on Old English and Anglo-Latin, and edited and co-wrote *Wirral and its Viking Heritage* (2000). His recent focus on the battle of Brunanburh has united his interests in Old English verse, place-names, language and history and has resulted in publications which have won widespread acceptance for Bromborough as the site of the battle.

**Richard Coates** is Professor of Linguistics at the University of the West of England, Bristol, a Research Professor at the University of Sussex, and a Fellow of the Society of Antiquaries of London. He specializes in proper names (from both the historical and the theoretical angles), and has been Hon. Director of the Survey of English Place-Names since 2003. He has also worked in English dialectology and the general philology of northern and western European languages.

**Robert Payson Creed**, Professor emeritus, University of Massachusetts, Amherst, has just completed a study of *Beowulf* based both on his analysis of the poem and many years of performing the poem at academic conferences and for the public. In 1979, his two-hour dramatization of *Beowulf* for National Public Radio, supported by a grant from the National Endowment for the Humanities, in which he performed the hero's three fights in Old English, received top awards. During his 45-year teaching career, he taught at Smith College, Brown University, and Stony Brook University. He has written many articles on *Beowulf* as a traditionally composed poem.

**Stephen Harding** was educated at Pembroke College, Oxford receiving a DSc. He was an Ernest Oppenheimer Fellow at Cambridge and is now Professor of Applied Biochemistry at Nottingham University. He is co-author of *Viking DNA* (with M. Jobling and T. King, 2010) and *Wirral and Its Viking Heritage* (with P. Cavill and J. Jesch, 2000), and is author of the popular texts *Ingimund's Saga* (2006) and *Viking Mersey* (2002). He is a medalist of the Royal Society of Chemistry.

**Marged Haycock**, Professor in Welsh Language and Literature at Aberystwyth University, is the author of *Legendary Poems from the Book of Taliesin* (2007), *Blodeugerdd Barddas o Ganu Crefyddol Cynnar* (1994), and co-editor of *Cyfoeth y Testun* (2003), a volume of textual criticism in memory of J.E. Caerwyn Williams. Her volume, *Prophecies from the Book of Taliesin*, will appear in 2012. Her interests include Welsh poetry to ca.1500, the literature of the Welsh borders, medieval women, aspects of material culture, particularly textiles, dress, food and drink, and the history of scholarship.

**Ulrike Hogg** completed an MA at the University of Düsseldorf, a PhD at the University of Aberdeen (in Scottish historiography), and now works as a curator in the Manuscripts Division of the National Library of Scotland, with special responsibility for Gaelic and early modern manuscripts.

**A. Keith Kelly** completed a PhD in Medieval Literature at Saint Louis University under the tutelage of Professors Tom Shippey and Paul Acker. In addition to his work with Old Norse language and literature, he has published material on medieval outlaw narratives, medievalism and film, and the works of J.R.R. Tolkien. He is currently an Assistant Professor of English at newly-founded Georgia Gwinnett College.

**Michael Livingston** holds degrees in History, Medieval Studies, and English. He currently serves as an Assistant Professor of English at The Citadel, is Associate Editor of the Secular Commentary Series of the Consortium for the Teaching of the Middle Ages (TEAMS), and holds a position on the Advisory Board of the TEAMS Middle English Texts Series. He is the author of scholarly editions of *Siege of Jerusalem* (2004), *In Praise of Peace* (2005), and *The Middle English Metrical Paraphrase of the Old Testament* (2011).

**Joanne Parker** is Lecturer in Victorian Literature at the University of Exeter. She specializes in nineteenth-century representations of the past, with a particular interest in Victorian Medievalism. Her previous publications include *England's Darling: The Victorian Cult of Alfred the Great* and *Written on Stone: The Poetry of Prehistory*. She is currently working on an AHRC-sponsored project, *Identity, Community and Victorian Medievalism in South-West England*.

**Robert Rouse**, having completed his doctorate at Bristol University in 2003, has taught medieval literature at the University of British Columbia (Vancouver, Canada) since 2005. The author of *The Idea of Anglo-Saxon England in Medieval Romance* (2005) and *The Medieval Quest for Arthur* (2005), he is currently completing a book that examines the pre-cartographic medieval geographical imagination. He has published on medieval romance and the law, Arthurian literature, the medieval erotic, the colonial ethics of medieval manuscript collection, the problem of the medieval "nation," and most recently, on issues of medieval geography and spatial theory.

**Scott Thompson Smith** is an Assistant Professor of English and Comparative Literature at the Pennsylvania State University. His research interests include Old English and Anglo-Latin literature, law and land tenure, and historicism. He also has teaching interests in comics and graphic novels, and the literature of horror and the supernatural. He has recently published articles in *The Journal of English and Germanic Philology* and *Anglo-Saxon England*, and has contributed to two essay collections, one dedicated to the *Anglo-Saxon Chronicle* and the other to critical theory in Anglo-Saxon studies.

# Abbreviations

Certain terms and works appear often enough that we have opted to abbreviate them.

| | |
|---|---|
| *ASC* | *Anglo-Saxon Chronicle* (in undifferentiated reference to the versions) |
| *BEASE* | Lapidge, et al., eds., *Blackwell Encyclopaedia of Anglo-Saxon England* |
| CC | Common Celtic (the ancestor of Welsh and Irish) |
| *DOE* | *Dictionary of Old English* |
| EETS | Early English Text Society |
| EPNS | English Place-Name Survey/Society |
| Gneuss | Gneuss, *Handlist of Anglo-Saxon Manuscripts* |
| *GP* | William of Malmesbury, *Gesta pontificum Anglorum* |
| *GR* | William of Malmesbury, *Gesta regum Anglorum* |
| ME | Middle English |
| *MED* | *Middle English Dictionary* |
| MGH | Monumenta Germaniae Historica |
| MW | Middle Welsh |
| OE | Old English |
| *OED* | *Oxford English Dictionary* |
| OF | Old French |
| ON | Old Norse |
| *PN Ch* | Dodgson, *The Place-names of Cheshire* |
| PrW | Primitive Welsh |
| S | Sawyer, *Anglo-Saxon Charters* (cited by charter number) |
| Scand. | Scandinavian (the ancestor of Danish and Norwegian) |
| Sharpe | Sharpe, *Handlist of the Latin Writers* |

**British Isles, ca. 937 CE**, showing important Roman roads and locations mentioned in the text.

Michael Livingston

# The Roads to Brunanburh

Anoche maté a un hombre en Brunanburh.
[Last night I killed a man in Brunanburh.]
— Jorge Luis Borges, "Brunanburh, 937 A.D.," line 13

Sometime late in the year 937, somewhere in Britain, rival armies of uncertain size from across the wide expanses of northern Europe — from London to Dublin, from Scotland to Scandinavia — met in a place called Brunanburh.

For centuries afterward, records of the Battle of Brunanburh, as it came to be known, spread far and wide, in poem and song, in chronicles and prayers, in sagas and charters, in Anglo-Saxon, Welsh, Latin, Old Norse, Middle English, and Anglo-Norman, to say nothing of post-medieval appearances in languages around the globe. It was, as Paul Hill has termed it, "the greatest showdown in Anglo-Saxon times," and while the details of that fateful event are nevertheless tantalizingly uncertain, its impacts are undeniable.[1] For generations afterward, the raging, bloody hours that culminated in a victory for the English forces under King Athelstan would be called "The Great Battle," and though it is perhaps misleadingly considered by some to be the moment in which a national vision of Englishness was born — a 2004 article in London's *Independent* called Brunanburh "The Cradle of English Civilisation"[2] — it would be no small stretch to consider the battle the moment when Englishness came of age. The men who fought and died on that field forged a political map of the future that remains with us today, arguably making the Battle at Brunanburh one of the most significant battles in the long history not just of England, but of the whole of the British Isles.

This book is the most comprehensive collection of sources related to the battle ever assembled, gathering, annotating, and translating into English every significant reference to Brunanburh in the Middle Ages, no matter the language of origin. In addition, this book includes essays not only putting those varied sources into context but also addressing many of our lingering questions about the conflict, including the controversial question of where it took place and the fascinating fate of its memory over centuries: Brunanburh, nearly forgotten in the late medieval period, went on to be reclaimed by Alfred, Lord Tennyson and the Victorians before it was re-reclaimed by writers as recent and far afield from England as Argentinian writer Jorge Luis Borges.

Alfred Smyth has observed that "Brunanburh was probably the greatest single battle in Anglo-Saxon history before Hastings, and yet in spite of a considerable amount of documentation relating to it, it is probably the most poorly understood."[3] What you have in your

[1] Hill, *Age of Athelstan*, p. 122.

[2] Jury, "Cradle of English Civilisation," p. 15.

[3] Smyth, *Scandinavian York and Dublin*, 2.62.

hands, therefore, stands as yet one more reclamation of its subject: an academic recollection determined to induce study and promote fresh understanding of the oft-forgotten but profoundly significant Battle of Brunanburh.

## THE BACKGROUND OF BRUNANBURH

To begin to understand the Battle of Brunanburh and its lasting significance, we must remember that while Brunanburh was an important (if hard-won) English victory and thus an essential moment in the history of what was becoming England, it was nevertheless a truly international battle. The roots of 937 began in the deep past of the British Isles, long before the coming of the Anglo-Saxons and those who would lead them. Indeed, one might view what happened at Brunanburh as the culmination of a long history of conquests and migrations, of shifting centers of power and population on the Isles.

From at least the ninth century, when the legend was included in the *Historia Brittonum*, commonly attributed to Nennius, most medieval writers thought the name *Britain* derived from Brutus, a descendant of Aeneas who, after many travails, was supposed to have brought a Trojan fleet to the Isles and there established a civilization with its capital at Troia Nova (London). According to Geoffrey of Monmouth's recounting of the tale, the islands were previously known as Albion, and at Brutus' arrival they were unoccupied save for a race of giants that the Trojans quickly dispatched. Hundreds of years later, according to these legendary accounts, the Picts arrived and occupied the Orkney Islands before wresting control of what came to be called Wales. Later still, the Scots came to the shores of Britain and took control of the north. And so things stood until the precarious balance between the three competing nations was disrupted by the conquering legions of the Romans, who overran Britain in several campaigns beginning with Julius Caesar's invasion in 55 BCE. This new state of affairs unraveled by slow decline until the Romans officially abandoned Britain in 410 CE. By invitation or invasion, loosely affiliated groups of Germanic peoples — most famous among them the Angles and Saxons — took advantage of the ensuing chaos and began to migrate to the eastern shores of Britain, where they established permanent settlements. Town by town they advanced, pushing the "native" Britons off their land in the so-called Anglo-Saxon invasion that would, ultimately, give its name to the cultural and political entity known as England (Angle-land).

We do not now think that all of the elements of this medieval history are true. We are relatively certain, for instance, that the earliest historically recorded inhabitants of the British Isles were not giants but Celts, a roughly defined cultural group that came to dominate northern Europe by the Iron Age. The name *Britain*, likewise, derives not from the legendary Brutus, but from one of the two primary native languages of the Celts living on the Isles. This language, called Brythonic, is the basis for modern Welsh and Cornish. The other Celtic language, Goidelic, is the basis for modern Irish, Gaelic, and Manx. And what Geoffrey and other medieval writers considered to be separate nations with separate arrival points on the British Isles — first the Britons, then the Picts, and later the Scots and Irish — instead appears to have originated as a mixed cultural entity whose national identities separated over the course of events across the varied geography of the Isles. On the other hand, it seems quite true that the Romans encountered what were by the Common Era distinguishably different groups of people within the Isles, just as the Angles and Saxons were clearly the latecomers to the British scene — though we think these Germanic groups began their own incursions across the Channel in the early part of the fourth century rather than the middle of the fifth. Such nitpicking of points, however, is to some degree culturally insignificant. While we might, from our distant, seemingly objective position, view some of this story as true, some as hazy remembrance, and some as myth or legend, we nevertheless cannot question that, for the men at Brunanburh, it was history in the most literal sense.

It is easiest to view the events leading to Brunanburh relative to events in England, in part because of its historical position as the "winner" in the struggle over possession of the British Isles: not only is history proverbially written by the victors, but its history has as a result become an integral part of the history of the West. Add in the broad linguistic familiarity with which most readers may approach English documentary evidence, and the common Anglo-centric view of history is, if not necessarily proper, at least understandable. While this book about Brunanburh to some degree refutes such a perspective by nature of its multi-cultural, multi-period, multi-lingual gathering of sources, it is nevertheless simplest to begin an historical overview of the events leading to Brunanburh through English eyes. To this we can add those events that brought (or failed to bring) to that fatefully bloodied field the adversaries of Athelstan, what Patrick Wormald has characterized as "a mighty coalition of Scots, Strathclyde Britons and Hiberno-Norse under the great-grandson of the Viking who had first created the Danelaw," all come to meet in "an encounter later viewed by the English as the climax of their struggle for the mastery of Britain."[4]

*The South*

As the Anglo-Saxon period in the British Isles progressed, kingdoms rose and fell, with different areas vying for dominance at one time or another. By the sixth century there were in England seven primary kingdoms, called the Heptarchy. Three of these kingdoms were identified with the Saxons: Essex (home of the East Saxons), Sussex (South Saxons), and Wessex (West Saxons). Three kingdoms were likewise associated with the Angles: East Anglia, Mercia, and Northumbria. A seventh kingdom, Kent, became the traditional home of the Jutes, another of the Germanic tribes to arrive in Britain. Roughly speaking, the power balance within the Heptarchy shifted by the century: Kent was the dominant kingdom in the sixth century, Northumbria in the seventh, and Mercia in the eighth (during which the Mercian king Offa built his 150-mile-long dyke to mark and defend the border between his kingdom and the Celt-controlled lands of Wales). The ninth century saw the rise of Wessex, due in no small part to the increasing success that Norse raiders had in infiltrating and occupying the lands of England.

The incursions of these sea-borne warriors, known popularly as the Vikings,[5] began simply enough, if the *Anglo-Saxon Chronicle* is to be believed, with the arrival of three ships in 787:

> Beorhtric took King Offa's daughter Eadburh. And in his days came first three ships of Northmen from Hordaland: and then the reeve rode there and wanted to compel them to go to the king's town because he did not know what they were; and then they killed him. These were the first ships of the Danish men which sought out the land of the English race.[6]

[4] Wormald, "Making of England," p. 28.

[5] The popular name — which occurs interchangeably in the chronicles alongside references to the Danes, Norse, Northmen, and so forth — is of uncertain meaning. Regardless of its origin, however, it is potentially misleading: it implies a political and cultural homogeneity that seems to little reflect reality, since the invaders came from across a wide swath of medieval Scandinavia.

[6] *Anglo-Saxon Chronicle*, Version E; trans. Swanton, p. 55. This event is now considered to have followed the attacks on Northumbria in 793–94; see Woolf, *From Pictland to Alba*, pp. 46–47.

As the chronicler, who was writing at a later date, notes, this was a precursor of things to come. Most scholars now date the expansion of the so-called Viking Age to the sacking of the twin monasteries at Lindisfarne and Jarrow in Northumbria in 793. After this sudden, precipitous blow, the rulers of the Heptarchy had not only their inter-regnal rivalries to trouble them, but they also had to contend with the ever-present foreign threat of the Norsemen.

A difficult situation for the Anglo-Saxons turned desperate less than a hundred years later, in 865, with the arrival in East Anglia of an invading force so massive that the writers of the *Anglo-Saxon Chronicle* often call it simply *se micel here*: The Great Army. While often characterized in the chronicles as a group of Danes, we now know the Great Army was actually arriving in Britain from ten years spent in Ireland.[7]

Not only more massive than previous Norse assaults (some have estimated it to have been several thousand strong), the Great Army was different from previous Norse forces in that it aimed not to raid and retreat, but "to exist parasitically upon the backs of established kingdoms in the Insular world."[8] It was, as Frank Stenton observes, "a momentous change in the character of the Danish attacks upon England," and it threatened "the whole fabric of English society."[9] They were led by Ivarr (Gaelic *Ímar*) Ragnarsson, more well known by his saga name Ivar the Boneless, who was aided by his brothers Halfdann and Ubbe. All three men were reported to be sons of the famed warrior Ragnar Lodbrok, who had been murdered by the king of Northumbria in 865. According to the saga *Ragnarssona þáttr* [*The Tale of Ragnar's Sons*], at least part of the goal of Ivar and his brothers was to avenge their father's death, which could go some way toward explaining why shortly after their arrival in East Anglia they turned their army toward Northumbria. Regardless of rationale, the Danes had captured that kingdom by 867 and placed it under the control of an English puppet-king. East Anglia itself followed in 870, and the Danes were already eyeing the rest of the Heptarchy as fruit ripe for the picking.

For two years King Æthelred of Wessex paid off the Danes to prevent an attack on his West Saxon lands, but that uneasy peace broke near the end of 870. The following year saw a long sequence of skirmishes and conflicts between the Wessexmen and the Danes, leading to a pitched battle at Ashdown where the Wessex forces, under Æthelred and his brother Alfred, won an impressive if short-lived victory. A fortnight later the forces met again at Basing, where Wessex was defeated, and eight weeks later the Danes won again at Meretune. Æthelred died in April 871, and Alfred — later to earn the epithet "the Great" — was crowned king.

The first few years of Alfred the Great's reign made the prospects of his kingdom's survival seem slim. Within a few years, Mercia followed Northumbria into the hands of the Danes, and Alfred's Wessex was becoming one of the final holdouts against the total loss of the

---

[7] Prior to their arrival in Ireland, there is a possibility not only that they had been a segment of the great fleet that had raided Frisia in 850 and taken control of Dorestad under the leadership of Rorik, but also that they might have been responsible for the sacking of Canterbury and London in 851. Alex Woolf points out that within the tenth- or eleventh-century *History of St. Cuthbert* an alternative name for the members of the Great Army is the "Scaldingi," which might well derive from the River Scheldt in Frisia. The connection, he observes, implies that "they had left Denmark nearly a quarter century before arriving in England. Many of them had presumably been born in Frisia. If this is the case then these 'Danes' had been cohabiting with Christians speaking a West Germanic dialect almost identical to Old English for a very long time" (*From Pictland to Alba*, pp. 71–72).

[8] Woolf, *From Pictland to Alba*, p. 73.

[9] Stenton, *Anglo-Saxon England*, pp. 245–46.

Heptarchy. He literally bought time by paying off the Danes for peace, but it would never last. In early 878 the peace was broken by a large "Danish" army headed by a new leader named Guthrum, who invaded and caught Wessex seemingly unaware. The kingdom collapsed into chaos, to the point that Alfred held secure little more than the Isle of Athelney in the Somerset marshes. From there Alfred gathered his surviving forces bit by bit, until he at last marched out and won a resounding victory — of which less is known than of Brunanburh — over Guthrum's Danes at Ethandun, or Edington. Alfred's success preserved Wessex from following the other Anglo-Saxon kingdoms into submission. Within weeks Guthrum had promised in the so-called Treaty of Wedmore to leave Alfred's lands in peace. Even more, he had agreed to be baptized as a Christian, with Alfred as his godfather. In so doing, Guthrum took the name of Alfred's eldest brother (some sources say uncle), who had died as king of Kent sometime before 855: Æthelstan. No one could have anticipated the eventual irony.

The survival of the Anglo-Saxon kingdom of Wessex had been a near thing, but survived it had. At the same time, Alfred's victory could hardly be categorized as a victory for the Anglo-Saxons as a whole. The Treaty of Wedmore and the subsequent Treaty of Alfred and Guthrum in 884 might have left Wessex secure, but it also codified the Danish possessions through a great swath of central and eastern England, which came to be called the Danelaw. When the proverbial dust had settled, Wessex held the lands south of the Thames, with Guthrum ruling the lands north of the Thames and east of a line running roughly along Watling Street. West of that treaty line, caught between Wessex, the Danelaw, and the Welsh lands, was what remained of Mercia, now under the rule of "Earl" Æthelred, who had taken control of the kingdom after the death of the Danes' puppet-king. Far to the northeast, Northumbria remained as a reduced coastal kingdom between the Tees and the Firth of Forth, flanked by the Celtic Britains of Strathclyde and hemmed in by the northern kingdom of Scotland. While the historical importance of Alfred's success is unquestionable, his was clearly not a victory for any greater entity we might call "England." As Wormald wryly observes, "There is evidence that Alfred came to see himself in some sense as a king of all Englishmen. There is almost no evidence that Englishmen beyond Wessex and perhaps the West Midlands would have agreed with him."[10]

King Alfred never ceased to push back against the border of the Danelaw, a struggle that was continued by his son Edward the Elder, who succeeded to the throne of Wessex upon Alfred's death in 899. Edward was much aided in this cause by Mercia. The bonds between Wessex and Mercia were strong from Alfred's time, largely due to the marriage, brokered by Alfred, between Earl Æthelred and Edward's sister, Æthelflæd. This close cooperation between the two Anglo-Saxon kingdoms on the southern border of the Danelaw was a significant threat to the Danish presence in Britain, a fact shown most dramatically in the summer of 910, when a large army of Northumbrian Anglo-Danes sailed up the River Severn and began to ravage the heart of Mercia in apparent retaliation for a campaign Edward and Æthelred had led into southern Northumbria the previous year. Edward reacted with lightning speed by amassing his strength with Æthelred and rapidly cornering the surprised invaders. In the Battle of Tettenhall (sometimes called Wednesfield), the Anglo-Saxons forced the Anglo-Danes into pitched battle, and the result was, by all accounts, a decisive victory for the Wessex-led allies. Casualties among the Anglo-Danes were heavy, with both their leading kings dead on the field. In one stroke, the combined might of Wessex and Mercia

[10] Wormald, "Making of England," p. 26.

had effectively ended the Anglo-Danish dynasty in the north, allowing Edward to turn against the remaining pockets of their presence in the south.

Æthelred died the year after Tettenhall — perhaps from wounds sustained in that battle — but Æthelflæd maintained control as the Lady of Mercia, and she continued the close ties between her lands and those of her brother. Indeed, after her own death in 918, rule of Mercia was given over directly to Edward and Wessex, and it seems hardly anyone blinked twice.[11] Close on the heels of this "annexation," Edward further stabilized his position by receiving the submission of the three most prominent kings of Wales, all grandsons of Rhodri Mawr: Hywel and Clydog, sons of Cadell and rulers of Dyfed and Seisyllwg in the south, and Idwal, son of Anarawd and ruler of Gwynedd in the north.

By the time Edward the Elder died in 924, the Danelaw had been pushed beyond the Humber, and the southern kingdoms were, for all intents and purposes, a united land. Despite his success, however, the final settling of accounts in the north, the final reduction of the Danelaw and the simultaneous solidification of a political entity that could truly be termed "England," would fall to Edward's son, who in a strange twist of history was named Æthelstan (hereafter Athelstan), the same name given to the man who had founded the Danelaw, his grandfather Alfred's enemy-turned-godson, Guthrum.[12]

Born around 895, Athelstan had been raised in Mercia by his aunt Æthelflæd, and he appears to have had particularly strong ties to the Mercian territories as a result.[13] These connections served him well in the course of a brief accession crisis after Edward's death: Mercia appears to have been unwavering in its support of Athelstan's claim to the throne over his half-brother, Edwin. Æthelflæd's influence also likely looms large in what appears to have been his sense of unfinished work, a vision of a united England that had yet to be realized. When Athelstan was consecrated as king of the great southern alliance that Edward had built, he did so as "rex Saxonum et Anglorum" [king of the Angles and Saxons], but there was no doubt he aimed at a higher goal. Janet L. Nelson has discussed the fact that Athelstan's coins feature the king crowned — itself a numismatic first — surrounded by the legend *rex totius Brittaniae* [king of all Britain].[14] Similarly, David N. Dumville finds in the king's cartulary record a consciousness on Athelstan's part "of the changed nature of English kingship. From the first his charters exhibit a latinity of Aldhelmian bombast and royal styles which bespeak imperial pretension."[15]

---

[11] This is not to say that there was not at least some intrigue to the union. Æthelred and Æthelflæd's daughter, Ælfwynn, was the clear and unquestioned heir to the Mercian seat, a point borne out in many of the chronicles, but she was quickly deposed after her mother's death and taken into Wessex. Her subsequent fate is unknown, though it is likely she entered holy orders and lived out her life in the nunnery of Wilton (Bailey, "Ælfwynn"). The tradition preserved in Caradoc's *History of Wales* that Ælfwynn was deposed because of a secret marriage to a Danish king is historically unlikely; see Laura Hibbard Loomis, *Medieval Romance in England*, p. 110.

[12] On the normalization of names commonly used in this volume, such as Athelstan, see the prefatory note on spellings, p. xi.

[13] Thus William of Malmesbury, *GR* 1.210; for opposing views on the historicity of this account, see Lapidge, "Some Latin Poems," pp. 62–71, and Wood, *In Search of England*, pp. 149–68.

[14] Nelson, "Earliest Surviving Royal *ordo*," pp. 44–46. On the king's coins, see Blunt, "Coinage," pp. 47–48. To be "king of all Britain" would have been a strikingly revolutionary idea in Athelstan's day, governing over both a people and a territorial polity that were historically un-unified.

[15] Dumville, *Wessex and England*, p. 149.

*The North*

The ultimate test of Athelstan's claim to rule "all Britain" would come at Brunanburh, but the seeds of that battle had been sown long before Athelstan's reign. It was, in a certain sense, an inevitable consequence of the history so briefly outlined here: the many rival cultural claimants for the land that would become England were not likely to part with their stakes without a fight. Even so, Hill is assuredly right in observing that the "immediate origins" for the battle occur "in the 920s when Rægnald (hereafter Ragnall), the Scandinavian leader from Ireland, had conquered the Danes of York, the Scots and the English of Bamburgh."[16]

Ragnall appears rather suddenly on the pages of history as one of several grandsons of a Viking leader known as Ímar, who has traditionally been identified as none other than Ivar the Boneless, the man who had led the Danes' Great Army to its original triumphs on Anglo-Saxon soil.[17] The first mention of Ragnall occurs in 914, when the *Annals of Ulster* record "a naval battle off the Isle of Man between Bárid son of Oitir and Ragnall grandson of Ímar, in which Bárid and nearly all of his army were destroyed." This was, apparently, a conflict "between Northmen driven out of Scotland by Constantín seeking new hunting grounds in the Irish Sea [under Ragnall], and the Hiberno-Norse settlers who had recently colonised the region [under Bárid]."[18] The "internal" nature of this battle speaks volumes for the unsettled history of both the northern lands and, in turn, those surrounding the Irish Sea in the long wake of the Danes' arrival in the Isles.

The history of the north is less certain than that of "England" in many respects, largely due to the relative paucity of reliable chronicle records from the period. That said, the broad strokes of its progress have been drawn by scholars. By the middle of the eighth century, nearly the whole of the modern lands of Scotland north of the Forth were under control of a broadly unified kingdom of Picts, a British culture differentiated from its southern counterparts by its refusal to settle in with the Romans in earlier centuries. By the ninth century, this Pictish kingdom held, too, the lands of Dál Riata, a Gaelic kingdom associated in the main with the western seaboard of modern Scotland, and those of Strathclyde, a British kingdom centered on Dumbarton. The political heart of this conglomeration, as Wessex was for the Anglo-Saxons in the south, lay in Fortriu, most probably situated on the Moray Firth.[19]

While Northumbria and the southern kingdoms of the British Isles suffered under the raids of the Danes, Pictavia (as it was then known) appears to have gone remarkably unscathed until 839, when the *Annals of Ulster* report that "the heathens" won a decisive victory in the north, in a battle of great historical significance but little specificity: "we know nothing of its details and even its location," Woolf notes, only that "the men of Fortriu . . . fighting against assailants of unknown origin . . . had been wiped out and their empire began to crumble."[20]

The fall of Fortriu likely enabled the rise of Cináed, son of Alpín, known more commonly by his Anglicized name Kenneth MacAlpin. Though popularly styled the first king of the Scots, who defeated the Picts and established a unified Scotland, he and several of his immediate successors carried only the title "king of the Picts." Indeed, there is a good chance that Ken-

[16] Hill, *Age of Athelstan*, p. 124.

[17] On the identification arguments, see Ó Cróinín, *Early Medieval Ireland*, pp. 250–54.

[18] Woolf, *From Pictland to Alba*, pp. 140–41.

[19] Woolf, "Dún Nechtáin."

[20] Woolf, *From Pictland to Alba*, pp. 66–67.

neth was himself a Pict, who had succeeded to the Gaelic throne of Dál Riata through matrilineal descent following the disaster of 839. Thence, around 842, he took control of Pictavia. The following half-century is a tangled sequence of kings and events, not least among the latter the incursion of part of the Great Army of the Danes into the southern lands of Pictavia after their victory over Northumbria in 867, with Ivar the Boneless himself sacking Dumbarton in 870. In the chaos of the following years, Pictavia was taken over completely by the Gaels.[21]

The history of the north grows far more certain with the reign of Constantín (hereafter Constantine), whose remarkably long reign (900–43) would see him fight and defeat two grandsons of Ímar, solidify the throne of the "new" kingdom of Alba, and contest against Athelstan both at home and at Brunanburh. The grandson of Cináed, Constantine was crowned king of a land now called Alba and increasingly taking the shape of modern Scotland. The kingdom he inherited was a troubled one, however, with borders under seemingly constant threat from the predatory Danes, who could strike from any direction. In the third year of his reign the chronicles report that an army of Danes managed to make deep incursions across his lands, occupying much of the Tay basin, not long after the expulsion of the Hiberno-Norse from Ireland in 902, which will be discussed in more detail below.[22] These forces were led, it seems, by another of the grandsons of Ímar: in 904 the *Annals of Ulster* report Constantine putting an end to the threat by winning a great victory over Ímar grandson of Ímar.

This was hardly the end of Constantine's engagement with the Danes; nor was it the end of the line for the grandsons of Ímar. In 917, two more grandsons of Ímar, Sihtric and the aforementioned Ragnall, landed fleets in Ireland, apparently determined to return the ports to the control of the Hiberno-Norse who had ruled there for over a generation. By late in the year they had succeeded in conquering Dublin. While Sihtric stayed to press his claims in Ireland, Ragnall sailed back across the Irish Sea to Britain, perhaps to coastal lands in the west of Northumbria that he had held from around the time of his sea battle near Man in 914. The exact path of Ragnall's subsequent actions are uncertain as a result of the vacuum in our sources, but we know that Ragnall eventually attacked eastern Northumbria, and that the English king of Northumbria, Ealdred, begged Constantine for assistance, a testament to the perceived strength of the Scots. The battle between Ragnall and the Scots took place remarkably far south, at Corbridge in Northumbria, and it ended with defeat for Constantine, who had to return north to lick his wounds.[23] Ragnall thus held sway over the whole of Northumbria (facing Edward the Elder's Mercian frontier to the south), along with the Isle of Man and, through his cousin's oversight, the Hiberno-Norse ports of Ireland.

Edward quickly fortified his Mercian border in response, and in 920 he gained at least some measure of peace by brokering an agreement with his many potential northern enemies in what must have been a striking act of diplomatic maneuvering. The Wessex-authored *Anglo-Saxon Chronicle* (Version A) reports:

---

[21] Duncan attempts to sort out an elusive pattern in the interesting tendency in this period to alternate between two lines of kings in *Kingship of the Scots*, pp. 16–22.

[22] The coincidence of this timing has led many to assume that Constantine's enemies had arrived from Ireland, but this is not necessarily so. See Woolf, *From Pictland to Alba*, pp. 133–34.

[23] For the political context of this and a second battle at Corbridge, see Smyth, *Warlords*, pp. 196–98. Woolf attempts to positively identify the battle's site in *From Pictland to Alba*, pp. 142–44.

> And then the king of the Scottas and all the people of the Scottas and Rægnald, and the sons of Eadwulf, and all who live in Northumbria, both English and Danish and Northmen and others, and also the king of the Strathclyde Welsh and all the Strathclyde Welsh, chose him as father and lord.[24]

As Hill points out, while Edward I would later use this event "as an excuse for his campaigns in Scotland in the late thirteenth century . . . nobody was in fact reduced to the feudal notion of vassalage." Quite to the contrary, each group was both biding its time and gaining its own immediate political security: "an achievement for each of the leaders in an age of migration, settlement, and warfare."[25] The players all had good reason for the agreement. Edward, of course, had cause to fear that Ragnall would move south into the old territories of the Danelaw, which were still newly won; he also must have feared that the Scots and the Strathclyde Britons might enter into an "active alliance" with a Dane-controlled York.[26] In return for promises to these ends, Ragnall appears to have gained both assurance that Constantine would not again attack him from the north and that York would pass without contention to his heirs. Constantine achieved security for Alba in the wake of his defeat at Ragnall's hands, and the unnamed king of Strathclyde caught between them all surely welcomed the chance to ensure the survival of his holdings in what was an increasingly contested part of the Isles.

Ragnall died in 920, and his cousin (or brother) Sihtric peacefully succeeded to the throne of Northumbria, sending yet another grandson of Ímar, Guthfrith, from Northumbria to rule in his now-vacant place in Dublin. In 926, the newly crowned Athelstan met with Sihtric at Tamworth, where he seems to have continued Edward's strategy of making deals with the Hiberno-Norse leaders by giving his sister to Sihtric in marriage.

Athelstan might well have thought to subsume Northumbria to his kingdom by marriage and eventual annexation, as Alfred had done with Mercia through Athelstan's aunt Æthelflæd, but Sihtric died within a year, apparently without producing an heir. Guthfrith set off at once from Dublin either to claim the British lands of his cousins or perhaps to support one of Sihtric's sons in his own claim (the sources are unclear), but Athelstan chose instead to make his own move for Northumbria and took York by force early in 927. There followed at Eamont a meeting in which the kings of Britain were forced to submit to the West Saxon crown: Hywel of the Welsh, Constantine of the Scots, Owain of Gwent (or perhaps of Strathclyde), and Ealdred the leader of Bamburgh. Defeated, Sihtric's son fled for Ireland, and Guthfrith followed, perhaps after first fleeing to Scotland and thence being captured by Athelstan's men and forced to swear an oath never to return to Britain. It is likely that the Latin poem *Carta dirige gressus* (Item 2 in this volume) was written to commemorate these events.

Athelstan surely had a right to feel pleased with his successes, and indeed it is after Eamont that the king's title in charters moves from "rex Saxonum et Anglorum" [king of the

[24] Quoted by Woolf, who observes this entry "is the first contemporary English use of the term Scottas to describe the inhabitants of the Alpínid kingdom. It is also the earliest recorded diplomatic exchange between a kingdom that can legitimately be regarded as ancestral to Scotland and one that can legitimately be regarded as ancestral to England" (*From Pictland to Alba*, p. 146). On Strathclyde's "permanent client relationship" with the Scots in this period, see Smyth, *Warlords*, pp. 205–06.

[25] Hill, *Age of Athelstan*, pp. 99–100. For more on this fascinating event and its political milieu, see Davidson, "(Non)submission."

[26] Smyth, *Warlords*, p. 199.

Angles and Saxons] to "monarchus totius Brittaniae" [high king of all Britain].[27] Things were looking good for the king on a foreign relations level, too. Both Alfred the Great and Edward the Elder had daughters married into Continental royalty through Flanders and France, respectively, and these connections enabled Athelstan to influence events across the Channel. Just a year before Eamont, any imperial leanings Athelstan might have had were given a measurable boost when Hugh, duke of the Franks, sent Adelulf, count of Flanders and Athelstan's first cousin, to meet with Athelstan at Abingdon. Athelstan was then raising in his court the exiled Louis d'Outremer, who had been only two when his father Charles III was deposed as king of France. The outcome of the meeting was Hugh's support for Louis, made fast by Hugh's marriage to Athelstan's famously beautiful sister Eadhild. Hugh also lavished Athelstan himself with gifts. In what amounted to a *translatio imperii* of Carolingian claims of regnal legitimacy, Athelstan was supposedly given more than just an expansive wealth of gems and coin and other treasures; Hugh presented to the English king the Lance of Charlemagne, which was thought to have pierced the side of Christ, the sword of Constantine the Great, which was said to have a nail from the True Cross in its hilt, and the banner of St. Maurice, which had been carried before the Theban Legion by the third-century saint (see, e.g., Item 36.42–73). As David Rollason observes, "it would be hard to imagine objects of greater value for giving tangible form to the ambitions and pretensions of the English kings."[28]

We have little record of Athelstan's actions in the immediate years after Eamont, though it is almost assuredly the case that with his north border secure he moved to shore up the west, where Idwal Foel, king of Gwynedd, and others among the Welsh were straining against their subservient position to the increasingly unified English. Athelstan campaigned through Dyfed, Gwynedd, Morgannwg, Gwent, and Brycheiniog, and the Welsh kings — including the powerful Hywel Dda of Deheubarth — were made to submit to him at Hereford in 927. Athelstan took similar action against the Welsh of Cornwall, pushing them out of Exeter and rebuilding the city there. In the English sources the tributes the king thus levied are often repeated as proof of the superiority of Athelstan and the English (see, e.g., Item 32.5566–81), but things were not viewed nearly so positively in the west lands. As Hill notes, "not every Welsh king was anti-Athelstan . . . yet there is something menacing in the notion expressed in Welsh poetry that the northmen would be welcomed if they were to ally with the Welsh against the over-proud English."[29] The Welsh poem *Armes Prydein Vawr*, Item 1 in this volume, was written either at this time or shortly after it, perhaps even in Deheubarth, where Hywel Dda took a relatively pro-Wessex position.[30] The taxes levied by Athelstan upon the Welsh weigh heavily on the anonymous poet's mind as he calls for a pan-Irish Sea alliance to drive the "foreign" Saxons back to the eastern sea: "As an end to their taxes," he writes, "they will know death" (Item 1.84). Resentment of Athelstan and his vision of a unified Britain under his rule was growing, but as yet no one had the strength to stand against him.

---

[27] Hill, *Age of Athelstan*, p. 210.

[28] Rollason, *Saints and Relics*, p. 160. Patrick Wormald opines that "It is barely conceivable that Æthelstan was unaware of the symbolism of his receipt of Charlemagne's cherished relics" (*Making of English Law*, p. 445). See also Wood, "Making of King Æthelstan's Empire," p. 267.

[29] Hill, *Age of Athelstan*, p. 126. On the specifics of the tribute, see Loyn, "Wales and England."

[30] See more on the dating and context of this poem, along with its connections to the Battle of Brunanburh, see John Bollard's essay in this volume, pp. 245–61.

The relative peace, festering though it was beneath the surface, was broken in 934 when Athelstan invaded Scotland. What had happened to cause this action is not known. Woolf speculates that Athelstan felt his position was suitably strengthened following three deaths: that of his half-brother and potential rival Edwin who drowned — one legend says at Athelstan's order[31] — in 933, and in 934 those of Guthfrith, the grandson of Ímar in Dublin, and of a king of Northumbria of uncertain name. This third death might also have produced the *casus belli* if the Scots and English "fell out either because they backed alternative competitors to the succession, or because Æðelstan now wished to do away with an autonomous sub-king altogether."[32] Whatever the cause, the effect is known with certainty: Athelstan drove a land army almost to Fortriu in Scotland, while his naval raiding force supposedly reached Caithness (see, e.g., Item 40.626–29, below). Smyth observes that if this latter fact is true, it could reveal a second northern target for Athelstan, since it would mean "that the naval force, at least, was directed as much against the Norwegian settlers of north-east Scotland as it was against the Scots."[33]

Athelstan exacted heavy tribute from the Scots, as he had from the Welsh earlier at Hereford, and he returned to the south in a more powerful position than ever. Again he turned his attention to the Continent, where Louis d'Outremer had been installed as king with the help of Hugh. No doubt the English king felt secure in his own lands, close to making good on his claim to be *rex totius Britanniae*.

Though he could hardly have known it, however, his greatest test was yet to come. The anti-English forces surrounding his kingdom were gathering, their resolve actually strengthened by Athelstan's latest foray north. By 937 they had agreed to set aside whatever political, cultural, historical, and even religious differences they might have had in order to achieve one common purpose: to destroy Athelstan.

*The West*

Of the negotiations leading up to the Battle of Brunanburh, with its alliance between the Scots, the men of Strathclyde, and the Hiberno-Norse of Dublin and the lands around the Irish Sea, no records have survived. This is unfortunate, if only from a sense of curiosity about what plans for attack and support they actually had, and who took the initiative in the alliance's formation. After all, the three kings who spearheaded the Brunanburh campaign — King Constantine of the Scots, King Anlaf Guthfrithson of the Hiberno-Norse, and King Owain of Strathclyde — had all been enemies of each other in living memory. Constantine and the Scots, the degradations of 934 still fresh in their minds, are perhaps instinctive candidates for planning a grand anti-English alliance in 937, but Anlaf was almost assuredly the mastermind behind the plan.[34] Indeed, while I have for the sake of familiarity presented the

---

[31] The evidence is uncertain; compare, e.g., Item 18.6 with the story in Item 40.605–12.

[32] Woolf, *From Pictland to Alba*, pp. 163–65.

[33] Smyth, *Scandinavian York and Dublin*, 2.65.

[34] Interestingly, Smyth separately attributes "overall" leadership to both Anlaf (*Scandinavian York and Dublin* 2.44) and Constantine, the latter of whom might have "stage-managed" the campaign (*Warlords*, p. 204). In the early sources, however, it is Anlaf who is the primary adversary of Athelstan (e.g., Items 4.26, 9.3, 12.2, 13.3). A Scots-led campaign first appears in *Egil's Saga*, though the "king of the Scots" named there (Item 25.1) is Anlaf (see also note 36 below). Accounts specifying Constantine as the alliance leader appear much later, perhaps starting with Anglo-Normans (see Item 28).

preceding historical overview of the British Isles largely in terms of the Anglo-Saxons, we should begin to see for the sake of accuracy that, as Smyth has argued, Brunanburh is most properly situated in the "wider context" of "the continuing struggle of the Dublin kings to control York, and of York's own desire to remain independent of Wessex."[35]

After Guthfrith's death in 934, which had perhaps helped to precipitate Athelstan's invasion of Scotland, his son Anlaf (ON *Óláfr*) inherited the lands of the Hiberno-Norse. Unlike his unlucky father — who had by the end of his days a long history of defeats and had, in fact, been the man to lose the important Hiberno-Norse claim to Northumbria when he was beaten by Athelstan in 927 — Anlaf opened his reign as king in Dublin by successfully attacking the other powers in Ireland: the kings of Southern and Northern Brega, the rich monastery of Clonmacnoise, and, in a stunning political move, the competing Hiberno-Norse king at Limerick, Anlaf Cenncairech, whom he soundly defeated in a naval engagement on Lough Ree in August of 937.[36] In only three short years Anlaf had taken complete control of the Hiberno-Norse settlements in Ireland; his subsequent rule is widely considered "the zenith of viking-power in Ireland."[37] As Smyth notes, Anlaf wasted no time in next turning his eye toward York:

> From Óláfr's point of view his right to rule Northumbria was greater than that of the West Saxon king. Athelstan was the first West Saxon prince to rule there, while four of Óláfr's relatives had been kings of York, and his father, Gothfrith, had been deprived of it by force. Furthermore, Óláfr might count on the support of the Danish *bændr* [farmers] in the Vale of York and the merchants of that city who were the traditional allies of his dynasty which had led them into England. In the very year in which he destroyed the ships of Limerick and took her king captive to Dublin, the triumphant Óláfr set sail to engage King Athelstan in one of the greatest battles in Anglo-Saxon history.[38]

Thus, while it is true that at the time of the battle Anlaf had only recently secured his own kingdom in Ireland, it is also almost assuredly true that as the great-grandson of the man

---

[35] Smyth, *Scandinavian York and Dublin*, 2.35–36.

[36] Much confusion over the years has arisen due to the fact that so many of the Hiberno-Norse leaders share in a common stock of names: Imar, Ragnall, Sihtric, Guthfrith, and Anlaf foremost among them. For our present purposes, in addition to Anlaf Cenncairech, it should be noted that Anlaf Guthfrithson's second cousin — the son of the Sihtric who had ruled at York prior to his death in 927 — was also named Anlaf, and that he, too, struggled for control of Northumbria and eventually ruled it. Much of Anlaf Sihtricson's career before 940 is uncertain, and it is possible that he spent the years after his father's death and leading up to that time in Scotland. It is even possible that he married the daughter of Constantine, which would explain why some of our sources term the Anlaf at Brunanburh the son-in-law of Constantine (though the same could be said for Anlaf Guthfrithson, too; Smyth argues that it was Guthfrithson's marriage into Constantine's family, in fact, that precipitated Athelstan's 934 attack on Scotland [*Warlords*, p. 203]). Indeed, it could be that *all three* King Anlafs — Guthfrithson, Sihtricson, and Cenncairech — were present at the battle. The *Annals of Clonmacnoise* strongly indicate that Anlaf Guthfrithson forced Anlaf Cenncairech to fight for him at Brunanburh (see Item 52 and notes), and both second cousins make explicit appearances at the battle in the sources (for Guthfrithson, see Items 13.3, 51.9; for Sihtricson, see Items 17.1, 53.2). Given the fundamental confusions between the careers of the two second cousins, however, we can prove little in the positive or negative regarding Anlaf Sihtricson before 940.

[37] Downham, *Viking Kings*, p. 41.

[38] Smyth, *Scandinavian York and Dublin*, 2.35.

who had led the Great Army and established the Danelaw he regarded Dublin as the lesser of his claims: from his perspective, Athelstan, the grandson of the man who had prevented the Great Army from overrunning the whole of the British Isles, had stolen his rightful place as king of Northumbria, a land conquered so long before by his forebears. Anlaf thus had the motive to attack Athelstan, and he also had the means: as king of the Hiberno-Norse he could summon ships and men from Dublin and the coasts of Ireland, from the Isle of Man and the western isles of Scotland, in addition, no doubt, to Celtic Gaels from across these same areas. After seeing what had happened to the Scots in 934 he would no doubt have suspected that he might also need the extra strength that other nations could provide, and the recently humiliated Constantine and Owain were logical allies to add to Anlaf Cenncairech and the other Vikings he had defeated and pressed into his service at Lough Ree.[39]

## THE GREAT BATTLE

### *When*

It is unlikely that we will ever know at what point the idea of this great alliance was first formulated. After all, even if Anlaf had pre-arranged plans for a grand invading alliance with Constantine and Owain and even the Hiberno-Norse of Man and the other island communities, plans perhaps made through the intermediary of his second cousin Anlaf Sihtricson, he could hardly have acted on them until he had secured his realm in Ireland.[40] The fact that he defeated Anlaf Cenncairech of Limerick in August of 937, and that the Battle of Brunanburh took place by the end of that year, however, speaks toward some measure of prior coordination. In a matter of only a few months, Anlaf and his allies were able to raise massive armies — the sources all agree that the forces amassed at Brunanburh were vast in number — and move them from across the British Isles into Athelstan's territory.

William of Malmesbury, in his *Gesta regum Anglorum*, preserves an allegedly older Latin poem about the battle that purports to relate what happened after the arrival of the alliance:

> For because our king, bold and spirited in his youth,
> had retired from war long ago and languished in sluggish leisure,
> they defiled everything in their relentless plundering,
> afflicting the wretched fields with spreading fires.
> Verdant grass had withered on all the plains;
> diseased grain had mocked the prayers of farmers;
> so great was the barbaric force of the footmen and riders,
> the charge of countless galloping steeds.[41]

The details here have the ring of truth about the readiness of England. Earlier, in his own prose account, William tries to mitigate any negligence on Athelstan's part by attributing

---

[39] On the presence of the Lough Ree Vikings and some number of Gaels among Anlaf's alliance, see the notes to Item 52.

[40] Murray Beavan has argued that Anlaf Sihtricson functions as first lieutenant for Anlaf Guthfrithson in the years following Brunanburh ("King Edmund," p. 6), and it is not hard to anticipate, as Kevin Halloran does ("Brunanburh Campaign," p. 140), such a relationship between them at the time of the battle itself. For more on the two Anlafs and Brunanburh, see note 36, above.

[41] Item 17.me12–19. On the dating of this poem, see Smith's essay, pp. 274–76.

the defensive delay to the fact that the king "purposely held back so that he might defeat an already insolent foe in a more glorious manner" (Item 17.pr2–3), but the truth of the matter seems plain indeed: Athelstan was far from ready for a fight. The campaign of 934 had clearly put him in a confident mood, and even if he had heard word of Anlaf's victory over Limerick and consequent eye on York, Athelstan would probably have thought it impossible for Anlaf to mount anything more than local raids before winter set in. The possibility that Anlaf would instead invade at the head of a grand alliance could hardly have occurred to him. The highlighting in William's poem of the destruction of crops by the invaders is also worth noting. The sheer weight of logistics would argue that Anlaf's surprise invasion could hardly have arrived before mid-September, by no small coincidence a crucial time in the seasonal planting schedule: "Not only were the crops at risk in an invasion at this season, but harvest-time saw the Mercian and West Saxon yeomen busy in the fields and unprepared for battle."[42] Anlaf's decision to invade quickly on the heels of his August victory was, therefore, a triple stroke of genius. Athelstan was unsuspecting, his army was in the fields, and a blow against the harvest would have profound effects beyond the initial campaign. Though we can do no more than guess, it is a sound assumption that Anlaf arrived on enemy soil in mid-September. Athelstan, unready for the fight, would have needed time to gather his own forces — several of our sources make clear that Anlaf's alliance had a relative freedom over the countryside for a time — which places the Battle of Brunanburh in early October.[43]

*How*

Smyth has rightly observed that the Latin poem that survives in William's text, in addition to helping us to date Anlaf's assault, might also help us to trace its path, though it must be emphasized that any notion of how these armies came together must be extremely speculative in nature. Preceding the quotation noted above come lines that allude to the co-operation of much of the north with the allied invasion:

> Now the savage barbarity of the north comes to ground,
> now the pirate has left the sea to take the field,
> as Anlaf rasps threats unlawful and grim.
> To this raving fury, welcome to the king of the Scots,
> the northern land lends clear support.
> Now they greatly swell with pride and terrify the air with their words;
> The people and the entire region yield to their arrogance. (Item 17.me5–11)

Taken together with the evidence from Anlaf's campaign three years later, in 940, when Northumbria readily submitted to him, Smyth argues that this passage "could well reflect a logical sequence, beginning with Óláfr's emergence from the Scottish Lowlands with Constantine's help, followed by the submission of Northumbria and his acceptance at York, and finally culminating in an invasion of Mercia and the ravaging of English crops which prompted

---

[42] Smyth, *Scandinavian York and Dublin*, 2.50.

[43] Smyth dates the battle as "October at the latest" (*Scandinavian York and Dublin* 2.49), while Philip Cronenwett likewise points to the month ("Basileos Anglorum," p. 43). For his part, Halloran also places the battle in October, with Anlaf's arrival in September ("Brunanburh Campaign," p. 138), though he speculates that this was preceded by the primary attack of Constantine and Owain "not later than August" (p. 143), a timing with which I disagree. See below.

Athelstan to immediate action."[44] Though I will reject some of the specifics of this sequence, the broad progression of Smyth's proposal — a movement down from the north, with the ravaging of crops and population only occurring once the "English" border was breached — makes a great deal of sense. While *Egil's Saga* (Item 25) preserves a tradition that Anlaf engaged in a brief battle with two Northumbrian earls of Athelstan, Godric and Alfgar, it also makes clear that the main engagement of the campaign occurred much farther to the south. The north fell, and the south lay open. Attempts to identify Brunanburh with locations in the north remain fundamentally flawed in light of the evidence at hand.[45]

Smyth's suggestion that Anlaf was accepted at York is an intriguing scene, and there is nothing to say that it did not happen. At the same time, there are reasons to think it unlikely. For one thing, we would expect more specific references to such an oath-breaking on the part of the Northumbrians if it did occur. To lend "clear support" (Item 17.me9) was one thing, but to rebel outright by officially accepting Anlaf's lordship at York would have been a notable event indeed. Even *Egil's Saga*, with its statement that Anlaf conquered "all of Northumberland" in the initial invasion, makes no reference to a triumphal entry at York (Item 25.6–7), a well known point of reference to Norse writers. In addition, it is probable that the success of Anlaf's invasion depended on speed. His biggest ally aside from the Scots and the Britons was surprise. And, as we have already seen, it appears that he used it well to his advantage, catching Athelstan "languished in sluggish leisure" (Item 17.me13). Similarly, it is unlikely that Athelstan, as Smyth postulates, would have awaited the incursion into Mercia before beginning the task of organizing a counter-attack. If there was to be any shred of credibility to his proclaimed role as king of all Britain, his lands were under attack from the moment Anlaf crossed into Northumbria.[46] That Brunanburh occurred much further south, almost assuredly after the allies had begun to pillage inside the border of Mercia, simply points once more to the surprising late-year timing of the attack and the speed with which it was carried out.

Any attempt to trace the course of the allied invasion must remain speculation, since the sources give us only enough to conjecture a broad north-to-south outline, but we can assume

---

[44] Smyth, *Scandinavian York and Dublin*, 2.49.

[45] For a recent example of a northern hypothesis, see the work of Halloran ("Brunanburh Campaign" and "Identity"), which is further discussed below (see especially notes 46 and 59). Halloran's proposal that Brunanburh is to be identified with Burnswark is discussed and rejected in Cavill's essay in this volume (pp. 340–41). William of Malmesbury calls the site "far into England" (Item 17.pr3–4), and Robert of Gloucester explicitly points out that the site of the battle was "south of the Humber" (Item 32.5507). Associated engagements may have occurred in the north in 937; indeed, it could be that an initial skirmish of the campaign occurred on or near Burnswark. Yet, while complete certainty must elude us, Smyth's 1975 dismissal of such northern-oriented theories for Brunanburh itself as being "very unlikely indeed" appears to remain quite true today (*Scandinavian York and Dublin* 2.42).

[46] Though Halloran rightly casts doubt on the seizing of York in 937, since it "would gain no permanent advantage for the coalition while the English army remained undefeated," his further supposition — that the invaders stayed in Northumbria, "raiding extensively" while they awaited Athelstan — is difficult to accept ("Brunanburh Campaign," p. 139). The alliance, drawn together in haste and in any event relying on speed and surprise — which the sources consistently say they achieved — would almost assuredly have followed in a long tradition, both medieval and for Anlaf familial, of provisioning off the land. To remain in Northumbria, therefore, would be to pillage the very land he meant to rule. Far more likely is a rapid advance south, pillaging Mercian lands and planning to catch Athelstan at a disadvantage rather than waiting and giving him time to gather his forces.

that an invading land force would have followed one of two logical courses south. The first avenue of attack would have been the traditional route into England: Dere Street, one of the primary Roman roads, led from the Antonine Wall straight to York. From there, an army could follow Ermine Street south to Lincoln, opening up avenues for attack against the whole breadth of Athelstan's lands. This had been the path followed by many armies over the years. It was on this road that Constantine had lost his struggle against Anlaf's relative Ragnall less than twenty years earlier at Corbridge, where Dere Street crossed Hadrian's Wall, and it was through this conduit that Athelstan almost assuredly moved his forces northward in 934.[47] That Dere Street to Ermine Street was the "traditional" invasion route could be used to argue for or against its use in 937, of course. The speed of the allies' attack might certainly have been aided by the heavily used Roman road and their general familiarity with it, yet at the same time its known quality would have worked quite against their need for surprise. In addition, while invading via this route might have been sensible for Constantine and his Scots, it would have been logistically difficult for Anlaf's Hiberno-Norse: it would have required the alliance to gather in the north, perhaps at Dumbarton, before they struck south, a difficult task to coordinate given the time constraints of the year. The same difficulty, of course, is only compounded in attempts to identify Brunanburh with an eastern location off the Humber following John of Worcester's account of the battle (Item 16), which Woolf wisely disregards as "fundamentally unlikely."[48]

The second immediate option for a land route out of the north would have had much to recommend it in 937: the old Roman road from Carlisle to Manchester across the Lancashire Plains, which became Watling Street as it extended down through Chester. While historically perhaps not as heavily traveled as Dere Street, it was nevertheless a centuries-old path. From Anlaf's perspective it would have had the additional advantage of keeping him and his allies close to the coast of the Irish Sea and the surrounding plains, which were dotted with small colonies of loyal Hiberno-Norse, many of whom had settled the shoreline from the Clyde to the Dee after their expulsion from Ireland in 902. Interestingly for our attempts to locate Brunanburh, it was at this same time that the Welsh *Annales Cambriae* record "Igmunt" arriving in Anglesey, which Woolf notes corresponds well with

> a short saga about "Hingamund" (both Igmunt and "Hingamund" seem to represent Old Norse Ingimundr), which survives in the so-called *Fragmentary Annals of Ireland*. . . . This story tells how Ingimundr was driven out of Anglesey by the local ruler and how he then settled near Chester, with the permission of the king and queen of Mercia (Æthelred, 879–911, and his wife Æthelflæd, who survived him until 918). After a while Ingimundr grew dissatisfied and persuaded other "Norwegians" and "Danes" who were settled nearby to rise up against their hosts and to seize Chester. The saga recounts their attempts to take the ancient Roman fortress which ultimately proved unsuccessful.[49]

---

[47] Woolf, *From Pictland to Alba*, pp. 162, 165–66.

[48] Woolf, *From Pictland to Alba*, p. 171. Cavill analyzes the Worcester account and its lack of geographical usefulness in his essay in this volume (pp. 337–39). It is possible that the Humber confusion is due to a second attacking fleet aimed more directly at York and led by Anlaf Sihtricson coming down from Scotland, but such a scenario, while intriguing for explaining a few stray facts in the sources, can be nothing more than fascinating (and rather doubtful) speculation.

[49] Woolf, *From Pictland to Alba*, pp. 131–32.

At any rate, a decision to stay close to the Irish Sea might well have been natural to Anlaf and his allies. It was relatively fast, safe, easy, and unexpected.

As near as we can determine, therefore, the campaign proper would have begun in early to mid-September, with Constantine and the amassed Scots moving south to be joined by the Strathclyde Britons before crossing Hadrian's Wall near Carlisle. It may be that Anlaf himself had sailed ahead of his own gathering forces to join Constantine and make certain their pact and plans, but more likely this role was given to a trusted lieutenant since many of our sources repeatedly imply an initial separation between the allied forces: Constantine came by land, Anlaf by sea.[50] It is logical that at least some organized local resistance was encountered by the Scots and Britons, perhaps in Cumbria; this struggle, presumably, gave rise to *Egil's Saga*'s account of Godric and Alfgar. Continuing south, the invading army would have gathered strength from the countryside: *Egil's Saga* reports a growing army due to the confidence of the Northumbrians — by which it is surely meant the Hiberno-Norse settlers in the area — that Anlaf would defeat the English (Item 25.12–14). This increase was likely slow at first, as the Hiberno-Norse trickled in from the coastal settlements, but at some point it would have increased the alliance significantly as Anlaf's main forces arrived from across the sea.[51] Even without the time pressure of an impending winter, the logistics of such an operation would be remarkable even by modern standards; for the Middle Ages, this rapid and organized international gathering of forces is extraordinary.[52]

Following a western route south from Scotland and gathering strength as they did so, Anlaf and his allies would have presented a strategic problem from Athelstan's perspective: once the English king had an army ready to take on his enemies — a process that our sources say took some time, perhaps even forcing Athelstan to make personal pleas for service (see Item 25.21–24) — where was he to send them? An initial assumption might have been that Anlaf's intent was to seize York. Aside from its traditional importance in the north, it was the object of Anlaf's ancestral claim. Common sense would have thus dictated that Athelstan should send his forces north with all speed, gathering perhaps at Lincoln before crossing the Humber and meeting Anlaf head-on. This would have been the obvious course of action if Anlaf had followed the route of Dere Street, but if he and his allies indeed chose the western route down toward Lancashire, Athelstan would no longer have been certain of their intent. Though less direct for the Scots than Dere Street, the route through Lancashire still allowed for the attack to fall on York via the "Aire Gap," a geographical break in the

---

[50] Halloran, "Brunanburh Campaign," pp. 138–42. See note to Item 4.37, however, for the chance that Constantine joined Anlaf in fleeing the field by ship. On the possibility that Anlaf Guthfrithson's man in Scotland was Anlaf Sihtricson, see note 40, above.

[51] Many possible landing points for this force present themselves, from as far north as the Solway Firth to as far south as the Dee, a matter greatly complicated by the strong possibility that Anlaf's forces could have come in multiple waves initially, only to disengage from shore to move to the Wirral if the notion of an "arranged" final battle at Brunanburh is accepted as true. Regardless, it is noteworthy that the Mersey estuary is known to have served as a conduit for messages, and perhaps men and materials, between the Norse kingdoms of Dublin and York: In the 920s Edward the Elder, Athelstan's predecessor on the throne, built or rebuilt a series of fortifications on the river and in Manchester to cut off this avenue. Given the Norse settlements across the Wirral and the Cheshire plain, Anlaf might have expected (and received) a warm welcome in these areas. See below.

[52] Smyth calls the rise of the allied assault "one of the most elaborate military preparations ever made in these islands by a Dark Age king" (*Scandinavian York and Dublin* 2.63).

Pennine Hills defended by Skipton. Indeed, for the bulk of Anlaf's Hiberno-Norse forces crossing the Irish Sea from Dublin and Man, the Gap would have been the most direct path to York, with the main surge of its naval component possibly riding up the River Ribble.[53] Owain's Strathclyde Britons were likely a relatively small contingent of the alliance, but for them either way would suit as well as another if York was the destination.[54] Athelstan would have been in a bind: if he hurried to York, the allies could continue south down the western road, bypassing the Gap and instead cutting their way through the fertile farmlands around Manchester en route to the exposed heart of Mercia. Athelstan would then be caught severely out of position, with Anlaf effectively threatening the whole of England to his rear. On the other hand, if he tarried before moving to York, he risked losing that important city to a quick allied strike through the Gap. There was, as we have seen, some delay before Athelstan met the allied invasion due to his own logistical troubles in calling out his forces, and to this we might add his uncertainty about the invaders' movements. Given the combination of factors, we might speculate that he mustered his own armies to High Cross in Leicestershire, at the intersection of Watling Street and the Fosse Way.

The invading forces were meanwhile harrying Athelstan's domains in Lancashire and the Cheshire plains at harvest time, living parasitically, as the earlier Great Army had, off the English lands. Anlaf's sea-borne forces had arrived, and the alliance was at full strength for the battle to come. At some point, if we are to believe the tradition in *Egil's Saga*, messages were exchanged between the invaders and Athelstan, and it was agreed that Anlaf would cease harrying the countryside and that the two armies would meet at a pre-arranged location.[55] Even setting aside the questionable particulars of the saga story, the "truth" of the matter seems clear enough: there would be one fight, and to the victor went England.[56]

By one road or another, what we know for certain is that Athelstan eventually met Anlaf's allied forces at a place called Brunanburh, and that a great many men died there. Perhaps our biggest question, therefore, is that which has long overshadowed all others concerning the battle: Where was Brunanburh?

*Where*

Paul Hill, writing in 2004, noted over thirty rival theories as to the location of Brunanburh, providing a useful examination of many of them.[57] Some of these locations have little to recommend them beyond a rough orthographic similarity to the word *Brunanburh* that fails to resolve itself into anything convincing on etymological grounds. Indeed, the uncertainties of the situation have led to the general feeling among most scholars that we will

[53] Woolf, *From Pictland to Alba*, p. 171. If Anlaf and his allies moved up the Ribble toward the Gap, it could well be that a 937 battle — perhaps that remembered in *Egil's Saga* with Godric and Alfgar — was fought near Burnley, one of the many candidates to have vied for the location of Brunanburh.

[54] Smyth, *Scandinavian York and Dublin*, 2.65.

[55] See Item 25.39–42. The rarity of the agreement to cease harrying is discussed by Margaret Ashdown in her dated but still intriguing "Single Combat," p. 121.

[56] If there is any truth to a spurious charter, Athelstan understood Anlaf's goal to be the eradication of the Anglo-Saxon dynasty. In S 406 Athelstan describes Anlaf as the king "qui me vita et regno privare disponit" [who attempted to take from me my realm and life]. On notions of truth in the saga tradition, see Kelly's essay in this volume, pp. 305–14.

[57] Hill, *Age of Athelstan*, pp. 141–42.

simply never know where the Battle of Brunanburh was fought. As Alistair Campbell noted after his own study of the possibilities in 1938, "Unless new evidence can be produced, an honest *nescio* is greatly to be preferred to ambitious localisations built upon sand."[58] Fortunately, our knowledge base has expanded significantly since Campbell, and even since the time of Hill's conclusions. In their sequence of essays in this volume, Paul Cavill, Stephen Harding, and Richard Coates make clear that the case for modern Bromborough (OE *Brunanburh*) on the Wirral as the rough location of the medieval battle is hardly built upon sand. Quite to the contrary, the Bromborough-Brunanburh connection is a multi-faceted argument built upon the "hard rock" of onomastics, linguistics, history, logic, folklore studies, and even a bit of genetics. It is currently the standard against which all other theories must be measured, and to date all other options have fallen short of its high mark. Put simply, the case for Bromborough is currently so firm that many scholars are engaged not with the question of whether Brunanburh occurred on the Wirral, but where on the peninsula it took place.[59]

That the confrontation between Athelstan and the allied forces under Anlaf should happen on the Wirral makes a great deal of sense in light of what we can ascertain about the allied campaign. Gathered in haste, no doubt gathered greatly en route, the allied armies had moved south along the western seaboard through the Lancashire Plains. Somewhere between Solway Firth and the Dee the northern Scots of Constantine and the Britons of Owain would have met with the Hiberno-Norse of Anlaf. While we cannot discount that they themselves gathered on the Wirral, awaiting the arrival of the northern forces before pushing at Chester and the central Anglo-Saxon lands beyond it, if the hypothesis of a surprise invasion with several optional targets is to be followed, then a reasonable landing point for Anlaf's sea-borne men could also have been the Lancashire coast, perhaps along the River Ribble. From there the coalition's two primary options — east to York or south to Mercia — would have remained open. Whether the invaders gathered on the Wirral or arrived there after a march from elsewhere, however, we can be reasonably certain that the decision to fight on that peninsula was their own. Athelstan was playing catch-up one way or another, and the Wirral could easily have been viewed from Anlaf's perspective as the closest thing to "home field" he was going to find in Athelstan's territories. We have already seen that there had been a significant re-settling of Hiberno-Norse along the coasts of the Irish Sea after their expulsion from Ireland in 902. In particular, the story about Ingimundr, who was driven from Anglesey only to settle near Chester and thereby unsettle the area, gives us a literary indication of how well known the Norse-leanings of this part of England were, a fact that finds corroboration in place-names and even genetic analyses.[60] The northern and western coasts of the Wirral peninsula show evidence of a strong and long-standing Norse

[58] Campbell, *Battle of Brunanburh*, p. 80.

[59] The most extensive effort to reject Bromborough is arguably that of Halloran, who locates the battle in the north. Essentially, Halloran regards Bromborough as too far south to be identified with the 937 campaign, arguing that the amount of time between the presumed September date for Anlaf's arrival and the October date of the battle would be insufficient for the invaders to penetrate so deeply into Athelstan's lands ("Brunanburh Campaign," p. 139). Not so. Gauging the speed of a marching army can be difficult, but fifteen miles per day is a suitable estimate on average; in fact, this is the slowest possible pace of Athelstan's own forces as they gathered and moved north toward Scotland in 934. Even if we measure the invasion as beginning in distant Scone, such a rate of advance would require less than three weeks to reach Bromborough, well within the campaign's assumed dates.

[60] For more on these studies, see Harding's and Coates' essays in this volume.

presence, and these areas would have provided opportunity for a boat-assisted quick getaway — no doubt a wise Hiberno-Norse preparatory instinct — if things down south metaphorically went south: between the Mersey and the Dee there were points of anchorage, a fact for which Anlaf himself would later have reason to give thanks.

For many reasons, then, the Wirral peninsula was a logical choice for the final showdown, especially if is true that the battle site was pre-arranged between the two armies after a sequence of harrying further north.

*What*

One of the earliest sources for the battle, and perhaps the most famous, is the lengthy poem traditionally titled *The Battle of Brunanburh*, which is included in several copies of the *Anglo-Saxon Chronicle* (*ASC*). In it, the anonymous poet reports the bloody results of the fight:

> Five lay still
> on that battlefield — young kings
> by swords put to sleep — and seven also
> of Anlaf's earls, countless of the army,
> of sailors and Scotsmen. There was put to flight
> the Northmen's chief, driven by need
> to the ship's prow with a little band.
> He shoved the ship to sea. The king disappeared
> on the dark flood. His own life he saved.
> So there also the old one came in flight
> to his home in the north; Constantine,
> that hoary-haired warrior, had no cause to exult
> at the meeting of swords: he was shorn of his kin,
> deprived of his friends on the field,
> bereft in the fray, and his son behind
> on the place of slaughter, with wounds ground to pieces,
> too young in battle. (Item 4a.28–44)

Æthelweard, in his *Chronicle*, reports that Brunanburh was "still called 'the great war' to the present day by the common folk" (Item 7.4), and it is the magnitude of the battle that is emphasized again and again throughout the records. The aftermath described by Henry of Huntingdon, for example, is one of utter devastation:

> Then the dark raven with horned beak,
> and the livid toad, the eagle and kite,
> the hound and wolf in mottled hue,
> were long refreshed by these delicacies.
> In this land no greater war was ever waged,
> nor did such a slaughter ever surpass that one. (Item 18.60–65)

Geoffrey Gaimar's description is even more succinct: "There so many were slain / I think it will be told forever" (Item 19.3527–28).

The majority of our sources are one way or another associated with the English victors, and they speak mainly to the uncountable losses suffered by Anlaf and his allies. The independent record in the *Annals of Ulster*, however, makes clear that the casualties were staggering on both sides of the fight:

> A huge war, lamentable and horrible, was cruelly waged between the Saxons and Norsemen. Many thousands of Norsemen beyond number died although King Anlaf escaped with a few men. While a great number of the Saxons also fell on the other side, Athelstan, king of the Saxons, was enriched by the great victory. (Item 50)

Of the actual course of this battle we can know very little with certainty. The Anglo-Saxon poem describes the battle as taking place "near Brunanburh" (Item 4a.5), but we can only make the roughest guesses about where. The reliability of the Norse source in *Egil's Saga* (Item 25) is questionable in regards to what it reports as the geography of Brunanburh, but there may be at least some measure of truth to its indication that the battle was fought on a field (or heath) near hills or perhaps a ridgeline.[61] This would, at the very least, be in keeping with medieval practice. Coates, in his essay within this volume, studies the folklore and history of the Wirral and is able to speculate that the primary engagement of the battle could have taken place on Bebington Heath, which is a compelling possibility. If there is any truth at all to *Egil's Saga*'s explanation that the site of the battle itself was arranged by common assent between the antagonists — as we have seen, a not wholly improbable possibility once Athelstan had mustered forces to meet with Anlaf — this area might even have been a natural choice. Anlaf's back would have been to the presumably sympathetic Hiberno-Norse settlements on the northern and western coasts. Athelstan's back would have been to the presumably loyal Mercian populations south and east. Those individuals seeking the battle site today might do best to seek out the heath along Red Hill Road. While local legends that the road was *named* for the blood that ran upon it are probably in error, there is nevertheless a decent chance that the paths here indeed ran red in 937.[62]

Whether it began at Bebington Heath or somewhere else in the vicinity of Bromborough, the sources are consistent in reporting that the battle was an all-day affair.[63] According to later stories, the fight actually began long before dawn, when Anlaf attacked the Anglo-Saxon encampment by surprise and killed a bishop there. More legendary accounts explain that this was preceded by Anlaf infiltrating Athelstan's tents disguised as a harper; having discovered the location of the king, he snuck away to prepare the nighttime assault. This plan was thwarted when one of Athelstan's men recognized Anlaf's presence and suggested that the king's tent be moved. The unnamed bishop who was killed simply had the misfortune of arriving later and pitching his own tent in the vacated spot. Another more fantastical tradition has Athelstan losing his sword at dawn under the press of his enemies on the field. Praying for help, Athelstan miraculously is delivered a sword from God which he uses to help rout his enemies. Many of these tales come together and are transferred down through the histories through William of Malmesbury's influential account (Item 17).

In *The Chronicle of Crowland* (Item 46), once attributed to Ingulf, the battlefield is described as being divided: Athelstan leads his loyal West Saxon forces against Anlaf's army of Hiberno-Norse, while Turketul leads the Mercian forces and the Londoners against Con-

---

[61] On the geographic unreliability of *Egil's Saga*, which has too often been the primary source for individuals aiming to locate Brunanburh, see Ian McDougall, "Discretion and Deceit," and Kelly's essay in this volume, pp. 305–14.

[62] The road instead seems to be named for the local red sandstone; see Harding's essay in this volume, p. 354.

[63] Indeed, it was miraculously so in Items 11 and 14.

stantine's army of Scots.[64] Hours into the fight, Turketul, with the help of a warrior named Singrin, pierces deeply into the allied forces and "Constantine" — if the tale has any basis in reality it ought rather to have been the *son* of Constantine — is killed. The Scots surrender, and the Hiberno-Norse are thus put to flight with Athelstan's men rushing after them. According to the poem in the *ASC*, Anlaf, after a long and bloody run, is able to reach the water and a waiting ship at a place called "Dingesmere" (Item 4a.54). From there he manages to escape to the sea "with a little band" (Item 4a.34; see also Item 50.3). The assumption has always been that it is Anlaf Guthfrithson who is so described, but the *ASC* is actually unspecific on the matter. William of Malmesbury's old poem also reports Anlaf's escape from the field — "alone of what were recently so many thousands," he writes (Item 17.me32) — but in his case he specifies the fleeing king to be Anlaf Sihtricson (Item 17.pr1), adding to our uncertainty about the multiple Norse "kings" at the battle named Anlaf (see note 34, above). It is interesting to note, at any rate, that the Irish annals do not report an immediate return of Anlaf Guthfrithson to Ireland; quite to the contrary, he is specifically noted for coming back to Dublin the year after his defeat. His whereabouts in the meantime are not recorded. Though the reliability of chronicle dates is subject to scrutiny, this could be another clue to the possibility that it was actually Sihtricson who fled the field via Dingesmere, for which Harding suggests two primary locations: Meols and Heswall, of which the latter may have the better claim due to its relative shelter on the Dee.[65] Regardless which Anlaf fled the field by this means, however, we can be sure that most of the remainder of the allied forces were probably forced to flee the battle by land. Some, if we believe *Egil's Saga*, fled south and west (see note to Item 25.157). Others probably beat a hasty retreat the way they had come: up the Roman roads toward Northumbria and Scotland. It is perhaps pertinent in this latter regard that such a path would immediately proceed across the plains at the foot of the Lyme, the location of the battle perhaps intended by the cryptic reference in the *Annals of Clonmacnoise* (see note to Item 52.4).

*Who*

Though the day's dead could not be counted, the sources do take note of a striking number of royalty who lost their lives. The *ASC* poem cites five kings and seven earls (Item 4a.28–32). Another recension of the *ASC* raises the count to eight earls (Item 12.3). William of Malmesbury later ups the ante further, listing among the dead "Constantine, king of the Scots, a man of treacherous spirit and vigorous old age, as well as five kings, twelve earls, and nearly the entire barbarian horde" (Item 17.pr31–34). Constantine, at least, certainly outlived Brunanburh: he abdicated the throne of Scotland in 943 and retired to religion at St. Andrews, a correction that Walter Bower is quick to point out in his account (Item 49.64–71). William appears to have mistaken what other sources make clear: Constantine's son, not Constantine himself, was among the dead at Brunanburh (see, e.g., Item 4a.42). The fate of King Owain of Strathclyde is not given in the sources, but it is quite possible that he, too, died on the field at Brunanburh; as Smyth observes, "no record survives" of him

[64] The heroic acts of Turketul, who would later become abbot of Croyland, are almost assuredly the spurious insertions of over-enthusiastic Croyland scribes. Likewise, the chronicle's description of him as Athelstan's "chancellor" is rather unlikely to be accurate.

[65] Guthfrithson's return is separately reported for late 938 in both the *Annals of Ulster* and *Annals of the Four Masters* (s.a. 936 [=938]). For Harding's discussion of Dingesmere, see pp. 355–62.

after this point.[66] The same is true of King Anlaf Cenncairech of Limerick. The anonymous *Eulogium historiarum* informs us that "Two nephews of King Athelstan also died there, namely Ælfwine and Æthelwyn" (Item 43.4). Walter Bower adds "Eligenius, subking of the Deirans" (Item 49.56–57). Our largest list of the dead comes from the *Annals of Clonmacnoise* (Item 52), which records the deaths of two sons of Sihtric named Sihtfrith and Audgisl, Anlaf the Fool (perhaps Anlaf Cenncairech of Limerick?), Máel-Muire the son of Cossa-Nara, Máel-Ísu, Gibhleachán the king of the Hebrides, Cellach the prince of Scotland, Hárekr Bárdarsson, Illugi the Stout, and Ívarr the prince of Denmark. Whether we can accept the accuracy of such a specific list, it clearly speaks to the lingering memory that Brunanburh was a monumental battle, bringing together a "who's who" of the British Isles if not much of northern Europe. It was, in this respect, not unlike the Troy that so many of the battle's participants no doubt believed lay in their own ancestral past: a contest of civilizations that left seemingly no one untouched.

Couched in such terms, the apparent absence of the Welsh from the field is striking. We cannot be certain of much about the Battle of Brunanburh — though we are certain of much more now than we were only a few years ago when this project began — but there is simply no certain record of their participation in an event that they ought, by all rights, to have taken part in.[67] Whether *Armes Prydein Vawr* (Item 1) was written in the years immediately preceding Brunanburh or a few short years later, its anti-English sentiment no doubt would have rung true for many of the Welsh at the time of the battle. Its vision of a grand anti-English alliance that would drive the Anglo-Saxons to the sea appears to be precisely in line with the alliance that Anlaf musters to Brunanburh. And that battle almost certainly happened on the Wirral, right on the doorstep of Wales. Brunanburh was, as near as we can tell, a close-fought engagement. Had the Welsh entered the fray, assaulting the Mercian border and drawing just a fraction of Athelstan's forces to shore up his flank, the battle might well have gone against the English. That they did not do so remains a lingering mystery, though a few explanatory theories present themselves. Beginning in 927, Athelstan had forced the Welsh kings to submit to his overlordship, which was clearly a chafing point for the poet behind *Armes Prydein Vawr*, and one might suppose that the kings simply did not feel confident enough in Anlaf's chances to break their oaths to the king of Wessex. Alternatively, it could be that Constantine refused to allow them a place in the alliance given their involvement in Athelstan's campaign into Scotland in 934: we know that Kings Hywel Dda of Deheubarth, Idwal Foel of Gwynedd, and Morgan ab Owain (Morgan Hen) of Morgannwg were compelled to march north alongside the Anglo-Saxon forces, a wound perhaps too recent to be set aside. One can only hope that further study of this important era will help to shed light on the matter.

---

[66] Smyth, *Scandinavian York and Dublin*, 2.40. See also Campbell, *Battle of Brunanburh*, p. 44n6.

[67] *Egil's Saga* records the presence of two "earls" at the battle named Hring and Adils who may be identified as being Welsh but quite possibly represent the agglomeration of other events onto the more famous Battle of Brunanburh (see note to Item 25.14). This same kind of process is almost assuredly behind the implausible Devonshire tradition that Axminster was founded by King Athelstan in honor of seven earls who died fighting the Danes at Calesdown (!) in 937 (see Worth, *History of Devonshire*, p. 60).

### THE IMPORTANCE OF BRUNANBURH

The Battle at Brunanburh lodged long in the minds of the participants, and there was no question that it was a momentous occasion for Athelstan in particular. He had faced a mighty alliance drawn from his enemies all across the Isles, and he had beaten them. Never again would he face such a threat, and his self-appointed role as king of a united Britain — more or less a modern England, in other words — was at last secure. As Sarah Foot has persuasively argued, his was a land not of separate West Saxons, East Saxons, and Mercian Angles, but of one "imagined community," a new identity envisioned by Alfred and at last made real by their victorious unity beneath King Athelstan.[68] Quite rightly Dumville thus sums up the king's importance with the simple statement that at Brunanburh Athelstan "became the father of mediaeval and modern England."[69]

The anonymous poet behind *Rex pius Athelstan*, likely writing in the immediate aftermath of Brunanburh, seizes the moment to compare the victorious king to the Old Testament, martial figure of Joshua, who had finally conquered the Promised Land for God's chosen people:

> O devout King Athelstan, famed across the widespread orb,
> whose glory thrives and whose renown endures everywhere,
> whom God made king of the English, resting on the foundation
> of the throne, and ruler over earthly beings,
> clearly so that this king himself, strong in war,
> might conquer defiant kings, treading upon their arrogant necks. (Item 3.1–6)

The poet here references the story of Israel's final defeat of the five kings of the Amorites, where Joshua has the defeated leaders of Canaan brought forth and instructs his men to "go and set your feet on the necks of these kings" before he executes them (Joshua 10:24). The association of Athelstan with Joshua is an obviously flattering one for both king and country, as it also associates the English with God's chosen people, the Israelites. At the same time, the particular biblical reference is strikingly fitting given the five young kings of Athelstan's enemies who were slain on the field at Brunanburh according to the *ASC* (Item 4a.28–30). Similar sentiments comparing these two unmarried warriors of faith, Athelstan and the Israelite leader who would in time become one of the famed "Nine Worthies" of the Middle Ages, quickly propagated (e.g., Items 10.9, 11.23–24).[70] Athelstan, whose royal styles after Brunanburh almost invariably mention God's support for his kingship, could hardly be faulted if he saw a future for himself in which his memory would be held akin to Joshua's,

---

[68] Foot, "Where English Becomes British," pp. 127–28; Foot here argues for the identity thus forged to be termed "British" rather than "English," an interesting but uncertain distinction when viewed across the sources. See also her "Making of *Angelcynn*," pp. 27–37, and "Remembering," pp. 197–99.

[69] Dumville, *Wessex and England*, p. 171.

[70] Both men also appear to have been childless, though the late twelfth-century *Liber Eliensis* (ed. Blake, p. 292) records an otherwise unknown "Æðida filia regis Æðelstani" [Ethida daughter of King Athelstan]. On the forces both political and personal that might have encouraged Athelstan's lack of an heir, see Dumville, *Wessex and England*, pp. 150–51.

> like the composition of a sweet smell made by the art of a perfumer: His remembrance shall be sweet as honey in every mouth, and as music at a banquet of wine. He was directed by God unto the repentance of the nation, and he took away the abominations of wickedness. And he directed his heart towards the Lord, and in the days of sinners he strengthened godliness. (Ecclesiasticus 49:1–4)

In light of such facts, it is not easy, especially on reading the repeated accounts of both Athelstan's battle-won glory and his devout piety contained in the sources collected here, to overemphasize the importance of Brunanburh, especially within the hard political realities of the time.[71]

At the same time, while it is true that Athelstan would control the whole of Britain until the end of his reign, that end came just three short years later. His eighteen-year-old brother Edmund, who had fought at Brunanburh, took up the throne and almost at once found himself under attack. Just as Athelstan in 934 had chosen the moment when the Hiberno-Norse and the Strathclyde Britons were weakened by the tumult of succession to strike his great northern campaign, so Anlaf, his Northumbrian claims far from forgotten, chose the succession of 940 to re-engage on British shores. Whatever his destination had been in 937, in this year his force struck out for York directly, and the city opened its gates wide to him, apparently without so much as a skirmish. Northumbria in hand, Anlaf blitzed south, crossing the Humber and raiding as far as Northampton. By the end of the year, he made terms with the young English king that effectively reestablished the Danelaw. It would take Edmund some four or five years to restore what Athelstan had won, and even then the struggles in the north would continue for generations, if not centuries.

The importance of Brunanburh, however, lies not in the land gains under Athelstan that were solidified — if transiently so — on that battlefield. To the contrary, Brunanburh was remembered as a rousing call for a nation. What Athelstan won in 937 was more than a kingdom of soil, it was a kingdom of the heart and mind: those who followed him to the throne ruled not as kings of Wessex, but as kings of Britain. Alfred the Great might have dreamed of a national entity we might call "England," but the battle had made it real.

It is strange, therefore, that Brunanburh has often been relegated to a footnote, an easily forgotten point on the marching timeline toward 1066 and the linguistically influential defeat of the English king Harold Godwinson by the Norman duke William the Bastard at Hastings, which eclipses so much of what came before it. This is strange, but it is strangely fitting, too: less than 130 years after the Battle of Brunanburh, what William conquers is no longer a realm in the making. Within only a few generations of Athelstan, the nation of England, the vision and the victory of Athelstan, had been forged.

By the later Middle Ages, only a couple of centuries after what Henry of Huntingdon had called "the greatest of battles" (Item 18.13), the details of the Battle of Brunanburh were fading. It was a marginalization wrought of time and shifting political power structures, but it was never complete. Though its location, its key figures, and even its name were being lost, the perilousness of the moment that Brunanburh represented was never forgotten. In the fourteenth-century *Stanzaic Guy of Warwick*, for instance, as the king faces Anlaf and an alliance that over time had become an army of Danes and a mighty and horrible African giant led deep into the south of England, Athelstan laments to his parliament at Winchester:

---

[71] On the Old Testament as a model for medieval kings, see Judith McClure, "Bede's Old Testament Kings."

> If he overcomes us in battle
> he will slay us all without doubt
> and destroy all our people.
> Then shall England evermore
> live in thralldom and in woe
> unto the world's end. (Item 37.2863–68)

Anglo-Norman sources had brought to long-dead Athelstan a new setting for the greatest of battles, and a new hero in Guy of Warwick to win a David-like victory, but the threat to England's existence remained the same. Whether imagined as unfolding across the *ASC*'s "slaughter-field" between armies (Item 4b.43), upon the deliberately pre-staked field of *Egil's Saga*, or in the relatively humane arrangement of a single combat as in the romantic vision of the *Stanzaic Guy of Warwick*, in one day, on one field, the fate of a nation was determined.

# ACCOUNTS OF THE BATTLE
## Texts and Translations

## ACCOUNTS OF THE BATTLE (TEXTS)

### 1. *ARMES PRYDEIN VAWR*

**Welsh**
**927–950 CE**

Dygogan awen — dygobryssyn;
maraned a meued a hed genhyn,
a phennaeth ehelaeth a ffraeth vnbyn,
a gwedy dyhed, anhed ym pop mehyn.
Gwyr gwychyr yn trydar, Kasnar degyn,
escut yg gofut, ryhyt diffyn,
gwaethylgwyr hyt Gaer Weir gwasgarawt allmyn.
Gwnahawnt goruoled gwedy gwehyn
a chymot Kymry a gwyr Dulyn.
Gwydyl Iwerdon, Mon, a Phrydyn,
Cornyw a Chludwys eu kynnwys genhyn.
Atporyon uyd Brython pan dyorfyn.
Pell dygoganhet amser dybydyn,
teyrned a bonhed eu gorescyn,
gwyr Gogled yg kynted yn eu kylchyn;
ym perued eu racwed y discynnyn.

Dysgogan Myrdin — kyferuydyn
yn Aber Perydon meiryon mechtëyrn,
a chyny bei vn reith, lleith a gwynyn.
O vn ewyllis bryt yd ymwrthuynnyn.
Meiryon eu tretheu dychynnullyn;
yg ketoed Kymry nat oed a telhyn.
Yssyd wr dylyedawc a lefeir hyn.
Ny dyffei a talei yg keithiwet.

Mab Meir, mawr a eir! Pryt na tharder
rac pennaeth Saesson ac eu hoffed?
Pell bwynt kechmyn y Wrtheyrn Gwyned!
Ef gyrhawt allmyn y alltuded.
Nys arhaedwy neb. Nys dioes dayar.
Ny wydynt py treiglynt ym pop aber.
Pan prynassant Danet trwy fflet called
gan Hors a Hegys, oed yng eu ryssed,
eu kynnyd bu y wrthym yn anuonhed.

## Accounts of the Battle (Translations)

### 1. *The Great Prophecy of Britain* See pp. 155–70

Inspiration prophesies — they will hasten;
treasure and wealth and peace with us,
and extensive dominion and ready chieftains,
and after strife, settlement in every place.
Courageous men in battle, mighty like Casnar,
swift in (battle's) hardship, stubborn in defence,
warriors (from) as far as Caer Weir will scatter foreigners.
They will bring about rejoicing after devastation
and reconciliation of the Cymry and the men of Dublin.
The Irish of Ireland, Anglesey, and Scotland,
the Cornish and the men of Strathclyde will be welcomed among us.
The Britons will rise again when they prevail.
Long was prophesied the time when they will come,
rulers by right of descent taking their possession,
men of the North in a place of honor around them;
in the center of their van they will advance.

Myrddin prophesies — they will meet
in Aber Peryddon agents of a "Great King,"
and though it be not in the same way, they will (all) lament death.
With a single will they will join battle.
The agents will collect their taxes;
in the treasuries of the Cymry was nothing they would pay.
It is a high-born man who says this.
No one would come who would pay under compulsion.

Son of Mary, great the Word! How is it that they do not burst forth
from the rule of the Saxons and their boasting?
Far off may the shitheads of Gwrtheyrn Gwynedd be!
The foreigners will be driven into exile.
No one will have them. They will have no land.
They will not know why they wander in every river mouth.
When they purchased Thanet with cunning falsehood
with Hors and Hengist, their power was constrained,
their gain at our expense, unworthy.

Gwedy rin dilein,  keith y mynuer.
Dechymyd meddawt  mawr wirawt o ved.
Dechymyd aghen  agheu llawer.
Dechymyd anaeleu  dagreu gwraged.
Dychyfroy etgyllaeth  pennaeth lletfer.
Dechymyd tristit  byt a ryher.
Pan uyd kechmyn  Danet an teyrned,
gwrthottit Trindawt  dyrnawt a bwyller —
y dilein gwlat Vrython  a Saesson yn anhed.
Poet kynt eu reges  yn alltuded
no mynet Kymry  yn diffröed.

Mab Meir, mawr a eir!  Pryt nas terdyn,
Kymry, rac goeir  breyr ac vnbyn?
Kyneircheit, kyneilweit  — vn reith cwynyn;
vn gor vn gyghor  vn eissor ynt.
Nyt oed yr mawred  nas lleferynt,
namyn yr hebcor goeir  nas kymodynt.
Y Dduw a Dewi  yd ymorchymynynt.
Talet, gwrthodet  flet y allmyn.
Gwnaent wy aneireu,  eisseu trefdyn.
Kymry a Saesson  kyferuydyn
y am lan ymtreulaw  ac ymwrthryn
o diruawr vydinawr  pan ymprofyn.
Ac am allt — lafnawr  a gawr a gryn,
ac am Gwy — geir kyfyrgeir  y am peurllyn,
a lluman adaw,  agarw discyn,
a mal bwyt balaon  Saesson syrthyn.
Kymry kynyrcheit  kyfun dullyn,
blaen wrth von granwynyon  kyfyng oedyn.
Meiryon, ygwerth eu geu,  yn eu creu creinhyn,
Eu bydin ygwaetlin  yn eu kylchyn.
Ereill ar eu traet  trwy goet kilhyn.
Trwy uwrch y dinas  ffoxas ffohyn.
Ryfel heb dychwel  y tir Prydyn.
Attor trwy law gyghor  mal mor llithryn.

Meiryon Kaer Geri  difri cwynant.
Rei y dyffryn a bryn  nys dirwadant —
y Aber Perydon  ny mat doethant.
anaeleu tretheu  dychynullant.
Naw vgein canhwr  y discynnant.
Mawr watwar! Namyn petwar,  nyt atcorant.
Dyhed y eu gwraged  a dywedant.
Eu crysseu yn llawn creu  a orolchant.
Kymry kyneircheit,  eneit dichwant,
gwyr Deheu, eu tretheu  a amygant.

After secret destruction, slaves in a crown.
Drinking of mead means great drunkenness.
Many a death means need.
Women's tears mean affliction.
Oppressive rule brings about grief.
A world that is overturned means sadness.
When the shitheads of Thanet will be our rulers,
let the Trinity ward off the blow that is intended —
to destroy the land of the Britons, with the Saxons in occupation.
May their departure into exile be sooner
than the Cymry becoming homeless.

Son of Mary, great the Word! How is it they did not burst forth,
the Cymry, because of the infamy of lord and chieftains?
Followers, leaders — in the same way they complain;
they are of one song, one counsel, one nature.
It would not be out of pride that they would not speak of it,
but to avoid infamy that they would not make peace.
To God and Dewi they commend themselves.
Let Him repay, let Him repel the cunning of the foreigners.
Let them perform shameful acts, lacking a dwelling place.
The Cymry and Saxons will meet
upon a bank to destroy and attack one another
with huge armies when they contend with one another.
And on a hill — blades and battlecry and thrusting,
and on the Wye — shout against shout upon the shining water,
and dropping of banners, fierce attacking,
and Saxons will fall as food for wild beasts.
The followers of the Cymry will line up as one,
front to rear the palecheeks would be constrained.
The agents, as payment for their deceit, will wallow in their blood,
their army in a flood of blood around them.
Others on foot will retreat through the wood.
Through the ramparts of the fortification the "foxes" will flee.
War will not return to the land of Britain.
Through wretched counsel, they will slip back again like the sea.

The agents of Cirencester will bitterly lament.
Some, in valley and on hill, will not deny it —
it was not fortunate that they came to Aber Peryddon.
The taxes they will collect — affliction.
Nine score hundred men will attack.
Great mockery! Except for four, they will not return.
A tale of strife they will tell to their wives.
They will wash their shirts full of blood.
The followers of the Cymry, reckless of their lives,
men of the South, will fight for their taxes.

Llym llifeit llafnawr   llwyr y lladant.
Ny byd y vedyc   mwyn or a wnaant.
Bydinoed Katwaladyr   kadyr y deuant.
Ry drychafwynt Kymry!   Kat a wnaant.
Lleith anoleith   ry dygyrchassant.
Yg gorffen eu tretheu   agheu a wdant.
Ereill arosceill   ry planhassant.
Oes oesseu eu tretheu   nys escorant.

Yg koet ymäes   ym bro ym bryn.
canhwyll yn tywyll   a gerd genhyn —
Kynan yn racwan   ym pop discyn.
Saesson rac Brython,   'Gwae!' a genyn.
Katwaladyr yn baladyr   gan y unbyn,
trwy synhwyr yn llwyr   yn eu dichlyn.
Pan syrthwynt eu clas   dros eu herchwyn,
yg custud a chreu rud   ar rud allmyn,
yg gorffen pop agreith   — anreith degyn.
Seis ar hynt hyt Gaer Wynt   kynt pwy kynt techyn.
Gwyn eu byt wy Gymry   pan adrodynt,
"Ry'n gwarawt y Trindawt   o'r trallawt gynt.
Na chrynet Dyfet   na Glywyssyg."
Nys gwnaho molawt   meiryon mechtëyrn,
na chynhoryon Saesson   keffyn ebryn.
Nys gwnaho medut   meddawt genhyn,
heb talet o dynget   meint a geffyn
o ymdifeit veibon   ac ereill ryn.
Trwy eiryawl Dewi   a seint Prydeyn,
hyt ffrwt ar Lego   ffohawr allmyn.

Dysgogan awen   — dydaw y dyd
pan dyffo Iwys   y vn gwssyl,
vn cor, vn gyghor,   a Lloegyr lloscit,
yr gobeith anneiraw   ar yn prydaw luyd.
A cherd ar alluro   a ffo beunyd.
Ny wyr kud ymda,   cwd a, cwd vyd.
Dychyrchwynt gyfarth   mal arth o vynyd
y talu gwynyeith   gwaet eu hennyd.
Atvi peleitral   dyfal dillyd.
Nyt arbettwy car   corff y gilyd.
Atui pen gaflaw   heb emennyd.
Atui gwraged gwedw   a meirch gweilyd.
Atui ubein vthyr   rac ruthyr ketwyr,
a lliaws llaw amhar   kyn gwascar lluyd.
Kennadeu agheu   dychyferwyd
pan safhwynt galaned   wrth eu hennyd.
Ef dialawr ar gwerth   y treth beunyd,

With keen sharpened blades they will strike to the fullest.
There will be no profit for a doctor from what they will do.
The armies of Cadwaladr, bravely will they come.
May the Cymry rise up! They will do battle.
They have raised up inescapable extinction.
As an end to their taxes, they will know death.
They had afflicted others. . . .
For ever and ever they will not (be able to) round up their taxes.

In wood, in field, in vale, on hill,
a candle in the darkness will go with us —
Cynan rushing forward in every attack.
Before the Britons, the Saxons will sing, "Woe!"
Cadwaladr — a spearshaft among his chieftains,
with wisdom seeking them out thoroughly.
When their people fall for their defender,
in sorrow with red blood on the cheeks of the foreigners,
at the the end of all defiance — immense spoils.
The Saxon will flee straightway to Winchester faster and faster.
Blessed will the Cymry be when they say,
"The Trinity has delivered us from the tribulation of the past.
Let neither Dyfed nor Glywysing tremble."
It will not bring praise to the agents of the "Great King,"
nor the champions of the Saxons, though they be fierce.
Drunkenness will not bring them joy at our expense,
without inevitably paying for as much as they get
in orphaned children and others shivering.
Through the intercession of Dewi and the saints of Britain,
as far as the stream by Caerleon(?) the foreigners will be put to flight.

Inspiration prophesies — the day will come
when the men of Wessex will come to one council,
one song, one counsel, with the Mercian arsonists,
hoping to bring shame upon our handsome hosts.
But the foreigner (will be) on the move and in flight daily.
He knows not where he will journey, where he will go, where he will stay.
They will rush to battle like a bear from the mountain
to avenge the blood of their companions.
There will be spear-thrusts, a fierce flood.
No friend will spare the body of his enemy.
There will be heads split open, without brains.
There will be women widowed and horses riderless.
There will be terrible wailing before the rush of warriors,
and a multitude wounded by hand before the hosts separate.
Messengers will meet Death
when corpses stand up against their companions.
Paying the tax will be avenged daily,

A'r mynych gennadeu   a'r geu luyd.
Dygorfi Kymry   trwy kyfergyr,
yn gyweir, gyteir,   gytson, gytffyd.

Dygorfi Kymry   y peri kat,
a llwyth lliaws gwlat   a gynnullant,
a lluman glan Dewi   a drychafant
y tywyssaw Gwydyl   trwy lieingant.
A gynhon Dulyn   genhyn y safant;
pan dyffont y'r gat   nyt ymwadant.
Gofynnant y'r Saesson   py geissyssant.
Pwy meint o dylyet   o'r wlat a dalyant?
Cw mae eu herwi?   Pan seilyassant?
Cw mae eu kenedloed?   Py vro pan doethant?
Yr amser Gwrtheyrn   genhyn y sathrant.
Ny cheffir o wir   rantir an karant.
Neu vreint an seint   — pyr y saghyssant?
Neu reitheu Dewi   — pyr y torrassant?
Ymgetwynt Gymry   pan ymwelant
nyt ahont allmyn   o'r nen y safant
hyt pan talhont seithweith   gwerth digonsant,
ac agheu diheu   yg werth eu cam.
Ef talhawr o anawr   Garmawn garant
y pedeir blyned   a'r petwar cant.

Gwyr gwychyr gwallt hiryon,   ergyr dofyd,
y dehol Saesson   o Iwerdon dybyd.
Dybi o Lego   lyghes rewyd.
rewinyawt y gat,   rwyccawt lluyd.
Dybi o Alclut gwyr   drut diweir
y dihol o Prydein,   virein luyd.
Dybi o Lydaw   prydaw gyweithyd,
ketwyr y ar katueirch;   ny pheirch eu hennyd.
Saesson o pop parth   y gwarth a'e deubyd.
Ry treghis eu hoes.   Nys dioes eluyd.
Dyderpi agheu   y'r du gyweithyd,
clefyt a dyllid   ac angweryt.
Gwedy eur ac aryant   a chanhwynyd,
boet perth eu disserth   ygwerth eu drycffyd.
Boet mor, boet agor   eu kussulwyr.
Boet creu, boet agheu   eu kyweithyd.
Kynan a Chatwaladyr,   kadyr yn lluyd,
etmyccawr hyt Vrawt   — ffawt ae deubyd —
deu vnben degyn,   dwys eu kussyl,
deu orsegyn Saesson   o pleit Dofyd,
deu hael, deu gedawl   gwlat warthegyd,
deu diarchar barawt,   vnffawt, vnffyd,

and the frequent messengers and the deceitful hosts.
The Cymry will prevail through battle,
ready, united in word, speech, and faith.

The Cymry will prevail to make battle,
and they will gather together the peoples of many countries,
and they will raise the holy banner of Dewi
to lead the Irish with a linen standard.
And the foreigners of Dublin will stand with us;
when they come to the battle, they will not refuse.
They will ask the Saxons what they had been seeking.
How much of the land they hold by right?
Where are their lands? Whence did they set out?
Where are their families? From what region did they come?
Since the time of Gwrtheyrn do they oppress us.
The patrimony of our kinsmen will not be got by right.
Or the privileges of our saints — why have they trampled upon them?
Or the rights of Dewi — why have they destroyed them?
The Cymry will take care when they come together
that the foreigners will not go from the place where they stand
until they pay seven times the value of what they have done,
with certain death as payment for their wrong.
Garmon's kinsmen will be repaid with vigor
for the four hundred and four years.

Courageous long-haired men, lords of blows,
will come from Ireland to expel the Saxons.
From Lego will come a spirited fleet.
It will wreak destruction in battle, it will tear apart hosts.
From Alclud will come reckless loyal men
to expel them from Britain, splendid hosts.
From Brittany will come a handsome company,
warriors on warhorses; they will not spare their adversaries.
The Saxons — from every side shame will come to them.
Their time has passed away. They have no territory.
Death will befall the black company,
sickness and flux and sorrow.
After gold and silver and adornments,
let a thicket be their retreat as payment for their bad faith.
Let sea, let anchor be their counselors.
Let blood, let death be their companions.
Cynan and Cadwaladr, with fine hosts,
will be praised until Judgment Day — good fortune will come to them —
two mighty chieftains, profound their counsel,
two tramplers of Saxons on the side of God,
two generous ones, two noble cattle-raiders of a country,
two ready fearless ones, of one fortune, one faith,

deu erchwynawc Prydein    mirein luyd,
deu arth nys gwna gwarth    kyfarth beunyd.

Dysgogan derwydon    meint a deruyd:
o Vynaw hyt Lydaw    yn eu llaw yt vyd.
O Dyuet hyt Danet    wy bieiuyd.
o Wawl hyt Weryt    hyt eu hebyr.
Llettawt eu pennaeth    tros Yrechwyd.
Attor ar gynhon    Saesson ny byd.
Atchwelwynt Wydyl    ar eu hennyd.
Ry drychafwynt Gymry    kadyr gyweithyd,
bydinoed am gwrwf    a thwrwf milwyr,
a theyrned Dews    ry gedwys eu ffyd.
Iwis y pop llyghes;    tres a deruyd,
a chymot Kynan    gan y gilyd.
Ny alwawr gynhon    yn gynifwyr,
namyn kechmyn Katwaladyr    a'e gyfnewitwyr.
Eil Kymro llawen    llafar a uyd.
Am ynys gymwyeit    — heit a deruyd.
Pan safhwynt galaned    wrth eu hennyd
hyt yn Aber Santwic,    swynedic vyd —
allmyn ar gychwyn    y alltudyd,
ol wrth ol attor    ar eu hennyd,
Saesson wrth agor  ar vor peunyd.
Kymry gwenerawl    hyt Vrawt goruyd.
Na cheisswynt lyfrawr    nac agawr brydyd;
arymes yr ynys hon    namyn hyn ny byd!
Iolwn-i Ri a grewys    nef ac eluyd:
poet tywyssawc Dewi    y'r kynifwyr.
Yr yg, Keli kaer    a'm Duw yssyd.
Ny threinc, ny dieinc,    nyt ardispyd,
ny wyw, ny wellyc,    ny phlyc, ny chryd.

### 2. *CARTA DIRIGE GRESSUS*

**Latin 927?**

Carta, dirige gressus
per maria nauigans
tellurisque spacium
ad regis palacium.

Rege primum salutem
ad reginam, clitonem,
claros quoque comites,
armigeros milites.

two defenders of Britain, splendid hosts,
two bears to whom daily battle brings no shame.

Wise men prophesy all that will happen:
from Manaw to Brittany will be in their hands.
From Dyfed to Thanet it will be theirs,
from the Wall to the Firth of Forth to their estuaries.
Their chieftaincy will spread across Erechwydd.
No return will there be for the Saxon foreigners.
The Irish will return to their companions.
May the Cymry rise up, a brave company,
armies about the ale and the tumult of warriors,
and God's rulers, who have kept their faith.
The men of Wessex in all their ships; the uproar will end,
and Cynan will be in concord with his fellows.
The foreigners will not be called warriors,
but Cadwaladr's shitheads and his pedlars.
The descendants of a Welshman will be merry of speech.
As for the tormentors of the island — a swarm of bees that will pass away.
When corpses stand up against their companions
as far as Aber Santwic, blessed will it be —
the foreigners setting out for exile,
one after the other, back again to their companions,
the Saxons at anchor on the sea daily.
The devout Cymry will be victorious until Judgment Day.
Let them not seek a bookman or a greedy poet;
there will be no prophecy for this island but this!
Let us pray to the Lord who created heaven and earth:
let Dewi be prince of the warriors.
Despite adversity, there is a heavenly fortress and my God.
He will not die, He will not escape, He will not retreat,
He will not wither, He will not reject, He will not waver, He will not diminish.

## **2. *Letter, Direct Your Steps***

**See pp. 170–72**

Letter, direct your steps
sailing across the seas
and an expanse of land,
to the king's burh.

Direct first of all your best wishes
to the queen, the prince,
the distinguished ealdormen as well,
the arm-bearing thegns.

Quos iam regit cum ista
perfecta Saxonia:
uiuit rex Æþelstanus
per facta gloriosus!

Ille, Sictric defuncto,
armat tum in prelio
Saxonum exercitum
per totum Bryttanium.

Constantinus rex Scottorum
aduolat Bryttanium:
Saxonum regem saluando,
fidelis seruitio.

Dixit rex Æþelstanus
per Petri preconia:
sint sani, sint longeui
saluatoris gratia!

### 3. *REX PIUS ATHELSTAN*

**Latin**
**937–939**

Rex pius AEÐELSTAN, patulo famosus in orbe,
Cuius ubique uiget Gloria lausque manet,
Quem Deus Angligenis solii fundamine nixum
Constituit regem Terrigenisque ducem,
Scilicet ut ualeat reges Rex ipse feroces
Vincere bellipotens, Colla superba terens.
Quisquis amore fluens rutilans hoc luce uolumen
Perspicis, eximia Dogmata sacra lege
Quod rex aureolis sacro spiramine fusus
Ornauit titulis Gemmigerisque locis,
Quodque libens Christi ecclesiae de more dicauit
Atque agiae sophiae Nobilitauit ouans.
Hoc quoque scematicis ornarier ora lapillis
Auxit ubique micans Floribus ut uariis.
Quisque sitit ueniat cupiens haurire fluenta:
Dulcia mella gerens Inueniat latices.
Ergo greges pastorque sacrae Dorobernicus aulae
Se caueant, ne quid Fraus inimica gerat:
Hunc quisquis textum diuino fonte refertum
Tollere praesumat, Finetenus pereat.

Whom he now rules with this
England [now] made whole:
King Athelstan lives
glorious through his deeds!

He, with Sihtric having died,
in such circumstances arms for battle
the army of the English
throughout all Britain.

Constantine, king of the Scots,
hastens to Britain:
by supporting the king of the English
[he is] loyal in his service.

King Athelstan said [these things]
through the announcements of Peter:
may they be well, live long,
through the Savior's grace!

### 3. *Devout King Athelstan*

**See pp. 172–73**

O devout King Athelstan, famed across the widespread orb,
whose glory thrives and whose renown endures everywhere,
whom God made king of the English, resting on the foundation
of the throne, and ruler over earthly beings,
clearly so that this king himself, strong in war,
might conquer defiant kings, treading upon their arrogant necks.
Whosoever examines this book flowing with love
and glowing with light, read its excellent sacred doctrines,
this book which the king, brimming with the holy spirit,
adorned with golden headings and bejeweled settings,
and which, according to custom, he gladly granted to Christ Church
and, rejoicing, ennobled it with sacred wisdom.
He also enhanced it everywhere by ornamenting its edges
splendidly with wrought stones as if with diverse blossoms.
Let him come, whosoever thirsts, longing to drink from these streams,
let him, bearing sweet honey, discover these waters.
Therefore let the flock and shepherd of the holy court of Canterbury
beware, lest inimical fraud bear its fruit:
Let whosoever presumes to steal this book,
filled at the divine font, be annihilated.

### 4A. *ANGLO-SAXON CHRONICLE* [VERSION A], *BATTLE OF BRUNANBURH*

**Old English**
**ca. 955**

**937.**

Her Æþelstan cyning,   eorla dryhten,
beorna beahgifa,   and his broþor eac,
Eadmund æþeling,   ealdorlangne tir
geslogon æt sæcce   sweorda ecgum
ymbe Brunanburh.   Bordweal clufan,
heowan heaþolinde   hamora lafan,
afaran Eadweardes,   swa him geæþele wæs
from cneomægum   þæt hi æt campe oft
wiþ laþra gehwæne   land ealgodon,
hord, and hamas.   Hettend crungun.
Sceotta leoda   and scipflotan
fæge feollan.   Feld dunnade
secga swate,   siðþan sunne up
on morgentid,   mære tungol
glad ofer grundas,   Godes candel beorht,
eces Drihtnes,   oð sio æþele gesceaft
sah to setle.   Þær læg secg mænig
garum ageted,   guma norþerna
ofer scild scoten,   swilce Scittisc eac,
werig, wiges sæd.   Wesseaxe forð
ondlongne dæg   eorodcistum
on last legdun   laþum þeodum,
heowan herefleman   hindan þearle
mecum mylenscearpan.   Myrce ne wyrndon
heardes hondplegan   hæleþa nanum
þæra þe mid Anlafe   ofer æra gebland
on lides bosme   land gesohtun,
fæge to gefeohte.   Fife lægun
on þam campstede   — cyningas giunge,
sweordum aswefede —   swilce seofene eac
eorlas Anlafes,   unrim heriges,
flotan and Sceotta.   Þær geflemed wearð
Norðmanna bregu,   nede gebeded
to lides stefne   litle weorode.
Cread cnear on flot,   cyning ut gewat
on fealene flod.   Feorh generede.
Swilce þær eac se froda   mid fleame com
on his cyþþe norð;   Costontinus,
har hilderinc,   hreman ne þorfte
mæca gemanan:   he wæs his mæga sceard,
freonda gefylled   on folcstede,
beslagen æt sæcce,   and his sunu forlet

## 4A. *ANGLO-SAXON CHRONICLE* [VERSION A], *BATTLE OF BRUNANBURH*

**See pp. 174–77**

**937.**

Here King Athelstan, lord of earls,
ring-giver of men, and his brother also,
Prince Edmund, age-long glory
won in strife with swords' edges
near Brunanburh. They split the shieldwall,
hewed the battle-wood with hammer-beaten blades,
Edward's sons, as it was their
birthright that they often in battle
against every enemy defended the land,
treasure, and homes. Their enemies perished.
The men of the Scots and the men of the sea,
fated, they fell. The field darkened
with the blood of men, from the rising of the sun
in the morningtime, when that glorious light
glided over the ground, bright candle of God,
of the eternal Lord, until that noble creation
sank to rest. There lay many warriors
destroyed by spears, men of the north
shot over shield, and so, too, the Scots,
weary, sated with war. The West Saxons thence
the length of the day in troops
pursued the hated peoples,
hewed the fugitive harshly from behind
with mill-sharpened swords. The Mercians did not deny
hard hand-play to any heroes
who with Anlaf over the sea-surge
in the belly of a ship had sought land,
fated to fight. Five lay still
on that battlefield — young kings
by swords put to sleep — and seven also
of Anlaf's earls, countless of the army,
of sailors and Scotsmen. There was put to flight
the Northmen's chief, driven by need
to the ship's prow with a little band.
He shoved the ship to sea. The king disappeared
on the dark flood. His own life he saved.
So there also the old one came in flight
to his home in the north; Constantine,
that hoary-haired warrior, had no cause to exult
at the meeting of swords: he was shorn of his kin,
deprived of his friends on the field,
bereft in the fray, and his son behind

on wælstowe, wundun forgrunden,
giungne æt guðe. Gelpan ne þorfte,
beorn blandenfeax bilgeslehtes,
eald inwidda, ne Anlaf þy ma.
Mid heora herelafum hlehhan ne þorftun
þæt heo beaduweorca beteran wurdan
on campstede, cumbolgehnastes
garmittinge, gumena gemotes,
wæpengewrixles, þæs hi on wælfelda
wiþ Eadweardes afaran plegodan.
Gewitan him þa Norþmen nægledcnearrum,
dreorig daraða laf, on Dingesmere;
ofer deop wæter Difelin secan,
eft Iraland, æwiscmode.
Swilce þa gebroþer begen ætsamne,
cyning and æþeling, cyþþe sohton,
Wesseaxena land, wiges hremige.
Letan him behindan hræw bryttian
saluwigpadan, þone sweartan hræfn,
hyrnednebban, and þane hasewanpadan:
earn æftan hwit, æses brucan,
grædigne guðhafoc, and þæt græge deor,
wulf on wealde. Ne wearð wæl mare
on þis eiglande, æfre gieta
folces gefylled beforan þissum
sweordes ecgum, þæs þe us secgað bec,
ealde uðwitan, siþþan eastan hider
Engle and Seaxe up becoman.
Ofer brad brimu Brytene sohtan,
wlance wigsmiþas. Wealas ofercoman,
eorlas arhwate, eard begeatan.

on the place of slaughter, with wounds ground to pieces,
too young in battle. He could make no boast,
that gray-haired warrior of the sword-slaughter,
the old deceitful one, no more than could Anlaf.
With the remnant of their army they had no reason to laugh
that they were better in the work of war
on the battlefield, of the clashing of banners,
of the meeting of spears, of the meeting of men,
of the exchange of weapons, when they on the field of death
played with the sons of Edward.
Departed then the Northmen in their nailed ships,
dreary survivors of the spears, on Dingesmere,
over deep water to seek Dublin,
back to Ireland, ashamed in spirit.
Thus the brothers both together,
king and prince, sought their home,
the West-Saxons' land, exultant from war.
They left behind to divide the corpses
the dark-coated one, the black raven,
the horn-beaked one, and the dusk-coated one:
the white-tailed eagle, to enjoy the carrion,
that greedy war-hawk, and that gray beast,
the wolf of the wood. Never was there more slaughter
on this island, never as many
folk felled before this
by the swords' edges, as those books tell us,
old authorities, since here from the east
the Angles and Saxons came ashore.
Over the broad salt-sea they sought Britain,
those proud war-smiths. They overcame the Welsh,
glory-eager earls, and took hold of this land.

**4B. *ANGLO-SAXON CHRONICLE* [VERSION B], *BATTLE OF BRUNANBURH***

**Old English**
**late 10th c.**

**937.** Her

Æþelstan cing,   eorla drihten,
beorna beaggifa,   and his broþor eac,
Eadmund æþeling,   ealdorlangne tir
geslogan æt sake   sweorda ecggum
embe Brunanburh.   Bordweall clufan,
heowan heaðolinda   hamora lafum,
eaforan Eadweardes,   swa him geæþele wæs
fram cneomagum,   þæt hie æt campe oft
wið laðra gehwane   land ealgodan,
hord and hamas.   Hettend crungon,
Scotta leode   and scipflotan
fæge feollan,   feld dennade
secga swate,   siþþan sunne upp
on morgentid,   mære tungol,
glad ofer grundas,   godes candel beorht,
eces drihtnes,   oð seo æþele gesceaft
sah to setle.   Þær læg secg manig
garum forgrunden,   guman norðerne,
ofer scyld sceoten,   swylce Scyttisc eac,
werig, wigges sæd.   Westsexe forð
andlangne dæg   eoredcystum
on last legdon   laðum þeodum,
heowan hereflyman   hindan þearle
mecum mylenscearpum.   Myrce ne wyrndon
heardes handplegan   hæleþa nanum
þara ðe mid Anlafe   ofer eargebland
on lides bosme   land gesohtan,
fæge to gefeohte.   Fife lagon
on ðæm campstede   ciningas geonge,
sweordum aswefede,   swilce seofone eac
eorlas Anlafes,   unrim herges,
flotan and Scotta.   Þær geflymed wearð
Norðmanna brego,   nede gebæded,
to lides stefne;   lytle weorode
cread cnear on flot,   cing ut gewat
on fealone flod,   feorh generede.
Swylce þær eac se froda   mid fleame com
on his cyþþe norð,   Constantinus,
har hilderinc,   hreman ne þorfte
mecea gemanan;   he wæs his maga sceard,
freonda gefylled   on folcstede,
forslegen æt sace,   and his sunu forlet

## 4B. *ANGLO-SAXON CHRONICLE* [VERSION B], *BATTLE OF BRUNANBURH*

**See pp. 174–77**

**937.** In this year,

King Athelstan — earls' lord,
warriors' ring-giver, and his brother also,
Prince Edmund — long-lasting glory
forged at the fighting with swords' edges
around Brunanburh. They cleft the shieldwall,
hewed battle-shields with well-hammered weapons —
Edward's sons, as was natural to them
from their birth, that they in battle often
against every enemy defended the land,
treasure, and homes. Enemies collapsed,
Scotsmen and sailors
fated to die, fell. The field grew dark
with men's blood, after the sun, up
in the morningtide, that splendid light,
glided over the ground — God's bright candle! —
until the eternal Lord's noble creature
sank to its seat. There lay many a man
cut down by spears, Northern men
shot over shields, and Scotsmen also,
weary, sated with warfare. West Saxons in the van
the whole long day held ranks,
harassing the hated hordes as they fled,
hewing them harshly from behind
with well-sharpened swords. Mercians did not refuse
hard hand-play to any warrior
who, with Anlaf, over the surging waves
in the bosom of a ship sought land,
fated to die in the fight. Five lay dead
on that battlefield — young kings
by swords put to sleep — and seven
of Anlaf's earls, unnumbered invaders,
sailors and Scotsmen. There was put to flight
the chief of the Northmen, driven by force
to his ship's stem; with a little band
he shoved the ship onto the sea; the king fled out
onto the dark flood, his own life he saved.
So there also the old one in flight came
to his native land in the north, Constantine;
that gray-haired warrior did not need to boast
of the encounter of swords; he was shorn of kinsmen,
of friends felled on the battlefield,
slain at the fight, and left his son behind

on wælstowe    wundum forgrunden
geongne æt guþe.    Gylpan ne þorfte
beorn blandenfex    billgeslyhtes,
eald inwitta,    ne Anlaf þe ma;
mid heora herelafum    hlihhan ne þorftan
þæt hie beadoweorca    beteran wurdan
on campstede    cumbolgehnastes,
garmittinge,    gumena gemotes,
wæpengewrixles,    þæs hie on wælfelda
wiþ Eadweardes    eaforan plegodan.
Gewitan him þa Norðmenn    nægledcnearrum,
dreorig daroða laf,    on Dyngesmere
ofer deop wæter    Dyflen secean,
eft Iraland,    æwiscmode.
Swylce þa gebroðor    begen ætsomne,
cing and æþeling,    cyþþe sohtan,
Westseaxna land,    wigges hremige.
Letan him behindan    hraw bryttigean
salowigpadan,    þone sweartan hræfn,
hyrnednebban,    and þone hasopadan,
earn æftan hwit,    æses brucan,
grædigne guþhafoc    and þæt græge deor,
wulf on wealde.    Ne wearð wæl mare
on þys eglande    æfre gyta
folces afylled    beforan þyssum
sweordes ecgum,    þæs þe us secggeaþ bec,
ealde uþwitan,    syþþan eastan hider
Engle and Sexe    upp becoman,
ofer brade brimu    Brytene sohtan,
wlance wigsmiþas    Wealas ofercoman,
eorlas arhwate    eard begeaton.

### 5. *GLASWAWT TALIESSIN*

**Welsh**
**late 10th c.**

*Glaswawt Taliessin*: xxiiii a tal

Kennadeu a'm dodynt    mor ynt anuonawc!
Dygawn y'm lletcynt    meint vyg keudawt.
Gnawt rwyf yn heli    — Beli wirawt;
gnawt yscwyt yscawn    ar gefyn yscawt;
gnawt gwyth ac adwyth    o yspydawt — gaer,
  a naw cant maer marwhawt.
Atvyd Mei ar Venei,    crei gyflogawt,
atvyd mwy ar Gonwy, gwynyeith gwnahawt.
Adoer lleith dyrreith,    anaw barawt,
o hëyrn erchwyrn    edyrn dyrnawt.

on the slaughter-field, by wounds cut down,
young in warfare. He could not boast,
that gray-haired warrior, of the sword-fighting —
evil old man! — nor could Anlaf either;
with the remnants of their armies, they could hardly pretend
that they were better in the work of battle,
on the field of combat, at the clashing of standards,
at spear-throwing, at the meeting of men,
at the exchanges of weapons, when they on the field of corpses
with Edward's sons played deadly games.
Then the Northmen left in their well-built boats,
sad survivors of spears, on Dingesmere,
over deep water, Dublin to seek,
back to Ireland, deeply disgraced.
Meanwhile, both brothers together,
king and prince, sought their homeland,
Westsaxons' land, exulting in warfare.
They left behind them to divide the corpses
the dark-plumaged black raven
horn-beaked, and the gray-coated one,
the white-tailed eagle, to share the carnage,
the greedy battle-hawk, and that gray beast,
the woodland wolf. Nor was there greater slaughter
on this island ever yet,
of folk felled, before this
by the sword's edges — as books tell us,
old but full of wisdom — since from the east hither
Angles and Saxons came ashore,
over broad seas sought the Britons,
proud war-smiths overcame the Welshmen,
earls eager for glory took over this land.

## 5. *Taliesin's Verdant Song*

**See pp. 177–82**

*Taliesin's Verdant Song*: worth 24 [points]

Messengers have come to me, how splendid they are!
The whole [preoccupation] of my mind causes me grief:
frequent, an oar in the brine — Beli's drink;
frequent, a light shield in the depth of night;
frequent, ferocity and destruction [emanating] from a fortress of feasting,
  and nine hundred stewards shall perish.
In May, on the Menai, there will be a place of carnage,
on the [River] Conwy there will be more [suffering] that will wreak vengeance.
Chilling the death which arose — ready reward —
by means of savage iron [weapons], an immense blow.

Tri dillyn diachor,   droch drymluawc,
teir llyghes yn aches   arymes kyn Brawt,
teir diwedyd kat   am tri phriawt — gwlat:
gwnahawt bat betrawt —
tri o pop tri tri phechawt —
ac Eryri vre varnhawt.
Llu o Seis, eil o Ynt,   trydyd dygnawt:
yg Kymry yd erhy   gwraged gwed-dawt.
Rac baran Kynan   tan tardawt.
Katwaladyr ae cwyn;
briwhawt bre a brwyn,
gwellt a tho tei, ty tandawt.
Atvyd ryfedawt:
gwr gan verch y vrawt.
Dyfynhyn durawt
o lin Anarawt:
ohonaw y tyfhawt
coch kattybrunawc:
nyt arbet na nawt
na chefynderw na brawt.
Wrth lef corn kadwr
naw cant yn afyrdwl,
O bedrydant dygnawt
dygorelwi lesni   o Laswawt —
ef ret wrth a gawd y geudawt.

## 6. *ANNALES CAMBRIAE*

**Latin**
**late 10th c.**

Annus CCCCXCIV Bellum Brune.

## 7. ÆTHELWEARD, *CHRONICON*

**Latin**
**ca. 980**

Anno etiam in quo imperii functus fuerat stefos Æthestan rex robustissimus, transacti sunt anni a gloriosa incarnatione saluatoris nostri DCCCC, supraque uiginti et sex. Igitur post annos tredecim facta est pugna immanis barbaros contra in loco Brunandune, unde et uulgo usque ad praesens bellum praenominatur magnum. Tum superantur barbarae passim turbae, nec ultra dominari; post quos ultra pellit oceani oris, nec non colla subdunt Scoti, pariterque Picti; uno solidantur Brittannidis arua, undique pax, omniumque foecundia rerum, nec usque ad istas motus adhaesit sine littora Anglorum foedere classicus.

Three trim invincible ones, heavily-laden in the water with hosts,
three fleets in the flood, a tribulation before Judgment,
three battles at dusk for/around three rightful land-rulers:
    death will necessitate a grave —
    all three, three transgressions —
    and will try the high ground of Eryri.
A host of Saxons, the second of Foreigners, the third a cruel one:
in Wales there will remain the widowhood of wives.
Before Cynan's tumult, fire will spread.
    Cadwaladr will scourge them;
    he will trample hill and rushes,
    thatch and the roofs of houses, a house conflagration.
A strange thing shall come to pass:
a man [consorting] with his brother's daughter.
They [the Cymry] shall summon a man of steel
from the line of Anarawd:
from him shall stem
a ruddy one of the battle for the settlement in Brun's region
who will spare neither kin
nor cousin nor brother.
At the call of the warrior's horn
nine hundred [shall be] sad.
Because of the powerful, harsh man
whom the verdancy of the 'Glaswawd' declaimed —
he will swoop on those who inflame his mind.

### 6. *ANNALS OF WALES* See pp. 182–83

**937.** War at Brune.

### 7. ÆTHELWEARD, *CHRONICLE* See p. 183

Nine hundred years plus twenty-six more had passed from the glorious Incarnation of our Savior when the all-powerful King Athelstan assumed the crown of empire. Thirteen years later there was a massive battle against barbarians at Brunandun which is still called "the great war" to the present day by the common folk. The barbarian hordes were then overcome on all sides and they held sway no longer. Afterwards he drove them from the shores of the sea and Scots and Picts alike bent their necks. The fields of Britain were joined as one; everywhere there was peace and abundance in all things. No fleet has since moved against these shores and remained without the consent of the English.

### 8. WULFSTAN OF WINCHESTER, *VITA S. ETHELWOLDI*

**Latin**
**ca. 996**

Contigit interea uictoriosissimum regem Ethestanum, quarto anno postquam hostilem paganorum exercitum maxima strage peremit, obisse et fratrem eius Eadmundum pro eo regni gubernacula suscepisse.

### 9. ÆLFRIC OF EYNSHAM, *EPILOGUE TO JUDGES*

**Latin**
**998**

On Engla lande eac oft wæron cyningas sigefæste þurh God, swa swa we secgan gehyrdon. Swa swa wæs Ælfred cining, þe oft gefeaht wið Denan, oþ þæt he sige gewann ond bewerode his leode. Swa gelice Æðelstan, þe wið Anlaf gefeaht ond his firde ofsloh ond aflimde hine sylfne, ond he on sibbe wunuðe siþþan mid his leode. Eadgar, se æðela ond se anræda cining, arærde Godes lof on his leode gehwaer, ealra cininga swiðost ofer Engla ðeode, ond him God gewilde his wiðerwinnan a, ciningas ond eorlas, þæt hi comon him to buton ælcum gefeohte friðes wilniende, him underþeodde to þam þe he wolde, ond he wæs gewurðod wide geond land.

### 10. *ATHELSTAN'S PRAYER*

**Old English**
**ca. 1000**

Æla þu Dryhten æla ðu Ælmihtiga God, æla Cing ealra Cyninga ond Hlaford ealra Waldendra, on þæs mihta wunaþ ælc sige, ond ælc gewin weorþ tobryt, forgif me Drihten þæt þin seo mihtigu hand mines unstrangan heortan gestrangie ond þæt ic þurh þine þa miclan mihte mid handum minum ond mihte stranglice ond werlice ongan mine fynd winnan mæge swa þæt hy on minre gisihþe feallan ond gereosan swa swa gereas Golias ætforan Dauides ansyne þines cnihtes, ond swa swa gereas ond wearþ besenct Faraones folc on þære Readan Sæ ætforan Moyses ansene, ond swa swa feollan Filistei beforan Israela folce, ond swa swa gerias Amaleh ætforan Moisen ond Chananei ætforan Iesu Naue. Swa feallan ond gereosan mine fynd under minum fotum, ond hi ealle samod þurh ænne weg ongan me cumen ond þurh seofan wegas hie fram me gewican. Forbryt Drihten heora wapna ond heora sweord tobrec ond do Drihten þæt hy formeltan on minre gesihþe, swa swa weax mylt fram fyres ansyne, þæt eall eorþan folc wite ond ongyte þæt ofer me is geciged noma ures Drihtnes Hælendes Cristes, ond þæt þin noma, Drihten, sy geweorþad on minum wiþerwinum, þu þe eart Drihten Israela God.

### 11. EADMER OF CANTERBURY, *VITA ODONIS*

**Latin**
**very late 11th c.**

Anno inter haec Domenicae incarnationis nongentesimo tricesimo octauo, regni autem Æthelstani uictoriosissimi regis quarto decimo, congregatus est aduersus regnum Anglorum immensus exercitus paganorum, profanis legibus suis subiugando eneruare, et eneruando uolens annichilare sacratissimas quas Angli seruabant leges

### 8. WULFSTAN OF WINCHESTER, *LIFE OF SAINT ETHELWOLD* See p. 184

Meanwhile it came to pass that Athelstan, the most victorious king, passed away in the fourth year after he had destroyed a hostile army of pagans in a great slaughter, and his brother Edmund assumed from him the guidance of the kingdom.

### 9. ÆLFRIC OF EYNSHAM, *EPILOGUE TO JUDGES* See p. 184

In the land of the Angles kings were also often victorious through God, just as we have heard said. Just so was Alfred the king, who often fought with the Danes, until he won the victory and protected his people. So, too, was Athelstan, who fought with Anlaf and slew his forces and drove him himself to flight, and who remained afterwards in peace with his people. Edgar, the noble and single-minded king, raised the love of God everywhere among his people, more than all other kings of the English nation; and God subdued his adversaries for him, kings and earls, so that they came to him without any struggle, desiring peace, submitted to him as he wished, and he was honored widely throughout the land.

### 10. *ATHELSTAN'S PRAYER* See pp. 185–86

O Lord God Almighty, King of Kings and Lord of Lords, in whose might lies every victory, and through whom every war is crushed, grant to me, Lord, that your might may strengthen my heart so that through your strength and through my hands and powers I may fight well and act manfully, so that my enemies may fall in my sight and may collapse just as Goliath collapsed before David your servant, and just as the people of Pharaoh collapsed in the Red Sea before Moses, and just as the Philistines fell before the people of Israel, and just as Amalek collapsed before Moses and the Canaanites before Joshua. Thus let my enemies collapse beneath my feet, and let them come by one path against me and let them by seven paths run away from me. And may the Lord burst their weapons and break their swords and melt them in my sight, just as wax melts before a flame, so that all the peoples of the earth may know that upon me is placed the name of Our Holy Lord Christ. And so let your name, Lord, be increased among my adversaries, O Lord God of Israel.

### 11. EADMER OF CANTERBURY, *LIFE OF ODA* See pp. 186–88

Meanwhile in the year of the Lord's Incarnation 938, the fourteenth year of the reign of the most victorious King Athelstan, an immense army of pagans assembled against the English kingdom. They wanted to weaken them by subjecting them to their own profane laws, and in weakening them to annihilate the most sacred Christian laws

Christianorum. Quibus nominatus princeps ualida armatorum manu stipatus occurrens, pugnae se dedit, et diutissime ac atrocissime pugnatum utrinque est. Duxerat autem secum in aciem rex sanctum Odonem, eius meritis se multo maxime quam militum copiis confidens hostem uicturum. Dum igitur hinc inde strages grauissima fieret et erumnosa, res luctuosa contigit. Quo etenim rex ipse pugnabat iuxta capulum gladius confractus est, et regem quasi inermem hostibus exposuit.

Inter haec Odo a pugna remotus longiuscule stabat, ore et corde pro salute Christiani exercitus Christo supplicans, et uultum, manus ac lumina caelestibus pro hoc ipso indefessus extendens. Quid itaque rex in tali euentu facere posset fluctuabat. Ut se armaret suorum quemquam exarmare nefas iudicabat. Pars igitur aduersariorum ubi regem fracto ense stare aduertit inermem, fugam quam inire caeperat uersis uultibus in pugnam acriori caede uindicare aggreditur. Tum subito intonat aether a clamore multitudinis, ut Deus succurreret et celeri gressu Odo uenerandus accurreret, uociferantis. Aduolat et quidnam sibi uelit rex a se fieri lassabundus interrogat. Audit et statim regi taliter inquit: 'Quid est hoc? Quo intendis? Ensis tuus in latere tuo integer pendet, et tu eum fractum esse conquereris? Redi ad te; ad uaginam manum extende; exere illum, et ecce dextera Domini erit tecum. Nec formides, quia non prius continget solis occubitus, quam aduersarios Domini tui qui contra te surrexerunt fuga inuoluat aut interitus.' Ad haec quique audientium grandi stupore attoniti, deflexis luminibus uiderunt quem prius non uiderant, ensem in latere regis pendentem. Quem rex in Domino confortatus arripiens, dextra leuaque cunctos occursantes aut debilitauit aut fugauit aut morti funditus tradidit.

Itaque iuxta uerbum famuli Dei factum est ut simul et sol occumberet et regi de hostibus uictoria proueniret. Quid hinc gratiarum, quid laudum, quid uotorum Deo per fidelem seruum suum Odonem, per regem, per uictorem exercitum, per totum regnum quo magnitudo istius uictoriae perlata est, sit persolutum quis enarret? Magnificentia facti docebit audientes, quia non facile quisquam. Gloriosus autem Odo magnae dehinc admirationis apud omnes habitus est, et uere praeclarus Isrelita comprobatus.

## 12. *ANGLO-SAXON CHRONICLE*, CANTERBURY VERSION (F) — Old English, Latin ca. 1100

**938.** Her Æðestan cing (ond Eadmund his broðer) lædde fyrde to Brunanbyri, ond þar gefeht wið Anelaf ond Criste fultumegende sige hæfde (ond þar ofslogan .v. cingas ond .viii. eorlas).

Hic factum est illud magnum et famosum bellum in Brunanbyri. Cum rex Æðestanus (et frater eius Eadmundus) pugnauit contra Anelaf et auxiliante Christo uictoriam cepit (et occiderunt .v. reges et .viii. comite[s] de sociis Anelafi).

kept by the English. Surrounded by a strong band of warriors as he rushed upon the English, their leader threw himself into battle, and for a great while the battle raged savagely on both sides. But the king had led holy Oda with him to the front line, trusting that he would defeat the enemy more through Oda's merits than with an abundance of soldiers. And while there was a most heavy and wretched slaughter all around, a grievous thing happened. The king's sword shattered near the hilt as he was fighting and exposed him as if he were unarmed before his enemies. Meanwhile Oda stood at a distance, removed from the battle, praying to Christ aloud and in his heart for the safety of the Christian army. Without tiring, he raised his face, hands, and eyes to the heavens to this end. The king was uncertain what to do in such an event. He considered it a crime to disarm any of his warriors in order to arm himself. An enemy group noticed where the king stood unarmed with a broken sword, and with their faces turned back to the fight they attacked in order to vindicate with violent murder the flight which they had begun to take. Then the ether thundered suddenly with the clamor of the multitude crying out that God should lend His aid and that the venerable Oda should come forth quickly. He flew forward and, though winded, asked the king what he wanted him to do. He listened and immediately answered the king in this way: "What is this? Why are you upset? Your sword hangs whole by your side, and you complain that is broken? Pull yourself together! Reach out your hand to the scabbard; draw the sword and, behold, the Lord's right hand will be with you. Fear not, because the setting of the sun will not come before flight or destruction overcomes your Lord's enemies who have risen against you." All those listening were thunderstruck in great astonishment at this, and as they turned their eyes they saw what they had not seen before, a sword a hanging by the king's side. Finding comfort in the Lord, the king took hold of the sword and maimed or routed or killed all the attackers left and right without exception.

And so it happened according to the word of God's servant that victory over his enemies came to the king just as the sun set. Who could tell what thanks, praises, and prayers were rendered to God for His faithful servant Oda, the king, the triumphant army, the entire kingdom, when the magnitude of the victory was announced? The magnificence of the deed will instruct those who hear of it, for no person can easily do so. And glorious Oda was afterwards held in great veneration by all and esteemed a truly illustrious Israelite.

## 12. *Anglo-Saxon Chronicle*, Canterbury Version (F) See p. 188

**937.** In this year Athelstan the king (and Edmund, his brother) led the levy to Brunanburh, and there fought against Anlaf and, with Christ helping, had the victory (and there slew five kings and eight earls).

Here happened that great and famous battle at Brunanburh. At that time King Athelstan (and his brother Edmund) fought against Anlaf and with Christ's help took the victory (and they killed five kings and eight earls among Anlaf's allies).

### 13. SYMEON OF DURHAM, *LIBELLUS DE EXORDIO*

**Latin**
**1104–1115**

Quarto post haec anno, hoc est dcccc$^{mo.}$ xxxvii$^{mo.}$ Dominicae Natiuitatis anno, apud Wendune, quod alio nomine Et Brunnanwerc uel Brunnanbyrig appellatur, pugnauit contra Onlaf Guthredi quondam regis filium, qui dc. et. xv. nauibus aduenerat, secum habens auxilia regum prefatorum Scottorum scilicet et Cumbrorum.

At ille sancti Cuthberti patrocinio confisus, prostrata multitudine infinita reges illos de regno suo propulit et gloriosum inde reportans triumphum; hostibus circumquaque tremendus, suis erat pacificus, et in pace postmodum uitam terminauit, fratri Eadmundo imperii monarchiam relinquens.

### 14. EADMER OF CANTERBURY, *VITA OSWALDI*

**Latin**
**ca. 1115**

Hic, ut fertur, Æthelstano uictoriosissimo regi Anglorum ualde carus erat et acceptus, ac pro illius praedicabili sanctitate rex idem illum secum habere, eiusque consiliis magnopere inniti solebat. Qui rex Deum diligens, aequitatis legibus seruiens, regnum strenue gubernabat. Is immenso paganorum exercitui quodam tempore armatus occurrens, memoratum Odonem cuius meritis se quam maxime credebat hostem uicturum in aciem duxit. Et commisso praelio, Odo, eminus a pugna stans, lumina ac manus in caelum tetendit, pro rege et suis Dominum intentius orans. Pugnatum hinc inde atrocissime, et dies ferme totus in certamine absumptus. Tandem iam sole in occasum uergente, sors lacrimabilis accidit; iuxta capulum confractus est regius ensis. Quid faceret? Ut se armaret nullum de suis exarmare uolebat. Quid tunc? Hostes qui iam uertere terga caeperunt, uidentes regem fracto ense factum quasi inermem, animati et in pugnam acrius reuersi sunt. Insonuit clamor, Odonem citius aduolare perurgens. Adest, et opem sua prece negotio ferat rex ipse ortatur et obsecrat. At ille: "Ope quam desideras, uti solummodo uelis, praesto est. Quid igitur agis? Ut quid eo qui in latere tuo pendet gladio parcis? Cur eum a Domini tui hostibus arces? Quid formidas? Nil dubitans arripe illum, et ecce manus Domini erit tecum. Nec prius solis continget occubitus, quam obsistentes aduersarios tuos fuga inuoluat aut interitus." Dixit, et rex, ad eius uerba attonitus, ilico uersa dextra ad uaginam extraxit gladium fulgidum, fortem et insignem. In quo cunctos occursantes deterrens, cedens seu prosternens, ad uerbum serui Dei iuxta factus est et solis occubitus et regis triumphus.

### 15. *ANGLO-SAXON CHRONICLE*, PETERBOROUGH VERSION (E)

**Old English**
**ca. 1121**

**937.** Her Æðelstan cyning lædde fyrde to Brunanbyrig.

**13. SYMEON OF DURHAM, *TRACT ON THE ORIGINS*** **See pp. 188–89**

Four years later, in the year 937 of the Lord's Nativity, at Wendun which is called by another name Et Brunnanwerc or Brunnanbyrig, Athelstan fought against Anlaf, son of former king Guthfrith, who came with 615 ships and had with him the help of the kings of the Scots and the Cumbrians.

But having trusted in the protection of St Cuthbert, Athelstan drove out those kings from his kingdom with their vast horde overthrown, thereupon obtaining a glorious victory. Terrible to his enemies on all sides, he was peaceable to his own people. Afterwards he ended his days in peace, leaving the rule of the empire to his brother Edmund.

**14. EADMER OF CANTERBURY, *LIFE OF OSWALD*** **See pp. 189–90**

As it is said, Oda was greatly beloved and well-liked by Athelstan, most victorious king of the English, and because of his known sanctity the king was accustomed to have Oda with him and to greatly rely upon his counsel. Loving God and devoted to just laws, this king actively guided the kingdom. On one occasion when he had armed for war to fight a vast army of pagans, he took the renowned Oda to the front line because he trusted most that the enemy would be conquered through Oda's merits. When the battle had begun, Oda, standing at a distance from the fight, raised his eyes and hands to heaven and intensely prayed to the Lord for the king and his men. The battle raged fiercely all around and nearly the entire day was spent in the combat. Finally when the sun was sinking in the west, woeful chance struck — the king's sword shattered at the hilt. What could he do? He was unwilling to disarm any of his men in order to arm himself. What then? The enemy who had already begun to flee, seeing the king as if unarmed with a broken sword, turned back more sharply determined to the fight. A shouting rang out, urging Oda to hasten forward more quickly. He arrived and the king urged and implored that he should provide help in this trouble through his prayers. But Oda answered: "The help you ask for is at hand if only you would use it. And so what are you doing? Why do you shun the sword that hangs by your side? Why do you hold it back from the enemies of your Lord? What do you fear? Put aside doubt, seize the sword and, behold, the Lord's hand will be with you. Nor will the setting of the sun come before flight or ruin overcomes the enemies opposing you." He said this, and the king, thunderstruck by his words, at once moved his right hand to the sheath and drew the shining sword, strong and glorious. With it he drove back, cut down, or laid low all the attackers, and both the setting of the sun and the king's triumph came according to the word of God's servant.

**15. *ANGLO-SAXON CHRONICLE*, PETERBOROUGH VERSION (E)** **See p. 190**

**937.** In this year Athelstan the king led the levy to Brunanburh.

### 16. JOHN OF WORCESTER, *CHRONICON* — Latin, early 12th c.

**937.** Hiberniensium multarumque insularum rex paganus Anlafus, a socero suo rege Scottorum Constantino incitatus, ostium Humbre fluminis ualida cum classe ingreditur. Cui rex Æthelstanus fraterque suus clito Eadmundus in loco qui dicitur Brunanburh cum exercitu occurrerunt, et prelio a diei principio in uesperum tracto, v. regulos viique duces, quos aduersarii sibi in auxilium conduxerant, interfecerunt, tantumque sanguinis quantum eatenus in Anglia nullo in bello fusum est fuderunt, et reges Anlafum et Constantinum ad naues fugere compellentes, magno reuersi sunt tripudio. Illi uero summam infelicitatem de interitu sui exercitus consecuti, cum paucis redeunt in sua.

### 17. WILLIAM OF MALMESBURY, *GESTA REGUM ANGLORUM* — Latin, 1127

Postremum illi bellum cum Analauo fuit, Sihtrici filio, qui spe euadandi regni cum supradicto Constantino iterum rebellante terminos transierat. Et Ethelstano ex consulto cedente, ut gloriosius iam insultantem uinceret, multum in Angliam processerat iuuenis audacissimus et illicita spirans animo, cui tandem magnis artibus ducum, magnis uiribus militum apud Bruneford occursum. Ille, qui tantum periculum imminere cerneret, astu exploratoris munus aggressus, depositis regiis insignibus assumptaque in manibus cythara ad tentorium regis nostri progreditur; ubi cum, pro foribus cantitans, interdum quoque quateret dulci resonantia fila tumultu, facile admissus est professus mimum qui huiusmodi arte stipem cotidianam mercaretur. Regem et conuiuas musico acromate aliquantisper deliniuit, cum inter psallendum omnia oculis scrutaretur. Postquam satietas edendi finem delitiis imposuisset, et seueritas amministrandi belli in colloquio procerum recrudesceret, abire iussus precium cantus accepit; quod asportare nausians sub se in terra defodit. Notatum id a quodam, qui olim illi militasset, et confestim Athelstano dictum. Ipse Adelstanus hominem incusans quod hostem pre oculis positum non prodidisset, hoc responsum accepit: "Idem sacramentum quod tibi nuper, o rex, feci, quondam Analauo dedi; quod si in ipso me uidisses uiolare, de te quoque posses exemplum simile cauere. Sed dignare famuli audire consilium ut hinc tentorium amoueas, alioque loco, usque dum partes relictae ueniant, manens inimicum petulanter insultantem modesta cunctatione frangas." Dicto probato, discessum est illinc. Analauus, nocte paratus adueniens, episcopum quendam, qui uespere ad exercitum uenerat, nesciusque rerum gestarum pro uiridantis campi aequore ibi tabernaculum tetenderat, cum tota familia occidit. Tum ultra progrediens regem ipsum imparatum offendit, quippe qui nichil tale hostem ausurum timens large quieti indulserat. Sed cum tanto fremitu stratis excussus suos, quantum per id noctis poterat, ad bellum

## 16. JOHN OF WORCESTER, *CHRONICLE* See pp. 190–91

**937.** Anlaf, the pagan king of the Irish and of many other islands, incited by his father-in-law Constantine, king of the Scots, entered the mouth of the River Humber with a strong fleet. King Athelstan and his brother, Prince Edmund, stood against him with an army at the place called Brunanburh. When the battle had drawn on from dawn into the evening, they had killed five under-kings and seven earls whom their adversaries had gathered as allies, and they had spilled more blood than was ever shed before then in any war in England. They forced kings Anlaf and Constantine to flee to their ships, and they then returned home in great jubilation. Having faced the greatest misfortune in their army's ruin, Anlaf and Constantine went back to their own lands with very few men.

## 17. WILLIAM OF MALMESBURY, *HISTORY OF THE ENGLISH KINGS* See pp. 191–95

Afterwards there was his war with Anlaf, son of Sihtric, who had crossed the borders in the hope of invading the kingdom with the aforementioned Constantine who was rebelling yet again. And since Athelstan purposely held back so that he might defeat an already insolent foe in a more glorious manner, Anlaf, a most audacious youth with a criminal-bent mind, had advanced far into England. In the end, however, he was opposed by the great skills of commanders and a great force of soldiers at Bruneford. Discerning the imminence of such great danger, Anlaf guilefully assumed the role of a spy, and having put off his regal trappings and taken a harp in his hands, he went to the tent of our king. There before the entrance he sang and sometimes plied the resounding strings in a sweet commotion, and he was easily admitted, claiming to be a performer who earned daily pay through such craft. For a time he charmed the king and his companions with pleasing music, and he studied everything with his eyes as he played. After the end of the meal had put a stop to entertainments and the serious matter of running a war was taken up again in the talk of great men, the singer was ordered to leave with his wage. Too disgusted to carry it away, he buried it in the earth beneath him. That was noticed by a man who once had soldiered for him and immediately related to Athelstan. Athelstan reproached the man because he had not given up the enemy when he was in sight. He received this answer: "The same oath that I recently made to you, O King, I once gave to Anlaf; if you had seen me break it with him, you would be wary of a similar thing happening with you. But deign to hear a servant's counsel. Move your tent away from here, and remaining elsewhere until the forces you left behind have arrived, you may with a short delay break the enemy who impudently mocks you." Accepting this advice, they moved away from there. A readied Anlaf arrived that night. A certain bishop had come to the army that evening, and being unaware of the state of things, had set a canopy there on account of the smooth surface of the verdant field. Anlaf murdered the bishop along with his entire household. Then he advanced further and came upon the unprepared king, who had fallen into a deep sleep since he had not feared such an emboldened enemy. But shaken from his bed by such an uproar, he was urging his men on to war as well as he could at that time of night when his sword

acueret, gladius eius fortuitu uagina excidit. Quocirca, cum omnia formidinis et ceci tumultus plena essent, inclamato Deo et sancto Aldelmo reductaque ad uaginam manu inuenit ensem, qui hodieque pro miraculo in thesauro regum seruatur. Est sane, ut aiunt, una parte sectilis, nec umquam auri uel argenti receptibilis. Hoc Dei dono fretus simulque quia iam illucescebat Noricum adorsus, tota die usque ad uesperam indefessus fugauit cum exercitu. Cecidit ibi rex Scottorum Constantinus, perfide animositatis et uiuacis senecte homo, aliique reges quinque, comites duodecim, omnisque barbarorum congeries; pauci qui euaserant pro fide Christi suscipienda conseruati.

. . .

De quo bello tempus est ut illius uersifici, de quo omnia haec excerpsimus, sententiam ponamus:

Transierat quinos et tres et quattuor annos
iure regens ciues, subigens uirtute tyrannos,
iure fideque regens hinc Anglos inde Britannos,
cum redit illa lues, Europae noxia labes.
Iam cubat in terris fera barbaries aquilonis,
iam iacet in campo pelago pirata relicto,
illicitas toruasque minas ANALAWUS anhelans.
Bacchanti furiae, Scottorum rege uolente,
commodat assensum borealis terra serenum.
Et iam grande tument, iam terrent aera uerbis;
cedunt indigenae, cedit plaga tota superbis.
Nam quia rex noster, fidens alacrisque iuuenta,
emeritus pridem detriuerat otia lenta,
illi continuis fedabant omnia predis,
urgentes miseros iniectis ignibus agros.
Marcuerant totis uiridantia gramina campis,
egra seges uotum deriserat agricolarum;
tanta fuit peditum, tam barbara uis equitantum,
innumerabilium concursus quadrupedantum.
Exsciuit tandem famae querimonia regem,
ne se cauterio tali pateretur inuri,
quod sua barbaricae cessissent arma securi.
Nec mora: uictrices ducentia signa cohortes
explicat in uentum, uexilla ferocia centum;
cruda uirum uirtus decies bis milia quina
ad stadium belli comitantur preuia signa.
Hic strepitus mouit predatorum legiones,
terruit insignis uenientum fama latrones,
ut posita preda proprias peterent regiones.
At uulgus reliquum, miseranda strage peremptum,
infecit bibulas tetris nidoribus auras.

accidentally fell from its scabbard. Wherefore, when all were full of alarm and blind confusion, he cried out to God and Saint Aldhelm and, reaching back to his scabbard, he discovered the blade which is still preserved today in the royal treasure-house on account of that miracle. It is, as they say, clearly engraved on one side but never inlaid with gold or silver. Inspired by this gift of God and by the coming of dawn, he tirelessly assailed the Norwegian all that day until evening and routed him with his army. There fell Constantine, king of the Scots, a man of treacherous spirit and vigorous old age, as well as five kings, twelve earls, and nearly the entire barbarian horde. The few who escaped were spared so that they might receive the Christian faith.

. . .

Regarding this battle, it is time that I offer the opinion of the versifier from whom I have taken all this matter:

He had passed twelve years
ruling his people justly and bravely putting down tyrants,
ruling both English and British in law and faith,
when that scourge, Europe's deadly canker, returned.
Now the savage barbarity of the north comes to ground,
now the pirate has left the sea to take the field,
as Anlaf rasps threats unlawful and grim.
To this raving fury, welcome to the king of the Scots,
the northern land lends clear support.
Now they greatly swell with pride and terrify the air with their words;
the people and the entire region yield to their arrogance.
For because our king, bold and spirited in his youth,
had retired from war long ago and languished in sluggish leisure,
they defiled everything in their relentless plundering,
afflicting the wretched fields with spreading fires.
Verdant grass had withered on all the plains;
diseased grain had mocked the prayers of farmers;
so great was the barbaric force of the footmen and riders,
the charge of countless galloping steeds.
Rumor's complaint finally roused the king,
lest he allow himself to be branded with the mark
that his armed men had submitted to the barbarian ax.
There was no delay: in the wind he unfolded
the standards that lead his victorious troops, one hundred defiant banners;
the raw power of his men, one hundred thousand soldiers,
follow the standards leading to the stadium of war.
This din shook the legions of pillagers,
the news of their approach so terrified the infamous brigands
that they dropped their plunder and made for their own lands.
But the remaining rabble, cut down in miserable slaughter,
infected the thirsty air with a foul stench.

Fugit ANALAFUS, de tot modo milibus unus,
depositum mortis, fortunae nobilae munus,
post ETHELSTANUM rebus momenta daturus.

### 18. HENRY OF HUNTINGDON, *HISTORIA ANGLORUM*

**Latin**
**ca. 1133**

Adelstan filius Edwardi electus est rex in Merce, et sacratus apud Kingestune. Qui regno quidem parum uixit, sed clare gestis non parum splenduit, qui a fortissimis lacessiri sed bello numquam potuit uinci. Curriculo siquidem sequentis anni, Gudfridum regem Dacorum patrem Reginaldi predicti regis, bello lacessitus bello reppulit, repulsum fugauit, fugatum perdidit. Nec multo post, aduersa perculsus fortuna fratrem suum Edwinum, magni uigoris et bone indolis iuuenem, maris fluctibus flebiliter amisit. At uero rex Adelstan his transactis gentem perfidam Dacorum, et infidam Scotorum, in exterminium traducere disponens, confertissimum duxit exercitum terra et mari in Nordhimbram et Scotiam. Cui cum non esset qui resistere inciperet, uel qui resistere persisteret, ubicumque terrarum progrediens, et pro libitu predans cum triumphali rediit lauro.

Adelstan rex, anno gratie dccccxlv, regni uero sui anno quarto, commisit prelium ad Brunebirih, preliorum maximum, contra Anlaf regem Hibernie. Qui uires suas gente Scotorum et Dacorum in Anglia conuersantium adauxerat. De cuius prelii magnitudine Anglici scriptores quasi carminis modo proloquentes, et extraneis tam uerbis quam figuris usi translatione fida donandi sunt. Ut pene de uerbo in uerbum eorum interpretantes eloquium ex grauitate uerborum grauitatem actuum et animorum gentis illius condiscamus.

Rex Adelstan, decus ducum, nobilibus torquium dator, et frater eius Edmundus, longa stirpis serie splendens, percusserunt in bello acie gladii apud Brunebirih. Scutorum muros fiderunt, nobiles ceciderunt, domestice reliquie defuncti Edwardi. Sic namque eis ingenitum fuerat a genibus cognationum, ut bellis frequentibus ab infestis nationibus defenderent patrie thesauros et domos, pecunias et exenia. Gens uero Hibernensium, et puppium habitatores fatales corruerunt, colles resonuerunt. Sudauerunt armati ex quo sol mane prodiit, micans ilariter, letificans profunda, Dei luminare, fax creatoris, usquequo idem nobilis ductor occasu se occuluit. Ibi uiri iacuerunt multi a Dacia oriundi, telis perforati, sub scutis lanceati, simul et Scotti

Anlaf, alone of what were recently so many thousands,
fled the deposit of death, Fortune's famous rite,
ready to start things again after Athelstan.

## 18. HENRY OF HUNTINGDON, *HISTORY OF THE ENGLISH* See pp. 195–200

Athelstan, son of Edward, was chosen king in Mercia and consecrated at Kingston. Although he did not live long in his reign, he shone brightly in his deeds a great deal as he was challenged by the very mighty but never conquered in war. Indeed, in the course of the following year he was challenged in war and in war he drove back Guthfrith, king of the Danes and father of King Ragnall; having driven him back he routed him, and having routed him he destroyed him. Not long after, struck by cruel fortune, he sadly lost his brother Edwin, a youth of great vigor and good character, to the waves of the sea. But when this had passed King Athelstan, determined to bring an end to the treacherous Danes and the faithless Scots, led a vast army by land and sea into Northumbria and Scotland. There were none who could begin to oppose him (or could continue to oppose him) as he overran all those lands and plundered as he wished, and he returned with the triumphal laurel.

In the year of grace 945, the fourth year of his reign, King Athelstan engaged in battle at Brunebirih, the greatest of battles, against Anlaf, king of Ireland, who had increased his own men with Scots and Danes living in England. English writers express the greatness of this battle in a poetic fashion, and they employ strange words and figures that require a faithful translation. As we render their eloquence nearly word for word, let us learn the dignity of the deeds and spirit of that people from the dignity of their words.

King Athelstan, a glory among leaders,
ring-giver to nobles, and his brother Edmund,
shining in a long ancestral line,
struck with point of sword in battle at Brunanburh.
The family descendants of deceased Edward
split shield-walls, struck down nobles.
For it had been instilled at the knees of kinsmen
that in many wars they must thus defend
the hoards and homes of their native land,
wealth and precious things, from hostile peoples.
But the Irish people and deadly ship-dwellers
descended. The hills resounded.
Armed men sweat from morning when the sun
rose shining cheerfully, gladdening the world below,
God's lamp, torch of the Creator,
until that noble guide hid itself in setting.
There many men born in Denmark lay,
pierced by spears, stabbed under their shields,
and the Irish, too, weary from war.

bello fatigati. Gens uero Westsexe tota simul die, prius electi, post indefessi, inuise gentis globos strauerunt, uiri elegantes hastas cedebant, uiri Mercenses acuta iacula mittebant duro manus ludo. Sanitas ibi nulla his, qui cum Anlauo trans maris campos in ligni gremio terram pecierunt, Marte morituri. Quinque occubuerunt in loco belli reges, iuuenes, gladiis percussi, ducesque .vii. regis Anlaui. Absque numero ceciderunt Scotti. Deperiitque Normannorum tumor. Nec enim paucos ad litem belli duxerant secum. Cum paucis uero in maris fluctus rex naui prouectus intrinsecus gemebat. Simul et Froda, ductor Normannus, cumque suis notis dux Constantinus, de Martis congressu iactare nequierunt, ubi cognationis sue fragmen apparuit, ubi amici sui corruerant in statione populi bello prostrati, et filium suum in loco prelii uulneribus demolitum carum reliquit. Nec Gude Dacus declamare potuit, licet uerbis blandus, et mente uetustus. Nec Anlaf ipse cum reliquiis suis mentiri potuit, quod ad hoc negotium sui prestiterint in campo belli ictuum inmanitate, telorum transforatione in concilio proborum. Matres uero et nurus planxerunt suos belli alea cum Edwardi filiis lusisse, cum Normanni nauibus clauatis et Anlaf tabefactus ultra profundum flumen terras suas mesto animo repetissent. Postea frater uterque rediit Westsexe belli reliquias post se deserentes, carnes uirorum in escam paratas. Ergo coruus niger ore cornutus, et buffo liuens, aquila cum miluo, canis lupusque mixtus colore, his sunt deliciis diu recreati. Non fuit bellum hac in tellure maius patratum, nec cedes tanta precessit istam, postquam huc

But the West Saxon people, first chosen,
afterwards unwearied, throughout the day
scattered the masses of the hateful race,
fine men gave up their spears,
Mercian men threw sharp javelins in hard hand-play.
There was no safety there for those fated to die,
those who with Anlaf had sought out the land
across the sea-fields in a bosom of wood.
Five lay dead in that place of war,
young kings, struck down by swords,
and seven earls of King Anlaf.
Irishmen died beyond number.
The pride of the Norsemen perished.
Indeed they had led not a few to the contest of war,
but sailing back onto the sea-waves
with only a few men the king grieved within.
And likewise Froda, leader of the Norsemen,
and with him the earl Constantine with his own comrades,
could not boast about the clash of war,
when only a scrap of their kinsmen remained,
when their friends came to ruin,
laid low by war at the nation's stand.
He abandoned his beloved son,
destroyed by wounds on the battlefield.
Nor was Guda the Dane able to bluster,
although easy with words and aged in mind.
Nor was Anlaf himself with his survivors
able to pretend that in this business
they had prevailed on the battlefield
with brutality of blows and stabbing of spears
at the meeting of tried men. Mothers and young wives
lamented that their men had played
at the game of war with Edward's sons
when the Norsemen in nailed ships
and a subdued Anlaf
had returned over the deep flood
to their own lands in low spirits.
Afterward both brothers returned to Wessex
leaving the flotsam of war behind them,
the flesh of men now become as food.
Then the dark raven with horned beak,
and the livid toad, the eagle and kite,
the hound and wolf in mottled hue,
were long refreshed by these delicacies.
In this land no greater war was ever waged,
nor did such a slaughter ever surpass that one,
since the Angles and Saxons, famous war-smiths,

uenerunt trans mare latum Saxones et Angli, Britones pulsuri, clari Martis fabri Walenses uicerunt, reges fugauerunt, regna susceperunt.

. . .

De regno uero Westsexe hec elucidatio adhibeatur. . . .

. . . Athelstan filius Edwardi xiiii annis. Qui fecit maximum preliorum apud Brunebirig.

### 19. GEOFFREY GAIMAR, *ESTOIRE DES ENGLEIS*

**Anglo-Norman**
**mid-12th c.**

Puis regnat son fiz Adelstan.
Quant out regné tresk'el quart an,
bataille tint contre Daneis;
si descunfist Gudfrid li reis.
Puis asembla mult grant empire
e en la mer mist grant navire.
Dreit en Escoce s'en ala;
icel pais forment preia.
Après un an, ne mains ne plus,
a Bruneswerce out le desus
sur les Escoz, e sur Combreis,
sur Gawaleis, e sur Picteis.
Iloc en furent tant oscis
crei ke parlé en ert tutdis.
Puis ne vesqui-il que treis anz;
il n'out ne fiz, ne altres enfanz.
De son frere firent donc rei,
Eadmund out nun; prodom, ço crei.

### 20. SYMEON OF DURHAM, *HISTORIA REGUM*

**Latin**
**mid-12th c.**

Anno dccccxxxxvii. Ethelstanus rex apud Wendune pugnauit, regemque Onlafum cum dc. et xv. nauibus, Constantinum quoque regem Scotorum, et regem Cumbrorum, cum omni eorum multitudine in fugam uertit.

. . .

Anno dccccxxxvi[i]. Hiberniensium multarumque insularum rex paganus Anlafus, a socero suo rege Scotorum Constantino incitatus, ostium Humbre fluminis ualida cum classe ingreditur. Cui rex Ethelstanus fraterque suus clito Eadmundus in loco qui dicitur Brunanburh cum exercitu occurrerunt, et praelio a diei principio in uesperum tracto, quinque regulos septemque duces, quos aduersarii sibi in auxilium

came here across the broad sea
to drive out the Britons; they conquered the Welsh,
routed kings, and took kingdoms.

. . .

This survey may be consulted for the kingdom of Wessex. . . .

. . . Athelstan, son of Edward, ruled for fourteen years. He fought the greatest of battles at Brunebirig.

### 19. GEOFFREY GAIMAR, *HISTORY OF THE ENGLISH*

**See pp. 200–02**

After that reigned Edward's son Athelstan.
When he had reigned to the fourth year,
he waged a battle against the Danes;
and he defeated Guthfrith the king.
After that he assembled a great army
and into the sea issued a great fleet.
Directly to Scotland he went;
he harried that country well.
One year later, no less or more,
at Brunanburh he had the upperhand
over the Scots, and over the men of Cumberland,
over the Welsh, and over the Picts.
There so many were slain
I think it will be told forever.
Afterwards he lived only three years;
he had no son, no other children.
His brother was then made king,
Edmund was his name; a good man, I believe.

### 20. SYMEON OF DURHAM, *HISTORY OF THE KINGS*

**See p. 202**

**937**. At Wendun King Athelstan fought King Anlaf with his 615 ships, as well as Constantine, king of the Scots, and the king of the Cumbrians, when he put their entire host to flight.

. . .

**937**. Anlaf, the pagan king of the Irish and of many other islands, incited by his father-in-law Constantine, king of the Scots, entered the mouth of the River Humber with a strong fleet. King Athelstan and his brother, Prince Edmund, stood against him with an army at the place called Brunanburh. When the battle had drawn on from dawn into the evening, they had killed five under-kings and seven earls whom their adversaries had gathered as allies, and they had spilled more blood than was ever

conduxerant, interfecerunt, tantumque sanguinis quantum eatenus in Anglia nullo in bello est infusum, fuderunt, et reges Anlafum et Constantinum ad naues fugere compellentes, magno reuersi sunt tripudio. Illi uero, summam infelicitatem de interitu sui exercitus consecuti, cum paucis redeunt in sua.

### 21. *CHRONICON RAMESIENSIS*

**Latin**
**ca. 1170**

Quodam ergo dierum contra Analafum, quendam barbarorum ducem strenuissimum, qui hostili inuasione partem iam Anglie turbauerat, exercitum ducens, uirum sanctum in comitatu habuit, ipsius meritis euentum belli prosperum sibi fieri posse confisus. Igitur hostibus castra regis sub ceca nocte callide inuadentibus, facta strictius partium congressione, dum se mutuis ictibus dilaniant, dum stridores lituorum fierent et fremitus armorum, forte regius ensis e uagina lapsus aduersariis quidem incrementum audacie, ipsi uero regi et suis plurimum formidinis, importauit. Quo cognito uir beatus orauit et uagine regis uacue alius diuinitus immissus est ensis, quo ad nutum uiri Dei educto populatores palantes cesi sunt, et de eis inopinata celeritate triumphatum. In argumentum diuine bonitatis et regie uictorie idem ensis in thesauris regum, ut fertur, usque hodie reseruatur.

### 22. *CHRONICA DE MAILROS*

**Latin**
**1173–74**

Anno DCCCC.xxxvij. Anlafus rex Hyberniae ostium Humbre fluminis cum DC. et XV. navibus ingreditur, cui rex Aðelstanus et frater eius Edmundus occurrit apud Brunanburch, et commisso proelio regulos v. et vij. duces occidunt et cum triumpho reversi sunt.

### 23. GWYNFARDD BRYCHEINIOG, *CANU Y DEWI*

**Welsh**
**late 12th c.**

*Canu y Dewi*: Gwynnuart Brycheinyawc a'e cant

. . .

Deu ychen Dewi ardderchawc — oetynt,
deu gar a gertynt yn gydpreinyawc
y hebrwg anrec yn redecawc
y Lasgwm. Nyd oet trwm tri urtassawc.
Edewid Bangu gu gadwynawc
a'r deu ereill ureisc y Urycheinyawc.
Ban del gofyn arnam-ny, ry bytwn ofnawc
rac gormes kedeirn Cad Dybrunawc.
Ar Duw a Dewi, deu niuerawc,
yd alwnn bressen bresswil vodawc.

shed before then in any war in England. They forced kings Anlaf and Constantine to flee to their ships, and they then returned home with great rejoicing. Having faced the greatest misfortune in their army's ruin, Anlaf and Constantine went back to their own lands with very few men.

### 21. *CHRONICLE OF RAMSEY* **See p. 203**

And so one day Athelstan was leading his army against Anlaf, a most vigorous leader of barbarians who had already disturbed part of England with hostile invasion. Athelstan had a holy man in his company through whose merits he was confident of success in war. During the dark night enemies cunningly invaded the king's camp, and as the parties clashed in close quarters they tore one another with mutual blows. During the clamor of horns and the clash of arms, the royal sword by chance slipped from its scabbard, causing increased daring among the enemy and the greatest alarm among the king and his men. Realizing this, the blessed man prayed and another sword divinely appeared in the king's empty scabbard and it was drawn at the man of God's command. The scattering ravagers were cut down and defeated with surprising swiftness. In token of divine munificence and royal victory, as it is said, that same sword is kept in the royal treasure-house up to the present day.

### 22. *CHRONICLE OF MELROSE* **See pp. 203–04**

In the year 937 Anlaf king of Ireland entered the mouth of the River Humber with 615 ships. Athelstan and his brother Edmund went to meet him at Brunanburh. Having engaged in battle, they killed five sub-kings and seven ealdormen and returned home in triumph.

### 23. GWYNFARDD BRYCHEINIOG, *SONG TO ST. DAVID* **See pp. 204–06**

*Song to St. David*: Gwynfardd Brycheiniog sang it

. . .

Dewi's two oxen were excellent,
two dear ones who would go yoked together
to bring a gift at a run
to Glascwm. The three noble [objects] were not heavy.
Bangu was left [there], a dear one on a chain,
and the two other splendid [ones went] to Brycheiniog.
When need may come upon us, we shall be fearful
in the face of the oppression of the mighty ones of the Battle of Brunanburh(?).
Upon God and Dewi, two with great hosts,
shall we on earth call continuously [and] steadfastly.

### 24. ROGER OF HOWDEN, *CHRONICA*

**Latin**
**ca. 1200**

[See notes.]

### 25. *EGILSSAGA*

**Old Norse**
**1220–40**

LII. Kapítuli — Af liðs samandrætti.

Óláfr Skotakonungr dró saman her mikinn ok fór síðan suðr á England, en er hann kom á Norðimbraland, fór hann allt herskildi. En er þat spurðu jarlarnir, er þar réðu fyrir, stefna þeir saman liði ok fara móti konungi. En er þeir finnask, varð þar orrosta mikil, ok lauk svá, at Óláfr konungr hafði sigr, en Goðrekr jarl fell, en Álfgeirr flýði undan ok mestr hluti liðs þess, er þeim hafði fylgt ok brott komsk ór bardaga. Fekk Álfgeirr þá enga viðstǫðu. Lagði Óláfr konungr þá allt Norðimbraland undir sik. Álfgeirr fór á fund Aðalsteins konungs ok sagði honum ófarar sínar.

En þegar er Aðalsteinn konungr spurði, at herr svá mikill var kominn í land hans, þá gerði hann þegar menn frá sér ok stefndi at sér liði, gerði orð jǫrlum sínum ok ǫðrum ríkismǫnnum. Sneri konungr þegar á leið með þat lið, er hann fekk, ok fór í mót Skotum.

En er þat spurðisk, at Óláfr Skotakonungr hafði fengit sigr ok hafði lagt undir sik mikinn hluta af Englandi, hafði hann þá her miklu meira en Aðalsteinn, en þá sótti til hans mart ríkismanna. En er þetta spyrja þeir Hringr ok Aðils, — hǫfðu þeir saman dregit lið mikit, — þá snúask þeir í lið með Óláfi konungi. Hǫfðu þeir þá ógrynni liðs.

En er Aðalsteinn spurði þetta allt, þá átti hann stefnu við hǫfðingja sína ok ráðamenn, leitaði þá eptir, hvat tiltœkiligast væri, sagði þá allri alþýðu greiniliga þat, er hann hafði frétt um athǫfn Skotakonungs ok fjǫlmenni hans. Allir mæltu þar eitt um, at Álfgeirr jarl hafði inn versta hlut af, ok þótti þat til liggja, at taka af honum tígnina. En sú ráðagørð staðfestisk, at Aðalsteinn konungr skyldi fara aptr ok fara á sunnanvert England ok hafa þá fyrir sér liðsafnað norðr eptir landi ǫllu, því at þeir sá elligar myndi seint safnask fjǫlmennit, svá mikit sem þyrfti, ef eigi drœgi konungr sjálfr at liðit.

En sá herr, er þá var þar saman kominn, þá setti konungr þar yfir hǫfðingja Þórólf ok Egil. Skyldu þeir ráða fyrir því liði, er víkingar hǫfðu þangat haft til konungs, en Álfgeirr sjálfr hafði þá enn forráð síns liðs. Þá fekk konungr enn sveitarhǫfðingja þá, er honum sýndisk. En er Egill kom heim af stefnunni til félaga sinna, þá spurðu þeir, hvat hann kynni at segja þeim tíðenda frá Skotakonungi. Hann kvað:

Áleifr of kom jǫfri,
ótt vas víg, á bak flótta,
þingharðan frák þengil
þann, en felldi annan.

## 24. Roger of Howden, *Chronicle*

See p. 206

[See notes.]

## 25. *Egil's Saga*

See pp. 206–12

Chapter 52. Of the gathering of the army.

Anlaf, king of the Scots, drew together a great army and then went south into England. When he came to Northumberland he began to harry everywhere. Upon hearing of this the earls who ruled there summoned troops and went out against the king. When they met each other there was a great battle, and in the end King Anlaf had victory, and Earl Godric fell, and Alfgar fled from the field with the majority of those troops that had accompanied them. Since Alfgar gave no further resistance, King Anlaf conquered all of Northumberland. Alfgar went to meet with King Athelstan and told him of their ill fate.

As soon as King Athelstan was informed that such a great host had come into his land he immediately sent out messengers, summoned troops and sent word to his earls and other powerful men. The king, with that force that he had gathered, set off on his way at once to oppose the Scots.

When it was learned that Anlaf, king of the Scots, had won a victory and had subjugated a large part of England, he rallied a much greater army than Athelstan, for many powerful men joined him. When they heard this, Hring and Adils, who had drawn together a large band of men, set out to join with King Anlaf's army; they then had a great number of troops.

When Athelstan heard all this he held a meeting with his chieftains and counselors to seek out the best course of action, telling them in detail all that he had learned of the doings of the Scottish king and his large band of men. All there agreed on one thing, that Earl Alfgar had the worst share of the blame, and they thought that it would be proper to take away his rank. But the plan that was resolutely made was that King Athelstan should turn back to the south of England and gather troops to himself from all the land as he moved north; for they saw that it would only be possible to gather the necessary men, so many were needed, if the king himself were there to lead the force.

As for the army that was already gathered there, the king placed over them as leaders Thorolf and Egil. They were also to be responsible for the forces that the Vikings had brought to the king; but Alfgar was to still have command of his own men. Then the king gave over command of the other troops as he saw fit. When Egil returned from the council to his fellows they asked him what tidings he could tell them about the king of the Scots. He said:

Anlaf put one earl to flight
through furious battle,
and another felled;
a hard man in fight is this ruler;

Glapstígu lét gnóga
Goðrekr á mó troðna.
Jǫrð spenr Engla skerðir
Alfgeirs und sik halfa.

Síðan gera þeir sendimann til Óláfs konungs ok finna þat til ørenda, at Aðalsteinn konungr vill hasla honum vǫll ok bjóða orrostustað á Vínheiði við Vínuskóga ok hann vill, at þeir heri eigi, á land hans, en sá þeira ráði ríki á Englandi, er sigr fær í orrostu, lagði til viku stef um fund þeira, en sá bíðr annars viku, er fyrr kemr. En þat var þá siðr, þegar konungi var vǫllr haslaðr, at hann skyldi eigi herja at skammlausu, fyrr en orrostu væri lokit. Gerði Óláfr konungr svá, at hann stǫðvaði her sinn ok herjaði ekki ok beið til stefnudags. Þá flutti hann her sinn til Vínheiðar.

Borg ein stóð fyrir norðan heiðina. Settisk Óláfr konungr þar í borgina ok hafði þar mestan hlut liðs síns, því at þar var út í frá heruð stór, ok þótti honum þar betra til atflutninga um fǫng þau, er herrinn þurfti at hafa. En hann sendi menn sína upp á heiðina, þar sem orrostustaðrinn var ákveðinn. Skyldu þeir taka þar tjaldstaði ok búask þar um, áðr herrinn kœmi. En er þeir menn kómu í þann stað, er vǫllrinn var haslaðr, þá váru þar settar upp heslistengr allt til ummerkja, þar er sá staðr var, er orrostan skyldi vera. Þurfti þann stað at vanda, at hann væri sléttr, er miklum her skyldi fylkja. Var þar ok svá, er orrostustaðrinn skyldi vera, at þar var heiðr slétt, en annan veg frá fell á ein, en á annan veg frá var skógr mikill.

En þar er skemmsk var milli skógarins ok árinnar, ok var þat mjǫk lǫng leið, þar hǫfðu tjaldat menn Aðalsteins konungs. Stóðu tjǫld þeira allt milli skógarins ok árinnar. Þeir hǫfðu svá tjaldat, at eigi váru menn í inu þriðja hverju tjaldi ok þó fáir í einu. En er menn Óláfs konungs kómu til þeira, þá hǫfðu þeir fjǫlmennt fyrir framan tjǫldin ǫll, ok náðu þeir ekki inn at ganga. Sǫgðu menn Aðalsteins, at tjǫld þeira væri ǫll full af mǫnnum, svá at hvergi nær hefði þar rúm lið þeira. En tjǫldin stóðu svá hátt, at ekki mátti yfir upp sjá, hvárt þau stóðu mǫrg eða fá á þykkðina. Þeir hugðu, at þar myndi vera herr manns. Óláfs konungs menn tjǫlduðu fyrir norðan hǫslurnar, ok var þangat allt nǫkkut afhallt. Aðalsteins menn sǫgðu ok annan dag frá ǫðrum, at konungr þeira myndi þá koma eða vera kominn í borg þá, er var sunnan undir heiðinni. Lið drósk til þeira bæði dag ok nótt.

En er stefna sú var liðin, er ákveðit var, þá senda menn Aðalsteins ørendreka á fund Óláfs konungs með þeim orðum, at Aðalsteinn konungr er búinn til orrostu ok hefir her allmikinn, en hann sendir Óláfi konungi þau orð, at hann vill eigi, at þeir geri svá mikit mannspell, sem þá horfðisk til, bað hann heldr fara heim í Skotland, en Aðalsteinn vill fá honum at vingjǫf skilling silfrs af plógi hverjum um allt ríki sitt ok vill, at þeir leggi með sér vináttu.

En er sendimenn koma til Óláfs konungs, þá tók hann at búa her sinn ok ætlaði at at ríða. En er sendimenn báru upp erendi, þá stǫðvaði konungr ferð sína þann dag, sat þá í ráðagørð ok hǫfðingjar hers með honum. Lǫgðu menn þar allmisjafnt

confounded on the field
Godric trod a dark path;
this foe of the English
has half of Alfgar's lands.

After that they sent messengers to King Anlaf, giving as their errand that King Athelstan would challenge him to combat in a field marked out by hazel wands, and offer battle at Vinheath by Vinwood; and he wished that they not harry his land. But the one who should rule over all of England was he who took victory in battle. He proposed that the battle be fought in one week, and that the one who came first should wait a week for the other. It was the custom then that when a king had marked out a battlefield with the hazel rods he should not shamelessly harry the land before the battle was over. Accordingly, King Anlaf did thus, and he ordered his army to halt and to harry not and wait until the chosen day. Then he moved his forces to Vinheath.

A fortified town stood to the north of the heath. King Anlaf settled himself in that town, and set the greater part of his army there because beyond it there was a large district that seemed to him better for the conveyance of provisions that the army needed. But he sent men of his own up to the heath where the appointed battle site was. They were to set up a camp there and ready themselves before the other army arrived. But when the men came to the place designated for the battle, the hazel rods had already been set up to mark the ground where the battle was to be. By custom the place ought to be level and large enough for armies to draw up in battle array. And this was so, for in the place chosen for the battle the heath was level and on one side a river flowed and on the other was a great forest.

But where the distance was least between the forest and the river, and that was a very long way, there King Athelstan's men had pitched camp; their tents stood in all the space between the forest and the river. They had made camp so that in every third tent there were no men, and only few in one of the three. Yet when King Anlaf's men came to them they had such a large number of men in front of all the tents that they could not go in to rest. Athelstan's men said that their tents were all full of men so that their army had no room anywhere nearby. But the tents stood so high that it was not possible to see over them, whether their numbers stood deep or few in depth; they thought that there was a host of men there. King Anlaf's men pitched their tents north of the hazel rods and there the ground had a slight downward slope. On each day, Athelstan's men said that their king would come, or had come to the town that lay to the south of the heath; meanwhile forces gathered to them both day and night.

But when that time came that was appointed, then Athelstan's men sent messengers to meet King Anlaf with these words: that King Athelstan is ready for battle and has a very great army, but he sends to King Anlaf word that he wishes that they should not cause such loss of men as they now faced; he asks rather that he return to Scotland, and Athelstan will give to him as a friendly gift a silver shilling for every plough in all his kingdom, and he wishes to establish a friendship between them.

When the messengers came to King Anlaf he was preparing to take his army and intended to ride out. However, when the messengers made known their errand, then the king did not set out that day, but sat in counsel with his chieftains. The men were

til. Sumir fýstu mjǫk, at þenna kost skyldi taka, sǫgðu, at þat var þá orðin in mesta fremðarferð, at þeir fœri heim ok hefði tekit gjald svá mikit af Aðalsteini. Sumir lǫttu ok sǫgðu, at Aðalsteinn myndi bjóða miklu meira í annat sinn, ef þetta væri eigi tekit, ok var sú ráðagørð staðfest.

Þá báðu sendimenn Óláf konung at gefa sér tóm til, at þeir hitti enn Aðalstein konung ok freistaði, ef hann vildi enn meira gjald af hendi reiða, til þess at friðr væri. Þeir beiddu griða einn dag til heimreiðar, en annan til umráða, en inn þriðja til aptrferðar. Konungr játtaði þeim því. Fara sendimenn heim ok koma aptr inn þriðja dag, sem á kveðit var, segja Óláfi konungi, at Aðalsteinn vill gefa allt slíkt, sem hann bauð fyrr, ok þar um fram til hlutskiptis liði Óláfs konungs skilling manni hverjum frjálsbornum, en mǫrk sveitarhǫfðingja hverjum þeim, er réði tólf mǫnnum eða fleirum, en mǫrk gulls hirðstjóra hverjum, en fimm merkr gulls jarli hverjum.

Síðan lét konungr þetta upp bera fyrir lið sitt. Var enn sem fyrr, at sumir lǫttu, en sumir fýstu, en at lykðum veitti konungr órskurð, segir, at þenna kost vill hann taka, ef þat fylgir, at Aðalsteinn konungr lætr hann hafa Norðimbraland allt með þeim skǫttum ok skyldum, er þar liggja.

Sendimenn biðja enn fresta um þrjá daga ok þess með, at Óláfr konungr sendi þá menn sína at heyra orð Aðalsteins konungs, hvárt hann vill eða eigi þenna kost, segja, at þeir hyggja, at Aðalsteinn konungr myndi láta fátt við nema, at sættin tœkisk. Óláfr konungr játtir því ok sendir menn sína til Aðalsteins konungs. Ríða þá sendimenn allir saman ok hitta Aðalstein konung í borg þeiri, er var næst heiðinni fyrir sunnan. Sendimenn Óláfs konungs bera upp ørendi sín fyrir Aðalstein konung ok sættaboð. Aðalsteins konungs menn sǫgðu ok, með hverjum boðum þeir hǫfðu farit til Óláfs konungs, ok þat með, at þat var ráðagørð vitra manna, at dvelja svá orrostu, meðan konungr kœmi eigi.

En Aðalsteinn konungr veitti skjótan órskurð um þetta mál ok sagði sendimǫnnum svá: "Berið þau orð mín Óláfi konungi, at ek vil gefa honum orlof til þess at fara heim til Skotlands með lið sitt, ok gjaldi hann aptr fé þat allt, er hann tók upp at rǫngu hér í landi. Setjum hér síðan frið í millum landa várra ok heri hvárigir á aðra. Þat skal ok fylgja, at Óláfr konungr skal gerask minn maðr ok halda Skotland af mér ok vera undirkonungr minn. Farið nú," segir hann, "aptr ok segið honum svá búit."

Sendimenn sneru aptr leið sína þegar um kveldit ok kómu til Óláfs konungs nær miðri nótt, vǫkðu þá upp konung ok sǫgðu honum þegar orð Aðalsteins konungs. Konungr lét þegar kalla til sín jarlana ok aðra hǫfðingja, lét þá sendimenn koma til ok segja upp ørendislok sín ok orð Aðalsteins konungs. En er þetta var kunnigt gǫrt fyrir liðsmǫnnum, þá var eitt orðtak allra, at þat myndi fyrir liggja, at búask til orrostu. Sendimenn sǫgðu ok þat með, at Aðalsteinn hafði fjǫlða liðs, ok hann hafði þann dag komit til borgarinnar, sem sendimenn kómu.

Þá mælti Aðils jarl: "Nú mun þat fram komit, konungr, sem ek sagða, at yðr myndi þeir reynask brǫgðóttir, inir ensku. Hǫfum vér hér setit langa stund ok beðit þess, er þeir hafa dregit at sér allt lið sitt, en konungr þeira mun verit hafa hvergi nær,

of various opinions on what to do. Some were eager to take this opportunity, saying that the glorious journey would have gone well if they were to return home having taken such a great payment from Athelstan. Some others were against it, saying that Athelstan might offer much more a second time if this offer was not taken. And this latter is what they decided to do.

The messengers asked King Anlaf to give them more time so that they could meet with King Athelstan and find out if he would pay yet more to keep peace. They asked for a truce of one day to ride home, and another for deliberation, and a third to return. The king agreed to this. The messengers went home and returned on the third day as had been settled and said to King Anlaf that King Athelstan would give as much as he had offered before with an additional share of one shilling for each of King Anlaf's freeborn men, a silver mark to every leader of a troop of twelve or more men, a gold mark to every captain of the king's men, and five gold marks to every earl.

Then the king set this offer before his forces. It was as before, some were opposed to it, others were in favor of it. In the end the king decided the issue, saying that he would take the terms, if in addition King Athelstan would let him have Northumberland with all the dues and tributes that went with it.

The messengers again asked for a respite of three days, and furthermore that King Anlaf should send his own men to hear King Athelstan's answer, whether or not he would accept the terms, saying that to their thinking King Athelstan would let little stand in the way of a settlement. King Anlaf agreed to this and sent his men to King Athelstan. The messengers all rode together and found King Athelstan in the town that was near the heath to the south. King Anlaf's messengers delivered their message to King Athelstan and written evidence of the agreement. King Athelstan's men also spoke of the offers they had made to King Anlaf, and that it had been the counsel of wise men thus to delay the battle, as the king had not yet arrived.

King Athelstan made a quick decision on the issue and spoke to the messengers thus: "Bear these my words to King Anlaf, that I will give him leave thus, to return home to Scotland with his troops, but let him repay all that property that he wrongfully seized here in the land. Then let us make peace between our lands, neither harrying the other. And further it shall be that King Anlaf shall become my vassal and hold Scotland for me, and be my underking. Go back now," he said, "and tell him this without more ado."

The messengers turned back at once that same evening and came to King Anlaf near the middle of the night. Then they woke up the king and at once told him the words of King Athelstan. The king immediately called together his earls and other captains, and had the messengers repeat the outcome of their errand and Athelstan's words. But when this was made known to the warriors, then they were all of one mind about what must lie before them: to prepare for battle. The messengers also said that Athelstan had a great number of troops and that he had just come to the fortress that same day that the messengers had arrived.

Then Earl Adils spoke out, "Now that has come to pass, King, which I have said before to you, that the English will prove to be cunning. We have sat here a long time and waited, while they have gathered together all their forces; but their king must not have been anywhere near when we came here. Now they will have gath-

þá er vér kómum hér. Munu þeir nú hafa safnat liði miklu, síðan vér settumsk. Nú er þat ráð mitt, konungr, at vit brœðr ríðim þegar í nótt fyrir með okkru liði. Má þat vera, at þeir óttisk nú ekki at sér, er þeir hafa spurt, at konungr þeira er nær með her mikinn. Skulum vit þá veita þeim áhlaup, en er þeir verða forflótta, þá munu þeir láta lið sitt, en ódjarfari síðan í atgǫngu at móti oss."

Konungi þótti þetta ráð vel fundit. "Munum vér búa her várn, þegar er lýsir, ok fara til móts við yðr."

Staðfestu þeir þetta ráð ok luku stefnunni.

LIII. Kapítuli — Um bardaga.

Hringr jarl ok Aðils bróðir hans bjuggu her sinn ok fóru þegar um nóttina suðr á heiðina. En er ljóst var, þá sá varðmenn þeira Þórólfs, hvar herrinn fór. Var þá blásinn herblástr, ok herklæddusk menn, tóku síðan at fylkja liðinu ok hǫfðu tvær fylkingar. Réð Álfgeirr jarl fyrir annarri fylking, ok var merki borit fyrir honum. Var í þeiri fylking lið þat, er honum hafði fylgt, ok svá þat lið, er þar hafði til safnazk ór heruðum. Var þat miklu fleira lið en þat, er þeim Þórólfi fylgði.

Þórólfr var svá búinn, at hann hafði skjǫld víðan ok þykkvan, hjálm á hǫfði allsterkan, gyrðr sverði því, er hann kallaði Lang, mikit vápn ok gott. Kesju hafði hann í hendi. Fjǫðrin var tveggja álna lǫng ok sleginn fram broddr ferstrendr, en upp var fjǫðrin breið, falrinn bæði langr ok digr, skaptit var eigi hæra en taka mátti hendi til fals ok furðuliga digrt. Járnteinn var í falnum ok skaptit allt járnvafit. Þau spjót váru kǫlluð brynþvarar.

Egill hafði inn sama búnað sem Þórólfr. Hann var gyrðr sverði því, er hann kallaði Naðr. Þat sverð hafði hann fengit á Kúrlandi. Var þat it bezta vápn. Hvárrgi þeira hafði brynju.

Þeir settu merki upp, ok bar þat Þorfiðr strangi. Allt lið þeira hafði norrœna skjǫldu ok allan norrœnan herbúnað. Í þeiri fylking váru allir norrœnir menn, þeir er þar váru. Fylkðu þeir Þórólfr nær skóginum, en Álfgeirs fylking fór með ánni.

Aðils jarl ok þeir brœðr sá þat, at þeir myndi ekki koma þeim Þórólfi á óvart. Þá tóku þeir at fylkja sínu liði. Gerðu þeir ok tvær fylkingar ok hǫfðu tvau merki. Fylkði Aðils móti Álfgeiri jarli, en Hringr móti víkingum. Síðan tóksk þar orrosta. Gengu hvárirtveggju vel fram.

Aðils jarl sótti hart fram, þar til er Álfgeirr lét undan sígask, en Aðils menn sóttu þá hálfu djarfligar. Var þá ok eigi lengi, áðr en Álfgeirr flýði, ok er þat frá honum at segja, at hann reið undan suðr á heiðina ok sveit manna með honum. Reið hann, þar til er hann kom nær borg þeiri, er konungr sat.

Þá mælti jarlinn: "Ekki ætla ek oss fara til borgarinnar. Vér fengum mikit orðaskak næst, er vér kómum til konungs, þá er vér hǫfðum farit ósigr fyrir Óláfi konungi, ok ekki mun honum þykkja batnat hafa várr kostr í þessi ferð. Mun nú ekki þurfa at ætla til sœmða, þar sem hann er."

-ered a great force since we set up camp. Now, my counsel is this, King, that we two brothers ride out at once this very night with our forces. It may be that they will have no fear for themselves since they have learned that their king is nearby with his army. We will set upon them, but if they turn and flee they must lose some of their men and then will be less bold in making attacks against us."

The King realized that this seemed to be good advice. "We will make our army ready here, as soon as it is light, and move to join you."

They made steadfast this plan and ended the council.

Chapter 53. Of the battle.

Earl Hring and Adils his brother made ready their army and immediately moved out into the night going southward toward the heath. But when dawn came, Thorolf's watchmen saw the army approaching. Then was blown a blast of trumpets and men put on armor and took to drawing up the army into two battle arrays. Earl Alfgar took command of one of the battalions and his standard was borne before him. In that group were those men of his own, as well as those forces who had joined them from the countryside. It was a much larger force than that which was commanded by Thorolf.

Thorolf was thus armed: he had a wide shield that was thick, and a very strong helm upon his head. He was girt with a sword that he called Long, a weapon large and good. He had in his hand a halberd. Its blade was two ells long and forged into a broad tapering spike. The socket was both long and thick. The shaft was made just so tall that a man might grasp the socket with his hand, and it was extremely thick. The socket was fitted with an iron spike, and it was wrapped with iron all about. These spears were called mail-piercers.

Egil had the same gear as Thorolf. He was girt with the sword he called Adder, the sword he had gotten in Courland; it was the best of weapons. Neither of them had on mail.

They raised up their standard, and it was borne by Thorfid the Strong. All of their forces had Norse shields and Norse weaponry, and in their battalion were all the Norsemen who were there. Thorolf's forces were arrayed near the wood, while Alfgar's moved along the river.

Earl Adils and his brother saw that they would not be able to come upon Thorolf unaware so they began to draw up their own forces. They formed up two groups as well and had two standards. Adils set his force against Earl Alfgar while Hring opposed the Vikings. Then battle began and both sides went forward valiantly.

Earl Adils pressed forward hard, until Alfgar gave ground. Then Adil's men pressed on much more boldly, and it was not long before Alfgar fled. Of him it is said that he rode away south over the heath with a troop of men with him. He rode on till he came near that town where the king was staying.

Then spoke the earl, "I do not think we will go into the town. We received a great scolding the last time we came before the king, after we were defeated by King Anlaf, and he will not think our condition is much improved by this coming. I do not think there is need to expect honor where he is concerned."

Síðan reið hann suðr á landit, ok er frá hans ferð þat at segja, at hann reið dag ok nótt, þar til er þeir kómu vestr á Jarlsnes. Fekk jarl sér þar far suðr um sæ ok kom fram á Vallandi. Þar átti hann kyn hálft. Kom hann aldregi síðan til Englands.

Aðils rak fyrst flóttann ok eigi langt, áðr hann snýr aptr ok þar til, er orrostan var, ok veitti þá atgǫngu.

En er Þórólfr sá þat, sneri hann í móti jarli ok bað þangat bera merkit, bað menn sína fylgjask vel ok standa þykkt, — "Þokum at skóginum," sagði hann, "ok látum hann hlífa á bak oss, svá at þeir megi eigi ǫllum megum at oss ganga."

Þeir gerðu svá, fylgðu fram skóginum. Varð þá hǫrð orrosta. Sótti Egill móti Aðísli, ok áttust þeir við hǫrð skipti. Liðsmunr var allmikill, ok þó fell meir lið þeira Aðils.

Þórólfr gerðist þá svá óðr, at hann kastaði skildinum á bak sér, en tók spjótit tveim hǫndum. Hljóp hann þá fram ok hjó eða lagði til beggja handa. Stukku menn þá frá tveggja vegna, en hann drap marga. Ruddi hann svá stíginn fram at merki jarlsins Hrings, ok helzk þá ekki við honum. Hann drap þann mann, er bar merki Hrings jarls, ok hjó niðr merkis tǫngina. Síðan lagði hann spjótinu fyrir brjóst jarlinum, í gegnum brynjuna ok búkinn, svá at út gekk um herðarnar, ok hóf hann upp á kesjunni yfir hǫfuð sér ok skaut niðr spjótshalanum í jǫrðina, en jarlinn sœfðisk á spjótinu, ok sá þat allir, bæði hans menn ok svá hans óvinir. Síðan brá Þórólfr sverðinu, ok hjó hann þá til beggja handa. Sóttu þá ok at hans menn. Fellu þá mjǫk Bretar ok Skotar, en sumir snerusk á flótta.

En er Aðils jarl sá fall bróður síns ok mannfall mikit af liði hans, en sumir flýðu, en hann þóttisk hart niðr koma, þá sneri hann á flótta ok rann til skógarins. Hann flýði í skóginn ok hans sveit. Tók þá at flýja allt lið þat, er þeim hafði fylgt. Gerðisk þá mannfall mikit af flóttamǫnnum, ok dreifðisk þá flóttinn víða um heiðina. Aðils jarl hafði niðr drepit merki sínu, ok vissi þá engi, hvárt hann fór eða aðrir menn. Tók þá brátt at myrkva af nótt, en þeir Þórólfr ok Egill sneru aptr til herbúða sinna, ok þá jafnskjótt kom þar Aðalsteinn konungr með allan her sinn ok slógu þá landtjǫldum sínum ok bjuggusk um.

Litlu síðar kom Óláfr konungr með sinn her. Tjǫlduðu þeir ok bjuggusk um, þar sem þeira menn hǫfðu tjaldat. Var Óláfi konungi þá sagt, at fallnir váru þeir báðir jarlar hans, Hringr ok Aðils, ok mikill fjǫlði annarra manna hans.

LIV. Kapítuli — Enn um bardaga. Fall Þórólfs.

Aðalsteinn konungr hafði verit áðr ina næstu nótt í borg þeiri, er fyrr var frá sagt, ok þar spurði hann, at bardagi hafði verit á heiðinni, bjósk þá þegar ok allr herrinn ok sótti norðr á heiðina, spurði þá ǫll tíðendi glǫggliga, hvernig orrosta sú hafði farit. Kómu þá til fundar við konung þeir brœðr, Þórólfr ok Egill. Þakkaði hann þeim vel framgǫngu sína ok sigr þann, er þeir hǫfðu unnit, hét þeim vináttu sinni fullkominni. Dvǫlðusk þeir þar allir samt um nóttina.

Aðalsteinn konungr vakði upp her sinn þegar um morgininn árdegis. Hann átti tal við hǫfðingja sína ok sagði, hver skipun vera skyldi fyrir liði hans. Skipaði hann

Then he rode into the southlands, and of his journey it is said that he rode day and night until he and his men came west into Earlsness. There the earl obtained a ship and traveled south, over the sea, and came to France, which was the place of origin of half his kin. He came never again to England.

Adils at first pursued the flying foe, but it was not long before he turned back to where the battle was and made an attack.

But when Thorolf saw this he turned to oppose the earl and ordered that the standard be borne there. He bade his men to follow bravely and stand fast. "Move along the wood," he said, "and let it cover our backs so that they may not attack us from all sides."

They did so, skirting the forest. The battle was fierce. Egil sought out and attacked Adils, and they exchanged hard blows. The odds were very great, but still more of Adils men fell.

Thorolf then fought so furiously that he cast his shield over his back and took his halberd in two hands. He leaped forward and hewed and thrust to either side. Men sprang away in both directions but he slew many. He cleared the path to Earl Hring's standard and nothing could stand against him. He slew the man who bore King Hring's standard and hewed down the standard pole. Then he thrust his spearhead into the earl's breast, through his mail and his body so that it came out between his shoulders, and lifted him up over his own head upon the great halberd and drove the other end into the earth. And all saw, both friend and foe alike, that he was defeated. Then Thorolf drew his sword and slashed about on either side as his men pressed the attack. Then many Britons and Scotsmen fell, but some turned and fled.

When Earl Adils saw the death of his brother, and the great number of men fallen from his army, and that some were fleeing, he deemed then that a harsh end was coming. He turned and fled, running into the forest with his men. Then all the forces that he had fled likewise. There were great casualties among the fleeing men and they were scattered widely across the heath. Earl Adils had dropped his standard and no one could tell him from the other men who fled. Soon the darkness of night fell and Thorolf and Egil turned back to their camp. At that moment King Athelstan arrived with all his army, and they set up their tents and made camp.

Soon after King Anlaf arrived with his army and they too set up their tents and settled into camp where their men had been before. King Anlaf was told that both his earls, Hring and Adils, had fallen along with a great many of his men.

Chapter 54. Still of the battle. Thorolf's fall.

King Athelstan had spent the night before in that town that was spoken of earlier, and there he heard that there had been battle on the heath. He and all his army made ready at once and set out north across the heath. There they heard clearly all the tidings concerning how things had fared in battle. The two brothers, Thorolf and Egil, came to meet with the king, and he thanked them for their bold charge and the victory that they had won; he promised to them his full friendship. They all stayed there together for the night.

King Athelstan quickly woke his men early the next morning. He spoke to his captains and told them just how his forces should be arrayed. He ordered his group

fylking sína fyrst, ok þá setti hann í brjósti þeirar fylkingar sveitir þær, er snarpastar váru.

Þá mælti hann, at fyrir því liði skyldi vera Egill, — "en Þórólfr," sagði hann, "skal vera með liði sínu ok ǫðru því liði, er ek set þar. Skal sú vera ǫnnur fylking í liði váru, er hann skal vera hǫfðingi fyrir, því at Skotar eru jafnan lausir í fylkingu, hlaupa þeir til ok frá ok koma í ýmsum stǫðum fram. Verða þeir opt skeinusamir, ef menn varask eigi, en eru lausir á velli, ef við þeim er horft."

Egill svaraði konungi: "Ekki vil ek, at vit Þórólfr skilimsk í orrostu, en vel þykkir mér, at okkr sé þar skipat, er mest þykkir þurfa ok harðast er fyrir."

Þórólfr mælti: "Látum vit konung ráða, hvar hann vill okkr skipa. Veitum honum svá, at honum líki. Mun ek vera heldr, ef þú vill, þar er þér er skipat."

Egill segir: "Þér munuð nú ráða, en þessa skiptis mun ek opt iðrask."

Gengu menn þá í fylkingar, svá sem konungr hafði skipat, ok váru sett upp merki. Stóð konungs fylking á víðlendit til árinnar, en Þórólfs fylking fór it efra með skóginum.

Óláfr konungr tók þá at fylkja liði sínu, þá er hann sá, at Aðalsteinn hafði fylkt. Hann gerði ok tvær fylkingar, ok lét hann fara sitt merki ok þá fylking, er hann réð sjálfr fyrir, móti Aðalsteini konungi ok hans fylking. Hǫfðu þá hvárirtveggju her svá mikinn, at engi var munr, hvárir fjǫlmennari váru, en ǫnnur fylking Óláfs konungs fór nær skóginum móti liði því, er Þórólfr réð fyrir. Váru þar hǫfðingjar jarlar skozkir. Váru þat Skotar flest, ok var þat fjǫlmenni mikit.

Síðan gangask á fylkingar, ok varð þar brátt orrosta mikil. Þórólfr sótti fram hart ok lét bera merki sitt fram með skóginum ok ætlaði þar svá fram at ganga, at hann kœmi í opna skjǫldu konungs fylkinginni. Hǫfðu þeir skjǫlduna fyrir sér, en skógrinn var til hœgra vegs. Létu þeir hann þar hlífa. Þórólfr gekk svá fram, at fáir váru menn hans fyrir honum, en þá er hann varði minnst, þá hlaupa þar ór skóginum Aðils jarl ok sveit sú, er honum fylgði, brugðu þegar mǫrgum kesjum senn á Þórólf, ok fell hann þar við skóginn, en Þorfiðr, er merkit bar, hopaði aptr, þar er liðit stóð þykkra, en Aðils sótti þá at þeim, ok var þar þá orrosta mikil. Œpðu Skotar þá sigróp, er þeir hǫfðu felldan hǫfðingjann.

En er Egill heyrði óp þat ok sá, at merki Þórólfs fór á hæl, þá þóttisk hann vita, at Þórólfr myndi eigi sjálfr fylgja. Síðan hleypr hann til þangat fram í milli fylkinganna. Hann varð skjótt varr þeira tíðenda, er þar váru orðin, þegar hann fann sína menn. Hann eggjar þá liðit mjǫk til framgǫngu. Var hann fremstr í brjóstinu. Hann hafði sverðit Naðr í hendi. Hann sótti þá fram ok hjó til beggja handa ok felldi marga menn. Þorfiðr bar merkit þegar eptir honum, en annat lið fylgði merkinu. Var þar in snarpasta orrosta. Egill gekk fram, til þess er hann mœtti Aðísli jarli. Áttusk þeir fá hǫgg við, áðr Aðils jarl fell ok mart manna um hann, en eptir fall hans þá flýði lið þat, er honum hafði fylgt, en Egill ok hans lið fylgði þeim ok drápu allt þat, er þeir náðu, því at ekki þurfti þá griða at biðja. En jarlar þeir inir

to advance first and placed in the front wave of that battalion the keenest of their men.

Then he said that Egil should be in command of these men. "But Thorolf," he said, "shall be with his own men and others that I place there. That shall be our other battalion, and he shall be in command of it, because the Scots are always in loose ranks and they run to and fro and come forward in various places. They are often apt to do damage if men are not on guard, but are unreliable in the field if you go against them."

Egil answered the king, "It is my will that Thorolf and I not be separated in battle; rather it seems well that we two be placed there, where there appears to be the most need and the hardest fighting."

Thorolf spoke, "Let the king determine where he will place us. We will support him as he wishes. I will hold that spot, if you wish, that was assigned to you."

Egil said, "You may decide now, but this arrangement I will often repent."

The men then formed into battle array, just as the king had ordered them, and the standards were raised. The king's battalion formed up on the plain towards the river, while Thorolf's force moved to the higher ground along the wood.

King Anlaf put his own forces into formation when he saw that Athelstan had arrayed his. He put them into two battalions as well, and commanded that his standard and the battalion that he commanded himself be opposed to King Athelstan and his forces. Both of them had great armies; there was no telling which had the larger number of men. But King Anlaf's second battalion moved near the wood to oppose the forces that Thorolf commanded. The captains there were Scottish earls. There were a great many men and they were mostly Scots.

Then the armies came together and there was at once great battle. Thorolf moved forward boldly and ordered his standard to be borne forward along the wood. He intended to advance there and come against the king's open shields. His own men had their shields before them, with the forest on the right, letting it protect them there. Thorolf charged forward boldly, so that few of his men were before him, but when he was least wary, out from the forest leapt Earl Adils and his troops who were with him. They immediately thrust at Thorolf with many halberds and he was felled there by the wood. But Thorfid, who bore the standard, retreated to where the forces stood thicker. Then Adils pressed against them and there was a great fight. The Scots raised a shout of victory when they had slain the enemy leader.

When Egil heard that shout and saw that Thorolf's standard was moving in retreat, then he felt sure that Thorolf must not be with his troops. He then leapt forward into the space between the two battalions. When he came to his own men there, he was quickly given tidings of what had occurred. He strongly urged his men to advance with courage, and he was foremost in the charge. He had his sword Adder in his hand, and he pressed forward, slashing to either side and felling many men. Thorfid bore the standard quickly after him, and behind the standard followed the rest of the troops. There was fierce combat. Egil advanced until he came up against Earl Adils. They exchanged few blows before Earl Adils was slain and many men around him. But after his fall many of the troops that had followed him fled, and Egil and his men pursued them and slew all they overtook; there was no need to beg for quarter. The

skozku stóðu þá ekki lengi, þegar er þeir sá, at aðrir flýðu þeira félagar, tóku þegar á rás undan.

En þeir Egill stefndu þá þar til, er var konungs fylkingin, ok kómu þá í opna skjǫldu ok gerðu þar brátt mikit mannfall. Riðlaðisk þá fylkingin ok losnaði ǫll. Flýðu þá margir af Óláfs mǫnnum, en víkingar œpðu þá sigróp. En er Aðalsteinn konungr þóttisk finna, at rofna tók fylkíng Óláfs konungs, þá eggjaði hann lið sitt ok lét fram bera merki, gerði þá atgǫngu harða, svá at hrǫkk fyrir lið Óláfs ok gerðisk allmikit mannfall. Fell þar Óláfr konungr ok mestr hluti liðs þess, er Óláfr hafði haft, því at þeir, er á flótta snerusk, váru allir drepnir, er nát varð. Fekk Aðalsteinn konungr þar allmikinn sigr.

LV. Kapítuli — Egill jarðaði Þórólf.

Aðalsteinn konungr sneri í brott frá orrostunni, en menn hans ráku flóttann. Hann reið aptr til borgarinnar ok tók eigi fyrr náttstað en í borginni, en Egill rak flóttann ok fylgði þeim lengi ok drap hvern mann, er hann náði. Síðan sneri hann aptr með sveitunga sína ok fór þar til, er orrostan hafði verit, ok hitti þar Þórólf, bróður sinn látinn. Hann tók upp lík hans ok þó, bjó um síðan, sem siðvenja var til. Grófu þeir þar grǫf ok settu Þórólf þar í með vápnum sínum ǫllum ok klæðum. Síðan spennti Egill gullhring á hvára hǫnd honum, áðr hann skilðisk við, hlóðu síðan at grjóti ok jósu at moldu.

. . .

Síðan váru grœddir þeir menn, er sárir váru ok lífs auðit. Egill dvalðisk með Aðalsteini konungi inn næsta vetr eptir fall Þórólfs, ok hafði hann allmiklar virðingar af konungi. Var þá með honum lið þat allt, er áðr hafði fylgt þeim báðum brœðrum ok ór orrostu hǫfðu komizk. Þá orti Egill drápu um Aðalstein konung, ok er í því kvæði þetta:

Nú hefr foldgnárr fellda,
fellr jǫrð und nið Ellu,
hjaldrsnerrandi, harra
hǫfuðbaðmr, þría jǫfra.
Aðalsteinn of vann annat,
allt's lægra kynfrægjum,
hér sverjum þess, hyrjar
hrannbrjótr, konungmanni.

En þetta er stefit í drápunni:

Nú liggr hæst und hraustum
hreinbraut Aðalsteini.

Scottish earls did not stand long then, as soon as they saw that their companions had fled, and took at once to their heels.

Then Egil and his men made for where King Anlaf's forces were arrayed and came against their open shields and a great many men were slain. The entire formation broke ranks and fell into disarray. Many of Anlaf's men fled and the Vikings let out a cry of victory. When King Athelstan realized that King Anlaf's forces were giving way then he urged on his army and commanded his standard to be borne forward, making such a fierce attack that Anlaf's forces retreated and many were slain in the field. King Anlaf fell there and the greater part of the forces that he had; because of those who turned and fled all were slain that were taken. King Athelstan won a very great victory there.

Chapter 55. Egil buries Thorolf.

King Athelstan turned away from the battlefield while his men pursued those who had fled. He rode back to the fortified town, taking no quarters for the night until he reached it. But Egil drove the routed forces, pursuing them long and killing every man that he could catch. Then he turned back with his troop and went again to the battlefield, and came upon his brother Thorolf, slain. He took up his body and yet prepared it according to custom. They dug a grave there and set Thorolf in it with all his weapons and garments. Then Egil clasped a gold ring upon either wrist before he parted from him. Then they heaped stones upon the grave and covered it with earth.

*[At this point the chapter goes on to describe the ring-giving ceremony between Egil and Athelstan, in which the King repays Egil for the death of his brother.]*

Then those men were healed, who were wounded and had hope for life. Egil dwelt with King Athelstan for the next winter after Thorolf's death, and received very great honor from the king. There were with him all those men who had followed the two brothers and who had come out of the battle. Then Egil composed a poem about King Athelstan, and in it was this verse:

Now has the earth-shield,
the battle messenger,
three earls felled,
all fallen under the kin of Ella.
Athelstan achieved more,
the kin-famous king conquers all,
this I swear, to the breaker
of the wave of fire, king of men.

But this is the refrain in the poem:

Now lie the high reindeer hills
under Athelstan's rule.

### 26. ROGER WENDOVER, *FLORES HISTORIARUM*

**Latin**
**before 1236**

[See notes.]

### 27. MATTHEW PARIS, *CHRONICA MAJORA*

**Latin**
**1259**

[See notes.]

### 28. *LIVERE DE REIS DE ENGLETERRE*

**Anglo-Norman**
**1274**

Adelstan, le fiz Eduuard, fu corune de Adelin, le erceveske de Cantorbirie, a Kingestone, e regna xvi. anz. Cestui Adelstan fist Vidual le rei de Waleis e Constantin le rei de Escoce veuder lour reaumes. E nekedent tost a pres par sa merci rendi a eus lur reaumes a tel covenant, ke il les tenissent de ly. E dist ke plus noble chose est fere rei ke estre rei.

Au derein le rei de Escoce avant dit ou le fiz le rei de Northumerlaunde ki soleit estre, ki filie le rei Adelstan avoit a femme, se mist contre lui. En un vespre kant il fu couche en soen lit vint sudeinement sur ly, kant il ne sucha si ben noun. E il meintenant tut effrae leva e se ceint de se espeie, e cria a ses genz ke chescon se armast e defendist al meuz ke il peust.

Estevus ke par kas le espee le rei chai hors del feure ke il ne sout; mes kant il fu venu alfort e il quidoit aver troue se espee, ne trova ren. E il tant tost se mist a prier Deu e Seint Aldelin. E estevus il mist la mein al feure e le trova meintenant. E il de ceo prist tant de hardement ke il combati si forciblement ke il les enchaca trestuz; e cel espee est unkore garde pur miracle el tresor des reis.

Le fu tue le rei de Escoce Costantin, e autre v. reis, ki vindrent oue li, e xii. contes, e pur poi tuz ceus ki la vindrunt, hors pris aucons ki demorerent e resceurunt la fei Crestiene.

### 29. BARTHOLOMEW OF COTTON, *HISTORIA ANGLICANA*

**Latin**
**ca. 1292**

Anno Domini DCCCCXLV et regni sui iiii., commisit proelium maximum apud Brunesberich contra Anlaf, regem Hiberniae, qui uenit in auxilium Scotorum et Dacorum conuersantium in Anglia . . . in quo bello v. reges occubuerunt . . . ducesque vii. regis Anlaui, et absque numero ceciderunt Scoti . . . Deinde rediit in Westsexe cum fratre suo Eadmundo, qui ei in auxilium in hoc bello praebuit.

### 30. *ANNALES DE WINTONIA*

**Latin**
**late 13th c.**

Iste unum regem Scottorum, et quinque reges Dacorum, et duodecim comites, cum copiis suis uno certamine vita privavit.

## 26. Roger Wendover, *Flowers of History* See p. 212

[See notes.]

## 27. Matthew Paris, *Great Chronicle* See p. 212

[See notes.]

## 28. *Genealogy of the Kings of England* See pp. 212–13

Athelstan, the son of Edward, was crowned by Adelen, the archbishop of Canterbury, at Kingston, and reigned for sixteen years. This Athelstan forced Idwal, king of Wales, and Constantine, king of Scotland, to abandon their realms. And yet soon after, out of his mercy, he gave them back their realms, on the condition that they should hold them of him. And he said it was a more noble thing to make a king than to be a king.

At last the aforesaid king of Scotland, with the son of the former king of Northumberland who had King Athelstan's daughter to wife, rebelled against him. One evening, when he was lying on his bed, he came suddenly upon him while he was thinking no harm. And at once, all alarmed, he rose up and girded on his sword and cried to his followers that every one should arise and defend himself as best he could.

Behold, by accident the king's sword fell out of its scabbard, and he knew it not; but when he was in danger, and thought to reach for his sword, he found nothing. And immediately he himself prayed to God and to Saint Aldhelm. And, behold, he put his hand to the scabbard, and at once he found it. And thus he received such great encouragement that he fought so stoutly that he drove them all away; and that sword is still kept in the king's treasury, in memory of the miracle.

There was slain Constantine the king of Scotland, also five other kings who came with him, and twelve earls, and nearly all those who came there, except some who remained and received the Christian faith.

## 29. Bartholomew of Cotton, *History of England* See p. 213

In the year of the Lord 945 and the fourth of his reign, Athelstan fought the greatest of battles at Brunesberich against Anlaf, king of Ireland, who had made an alliance with the Scots and Danes living in England . . . in that war five kings lay dead . . . and seven earls of King Anlaf, and Scots beyond number died . . . Then Athelstan returned to Wessex with his brother Edmund who provided aid in that war.

## 30. *Annals of Winchester* See p. 213

In a single battle he deprived one king of the Scots, five kings of the Danes, and twelve earls of life, along with many of their men.

### 31. JOHN OF OXNEAD, *CHRONICA*

**Latin**
**before 1293**

Anno Dominicae Incarnationis nongentesimo xxiiij°, Æthelstanus, filius Edwardi, electus rex in Merce, et sacratus apud Kingestone, qui regno quidem parum uixit, sed belli gestis non parum splenduit; qui a fortissimis lacessiri, sed bello nunquam potuit uinci. Qunique reges in loco belli occuberunt gladiis percussi, duces septem; absque numero ceciderunt Scoti. Non fuit bellum hac in tellure majus paratum, nec caedes tanta praecessit istam postquam hic uenerunt Angli et Saxones [Britones] pulsuri, clari martis fabri, Walenses uicerunt, reges fugauerunt, regna susceperunt.

### 32. ROBERT OF GLOUCESTER, *METRICAL CHRONICLE*

**Middle English**
**late 13th c.**

Athelston was tho king  that was Edwardes sone:
ond thoru the heymen of the lond  ycrouned at Kingestone
in the nyen hundred yer ond four one tuenty  of grace ycrouned he was,
ond bote aboute vourtene yer  king ther after he nas.
Holi Chirche he lovede wel  ond rerde manyon.
The verste yer of is kinedom  ybore was Seint Dunston.
Nywe abbeys he made vaste,  the gode Athelston,
ond ther nas of olde house  in the londe non
that he ne amendede with som lond  other mid buldinge
other mid boc other riche cloth  other som other riche thinge.
Northhomberlond he wan,  ond Walis ond Scotland;
ond the kinges ond her lond  heold al in is hond.
Him thohte it was more nobleye  tho he adde an honde al this
vor to maky kinges  than to be king ywis.
Ayen he made kinges  that kinges er were,
bote that hii were under him  ond truage him bere.
Tho hii adde hor lond ayen:  the king of Scotlond
Constantin, ond Analaf  king of Homberlond.
Upe this king Athelston  gaderede men ynowe,
ond here bisouthe Humber  mid hor ost drowe.
Analaf was god kniht  ond stalwarde ond quoynte:
menestral he was god ynou  ond harpare in eche poynte.
To Athelstones pavylon  mid is harpe he wende
ond so wel withoute harpede  that me after him sende.
There he harpede so wel  that he payde al the route.
Ac evere were is eyen  in eche hurne aboute.
After mete tho hii nolde  nammore of is pley:
hii yeve him silver vor is glé  ond lete him go is wey.
Of the silver he adde hoker  vor he ne com thuder vor non,
ac is wille he adde tho he sey  the stat of is fon.
On that adde ybe mid him  the king tolde ther.
The king him blamede tho  that he nadde ytold him er.

## 31. JOHN OF OXNEAD, *CHRONICLE*

**See p. 214**

In the year of the Lord's Incarnation 924, Athelstan, son of Edward, was chosen king in Mercia and consecrated at Kingston. Indeed he lived a short while during his reign but he shone a great deal in deeds of war; he was challenged by the very mighty but never conquered in war. Five kings met their death on the battlefield, struck down by swords, as well as seven earls. Irishmen died beyond number. No greater war was ever waged in this land, nor did such a slaughter surpass that one since the Angles and Saxons, famous war-smiths, came here to drive out the Britons; they conquered the Welsh, routed kings, and took kingdoms.

## 32. ROBERT OF GLOUCESTER, *METRICAL CHRONICLE*

**See pp. 214–15**

Athelstan, who was Edward's son, was then king:
through the nobles of the land he was crowned at Kingston
in the year of Our Lord nine-hundred and twenty-four,
and there was no other king for about fourteen years thereafter.
Holy churches he loved well and built many of them.
The first year of his reign Saint Dunstan was born.
New abbeys he made secure, the good Athelstan,
and there was no old house [of God] in the land
that he did not aid with some land or building
or book or rich cloth or some other rich thing.
Northumberland he won, and Wales and Scotland;
and he held the kings and their lands all in his power.
He thought it was more noble since he had control
to make kings than to be a king.
So he made them kings again who kings were before,
on the condition that they were under him and owed him tribute.
Then they had their lands again: the king of Scotland
Constantine, and Anlaf the king of Northumbria.
Against this King Athelstan [they then] gathered men enough,
and here south of the Humber they came with their army.
Anlaf was a good knight, stalwart and clever:
in minstrelsy he was well-versed, and a harper in every way.
To Athelstan's tent with his harp he went
and played so well outside that men were sent after him.
Inside he harped so well that he gladdened all the men.
But always were his eyes in each corner around him.
After their meal they would have no more of his playing:
they gave him silver for his reward and let him go his way.
He disdained the silver because he did not come there for that,
but his desire he had accomplished when he saw the state of his foe.
One man that had been with him told the king [about this].
The king blamed him then, that he had not told him earlier.

"Sire," he sede, "Ich was ysuore to him ar to thee.
One yif ichadde him bisuike the wors thou wost leve me.
Ac remwe into another stude thi pavilon bi mi rede:
other thou miht yut to niht of som treson drede."
The pavilon was remewed tho, ond the king ond alle his.
Ac a bissop ond is men ther vorth come ywis
and pihte there hor pavylon ond bilevede al niht there.
Ond this luther men come aniht ond wende the king it were
ond slowe the bissop ond al is men that gult nadde non.
Ond suththe hii wende vorthore mo ond sohte Athelston.
Of hom nas he nohte ywar ar tho atte laste,
ac sone he ond is men armede hom wel vaste,
ond Edmund is brother mid him ond tho hii preste were echon.
Hii wende vorth to this batayle ond mette mid hor fon.
The king to is suerde drou ond tho ne vond he non
ac was mid treson him binome. Hard cas was that on!
On God Almihti ond Seint Aldelm the king cryde vaste tho,
ond hii sende him bi vair miracle bote of is wo:
to is scauberc he pulte is hond al prest a suerd he vond,
Therinne thoru God ysend. No betere nas in the lond.
In the kinges tresorie that suerde iwust ys
as vor noble relike yut to this daye ywis.
Yegged it is in the on half ond in the other noht,
ther ne mihte nevere gold ne selver ther on ben ybroht.
This noble king Athelston, tho this gode suerd to him com,
nobliche ond wel he faht. Ond so God ernest to him nom
that fram that the sonne aros vorte hit derc niht was
the batayle ylaste ond nevere wery he nas.
Wat thoru is stalwardhede, wat thoru Godes grace,
mony was the gode body that he slou in the place.
The batayle was at Brymesbury, ond ther were of Deneys
ond of Scottes aslawe — ond also of Yreis —
vif yonge kinges proute thoru alle thing,
ond the proute Constantin that of Scotlond was king.
Ond of othere that were aslawe me ne mihte non ende ysé.
Hii that of scapede alive bigonne vaste to flé.
Thus the king Athelston agaste tho is fon.
Ond vor hii ne ssolde in is lond abbe recet non,
the castel of Everwik to grounde he let caste —
vor is fon were ofte ther inne the wule he ylaste —
that hii nadde no recet vor to grevy is lond.
Also of ech maner purchas that com in is hond,
other that eny of is as in purchas nome,
he vorbed that nevere more among is spence ne come
ac to hous of religion that me hit al clene bere
ond to poueremen aboute that meseyse were.
Alle the kinges of Walis he brohte al to lawe:

"Sire," he said, "I was sworn to him before I was sworn to you.
If I had betrayed him you would have thought me capable of worse.
But take my advice and move your tent to another place:
otherwise you might suffer tonight some dreadful danger."
The tent was removed then, along with the king and all his household.
But a bishop and his men came there
and set up their tent in that same place and there stayed the night.
Thus the wicked men came at night and thought that tent was the king's
and slew the bishop and al his men who were innocent.
Then they went further into the camp seeking Athelstan.
He was not aware of them until the last moment,
but quickly he and his men armed themselves well,
and Edmund, his brother, and the others with him were pressured.
They went forth to this battle and met with their enemy.
The king reached for his sword and then found that he had none
but was beset with danger. A difficult situation that was!
To God Almighty and Saint Aldhelm the king then cried,
and they sent him through a beautiful miracle a cure for his woe:
to his scabbard he again put his hand and touched a sword he found there,
sent by God. There was no better [blade] in the land.
I know that sword remains in the king's treasury
taken as a noble relic still to this day.
Etched it is on one side and not on the other,
there is neither gold nor silver upon it.
This noble King Athelstan, after this good sword came to him,
fought nobly and well. And so God gave him such ardor
that from the time that the sun arose until the dark of night fell
the battle lasted yet he never grew weary.
Skilled through his stalwartness, skilled through God's grace,
there were many good men that he slew in that place.
The battle took place at Brymesbury, and there of the Danes
and of the Scots were slain — and also of the Irish —
five young kings who were proud in all their works,
along with the proud Constantine who of Scotland was king.
And of the others who were slain men could not count them.
Those who escaped alive fled quickly.
Thus the king Athelstan confounded those who were his foes.
And so that they should not have shelter in his land,
the fortress of York he cast to the ground —
because his foes were often therein during his time —
so that they had no harbor from which to harm his land.
Also of every kind of wealth that came into his hand,
or that he had himself seized as booty,
he swore that it should never into his treasury come
but that men should bear it wholly to the houses of religion
and to the poor who suffered in the land.
All the kings of Wales he brought completely to order:

to Hereford al under him    to is wille vawe
that tuenty pound of golde    ech of hom hym bere,
ond thritti pound of selver    fram yere to yere,
ond tuenti thousend oxen    ek to his yolde,
ond hauekes ond houndes    as mony as he wolde.
To certein woniinge he hom brohte,    bothe lowe ond heye,
so that hor woniinge were    al bi weste weye
ond nothing in the est alf.    So that weye ywis
yut to this day to delth    Engelond ond Walis,
ond thoru King Athelston    that was verst ydo.
Men of Cornwayle he brohte    to certeyn stude also,
vor biyonde the water of Tamer    he hom adde alle ybroht
to wonye ther as in hor owe    ond a this alf noht,
vor hii wonede ther bivore    anon to Excestre riht,
ond the welisse ver in Engelond    vorte he it adde ydiht.
King Athelston lovede moche    Malmesbury ywis:
he yef hom of the Holy Croys    som that yut there is.
Ond he was at is ende day    vaire ybured ther.
King he arst adde ybe    aboute an viftene yer.

### 33. *ANNALES DE WAVERLEIA*

**Latin**
**late 13th c.**

DCCCCXXII Edwardo filio Alfredi rege Anglorum mortuo, successit filius ejus Athelstan, et regnauit annis xiv; qui fecit maximum praelium apud Bruneberi.

### 34. *BRUT Y TYWYSOGION*

**Welsh**
**late 13th c.**

Deg mlyned ar hugein a nawcant oed oet Crist pan las Gruffud ab Ywein y gan wyr Keredigyawn. Ac y bu ryfel Brun. Ac y bu varw Hennyrth vab Clydawc a Meuryc y vrawt. Ac y bu varw Edelstan, brenhin y Saeson.

### 35. *BRENHINEDD Y SAESSON*

**Welsh**
**ca. 1300**

Anno Domini .ix.$^{c}$xxiiij. y bu varw Edward vrenhin, ac y clathpwyt ef yn y vanachlawc a wnathoed y dat yn Gaer Wynt.

Ac yna y gwnaethpwyt Edelstan vab Edward yn vrenhin yn Lloegyr. Ac y doeth gwyr Denmarc y geisiau goresgyn yr ynys y arnaw. Ac y rodes yntev kyffranc ydunt. Ac yn y kyffranc hwnnw y llas brenhin yr Yscottieit a phymp brenhin o Denmarc a deudeng ieirll ac ev lluoed. Ac ef a ystyngawd ydaw holl brenhined Kymre ac y berys

at Hereford all under him at his bidding they made a vow
that twenty pounds of gold each of them would bear to him,
and thirty pounds of silver from year to year,
and also to yield to him twenty thousand oxen,
and as many hawks and hounds as he desired.
To a certain dwelling place he brought them, both the rich and poor,
so that their dwellings were all moved to the west
and nothing remained in the east half. This was done, I know,
and continues to this day, to separate England and Wales,
and through King Athelstan this was first done.
The men of Cornwall he brought to a certain place, too:
far beyond the River Tamar he had them all brought
to dwell there in their own place not in this part,
for they lived there before even as far as Exeter,
like the Welsh far into England until he had governed it.
King Athelstan greatly loved Malmesbury, it is known:
he gave them of the Holy Cross that part that remains there.
And he was after his final day royally buried there.
King he had been about fifteen years.

## 33. *Annals of Waverley*

**See pp. 215–16**

**922**. After Edward, son of Alfred and king of the English, died, his son Athelstan succeeded him and ruled for fourteen years. He fought the greatest battle at Bruneberi.

## 34. *Chronicle of the Princes*

**See p. 216**

**[934/5.]** Nine hundred and thirty was the time of Christ when Gruffudd son of Owain was killed by the men of Ceredigion. **[937.]** And there was the battle of Brun. **[938.]** And Hyfaidd son of Clydog and Meurig his brother died. **[939.]** And Athelstan, king of the Saxons, died.

## 35. *Kings of the English*

**See pp. 216–19**

**[925.]** Year of Our Lord 924: King Edward died, and he was buried in the monastery his father built in Winchester.

And then Athelstan, the son of Edward, was made king in England. And men of Denmark came to try to conquer the island from him. And he gave battle to them, and in that battle the king of the Scots was killed, and five kings of Denmark and twelve earls and their hosts. And he subdued to him all the kings of Wales, and he

ydunt talu teyrnget ydaw megys y talawd brenhin Nortwei ydaw. Sef oed hynny — try chant pvnt o areant ac vgeint pvnt o eur a phymp mil o warthec pob blwydyn.

Ac ydaw yd oed chwaer, Hilde oed y henw, a theckaf morwyn o'r byt oed. Ac y doeth Edulf, iarll Boloyn, a Baudewine, iarll Flandrys, ac anrec y gan Huges, brenhin Freinc, y Edelstan, brenhin Lloegyr, hyt yn Abyndon — nyt amgen try chant emmys ac ev gwisgoed yn gyweir arnadunt, a chledyf Constans amheraudyr a'r wein yn eur coeth, ac vn o'r kethreu a uu mewn traet Yessu Grist pan diodefaut, yn gaeyedic yn y cledyf, a'r gwayw a uuassey gan Charlemaen vrenhin yn ymlad a Sarassinieit gynt, a choron Seyn Moris, a pheth o bren y Groc y diodefaut Crist, mewn maen krissiant yn gayedic, a phet o'r goron drein a uu ar benn Crist pan diodefaut, a choron vrenhiniaul o eur coeth a meyn gwyrthuaur o amryuaylion gwyrthyeu. Ac ef a'y derbynnws yn enrydedus, ac a anvones y chwaer y vrenhin Freinc, yr honn y buassei yn y damvnaw ys llawer o amser kyn no hynny.

Ac ef a gynhelijs yr ynys yn gyn gadarnhet pei edewyt torch o eur ar fford na lauassey neb y dwyn y lledrat. Ac ef a rodes y eglwys Caer Wynt penn Seyn Justi merthyr a their llys, nyt amgen, Childboldintone, Euedford, ac Eismereswordham. Ac a rodes llawer y uanachloc Malmesburie.

Anno .ix.$^{c}$xxvi. yd aeth Howel Da vab Cadell y Ruvein. Ac y bu varw Elen.

Anno Domini .ix.$^{c}$xxxiij. y llas Grufud vab Oweyn y gan wyr Keredigyawn.

Anno .ix.$^{c}$xxxv. y bu ymlad y Brune.

Anno .ix.$^{c}$xxxvi. y bu varw Hymeith vab Clydauc a Meuric.

Anno .ix.$^{c}$xxxix. y bu varw Edelstan, vrenhin Lloegyr; ac y clathpwyt ef yn Malmesburie.

## 36. PETER OF LANGTOFT, *CHRONIQUE*

**Anglo-Norman**
**ca. 1300**

Anno Domini d.cccc.xxiiij.

Après le ray Eduuard comença regner
Adelstan sun fiz, molt vailliaunt chuvaler.
Countes et barouns et clers de bon quer
s'en vount à Kingestoun ly rays corouner.
Les raytels de Gales ne sevent pes aver,
l'an secounde de sun regne of ly volent medler;
mès il les venquist; de pees en vount parler.
Le rays Adelstan Northwales fet charger
de xxiiij. livres d'or par an, ccc. de argent cher,
de x. mil vaches par an à sun larder;

had them pay tribute to him as the king of Norway had paid him, that is — three hundred pounds of silver and twenty pounds of gold and five thousand cattle each year.

And he had a sister, Eadhild was her name, and she was the fairest maiden in the world. And Adelolf, earl of Boulogne, and Baldwin, earl of Flanders, came with gifts from Hugh, king of France, to Athelstan, king of England, as far as Abingdon — none other than three hundred steeds with their trappings complete upon them, and the sword of Emperor Constantine with a scabbard of refined gold, with one of the nails which had been in the feet of Jesus Christ when He suffered set in the sword, and the spear that had been with King Charlemagne fighting with the Saracens long ago, and the crown of Saint Maurice, and part of the tree of the Cross on which Christ suffered, set in a crystal stone, and part of the crown of thorns that was on the head of Christ when He suffered, and a royal crown of refined gold, and precious stones of various virtues. And he received them honorably, and he sent his sister to the king of France, she whom he had been desiring for a good while before that.

And he held the island so strongly that if a torque of gold were left on the road, no one would dare take it by stealth. And he gave the head of Saint Justin the Martyr to the church of Winchester, and three courts — none other than Chilbolton, Alvesford, and Ashmansworth. And he gave much to the monastery of Malmesbury.

**[929.]** Year 926: Hywel Dda, son of Cadell, went to Rome. And Elen died.

**[934.]** Year of Our Lord 933: Gruffudd son of Owain was killed by men of Ceredigion.

**[937.]** Year 935: There was the battle of Brune.

**[938.]** Year 936: Hyfaidd son of Clydawg and Meurig died.

**[939.]** Year 939: Athelstan, king of England, died, and he was buried in Malmesbury.

## 36. PETER OF LANGTOFT, *CHRONICLE*

**See pp. 219–21**

Year of Our Lord 924.

After Edward the king began to reign
Athelstan his son, a very valiant knight.
Earls and barons and clergy with good will
journeyed to Kingston to crown the king.
The under-kings of Wales know not how to keep peace:
the second year of his reign they make war,
but he vanquishes them; for peace they go to parley.
Athelstan the king charges North Wales
with 24 pounds of gold each year, 300 of pure silver,
and 10,000 cows a year for his larder.

Pur trewe de Suthwales ne payent nul dener,
fors mil et cc. vaches, dount fu tributer.
Le iiij. an de sun regne, Owal, un guerrayere,
et Constantyn, d'Escoce rays et justiser,
Onvere rays de Venz, s'en vount batailler
of le ray Adelstan; molt graunt fu lur poer.
Li rays, of l'aide Deu, les va rechacer;
si dure al darayn les mene k'il les fet jorer
ke leals ly serraynt et par terre et par mer.
Le disme an après ke ly rays fu corounez,
fust Edwyn, sun frere, devaunt sun barné
a Loundres en sa court attaynt de malveysté.
Adelstan le fist lyer et mayn et pé,
et jettre en Tamyse, où il fu tost nayé.
Constantyn de Escoce, dount fu ray clamé,
rompist tost la pes ke fust affermé.
Genz de Danemark lur poer l'ount doné,
tuent les Englays, wastent terre et pré.
Adelstan l'oit dire, s'en vayt à Beverlé,
a saint Jon le eveske, où ore gist enfertré,
ke aider ly voylle devers la Trinité
devotement ly prie, si l'ad confermé
terres et fraunchises le eglise en est feffé.
Puys vayt à Dureme, Saint Chutbert ad dowé
des terres et de rentes, et graunt digneté;
le eveske de sun doun tent regalté.
Puys vayt à la bataylle de Deu ben conforté.
La guere de Escoce est prise, et Katenesse wasté.
Constantyn est rayns, sun fiz est liveré,
est en hostage al ray Adestan clamé,
ke est of la victore à Loundres retorné.
En le honur nostre Dame à l'Assumpcioun,
se mist le ray de Loundres devers Abendoun;
où messagers ly venent du riche ray Karloun.
Le counte de Boloyne, Aldulphe fu sun noun,
le duk de Burgoyne, Rayner fiz Edmoun,
al rays Adelstan presentent ryche doun,
par Charles ray de France; il memes l'enveit gonphanoun
ke Saint Marie portait devaunt la legioun;
la launce dount Jhesus kant sanz achesoun
fu naffrez al quer en sa passioun;
un espeye de fyn or, plus ryche del regioun;
deus clowes sunt dedenz dount ly Jeu feloun
tacha les pez Deu, kant pendist cum laroun;
partye des espynes dount fu sa coroun;
une pece de la Croyce ke ly bon baroun
Constantyn conquist à l'occiscoun

For the tribute of South Wales they pay not a coin,
except 1200 cows, which was their tribute.
The fourth year of his reign, Idwal, a warrior,
Constantine, the king and ruler of Scotland,
and Onwer, king of Gwent, go to fight
with King Athelstan; very great was their strength.
The king, with the aid of God, puts them to flight.
So hard he presses them that at last they swear
that they will be loyal both by land and by sea.

The tenth year after the king was crowned,
was Edwin, his brother, in the sight of his baronage
in his court at London convicted of treachery.
Athelstan ordered him bound hand and foot
and thrown into the Thames, where he was quickly drowned.
Constantine of Scotland, of which he was proclaimed king,
soon broke the peace that had been confirmed.
The Danish people have given their power to him,
[and together] they kill the English, lay waste land and field.
Athelstan of that hears word, he journeys to Beverley,
to St. John the archbishop, where he now lies interred.
Asking that he help him by interceding with the Trinity,
he prays to him devoutly, and has confirmed to him
land and privileges that are given to the church.
Next he goes to Durham, has St. Cuthbert endowed
with lands and with rents and great dignity;
the bishop by his gift holds royalty.
Then he goes to the battle with the comfort of God.
The war with Scotland is decided, and Caithness is laid waste.
Constantine is ruined, his son is delivered
as a hostage claimed by King Athelstan,
who returns to London with the victory.

For the feast of the Assumption of Our Lady
the king travels from London to Abingdon,
where messengers from the rich king Charles come to him.
The earl of Bologne, Adelolf was his name,
[with] the duke of Burgundy, Rayner the son of Edmund,
to King Athelstan present rich gifts
on behalf of Charles the king of France. He himself sends the pennant
that St. Maurice carried before the legion,
the lance with which Jesus without cause
was cut to the heart in His Passion,
a sword of find gold more valuable than a kingdom
(two nails are inside it, with which the wicked Jew
tacked the feet of God, when He was hanged like a thief),
a part of the thorns from which His crown was made,
a piece of the Cross which the good baron
Constantine conquered at the slaughter

del graunt soudan Maudans de Scaloun.
Le present est resceu of graunt devocioun.
Lors s'en vent le cosyn, le rays, of sun menage,
descendist en la sale of molt fere corage;
Rayner fiz Edmoun li dist en sun langage,
"Sir rays Adelstan, Karles, de halt parage,
ke ço present te envayt, te maunde sun message,
ke lyer se volt à tay, en ton lynage,
de Hilde, ta bele sor, te prie le mariage."
Hilde est si venue, tant bele de visage,
tant cortayse en parole, tant gent en corsage,
plus bele creature vist unkes home en age.
La damoysele s'assent, le rays et sun barnage
of molt grant richesce atyrent sun passage.
Hilde s'en va vers Fraunce, fet est le passage;
Adelstan demort garder sun heritage.
L'an primer ke Hilde esposez estait,
Constantyn de Escoce en Humbre aryvayt,
un rays paen, Analphe, of ly amenait;
d. cc. et xv. nefs le ray Anlaphe avayt.
Ly bon ray Adelstan, ke drayture amayt,
of Edmoun sun frere, dount ben s'affyait,
a Bruneburge sur Humbre les feluns encountrait.
Del matyn jekes al vespre la bataylle durait.
Le rays Adelstan les ij. rays enchascait;
chescun en sa terre enfuaunt s'en vayt;
Pur veir lur remisaille Adelstan tuait.
Kant le rays Anlaphe avait perdu sa gent,
il mesmes à grant payne passa del thorment;
vers Danemarche s'en va al sigle et la vent.
A la Paske après aryve en l'orient,
al porte de Sanwyce, of pople à talent.
Colebrand vint of ly, Anlaphe avaunt se tent
tut drait à Wyncestre où Adelstan attent.
Anlaphe saunz demore ly maunde apertement,
par ses messagers, ke la terre ly rend,
ou encountre Colebrand par un home la defent.
Ly rays Adelstan tynt sun parlement,
ne trova chuvaler de tel hardyment,
ke of ly combaterayt pur tut le tenement.
Adelstan priait à Deu omnipotent,
ke aider ly vousist, et Deu benignement
en sounge of ly parlait, et dist ke prestement
ke al matyn troverayt un velz palmer et lent,
a la porte del seu, et cely seurement
parfrait la bataille, pur Deu omnipotent,
si pur Deu ly priast; ço fu verrayment

of the great sultan Maudans of Ascalon.
This gift is received with great devotion.
Then blew the trumpets, [and] the king, with his household,
descended into the hall with very proud bearing;
Rayner, son of Edmund, says to him in his language,
"Sir King Athelstan, Charles, of high descent,
who sends you this gift, sends you this message:
that he wishes to ally himself with you and your lineage,
of Eadhild, your beautiful sister, he asks for marriage."
Eadhild is introduced at once, so beautiful of face,
so courteous in speech, so elegant in body,
such a perfect creature no man had ever seen.
The damsel assents to it; the king and his baronage
with very great riches provider her passage.
Eadhild journeys to France, the bond is thus made;
Athelstan remains to protect his inheritance.
The first year after the marriage of Eadhild,
Constantine of Scotland arrived on the Humber,
a pagan king, Anlaf, came with him.
Anlaf the king had 715 ships.
The good king Athelstan, who loved justice,
with Edmund his brother, in whom he trusted,
at Brunanburh on the Humber encountered the wicked men.
From morning to night the battle raged.
King Athelstan chased away the two kings,
each in flight returned to his land.
In truth, Athelstan slew those who remained.
After King Anlaf had lost his men,
he himself passed with great trouble from the turmoil;
toward Denmark he flees with sail and wind.
The following Easter he arrives in the east,
at the port of Sandwich, with people in abundance.
Colbrand came with him, Anlaf advanced with him
directly to Winchester where Athelstan awaited.
Anlaf without delay openly calls on him,
by his messengers, to give up the land to him,
or to defend his home in a fight with Colbrand.
King Athelstan held his parliament,
found no knight of such bravery
who would fight with him for the whole domain.
Athelstan prayed to Almighty God,
that He would vouchsafe to help him, and God benignly
in a dream talked to him, and said that immediately
in the morning he would find an old and slow palmer
at the south gate, and he assuredly
would perform the battle for Almighty God
if he prayed him for God's sake. This was truly

Guy de Warwik, sun livre dist coment
il tuayt Colebrand, par quai tut quitement.
Anlaphe rethorna à cel fez dolent.
    Le rays Adelstan, pur ky Deu molt fist,
xvj. aunz et xvj. jours ray regnaunt vesquit.
La maladye mortele à Gloucestre ly prist;
mès hors de la cyté, pur veirs, s'en partist,
si ne sait à Mauncestre, ne say quel par se prist.

### 37. *Stanzaic Guy of Warwick*

**Middle English**
**early 14th c.**

God graunt hem heven-blis to mede
that herken to mi romaunce rede
al of a gentil knight;
the best bodi he was at nede
that ever might bistriden stede
and freest founde in fight.
The word of him ful wide it ran
over al this warld the priis he wan,
as man most of might.
Balder bern was non in bi,
his name was hoten Sir Gii
of Warwike wise and wight.

Wight he was for sothe to say
and holden for priis in everi play
as knight of gret boundé.
out of this lond he went his way
thurth mani divers cuntray
that was biyond the see.
Sethen he com into Inglond
and Athelston the king he fond
that was bothe hende and fre.
For his love ich understond
he slough a dragoun in Northhumberlond
ful fer in the north cuntré.

. . .

Now went Gii forth in his way
toward the see so swithe he may,
for Tirri he siked sare.
into schip he went bilive,
over the se he gan drive,
into Inglond he gan fare.
The lond folk he axed anon

Guy of Warwick; his book tells how
he killed Colbrand, whereby all quit:
Anlaf returned that time in sorrow.
    King Athelstan, for whom God did much,
16 years and 16 days lived and reigned as king.
The mortal disease took him at Gloucester;
but out of the city, in truth, he departed.
If it were not at Manchester, I know now where he went.

## 37. *Stanzaic Guy of Warwick*

**See pp. 221–25**

God grant them the rewards of Heaven
who listen to my romance read
all about a noble knight;
the best man he was in times of trouble
that ever might ride a horse
and the most noble fellow in a fight.
His reputation was known widely
over all this world he won rewards,
as the man of greatest strength.
A bolder man was there none to be found,
his name was Sir Guy
of Warwick clever and courageous.

Brave he was to tell the truth
and considered most excellent in every tournament
as a knight of great valor.
Out of this land he went his way
through many diverse countries
that are beyond the sea.
Then he returned to England
and Athelstan the king he found
who was both noble and proper.
For his love I understand
he killed a dragon in Northumberland
very far in the north country.

. . .

Now Guy went forth on his way
toward the sea as quickly as he can,
for Tirri he sighed in sorrow.
Into a ship he went at once,
over the sea he set sail,
into England he did go.
The land's folk he asked at once

after King Athelston
in what cuntré he ware.
"At Winchester verrament
and after his barouns he hath sent,
bothe lasse and mare.

"Erls, barouns, and bischopes,
knightes, priours, and abbotes
at Winchester thai ben ichon
and han purvayd withouten lesing
thre days to ben in fasting
to biseke God in tron
He sende hem thurth His swet sond
a man that were douhti of hond
ogain Colbrond to gon.
Ther is the king and the barnage, ywis,
for doute of her enemis
that wayt hem forto slon.

"For Sir Anlaf the king of Danmark
with a nost store and stark
into Inglond is come
with fiften thousend knightes of pris,
alle this lond thai stroyen, ywis,
and mani a toun han nome.
A geaunt he hath brought with him
out of Aufrike stout and grim,
Colbrond hat that gome.
For him is al Inglond forlore
bot Godes help be bifore
that socour sende hem some.

"To the king he hath sent his sond
forto yeld him al Inglond
and gif him trowage outright
yif he no wil nought finde a baroun,
a geaunt other a champioun,
ogain Colbrond to fight,
and therof thai han taken a day.
Ac our king non finde may
erl, baroun, no knight,
no squier, no serjaunt non
ogain the geaunt dar gon
so grim he is of sight."

Than seyd Sir Gii, "Whare is Herhaud?
That in his time was so bald?"

about King Athelstan
in what part of the country he was.
"Truly at Winchester
and after his baronage he has sent,
both the lesser and the greater.

"Earls, barons, and bishops,
knights, priors, and abbots
at Winchester they are altogether
and have arranged without lie
to spend three days fasting
to beseech God in majesty
to send them through His sweet ordinance
a man who is of great fighting ability
against Colbrond to fight.
There is the king and the baronage, truly,
for fear of their enemies
that wait to slay them.

"For Sir Anlaf the king of Denmark
with an army powerful and strong
into England has come
with fifteen thousand excellent knights,
all this land they ravage, it is true,
and many towns have seized.
A giant he has brought with him
out of Africa stout and grim,
Colbrond is that creature called.
Because of him all England is lost
unless God's help is forthcoming
that sends them some relief.

"To the king Anlaf has sent his message
to yield to him all England
and give him tribute outright
if he can not find a baron,
a giant or a champion,
against Colbrond to fight,
and for that they have set a day.
But our king cannot find
earl, baron, knight,
squire, or any servant
who against the giant would dare go
because he is so terrifying to see."

Then said Sir Guy, "Where is Herhaud?
who in his time was so bold?"

And thai answerd ful swithe.
"To seche Gyes sone he is fare
that marchaunce hadde stollen thare,
for him he was unblithe."
"And where is th'erl Rohaut of pris?"
And thai answerd, "Dede he is —
a gode while is go sithe —
and Feliis his douhter is his air,
so gode a levedi no so fair,
ywis, nis non olive."

Gii went to Winchester a ful gode pas
ther the king that time was
to held his parlement;
the barouns weren in the halle.
The king seyd, "Lordinges alle,
mine men ye ben verrament,
therfore ich ax withouten fayl
of this Danis folk wil ous aseyl
ich biseche you with gode entent,
for Godes love Y pray you
gode conseyl give me now
or elles we ben al schent.

"For the king of Danmark with wrong
with his geaunt that is so strong
he wil ous al schende.
Therfore ich axi you ichon
what rede is best forto don
ogaines hem forto wende?
Yif he overcom ous in batayle
he wil slen ous alle saunfeyle
and strouen al our kende.
Than schal Inglond evermo
live in thraldom and in wo
unto the warldes ende.

"Therfore ich axi you now right
yif ye knowe our ani knight
that is so stout and bold
that the batayle dar take an hond
to fight ogain Colbrond.
Half mi lond have he schold
with alle the borwes that lith therto,
to him and to his aires evermo
to have yive he wold."
Stil seten erls and barouns

and they answered quite quickly.
"To seek Guy's son he has gone,
who merchants had stolen away;
for him he was sorry."
"And where is the earl Rohaut of renown?"
And they answered, "Dead he is —
a good while ago it was —
and Felice his daughter is his heir,
so good a lady nor so fair,
in truth, there is none alive."

Guy went to Winchester at great speed
where the king was at that time
to hold his parliament;
the barons were in the hall.
The king said, "Lords all,
my men you truly are,
therefore I ask without doubt
regarding this Danish people who will assail us
I beseech you in good faith,
for God's love I pray you
good counsel give me now
or ellse we are all ruined.

"For the king of Denmark with wickedness
with his giant that is so strong
he will us all destroy.
Therefore I ask you each one
what counsel is best to follow
against them to struggle?
If he overcomes us in battle
he will slay us all without doubt
and destroy all our people.
Then shall England evermore
live in thralldom and in woe
unto the world's end.

"Therefore I ask you now directly
if you know any knight among us
who is so stout and bold
that the battle dare take on hand
to fight against Colbrond.
Half my lands he should have
with all the towns that belong to it,
to him and to his heirs evermore
to have if he would do so."
As silent sat the earls and barons

as men hadde schaven her crounes;
nought on answere nold.

"Allas," seyd the king, "that Y was born.
Al mi joie it is forlorn,
wel wo is me olive.
Now in al mi lond nis no knight
ogains a geant to hold fight
mine hert wil breken on five.
Allas of Warwike Sir Gii
Y no hadde geven thee half mi lond frely
to hold withouten strive;
wele were me than bifalle.
Ac certes now the Danis men alle
to sorwe thai schul me drive."

When it was night to bedde thai yede;
the king for sorwe and for drede
with teres wett his lere.
Of al that night he slepe right nought
bot ever Jhesu he bisought
that was him leve and dere
He schuld him sende thurth His sond
a man to fight with Colbrond
yif it Is wille were.
And Jhesus Crist ful of might
He sent him a noble knight
as ye may forward here.

Ther com an angel fram heven-light
and seyd to the king ful right
thurth grace of Godes sond.
He seyd, "King Athelston, slepestow?
Hider me sent thee King Jhesu
to comfort thee to fond.
Tomorwe go to the north gate ful swithe,
a pilgrim thou schalt se com bilive
when thou hast a while stond.
Bid him for Seynt Charité
that he take the batayl for thee
and he it wil nim on hond."

Than was the king glad and blithe,
amorwe he ros up ful swithe
and went to the gate ful right.
Tuay erls went with him tho
and tuay bischopes dede also.

as men who had shaved their heads;
not one would answer.

"Alas," said the king, "that I was born.
All my joy is utterly lost,
much woe it is to live.
Now that in all my land there is no knight
against a giant to hold fight
my heart will break into five pieces.
Alas, Sir Guy of Warwick,
if only had given you half my land freely
to hold without dispute;
then I would do well.
But surely now the Danish men all
to sorrow they shall drive me."

When it was night to bed they went;
the king for sorrow and for dread
with tears wet his cheek.
Through all that night he slept not at all
but always prayed to Jesus
who was to him beloved and dear,
that He should send him through His grace
a man to fight with Colbrond
if it was His will.
And Jesus Christ full of might
sent him a noble knight
as you will hereafter hear.

There came an angel from Heaven
and spoke to the king at once
through the grace of God's power.
He said, "King Athelstan, do you sleep?
Here I am sent to you by King Jesus
to try to comfort you.
Tomorrow go to the north gate right away,
a pilgrim you shall see come there
when you have stood there awhile.
Bid him for Saint Charity
that he undertake the battle for you
and he will take it in his hand."

Then was the king glad and joyful,
the next morning he rose up at once
and went to the gate directly.
Two earls went with him then
and two bishops did also.

The weder was fair and bright.
Opon the day about prime
the king seighe cum the pilgrim
bi the sclavayn he him plight.
"Pilgrim," he seyd, "Y pray thee
to court wende thou hom with me
and ostel ther al night."

"Be stille, sir," seyd the pilgrim.
"It is nought yete time to take min in,
also God me rede."
The king him bisought tho
and the lordinges dede also,
to court with hem he yede.
"Pilgrim," quath the king, "par charité,
yif it be thi wil understond to me,
Y schal schewe thee al our nede:
the king of Danmark with gret wrong
thurth a geaunt that is so strong
wil strou al our thede.

"And whe han taken of him batayle
on what maner, saunfayle,
Y schal now tellen thee.
Thurth the bodi of a knight
ogains that geaunt to hold fight
schal this lond aquite be.
And pilgrim for Him that dyed on Rode
and that for ous schadde His blod
to bigge ous alle fre,
take the batayle now on hond
and save ous the right of Inglond
for Seynt Charité."

"Do way, leve sir," seyd Gii.
"Icham an old man, a feble bodi;
mi strengthe is fro me fare."
The king fel on knes to grounde
and crid him merci in that stounde
yif it his wille ware.
And the barouns dede also,
o knes thai fellen alle tho
with sorwe and sikeing sare.
Sir Gii biheld the lordinges alle
and whiche sorwe hem was bifalle,
Sir Gii hadde of hem care.

The weather was fair and bright.
Upon the day about prime
the king saw the pilgrim come
and by his cloak he grabbed him.
"Pilgrim," he said, "I pray that you
go home with me to court
and lodge there all night."

"Be still, sir," said the pilgrim.
"It is not yet time to take my lodging,
as God directs me."
The king begged him then
and the lords did also,
and to court with hem he went.
"Pilgrim," said the king, "for charity,
if it be your will understand me,
I shall show you all our need:
the king of Denmark with great wrong
through a giant who is so strong
will destroy all our nation.

"And we have agreed to fight with him
in the manner, truly,
I shall now tell you.
Through the strength of a single knight
against that giant to hold fight
shall this land be free.
And, pilgrim, for Him who died on the Cross
and who for us shed His blood
to buy all our salvation,
take the battle now in hand
and save us the right of England
for Saint Charity."

"Enough, dear sir," said Guy.
"I am an old man, a feeble body;
my strength is gone from me."
The king fell to his knees on the ground
and cried him mercy in that place
if it was his will.
And the barons did also,
on knees they fell all those
with sorrow and terrible sighs.
Sir Guy beheld the lords all
and what sorrow had befallen them,
Sir Guy had concern for them.

Sir Gii tok up the king anon
and bad the lordinges everichon
thai schuld up stond,
and seyd, "For God in Trinité
and forto make Inglond fre
the batayle Y nim on hond."
Than was the king ful glad and blithe
and thonked Gii a thousend sithe
and Jhesu Cristes sond.
To the king of Danmark he sent than
and seyd he hadde founden a man
to fight for Inglond.

The Danismen busked hem yare
into batayle forto fare,
to fight thai war wel fawe.
And Gii was armed swithe wel
in a gode hauberk of stiel
wrought of the best lawe.
An helme he hadde of michel might
with a cercle of gold that schon bright
with precious stones on rawe.
In the frunt stode a charbukel ston
as bright as ani sonne it schon
that glemes under schawe.

On that helme stode a flour
wrought it was of divers colour,
mirie it was to bihold.
trust and trewe was his ventayle,
gloves and gambisoun and hosen of mayle
as gode knight have scholde;
girt he was with a gode brond
wele kerveand biforn his hond;
a targe listed with gold
portreyd with thre kinges corn
that present God when He was born,
mirier was non on mold.

And a swift-ernand stede
al wrin thai dede him lede,
his tire it was ful gay.
Sir Gii opon that stede wond
with a gode glaive in hond
and priked him forth his way.
And when he com to the plas
ther the batayl loked was

Sir Guy took up the king anon
and asked alle the lords
to stand up,
and said, "For God in Trinity
and to make England free
the battle I will take in hand."
Then was the king very glad and joyful
and thanked Guy a thousand times
and Jesus Christ's grace.
To the king of Denmark he sent then
and said he had found a man
to fight for England.

The Danish prepared themselves quickly
into battle to fare,
to fight they were very eager.
And Guy was armed exceedingly well
in a good hauberk of steel
wrought in the best way.
A helm he had of much strength
with a circlet of gold that shone bright
with precious stones in a row.
In the front stood a carbuncle stone
as bright as any sun it shone
that it gleamed in the dark.

On that helm stood a flower
wrought of diverse colors,
beautiful it was to behold.
Trusty and true was his face-guard,
gloves and jacket and breeches of mail
as a good knight should have.
Armed he was with a good sword
sharp-edged in his hand;
a shield bordered with gold
adorned with the three kings
who offered gifts to God when He was born,
none was more beautiful in the world.

And a swift-footed steed
all outfitted they did lead to him,
his attire was very handsome.
Sir Guy upon that horse went
with a good sword in hand
and spurred him forth his way.
And when he came to the place
where the battle was decreed

Gii light withouten delay
and fel on knes doun in that stede
and to God he bad his bede
He schuld ben his help that day.

"Lord," seyd Gii, "that rered Lazeroun
and for man tholed Passioun
and on the Rode gan blede,
that saved Sussan fram the feloun
and halp Daniel fram the lyoun,
today wisse me and rede.
Astow art mighti Heven-king
today graunt me Thi blisseing
and help me at this nede;
and Levedi Mari ful of might
today save Inglondes right
and leve me wele to spede."

When the folk was samned bi bothe side
the to kinges with michel pride
after the relikes thai sende,
the corporas and the Messe gere.
On the halidom thai gun swere
with wordes fre and hende.
The king of Danmarke swore furst, ywis,
yif that his geant slayn is
to Danmarke he schal wende
and never more Inglond cum withinne
no non after him of his kinne
unto the warldes ende.

Sethen swore the king Athelston
and seyd among hem everichon
bi God that al may weld,
yif his man ther slayn be
or overcomen that men may se
recreaunt in the feld,
his man he wil bicom an hond
and alle the reme of Inglond
of him forto helde
and hold him for lord and king
with gold and silver and other thing
gret trowage him forto yelde.

When thai had sworn and ostage founde
Colbrond stirt up in that stounde,
to fight he was ful felle.

Guy dismounted without delay
and fell down on his knees in that place
and to God he prayed his prayer
that He should be his help that day.

"Lord," said Guy, "who raised Lazarus
and for man suffered the Passion
and on the Cross did bleed,
who saved Susan from the criminal
and helped Daniel from the lion,
today guide me and advise.
As You are mighty king of Heaven
today grant me Your blessing
and help me in this time of need;
and Lady Mary full of power
today save England's right
and enable me to attain success."

When the folk were assembled on both sides
the two kings with much pride
after the holy relics they sent,
the altar cloth and the implements of the Mass.
On the sacred relics they did swear
with words free and proper.
The king of Denmark swore first,
that if his giant was slain
to Denmark he would go
and nevermore return to England
nor would any of his kin do so
unto the world's end.

Then swore King Athelstan
and said among them all
by God who rules everything,
that if his man was there slain
or overcome that men may see
defeat in the field,
Anlaf's vassal he will become in hand
and all the realm of England
would submit to him
and hold him for lord and king,
with gold and silver and other things
great tribute to yield to him.

When they had sworn and exchanged hostages
Colbrond leapt up in that place,
to fight he was very fierce.

He was so michel and so unrede
that non hors might him lede
in gest as Y you telle.
So mani he hadde of armes gere
unnethe a cart might hem bere
the Inglisse forto quelle.
Swiche armour as he hadde opon,
ywis, no herd ye never non
bot as it ware a fende of Helle.

Of mailes was nought his hauberk,
it was al of another werk
that mervail is to here.
Alle it were thicke splentes of stiel,
thicke yjoined strong and wel,
to kepe that fendes fere.
Hossen he hadde also wele ywrought
other than splentes was it nought
fram his fot to his swere.
He was so michel and so strong
and therto wonderliche long
in the world was non his pere.

An helme he hadde on his heved sett
and therunder a thicke bacinet;
unsemly was his wede.
A targe he had wrought ful wel —
other metel was ther non on bot stiel —
a michel and unrede.
Al his armour was blac as piche
wel foule he was and lothliche,
a grisely gom to fede.
The heighe king that sitteth on heighe
that welt this warld fer and neighe
made him wel ivel to spede.

A dart he bar in his hond kerveand
and his wepen about him stondand
bothe bihinde and biforn
axes and gisarmes scharp ygrounde
and glaives forto give with wounde
to hundred and mo ther worn.
The Inglis biheld him fast.
King Athelston was sore agast
Inglond he schuld have lorn
for when Gii seighe that wicked hert

He was so great and so monstrous
that no horse might carry him
in the tales as I tell you.
So many armaments he had
hardly a cart might bear them
to use to kill the English.
Such armor as he wore,
you have never heard of it
unless it belonged to a devil from Hell.

His hauberk was not made of mail,
it was all constructed of another method
that it is astonishing to hear about it.
The whole of it was thick with plates of steel,
tightly set together for strength,
to protect that brother of demons.
Leg-guards he had also well-crafted
so that it was nothing but steel plates
from his foot to his neck.
He was so great and so strong
and also incredibly tall
that in the world there was none his peer.

A helm he had set upon his head
and under it a thick subhelmet;
unnatural were his clothes.
A shield he had wrought very well —
made of no metal other than steel —
a massive and mighty thing.
All his armor was black as pitch
very foul he was and loathsome,
a grisly creature to sustain.
The high king who sits on high
who rules this world far and near
made him difficult to beat.

A sharp-pointed spear he carried in his hand
and his weapons stood around him
both behind and before
axes and halberds sharply whetted
and swords to give wounds
two hundred and more there were.
The English stared intently at him.
King Athelstan was sorely terrified
England he should have lost
for when Guy saw that wicked heart

he nas never so sore aferd
sethen that he was born.

Sir Gii lepe on his stede fot-hot
and with a spere that wele bot
to him he gan to ride.
And he schet to Gii dartes thre,
of the tuay than failed he,
the thridde he lete to him glide,
thurth Gyes scheld it glod
and thurth his armour withouten abod
bituene his arme and side
and quitelich into the feld it yede
the mountaunce of an acre brede
er that it wald abide.

Sir Gii to him gan to drive
that his spere brast afive
on his scheld that was so bounde;
and Colbrond with michel hete
on Gyes helme he wald have smite,
and failed of him that stounde;
bituix the sadel and the arsoun
the strok of that feloun glod adoun
withouten wem or wounde.
That sadel and hors atuo he smot,
into the erthe wele half a fot
and Gii fel doun to grounde.

Sir Gii as tite up stirt
as man that was agremed in hert,
his stede he hadde forlore.
On his helme he wald hit him tho
ac he no might nought reche therto
bi to fot and yete more,
bot on his schulder the swerd fel doun
and carf bothe plates and hauberjoun
with his grimli gore.
Thurth al his armour stern and strong
he made him a wounde a spanne long
that greved him ful sore.

Colbrond was sore aschame
and smot Gii with michel grame.
On his helm he hit him tho
that his floures everichon
and his gode charbukel ston

he was never so sorely afraid
since he was born.

Sir Guy leapt on his steed quickly
and with a spear that cut well
towards him he began to ride.
And he threw at Guy three spears,
with the first two he missed,
the third he shot to him,
through Guy's shield it pierced
and through his armor without pause
between his arm and side
and completely into the field it went
the distance of the breadth of an acre
before it would stop.

Sir Guy to him began to drive
until his spear broke in five pieces
on his shield that was so ready;
and Colbrond with much fury
on Guy's helm he would have struck,
but he missed him that moment;
between the saddle and the pommel
the stroke of that wicked creature cut down
without injury or wound.
That saddle and horse he cut in half,
smashed into the earth at least half a foot,
and Guy fell down to the ground.

Sir Guy got up right away
as a man that was incensed in heart,
his steed he had lost.
On his helm he would have hit him then
but he could not reach it
by two feet and yet more,
but on his shoulder the sword fell down
and carved both plates and jacket
with his deadly weapon.
Through all his armor hard and strong
he made him a wound a hand's breadth long
that grieved him very sorely.

Colbrond was very ashamed
and struck Guy with much rage.
On his helm he hit him then
so that all his flowers
and his good carbuncle stone

wel even he carf atuo.
Even ato he smot his scheld
that it fleyghe into the feld.
When Gii seyghe it was so
that he hadde his scheld forlorn,
half bihinde and half biforn,
in hert him was wel wo.

And Gii hent his swerd an hond
and heteliche smot to Colbrond —
as a child he stode him under.
Open the scheld he yave him swiche a dent
bifor the stroke the fiir out went
as it were light of thonder.
The bondes of stiel he carf ichon
and into the scheld a fot and half on
with his swerd he smot asunder,
and with the out-braiding his swerd brast.
Thei Gii were than sore agast
it was litel wonder.

Tho was Gii sore desmayd
and in his hert wel ivel ypayd
for the chaunce him was bifalle,
and for he hadde lorn his gode brond
and his stede opon the sond
to our Levedi he gan calle.
Than gun the Danis ost
ich puken other and make bost
and seyd among hem alle,
"Now schal the Inglis be slain in feld;
gret trouage Inglond schal ous yeld
and evermore ben our thral."

"Now, sir knight," seyd Colbrond,
"thou hast lorn thi swerd in thine hond,
thi scheld and eke thi stede.
Do now wele, yeld thee to me
and smertlich unarme thee;
cri merci Y thee rede.
And for thou art so douhti knight
thou durst ogain me held fight
to mi lord Y schal thee lede
and with him thou schalt acorded be,
in his court he wil hold thee
and finde that thee is nede."

he split in two.
He even broke his shield in two
so that it flew into the field.
When Guy saw that it was so
that he had his shield lost,
half behind and half before,
in his heart he had woe.

And Guy took his sword in hand
and fiercely struck Colbrond —
as a child he stood under him.
Upon the shield he gave him such a blow
that sparks of fire went out from the strike
as if it were lightning before thunder.
The bands of steel he cut each one
and into the shield a foot and a half
with his sword he broke it asunder,
and when he was pulling out his sword it shattered.
If Guy was then intensely afraid
it would be little wonder.

Then was Guy very afraid
and in his heart had much misgiving
because of the luck that had befallen him,
and because he had lost his good blade
and his steed upon the ground.
To Our Lady he began to call.
Then began the Danish army
to poke each other and make boast
and say amongst themselves,
"Now shall the Englishman be slain in the field;
great tribute England shall yield to us
and evermore be our thrall."

"Now, sir knight," said Colbrond,
"You have lost your sword from your hand,
your shield and also your horse.
Do the right thing, yield yourself to me
and quickly unarm yourself;
cry for mercy I advise you.
Because you are so brave a knight
that you dared fight against me
to my lord I will lead you
and with him you shall be accorded,
in his court he will protect you
and give you whatever you need."

"Do way," seyd Gii, "therof speke nought.
Bi Him that al this world hath wrought
ich hadde lever thou were anhong.
Ac thou hast armes gret plenté,
ywis, thou most lene me
on of thine axes strong."
Colbrond swore bi Apolin,
"Of al the wepen that is min
her schaltow non afong.
Now thou wilt nought do bi mi rede
thou schalt dye on ivel dede
er that it be ought long."

When Gii herd him speke so
al sone he gan him turn tho
and to his wepen he geth
ther his axes stode bi hemselve;
he kept on with a wel gode helve
the best him thought he seth,
to Colbrond ogain he ran
and seyd, "Traitour," to him than,
"thou schalt han ivel deth.
Now ich have of thi wepen plenté
wherewith that Y may were me
right maugré al thin teth."

Colbrond than with michel hete
on Gyes helme he wald have smite
with wel gret hert tene
ac he failed of his dint
and the swerd into the erthe went
a fot and more, Y wene.
And with Colbrondes out-draught
Sir Gii with ax a strok him raught
a wounde that was wele sene.
So smertliche he smot to Colbrond
that his right arme with alle the hond
he strok of quite and clene.

When Colbrond feld him so smite
he was wel wroth ye may wel wite,
he gan his swerd up fond
and in his left hond op it haf
and Gii in the nek a strok him gaf
as he gan stoupe for the brond
that his heved fro the bodi he smot
and into the erthe half a fot

"Enough," said Guy, "I will speak it not.
By Him who all this world has wrought
I would rather you were hung.
But you have a great many arms,
truly, you must give me
one of your strong axes."
Colbrond swore by Apollo,
"Of all the weapons that are mine
here you shall have none.
Now if you will not follow by my counsel
you will die a painful death
before long."

When Guy heard him speak so
all at once he turned then
and to Colbrond's weapons he goes
where his axes stood by themselves;
he took one with a very good heft
the best he thought he saw,
to Colbrond again he ran
and said, "Traitor," to him then.
"You shall have a painful death.
Now I have enough of your weapons
to defend myself
in spite of your chattering teeth."

Colbrond then with much fury
on Guy's helm he would have struck
with much anger in his heart
but he missed in his blow
and the sword went into the earth
a foot and more, I believe.
And with Colbrond's strike overextended
Sir Guy with his axe struck him hard
a wound that was clearly seen.
So quickly he struck Colbrond
that his right arm with hand and all
he struck off completely.

When Colbrond felt himself so struck
he was very angry you might well know,
he began to take up his sword
in his left hand he heaved it up
and Guy gave him a blow to the neck
as he bent down for the blade
that his head from the body he smote
and into the earth half a foot

thurth grace of Godes sond.
Ded he feld the glotoun thare.
The Denis with sorwe and care
thai dight hem out of lond.

Blithe were the Inglis men ichon.
Erls, barouns, and King Athelston,
thai toke Sir Gii that tide
and ladde him to Winchester toun
with wel fair processioun
over al bi ich a side.
For joie belles thai gun ring
*Te Deum laudamus* thai gun sing
and play and michel pride.
Sir Gii unarmed him and was ful blithe;
his sclavain he axed also swithe,
no lenger he nold abide.

"Sir pilgrim," than seyd the king,
"whennes thou art withouten lesing?
Thou art douhti of dede,
for thurth douhtines of thin hond
thou hast saved al Inglond.
God quite thee thi mede,
and mi treuthe Y schal plight thee,
so wele Y schal feffe thee
bothe in lond and lede
that of riches in toun and tour
thou schalt be man of mest honour
that woneth in al mi thede."

"Sir King," seyd the pilgrim,
"of alle the lond that is tin
Y no kepe therof na mare
bot now ichave the geant slain,
therof, ywis, icham ful fain,
mi way ichil forth fare."
"Merci, sir," the king seyd than,
"tel me for Him that made man —
for nothing thou ne spare —
tel me what thi name it be,
whennes thou art and of what cuntré
or Y schal dye for care."

"Sir King," he seyd, "Y schal tel it thee.
What mi right name it be
thou schalt witen anon;

through grace of God's ordinance.
Dead he slew the glutton there.
The Danes with sorrow and care
took themselves out of the land.

Joyful were all the Englishmen.
Earls, barons, and King Athelstan,
they took Sir Guy at that time
and led him to Winchester
with a very fair procession
with people gathered at each side.
For joy bells began to ring
*Te Deum laudamus* they began to sing
and played and had much pride.
Sir Guy unarmed himself and was very glad;
his pilgrim's cloak he asked for soon,
no longer would he stay.

"Sir pilgrim," then said the king,
"Why would you leave?
You are brave at arms,
for through strength of your hand
you have saved all England.
May God reward you,
and my word I shall pledge to you,
so well I shall endow you
both in land and people
that of riches in town and tower
you shall be the man of most honor
who lives in all my realm."

"Sir King," said the pilgrim,
"Of all the land that is yours
I desire none of it at all
but now that I have the giant slain,
for which I am very glad,
I will go my way."
"Mercy, sir," the king said then,
"Tell me for Him who made man —
for nothing hold back —
tell me what your name is,
who you are and from what country you came
or I shall die for care."

"Sir King," he said, "I shall tell it to you.
What my right name is
you shall know soon;

ac thou schalt go with me yfere
that no man of our conseyl here
bot thou and Y alon."
The king him graunted and was blithe,
he comand his folk also swithe
no wight with him to gon.
Out of the toun than went he
wele half a mile fram that cité
and ther made Gii his mon.

"Sir King," seyd Gii, "understond to me.
O thing Y schal now pray thee
astow art curteys and hende:
yif Y mi name schal thee sayn
that to no man thou no schalt me wrayn
to this yere com to th'ende.
Gii of Warwike mi nam is right,
whilom Y was thine owhen knight
and held me for thi frende;
and now icham swiche astow may see.
God of Heven biteche Y thee,
mi way Y wil forth wende."

When the king seighe sikerly
that it was the gode Gii
that fro him wald his way
on knes he fel adoun to grounde,
"Leve Sir Gii," in that stounde,
"merci," he gan to say.
"For Godes love bileve with me
and mi treuthe Y schal plight thee
that Y schal this day
sese and give into thine hond
half the reme of Inglond;
for Godes love say nought nay."

"Sir King," seyd Gii, "Y nil nought so.
Have thou thi lond for evermo
and God Y thee biteche;
ac yif Herhaud to this lond com
and bring with him Reynbroun mi sone
help him Y thee biseche.
For thai er bothe hende and fre,
on Herhaud thou might trust thee
to take of thine fon wreche."
Thai kisten hem togider tho

but you must go with me so far
that no man of our words may hear
but you and me alone."
The king granted him this and was ready,
he commanded his folk quickly
no man with him to go.
Out of the town than he went
at least half a mile from that city
and there made his entreaty to Guy.

"Sir King," said Guy, "understand me.
One thing I shall now ask of you
since you are courteous and noble:
if I shall tell you my name
that to no man you shall reveal me
until this year comes to an end.
Guy of Warwick my name is truly,
I once was your own knight
and considered myself your friend;
and now I am such as you can see.
By God of Heaven I swear to you,
I will go my way."

When the king saw assuredly
that it was the good Guy
who from him would go his way
he fell down to the ground on his knees,
"Dear Sir Guy," in that place,
"Mercy," he began to say.
"For God's love remain with me
and my promise I will make to you
that I shall this day
give into your hand
half the realm of England;
for God's love don't say no."

"Sir King," said Guy, "I will not do it.
Keep your land forevermore
and I commend you to God;
but if Herhaud to this land comes
and brings with him Reynbroun my son
I ask you to help him.
For they are both noble and free,
you can trust on Herhaud
to take care of your wretched foes."
They kissed each other then

al wepeand thai wenten ato
withouten ani more speche.

The king wel sore wepe for pité
and went him hom to his meyne
with a mournand chere.
His folk ogaines him gan gon
and asked the king sone anon
what man the pilgrim were.
Thai seyd, "He is a douhti knight.
Wald Jhesu ful of might
he wald leve with ous here."
The king seyd, "Al stille ye be.
What he is your non schal wite for me,
iwis, of al this yere."

Sir Gii went in his way forth right,
oft he thonked God Almight
that the geaunt was slawe.
To Warwike he went to that cité
ther he was lord of that cuntré
to hold with right lawe.
He nas knowen ther of no man
when he to the castel gates cam,
therof he was ful fawe.
Among the pouer men he him dede
ther thai weren up in a stede
and sett him on a rawe.

### 38. *ANONYMOUS SHORT ENGLISH METRICAL CHRONICLE*

**Middle English**
**ca. 1330**

Edward king regned here
four ond tuenti ful yer.
At Winchester lith his bon
wel fair in a marbel ston.
After him regned King Athelston,
a gode kniht ond an hardi mon,
bothe bi day ond bi niht.
Wele he held his lond in riht.
Al the knihtes of Wales lond
he made hem bowe to his hond;
he leyd swiche trowage on hem
ond on al the Walismen
that thre hundred pounde of sterling
thai yoven to Athelston the king,
ond eke tuenti pounde of gold.

all weeping they went their separate ways
without any words more.

The king wept bitterly for pity
and went home to his household
with a mourning expression.
His people came to him
and asked the king at once
who the pilgrim was.
They said, "He is a brave knight.
If only by Jesus full of might
he would remain with us here."
The king said, "Be silent.
Who he is none of you shall learn from me,
truly, until this year is done."

Sir Guy went his way directly,
often he thanked Almighty God
that the giant was slain.
To Warwick he went to that city
where he was lord of that region
to hold with right law.
He was recognized by no man there
when he came to the castle gates,
of that he was very glad.
Among the poor men he placed himself
where they were arranged in one place
and sat himself in a group of them.

## 38. *Anonymous Short English Metrical Chronicle*

**See pp. 225–26**

King Edward reigned here
twenty-four years.
At Winchester lie his bones
enclosed in a beautiful marble tomb.
After him reigned King Athelstan,
who was a good knight and a strong man
all the days of his life.
He held his land by right.
All the knights of the lands of Wales,
he made them bow to his hand;
he set upon them such tribute —
and indeed upon all the Welshmen —
that three hundred pounds of silver
they had to give to King Athelstan,
along with twenty pounds of gold.

Scotlond him yeld sold,
yete Wales yelt more to him:
fif thousand of fat kin
to the king iche yere
er thai most be quic ond skere.
Thilke king Athelston
hadde a soster white so swan.
In al the warld men wist non
so fair a leuedi of flesche ond bon.
Ilde hiht that maiden fre,
that hadde so michel of beauté,
men nist non in this kingriche,
leuedi of beauté hir liche.
The king of Fraunce, that hiht Howe,
herd tel of that maiden trowe
that was so fair ond so hende,
ond after hir he gan sende
th'erl Edulf of Boloyne,
th'erles sone Baldwine of Coloine.
He was the kinges messanger
in his lond fer ond ner.
Tho he was to this lond ycome
the king he fond at Abindone.
Ther the king he mett
ond swithe fair he him gret.
A noble present he him brouht
ond of his soster him bisouht
to his lord the king
that is in Fraunce woniing.
Ond fro him verrament
he brouht a noble present
that was precious ond dere.
Wiche it was ye mow now here:
thre hundred stedes milke white,
in al this world nas her like;
the bridles wer for the nones
ful of precious stones.
Yete he present him also
other riches mani mo:
th'emperour swerd Costentin,
the schawberk was of gold fin,
therin was closed a nail gret
that was ydriven thurth Godes fet.
    Yete he present him the spere
that Charlmain was won to bere
oyaines Sarrazines in bataile.
Mani swore ond seyd, saunfaile,

Scotland also yielded tribute to him,
but Wales yielded more to him:
five thousand fat cattle
to the king each year
if they wanted to remain alive and unharmed.
This King Athelstan
had a sister white as a swan.
in all the world men knew no one
so fair a lady of flesh and bone.
Eadhild was the name of that maiden free,
who had so much beauty,
men knew not in this kingdom,
a lady of beauty like hers.
The king of France, who was called Hugh,
heard word of that maiden true
who was so fair and so well-bred,
and to pursue her he sent
the earl Adelolf of Boulogne,
who was the son of Baldwin, the earl of Cologne.
He was the king's messenger
in his land far and near.
Though he was to this land come
he found the king at Abingdon.
There he met the king
and very courteously greeted him.
A noble present he brought him
and of his sister him besought
to his lord the king
who is in France living.
And from him truly
he brought a noble present
that was precious and costly.
What it was you may now hear:
three hundred milk-white horses,
in all this world there wasn't their like;
the bridles were for the nones
full of precious stones.
Yet he presented him also
many additional riches:
the sword of Emperor Constantine,
the hauberk of it was made of fine gold;
therein was closed a large nail
that had been driven through the feet of God.

He presented him also with the spear
that Charlemagne liked to carry
against the Saracens in battle.
Many people swore and said, without doubt,

that with that spere smert
Jhesu was stongen to the hert.
Yete he present him, ywis,
the baner of Seyn Moris
that he was won to bere
oyain the Sarrazines here,
ond a parti of the Holy Crois
in a cristal don inclos,
ond thre of the thornes kene
that were in Godes heued y wene,
ond a riche croun of gold —
non richer king wer no schold —
ymaked within ond without
with precious stones al about.
To make frendes that wer fon
a better croun nas never non
to non erthelich man ywrouht
seththe this warld was made of nouht.
King Athelston was glad ond blithe
ond thonke the king of Fraunce swithe
of this yiftes noble ond riche.
In al this warld was non swiche.
In Athelstonis time, ich understond,
was Gii of Warwike in Inglond
ond for Athelston he dede a bateyle
with a geaunt gret, saunfaile.
The geaunt hiht Colbrond,
Gii him slouh with his hond.
At Winchester the bataile was don
ond seththe dede Gii never non.
Seven yer King Athelston
held this iche kingdom.
In Inglond that is so miri
he dyed ond lith at Malmesbiri.

### 39. Ranulf Higden, *Polychronicon* — Latin 1327–1352

[See notes.]

### 40. Robert Mannyng of Brunne, *Chronicle* — Middle English 1338

After Edward the olde regned Athelstan
that was his eldest sonne ond a noble man.
The baronage ond the clergie were somond to Kyngeston;
ther wes his fest holden ond gyven him the croune.

that with a strike of that spear
Jesus had been cut to the heart.
He also presented him, indeed,
with the banner of St. Maurice
that he liked to carry
against the Saracens here,
and a relic of the Holy Cross
enclosed in a crystal,
and three of the sharp thorns
that were stuck in God's head,
and a rich crown of gold —
there was none richer worn by a king —
crafted within and without
with precious stones all about.
To make friends that were foes
a better crown has never been
wrought by any earthly man
since this world was created.
King Athelstan was glad and pleased
and thanked the king of France greatly
for these gifts noble and rich.
in all this world there was not their equal.
In Athelstan's time, I understand,
was Guy of Warwick in England
and for Athelstan he fought a battle
with a great giant, without doubt.
The giant was called Colbrond,
Guy killed him with his hand.
At Winchester the battle was fought
and since then Guy never [fought] again.
Seven years King Athelstan
held this same kingdom.
In England that is so merry
he died and lies at Malmesbury.

### 39. RANULF HIGDEN, *POLYCHRONICON*

See p. 226

[See notes.]

### 40. ROBERT MANNYNG OF BRUNNE, *CHRONICLE*

See pp. 226–30

After Edward the Old, Athelstan reigned,
who was his eldest son and a noble man.
The baronage and the clergy were summoned to Kingston;
there his feast was held, and the crown given to him.

The next yere after his coronment,
the Walsh men that luf no pes on him ran ond brent.
Bot Athelstan the maistrie wan ond did tham mercie crie,
ond alle Northwales he set to treuage hie:
tuenti pounde of gold be yere, thre hundreth of silver clere,
ond ther to fyve hundreth kie ilk yere to his lardere.
Silver for Southwales, not a ferthing noke;
other treuage he sette, a thousand kie he toke.
The ferth yere of the regne, Owald, a werreoure,
Constantyn, of Scotland kyng was ond traitoure,
Onwer, kyng of Wentland, these thre with ther powere
werred on Athelstan with oste fulle austere.
Bot Athelstan thorgh Godes grace so with tham fore
thei were fayn to ask pes ond feauté thei him suore.
The tend yere of his regne sen he was crouned kyng,
of Edwyn his brother bifelle suilk a thing:
at London in his courte with wiknes men him fond.
Athelstan did him bynd both fote ond hond
ond kast him in tille Temse whan it was most brym;
to chastise all other, he tok vengeance on him.
At myn understandyng, he wild take no mede
that was ateynt of wikkednes, his brother to dede yede.
Constantyn of Scotland that I are of spak,
brak his feauté (of treson it is lak)
ond alle folk of Danmark with Constantyn held
ond slouh our Inglish men, wasted toun ond feld.
Athelstan herd say, he went to Beverlay
ond praied the Bisshop Jon, in fertre ther he lay,
that he wild bede his bone untille the Trinité,
ond he suld gyve his kirke franchise ond fe
to haf ond to holde, als he was kyng leale;
of him haf thei chartre seled with his seale.
Sithen he went to Durham ond gaf Saynt Cutbert
londes ond lithes with chartir aperte;
the bisshop of his gift holdes his fe.
Sithen he went to bataile, Constantyn to fle;
Constantyn he reymed ond did full stress
ond wan the lond ilk dele ond wasted alle Cathenesse,
ond his son yolden unto his ostage;
sithen he turned to London ond his baronage.
Athelstan in Scotland a selcouth ded he one,
he smote depe at Donbarre an elne in the stone.
At the feast of our Lady, the Assumpcion,
went the kyng fro London toward Abindon;
thider out of France fro Charles, kyng of fame,
com the erl of Boloyn, Adulphus was his name,
ond the duke of Burgoyn, Edmunde sonne, Reynere.

The next year after his coronation,
the Welsh, who do not love peace, attacked and burned his lands,
but Athelstan won the victory and made them cry mercy,
and he imposed a high tribute on all North Wales:
twenty pounds of gold a year, three hundred of pure silver,
and in addition five hundred cattle each year for his larder.
Not a bit of silver for South Wales;
he imposed a different tribute — he took a thousand cattle.
In the fourth year of his reign, Owald, a warrior,
Constantine, who was king of Scotland and a traitor,
Onwer, king of Wentland — these three with their power
warred against Athelstan with a very fierce host.
But Athelstan, through God's grace, so advanced against them
they were fain to ask for peace, and they swore fealty to him.
The tenth year of his reign after he was crowned king
a remarkable thing happened because of Edwin, his brother:
at London in his court, men discovered him [Edwin] intent on wickedness.
Athelstan had him bound both foot and hand
and cast him into the Thames when it was most turbulent.
To warn all others, he took vengeance on him.
It is my understanding that he would take no compensation
that was tainted with wickedness — his brother went to his death.
Constantine of Scotland, of whom I spoke before,
broke his fealty (that is a fault of treason),
and all the folk of Denmark held with Constantine
and slew our Englishmen, laid waste to town and field.
Athelstan heard of that. He went to Beverley
and prayed to Bishop John, in the shrine where he lay,
that he [John] would offer his [Athelstan's] prayer to the Trinity,
and he [Athelstan] should give his [John's] church franchise and fee
to have and to hold, as he was a loyal king.
They have a charter from him, sealed with his seal.
Afterwards he went to Durham and gave St. Cuthbert
lands and estates with a letter patent;
the bishop holds his fee through his [Athelstan's] gift.
Afterwards he went to battle, to put Constantine to flight.
He seized and imprisoned Constantine
and won the land entirely and laid waste to all Caithness,
and his [Constantine's] son was surrendered as his hostage.
Afterwards he returned to London and his baronage.
In Scotland Athelstan did a wondrous thing —
at Dunbar he smote deeply an ell into the stone.
At the Feast of the Assumption of Our Lady,
the king went from London toward Abingdon.
Thither out of France from Charles, the famous king,
came the earl of Boulogne, Adelolf was his name,
and the duke of Burgundy, Edmund's son, Rayner.

Thei brouht Kyng Athelston present withouten pere;
fro Charles, kyng sanz faile, thei brouht a gonfaynoun
that Saynt Morice bar in bataile before the legion,
ond scharp lance that thrilled Jhesu side,
ond a suerd of gold; in the hilte did men hide
tuo of tho nayles that war thorh Jhesu fete
tached on the Croyce, the blode thei out lete,
ond som of the thornes that don were on His heued,
ond a fair pece that of the Croyce leuued
that Saynt Helen sonne at the bataile wan
of the soudan of Askalone, his name was Madan.
Than blewe the trumpes fulle loud ond fulle schille;
the kyng com in to the halle that hardy was of wille.
Than spak Reyner, Edmunde sonne, for he was messenger.
"Athelstan, my lord thee gretes, Charles that has no pere.
He sendes thee this present ond sais he wille him bynde
to the thorh Ilde, thi sistere, ond tille alle thi kynde."
Befor the messengers was the maiden brouht;
of body so gentille was non in erth wrouht,
no non so faire of face, of speche so lufly;
scho granted befor tham alle to Charles hir body,
ond so did the kyng ond alle the baronage.
Mykelle was the richesse thei purveied hir passage
ond led hir unto France, spoused forto be.
Athelstan leves stille ond passed not the se.
  In the yere after that Ilde wedded was,
Constantyn of Scotlond did yit more trispas.
He brought the Kyng Anlaf, aryved up in Humbere,
seven hundreth schippes ond fiftene, so fele were the numbere.
Athelstan herd say of ther mykelle oste;
he ond Edmunde, his brother, dight tham to that coste.
At Brunesburgh on Humber thei gan tham assaile;
fro morn unto even lasted that bataile.
At the last, to ther schippes the kyng gan tham chace,
alle away thei fled, that was of Godes grace,
bot the most partie algate was slayn;
that with the life fled, I trowe thei were fulle fayn.
Whan the Kyng Anlaf sauh his folk lorn,
he fled unto Danmark ther there he was born.
  At the Pask after, he ryved in the south
at a haven of Sandwich in the portis mouth.
Whan he was aryved, the folk was affray
ond com unto Wynchestre ther the kyng lay.
He brouht with him a develle, a hogge geant;
wele haf ye herd telle, he hight Colibrant.
Anlaf sent messengers unto Athelstan
ond bad him yeld the lond or fynd another man

They brought King Athelstan a present without peer:
from Charles, king without fault, they brought a standard
that St. Maurice carried in battle before the legion,
and the sharp lance that pierced Jesus' side,
and a sword of gold — in the hilt men set
two of the nails that were attached on the Cross
through Jesus' feet; they let out the blood —
and some of the thorns that were placed on His head,
and a fair piece that survived of the Cross
that St. Helena's son won in battle
from the sultan of Ascalon — his name was Madan.
Then the trumpets blew very loud and very shrill;
The king, who was strong of will, came into the hall.
Then Rayner, Edmund's son, spoke, for he was the messenger,
"Athelstan, my lord, Charles, who has no peer, greets you.
He sends you this present and says he will bind himself
to you through Eadhild, your sister, and to all of your kin."
The maiden was brought before the messengers.
There was none on earth made so refined in form,
none so fair of face, of speech so lovely.
Before them all she granted her person to Charles,
and so did the king and all the baronage.
Great was the treasure they provided for her passage
and they led her into France to be wed.
Athelstan remained still and did not cross the sea.
In the year after Eadhild was married,
Constantine of Scotland committed yet more trespass.
He brought King Anlaf, arrived in the Humber,
seven hundred and fifteen ships, so great was their number.
Athelstan heard word of their great host;
he and Edmund, his brother, prepared themselves for that coast.
At Brunesburgh on Humber they attacked them;
that battle lasted from morning until evening.
At the last the king chased them to their ships.
They all fled away — that was by God's grace —
but the great majority was entirely slain.
Those who fled with their lives, I dare say they were quite glad.
When King Anlaf saw his folk were beaten,
he fled to Denmark, there where he was born.
At the following Easter, he arrived in the south
at a haven of Sandwich, in the port's mouth.
When he was landed, the folk were afraid
and came to Winchester, where the king lay.
He [Anlaf] brought with him a devil, a huge giant.
Well have you heard tell, he was called Colibrant.
Anlaf sent messengers to Athelstan
and bade him yield the land or find another man

to fight with Colibrant that was his champion.
Who felle to haf the lond, on tham it suld be done.
Athelstan tok a day, a parlement did make,
if any ageyn Colibrant the bataile durst take.
He fond no man that durst, for non had myght
with Colibrant alone in bataile to fight.
Than praied Athelstan to Criste ond sore wepe,
ond God sent him tokenyng on nyght as he slepe
that he suld fynd a palmere orly at morn
at the south gate, alone as he was born,
ond if he wild praie him for Jhesu Cristes love,
he wild do the bataile ond thei suld be above.
That was Guy of Werwik as the boke sais;
ther he slouh Colibrant with hache Daneis.
Anlaf turned agayn (I trowe him was wo),
he ond alle his to schippe gan thei go.
God delyverde Athelstan of many hard affraies;
sextene yere was he kyng ond seventene daies.
Sithen at Gloucestre, did evelle him tok,
bot quik he out went, so sais my boke.
(Pers can not say where he lies,
bot as I herd telle, I say myn avys.)
Men say he was fonden in the north cuntré
at Hexham now late, I wene it soth be.
The date whan he died, of god men tellis by,
nien hundreth wynter ond fulle fourty.

### 41. *Scottish Chronicle* (alias *Pictish Chronicle*)

**Latin**
**mid-14th c.**

Et bellum Duinbrunde, in xxx.iiij. eius anno ubi cecidit filius Constantini et post unum annum mortuus est.

### 42. John of Fordun, *Chronica Gentis Scotorum*

**Latin**
**mid-14th c.**

[See Item 49, below, and notes.]

### 43. *Eulogium Historiarum*

**Latin**
**ca. 1367**

Hic etiam contra Pictos et Scottos plura bella commisit; anno regni sui xii. congressus est cum rege Norhumbrorum, Arnalafo nomine, apud Donelew in Wilthschire. Ibi enim tot ceciderunt Pictorum, Scottorum, Danorum, quod numerari non possent; ceciderunt autem ibi duo nepotes regis Athelstani, scilicet, Elwyn et Athelwyn. Gesta autem Britonum dicunt Angelum de caelo missum gladium suum de manu

to fight with Colibrant, who was his champion.
Who happens to have the land, to them it should be given.
Athelstan took a day and called a parliament
[to see] if any dared take the battle against Colibrant.
He found that no man dared, for none had the might
to fight alone with Colibrant in battle.
Then Athelstan prayed to Christ and sorely wept,
and God sent him a sign at night as he slept
that he should find a palmer early in the morning
at the south gate, alone as he was born,
and if he would pray him for Jesus Christ's love,
he would fight the battle and they should prevail.
That was Guy of Warwick, as the book says;
there he slew Colibrant with a Danish battle-ax.
Anlaf turned back (I dare say he was woeful);
he and all his [men] — to ship they went.
God delivered Athelstan from many hard assaults;
he was king for sixteen years and seventeen days.
Afterwards at Gloucester illness took him,
but he went out quickly — so says my book.
(Pierre cannot say where he lies,
but just as I heard tell, I give my opinion.)
Men say that he was found in the north country
at Hexham lately — I believe it to be the truth.
The date when he died, as good men relate,
was fully nine hundred and forty winters.

### 41. *SCOTTISH CHRONICLE* (ALIAS *PICTISH CHRONICLE*)

**See p. 230**

And there was war at Duinbrunde in his thirty-fourth year when the son of Constantine fell. He died one year later.

### 42. JOHN OF FORDUN, *CHRONICLES OF THE SCOTTISH PEOPLE*

**See p. 230**

[See Item 49, below, and notes.]

### 43. *EULOGIUM HISTORIARUM*

**See pp. 230–31**

Here he also engaged in many wars against the Picts and the Scots; in the twelfth year of his reign he contended with the king of the Northumbrians, Anlaf by name, at Dunlow in Wiltshire. Indeed so many Picts, Scots, and Danes fell there that they cannot be numbered. Two nephews of King Athelstan also died there, namely Ælfwine and Æthelwyn. The deeds of the Britons moreover say that an angel sent

sua lapsum incontinenti regi dedisse. Sancta autem crux quod circa collum sum in bellis gestabat adhuc Malmesburiae inter sacras reliquas, ut decet, ueneratur.

### 44. *BRUT Y SAESSON* — **Welsh 1383–1387**

Gwedy hwnnw y gwledychawd Edylstan, y vab ynteu, yr hwnn a gawssoedit o orderchyat. Hwnnw dewr a doeth oed. Ac ef a gymerth yn dreth o Wyned vgein punt o eur a thrychant pvnt o aryant, ac ugein mil o warthec.

Ac un o'e chwioryd a rodes ef y vrenhin Nordhwmbyrlont. A gwedy marw hwnnw, ef a darestyngawd y holl gyuoeth idaw ehun. A chwaer arall idaw, Hild oed y henw, diruawr y thegwch, a gymerth Hu urenhin Ffreinc yn wreic idaw.

Hwnnw a oruv ar wyr Denmarc a'r Gwydyl a'r Ysgottyeit.

Hwnnw a deholes Idwal vrenhin Kymry, a Chustennin vrenhin Ysgotlont oc eu teyrnassoed. Chwe blyned ar hugeint a naw cant oed oet Crist yna. A gwedy hynny ef a'e gadawd wynt y wledychu drach eu kefyn, ac a dywawt mae mwy ogonyant oed wneuthur brenhin no bot yn vrenhin.

Damchwein oed uot hen uanachlawc yn Lloegyr nys teckaei yn y oes ef ac ar nys anrydedawd ef o adeilyadeu ac anreithyeu ac adurn tec.

Ef a dyrchafawd mab y Gustennin vrenhin Ysgotlont o'r bedydlestyr, ac a'e dalyawd wrth vedyd yn arwyd tangnefed y ryngthunt.

Ef a vynnassei rei ac Elret o Winsestyr yn dywyssawc arnadunt y dallu ef. Ac yna y dalpwyt Elret ac yd anuonet y Ruuein wrth y amdiffyn drwy ger bronn y pab. A gwedy tyngu ohonaw geyr bronn allawr Bedyr, ef a digwydawd y'r llawr. Ac y rwng dwylaw y weissyon y ducpwyt ef odyno, a'r dryded nos y bu uarw.

A'r Edylstan hwnnw a wledychawd vn vlwydyn ar bymthec ac a gladwyt y Malmesburi.

### 45. RICHARD OF CIRENCESTER, *SPECULUM HISTORIALE* — **Latin late 14th c.**

[See notes.]

### 46. PSEUDO-INGULF, *INGULFI CROYLANDENSIS HISTORIA* — **Latin ca. 1400**

[p. 29]

Anno uero regni sui xxiii. obiit iste Edwardus, et cum patre suo Wyntoniae tumulatus est. Cui successit filius suus primogenitus Athelstanus: contra quem cum Dani de Northumbria, Norfolchia conspirassent, associatis sibi Constantino Rege Scottorum, multisque aliis; ipse collectum exercitum ducens in Northumbriam, obuios habuit plures peregrinos de Beuerlaco ad propria uenientes. . . .

from heaven gave the careless king the sword that had fallen from his hand. A holy cross that he wore around his neck in war also is still venerated (as it should be) among the holy relics of Malmesbury.

### 44. *CHRONICLE OF THE ENGLISH* See pp. 231–33

After him [i.e., Edward], Athelstan, his son, ruled — the one who had been got in adultery. He was brave and wise. And he took as a tax from Gwynedd twenty pounds of gold and three hundred pounds of silver and twenty thousand cattle.

And one of his sisters he gave to the king of Northumberland. And after he [Edward] died, he [Athelstan] subdued the entire kingdom for himself. And another sister of his — Eadhild was her name, very great her beauty — Hugh the king of the Franks took as his wife.

He [Athelstan] conquered the men of Denmark and the Irish and the Scots.

He exiled Idwal king of Wales and Constantine king of Scotland from their kingdoms. Nine hundred and twenty-six was the time of Christ then. And after that he allowed them back to rule and said that it was better to make a king than to be a king.

It was [only] by accident that there would be an old monastery in England that he would not beautify during his life and that he did not honor with buildings and wealthy and fair adornment.

He raised the son of Constantine king of Scotland from the baptismal font and held him through baptism as a sign of peace between them.

Some, with Elred of Winchester as leader over them, had wished to blind him. And then Elred was caught and sent to Rome for his defense by [...] before the pope. And after he swore before the altar of Peter, he fell to the floor. And in the arms of his servants he was carried from there, and the third night he died.

And that Athelstan ruled for sixteen years and was buried at Malmesbury.

### 45. RICHARD OF CIRENCESTER, *MIRROR OF HISTORY* See p. 233

[See notes.]

### 46. PSEUDO-INGULF, *CHRONICLE OF CROWLAND* See pp. 233–34

[p. 29]

Edward died in the twenty-third year of his reign and was buried with his father at Winchester. His firstborn son Athelstan succeeded him. The Danes of Northumbria and Norfolk conspired against him in alliance with Constantine, king of the Scots, and many others. As he led his assembled army into Northumbria, Athelstan met on the way many pilgrims coming home from Beverley. . . .

Ceciderunt siquidem in illo praelio Constantinus Rex Scottorum ac alii Reges numero quinque, Comites duodecim, Barbaries popularium infinita. Hoc bello prospere consummato, non erat qui de cetero Regem auderet offendere in aliquo.

[p. 37]

Compleuit itaque dies suos inclytus Rex Edwardus, Ethestanusque filius ejus successerat. Contra quem cum Analaphus filius Sitrici, quondam Regis Northanhumbrorum insurgeret, et bellum ferocissimum multorum uiribus moliretur, conspirantibusque cum dicto Analapho, Constantino Rege Scotorum, et Eugenio Rege Cumbrorum, ac aliorum Regum Comitumque barbarie infinita, omnes, cum subjectis nationibus ad Brunford in Northanhumbria contra Athelstanum Regem conuenissent, arctissimo foedere conjurati, et dictus Rex Anglorum cum suo exercitu occurrisset, licet praefatus barbarus infinitam multitudinem Danorum, Norreganorum, Scotorum, ac Pictorum contraxisset, uel uincendi diffidentia, uel solita gentis suae uersutia, maluit nocturnis tenebris insidias tendere, quam aperto praelio dimicare. Irruit ergo subito super Anglos nocturno tempore; peremptoque quodam Episcopo, qui praecedente uespere ad exercitum Regis Athelstani accesserat, cum clamor morientium longius personaret, ut Rex ipse, qui plus uno milliari a loco distabat, suusque totus exercitus, qui circa illum in tentoriis sub dio dormiebat, euigilans atque intelligens citius armarentur aurora jam illucescente, ad locumque caedis appropinquans, paratus et promptus fieret ad inuadendum contra barbaros, qui tota nocte laborauerant, et jam lassos, et laxatos, ab ordine offendentem contigit Regem Athelstanum, qui Westsaxones omnes ducebat, contra aciem Analaphi occurrisse, ac Cancellarium suum Turketlum, qui Londonienses, et omnes Merciores trahebat, contra aciem Constantini obuiasse: cessantibus cito ferentariis armis, pede pes, et cuspide cuspis, umboque umbone pellebatur. Caesi multi mortales, confusasque cadauera Regum et pauperum corruebant. Cumque diutissime ac dirissime dimicaretur, et neutra pars cederet, (tanta erat Paganorum multitudo) Cancellarius Turketlus assumptis secum paucis Londoniensibus, quos fortissimos nouerat, et quodam centurione Wicciorum, Singrino nomine, qui spectata fortitudine pollebat, ipse prae cunctis et statura procerus, ossibus et neruis solidus et torosus, ac inter omnes heroes Londonienses uiribus robustissimus, praeuius ipse inuolat in aduersos; penetransque cuneos hostiles prosternit a dextris et a sinistris. Jam Orcadensium, ac Pictorum globos pertransierat, syluamque jaculorum et telorum, quae thorace fidelissima sufflauerat, in se projectam circumferens, jam cuneos Cumbrorum ac Scotorum cum suis sequacibus perforabat. Tandem multo sanguine ad ipsum Regem perueniens, equo dejecit, dejectumque cum uiuum capere omnimodis conaretur, et Scoti constipati Regem suum totis saluare uiribus insisterent, et plures in paucos niterentur, praecipueque omnes unum Turketlum appeterent, prout saepius postea fatebatur, tunc primum temeritatis suae poenitebat. Jam jamque opprimen-

[Here follows the story of Athelstan offering his dagger on the altar of St. John and redeeming it richly after the battle.]

And so Constantine, king of the Scots, was slain in that battle, as well as five other kings, twelve earls, and an infinite number of the barbarian masses. After this battle had come to its prosperous end, there were none left who dared to cross the king in anything.

[p. 37]

And so the renowned King Edward ended his days and his son Athelstan succeeded him. Anlaf, son of Sihtric, former king of the Northumbrians, rose against him, and made most savage war with a force of many men, conspiring with Constantine, king of the Scots, and Eugenius, king of the Cumbrians, as well as other kings and earls and an untold number of barbarians. Joined in close league, they all came together with their subject peoples against King Athelstan at Brunford in Northumbria, and the king of the English opposed [them] with his own force. Although the barbarian [Anlaf] had assembled a countless number of Danes, Norwegians, Scots, and Picts, either through uncertainty of success or through the customary guile of his people, he preferred to commit treachery in nocturnal darkness rather than engage in open war. He rushed upon the English unexpectedly in the night and a certain bishop was killed who had come to King Athelstan's army the previous evening. When the cries of the dying were heard from a distance, the king awakened and became aware more than one mile away from that place, and his entire army which slept around him in their tents in the open air quickly roused themselves. They approached the place of slaughter in the already quickening dawn, ready and eager for an attack against the barbarians who had struggled through the entire night and were already weary and worn from fighting in the line. King Athelstan, who commanded all the West Saxons, stood against Anlaf's force, while his chancellor Turketul, who led the Londoners and all the Mercians, met Constantine's force. The exchange of missiles soon ended, and it was toe to toe, point to point, and shield to shield. Many men died, and the corpses of kings and paupers fell together in confusion. And when they had fought hard for a long while and neither side had yielded (so great was the number of pagans), chancellor Turketul, with a few select Londoners he knew to be the most steadfast, as well as a captain of the Wicci by the name of Singrin — he was strong in proven fortitude, tall in stature above the rest, solid and muscular in bone and sinew, and the hardiest in strength among all the London heroes — led a charge into the enemy, and penetrating the enemy ranks cut them down right and left. He had already gone through the troops of the men of Orkney and the Picts, carrying about him a jutting forest of javelins and spears amassed upon his trusty cuirass, and with his followers he now pierced the ranks of the Cumbrians and Scots. Finally, amidst great bloodshed he came to King Constantine and threw him from his horse and as he was thrown tried to take him alive in any way possible. The Scots crowded together and tried to save their king with all their might. The many struggled against a few, and they all especially sought out Turketul alone, [who], as he often confessed later, was then beginning to regret his own daring. He had just

dus erat a Scotis, et Rex e manibus ejus eripiendus, cum Singrinus centurio gladio confodit eum. Sic Rege Scotorum Constantino perempto, Scoti se retrahentes, viam apertiorem Turketulo, suisque militibus concedebant. Cognita ergo morte Constantini per universum exercitum, Analaphus fugam facit, fugiuntque universi. Cecidit ibi Paganorum copia inaudita. In tam dura certamine saepius se gloriabatur a Domino conservatum Turketulus et se foelicissimum et fortunatum, quod nunquam hominem occiderit, neminem mutilaverit, cum pugnare pro patria, et maxime contra Paganos, licit quisque possit.

### 47. *Prose Brut*

**Middle English**
**1419**

Of Kyng Athelstone, ond of Edmunde, Eldrede, ond of Edwynne his brother. Capitulo Centesimo Undecimo.

After this Edward, regnede Athelston his sone; ond when he hade regnede iiij yere, he helde bataile ageynes the Danois, and drof Kyng Gaufride, that was kyng of the Danois, and al his hoste unto the see, ond restede by Scotland, ond nomen strongliche the contrey al a yere. And after that, tho of Cumberland, ond the Scottes of Westmerlande, bigonne to werre oppon Kyng Athelston; and he ham gaf so strong bataile that he quellede so meny of ham that no man couthe telle the nombre of ham. And after that he ne regnede but iij yere; ond he regnede in al xxv yere and lith at Malmesbury. And after this Athelston, regnede Edmund his brother, for as miche as Kyng Athelston hade none sone.

### 48. *Book of Hyde*

**Latin**
**mid-15th c.**

[See notes.]

### 49. Walter Bower, *Scotichronicon*

**Latin**
**1441–1445**

De Constantino filio Heth qui Cumbriam dedit Eugenio.

Constantinus filius regis Heth Alipedis, Donaldo succedens, anno Domini nongenesimo iii$^{o}$, Ludovici primo, regnavit annis xl. Ipso regnante duo reges Anglorum, supradictus videlicet Eadwardus et suus filius nothus Athelstanus, successive regnantes adversus eum frequenter bellabant, tum propter opem Danis adhibitam, tum quia terrarum Cumbrorum videlicet ac ceterarum in Anglia possessionum indigenas sibi fideliter et usque bellum de Brounnyngfelde adherentes omni virtute protegebat.

been overwhelmed by the Scots and the king had been wrested from his hands when the captain Singrin stabbed [Constantine] with his sword. And so with Constantine, king of the Scots, killed, the withdrawing Scots surrendered the open way to Turketul and his soldiers. And as Constantine's death was made known throughout the entire army, Anlaf and all the rest took flight. An unheard-of multitude of pagans was cut down in that place. Turketul often boasted that he been preserved by the Lord in such a hard combat and that he was most blessed and fortunate that he had never killed or maimed a man, though anyone could [do so] when fighting for his homeland, and most especially against pagans.

**47. *PROSE BRUT*** **See pp. 234–35**

Chapter 111. Of King Athelstan, and of Edmund, Eldred, and of Edwin, his brother.

After this Edward, Athelstan, his son, reigned. And when he had reigned four years, he fought a battle against the Danes and drove King Guthfrith, who was king of the Danes, and all his host into the sea and halted near Scotland and took the country by force all in a year. And after that, those of Cumberland and the Scots of Westmorland began to war upon King Athelstan, and he gave them such fierce battle that he killed so many of them that no one could tell the number of them. And after that he only reigned reigned three years, and in all he reigned twenty-five years and lies at Malmesbury. And after this Athelstan, Edmund, his brother, reigned, because King Athelstan had no son.

**48. *BOOK OF HYDE*** **See p. 235**

[See notes.]

**49. WALTER BOWER, *SCOTICHRONICON*** **See pp. 235–36**

Constantine son of Aed who gave Cumbria to Eochaid.

Constantine son of King Aed Wing-foot succeeded Donald in 903, the first year of the emperor Louis, and he reigned for forty years. During his reign two kings of the English, namely the above-mentioned Edward and his illegitimate son Athelstan, in their successive reigns fought frequently against him, both on account of the assistance he gave to the Danes and because he protected with all valor the inhabitants of the territory of the Cumbrians and the rest of his dominions in England, who loyally acknowledged allegiance to him right up to the Battle of Brunanburh.

Danice vero gentis mobiliores vento reges sibi sicut et predecessoribus suis, sub eadem conjuracione federis et amicicie forma juncti sunt, sed duobus annis vix fide manentes pacem cum Eadwardo subdolis seducti promissis ad propriam fecerunt perniciem contra Scotos. Neque diu contractus huiusmodi condicio tenuit quin post quadriennium exorta quedam inter eos discordia, dubium quo casu, sed opinatur Eadwardi scelere, qui terras eorum hostiliter invadens, per mensem integrum miserabili strage devastavit. Illi quidem necessitate coacti nullam alicubi sperantes opem quam reconsiliandos ad priorem federis amiciciam Scotos discernunt, a quorum contubernio nuper Eadwardi dolo recesserunt. Igitur ad mitigandum quod in eis rex Constantinus fixerat odium nuncios mittunt, veniam humiliter imprecantes et pacem nec uncquam de cetero foedus quodcunque, si tandem hoc reficere placuerit, suis rumpendum demeritis sacramento pollicentur. Sic quidem exacta queque negocia nuncii secum pro voto leti reportant, ira regis in pietate reformata.

Constantinus autem anno regni sui xvi dedit Eugenio filio Donaldi proximo sibi successori sperato regendum Cumbriae regionis dominium usque quo regni diadema post eius mortem fuerit optentus, ac eo rege coronato, suus heres proximus ad idem succedat dominium, et sic ab herede semper in regem coronato statim suo successori proximo dominium huiusmodi successionis ritu deinceps transferatur.

Anno regni sui xxii mortuus est Eadwardus et illi successit filius eius nothus Athelstanus ex opilionis filia genitus postposito fratre, qui de jure regnasset, Edwino miserabili postea morte tradito. Nam in navi sine remige vetustate consumpta solus unius hominis excepto comitatu, mari missus fuerat et demersus. Huiusmodi factis invidens quidem princeps Elfredus adversus Athelstanum regi Constantino prefatoque Sithrico se mox in omni fidelitatis societate colligavit.

. . .

De eodem Constantino, et de crudeli bello de Brounyngfelde.

Cum autem Athelstanus pretacte confederacionis rumores audisset motus immodice, nam adverse partis vires augeri suasque minui noverat, excogitare cepit rem pocius in occulto clam agere, quam in aperto dubios bellorum eventus experiri, emissis latenter suis susurronibus, in aure Sithrici dolose fraudem instillantibus, ipsum sacramenti prioris immemorem sed et filiis suis hoc omnino prohibentibus sororis sue fallaci connubio circumvenit. Unde contigit quod novem minime postea vixerit mensibus sed nequiter extinctus estimatur. Refert autem Willelmus quod Sithricus post annum vita deturbatus occasionem Adelstano dedit ut Northumbriam

The kings of the Danish race, more changeable than the wind, were allied to him as to his predecessors under the same sworn treaty and form of friendship, but they kept their pledged word for scarcely two years, making peace with Edward against the Scots to their own destruction, having been led astray by false promises. Nor did the terms of this kind of agreement hold for long, for after four years discord arose between them — from what incident is not clear — but it is thought that it arose from the villainy of Edward, who invaded their lands with hostile intent and ravaged them for a whole month with pitiful devastation. The Danes were compelled by necessity and had no hope of help from any other quarter except to make up their minds to win back to their former treaty of friendship the Scots from close ties with whom they had recently withdrawn through the trickery of Edward. Therefore to assuage the hatred which King Constantine had conceived against them, they sent envoys humbly requesting pardon and peace and promising on oath that they would never in future break any treaty whatsoever by their misdeeds, if he would consent to renew this one. The envoys joyfully took back with them the news that their mission had been accomplished as they desired, after the king's anger had turned to pity.

In the sixteenth year of his reign Constantine gave to Eochaid son of Donald, his intended successor next in line, rule over the lordship of the region of Cumbria until such time as he should obtain the crown of the kingdom after the death of Constantine. After he had been crowned king his own heir next in line was to succeed to the same lordship, and in this way the lordship should be immediately transferred by the heir in his turn in perpetuity, after he had been crowned king, to his successor next in line according to the custom of this kind of succession.

In the twenty-second year of his reign Edward died and was succeeded by his illegitimate son Athelstan whose mother was the daughter of a shepherd. He was preferred to his brother Edwin who should by rights have reigned and who was later given over to a pitiful death. For he had been set adrift in a boat without oars which was old and rotten, alone except for the company of one man, and drowned. In hatred of deeds of this kind a certain chief Elfred soon bound himself in a total alliance of loyalty to King Constantine and the aforesaid Sihtric against Athelstan.

. . .

More about Constantine and the savage battle of Brunanburh.

When Athelstan heard rumors of the afore-mentioned alliance, he was greatly disturbed, for he realized that the strength of the opposing side was being increased, while his own was diminishing. He began to reflect that it would be better to proceed secretly and stealthily rather than openly to test the doubtful results of battles. He secretly sent out his undercover agents treacherously to instill deception in the ear of Sihtric and so tricked him into forgetting his former oath and into a deceitful marriage with [Athelstan's] sister, although his sons were utterly opposed to it. Hence it came about that he lived scarcely nine months afterwards, but it is thought that he was killed by villainy. William [of Malmesbury] records that the fact that Sihtric departed this life a year later gave Athelstan the opportunity to attach Northumbria to his side.

parti sue jungeret et mox Eboracum obsidens opidanosque nunc precibus, nunc minis ad dedicionem sollicitans et pro voto neutrum expediens abcessit.

Northumbrie quidem gentes et Cumbrie Scotis et Danis iam diu fideliter tamquam una gens conglutinate libencius sibi quam Anglis subici curabant. Sithrico quidem, ut supra, de medio sublato, filios eius Analafum et Godefridum in principes sibi Northumbri libenter suscipiunt qui statim Constantino juncti totis viribus impugnabant Athelstanum. Igitur anno regni sui xxxvi rex Constantinus, Analafus et Godefridus grandi nimis exercitu collecto, partes Anglorum australes invadunt, cuncta vastando per que transiebant quoadusque locum quo tentoria fixerat Athelstanus, qui Bronnyngfelde dicitur, advenissent.

Willelmus: "Postremum Adelstano bellum fuit cum Analafo Sithrici filio Scotorumque rege Constantino qui spe invadendi regni terminos transierant, Adelstano ex consultu cedente ut gloriosius vinceret, iam insultantes multum in Anglia transierant." Nec mora, phalangis utriusque partis et aciebus intermixtis crudelissimum commissum est bellum et longe pre ceteris sevissimum vel antiquorum scriptis traditum sive presencium memorie commendatum. Cesi sunt autem ex parte victoris Athelstani precipue duces Elwinus et Ethilwinus aliique duces duo. Duo siquidem episcopi cum multis nobilibus. Ex altera vero parte regulus Deireiorum Eligenius cum aliis tribus, duces novem ac vulgi partis utriusque populus innumerus.

. . .

De morte Constantini et de belli huius dampnis Scotis illatis.

Infaustus enim erat Scotis ille dies nam queque dominia temporibus Gregorii vel actenus conquesta necnon quinquaginta iv$^{or}$ annis possessa vel amplius hoc in die jure bellico sunt amissa. Willelmus: "Cecidit ibidem rex Scotorum Constantinus magne quidem animositatis et vivacis senecte vir, reges quinque et c." Huius Willelmi posicionis contrarium veraces et varie produnt cronice, quia post huius belli funestum excidium regni sceptrum quatuor regebat et ultra annis ac deinde, regno sponte dimisso, religionis in habitu Deo serviens apud Sanctum Andream killideorum abbas effectus annis quinque vixit ibique moriens sepultus est. Hiennenses deinde monachi sua statim et de licencia effodientes ossa tulerunt et in basilica beati Orani patrum tumilo condiderunt anno domini nongentesimo xlvii$^{o}$. Non tenet ergo quod in bello Brounnyngfelde occisus fuerat, cum post bellum annis fere decem supervixerit. De quo habentur huiusmodi metra:

He was soon laying siege to York and trying to persuade the townspeople to surrender, at times by entreaties and at other times by threats. Succeeding in neither method, he departed.

The peoples of Northumbria and Cumbria who had for a long time now been faithfully united to the Scots and Danes, as if forming one people with them, preferred to be subject to them rather than to the English. When Sihtric, as described above, disappeared from the scene, the Northumbrians gladly adopted his sons Anlaf and Guthfrith as their princes. They immediately joined Constantine and attacked Athelstan with their whole strength. So in the thirty-sixth year of his reign King Constantine, Anlaf and Guthfrith gathered together an extremely large army and invaded the southern regions of the English, laying waste all the land through which they passed, until they reached the place which is called Brunanburh, where Athelstan had pitched his tents.

William [of Malmesbury] says: "Athelstan's final battle was with Anlaf son of Sihtric and Constantine king of the Scots, who had crossed the frontier in the hope of seizing his kingdom; since Athelstan was deliberately giving ground in order to win a more glorious victory, they had now insolently passed deep into English territory." Without delay the squadrons and battle lines of each side clashed and a savage battle was joined, fiercer by far than all other battles that were either recorded in the writings of the ancients or have been entrusted to the recollection of the present generation. There were slain on the side of the victorious Athelstan most notably the ealdormen Ælfwine and Æthelwyn, two other ealdormen, and also two bishops along with many nobles. On the other side Eligenius subking of the Deirans was killed along with three others, also nine ealdormen and countless numbers of the common folk on both sides.

. . .

The death of Constantine and the losses inflicted on the Scots by this battle.

Unlucky was that day for the Scots for all the dominions acquired in the time of Giric or earlier, which had been held for fifty-four years or more, were lost on that day by the right of conquest. William [of Malmesbury] writes: "There fell on that same field Constantine king of the Scots, a man of great spirit and vigorous old age, five kings etc." But the lie is given to this statement of William's by various reliable chronicles, because after the tragic destruction of this battle Constantine held sway over the kingdom for four and more years. Then giving up the kingship of his own accord, he put on the monk's habit and devoted himself to God. He lived for five years after becoming abbot of the culdees at St. Andrews. He died and was buried there. Then the monks of Iona immediately with permission dug up his bones, took them and buried them in the tomb of his fathers in the church of blessed Oran in 947. Therefore it is not tenable that he was killed in the battle of Brunanburh, since he survived for about ten years after the battle. The following lines of verse are about him:

Constantinus idem cuius pater Edh fuit Albus,
tris deca rex annis vixerat atque decem.
Andree Sancti fuit quinquennis in urbe
religionis ibi jure fruens obiit.

De predicto quidem Athelstano rege in *legenda miraculorum Sancti Johannis Berlaci* quod sequitur inter cetera scriptum repperi:

> Rex Athelstanus proficiscendo bellandum contra Scotos beatum Johannem Beverlaci visitavit, super cuius altare cultellum pro vadio posuit, promittens quod si victor redierit cultellum digno precio redimeret. Quod et implevit. Nam in dimicando contra Scotos rogavit Deum ut prece Sancti Johannis aliquod signum evidens ostenderet quo presentes et futuri cognoscere possent Scotos de jure Anglis subjugari. Unde rex cum gladio suo percussit scopulum quendam lapideum juxta castrum de Dunbar cuius ictu scopulus ad mensuram ulne cavatur, quod usque diem patet hodiernum.

Hec ibi. Verum ex relacione nugarum veterum consimilem trufam audivimus Arthuri regis militi Kaio dapifero cum quodam enormi cato dudum pugnaturo contigisse. Videns namque catus militem pugnaciter secum bellare paratum, magne rupis scandebat ad summum atque deorsum descendens ad pugnam mirabiliter ungues acuendo variis et incredibilibus fissuris rupem cavat et anfractibus. Catum tamen, ut aiunt, Kaius interfecit. . . . Athelstani vero rupis fissure non habetur in populo memoria vel noticia, ergo c'.

Ipso quoque anno belli obiit Henricus et filius eius Otho primus in regem coronatur. Et imperavit in Almannia annis xxxvi. Huius autem anno iii$^{o}$ domini videlicet ix$^{c}$ xl$^{o}$ mortuus est Athelstanus. Et frater eius Edmundus successit tenuitque regnum annis pene vii.

## 50. *Annals of Ulster*

**Latin**
**late 15th c.**

Bellum ingens lacrimabile atque horribile inter Saxones atque Norddmannos crudeliter gestum est, in quo plurima milia Nordmannorum que non numerata sunt, ceciderunt, sed rex cum paucis euassit, id est Amlaiph. Ex altera autem parte multitudo Saxonum cecidit. Adalstan autem, rex Saxonum, magna uictoria ditatus est.

Constantine, whose father was Aed Albus,
was king for thirty and ten years.
For five years he was in the city of St. Andrews.
There he died, living under religious rule.

Concerning the aforesaid King Athelstan I have found the following account written among other matters in the *Legend of the Miracles of St. John of Beverley*:

> King Athelstan, as he was setting out to fight against the Scots, visited the shrine of blessed John of Beverley and placed a dagger on his altar as a pledge, promising that if he returned victoriously he would redeem the dagger for a suitable price. This he accomplished. For in fighting against the Scots he asked God through the prayer of St. John that he would show some clear sign by which present and future generations could realize that the Scots were justly subject to the English. So the king struck a certain craggy rock near Dunbar castle with his sword by whose stroke the cliff was hollowed out to the depth of an ell, and this can be seen right to the present day.

But we have heard in the silly tales of old men that a similar trick happened long ago when King Arthur's knight, the seneschal Kay, was about to fight against a huge cat. The cat, seeing that the knight was ready to battle fiercely with it, climbed to the top of a huge crag and, as it climbed down sharpening its claws for the fight, it hollowed out the crag with various incredible cracks and tortuous windings. The cat, however, so they say, was killed by Kay. . . . There is no memory or knowledge of Athelstan's splitting of the rock popularly preserved. Therefore etc.

In the same year also as the battle Henry died and his son Otto I was crowned king and he reigned in Germany for thirty-six years. In 940 in the third year of his reign Athelstan died and his brother Edmund succeeded him and held the kingdom for almost seven years.

## 50. *Annals of Ulster* See p. 236

A huge war, lamentable and horrible, was cruelly waged between the Saxons and Norsemen. Many thousands of Norsemen beyond number died although King Anlaf escaped with a few men. While a great number of the Saxons also fell on the other side, Athelstan, king of the Saxons, was enriched by the great victory.

### 51. HECTOR BOECE, *HISTORIAE* — Latin 1527

Donaldo successit in Scotorum regnum Constantinus tertius filius Ethi Alipedis, anno virginei partus tertio supra noningentesimum: Vir ad urbanas res ac religiosas accommodato potius quam ad militiam ingenio. Hunc Edvvardus post patris Alarudi obitum Anglorum dictus rex bello petiturus, per fetialem monet Northumbriam Cumbriam, & Vestmariam, quas regiones Gregorius olim turbulento tempore vi occupaverat Anglis restitueret: alioqui sciret in quadragesimum diem bellum Scotis indictum. Constantinus ad fetialem, Impium, inquit, bellum quod rex Edvvardus ab optimi patris Alarudi instituto longissime diversus nulla lacessitus iniuria regiones nostras nobis adimendi cupidine, indicit: domum renuncia ingentibus animis nos suscipere, eisdemque caeli numinis favore ad exitum perducturos: superos praecantes cladem ex eo venturam, in eum vertant penes quem movendi belli tum esset culpa. Sequutae Scotorum in Anglos, & Anglorum in Scotos incursus direptionesque utramque gentem habuere sollicitam. Ita annus absque totarum virium concursu, ne alterum regnorum fieret Danorum iniuriae obnoxium levibus frequentibusque praeliis est consumptus. Anglorum maiores id bellum laboriosum magis quam utile intelligentes suasere Edvvardo ut facta cum Scotis pace omnem belli vim in Danos quorum iam opes plus quam Anglis tutum videbatur excreverant in Albione, converteret. Cuncta se armis, viris, telis, opisbusque eo bello facturos polliciti. Nihil consilium aversatus Edvvardus legatis ad Constantinum missis facile obtinuit apud eum utpote hominem quietis magis cupidum quam belli ut reparatis undique iniuriis veteri foedere utrinque staretur.

Insperatus casus brevi post tempore belli in Danos movendi ansam Edvvardo obtulit quam ipse quaesiverat diutius. Anglorum enim egentissimos quosdam & multo scelere insignes latrocinii insimulatos victosque in Danorum agris Cithricus dux Danicae gentis, furcis admovit. Id Angli summae loco iniuriae habentes, nonnullos Danos negociationis causa Londini diversatos, foede caesos interfecerunt. Sequutae haec direptiones ac depraedationes bonorum hominumque caedes quas Dani in Anglorum agris, & Angli in Danorum agrestes, invicem agebant, bellum ocyus ciebant inter populos. Et quum hostiles copiae stricto ferro paratae ad pugnam sub signis starent, pontificum sacerdotumque interventu bellum omne est diremptum, odiumque depositum: salutatioque ducum primum, inde militum dextris interiunctis mutua sequuta est amicitia. Pax ita parta, sequuta affinitate Beatrice Eduardi filia Cithrico Danorum duci matrimonio devincta, diutissime longaque in secula firmanda apparebat. Inter pacis conditiones ea caeteris insignior erat ut si quis ex eo connubio virilis sexus nasceretur in regnum succederet Anglorum.

**51. HECTOR BOECE, *HISTORIES*** **See p. 237**

In the year of the Virgin birth nine hundred and three, Constantine III, son of Aed Wing-Foot, succeeded Donald to the realm of Scotland: a man whose nature was suited better to cultural and religious matters than to warfare. Edward, the said king of the English, after the death of his father Alfred wished to make war on him, and demanded that he return to the English the regions of Northumberland, Cumbria and Westmoreland, which Giric had in the past, in troublesome times, forcefully taken into his own possession; otherwise he would find that on the fortieth day, war would be declared on the Scots. "That is an unjust war," said Constantine to the messenger, "that Edward is declaring on us out of greed to take our lands away from us, provoked by no injustice, and very much in contrast to what was established by his excellent father Alfred. Report at home that we are supported by great courage and that through it, by the goodwill of the God of heaven, we will be guided through to the end, and we will pray to those above that they will help to turn the resulting battle against him who was guilty of starting this war." The ensuing invasions and plunderings of Scots against English and English against Scots had each nation troubled. And so, without any encounter of their entire forces, so that neither realm would be rendered vulnerable to attacks of the Danes, the year was spent in light and frequent combat. Seeing that this war was troublesome rather than useful, the leaders of the English persuaded Edward to make peace with the Scots and then to turn all military power against the Danes, whose forces in Albion had already increased more than seemed safe to the English. In that war, they promised, they would provide everything: weapons, men, missiles and power. Not rejecting their advice, Edward sent messengers to Constantine and agreed with that man, who was longing for peace rather than war, to make compensation for all mutual damage, and then to adhere to the old alliance again.

Shortly afterwards, an unforeseen event offered Edward the long-awaited opportunity to make war on the Danes. For Sihtric, leader of the Danes, put to the yoke some very poor English people who were well known for many crimes, after they had been charged with robbery and defeated in the fields of the Danes. The English took this as the greatest insult, and shamefully set upon and murdered a fair number of Danes who in order to attend negotiations had taken up lodgings in London. The ensuing pillaging and plundering and the slaughter of good people which the Danes inflicted on the fields of the English, and the English upon the lands of the Danes, quickly gave rise to war between the peoples. And when the hostile troops were standing under their standards, ready with their swords drawn, the whole war was called off through the intervention of bishops and priests and all hatred laid aside, and the greeting by handshake first of the leaders, then of the soldiers was followed by mutual friendship. The peace that had been brought about in this way, with an alliance achieved when Edward's daughter Beatrice was joined in marriage with Sihtric, leader of the Danes, seemed set to last for a long time. Among the conditions of the peace, this one was more noteworthy than the others, namely that if somebody of male sex was born out of that marriage, he would succeed to the realm of the English.

Erat Eduardo germanus Eduinus haud mediocri inter Anglos virtutis opinione. Is Cithrici suasu solutili navi consulto missus ab Eduardo in Flandriam ne ad regnum aspiraret passus naufragium mari absorptus interiit. Sub idem tempus Athelstanus Eduardi Nothus sponte exulat ne Danorum insidiis circumventus cogeretur qualem Eduinus patruus & ipse exitum sortiri. Laetari secum inter haec Dani erecti in spem certam post Eduardi interitum quod praeter Beatricem nulli ei superessent liberi qui Anglorum regno succederent. Dumque Angli & Dani paci intenti & ocio animos a bello adeo haberent alienatos ut neutra gentium alterius exinde futuram speraret iniuriam, Eduardus filiae quam Cithrico matrimonio vinxerat secretiori nuncio admonitus est generi caveret insidias, fore ut Danorum perfidiam si illis ut antea familiarius uteretur brevi in caput esset experturus. Ad nuntium Anglus vehementer dolens fratrem Eduinum extinctum, quoque sanguinem cum Danis miscuisset, actus paene in amentiam personae atque dignitatis oblitus vix cohiberi ab astantibus amicis potuit quin vim sibi inferret. Ad se tandem rediens dolore in iram verso paratum a genero in se dolum in eum convertens filiae opera hominem veneno sustulit.

Duo Cithrico erant filii, Avalassus & Godofredus arte militari insignes. Hos Danorum maiores natu ut in patris locum succederent aequa potestate rei summam administraturi illico sufficiunt in principes. Avalassus itaque & Godofredus summum omnium suffragiis adepti inter Danos magistratum in Albione, armati in paternae necis ultionem, rem omnem ex aulicis & ancillis de noverca per quaestiones extorquent. Mox comperto Beatricem Cithrici consilium prodidisse genitori, patrisque suasu veneno extinxisse maritum, ovis calentibus assis super prunas alis sub humeris admotis (eas homines partes axellas appellant) brachiis thoraci alligatis fune, incudi algenti nudam insidere quoad animam exhalaret coegerunt. Talique supplicii genere ad id usque tempus inexcogitato summa cum ignominia subegerunt finire vitam. Bella secundum haec Dani adversus Anglos varia saepius fortuna spe omni ineundae cum illis pacis sublata, gesserant. Atroci tandem certamine ad Ovvsam fluvium gesto profligatis Danorum copiis Anglos victoria sed haud laeta, Edvvardo rege desiderato, est sequuta. Vulgata Anglorum regis caede Dani tametsi victi hostis vincendi a caeso capite magnum capientes omen, copiis denuo collectis ingenti alacritate animos resumpsere: consilioque habito quo potissimum modo rebus consulerent, Avalassus Godofredo germano ad gentis moderamen relicto in Anglia, ad Constantinum Scotorum regem celerrime est profectus. Apud quem partim largitionibus partim ingenti pecuniae & aliarum rerum pollicitatione corruptum obtinuit ut violato foedere cum Danis adversus Anglos in aciem descenderet. Naviter ergo & Scoti & Dani comparare quae in bello

Edward had a brother Edwin, whose virtue was held in more than average esteem among the English. On the instigation of Sihtric, so that he would not lay claim to the kingship, he was sent by Edward to Flanders in a ship that was known to be falling apart, and suffered shipwreck and perished, swallowed by the sea. At the same time Athelstan, Edward's illegitimate son, voluntarily went into exile so that, surrounded by the treachery of the Danes, his uncle Edwin and he would not have to share the same fate. Meanwhile the Danes were rejoicing amongst themselves, encouraged by the certain hope that after the death of Edward there would be no children of his left, apart from Beatrice, that might succeed to the kingdom of the English. And while the English and the Danes, intent on peace and quiet, were in their minds so far removed from war that neither nation was expecting any future attack from the other, Edward was warned by a secret messenger of his daughter, whom he had joined with Sihtric in marriage, that he should beware of the plots of his son-in-law, and that if he associated with the Danes very closely as before, he would soon experience their treacherousness very close to home. The Englishman grieved severely at the news of the death of his brother Edwin, also that he had mingled his blood with the Danes, and while he worked himself up almost into a frenzy, oblivious of his person and dignity, his friends who were standing by were barely able to prevent him from harming himself. When he finally came to his senses and his sorrow had turned into anger, he turned the deceit that had been committed against him by his son-in-law towards Sihtric himself, and through the help of his daughter killed the man with poison.

Sihtric had two sons, Anlaf and Guthfrith, who were outstanding in the military arts. The elders of the Danes instantly made these their leaders so that by right of birth they succeeded to their father's position with equal power to govern the state. Thus Anlaf and Guthfrith, having by vote obtained the highest office of all among the Danes, and armed for the revenge of their father's death, through questioning extorted from courtiers and maids in Albion the whole story about their mother-in-law. When soon they found out that Beatrice had betrayed the trust of their father and on the advice of her own father had killed her husband, they forced her to sit naked in a cold anvil, with red-hot eggs that had been roasted over burning coals attached to the underarms under her shoulders (the parts of the human body that they call the armpits) and her arms tied to her chest with a rope, until she exhaled her soul. And through this sort of torture, never hitherto imagined, they forced her to end her life with the greatest shame. After that, when all hope of making peace with them had gone, the Danes fought wars of varying outcome against the English. At last a dreadful battle was fought by the river Ouse, and when the troops of the Danes were destroyed, victory fell to the English, but not a joyful one, for King Edward was lost. When the death of the king of the English was known, the Danes, although defeated, took the death of the leader as a great omen of victory over the enemy and with their troops reassembled, recovered their spirits with enormous alacrity. And after they had deliberated as to how they might possibly deal with this situation, Anlaf left his brother Guthfrith behind in England to govern the people, and very quickly set off to Constantine, king of the Scots. He enticed him partly through gifts and partly through the promise of immense amounts of money and other things and thus ensured that Constantine would lower himself, in violation of the pact, to go into battle with the Danes against the English. And thus both Scots

gerendo usui forent, frumentum ingens, iumentorum carrorumque quibus arma ac commeatus veherentur, quam maximum numerum. Haud pro difficili negocio habentes Anglos ad exitium ducere in Albione. Sed ut sunt hominum res qui tum potissimum alienae patent iniuriae, quum maxime suis confidunt viribus: tantum rerum ad bellum gerendum apparatum tantosque tumentium conatus, vanum fragilesque infoelix exitus ostendit. Scotorum exercitui viginti ex hominum millibus conflato Constantinus Malcolmum Donaldi regis filium, qui post eum regnavit, Donatum Cumbria praefecit: sanciens qui secundum regem vita defunctum Scoticarum rerum esset potiturus, illi regioni in posterum dominaretur. Huic iuncti Avalassus Godofredusque cum Danorum haud exigua manu, totum infestum agmen in Anglorum agros ducunt ubi vastantes omnia, nullum belli iraeve exemplum non edunt. Infestum enim immiserunt in Anglos militem innocentum caede, civilium sacrarumque aedium ruinis & incendiis debacchantem, si qua indignitate Anglos quos viribus sibi impares sciebant, ad secum conferenda signa possent elicere. Sed quo impudentius in omne scelus ruebant, eo celerius sequuta est ultio. Athelstanus enim Anglorum rex (erat is Edvvardi regis Nothus quem secundum patris mortem virtutis praestantia regem effecerat) videns Anglorum agros igne ferroque plenos, virgines dicatas deo oppressas, mulierum expugnatam pudicitiam & cuncta resonare ploratu puerorum viduarumque eiulatu per quatriduum continuum nullis religionis partibus omissis, foelici pro rei successu deum praecatus subitario exercitu numinis praesidio fisus hostibus occurrit. Ad Broningfeldum atroci pugna certatum est. Primo congressu Angli victis similes aliquantulum pugnae loco consulto cessere. Unde Dani & Scoti ut iam tum victores, victis superbe insultantes solutis ordinibus ad praedam convertuntur. Angli re animadversa uti imperia a duce acceperant in pugnae locum composito agmine reversi ingenti caede edita in hostes victoriam facile sunt assequuti. Probavit funesta dies Scotis Danisque plus virium quam prudentiae fuisse, qui quum ea fuissent multitudine ut hostes poene sine pugna in vincula coniicere potuissent, praedae magis quam salutis memores victoriam quae in manibus erat summa cum ignominia & reipublicae iactura amiserint. Caesi sunt eo praelio ex Scotis Danisque quot vix aliquo priori: & inter eos Scotorum nobilitas (ea enim suo more ne turpis fugae in posterum insimularetur, in praelio usque ad extremum duravit) poene tota consumpta. Athelstanus visus victoria in Northumbriam cum victricibus Anglorum copiis extemplo abiit: qua regione quia praesidio vacua facile occupata, arces omnes & oppida in fidem recepit. Nihil inde ibi moratus movit in Vestmariam Cambriamque. Incolae autem illuc venienti regi inermes nudatis pedibus capitibusque, quod apud eos sanctioris deditionis argumentum erat, sese dedidere. Victi eo praelio exercitus, Malcolmus vulneribus sautius vehi-

and Danes diligently assembled the things that were useful in warfare, huge amounts of grain, and the largest possible number of drawing beasts and carts with which weapons and supplies were to be transported. They did not think it would be a difficult business to bring the English to ruin in Albion. But as can happen in the affairs of men, they will suffer from hostile injuries just when they have the greatest trust in their own powers: the unhappy outcome showed such magnificent preparations for warfare, such efforts of the proud, to be futile and frail. When the army of the Scots had increased to twenty thousand men, Constantine appointed Malcolm, the son of King Donald, who reigned after him, as ruler of Cumbria as heir-designate, ordaining that whoever was to govern Scottish affairs after the king had ended his life, should in future be the lord of that region. Joined with him, Anlaf and Guthfrith, with a sizeable force of Danes, led the entire hostile army into the lands of the English, where they laid waste to everything and there was no act of hostility or rage that they did not carry out. For they let loose on the English a hostile army that revelled in the killing of innocent people and the destruction and burning of private and sacred buildings, as if by this indignity they could draw out the English, whom they knew to be inferior in forces to themselves, to engage in battle with them. But the more shamelessly they rushed into all these crimes, the more quickly followed the revenge. For when Athelstan, the king of the English (he was the illegitimate son of King Edward, whose distinction in virtue had made him king after his father's death), saw that the fields of English people were full of fire and sword, virgins consecrated to God were overwhelmed, the virtue of women conquered, everything was resounding with the crying of children and wailing of widows for four successive days, and no places of religion were spared, he prayed to God for a successful outcome, put his trust in the protection of God, and, with a hastily assembled army, went to meet the enemies. At Broningfeld [Brunanburh] they fought in a terrible battle. At the first encounter the English, as if defeated, deliberately ceded a little ground on the battlefield. Thereupon the Danes and the Scots, as if they had already won, proudly taunted the defeated, and with their ranks dissolved, turned to looting. When they noticed this, the English, just as they had been instructed by their leader, returned to battle in an orderly battle-line, and after they had inflicted an enormous slaughter on the enemy, easily obtained victory. This calamitous day proved to the Scots and Danes that they had been stronger in forces than in wit; for although they had been in such numbers that they could have taken their enemies captive almost without a battle, they had thought of loot rather than their own safety, and with the utmost shame and disaster for the state lost a victory that was already so close. There were more men of the Scots and Danes killed in this battle than hardly anywhere before: and among these the nobility of the Scots was almost entirely destroyed, for according to custom, so that they would not afterwards be blamed of shameful flight, they had held out in battle to the very last. When Athelstan realized his victory he at once moved away to Northumberland with his victorious troops of Englishmen, and after he had easily taken possession of this region, since it was without a ruler, he received all fortresses and towns into his peace. From there, he moved without delay to Westmoreland and Cumbria. But the inhabitants gave themselves up to the arriving king unarmed and with naked feet and uncovered heads, which among them was a sign of a more holy surrender. Sick with

culo lecticario inter duos equos ne corpus quateretur devectus, Constantino erat nuncius. Rex cognito quam infoeliciter Dani ac Scoti ad Broningfeldum depugnassent, & quibus viribus Athelstanus invasisset Northumbriam, Cumbriam & Vestmariam, consessum primorum gentis Abbernethi habendum publicae saluti consulendi causa indixit. Ubi quae eo convenerat nobilitate conspecta inepta per aetatem ad regnum vel tutandum bello, vel pace regendum, nam iuventutem idoneam ad arma recens clades absumpserat, ut procul a domestico vitae splendore deinceps esset summo deposito magistratu in piorum coetum qui in divi Andreae Apostoli tum aedibus erant (cultores dei ea aetate) migrans, tonsus coenobio se sacrauit.

### 52. *ANNALS OF CLONMACNOISE* — **Early Modern English 1627**

**931**. The Danes of Loghrie, arrived at Dublin. Awley with all the Danes of Dublin and north part of Ireland departed and went over seas. The Danes that departed from Dublin arrived in England, & by the help of the Danes of that kingdom, they gave battle to the Saxons on the plaines of othlyn, where there was a great slaughter of Normans and Danes, among which these ensueing captaines were slaine, viz$^{t}$. Sithfrey and Oísle y$^{e}$ 2 sones of Sithrick Galey, Awley ffroit, and Moylemorrey the sonn of Cosse Warce, Moyle Isa, Gebeachan king of the Islands, Ceallagh prince of Scottland with 30000 together with 800 captives about Awley m$^{c}$Godfrey, and abbot of Arick m$^{c}$Brith, Iloa, Deck, Imar, the king of Denmarks owen son with 4000 souldiers in his guard were all slaine.

### 53. *ANNALA NA GCEITHRE MHÁISTRÍ* — **Irish 1632–1636**

**938**. Cathraoinedh ria righ Saxan for Constantin mac Aedha, for Anlaf no Amhlaoibh mac Sitric, & for Breathnaibh.

injuries and carried on a litter between two horses so that his body would not be shaken, Malcolm acted as messenger to Constantine, bearing the news of the army defeated in this battle. Once it was known how unluckily the Danes and Scots had fought at Broningfeld, and with what forces Athelstan had invaded Northumberland, Cumbria, and Westmoreland, the king ordered an assembly of the most eminent men of the people to take place at Abernethy, in order to discuss the public welfare. The nobility gathered there was deemed to be incapable of reigning, either as protectors in war or as rulers in peace because of their age, for the recent battle had wiped out all the youth capable of bearing arms. And therefore Constantine resigned the highest of offices, so that he would be far away from the splendor of life in his household, and moved into a community of religious people who were then in the buildings of the divine apostle Andrew (the culdees in these days); and taking the tonsure, he consecrated himself to the monastery.

### 52. *Annals of Clonmacnoise* See pp. 237–40

**937**. The Danes of Lough Ree arrived at Dublin. Anlaf, with all the Danes of Dublin and the north part of Ireland, departed and went overseas. The Danes who departed from Dublin arrived in England, and by the help of the Danes of that kingdom, they gave battle to the Saxons on the plains leading to the Lyme, where there was a great slaughter of Northmen and Danes, among which these ensuing captains were slain, namely: Sihtfrith and Audgisl (the two sons of Sihtric Gale), Anlaf the Fool, and Máel-Muire the son of Cossa-Nara, Máel-Ísu, Gibhleachán the king of the Hebrides, Cellach the prince of Scotland, with 30,000, together with 800 captives about Anlaf Guthfrithson, and abbot of Hárekr Bárdarsson, Illugi the Stout, Ívarr the king of Denmark's own son, with 4,000 soldiers in his guard were all slain.

### 53. *Annals of the Four Masters* See pp. 240–41

**937**. A victory was gained by the king of the Saxons over Constantine, son of Aedh, Anlaf (or Amhlaeibh) son of Sihtric, and the Britons.

# NOTES TO THE TEXTS

## 1. *ARMES PRYDEIN VAWR*

Ed. and trans. John K. Bollard.

*Manuscript*: National Library of Wales, Peniarth MS 2 (*The Book of Taliesin*), fols. 6r–8v.

For more information on this item, see pp. 245–62.

Title MS: *Arymes Prydein Vawr* [*The Great Prophecy of Britain*]. The title is rubricated by the scribal hand. The *-y-* of *arymes* [prophecy] in the manuscript title and in line 194 of the poem is epenthetic or intrusive; the more familiar spelling *Armes* has been adopted for the title throughout this book. *Vawr* [< *mawr*, meaning "great, large"] modifies *Arymes*, not *Prydein* [Britain]. Other pairs of poems in the *Book of Taliesin* are similarly distinguished by length, as *Gwawt Lud y Mawr* [*The Great* (or *Large*) *Praise Poem of Lludd*], *Ymarwar Llud Bychan* [*The Lesser* (or *Small*) *Discussion of Lludd*], and *Kanu y Byt Mawr* [*The Great* (or *Large*) *Song of the World*], *Kanu y Byt Bychan* [*The Lesser* (or *Small*) *Song of the World*]. An untitled prophetic poem of twenty-six lines begins with the same four lines as *Armes Prydein*, and Williams has plausibly suggested that this is in all likelihood the matching *Lesser Prophecy of Britain* (*Armes Prydein*, trans. Bromwich, pp. xl–xliii).

1 *Dygogan*. The first *-g-* is a remnant of Old Welsh orthography and is not pronounced here or in *dygobryssyn*.

*awen*. *Awen* is an ancient technical poetic term, cognate with the synonymous Irish *aí*. *Geiriadur Prifysgol Cymru* glosses *awen* as "poetic gift, genius or inspiration, the muse," though Bromwich adds that "its nuances are virtually untranslatable in English" (*Armes Prydein*, pp. 16–17). It implies the arcane, even occult, knowledge and prophetic powers imputed to poets in early Celtic societies.

The "they" of lines 1, 14–17, 20, 22, et passim, may be Cynan and Cadwaladr, who are named in lines 89 and 91. Alternatively, Isaac translates the nouns of lines 2 and 3 as subjects of the third plural verb in line 1 ("'Armes Prydain Fawr' and St. David," p. 171).

2 *meued*. In the poem identified as the likely *Lesser Prophecy of Britain* (see the title note above), this word, translated here as "wealth," occurs in the corresponding line with the spelling *meuued* (*Book of Taliesin*, ed. Evans, 70.17, also at 32.18), representing the Modern Welsh form *meufedd*. Both this form and *meuedd*,

without the /v/ sound, are well attested. It is a compound of *mau* [(what is) mine, property] + *medd* [authority, power; possession(s)].

5 *Kasnar degyn*. The meaning of *kasnar* is uncertain. It occurs as a name, for instance, in the first branch of *The Mabinogi*, where Casnar Wledig is named as a forebear of Cigfa, Pryderi's wife (*Mabinogi*, trans. Bollard, p. 40). Other examples of *casnar* in medieval Welsh poetry suggest that Casnar may be being invoked as a standard of comparison, much as we might call someone a Samson. Alternatively, the name Casnar may have developed into a generic noun for a "warrior, a fierce enemy or opponent," or even an adjective meaning "fierce, mighty."

7 *gwaethylgwyr hyt Gaer Weir* [warriors (from) as far as Caer Weir]. I.e., the Welsh and their allies. Or possibly, following Bromwich, "warriors will scatter foreigners as far as Caer Weir" (*Armes Prydein*, p. 3). Caer Weir was identified by Williams as Durham, on the river Wear; Koch suggests Chester-le-Street or Binchester, both Roman forts on the Wear (cited in *Legendary Poems*, ed. Haycock, p. 495). Haycock also presents several possible southwestern locations, including perhaps a connection with the Isle of Wight (*Ynys Weir*), and notes that "southeastern locations merit further investigation" (p. 495). The poet's main point, of course, is the great distance over which this struggle will be felt. Caer Weir is similarly used as a distant referent in *Mydwyf Taliesin*, a poem to Cunedda in the *Book of Taliesin*: "Because of Cuneddaf's wasting away shock is felt / in Caer Weir and Carlisle" (*Legendary Poems*, ed. Haycock, p. 491, lines 5–6). Haycock plausibly situates this poem in the twelfth or thirteenth century, though Koch proposes a fifth-century date. For the present reading and references to other sources, see the discussion in *Legendary Poems*, ed. Haycock, pp. 488–502, especially the note on Caer Weir, pp. 495–96.

*allmyn* [foreigners], sg. *allmon*, is a compound of *all-* [other] + OE *mon*, *men* [man, men]. For a similar all-Welsh compound which clarifies the dry humor of *allmyn*, compare *alluro*, line 111. Two other derogatory terms with English origins are used to describe the Saxons: *kechmyn* (see the note on line 27, below), and *ffoxas* [foxes] (line 66).

9 *Kymry* (*Cymry*, sg. *Cymro*). The eleven instances of *Cymry* in this poem are among the earliest occurrences of this word, which designates the people now known in English as "Welsh." *Cymry* also refers, though not in this poem, to the regions where they lived, including — for the early period — both Wales and Cumbria in the north. The earlier term *Brython* continued to be used as well; see lines 12, 42, 90. It was not until the sixteenth century that the spelling was differentiated to distinguish *Cymru* [Wales] from the *Cymry* [the people of Wales].

*gwyr Dulyn*. Literally, "the men of Dublin," i.e., the Norse who established the town there, as distinct from the *Gwydyl Iwerdon* [the Irish (or Goidels) of Ireland] in the next line. The need for reconciliation is made clear in a passage in the Welsh chronicles for the period 910–20: "Ac y diffeithwyt Iwerdon a Mon y gan y bobyl Dulyn" [And Ireland and Anglesey were ravaged by the folk of Dublin] (*Brut y Twysogion*, ed. and trans. Jones, pp. 10–11).

10 *Mon*. Anglesey (*Môn* in Modern Welsh), or less likely the Isle of Man (*Manaw*). It is uncertain who is meant by the "Gwydyl . . . Mon" [the Irish (or Goidels) of Mon]. Colmán Etchingham has presented evidence suggesting Viking trade and settlement in Anglesey with possible connections to the Dublin Scandinavians in the ninth and tenth centuries ("Viking-age Gwynedd," pp. 152–54). However, it is doubtful whether these would have been described as *Gwydyl*. A similar doubt can be raised in regard to Williams' suggestion that the Isle of Man (usually *Manaw*) may be meant, if that island, too, was originally Brythonic (*Armes Prydein*, trans. Bromwich, p. 21; Etchingham, "Viking-age Gwynedd," p. 165).

*Prydyn* [Pictland, Scotland]. *Prydyn* (cognate with Irish *Cruthne* [Pictland]) and *Prydein* [Britain] (< *Britannia*) are frequently confused in Welsh texts throughout the medieval period; compare line 67, where *Prydyn* refers to Britain.

11 *Cornyw* [Cornwall or the Cornish]. Usually spelled *Cernyw*; this is the only known example with *-o-*.

*Chludwys*. (The *C-* mutates to *Ch-* following *a* [and].) The men of Strathclyde, the Brythonic kingdom in southwestern Scotland; compare line 151.

12 *Atporyon*. Plural of *atbor*, *atbawr*, which generally means "leavings, remnants, scraps" (*Geiriadur Prifysgol Cymru*). However, Foster suggested that a closer etymological reading gives a better understanding of the line's implications (see *Armes Prydein*, trans. Bromwich, p. 22). *Atbor* derives from *ad-* [re-] + *pawr* [pasture, grass, a grazing] (*Geiriadur Prifysgol Cymru*); thus it is comparable in sense to Welsh *adladd*, Irish *athbronnad*, and English *aftermath*, *aftergrass*, and *afterpasture* in their literal senses [the grass that grows up after mowing]. Thus, this line may be rendered more literally as "The Britons will be the remains (who will flourish again) when they prevail."

13 *dygoganhet* [was prophesied] (subjunctive imperfect passive). MS: *dygoganher*. The usual sense of *dy(s)gogan* is "to prophesy," thus a past tense seems to fit the context better. Or possibly, retaining *dygoganher* (subjunctive present passive), we might read, "Long will the time when they come be spoken of"; see *Armes Prydein*, trans. Bromwich, p. 23.

15 *gwyr Gogled* [the men of the North]. I.e., the early Brythonic kingdoms of Rheged, Strathclyde, and Manaw Gododdin, in what is now northern England and southern Scotland.

16 *eu racwed*. The scribe is careful to distinguish *n* and *u*, and the manuscript reading is clear, but we might emend to *en racwed*, assuming that the scribe's exemplar used *e* for *y*, as in, for example, nine instances of *en* = *yn* in the *Black Book of Carmarthen* (see *Llyfr Du Caerfyrddin*, ed. Jarman, Index, s.v. *yn*). This would give the sense "in the center, in the van, they will advance"; i.e., the entire troop of leaders and men from the North will advance together. For similar referencing of the locations within an army, compare "ef lladei a pherued / ac eithaf a diwed" [he slashed the centre [of the army], / and the wing, and the rear] from the poem *Cad Godeu* [*The Battle of the Trees*], also in the *Book of Taliesin* (*Legendary Poems*, ed. Haycock, p. 179, lines 104–05).

17 *Dysgogan Myrdin*. A red capital *D* suggests that the scribe may have considered — or expected — this to be the beginning of a new *awdl* or stanza. The phrase "Dysgogan Myrddin" is also typical of opening lines (compare lines 1, 107, and 171). However, it is unusual for adjoining *awdlau* (pl.) to have the same rhyme; thus we might better consider lines 1–23 to constitute a single *awdl*. See notes to 24 and 25, below.

*Myrddin*. Whether Myrddin was an historical poet remains an open question, but there is no doubt that, like the sixth-century poet Taliesin, he became a figure of legend renowned for his prophetic powers. Full translations of the prophetic poetry attributed to Myrddin can be found in Bollard, "Myrddin"; for discussions of this material, see also Jarman, *Legend of Merlin* and "The Welsh Myrddin Poems." For the development of Myrddin into the Merlinus of Geoffrey of Monmouth, see Parry and Caldwell, "Geoffrey of Monmouth."

*kyferuydyn*. MS: *kyferu~~e~~yd hyn*. Scribal deletions, marked in the manuscript by underdotting, are indicated in these notes with a strike-through.

18 *Aber Perydon*. The location of the river Peryddon is uncertain; see pp. 258–59.

*mechtëyrn*. Meaning "great king," the word has three syllables; *-yrn* makes an "Irish rhyme" (see p. 262) with *gwynyn* (line 19) and with *Glywysy(n)g* (line 99) and *ebryn* (line 101). For a discussion of its meaning and possible connotations, see pp. 251–53.

24 Arguing from the irregularity of rhyme in lines 23–26, Williams suggests that line 24 was originally a marginal gloss on line 22 that was subsequently incorporated into the poem, as happens elsewhere in the *Book of Taliesin* (*Armes Prydein*, trans. Bromwich, pp. li–lii).

25 *Mab Meir*. Though it is not so rubricated in the manuscript, "Mab Mair, mawr a eir!" clearly begins a new *awdl* or stanza, as it does in line 45, which does have a red capital *M*.

*na tharder*. MS: *na tardet*. Williams emends the preterite indicative impersonal (passive) *na thardet* to the present subjunctive impersonal *na tharder* to match the "Irish rhymes" in *-ed*/*-er* in lines 26–44. The *-et* may thus be understood as a scribal attempt to provide a rhyme for the preceding line. A subjunctive form also better fits the "contrary-to-fact" sense of the line.

26 *Saesson*. Saxons, English; sg. *Seis* (line 96). *Sais*, *Saeson* is now the general term for "an Englishman, the English," but because *Armes Prydein* was written on the cusp of the appearance of a unified English nation, the terms have been translated throughout as "Saxon(s)."

27 *kechmyn*. MS: *kychmyn*. The word *kechmyn* occurs three times in this poem and is not known elsewhere. It is a regular plural by vowel affection and vowel mutation of a fairly transparent compound, *cach* [dung, excrement] + OE *mon* [man], and it is clearly compounded using the English base in order to be as demeaning as possible — hence the present translation. In Old Welsh and early Middle Welsh, *e* represents both /e, e:/ and /ə/; in later Middle Welsh the latter

is spelled *y*; thus, the manuscript hypercorrection *kychmyn* is here emended to *kechmyn* (compare lines 40 and 184).

*Wrtheyrn*. *Gwrtheyrn* is the Welsh form of Vortigern. (In the system of initial mutations in Welsh, *g-* /g-/ is dropped in certain contexts.) Traditionally Gwrtheyrn/Vortigern was the Brythonic ruler who invited the first Saxons, Hengist and Horsa, to Britain, where they settled on the Isle of Thanet, as recounted in the *Historia Brittonum* (*Nennius: British History*, ed. Morris, pp. 26, 66–67). This tale of the coming of the Saxons is the subject matter of this *awdl*; see also line 137.

29 *Nys dioes dayar*. Compare line 156: "Nys dioes eluyd."

32 *Hegys*. The *-g-* of *Hegys* represents *-ng-*, and there is thus consonance between *Heng-* and *yng*.

34 *rin dilein*. This "secret destruction" may be a reference to the "Night of the Long Knives" as recounted in the *Historia Brittonum*, ch. 46: "But Hengist told his followers to hide their daggers under their feet in their shoes, saying 'When I call out to you and say "English, draw your knives," take your daggers from your shoes and fall upon them, and stand firm against them.' . . . and all three hundred Seniors of King Vortigern were murdered. . . . To save his life, he [Vortigern] ceded several districts, namely Essex and Sussex, together with Middlesex and other districts that they chose and designated" (*Nennius: British History*, ed. Morris, p. 32).

35 *meddaut*. MS: *meddaw*; the Modern Welsh form is *medd-dod* or *meddwdod*.

37 *Dechymyd*. MS: *decymyd*.

44 The diaeresis here and elsewhere is editorial and indicates that the two vowels are separate, not a diphthong.

47 *cwynyn*. MS: *cwynnyn*.

51 *Dduw*. This is a relatively rare early example of *dd* representing [ð], as is now standard in Modern Welsh.

*Dewi*. *Dewi* is an early Welsh form derived through Brythonic from Latin *Davidus*. Before the nineteenth century, *Dewi* was restricted to refer to *Dewi Sant*, St. David (now regarded as the patron saint of Wales), who established his seat in Dyfed in southwest Wales in the sixth century. For other Davids, the form *Dafydd*, a somewhat later borrowing from Latin, was used as a forename. On St. David, see Evans and Wooding, eds., *Saint David of Wales*, especially ch. 8, and Isaac, "'Armes Prydain Fawr' and St. David," pp. 161–81.

53 *Gwnaent*. Third person plural imperative ("Let them do/perform"), or possibly imperfect ("They used to do"). Williams suggests that the present indicative *gwnaant* [they are doing/performing] might better suit the context (*Armes Prydein*, trans. Bromwich, pp. 37–38); compare lines 80 and 82.

58 *peurllyn*. The word probably derives from *pefr/pebr* (MW *peuyr/pebyr*) [bright, sparkling] + *llyn* [lake, pool].

60 *mal bwyt balaon*. MS: *mal balaon*. *Balaon/balawon* is the plural of *belau*, specifically "marten" (a cat-sized, carnivorous mammal of northern Europe related to the weasel), but the term may be used in a more general sense of "wild beast" or even "wolf" in some early Welsh contexts, though *blaidd* is the more usual and specific term for a wolf. Williams suggests the addition of *bwyt* [food] on the basis of a line from an early poem in the *Black Book of Carmarthen*: "ac am gewin yr aeluid bvid balawon" [And around Cefn yr Aelwyd, food for wild beasts] (*Armes Prydein*, trans. Bromwich, p. 40; the text is printed in *Llyfr Du Caerfyrddin*, ed. Jarman, p. 25, line 12; trans. in Bollard, "Myrddin," p. 22, stanza 2, line 12).

62 *von*. From *bon*, literally "root (of a tree or plant)" or the "hindquarters of an animal, including man"; here it has connotations not unlike those of English "rear (end)," as the enemy is fleeing.

*granwynyon*. From *gran* [cheek] + *gwyn* [white] + plural ending *-ion*. Williams suggests that "it was in the first place a nickname, given by the Welsh, who were dark, to their fair-haired English opponents, just as the American Indians called their enemies 'Palefaces'" (*Armes Prydein*, trans. Bromwich, pp. 40–41). The form *garanwynnyon* [emended to *granwynyon*] occurs in the poem *Arwyre gwyr Katraeth gan dyd*, attributed to the historical Taliesin: "Vn ynt tanc gan aethant golludyon / llaw yg croes gryt ygro g(a)ranwynyon" [They desired peace, because they had come up against obstacles, / with hands crossed (as a sign of surrender?), on the shingle, the palecheeks] (*Poems of Taliesin*, ed. Williams, p. 2, lines 19–20; my translation).

63 *ygwerth* [as payment for]. The scribe wrote *yg werth* here and *ygwerth* in line 160; both represent the same phonetic phrase, *yng ngwerth* in Modern Welsh spelling.

*yn eu creu creinhyn*. MS: *yn eu creinhyn*. To make sense of the line, Williams suggests emending the MS *yn eu* either to *yn creu* [in blood] or to *yn eu creu* [in their (own) blood] (*Armes Prydein*, trans. Bromwich, p. 41). This also adds alliteration and internal rhyme to the line.

64 *ygwaetlin* [in a flood of blood]. In Modern Welsh *yng ngwaedlin*, from *yn* [in] + *gwaed* [blood] + *llin* [a flow, a discharge (of blood)]; compare the note to *ygwerth* in the line above.

66 *uwrch*. I.e., *bwrch*, from OE *burh* [fortified enclosure, fort, castle], as in — coincidentally — *Brunanburh*. (In the system of initial mutations, *b-* /b-/ becomes *f-*, *u-* /v-/ in certain contexts.)

*ffoxas*. This is the plural of OE *fox*, applied derogatorily to the English themselves.

67 *Prydyn*. Here "Britain"; see the note to line 10, above.

70 The *y* could represent either Modern Welsh *i* [to] (*i ddyffryn*) or *yn* [in] (*yn nyffryn*). The sense is "everywhere," thus implying ironically that by *Rei* [Some] the poet really means "most," if not "all."

72 *anaeleu tretheu*. MS: *anaeleu ~~eu~~ tretheu*.

73 *Nau vgein canhwr* [Nine score hundred men]. Nine, nine score, nine hundred, and nine score hundred, as here, are conventional numbers used throughout much early Welsh verse, and the larger numbers are frequently used in describing numbers in battle; see also Item 5.6 and 32.

74 *Namyn petwar, nyt atcorant*. Of the 18,000 mentioned in line 73, "Except for four [or perhaps 'four score'], they will not return." This may echo — or prefigure, depending on the relative dates of composition — the repeated refrain in the mythological Arthurian poem, *Preideu Annwfn* [*The Spoils of Annwn*], also in the *Book of Taliesin*: "namyn seith, ny dyrreith" [except for seven, none will return] (*Legendary Poems*, ed. Haycock, pp. 433–51; trans. Bollard, "Arthur," pp. 20–21).

75 *Dyhed*. From *dy-* [negative prefix] + *hed* [peace, calm], usually means "war, commotion, tumult, adversity, misery" (*Geiriadur Prifysgol Cymru*, s.v. *dyedd*), but the context here suggests the sense of "a tale or account of war, disaster, or strife"; see *Armes Prydein*, trans. Bromwich, p. 43.

80 *a wnaant*. Line 82 employs the same rhyme in a common collocation, *gwneuthur kat* [to do battle] ([*g*]*wna*[*a*]*nt* is third person pl., present/future indicative of *gwneuthur* [to do]). Jones argues that identical rhymes would be unlikely to fall so close together in the same *awdl*, and he suggests emending *a wnaant* [they do] to *a wana(a)nt*, from *gwanu* [to pierce, strike], i.e., no doctor will profit from whom they pierce, for they will be dead (see *Armes Prydein*, trans. Bromwich, p. 44). From a metrical perspective, this would change the line from a fairly regular syllable count of 6/4 to the less common 6/5; however, metrical practice in the poem is not so rigid as to weigh decisively against this emendation.

82 *Ry drychafwynt*. *Ry* is most frequently a perfective (as in line 98) or often a simple affirmative particle, but with a present subjunctive verb, as *drychafwynt*, it may also express a wish.

*a wnaant*. MS: *a wnant*. Emending to *a wnaant* seems warranted here to improve the meter (*Armes Prydein*, trans. Bromwich, p. 45), giving the line a syllable count of 6/4; a three-syllable second halfline would be very unusual. Note that the *w-* is non-syllabic.

85 *arosceill*. Possibly *ar osceill*; either reading is obscure. Williams suggests that it may be a plural adjective describing the "others" who were afflicted or an adverb describing the manner of affliction (*Armes Prydein*, trans. Bromwich, p. 45). Isaac translates "Others, who were wise enough to bide their time, have struck" ("'Armes Prydein Fawr' and St. David," p. 175).

87 *ymäes [ym bro] ym bryn*. MS: *ymaes ym bryn*. Emended by Williams to fill out the line and the meter (*Armes Prydein*, trans. Bromwich, p. 8). Modern Welsh orthography gives a better visual impression of the consonance of the line: *Yng nghoed, ym maes, ym mro, ym mryn*.

89, 91 *Kynan . . . Kadwaladr*. Cynan and Cadwaladr are named together as deliverers of the Britons in various early and medieval prophetic poems, including *Glaswawt Taliessin* in the *Book of Taliesin* (Item 5), and *Yr Afallenau* [*The Apple Tree Stanzas*] and *Yr Oianau* [*The Little Pig Stanzas*] attributed to Myrddin in the *Black*

*Book of Carmarthen*. The Myrddin poems have been edited in *Llyfr Du Caerfyrddin*, ed. Jarman, pp. 26–35, and translated in Bollard, "Myrddin," pp. 19–30. Cadwaladr was, in all likelihood, Cadwaladr Fendigaid ap Cadwallon [Cadwaladr the Blessed, son of Cadwallon], who is mentioned in the *Historia Brittonum* (ch. 64) and in *Annales Cambriae*, s.a. 682 (see *Trioedd*, ed. Bromwich, pp. 298–99, and *Glaswawt Taliessin*, Item 5.19–20 and note, below). In his *History of the Kings of Britain*, Geoffrey of Monmouth confuses him with Ceadwalla, the king of Wessex. There are several early figures named Cynan, each of whom or a conflation of whom may have become the "Cynan of the Prophecies," as Bartrum calls him. Among these are the fourth-century Cynan ab Eudaf Hen (Geoffrey's Conan Meriadoc) and the sixth-century prince of Powys, Cynan Garwyn ap Brochwel (see Bartrum, *Welsh Classical Dictionary*, pp. 80–81, 162–68). As *Armes Prydein* is the earliest datable poem naming these two redeemers, we cannot know how much older this tradition might be, though the poem clearly expects the listener to recognize them.

92 *eu* [them]. I.e., the Saxons, not the chieftains of line 91; or alternatively, "having picked them [i.e., his chieftains] with complete wisdom" (Isaac, "'Armes Prydein Fawr' and St. David," p. 175).

93 *clas*. *Clas* generally refers to a religious or monastic community, especially a collegiate clerical community common in Wales before the coming of the Normans; here it is used in an extended sense of "a community of people."

*eu herchwyn*. *Erchwyn*, literally "bedside, edge (of grave, precipice, wagon, &c.), side, border, *also fig*." (*Geiriadur Prifysgol Cymru*, s.v. *erchwyn*), also has a secondary sense of "defense, protection, defender, protector" (see *Armes Prydein*, trans. Bromwich, p. 46). Isaac translates "When their troops [i.e., the Welsh] fall into bed, / after hard work" ("'Armes Prydein Fawr' and St. David," p. 175, line 23).

96 *Seis* [Saxon]. *Seis* is singular, but here is used collectively with a plural verb, *techyn* [they flee]; see note to line 26.

97 *Gwyn eu byt wy Gymry*. Literally "Blessed their world, the Cymry"; *Gwyn eu byd* was a common idiom in Middle Welsh expressing great joy or happiness.

99 *Dyfet . . . Glywyssyg*. Dyfed was a kingdom in southwest Wales, roughly contiguous with the former county of Pembrokeshire. Glywysing was a kingdom to the east, between the rivers Tawe and Usk; see the discussion on pp. 256–58.

100 *Nys gwnaho*. The subjunctive *gwnaho* here and in line 102 (as emended) may be read either as future, "will not make/do/cause/bring," or as optative, i.e., expressing a wish: "may it not make/do/cause/bring."

*mechtëyrn*. See note to line 18.

102 *gwnaho*. MS: *g6na6*; *-6* retraced? The underlying original script is unclear; *6* is a form of *u/v* used in *The Book of Taliesin* and other Middle Welsh manuscripts to represent *w*.

*meddawt* [drunkenness]. A reference to warriors being feasted by their lord, which they repay by fighting his battles; this motif is familiar in both Welsh and

Old English verse. The point, of course, is that a warrior ought to be able to hold his mead.

*genhyn*. Literally "with us" (compare lines 2, 11), but here in the sense of "at our expense."

103 *o dynget*. The translation "inevitably" comes from *o* [from, by, by means of] + *tynged* [fate, destiny, fortune]. Alternatively we might read "without [them] paying, because of fate/destiny, for as much as they get."

104 *veibon*. I.e., *meibon*, *meibion*, pl. of *mab* [son, child (of either sex)].

106 *ar Lego*. Williams prints *Ailego* and notes, "Gwenogvryn Evans . . . reads *arlego*, but I can only distinguish *i*, although the stroke that would turn it into *r* has been added, across the *l*, but higher up" (*Armes Prydein*, trans. Bromwich, p. 49). Williams may in this case have been looking at the facsimile printed in *The Book of Taliesin*, ed. Evans, facing page 16, which seems to bear out his statement; however, digital imagery of fol. 7v clearly supports Evans' reading. The difficulty comes in the interpretation; there is no known river Arlego or anything like it. To preserve the syllable count for the line, Williams suggests reading *ffrwt o Lego* (*o* = "from"), as we find in "Dybi o Lego" (line 149), syntactically congruent with "Dybi o Alclut" (line 151) and "Dybi o Lydaw" (line 153). There is no known *Arlego or *Llego, either. On the basis that *The Book of Taliesin* frequently reproduces forms without rather than with non-syllabic *-i-*, Isaac suggests that *Lego* may be a variant of *Legio*, which he identifies as either Chester or Caerleon, with a strong preference for the latter ("'Armes Prydein Fawr' and St. David," p. 165n8); compare *Historia Brittonum*, ch. 66a, which lists *Caer Legion* and *Caer Legeion Guar Usic* [sic] (*Nennius: British History*, ed. Morris, p. 80). Caerleon is certainly within the southeastern geographic sphere of interest of the poem. Accepting this, the *ffrwt* [swift stream, current] would be the Usk or perhaps the Bristol Channel, some five miles away as the crow flies. Elsewhere, especially lines 188–89, the poet envisions the Saxons fleeing much farther east than the Usk or the Wye, but perhaps the dominant image is of driving them into the sea; compare lines 30, 191. Invoking a more complex etymological development, Breeze compares *lego* and *arlego* to *Ligorensis civitas* and *Ligora ceaster*, earlier forms of the name Leicester ("*Armes Prydein*, Hywel Dda, and Edmund," p. 216).

*allmyn*. MS: *allan*. The emendation of *allan* [out, outside] to *allmyn* [foreigners] is based on the end rhyme as well as the sense; on *allmyn*, see the note to line 7.

108 *Iwys*. On this archaic name for Wessex, also appearing in line 181, see pp. 249–50. *Gwssyl* (= *gussyl* < *kussyl* [advice, counsel, council]) rhymes with *-yd* and *-yr* by "Irish rhyme" (see p. 262), as it does in line 165.

109 *Lloegyr*. There has been much discussion of the meaning of *Lloegr*, which became a generalized Welsh term for England, as well as the Franco-Arthurian *Logres*. Hamp deduces from his etymological analysis that *Lloeg(y)r* carries the sense "having a nearby border, being from near the border," and he concludes that "the Celtic term *Lloeg(y)r* is the exact opposite of the Germanic term in

English, *Welsh*, originally singling out not the foreignness but the nearness of the neighbour" ("*Lloegr*," p. 85). While *Lloegr* may not necessarily correspond in precise geographic or political terms with the extent of Mercia, there is little doubt that in this passage, contrasted with *Iwys*/Wessex, it is the functional equivalent of Mercia, i.e., the region to the east of much of the Welsh border and the kingdom now under Athelstan's control.

*lloscit*. Here *-it* is an earlier spelling of *-yd*, *-ydd*. *Llosgydd*, from the root of *llosgi* [to burn] + nominative agent suffix *-ydd*, hence "one who burns or sets fire." The reference is to the frequent practice of burning houses and crops in warfare. Williams draws attention to the instances of *Fflamddwyn* [Flame-bearer] as a name or nickname of a Saxon leader in two of the poems of the historical Taliesin (*Armes Prydein*, trans. Bromwich, p. 50; *Poems of Taliesin*, ed. Williams, poems 6.3, 6, 18, and 10.11). Isaac interprets *lloscit* as a 3 sg. present verb form and translates "and England will burn" ("'Armes Prydein Fawr' and St. David," p. 177).

111 More literally, "And a journey/movement upon (the) foreigner and flight daily." *A* [and] also often carries the sense of "but"; interpreting it as such here obviates the need to assume some lost text shifting the sense away from the hopes of the Saxons to those of the Welsh (see *Armes Prydein*, trans. Bromwich, p. 51).

*alluro*. The rare term *allfro* [foreigner], literally "(one) of another region," is the semantic opposite of *Cymro* [Welshman], literally "(one) of the same region"; see notes to *Cymry*, line 9, and *allmyn* [foreigner], line 7.

112 *kud*. Here *-u-* represents an alternative orthographic representation of *-w-*, perhaps reflecting the earlier orthography of the scribe's exemplar; compare *cwd . . . cwd* later in the line. *Cw*, *cwd*, *cwt* is an interrogative pronoun meaning "where?, whence?, whither?"; see also lines 135–36.

113 "They" refers to the Welsh in general, or perhaps to the deliverers Cynan and Cadwaladr.

*gyfarth*. *Cyfarth*, from *cyf-* [com-, with] + *arth* [bear], means "a barking or baying," originally a hunting term used particularly of an animal being held at bay, with reference to the sound of the hounds barking around it. Thus it was applied figuratively to warriors standing their ground and developed a more general sense of "resistance, opposition," and then simply "battle." It also is used as a verb, "to bark, to threaten." Undoubtedly influenced by the internal rhyme, all three instances of *cyfarth* in *The Book of Taliesin* are accompanied by *arth* [bear], used figuratively for a warrior (see line 170 below and *Book of Taliesin* 77.19: "Arth o Deheubarth yn kyfarth Gwyned" [A bear from Deheubarth threatening Gwynedd] — ed. Evans, trans. mine).

116 *arbettwy*. 3 sg. present/future subjunctive of *arbed* [spare, save, preserve, deliver] (*Geiriadur Prifysgol Cymru*, s.v. *arbedaf*, *arbed*).

*gilyd*. *Cilydd* usually means "companion," but it can also mean "enemy." Thus the line might alternatively be rendered "No friend/kinsman (*car*) will save the body of his fellow"; or "No friend/kinsman (*car*) will have pity on (or compassion for) the body of his fellow" (see *Armes Prydein*, trans. Bromwich, p. 53n116).

In other words, the Welsh will fight with such fury that they will not even stop to retrieve the bodies of their fallen comrades. The recovery of bodies is a theme as important in heroic literature as it is in the idealized ethic of modern warfare (compare Homer, *The Iliad*, 16.847–902, Patroclus and Hector's fight over the body of Kebriones; Book 17, The fight over Patroclus' body; Book 24, Priam begs for the body of Hector).

117 *gaflaw*. Literally, "forked," from *gafl* [fork] + adj. suffix *-aw*; hence "split open."

119 *ubein*. MS: *obein*. *Ubein* is a verbnoun with a range of meaning from "sigh, moan, sob" to "yell, wail, howl," from the interjection *wb*, *ub* [oh, woe, alas].

121 For the word order subject–object–verb in 121, compare line 21 and see Evans, *Grammar*, pp. 181–82; this has the advantage of equating the two instances of *kennadeu* [messengers] in 121 and 124. An alternative rendering of these lines is based on understanding *kennadeu agheu* as "the messengers of death": "many wounded by hand; before the hosts separate / the messengers of death will meet / when corpses stand up" (*Armes Prydein*, trans. Bromwich, p. 11). The collocation *kennadeu agheu* occurs in a thirteenth-century poem by Einion ap Gwalchmai (fl. 1203–23): "Before the time comes which is without assistance, / The messengers of death as guides (*kennadeu agheu yn gyuarwyt*), / Before I have a cold grave" (McKenna, *Medieval Welsh Religious Lyric*, 8.15–17, pp. 186–87).

122 This line, repeated in line 187, contains one of the most striking images in the poem — the press of the fleeing Saxons will be so great that the dead will not even have room to fall down.

123 *ar gwerth y treth*. MS: *"y treth "ar gwerth*, with transposition marks before *y treth* and before *ar gwerth*. Thus, transposing as marked by the scribe and assuming that, as was common in the early Middle Welsh period, the lenition of the *g* was not shown in the scribe's exemplar, we can understand *ar gwerth* as *arwerth*, *arwerthu* [to pay, make payment]. Whether or not there is a space between *ar* and *gwerth* is difficult to decide and would not be conclusive in either case. Ignoring the transposition marks gives *y treth a'r gwerth* [the tax and the payment]. With either reading we can understand lines 123–24 to be saying that the paying of the tax will be avenged daily, as will the frequent missions of the tax collectors and the lying hosts (of their enforcers) in the next line.

124 *gennadeu*. See the note on 121. Here *kennadeu* (Modern Welsh *cenhadau*; sg. *cennad*) might mean "expeditions, missions, messages" as well as "messengers."

125 *Dygorfi Kymry*. MS: *Dygorfu kymry ~~y peri~~*. In the manuscript *Dygorfu*, beginning in the middle of a line, has a large red *D*, with a small *d* guide letter visible in its middle, and following *kymry* the words *y peri* have been cancelled. The scribe's eye clearly skipped ahead in his exemplar to line 127, which he began before catching his mistake. Line 127 begins a new *awdl* with a *D* with a center dot, but no rubrication. Surely the large capital was meant to begin the new *awdl* on line 127.

*Dygorfi*. MS: *Dygorfu*. *Dygorfu* in both lines 125 and 127 is past tense, which Williams points out makes no sense in a prophecy (*Armes Prydein*, trans. Bromwich, pp. 55–56). The exemplar may have read *dygorui* or *dygoriu*, which could both account for the manuscript reading and give us a present/future verb *dy(g)orfi* or *dy(g)oriu/dy(g)oryw*. Arguing that the scribe accurately copied other future verb forms in the poem, Isaac retains the past tense here and in line 127, translating "The Welsh [ever] triumphed" ("'Armes Prydein Fawr' and St. David," p. 177; brackets in original). On the other hand, we have evidence in the manuscript that the scribe initially miscopied right at this point; thus his concentration might not have been at its best at that moment.

*kyfergyr*. An "Irish rhyme" (see p. 262) with *geu luyd* and *gytffyd*; compare *ketwyr*, line 119.

126 The poet is fond of using close synonyms and has outdone himself here, making translation difficult. *Gyweir* in reference to warriors means "ready, in proper order or array, equipped." *Gyteir* [agreed, united, unanimous], *gytson* [united in speech], and *gytffyd* [united in faith] are compounds of *cyd-* [co-, fellow-, common, united together, mutual] + *geir* [word], *son* [sound, noise], and *ffyd* [faith].

127 *Dygorfi*. MS: *Dygorfu*. For the emendation, see the note to line 125. The sense of the line is that the Cymry will survive to engage in battle once again; compare line 12. This line begins a new *awdl* rhyming in *-ant*, though line 127 itself rhymes internally with *gwlat* in line 128; compare line 151.

128–44 The antecedents to the various instances of "they" in this *awdl* can be distinguished as follows: the Cymry (or perhaps more specifically, Cynan and Cadwaladr), lines 128, 129; the Dublin Danes, lines 132, 133a; the Saxons, lines 133b–37, 139–40, 142–44; and the Cymry and the Saxons, line 141.

130 *lieingant*. A *hapax legomenon* from *lliain* [linen, canvas] + *cant* [circle, edge, partition], hence probably meaning "banner, standard."

134 *o dylyet*. MS: *eu dylyet*; perhaps in anticipation of *eu* [their] in the following lines.

135 *herwi*. MS: *herw*. The manuscript reading *herw* means "an attack, incursion, raid, pillaging" or possibly here "a wandering, exile," giving "Where is their wandering?" — i.e., "Where do they wander in exile?" Williams suggests that better sense can be made by emending to *herwi*, the plural of *erw* [acre], thus by extension, "lands." In this case, the *h-* would be a sandhi *h* generated by the prefixed pronoun *eu* [their]; see D. Evans, *Grammar*, pp. 22–23.

137 *Gwrtheyrn*. See the note to line 27.

140 *reitheu*. MS: *r . . . theu*; only faint remains of the bow of the first *e* are visible.

144 *cam*. *Cam* is an "Irish rhyme" (see p. 262) with *digonsan(t)*, *garan(t)*, *can(t)*, etc. A phonetic change from *-nt* to *-n(n)* is evidenced in early Middle Welsh and even in Old Welsh. Though he regularly writes *-ant*, the scribe of our poem frequently records *-yn* rather than the historical *-ynt* for third person plural verbs; e.g., *dygobryssyn* (line 1), *dyorfyn* (line 12), *dybydyn* (line 13), etc. Note, too, *-ynt* in lines 51 and 52 rhyming with *-yn* and *-yn(t)* in the third *awdl*.

145–46 The interpretation and translation of these lines depends on our understanding of which Garmon (Germanus) is intended and what is meant by "the four hundred and four years." The influence of the *Historia Brittonum* is likely. Garmon is probably the continental St. Germanus of the *Historia*, rather than one of the Irish saints of that name, and chapter 66 states that the Saxons came to Britain in the fourth year of the reign of Vortigern, in the four-hundredth year from the Incarnation (*recte* Passion?) of Jesus Christ (*Armes Prydein*, trans. Bromwich, pp. 59–61; *Nennius: British History*, ed. Morris, pp. 39, 80).

148 *y dehol*. MS: *o dehol*. The manuscript *o* is a mistake for *y*; compare *y dihol*, line 152. Though the *e* is somewhat irregular (and is even less clear in Evans' facsimile), the manuscript reads *dehol*. Evans mistakenly prints *dihol* in his diplomatic typescript, and this is reproduced without comment in Williams' edition. Though the earliest citations have *i/y*, *dehol* also occurs by the thirteenth century and the two forms remain in free variation; see *Geiriadur Prifysgol Cymru* s.v. *deholaf*, *diholaf*.

149 *Lego*. While Caerleon may be a possibility, it seems, somehow, less likely than in line 106, and Chester even less so, hence it has been left untranslated here; see the note to line 106.

*rewyd*. Though as an adjective *rhewydd* usually carries the pejorative sense of "lascivious, wanton, lustful," *Geiriadur Prifysgol Cymru* also suggests the more positive connotations of "spirited, lively, ardent, fervent"; Bromwich translates "rapacious" (*Armes Prydein*, p. 13).

151 *Alclut*. Dumbarton on the Clyde, capital of the kingdom of Strathclyde; compare line 11.

*diweir*. This makes an "Irish rhyme" (see p. 262) internally with *Prydein* and *virein*.

152 *virein luyd*. < *mirein luyd* [splendid hosts]; this is not the object of the verb, but a phrase descriptive of the men of Alclud. Compare line 169.

154 *hennyd*. This can mean "friend, companion," as in lines 114, 122, 177, 187, and 190, "other," or "enemy, adversary," as here and in Aneirin's *Gododdin*: "Ennaint crau ac angau o'i hennydd" [A blood-bath and death for his adversary] (ed. Jarman, line 112). It is cognate with Cornish *hynse* and Breton *hentez* [other, next, neighbor].

156 Compare line 29.

158 *dyllid*. The sense is obscure. As noun and verb it means "flow" or "flood," as in line 115. For this occurrence, Williams suggests a parallel with English *flux* [a flow of fluid from the body, as in diarrhea and dysentery]. Isaac translates as "pursuit" ("'Armes Prydein Fawr' and St. David," p. 179).

159 *a chanhwynyd*. The meaning of *canhwynydd* is uncertain; perhaps emend to *chanhwyllyd* [candle-bearers](?); see *Armes Prydein*, trans. Bromwich, pp. 63–64.

161 *kussulwyr*. MS: ~~*kussywy*~~ *kussulwyr*.

163 For Cynan and Cadwaladr, see the note to lines 89, 91.

165 *dwys eu kussyl*. Compare "Manawidan ab llyr, / oet duis y cusil" [Manawydan son of Llŷr, profound was his counsel], in the early Arthurian poem, "Pa ŵr yw'r Porthor?" ("Who is the Porter?") (see *Llyfr Du Caerfyrddin*, ed. Jarman, 31.19–20; trans. Bollard, "Arthur," pp. 16–18).

169 *mirein luyd*. See the note on line 152.

170 *kyfarth*. See the note on line 113.

171 *Dysgogan*. MS: *d ysgogan*. A small guide letter *d* appears, but a red capital was never inserted.

*derwydon* [wise men]. This is perhaps the earliest known example of this word; it occurs four more times in the *Book of Taliesin*, but in poems that are difficult to date. One of these, *Gwiail Jesse* [*The Rods of Jesse*], refers to the biblical wise men from the East (edited in Welsh in Haycock, *Blodeugerdd Barddas*, pp. 92–103). The remaining examples in the *Hengerdd*, the "Early Poetry," all appear in the *Book of Taliesin*, and they show a close connection with the singing of poems of prophecy (see *Legendary Poems*, ed. Haycock, p. 237). *Derwydd, derwyddon* was not connected with the druids until Wiliems proposed this derivation, via Davies in his *Dictionarium Duplex*, 1632. Wiliems and Davies posited Greek *δρυς* [oak] (Welsh *derw*) as the etymon, and this derivation caught the popular imagination. Morris-Jones proposed a derivation from the element *-derw* [certain, true], cognate with Old Irish *derb* [certain] (*Welsh Grammar*, p. 224). But Lloyd-Jones, followed by *Geiriadur Prifysgol Cymru*, rejects these and derives it from the intensifying prefix *der-, dar-* + *gwyd* , from *gwybod* [to know] (*Geirfa*, s.v. *derwŷδ*).

On the basis of rhyme, lines 147–99 might be considered as a single *awdl*; however, the formulaic *Dysgogan derwydon* in line 171 suggests that lines 171–99 form a separate *awdl*; see the note on line 17.

172 *o Vynaw* [from Manaw]. The reference could be to either the Isle of Man or Manaw Gododdin in southeast Scotland. The latter might better fit the implication of the north-to-south extent of Brythonic (i.e., Welsh) territory, where Dyfed to Thanet in the next line delimits the east-to-west extent.

174 *o Wawl. Gwawl*, literally, "Wall"; Williams suggests this is a reference to Hadrian's Wall; Bromwich proposes the Antonine Wall on the basis of the opposition between *Gwawl* [the Wall] and *Gweryt* [the Firth of Forth] (*Armes Prydein*, trans. Bromwich, p. 66).

175 *Llettawt*. MS: *Lletatawt*.

*Yrechwyd*. MS: *yr echwyd*. Modern Welsh *Erechwydd*. A region in the Brythonic kingdom of the Old North, ruled in the sixth century by Urien Rheged, who is praised in the poems of the historical Taliesin; see *Poems of Taliesin*, ed. Williams, 3.1: "Uryen yr Echwyd, haelaf dyn bedyd" [Urien of Yrechwydd, most generous Christian (lit. 'baptised man')]; 6.13: "Vryen, vd yr Echwyd" [Urien, lord of Yrechwydd]. The form derives from *ar* [on, alongside, by] + *echwydd* [(fresh) water]; *ar-*, in compound, was affected to *er-*, giving *erechwydd*. The *er-* was then assumed to be the definite article *yr*, written *er* in some early orthographic styles (see *Armes Prydein*, trans. Bromwich, pp. 67–68). Williams speculates that Erechwydd is the region of Swaledale, with its chief fort at Catraeth (Catterick), the site of the battle lamented in *The Gododdin* of Aneirin (*Poems of Taliesin*, pp. xlii–xliii). For the poet of *Armes Prydein*, it may have been simply an evocative name for "somewhere in the Old North" (*Armes Prydein*, trans. Bromwich, p. 67).

180 *Dews*. *Dews*, usually disyllabic, is a borrowing from Latin *Deus*; the Celtic-derived Welsh cognate is *Duw*.

181 *Iwis*. See the note to line 108 and pp. 249–50.

184 *gyfnewitwyr*. *Cyfnewidwyr* [merchants, dealers, hucksters], here used pejoratively.

188 *Aber Santwic*. Probably the estuary of the Stour, below the Sandwich Haven, is meant, if indeed the poet has any detailed knowledge of Kentish geography at all. He may simply know that Sandwich is near Thanet and about as far east as you can get from southeast Wales. He undoubtedly envisions a reversal of the traditional tale of the arrival of the Saxons with Horsa and Hengist.

193 *lyfrawr* [one who knows books]. A borrowing from Latin *librarius* [a copier of books]; hence, according to Jones, by extension, "a sorcerer, magician" (*Armes Prydein*, trans. Bromwich, pp. 70–71). Whether we understand it as "one who knows books," as "librarian" (Isaac, "'Armes Prydein Fawr' and St. David," p. 167n12), or as "sorcerer," the sense is that no one should seek any other source of wisdom in the matter of the future for Wales than this poem.

197 *Yr yg, Keli kaer a'm Duw yssyd*. MS: *yn yr yg ge-/lli kaer am duw yssyd*. The line is problematic or ambiguous at several points. As written it is ten syllables, and is thus not resistant to the following possible emendations on metrical grounds.

*Yr yg* [Despite adversity]. For *yg*, *yng*, see line 32 above and *Geiriadur Prifysgol Cymru*, s.v. *ing*, *yng* [strait(s), extremity, press of battle, crisis, distress, dire adversity, affliction; anguish, excruciating pain, agony, pain]. The construction *yn yr yg* occurs several times in the early period and can be analyzed as *yn* [in] + *yr* [the] + *yng/ing* (see *Geiriadur Prifysgol Cymru* for examples, alongside citations for *yn yg*). Williams' edition of *Armes Prydein* (p. 71) notes "Read *yn yg*," deleting the *yr*, and translates "In straits." Alternatively, deleting the *yn* and interpreting *yr* as the preposition (Modern Welsh *er*) with the sense "despite, notwithstanding," yields the translation adopted above: "Despite adversity/ distress" (Haycock, personal communication). In this case, the *yn* may have crept into the text under the influence of the set phrase *yn yr yng*. Isaac understands the preposition *yr* to mean "for the sake of" and translates "for the sake of those who are in the Kingdom of Heaven with my God" ("'Armes Prydein Fawr' and St. David," pp. 167, 180–81). Another possibility, though less likely in the context of the poem's closing prayer, is that, given the overall martial context of the poem, the "press (of battle)" sense may also be apt here, rather than the more general and abstract "adversity, strait(s)," giving us "In the press (of battle), there is a heavenly fortress and my God"; compare Iolo Goch's "Prudd yn yr yng, gyfyng gae" [sombre in the fray, constricted field] (*Iolo Goch*, ed.

Johnston, 11.72). Compare also *cyfyng* [narrow, confined, constrained], line 62 above, from *cyf-* [com-, con-] + *yng, ing*.

*Keli kaer*. MS: *gelli kaer*. *Keli/Celi* [heaven], from Latin *celi, caelum*; *caer* [fortress]. Semantically parallel to *Celi gaer* are *nef kaereu* [the fortresses of Heaven] (Haycock, *Blodeugerdd Barddas*, p. 83), and *caereu nef* (*Llawysgrif Hendregadredd*, ed. Morris-Jones, 33.24). If we retain the manuscript reading *Gelli Kaer* [Fort of the Grove], it may be a (mistaken?) reference to the town of Gelli-gaer, the site of a Roman fort in the Rhymni Valley, in what was Glywysing (see p. 259). The context, however, seems to call for the emended reading.

*a'm Duw*. The phrase means "and my God" or, alternatively, could be read *am Duw* [around/surrounding/encircling God].

## 2. *CARTA DIRIGE GRESSUS*

Ed. and trans. Michael Lapidge ("Some Latin Poems," p. 98). Notes by Scott Thompson Smith.

*Manuscript*: London, British Library, MS Cotton Nero A.ii, fols. 10v–11v.

This poem occurs in two manuscripts, the fuller of which, presented here, is London, British Library, MS Cotton Nero A.ii (Gneuss 342). The poem was noted by Stubbs, *Memorials of Saint Dunstan*, p. xiiin1, but the text given by Stubbs differs from that of the manuscript in significant ways. Lapidge ("Some Latin Poems," pp. 86–93) gives a reconstruction of the poem and a full account of its several difficulties.

London, British Library, MS Cotton Nero A.ii is 152 x 110 mm, and the poem, written in a large, bold script of the tenth or eleventh century, occupies fols. 10v–11v. There are no line breaks in the manuscript, but the end of each stanza is marked with a *punctus versus*. The poem also appears in the gospel-book Durham, Cathedral Library, MS A.II.17, fols. 2–102 (dated vii ex. / viii inc.) where it was written on 31v in a late tenth-century hand (Gneuss 220).

The poem is written in the form of a letter with a salutation (lines 1–8) and message (lines 9–24). Lapidge identified the poem's meter as iambic dimeter catalectic arranged in four-line stanzas with a rhyme-scheme of *aabb* or *abcd* ("Some Latin Poems," pp. 87–88; see also Stevenson, "Latin Poem," pp. 483–84).

2–3 Stevenson suggested that the poem was "a greeting from some oversea[s] poet, probably a resident in Frankland" ("Latin Poem," p. 486). Lapidge argued instead that the poem was composed near Penrith after Athelstan's northern victory in July 927 and sent south to Winchester to report the good news to the royal household. Such a route of travel would have involved passage over sea and land; *per maria*, then, does not by necessity indicate passage from the continent (Lapidge, "Some Latin Poems," pp. 91–92).

3–4 *tellurisque spacium / ad regis palacium*. Compare to *Poetae Latini Aevi Carolini*, ed. Dümmler, no. 4: "*Carta*, Christo comite, *per telluris spatium / ad* Caesaris splendidium nunc perge *palatium*" (lines 1–2, emphasis added).

6 *reginam.* MSS: *regem* (Durham A.II.17) and *reginem* (Cotton Nero A.ii). Both manuscript readings present textual difficulties in understanding this stanza. Within the context of the poem Durham's *regem* [king] would result in the king both addressing and claiming to rule himself. Against this, Nero's *reginem* [queen] seems far more reasonable aside from the need for a minor grammatical adjustment, and it is indeed this emendation that Lapidge chose for his edition (and which thus appears here). That Athelstan had a queen, however, is nowhere recorded. If we are to accept *reginam*, we must explain her appearance in this text, a problem for which several solutions might be proposed. (1) Athelstan did have a queen but this poem is the only record of her existence. The twelfth-century *Liber Eliensis* mentions an otherwise unrecorded daughter for Athelstan, "Æðida filia regis Æðelstani," in a catalogue of treasures at Ely (ed. Blake, p. 292). Could this reference be a later confusion for Athelstan's half-sister Eadgyth (Edith)? (2) The *regina* in question was a queen mother. King Edward the Elder had three wives, all of them mothers of kings. Edward's first wife and Athelstan's mother, Ecgwynn, appears in no surviving contemporary documents (charters, wills, manumissions, etc.) and in later sources she is rumored to have been a concubine (William of Malmesbury, *GR*, 2.131 and 139). Edward's later wives, however, do appear prominently in charter witness lists. Ælfflæd, Edward's second wife and mother to Ælfweard (king for less than a month in 924) and Edwin, appears third in a charter witness list (S 363, dated 901) after "Edward rex" and "Ealhswið mater regis." This charter, however, is much too early to have any relevance to *Carta dirige gressus*. Eadgifu, Edward's third wife and mother of kings Edmund and Eadred, has a more prominent and sustained presence in the historical record. Eadgifu appears as "regis mater" in several of Edmund's charters, including S 465, 470 (both dated 940), and 475 (dated 941); as "regina" in S 477 (dated 941); as "regis genetrix" and "regina" in S 546 (dated 949); and as "regina et mater Eadmundi et Eadredi" in S 1212 (dated 961). These documents are all dated after Athelstan's kingship (924–39), but it may be possible that Eadgifu's long career of political influence had already begun in Athelstan's reign. Additionally, MS Coburg, Landesbibliothek 1 (Gneuss 809), also known as "the Gandersheim Gospels" but written in Metz during the mid-ninth century, contains an inscription in Anglo-Saxon square minuscule which reads "+ eadgifu regina :- æþelstan rex angulsaxonum et mercianorum :-." Eadgifu's identity here is uncertain. It could refer to Athelstan's stepmother, but Keynes points out that Eadgifu does not appear in any of Athelstan's charters, which suggests "that she may have remained in the background during her stepson's reign" ("King Athelstan's Books," p. 190). (3) The *regina* here could also refer to Athelstan's half-sister Eadgifu, daughter of Edward and Ælfflæd. This Eadgifu (d. 951) married King Charles III, ruler of the West Franks, sometime between 917 and 919. Eadgifu sent her son Louis to England after Charles was deposed in 923, but it is unclear whether or not she returned to England with him. Louis returned to France to become king in 936. See Keynes, "King Athelstan's Books," pp. 189–93; Nelson, "Eadgifu"; and Stenton, *Anglo-Saxon England*, pp. 344–47. (4) The emendation to *reginam* is incorrect. For further discussion of the emendation issue, see Bobrycki, "Æthelstan, 'King of All Britain,'" pp. 47–48 and 102–05. None of the four explanations above are entirely satis-

factory, however, a problem which speaks to the highly corrupt state of the poem as it survives in the two manuscript witnesses.

*clitonem*. Lapidge identifies the *clitonem* [prince] as Edwin, son of Edward the Elder and Ælfflæd ("Some Latin Poems," p. 91n136). Edwin appears as *cliton* (just after Athelstan *rex*) in the witness list of a Winchester charter (S 1417) dated 924–933. *ASC* E states that Edwin drowned at sea in 933 (see also Stenton, *Anglo-Saxon England*, pp. 355–56). The range of possible dates for the Winchester charter and the record of Edwin's death in 933 suggest that Edwin was indeed the *clito* named in the poem. Edmund appears as *clito* only in charters apparently written *after* Edwin's death: S 387 (924–939), S 433 (937), and S 455 (934–939).

17, 19 These two lines have eight syllables whereas all others have seven.

21–24 The final stanza shows an *abcb* rhyme-scheme rather than the *aabb* rhyme-scheme typical to the first six stanzas. The stanza features notable repetitions of the sounds *p* and *s*. Compare to *Poetae Latini Aevi Carolini*, ed. Dümmler, no. 4: "dic, ut Caesar Karolus per Petri praeconia / Sit sanus, sit longaevus sit felix victoria" (lines 7–8) and "Salvatoris gratia" (line 14).

22 *Petri*. Since *Petrus* was a rare name during this period in England, the Peter named here may have been a continental clerk within Athelstan's retinue (Lapidge, "Some Latin Poems," pp. 92–93). One *Petrus* does appear in S 1417 (924–933), a lease from the New Minster at Winchester (the same charter witnessed by Edwin as *clito*). This single-sheet charter, the upper portion of a chirograph written in Anglo-Saxon square minuscule, can be dated to the middle of the tenth century. The name *Petrus* appears both in the witness list and in an endorsement later added in an eleventh-century hand. See *Charters*, ed. Miller, no. 9 at pp. 49–54. It should also be noted, however, that a *Petrus* also appears in the Carolingian poem (*Poetae Latini Aevi Carolini*, ed. Dümmler, no. 4, line 7). Samantha Zacher has also made the case that the word was intended as a cross-language pun on Athelstan's name (Latin *Petrus/petra* [stone] for OE *stan*). See Zacher, "Multilingualism."

### 3. *REX PIUS ATHELSTAN*

Ed. Paul Cavill. Trans. Scott Thompson Smith.

*Manuscript*: London, British Library, MS Cotton Tiberius A.ii, fol. 15r.

The unique manuscript is composite and very fragile. The manuscript is 230 x 178 mm, and the poem occupies the whole of folio 15r. The poem, recording Athelstan's donation of this gospel-book and another manuscript to Christ Church, Canterbury, is written in a slightly untidy hand of continental origin from the early part of the tenth century; this is not the main hand of the manuscript. For details of the manuscript, previous editions, and a new edition of the poem (which differs slightly from the text here), see Lapidge ("Some Latin Poems," pp. 94–96).

A prose preface, written in an English hand, appears on fol. 15v, opposite the poem:

> Volumen hoc euuangelii . ÆÐELSTAN . Anglorum basyleos . et curagulus totius Bryttanniæ . devota mente . Dorobernensis cathedre primatui . tribuit ecclesiæ Christo dicatæ . quod etiam archiepiscopus . hujus ac ministri ecclesiæ . presentes successoresque . curiosis affectibus perenitter agnoscant . scilicet et custodire studeant . prout Deo rationem sunt reddituri . Ne quis in æternum furva fruada [*recte* frauda] deceptus . hinc illud arripere conetur . Sed manens hic maneat . honoris exemplumque cernentibus . perpetue sibi demonstret . Vos etenim obsecrando postulo . memores ut vestris mei mellifluis oraminibus . consonaque voce fieri prout confido . non desistatis. (*Cartularium Saxonicum*, ed. Birch, no. 711, 2.417–18)
>
> [Athelstan, king of the English and guardian of all Britain, with a devout mind gave this book to the primatial see of Canterbury, a church dedicated to Christ. May the archbishop and his servants of the church, present and future, forever regard that book with diligent goodwill, and may they especially strive to keep it safe, as they are to render account to God, lest anyone hereafter, ensnared by dark deceit, should attempt to steal the book from here. But may it continue to remain here, and may it always provide an example of honor to those looking upon it. And I ask and pray that you will not cease to remember me in your sweet prayers, as I am sure will be made in harmonious voice.]

The poem is written in elegiac couplets. The manuscript marks the alternating pentameter lines with a medial space for the central caesura and a rubricated capital for the second half of the line. Several lines show leonine rhyme, or rhyme between the word immediately preceding the caesura and the final word of the line (lines 2, 4, 5, 6, 10, 13, 19 and 20).

1–12 These lines contain two full sentences, each six lines in length (lines 1–6 and lines 7–12). Both sentences have a parallel structure: each begins with a nominative singular noun or pronoun (*Rex*, *Quisquis*) and ends with a present participle (*terens*, *ouans*).

4 In the right margin between this and the next line is written, in a different hand, "Eawyn."

5–6 *Rex ipse feroces / Vincere bellipotens, Colla superba terrens*. For the flattering Old Testament reference being made in these lines, see Introduction, pp. 24–25.

6 The hermeneutic style popular in the later tenth century frequently employs compound adjectives ending in *-potens* (*bellipotens*, line 6), *-genus* (*Terrigenis*, line 4), and *-gerus* (*Gemmigeris*, line 10). See Lapidge, "Some Latin Poems," p. 96.

11 *de more*. MS: *demore*.

12–13 These lines contain a small cluster of grecisms: *agia*, *sophia*, *scematicus*.

18 *ne quid*. MS: *nequid*.

19–20 These lines show significant sound-play on *f* and *t*.

## 4. *ANGLO-SAXON CHRONICLE, BATTLE OF BRUNANBURH*

Version A: ed. and trans. Michael Livingston.
Version B: ed. and trans. Robert P. Creed.

*Manuscripts*: **A**: Cambridge, Corpus Christi College, MS 173, fols. 26r–27r; **B**: London, British Library, MS Cotton Tiberius A.vi, fols. 31r–32r; **C**: London, British Library, MS Cotton Tiberius B.i, fols. 141r–41v; **D**: London, British Library, MS Cotton Tiberius B.iv, fols. 49r–50r.

*The Battle of Brunanburh*, a 73-line poem preserved in four of the surviving manuscripts of the *Anglo-Saxon Chronicle*, is undoubtedly the most famous accounting of the battle that survives today, yet it remains a mystery in many essential ways. A number of its words (among them the name of the battle site and other geographical references) are now uncertain in meaning, and scholars are sharply divided about whether the poem pre-existed its present, chronicle-situated form. In light of these facts — and because it has long held such a vital place at the heart of the Brunanburh corpus — the poem is here presented in two editions and translations: the first based on the poem as preserved in manuscript A (the base text for most modern editions of the *Battle of Brunanburh*), the second based on manuscript B, which perhaps has much to recommend it as a reading of this poem in particular (see pp. 295–97). Aside from all other concerns, we hope that these two independent views of the poem, which make different decisions on some key issues (like inclusion of the first-line "Her") and are associated with two different translations, will bring readers into the process, not just the result, of editing and translating.

The notes below are keyed to both texts. Variants across all four manuscripts of the poem are kept to a minimum here; scholars seeking such information can consult the full edition presented by Campbell (*Battle of Brunanburh*, pp. 82–95) or the critical edition in the Anglo-Saxon Poetic Records series (*Anglo-Saxon Minor Poems*, ed. Dobbie, pp. 16–20).

For more information on the text of Version B, see pp. 285–304.

1/before 1 The adverb *Her* [here], which follows the number indicating the year and is usually translated "In this year," is not a metrical part of the first line of the poem according to the prosody incorporated in this volume (pp. 300–04). The same is not true, Campbell points out, for the two Edgar poems in *ASC* (*Battle of Brunanburh*, p. 36n2). For further discussion of whether the word belongs to the poem, and some of the ramifications of the editorial decision, see Thomas Bredehoft's essay in this volume (pp. 285–94).

1 *cyning* (A, D) / *cing* (B, C). B and C's late spelling forecasts Modern English *king*. To many modern Anglo-Saxonists, who prefer *cyning*, the spelling *cing* is unacceptable, even though the B and C texts also use *cing* in lines 35 (B only) and 58.

4 *sæcce* (A, C) / *sake* (B) / *secce* (D). B's spelling perhaps indicates the short form, usually spelled *sace*, as in line 42. If the form with doubled consonant is used, and the doubled consonant is taken to indicate a long first syllable, there will not be two but three measures in this halfline.

5 *Brunanburh*. A: *brunanburh*, corrected by a later hand to *brunnanburh*. C: *brunnanburh*. The line is partially disfigured in B: *emb-*, followed after a space by three or four minims that could be *-un-* or *-nn-*. Campbell reads *brunnanburh*, though Taylor's more recent edition of *ASC* B reads *brunanburh*. For an attempt to identify this site, see Cavill's essay in this volume, pp. 327–49.

6 *heaþolinde* (A) / *heaðolinda* (C, D [corrected from *heaðolinga*]) / *heaðolina* (B, with a possible deletion mark under the *o*). The word literally translates as "battle-linden": items made of linden wood that are used in battle; i.e., shields.

*hamora lafan* (A) / *hamora lafum* (B, C) / *hamera lafum* (D). This kenning literally translates as the "leavings of hammers"; i.e., swords.

12 *dunnade* (Campbell) / *dænnede* (A, $n_2$ inserted above line) / *dennade* (B, C) / *dennode* (D). The word is a notorious crux. Campbell devotes four and a half pages toward an attempt at deciphering it (*Battle of Brunanburh*, pp. 98–102). His translation, "became dark," is accepted by both editors here, though Creed does not accept his emendation to *dunnade* for the B-text. Dobbie (*Anglo-Saxon Minor Poems*, p. 147) admits as "defensible" either Campbell's emendation or that of Sedgefield (*ðanode* [became wet]; *Battle of Maldon*, p. 39), but in light of the uncertainties leaves the reading from A.

13 *secga swate* (B, C, D, followed by Campbell, Dobbie). A's reading, *secgas hwate* [men brave], is a perfectly acceptable reading but one that makes less sense in this context than the reading from the other manuscripts.

15 *candel*. So B, C, D. A: *condel*, followed by Dobbie.

16 *oð* (A, C, D). B simply writes a crossed thorn, *þæt*. The source may have been *oðþæt* (*Anglo-Saxon Minor Poems*, ed. Dobbie, p. 147).

18 *ageted* (A, C, D) / *forgrunden* (B). Both words provide double alliteration in this halfline. The verb utilized in B also occurs at line 43, from which it was taken if the original reading is, in fact, *ageted*. On the other hand, it is just within the realm of possibility that *ageted* represents an early emendation reacting to the fact that the same forceful verb was used twice in such close proximity.

*guma norþerna* (A) / *guman norðerne* (B, C) / *guman norþærne* (D). Dobbie argues that A's reading "agrees better" with the singular verb form in line 17 (*Anglo-Saxon Minor Poems*, p. 148; see, too, Campbell, *Battle of Brunanburh*, pp. 8, 103), but B's reading can fit syntax if, as in this translation, the plural forms in lines 18 and 19 function within a parenthetical clause expanding on the singular antecedent governed by line 17's *manig*.

25 *heardes*. So B, C, D, followed by Campbell, Dobbie. A's *he eardes* makes little sense.

26 *þara ðe* (B, C) / *þæra þe* (D, followed by Campbell, Dobbie) / *þæ* (A).

*æra gebland* (A, followed by Dobbie) / *eargebland* (B, C, D, followed by Campbell).

29 *cyningas* (D, followed by Campbell, Dobbie) / *ciningas* (B) / *cyninges* (A) / *cingas* (C).

32–36 As Cavill notes in his essay in this volume (p. 338n38), the verbs in this section are noticeably singular rather than plural. Given that Anlaf cannot literally be alone — he is accompanied, after all, by a "little band" whose help was no doubt necessary to launch his ship — the metaphoric singulars must be intended to emphasize Anlaf's aloneness relative to both the heavy losses suffered by his army and the specific means of fleeing the battlefield: Anlaf leaves metaphorically alone (relative to his once-large horde of allies) and in so doing follows a physical path separate from most of the Northmen, whose flight is detailed late in the poem at lines 53–56.

32 *flotan*. So B, A, C, D. Campbell emends to *flotena*; against this emendation, see *Anglo-Saxon Minor Poems*, ed. Dobbie, p. 148.

*Sceotta* (A) / *Scotta* (B, C, D). The word is ambiguous within its medieval context, meaning either (or both) men of Scotland or Ireland.

35 *cnear on*. So B, C, D, followed by Campbell, Dobbie. A: *cnearen*.

37 Depending on the meaning of *Swilce þær eac*, this line could be read to indicate that Constantine also fled Brunanburh by ship.

39 *hilderinc*. So B, C, followed by Dobbie. A: *hildering*. D: *hylderinc*.

40 *mæca* (Dobbie) / *mecea* (B) / *mæcan* (A) / *meca* (C) / *in ecga* (D). Campbell emends to *mecga*, attributing it (erroneously) to D. The B-reading is understood here to be the genitive plural of *mece* [sword], not, as Campbell (*Battle of Brunanburh*, pp. 110–11) has it, of *mæcg* [man].

41 *gefylled*. So B, A, C, D, followed by Dobbie. Campbell emends to *befylled*.

43 *forgrunden*. So B, C, D, followed by Campbell, Dobbie. A alone reads the unusual *fergrunden* here. See also line 18.

49 *cumbolgehnastes*. So B, C, D, followed by Campbell, Dobbie. A has the puzzling *culbodgehnades*, later corrected to *cumbelgehnades*.

53 *Norðmenn*. So B, C. A: *normen*, corrected to *norþmen*. D: *norðmen*.

54 *Dingesmere* (A, C) / *Dyngesmere* (B) / *dynigesmere* (D). For an attempt to identify this site, see Cavill's essay in this volume, pp. 346–47.

56 *eft Iraland*. So B, followed by Campbell, Dobbie. A: *7 eft hira land*. C, D: *eft yraland*. Clearly, A heard something like *hira land* [their land] after *eft*, but, since this did not seem quite right metrically, added the "and" sign, 7, just above the point between halflines.

59 *hremige* (B, C, D, followed by Dobbie). A: *hramige*, corrected to *hremige*. Campbell emends to *hremge*.

60 *hræw* (A, corrected from *hræ*) / *hraw* (B) / *hra* (C, D). Campbell emends to *hræ*.

62 *hasewanpadan* (A, followed by Dobbie) / *hasopadan* (B) / *hasupadan* (C, followed by Campbell) / *hasuwadan* (D).

66 *æfre*. So B, C, D, followed by Campbell, Dobbie. A: *æfer*.

70 *Seaxe* (A, D) / *Sexe* (C). Following the other manuscripts, B's plural *sexan* has been normalized to *-e*.

72 *Wealas*. So B, C, D, followed by Campbell, Dobbie. A has the puzzling *weealles*.

**5. *GLASWAWT TALIESSIN***

Ed. and trans. Marged Haycock.

*Manuscript*: National Library of Wales, Peniarth MS 2 (*The Book of Taliesin*), fols. 14v–15r.

For more information on this item, see pp. 262–64.

1 *Kennadeu a'm dodynt mor ynt anuonawc*. The announcement of the arrival of tidings, often bad, for relayal by the speaker is found in a variety of verse, including court poetry and prophecy. The use of *kennat* [message, messenger] is, however, far less common than *chwedyl* and its compound *kychwedyl* [account, news]. The use of the adjective *anuonawc* [noble] suggests "messengers," possibly horse-messengers or mounted envoys; since they are "sent" there may be intentional word-play on the homophone verb *anfon* [to send].

3 *Gnawt rwyf yn heli — Beli wirawt*. Runs of nominal statements beginning with *gnawt* [usual (is)] are found in gnomic verse and in another prophecy, "Peiryan Faban." Lines 3–5 are understood as describing current woes which cause the distress alluded to in line 2 rather than future tribulations. *Rwyf*, understood here in its literal meaning "oar," is most often used in poetry metaphorically for "leader," including God. The *gwirawt* [alcoholic drink] of Beli appears to be a kenning for the sea, Beli being either the legendary ancestor figure Beli Mawr ap Mynogan (see *Trioedd*, ed. Bromwich, pp. 288–89), or else Beli son of Rhun and grandson of Maelgwn Gwynedd. Twelfth- and thirteenth-century court poets freqently refer to Gwynedd rulers as being of Beli's lineage, and to the region as "Beli's land."

4 *yscwyt yscawn ar gefyn yscawt*. *Yscawn* is a variant of disyllabic *yscafyn* [light], which is perhaps to be restored here, providing a better correspondence, though not full rhyme, with monosyllabic *cefyn*; the final vowel in both words is epenthetic. *Yscwyt yscawn* can also be interpreted as "one(s) bearing light shields." *Ar gefyn* is most commonly used in the literal sense of "on the back of" (a horse, etc.), and therefore "on the back of an apparition" is not impossible; the meaning "in addition to, as a consequence of, with regard to" is attested only from the fifteenth century. *Cefn* is also found in toponyms where it means "ridge." Here *ar gefyn yscawt* is tentatively understood as "in the depth of darkness" (literally "on the back of the night"), comparing the idioms *cefn nos* and *cefn dydd*.

6 *naw cant* [nine hundred]. Nine hundred is frequently used in early Welsh verse to describe large numbers in battle; see also line 32 and Item 1.73.

7 *Atvyd Mei ar Venei*. *Menei* is rhymed with *Mei* "the month of May" in a short poem attributed to Hywel ab Owain Gwynedd, "Hawd gwelet goleulosc arnei / O gaer wenn geir emyl Menei. / Treghissyant trydydyd o Uei — trychanllog / Yn y llyghes 6ordei, / A deckant kynran a'y kilyei" [It was easy to see a blazing conflagration there (Rhuddlan) from the fair fort on the bank of the Menai. On the third day of May there foundered three hundred ships of the ?stately fleet, and a thousand soldiers sent it packing] (Llywelyn Fardd I, et al., poem 12.7–11). This poem appears to celebrate a Gwynedd victory in the struggle between Owain Gwynedd and Henry II, and its editors suggest it is more likely to refer to the events of 1157, the year of the Tal Moelfre victory in Anglesey (vividly celebrated by Gwalchmai [Meilyr Brydydd, et al., poem 8]), and the fall of Rhuddlan, rather than to those of 1167 when Rhuddlan was recaptured (Llywelyn Fardd I, et al., p. 168). But the same rhyme may have been used in referring to any one of a number of earlier battles fought in or near Anglesey such as those recorded for 853, 874, 877, 918, 989, 993, etc. If the mention of Conwy in line 8 refers to the battle of 880 which avenged the death of Rhodri Mawr (see below), it is likely that the battle in question is the "Sunday battle in Anglesey" in 877 which may have precipitated Rhodri's flight to Ireland; the place of his subsequent slaying at the hands of the Saxons in the following year is not known.

8 *atvyd mwy ar Gonwy, gwynyeith gwnahawt*. The *gwynyeith* [vengeance] brings to mind especially the Battle of Conwy in 881 that avenged the killing of Rhodri Mawr of Gwynedd by the English (probably the Mercians, under Ceolwulf in 878 [*Annales Cambriae*, line 880: "*Gueit Conguoy. Digal Rotri a Deo*" (The battle of Conwy. Vengeance for Rhodri at God's hand); *Nennius*, ed. Morris, pp. 90, 48]). Ceolwulf's successor, Ealdorman Æthelred, was defeated at the battle of Conwy which seems to have brought about the collapse of Mercian authority in Wales for the time being. Lloyd (*History of Wales* 1.328) states that Rhodri's son, Anarawd, arrested a raid on Snowdonia (see note to lines 25–26) by Æthelred. Further on the context, see Charles-Edwards, "Wales and Mercia," p. 101, and Keynes, "King Alfred and the Mercians," pp. 19–20.

But other battles were fought on the Conwy, including, in the early period, in 954, the battle of Conwy Hirfawr at the place called *Gwrgystu* (the element in Llan-rwst), between the sons of Idwal and the sons of Hywel in which Anarawd ap Gwri was slain. Other attacks on sites on the Conwy include the Saxon destruction of Degannwy in 823 and later incidents there (see *Legendary Poems*, ed. Haycock, pp. 283–85).

*gwynyeith*. MS: *creith gwynyeith*; delete hypermetrical *creith*, wrongly added under the influence of *crei* in line 7 and the ending of *gwynyeith*.

13 *teir diwedyd kat*. MS: *tri diwedyd kat*. Since *kat* in both meanings "battle" and "army" is a feminine noun, *tri diwedyd* would have to be understood separately, as adverbial, "at/over [?a period of] three dusks." It is more likely that *tri* [three] (masculine) is a mistake for *teir* [three] (feminine), arising from anticipating *tri phriawt gwlat*; this provides a more natural diction in the pre-caesura section, as well as correspondence with the preceding line.

17 *eil o Ynt. Gynt* ( < Latin *gentes*) [tribe, people] is used most often of the nations harrying the Welsh, especially Vikings and Danes, but also the English and the Normans.

19–20 *Kynan . . . Katwaladyr*. The two heroes who will lead the Welsh to victory, mentioned together several times in *Armes Prydein Vawr* (Item 1, above) and other prophecies, and once in court poetry (Meilyr Brydydd, et al., poem 6.21– 22, before 1160). Because both names were in common use, their identity is not entirely certain: Cynan has been equated with Cynan son of Eudaf (Geoffrey of Monmouth's Conanus Meriadocus, founder of Brittany (see *Trioedd*, ed. Bromwich, pp. 320–21), and Cadwaladr with the son of the famous Cadwallon, ruler of Gwynedd who was slain by the Angles at the battle of Hefenfelth in 634. The *Annales Cambriae* record Cadwaladr's death in the plague of 682; the *Historia Brittonum*, ch. 64, however, puts it before 671 (see *Trioedd*, ed. Bromwich, pp. 298–99).

25–26 *durawt / o lin Anarawt*. *Durawt* (adjective) used nominally here for "a harsh or cruel man." Rhymed, as here, with *Anarawt* by Meilyr Brydydd (early twelfth century) (Meilyr Brydydd, et al., poem 3.23–24). Anarawd ( < Latin *honoratus*), was a son of Rhodri Mawr of Gwynedd, and is likely with his brothers to have been victorious against the Mercians at the Battle of Conwy in 881 (see note to line 8). Subsequently he formed alliances in turn with the Scandinavian kingdom of York, and with Alfred of Wessex. In 895 his attacks on Ceredigion and Ystrad Tywi were aided by the English, not necessarily the West Saxons, however. During the second half of Anarawd's reign, Gwynedd suffered a series of Viking incursions — in 892 from the direction of Ireland, and in 894 from the Wirral. It was probably Anarawd who was instrumental in defeating the Viking lord Ingimundr (who had arrived in Anglesey in 903), and causing him to move east to Chester. Anarawd was remembered in poetry as victor at the battle of Conwy, as a skilful soldier (*Blodeugerdd Barddas*, ed. Haycock, 31.19, and Meilyr Brydydd, et al., poem 3.23–24], and, in a poem in praise of Rhys ap Gruffudd (d. 1197), as an illustrious forebear: "Gweleis-y hael o hil Anarawd, / A'e gweles, gwelei ryuetawd" [I saw a generous one of Anarawd's line; whoever saw him could see a wonder] (Cynddelw, poem 9.33).

Anarawd died in 916 and was succeeded by his son, Idwal Foel [the Bald]; other sons were Elise and perhaps Meurig. On his death in 942, Idwal Foel's sons, Iago and Ieuaf, were expelled from Gwynedd by Hywel Dda of Deheubarth in south Wales, but from 950–55, they retaliated against Hywel's sons. Rivalry between the brothers led to Ieuaf being imprisoned (and possibly hanged) by Iago in 969. Ieuaf's son, Hywel, continued the struggle against his uncle, wresting intermittent rule of at least parts of the kingdom during the 970s. A period of instability ensued between Hywel's death in 985 and 999 when his son, Cynan, came to power.

The phrase *o lin*, like the synonymous *o hil* (both common, especially in the court poetry), is most frequently used in conjunction with a figure from the fairly distant past, although some examples are used to refer to the issue of a father or grandfather. The identity of the "harsh man" from the line of Anarawt can only be guessed at: he is perhaps most likely to have been one of the direct line outlined above.

27 *ohonaw y tyfhawt*. *Ohonaw*, either "from him," or "because of him." *Tyfu* [to grow, sprout; to (cause to) grow, increase; to heal, make, become better, etc.], future 3sg (although note Evans, *Grammar*, p. 119, for the comment that a few forms in *-(h)awt* appear to be passive). The most straightforward interpretation here is "from him [i.e., the 'harsh man'] will stem" — followed by mention of another person, a man who "spares neither kin nor cousin nor brother" (lines 29–30). But not wholly impossible is "because of him will grow/increase" or (if passive), "by his agency will be increased."

28 *coch*. An adjective meaning "red, scarlet," most frequently used in poetry in the sense of "blood-stained," qualifying words for weapons, sullied waters, bodies, etc., and sometimes collocated with *kat* [battle]. It is also used of people to mean "red-haired" (and possibly "florid of face"), as seen in cognomina (Iorwerth Goch ap Maredudd, Iolo Goch, etc.). Another meaning, although somewhat uncommon, is "redness, red color": this is adopted by Downham, *Viking Kings*, p. 214n92, who translates *coch kat* as "the redness of battle (i.e., bloodshed)." *Coch* is understood here as "the red or blood-stained one" most natural with line 29; "bloody" (qualifying *kat* [battle]) with poetic inversion is not impossible.

*kattybrunawc*. MS: *kattybrudawt* (?recte *kat dybrudawt*). Although the *Book of Taliesin* scribe regularly uses *-tt-* to indicate provection of [d] before [h] — e.g., *Armes Prydein*, line 68, *attor* ( < *ad* + *hor*), and *Book of Taliesin* 24.5, *attebwys* ( < *ad* + *hebwys*), and 66.13, *brattau* ( < *brad* + *hau*) — it is unlikely that *hy-* is present here (in the medieval language, adjectives in *hy-* are compounded with nouns or verbal stems). The combination of *-d* and *d-* is more likely, paralleled before a consonant in *Book of Taliesin* 69.5, *attrefna* (but compare the spelling in *Book of Taliesin* 73.10, *atrefnwy*), and compare the *Red Book* spellings, *kattarw* [bull of battle] (*cad-darw* < *tarw*), *lletty* (*lled-dy* < *ty*), etc.

In poetry especially, feminine nouns, such as *kat* [battle; army, throng], very often cause lenition to a following proper genitive noun (compare *stauell Gyndylan* [Cynddylan's hall]; *bydin Ododin* [Gododdin's warband], *hudlath Vathonwy* [Mathonwy's magic staff], etc.), in which case a name beginning with *Ty* or *Tybr-* might be sought; this would also be the case if *kat* is used as an intensifying (and leniting) element (see *Geiriadur Prifysgol Cymru*, s.v. *caterwen*, and later attested *catperth*).

A place-name **Tybrudawt* is most unlikely because of the unsuitability of the *prud* (Modern Welsh *prudd*) element, the lack of early evidence for *brut* (Modern Welsh *brud*), and for a word **brud* (Modern Welsh **brudd*). A radical emendation to **Tybrunawc* (on which see further below) would, however, yield a plausible formation. The Anglo-Saxon personal name *Brūn* (or ON *Brūnn*) could be the base of a regional name "the territory of Brun" since the Welsh suffix *-iawc* (Modern Welsh *-iog*) is well-attested with personal names (Rhufoniog [the land of Rhufawn], Anhuniog, Peuliniog, and others, discussed by Richards, "Early Welsh Territorial Suffixes," p. 208). *The Book of Taliesin* is notoriously yod-shy so the lack of the semivowel -*y*- here is not an obstacle. The preceding *Ty* [house] would refer to a settlement in the region, possibly a caput (very roughly approximating to the *burh* of *Brunanburh*), or a religious settlement (comparing *Tyddewi*; *esgobty*).

The emendation of the ending from -*awt* to -*awc* is not problematic: the letter forms *c* and *t* are easily confused, and the generic rhyme that would be produced is paralleled in the poem, between lines 1 and 2. Given the poem's dominant rhyme in -*awt*, the emendation has the *lectio difficilior* principle in its favor. It is more difficult to account for the copying of -*rud* instead of the suggested -*run* since the two letters *d* and *n* are not confused (similarly with *t*, used in some orthographies for [ð], and *n*). One answer is that the scribe balked at writing a segment -*brun*- which for him had no meaning, being unparalleled in the Welsh language; he substituted -*brud*- presumably because *prud* (see below) was the only word known to him in *pru*- (or *bru*-). This implies he had no exact knowledge of the name. On the other hand, his writing of *kattybrudawt* as one word suggests that he was aware of a battle-name which had become merged into one phrase, or at least that he was prepared to follow his exemplar in treating it as such, but it may be worth mentioning the (albeit fifteenth-century) degradation of *Cad Gamlan* [the Battle of Camlan] into a common noun *cadgamlan* [mixed multitude, rabble, confused mob]. Is it possible that the Welsh name for the decisive encounter at Brunanburh became virtually a term for a major battle, and for the fourteenth-century *Book of Taliesin* scribe (if not the *Red Book* and *Hendregadredd* copyists), one which was open to corruption because its origin was not known to him?

The whole interpretation outlined above (with emendation to *kattybrunawc*) has in its favor, as Lloyd-Jones obviously thought, the alignment with *Red Book*'s *kattybrunawc* and *Hendregadredd*'s *cad dybrunawc* addressed elsewhere in this volume (see pp. 264–65); furthermore, it respects the copyist's compound format. It also has the attraction that a reference to Brunanburh (especially if the site is to be equated with Bomborough on the Wirral) sits well with the figures and north Wales battles of the late ninth and early tenth centuries (Conwy, Anarawd). The main problem, as explained above, is accounting for -*brud*- rather than -*brun*-.

We may now turn to another possibility. The -*tt*- could conceivably be the product of *kat* + *dy*- with the unusual merging into one word coming about through scribal error, possibly under the influence of the battle-name already discussed. The only contender here would be the verbal form *dybrud(h)awt*, 3sg future of *prudhau* [to make/grow wise; to sadden, grieve], a verb first attested in the fourteenth century (*Geiriadur Prifysgol Cymru*), although the adjective *prud* [wise, prudent, earnest, etc.] is commonly used in court poetry (the meaning "sad, sorrowful" becoming more evident from the fourteenth century onwards). If the latter meaning was already in existence, then "who will cause grief." If the primary meaning, then "who will bring sense/wisdom" or "who will become wise/grow in wisdom." Somewhat problematic is the lack of evidence for the suggested compound verb **dybrudhau*, but compare other hapax verbs in *dy*-

such as *dysaethu* (*Legendary Poems*, ed. Haycock, poem 23.14). It may be noted that the verbal form is favored since there is no evidence for an abstract noun formed from *prud* (i.e., Modern Welsh **prudd-dod*, MW **pruddawt*). The verb *brudyaw* [to prophesy] ( < *brud/brut* [chronicle; prophecy], fourteenth century onwards < French *brut* < *Brutus*) is attested first in the sixteenth century, according to *Geiriadur Prifysgol Cymru*, and is unlikely to be relevant, especially since no **dybrudyaw* is attested. This second interpretation has the advantage of needing less editorial intervention than the first, and of providing an equally convincing lead-in to lines 29–30. It has against it the compound format, and a lack of comparanda for the suggested verbal form, neither of which are insuperable objections, however.

A third possibility with minimal emendation of *-u-* to *-y-* would provide a formation from the productive adjective *dybryt* [deformed, ugly; hideous, terrible, etc.], positing **dybrydawt* alongside the known abstract nouns *dybrydrwyd*, *dybrydwch*. This would give "a florid one of grievous battle."

On balance, the first interpretation — the Battle of Brunanburh (more exactly "the battle for/at the settlement in Brun's territory") — is perhaps the most persuasive. But as stressed in the discussion on page 263, the uncertain dating of the poem means that it is not necessarily an early reference to the battle; and if the comments on the scribal treatment of the phrase are correct, then the *Book of Taliesin* scribe at least was somewhat in the dark about its origin.

29 *nyt arbet na nawt*. The verb *arbet* becomes more frequent in the court poetry. But compare especially *Armes Prydein*, "nyt arbettwy car corff y gilyd" [relatives shall not spare each other's bodies] (Item 1.116) for the verb and the sentiment. *Nawt* (perhaps from Latin *natio*, see *Geiriadur Prifysgol Cymru*) is most naturally interpreted as an example of the word meaning "kin, relation" rather than "nature, quality, trait, etc." (in which cases it may derive from or be influenced by *gnawt*).

## 6. *ANNALES CAMBRIAE*

Ed. Paul Cavill. Trans. Scott Thompson Smith.

*Manuscript*: London, British Library, MS Harley 3859, fol. 193r.

The only manuscript of this text to make mention of the Battle of Brunanburh is a composite containing the *Historia Brittonum* and other texts. The manuscript is Welsh, s. $x^2$, 265 x 155 mm. For a recent edition and discussion, see *Annales Cambriae*, ed. Dumville.

The Brunanburh entry is on fol. 193r, which is divided into three irregular columns.

1 *CCCCXCIV*. The date 937 and annal number are deduced: four lines further up the middle column is "Annus CCCC.XC." For the chronicle's dating system, see Dumville, *Annales Cambriae*, pp. xii–xiv. Dumville notes, "For anyone not used to Insular Celtic chronicles, the absence of an A.D. dating system will no doubt

seem odd. *Annales Cambriae* before 1097 lacks reference to any absolute, externally defined, chronology. The system found in [the present text] is simply to number the years sequentially, this being marked by decimal counting, a practice probably ultimately derived from the chronicle of Eusebius-Jerome via that of Prosper of Aquitaine, both of whom gave a number every ten years" (*Annales Cambriae*, p. xiii). The *Annales* begin at *annus* 238, which is 682 CE; thus *annus* ccccxciv [494] is 937 CE.

## 7. ÆTHELWEARD, *CHRONICON*

Ed. Paul Cavill. Trans. Scott Thompson Smith.

*Manuscript*: London, British Library, MS Cotton Otho A.x.

The original, London, British Library, MS Cotton Otho A.x (Gneuss 349), was almost completely destroyed in the 1731 Cottonian Library fire. All modern editions and translations, including Campbell's, are therefore dependent on Savile's publication of the manuscript in 1596. The following excerpt reproduces Savile's text; none of the surviving fragments of the original manuscript relate to this passage.

1 *stefos*. A grecism; such conspicuously learned words — often culled from glossaries — are typical of the hermeneutic style. For further discussion of the issue, see Lapidge, "Hermeneutic Style."

3 *post annos tredecim*. 939 for 937.

5 *barbarae passim turbae*. Æthelweard here uses apposition rather than the genitive to define or limit a group. He uses both methods in the *Chronicon*. Under 871, for example, he writes both *barbarorum exercitus* [an army of barbarians] and *paganum exercitum* [a pagan army].

5–6 The detail that Athelstan drove his enemies from the shores of the sea underscores the unlikelihood of a non-coastal location for the Battle of Brunanburh.

7–8 *nec usque . . . classicus*. This phrase has a particularly strained word order. Note, for example, the distance between the past participle *motus* and the noun which it modifies, *classicus*. Furthermore, the adjective *istas* (accusative plural feminine) does not agree with its noun, *littora* (accusative plural neuter). Campbell suggests that Æthelweard may have been thinking of *oras* (accusative plural feminine) but mistakenly supplied *littora* (Æthelweard, *Chronicle*, p. li n3).

## 8. WULFSTAN OF WINCHESTER, *VITA S. ETHELWOLDI*

Adapted by Paul Cavill, from Wulfstan, *Life*, ed. Lapidge and Winterbottom, p. 16. Trans. Scott Thompson Smith.

The text of Wulfstan's *Life* is edited from five witnesses, none earlier than the twelfth century, by Lapidge and Winterbottom. The present extract is taken from chapter 10.

2 *maxima strage*. Eadmer and William of Malmesbury both use similar language to describe the battle's casualties: *strages grauissima . . . et erumnosa* (*Vita Odonis*, Item 11.9) and *uulgus reliquum, miseranda strage peremptum* (*GR*, Item 17me30).

## 9. ÆLFRIC OF EYNSHAM, *EPILOGUE TO JUDGES*

Adapted by Michael Livingston, from Aelfric, *Old English Version of the Heptateuch*, ed. Crawford, pp. 416–17. Trans. Michael Livingston.

*Manuscript*: Oxford, Bodleian Library, MS Laud Misc. 509.

Ælfric of Eynsham (ca. 955–ca. 1010), who lived first at the monastery at Cerne and later at Eynsham, is known primarily for being the most prolific writer in Old English. Over his long career he wrote homilies, hagiography, biblical commentary, and scriptural translations. His *Epilogue to Judges*, a part of which is extracted here, is a part of the latter undertaking: an attempt to paraphrase the Latin Bible into Old English, which Ælfric reluctantly executed at the request of Earl Æthelweard (author of Item 7). The martial exploits of the Judges led Ælfric to observe in his epilogue that similar martial kings could be found among the English, and his brief summary of the reigns of three of them — Alfred, Athelstan, and Edgar — serves as a testament to the importance ascribed to these kings in the formative years of the English kingship.

3–4 Athelstan's reign is essentially defined by his victory at the Battle of Brunanburh, though the fight was apparently so well known in Ælfric's time that he feels no need to name it.

5–8 Ælfric skips over the reigns of Edmund, Edred, and Edwy in order to move from the glory of Athelstan to the rule of Edgar (r. 959–75). His decision to highlight Edgar in particular might be attributable to the fact that the whole of Ælfric's writing career had occurred under Edgar or one of his two sons: Edward the Martyr (r. 975–78) and Æthelred II (r. 978–1014).

**10. *ATHELSTAN'S PRAYER***

Adapted by Michael Livingston, from *Cartularium Saxonicum*, ed. Birch, no. 657, 2.332–33. Trans. Michael Livingston.

*Manuscript*: London, British Library, MS Cotton Galba A.xiv, fol. 4v.

While the text provided here survives in only a single manuscript in its Old English form, which has been dated close to the turn of the first millennium by Ker (*Catalogue of Manuscripts*, pp. 198–99), two Latin copies of it survive. The first immediately precedes the Old English version (fol. 3v):

> Domine Deus omnipotens rex regum et dominus dominantium in cujus manu omnis victoria consistit et omne bellum conteritur concede mihi ut tua manus cor meum corroboret ut in virtute tua in manibus viribusque meis bene pugnare viriliterque agere valeam ut inimici mei in conspectu meo cadent et corruant sicut corruit Golias ante faciem pueri tui David et sicut populus Pharaonis coram Moysi in mare rubro. Et sicut Philistini coram populo Israhel ceciderunt. Et Amalech coram Moysi et Chananei coram Jesu corruerunt sic cadant inimici mei sub pedibus meis et per viam unam conveniant adversum me et per septem fugiant a me et conteret Deus arma eorum et confringet framea eorum et eliquisce [Cotton Nero: liquiscent] in conspectu meo sicut cera a facie ignis ut sciant omnes populi terre quia invocatum est nomen domini nostri Jhesu [Cotton Nero: Jhesu Christi] super me et magnificetur nomen tuum domine in adversariis meis domine Deus Israhel.

The second, with only two minor differences (bracketed above), can be found in Cotton Nero A.ii, where it appears alongside *Carta dirige gressus* (Item 2, above). Birch was the first to associate this prayer with Athelstan, largely based on its association with the latter document; there is nothing in the text itself to confirm the relationship, and subsequent critics have found it unlikely (see, e.g., Lapidge, "Some Latin Poems," p. 84n111).

Whether or not the text can be positively identified with Athelstan himself, it is clear that at least one early scribe thought it a fitting association: Its concentration on martial prowess, and particularly its many direct connections to Old Testament notions of strength in battle, certainly mesh well with the kind of hagiography associated with Athelstan and his defeat of Anlaf in other sources, such as *Rex pius Athelstan* (Item 3 in this volume), Ælfric's *Epilogue to Judges* (Item 9), and the work of Eadmer (Items 11 and 14).

6 David's defeat of Goliath is told in 1 Kings [1 Samuel] 17.

7–8 Moses' defeat of Pharaoh at the Red Sea is told in Exodus 14.

8 Israel's defeat of the Philistines could refer to any number of battles told in the Bible. See, e.g., 1 Kings [1 Samuel] 7:3–14, 14, or 17 (the last being David's defeat of the Philistine Goliath; see line 6, above). The term "Philistine" subsequently became a stand-in for "unbeliever," thus making them a particularly fitting reference given the early religious associations given to Athelstan's struggle against Anlaf.

8–9 Moses' defeat of the Amalekites is recounted in various places in the Bible, but the tale undoubtedly in mind here is Exodus 17:8–16, in which the power of God stands against Israel's enemies whenever Moses raises his hands. With the help of Aaron and Hur, Moses holds his hands up for the length of the day, at which point Amalek is defeated. Oda, in Eadmer of Canterbury's account of Brunanburh, similarly promises that the sun will not set until Athelstan has victory upon the field (Item 11.23–24).

9 Joshua's defeat of the Canaanites is a lengthy campaign in the Bible, but the particular battle intended here is likely Joshua 10:5–28, where Israel fights against the five Canaanite kings of the Amorites. In the climactic battle God lengthens the day at Joshua's bidding in order to give the Israelites time to rout their enemies, a parallel to Moses' defeat of the Amekites (see note above). It is the aftermath of this same event that the anonymous poet of *Rex pius Athelstan* references in associating Athelstan and Joshua (see the note to Item 3.5–6).

10–11 The hope that "Athelstan's" enemies will fall to his feet, and that they will come against him by one path and flee from him by seven, is rooted in God's promise to the Israelites: "dabit Dominus inimicos tuos qui consurgunt adversum te corruentes in conspectu tuo per unam viam venient contra te et per septem fugient a facie tua" [The Lord shall cause thy enemies, that rise up against thee, to fall down before thy face: one way shall they come out against thee, and seven ways shall they flee before thee] (Deuteronomy 28:7).

11–12 Compare Vulgate Psalm 75:4, where it is said that God resides in Israel: "ibi confringet volatilia arcus scutum et gladium et bellum semper" [There hath he broken the powers of bows, the shield, the sword, and the battle].

12–13 Compare Vulgate Psalm 67:2–3: "exsurgat Deus et dissipentur inimici eius et fugiant qui oderunt eum a facie eius sicut deficit fumus deficiant sicut tabescit cera a facie ignis pereant impii a facie Dei" [Let God arise, and let his enemies be scattered: and let them that hate him flee from before his face. As smoke vanisheth, so let them vanish away: as wax melteth before the fire, so let the wicked perish at the presence of God].

## 11. Eadmer of Canterbury, *Vita Odonis*

Ed. Paul Cavill. Trans. Scott Thompson Smith.

*Manuscript*: Cambridge, Corpus Christi College, MS 371, fol. 46r (p. 91).

This manuscript, written before 1116, is probably Eadmer's autograph. A full account of the manuscripts is given in their edition by Turner and Muir.

The manuscript is 225 x 155 mm, written in single columns. Titles and decoration are in blue or green, incipits and explicits in red. New paragraphs begin with a capital in the margin. The *Vita Odonis* passage begins halfway down p. 91 (also numbered fol. 46r).

3 *paganorum*. Eadmer explicitly frames the battle as a conflict between pagans and Christians. The pagans seek to impose their *profanas leges* over the *sacratissimas leges Christianorum* held by the English. Patrizia Lendinara claims an "insistence on the opposition of Christian and pagans" at Brunanburh as common to "all the Latin chronicles" ("Brunanburh," p. 211), but this point is overstated. Of the texts surveyed in this study several do specify that Anlaf and/or the invaders are pagan: Wulfstan of Winchester, *Vita S. Æthelwoldi*; Eadmer of Canterbury, *Vita Odonis* and *Vita Oswaldi*; John of Worcester (as well as those texts that derive from John, such as the *Historia regum*, Roger of Wendover, et al.); and Pseudo-Ingulf, *Chronicle of Crowland*. Many other texts, however, simply indicate geographic origin (Henry of Huntingdon, *Eulogium Historiarum*) or designate the invaders only as "barbarians" (Æthelweard's *Chronicle*, the *Chronicle of Ramsey*, William of Malmesbury). Pseudo-Ingulf's *Chronicle of Crowland* calls the invaders both "pagans" and "barbarians." It should also be noted that while Anlaf was heathen, Constantine II was a Christian king who retired to a monastery upon leaving office in 943. See Smyth, *Warlords*, pp. 189 and 207–10.

5 *Christianorum*. Here and elsewhere, the scribe uses the *xp* abbreviation for *Christ-*.

10 *exposuit*. Page 92 begins after *exposuit*.

23–24 Compare to Joshua 10:12–14, in which Joshua petitions God to stop the movement of the sun until the Israelites have defeated the Amorites:

> tunc locutus est Iosue Domino in die qua tradidit Amorreum in conspectu filiorum Israhel dixitque coram eis sol contra Gabaon ne movearis et luna contra vallem Ahialon steteruntque sol et luna donec ulcisceretur se gens de inimicis suis nonne scriptum est hoc in libro Iustorum stetit itaque sol in medio caeli et non festinavit occumbere spatio unius diei non fuit ante et postea tam longa dies oboediente Domino voci hominis et pugnante pro Israhel.
>
> [Then Josue spoke to the Lord, in the day that he delivered the Amorrhite in the sight of the children of Israel, and he said before them: Move not, O sun, toward Gabaon, nor thou, O moon, toward the valley of Ajalon. And the sun and the moon stood still, till the people revenged themselves of their enemies. Is not this written in the book of the just? So the sun stood still in the midst of heaven, and hasted not to go down the space of one day. There was not before nor after so long a day, the Lord obeying the voice of a man, and fighting for Israel.]

26 Rhetorical repetition of *aut* in this sentence shows polysyndeton, or the repetition of conjunctions.

27–28 The passive voice here underscores divine agency in the English victory. *Victoria* comes to Athelstan through the intervention of God's servant (*uerbum famuli Dei*).

28–30 Rhetorical repetitions of *quid* (with attendant genitives) and *per* (with accusative objects).

32–33 *praeclarus Isrelita*. Byrhtferth's *Vita S Oswaldi*, one of Eadmer's main sources for the *Vita Odonis*, at one point describes Oswald as "egregius Israhelita" (*Lives*, ed. Lapidge, p. 40). Byrhtferth recounts three of Oda's miracles, but none of them involve his presence at Brunanburh. For Eadmer's use of Byrhtferth, see Eadmer, *Lives and Miracles*, ed. Turner and Muir, pp. xxxvi–xli; and Byrhtferth, *Lives*, ed. Lapidge, pp. lxxviii–lxxx.

## 12. *ANGLO-SAXON CHRONICLE* [VERSION F]

Ed. and trans. Michael Livingston.

*Manuscript*: London, British Libary, MS Cotton Domitian A.viii, fol. 58r.

This copy of the *ASC* was written around the year 1100 at Christ Church, Canterbury, and it is thus often termed simply the Canterbury Version. Like a string of other documents produced there at the time, it was written both in Old English and in Latin (for more on which see Smith's essay in this volume, p. 273n26). The annal dating of 938 is in error, just as it was in the original text of *ASC* A before it was corrected to 937. On the source of this error, which appears to be rooted in Winchester, see the collaborative edition by Bately, pp. xcviii–ix.

2 *Criste*. MS: *Xpe*, which is often understood to be the Greek "chi-rho," to which the Old English ending *-e* has been added.

3, 6 *.viii*. The majority of accounts, including all other versions of the *ASC* that include the detail, give the number of dead earls as seven (see Item 4a.30–31). The difference here is almost assuredly scribal error.

5 *comites*. MS: *comite*.

## 13. SYMEON OF DURHAM, *LIBELLUS DE EXORDIO*

Ed. Paul Cavill. Trans. Scott Thompson Smith.

*Manuscript*: London, British Library, MS Cotton Faustina A.v, fol. 61v.

Carrying the full title *Libellus de exordio atque procursu istius hoc est Dunhelmensis ecclesie*, this text is here edited from a compendium of various texts from different periods. The manuscript is 242 x 180 mm, written in a large hand of s. xii$^{2}$, thought by Rollason (Symeon of Durham, *Libellus de exordio*, pp. xxii–xxiii) to be that of a Durham scribe. Rollason's is the standard discussion and edition of the *Libellus de exordio* and uses an earlier version of the text, Durham, University Library, MS Cosin V.II.6; significant variations from this text and edition (Rollason 2.18) are noted below.

1 *dcccc*$^{mo.}$ *xxxvii*$^{mo.}$. I.e., *nongentesimo tricesimo septimo*.

3 *Onlaf*. *Libellus de exordio* and *Historia regum* in its passage beginning at fol. 75v share this spelling variation on *Anlaf*. The *Historia regum* passage beginning at fol. 84v (taken from the Worcester chronicle) has *Anlaf*.

*dc. et. xv. nauibus*. The detail that 615 ships took part in the invasion, which subsequently appears in a number of sources, first appears here.

4 *habens auxilia*. Rollason: *habens contra Aethelstanum auxilia*.

*regum Cumbrorum*. Owain, king of Strathclyde, c. 925–37 (Symeon of Durham, *Libellus de exordio*, ed. Rollason, p. 138n104).

*Scottorum scilicet*. Rollason: *scilicet Scottorum*.

5 The *A* is a large capital placed in the left margin.

6 *et gloriosum inde*. Rollason: *suisque gloriosum*.

## 14. EADMER OF CANTERBURY, *VITA OSWALDI*

Ed. Paul Cavill. Trans. Scott Thompson Smith.

*Manuscript*: Cambridge, Corpus Christi College, MS 371, fol. 108r (p. 215).

For more information, see notes to Item 11, above. The *Vita Oswaldi* passage begins two-thirds of the page down on p. 215 (also fol. 108r).

4 *immenso paganorum exercitui*. Eadmer again calls attention to the fact that the invaders are pagans. The word order here also shows an envelope pattern in which a noun is separated from its adjective by an intervening word (compare to *immensus exercitus paganorum* in *Vita Odonis*, line 3). In this revision of his earlier account of Brunanburh, Eadmer generally uses more hyperbaton, or the arrangement of words in an uncommon or arresting order.

9 *iuxta*. Page 216 begins after *iuxta*.

13–14 This sentence compresses the action into a fast series of short phrases. Such a narrative quickening is all the more effective after the dramatic pause established by the two rhetorical questions in lines 10 and 11.

17 *solis continget occubitus*. This phrase employs another envelope pattern in which a noun is separated by a modifying word (in this case an attendant genitive). Compare to *continget solis occubitus* in *Vita Odonis*, line 23.

18 *fuga inuoluat aut interitus*. Eadmer reuses this phrase verbatim from his *Vita Odonis*, line 24.

18–19 Eadmer here sharpens the focus on Athlestan and Oda by stating that the king alone was "thunderstruck" (*attonitus*) by Oda's words. In *Vita Odonis*, *everyone* (*quique audientium*) is shaken (*attoniti*) by his words and the sight of the restored sword. Eadmer uses the same adjective in both texts to describe the reaction to the miracle.

19–20 Three adjectives follow and modify the noun *gladium*. The phrase shows homoeoteleuton, or the occurrence of similar or identical endings in adjacent words (*gladium* and *fulgidum*, *fortem* and *insignem*).

20 Three nominative present participles follow their object *occursantes* in another example of homoeoteleuton.

21 *iuxta*. A post-position preposition preceded by its object (*uerbum serui Dei*). Compare to *Vita Odonis*, line 29 (*iuxta uerbum famuli Dei factum est*).

## 15. *ANGLO-SAXON CHRONICLE* [VERSION E]

Ed. and trans. Michael Livingston.

*Manuscript*: Oxford, Bodleian Library, MS Laud Misc. 636, fol. 35v.

This late text of the *ASC* was written at Peterborough, perhaps to replace a copy lost when the monastery burned in 1116. It is for this reason that it is often termed the Peterborough Version. The entries up to the year 1121 were all written at the same time, in the same scribal hand. It has been speculated that the exemplar used in that initial copying passed into the hands of Geoffrey Gaimar, who utilized it his *Estoire* (Item 19; see Short, "Gaimar's Epilogue," p. 331).

## 16. JOHN OF WORCESTER, *CHRONICON*

Ed. Paul Cavill. Trans. Scott Thompson Smith.

*Manuscript*: London, Lambeth Palace, MS 42, fol. 119v.

The manuscript was copied (s. xii$^{2}$) at Abingdon, possibly via Evesham, Almonry Museum MS (of which only a single leaf remains), but ultimately from Oxford, Corpus Christi College, MS 157, which was plausibly corrected and added to by John himself. As the version closest to John, this latter manuscript is the basis of the standard edition by Darlington and McGurk. For a full discussion of the manuscripts and the composition of the *Chronicon*, see Darlington and McGurk, 2.xxii–lxxxi. The Lambeth Palace manuscript is 370 x 260 mm, and is written in two columns, the text beginning on the last line of col. 1.

1 *937*. MS: *DCCCCXXXVII*. Rubricated, with *VII* above the *XXX* in the number.

*socero*. That Constantine was Anlaf's father-in-law is a detail original to John's account. While absent from the historical record, such a marriage might well be understandable; Smyth opines that it "is very unlikely to have been invented" by the writer, and that it makes a great deal of sense since, whatever pact Anlaf and

Constantine had reached in their agreement to fight Athelstan together, it might well have been "cemented" by the younger Anlaf marrying into Constantine's family (*Scandinavian York and Dublin* 2.79). It is also possible that the Anlaf mentioned here is Anlaf Sihtricson, though this is arguably less likely.

2 *Humbre fluminis*. John's account is the first to specify the invasion as occurring from the Humber, which has led to a great deal of confusion in our attempts to identify the location of the battle. For more on the issue, see Cavill's essay in this volume, especially pp. 337–39.

3 *clito*. For this term, equivalent to OE *æþeling*, see Dumville, "Ætheling," pp. 7–12.

3–4 *cui . . . occurrerunt*. The language in this phrase resembles that found in a statement in William of Malmesbury's *GR*: *cui tandem magnis artibus ducum, magnis uiribus militum apud Bruneford occursum* (lines 4–5).

4 *exercitu*. MS: *exercito*.

5 *v. regulos viique duces*. Consensus: *quinque regulos septemque duces*.

8–9 Even though John dramatically condenses *Battle of Brunanburh* as a whole, he does maintain its contrast between the victorious homecoming of the West Saxons and downcast retreat of the invaders (compare Item 4a.53–59).

## 17. WILLIAM OF MALMESBURY, *GESTA REGUM ANGLORUM*

Ed. Paul Cavill. Trans. Scott Thompson Smith.

*Manuscript*: London, British Library, MS Arundel 35, fols. 45r–45v (prose), 47v–48r (poem).

For a brief discussion of the textual tradition and manuscript families, see the standard edition of Mynors, Thomson, and Winterbottom, 1.xiii–xxvi. Significant variants from this edition are noted below.

The present manuscript, composed in Winchester (s. xii$^{2/4}$), is 300 x 200 mm, with paragraph capitals in green; there are no chapter numbers or titles, but a later hand inserts the names of kings in the lower margin. The manuscript is written in two columns, and the excerpt begins at fol. 45r, col. 1. In Mynors, Thomson, and Winterbottom the account is Book 2.131.4, and the verse is Book 2.135.6; the verse is written in a smaller script, with rubricated capitals at the beginning of each line.

*Prose*

1 William's first account of Brunanburh does not provide a date for the battle.

*Sihtrici filio*. William here apparently confuses Anlaf Guthfrithson, the Norse leader at Brunanburh, with his cousin Anlaf Sihtricson. See Campbell, *Battle of Brunanburh*, pp. 44–52, and the Introduction to this volume, p. 12n36, above.

*euadandi*. Consensus: *inuadendi*.

4 *iuuenis audacissimus*. I.e., Anlaf.

4–5 *cui . . . occursum*. *Occursum* (a nominative singular neuter past participle of *occurrere*) here functions as an impersonal verb in the passive with an understood *est*. *Occurrere* takes a dative object (in this case *cui*, referring back to Anlaf, the *iuuenis audacissimus*).

5 *Bruneford*. Consensus: *Brunefeld*.

8 *pro foribus*. MS: *proforibus*.

*dulci resonantia fila tumultu*. An example of chiasmus, or an "envelope" structure of ABBA (in this case: ablative adjective, accusative adjective, accusative noun, ablative noun).

11 *delitiis*. I.e., *deliciis*.

13 *accepit*. Column 2 begins after *acce-*.

14–15 *Adelstanus* is added above *ipse*.

15 *pre oculis*. MS: *preoculis*.

17 *uidisses*. MS: *uidisset*.

19 *insultantem*. William applies the same adjective to Anlaf in line 3.

19–20 The recommendation of a short delay in order to allow time for the arrival of reinforcements resembles the series of delaying tactics employed by the English at the battle of Vinheath in *Egil's Saga* (Item 25.40).

20 *Dicto probato, discessum est illinc*. The compressed syntax speeds the narrative.

21 *adueniens*. Not in manuscript.

22 *tabernaculum*. This word choice for "tent" (common in the Old Testament Vulgate) carries obvious religious connotations. This connotation compounds the villainy of Anlaf as he violates a holy site in his act of murder.

27 *sancto Aldelmo*. That Athelstan called specifically on Saint Aldhelm (d. 709) in the midst of his fight is a detail original to William's account. Aldhelm was abbot of Malmesbury, and his body was entombed there. Given his importance to the abbey both spiritually and — given pilgrim veneration of his tomb after his burial — monetarily, the inclusion is hardly surprising.

29 Fol. 45v, column 1 begins after *sane*.

*uel*. Consensus: *aut*.

30 *usque ad*. MS: *ad usque*.

32 *perfide animositatis et uiuacis senecte homo*. Genitives of quality (Classical Latin *-ae* commonly appears as *-e* in medieval orthography). The statement that Constantine died in the battle suggests that William did not use as a source the Old English poem, which prominently includes Constantine among the shamed survivors who flee England.

32–33 William numbers the slain *comites* (equivalent to OE *eorlas*) at twelve. The poem in the *ASC*, however, numbers the slain *eorlas* at seven (Item 4a.30–31), a figure repeated by both Henry of Huntingdon and John of Worcester. Several later sources, including the *Polychronicon* and Book of Hyde, repeat William's apparent error. Lendinara has suggested that the incongruity may be "owing to a misreading of vii or its alteration to xii" ("Battle of Brunanburh," p. 211).

33 *omnisque barbarorum*. Consensus: *omnisque pene barbarorum*.

*euaserant*. MS: *euaserat*.

*Poem* The verse included here by William is written in a combination of *caudati* (in which the words at the end of successive lines rhyme) and *leonini* (in which the word before the caesura rhymes with the word at the end of the line) hexameters. Lapidge had argued that the poem's diction, meter, and rhyme display none of the distinctive qualities common to the hermeneutic style popular in England during the tenth century, but rather show qualities indicative of composition in the late eleventh or early twelfth century ("Some Latin Poems," pp. 64–69). See also William, *GR*, ed. Mynors, Thomson, and Winterbottom, 2.116–18.

1 Since Athelstan was consecrated in 925, this line would accurately date the battle to 937.

1–3 Bisyllabic tail-rhyme on *-annos* (*caudati* rhyme) across three consecutive lines.

2–3 Anaphora on *iure*.

3 Supplied from the edition of Mynors, Thomson, and Winterbottom. The manuscript is garbled and reads:

> Transierat ~~regens~~ ciues — subigens uirtute tyrannos
> Iure regens ciues — subigens uirtute tyrannos
> Cum redit [etc.],

thus omitting line 3, *iure fideque regens hinc Anglos inde Britannos*.

4–6 These lines change from *caudati* to *leonine* rhymes (*cum redit illa lues*, || *Europę noxia labes*).

5–6 Anaphora on *iam*.

5 *in terris*. MS: *interris*.

8 *Bacchanti*. MS: *Bachanti*.

10–11 Bisyllabic tail-rhyme on *-erbis*.

11 *cedunt* and *cedit*. An example of polyptoton, or the repetition of the same word in different morphological forms.

12 *fidens alacrisque iuuenta*. The feminine noun *iuuenta* here could be in either the nominative or ablative case. If nominative, the phrase would indicate that Athelstan was a "bold and spirited" youth at the time of the battle; if ablative, the noun would express *time when* and the phrase would thus mean "bold and spirited in his youth." Since William has earlier stated that Athelstan was thirty

years old at the time of his succession (*GR* 2.133), the king would have been forty-two years old at the time of Brunanburh (clearly no longer a youth). Consequently, the ablative makes better sense in the larger context of the work.

12–13 Bisyllabic tail-rhyme on *-enta*.

15 Chiasmus in *miseros iniectis ignibus agros*.

16 Chiasmus in *totis uiridantia gramina campis*.

17–19 Tail-rhyme on *-um* with bisyllabic tail-rhyme in lines 18 and 19 (*-antum*). The three lines include a notable cluster of five genitive plural nouns and adjectives.

18 *barbara uis*. Compare to *barbaries* in line 5 and *barbaricae securi* in line 22.

19 *quadrupedantum*. The poet uses a five-syllable word to complete the last two feet of a hexameter (Lapidge, "Some Latin Poems," pp. 65–66). Compare *agricolarum* in line 17.

20 *Exsciuit*. I.e., *exciuit*.

21 *ne se*. MS: *Nese*.

22 The line shows hyperbaton (note the separation of *sua* from *arma* and of *barbaricae* from *securi*).

23 Chiasmus in *uictrices ducentia signa cohortes*.

23–26 Sound-play on initial *u* and initial and internal *c*.

24 *in uentum*. MS: *inuentum*.

25 Fol. 48r begins after *quina*.

25–26 Extended tail-rhyme on *milia quina* and *preuia signa*. Furthermore, Lapidge points out that *quina* would have rhymed with *signa* for an Old French speaker, thus creating bisyllabic tail-rhyme ("Some Latin Poems," p. 69).

27–29 Bisyllabic tail-rhyme on *-ones*.

28 *fama*. Not in manuscript; a ?later hand has made an illegible insertion above the line.

29 Alliteration on a chiastic pattern in *posita preda proprias peterent*.

29–33 The content of these lines — the fleeing invaders and the carcasses left behind — recalls lines 53–56 and 60–65 from *Battle of Brunanburh* (Item 4a). The phrase *depositum mortis*, or "the deposit of death," applied to Anlaf, is specifically reminiscent of OE *daroða laf* (line 54a), or "what is left by spears."

I have translated both *depositum* and *munus* as appositive objects (both accusative singular) of transitive *fugit* (*fugere*). That is, Anlaf fled both the dead bodies (*depositum mortis*) and death itself (*fortunae nobilae munus*) in order to save his own life. For the sense of *munus* as "last rites" or "burial" see Virgil, *Aeneid*, 11.26. Mynors, Thomson, and Winterbottom, however, translate *depositum* and *munus* as nominatives in apposition with *Analafus* (*GR* 1.223). Thomson and

Winterbottom explain, "The sense seems to be that Death allowed Anlaf to remain on earth as a special favour" (*GR* 2.126).

30 Chiasmus in *reliquum, miseranda strage peremptum*.

31 Chiasmus in *bibulas tetris nidoribus auras*.

32–34 Tail-rhyme on *-us* with bisyllabic tail-rhyme in lines 32 and 33 (*-unus*). Compare to lines 1–3, 17–19, and 27–29. Lines 32–34 also show significant alliteration on *m*.

34 *post ETHELSTANUM*. Anlaf again invaded England, this time far more successfully, after the death of Athelstan during the reign of his brother, Edmund.

## 18. HENRY OF HUNTINGDON, *HISTORIA ANGLORUM*

Ed. Paul Cavill. Trans. Scott Thompson Smith.

*Manuscript*: National Library of Scotland, Advocates' MS 33.5.4, fols. 58v–59v.

This manuscript, written in England (s. xii[med]), is the only witness to the earliest version, 1, of the text of *Historia Anglorum*, ending at the year 1129. The continuation (from fol. 88v) takes the history to 1138 and represents version 3 of that part of the text. For a full discussion of the versions and manuscripts of the text of the *Historia*, see Henry, ed. Greenway, pp. lxvi–clx. The present MS is 215 x 145mm, written in a neat upright hand without rubrics.

The standard modern edition of the *Historia Anglorum* naturally aims to "reconstruct the author's final text" (ed. Greenway, p. clxii), and is a composite, taking as its exemplar for the section of the text with which we are concerned a representative of version 3 which ends at the year 1138. This text is London, British Library, MS Egerton 3668 (s. xii[med]). The manuscript used by Arnold, London, British Library, MS Arundel 48 (s. xiii[1]), is a "corrupt and contaminated manuscript of version 5 of the text" (ed. Greenway, p. clxi), and is idiosyncratic, not least in the spelling of the place-name *Brunanburh* as *Brunesburith* (see further Cavill's essay in this volume, p. 349).

The value of the version edited here is that it demonstrates the considerable continuity between early and late versions of the text. The variants are essentially scribal and circumstantial: significant departures from the consensus text, as edited by Greenway, are indicated in the notes.

4 *lacessitus*. An echo of Henry's previous statement that Athelstan had been *a fortissimis lacessiri* (lines 2–3) during his reign.

4–5 *bello lacessitus bello reppulit*. Repetition of *bello*, in each case an ablative of respect preceding the word which it modifies.

The phrase *reppulit, repulsum fugauit, fugatum* shows polyptoton. Also noteworthy is the parallel syntax in *repulsum fugauit, fugatum perdidit* (twin phrases in which an accusative singular past participle is followed by a third-person singular perfect verb in the indicative).

5–6 *aduersa perculsus fortuna*. Envelope pattern in which a noun (*fortuna*) is separated from its adjective (*aduersa*) by an intermediate word (*perculsus*).

6 *fratrem suum Edwinum*. Athelstan's brother Edwin drowned at sea in 933 (*ASC* E). William of Malmesbury reports the story that Athelstan exiled Edwin because of accusations that he had conspired against him. Edwin was set adrift in a boat without oars; overcome by despair, he threw himself into the sea and drowned. Athelstan later undertook a seven-year penance and mourned his brother's loss after he learned that the accusations against Edwin were false. William, however, notably doubts the story's veracity (*GR* 2.139–40). See also Stenton, *Anglo-Saxon England*, pp. 355–56.

7–8 *perfidam Dacorum, et infidam Scotorum*. Repetition on *-fidam*, in both cases followed by a genitive plural.

10 *ubicumque*. Consensus: *ubique*.

11 *cum triumphali rediit lauro*. An instance of hyperbaton in which the envelope pattern of *triumphali rediit lauro* embeds the finite verb within a prepositional phrase.

12 *anno gratie dccccxlv, regni uero sui anno quarto*. The dating here is doubly inaccurate, first providing the year of grace at 945 and then 928/29 as the regnal year.

13 *prelium*. I.e., *praelium*, with the common medieval spelling of *e* for Classical Latin *ae*.

14 MS: fol. 59r begins after *Dacorum*.

*adauxerat*. MS: *ad auxerat*.

15 *scriptores*. MS: *sciptores*.

17–18 Polyptoton in *grauitate uerborum grauitatem actuum*.

19 For Henry's translation of the Old English poem with specific attention to stress patterns, alliteration, and rhyme, see Rigg, "Henry of Huntingdon's Metrical Experiments." The translation offered here approximates the line breaks proposed by Rigg. For Henry's translation of Old English poetic compounds, see also Cavill, "*Eorodcistum*," pp. 7–9.

*decus decum*. Shows the alliterative stress pattern of a Type A verse in Old English poetry (lift, drop, lift, drop).

*nobilibus torquium dator*. An envelope pattern; compare OE *beorna beahgifa* (Item 4a.2)

19 *frater*. MS: "Corrected" in the margin in a sixteenth-century hand to *filius*.

20 *longa stirpis serie*. An envelope pattern; compare OE *ealdorlangne* (Item 4a.3), a hapax legomenon.

*splendens*. Consensus: *splendentes*.

21 Henry mistranslates OE *hamora lafan* (Item 4a.6) [remnants of hammers] as *domestice reliquie* [household survivors or family descendants], misconstruing *hamora* as "homes." Rigg presents *domestice reliquie defuncti Edwardi* as a separate line of verse in which the two half lines are linked by alliteration on *d*.

*defuncti Edwardi*. For OE *afaran Eadweardes* (Item 4a.7) [Edward's heirs] "Henry recognizes ME *afaren* 'to depart'" (Cavill, "*Eorodcistum*," p. 8).

22 *namque*. MS: *nanque*.

Henry translates OE *cneomægum* (Item 4a.8) [kinsmen, ancestors] as *a genibus cognationum* [at the knees of kinsmen]. Presumably unaware of *cneow*'s secondary sense in Old English as "generation" or "degree of blood-relationship or affinity" (*DOE*, s.v. *cneow* 2 and 2a), Henry understandably uses the more common meaning current in his lifetime.

22–23 Half-lines doubly linked by rhyme in *ut bellis frequentibus ab infestis nationibus*.

23 Linking alliteration in *defenderent patrie thesauros et domos, pecunias et exenia* (Rigg, "Henry of Huntingdon's Metrical Experiments," p. 67).

*patrie thesauros et domos*. Compare OE *land, hord,* and *hamas* (Item 4a.9 and 10).

24 Half-lines linked by rhyme in *fatales corruerunt, colles resonuerunt* (Rigg, "Henry of Huntingdon's Metrical Experiments," p. 68).

*colles resonuerunt*. Compare OE *feld dunnade* (Item 4a.12). The difficult Old English verb *dennian* is of uncertain meaning with its sole appearance in the *ASC* poem (see *DOE*, s.v. *dennian*; and Campbell, *Battle of Brunanburh*, pp. 98–102). Henry clearly understood the verb to be a form of *dynian* [to resound].

25 *sudauerunt armati*. Compare OE *secga swate* (Item 4a.13).

Chiastic sound-play in *prodiit, micans ilariter, letificans profunda* (with a possible linking repetition of *l* and *f*).

*ilariter*. Henry mistranslates OE *glad* (Item 4a.15, from the strong verb *glidan* [to glide]) as the adverb *hilariter* [gladly] (Cavill, "*Eorodcistum*," p. 8).

26 *occasu se occuluit*. Compare OE *sah to setle* (Item 4a.17).

27 *sub scutis*. MS: *subscutis*.

Half-lines doubly linked by rhyme in *telis perforati, sub scutis lanceati* (Rigg, "Henry of Huntingdon's Metrical Experiments," p. 68).

28 Alliteration and rhyme link half-lines in *prius electi, post indefessi*.

*prius electi*. Compare OE *eorodcistum* (Item 4a.21). The noun *eorodcyst* [band of chosen men] (*DOE*, s.v. *eorodcyst*), appears only four times in the Old English poetic corpus, always in the dative plural. Henry's translation approximates the sense of the compound but renders it in the nominative in apposition to *Wesseaxe forð* (Item 4a.20). See Cavill, "*Eorodcistum*," pp. 8–9.

28–29 *inuise gentis*. Compare OE *laþum þeodum* (Item 4a.22). An example of Henry's "nearly word for word" rendering of a half-line from the *ASC* poem.

29 Following Rigg's line divisions, anaphora in *uiri elegantes hastas cedebant, / uiri Mercenses acuta iacula*.

*acuta iacula*. Compare OE *mecum mylenscearpan* (Item 4a.24). Henry seems to have had difficulties with both *mece* [sword], and *mylenscearp*, a hapax legomenon meaning "sharpened on a grindstone" (see Campbell, *Battle of Brunanburh*, pp. 105–06). Henry later translates *mecga gemanan* (Item 4a.40) as *Martis congressu* (line 36), further indicating that he was uncertain about the meaning of OE *mece*.

30 Alliteration and rhyme link half-lines in *mittebant duro manus ludo*.

*duro manus ludo*. An envelope pattern; compare OE *heardes hondplegan* (Item 4a.25), another example of an accurate "word-for-word" rendering of an Old English half-line.

*sanitas . . . nulla*. Henry here mistranslates OE *hæleþa nanum* (Item 4a.25) [to none of the warriors], mistaking the noun *hæleþ* for "health" (ME *hælþ*).

*Anlauo*. MS: *Alano*.

32 *.vii. septem* in several manuscripts.

33 *Normannorum*. While Henry calls the invaders Danes (*Daci*) or Scots (*Scoti*) prior to his translation of the *ASC* poem, he renders OE *Norðmanna* and *Norþmen* (Item 4a.33 and 53) as *Normanni*, the same word he will later use for the Normans (beginning in Book VI). Prior to the Brunanburh episode, Henry primarily names Scandinavian invaders as *Daci*, *pagani*, or simply *exercitus* (following the *ASC*'s use of OE *here*).

35 *Froda, ductor Normannus*. Henry misconstrues OE *se froda* (Item 4a.37), modifying *Costontinus* (Item 4a.38), as a separate proper name. He apparently adds *ductor Normannus* to specify the identity of this "Froda."

36–37 Following Rigg's line divisions, anaphora in *ubi cognationis sue fragmen apparuit, / ubi amici sui corruerant*.

37 Alliteration links half-lines in *in statione populi bello prostrati*.

*in statione populi*. Compare OE *on folcstede* (Item 4a.41).

38 *in loco prelii*. Compare OE *on wælstowe* (Item 4a.43).

*Gude Dacus*. Henry misconstrues the dative singular noun *guðe* (Item 4a.44) as a proper name.

39 Rhyme doubly links half-lines in *licet uerbis blandus, et mente uetustus*.

*mente uetustus*. Compare OE *eald inwidda* (Item 4a.46).

*reliquiis suis*. Compare OE *herelafum* (Item 4a.47). Henry gives an accurate enough translation, but in this case he compresses an Old English compound into a single Latin word (in contrast, for example, with his more usual practice as represented in lines 37 and 38 above).

40 *hoc negotium*. Compare OE *beaduweorca* (Item 4a.48). As with *reliquiis suis* above, Henry here translates a Old English poetic compound with a single Latin word. *Beaduweorc* occurs only three times in the Old English corpus (and always in verse). Henry must have been uncertain of the word's specific sense and opted for a general approximation.

*in campo belli*. Compare OE *on campstede* (Item 4a.49).

40–41 Rhyme doubly links half-lines in *ictu<u>um</u> inmanitat<u>e</u>, telor<u>um</u> transforation<u>e</u>*.

Henry renders OE *cumbolgehnastes* (Item 4a.49), a hapax legomenon meaning "clash of banners," as *ictuum inmanitate*. This seems to be another case of Henry rendering an uncertain poetic compound in more general terms appropriate to context.

41 MS: fol. 59v begins after *transforatione*.

*nurus*. MS: *nurdus* with *d* underdotted for deletion.

41–42 *Matres uero et nurus planxerunt suos*. This seems to be Henry's addition.

42 Following Rigg's line divisions, anaphora in <u>*cum*</u> *Edwardi filiis lusisse, /* <u>*cum*</u> *Normanni nauibus clauatis*.

Chiastic alliteration in ***c**um **N**ormanni **n**auibus **c**lauatis*.

*nauibus clauatis*. Compare OE *nægledcnearrum* (Item 4a.53). Whereas Henry earlier omits *cread cnear* (Item 4a.35) from his translation, here he accurately renders the rare noun *cnear*: the word appears only three times, twice in the *ASC* poem and once as a gloss for *nauis acturia* (*DOE*). See also Campbell, *Battle of Brunanburh*, pp. 108–09 and 114.

42–43 Henry omits all the place-names in the *ASC* poem in these lines: *Dingesmere* (Item 4a.54), *Difelin* (Item 4a.55), and *Iraland* (Item 4a.56). It is possible that in desperation he reconstructs *Anlaf* from the OE *dreorig darað<u>a laf</u>* (Item 4a.54), supplying what he might have supposed was a missing macron over the genitive plural *-a* and *laf*, thus *daroð anlaf*.

43 Rhyme within half-lines in *terr<u>as</u> su<u>as</u> mest<u>o</u> anim<u>o</u>*.

*mesto animo*. Compare OE *æwiscmode* (Item 4a.56). Henry here accurately renders an Old English compound which occurs only four times in the corpus. The adjective *mesto* [mournful] has the medieval spelling of *e* for Classical Latin *ae*.

44 *Postea frater uterque rediit Westsexe*. Henry here notably compresses Item 4a.57–59.

44–45 *belli reliquias post se deserentes, carnes uirorum in escam paratas*. Henry notably expands Item 4.60: *Letan him behindan hraw bryttigean*. He has perhaps erroneously construed OE *wiges hremige* (Item 4a.59) as *belli reliquias*.

45 Alliteration and rhyme link half-lines in ***E**rgo **c**oru<u>us</u> niger **o**re **c**ornut<u>us</u>*.

Henry translates OE *hasewanpadan* (Item 4a.62), a hapax legomenon, as *buffo liuens*, construing *pade* as "toad," a meaning well attested in both Old and Middle English (*MED*, s.v. *pade*; compare OE *pād* [covering, coat]). See also Cavill, "*Eorodcistum*," p. 8.

46 Chiastic alliteration and rhyme link half-lines in *canis lupusque mixtus colore*.

47 Henry omits entirely Item 4a.68–69 (*þæs þe us secgað bec, / ealde uðwitan*).

48 *trans mare latum*. Compare OE *ofer brad brimu* (Item 4a.71). A close "word-for-word" translation.

*clari Martis fabri*. Compare OE *wlance wigsmiþas* (Item 4a.72). Henry's rendering of *wlanc* as *clarus* (meaning "renowned" or "illustrious" rather than the Old English sense of "bold" or "proud") accurately represents the word's sense in Middle English. In addition to the traditional sense of "haughty, arrogant; high-spirited, bold" (*MED*, s.v. *wlonk* 2), the word increasingly came to signify a general notion of excellence: "Of a person: distinguished by birth or character, noble; also, physically beautiful, fair or handsome; also, as a noun: a person of noble character" (*MED*, s.v. *wlonk* 1).

48–49 Rhyme across half-lines in *Saxones et Angli, Britones pulsuri, clari Martis fabri Walenses*.

49 Homoeoteleuton, rhyme, and alliteration in *Walenses uicerunt, reges fugauerunt, regna susceperunt*.

Henry replaces OE *eorlas arhwate* (Item 4a.73) with *reges fugauerunt*. Henry may have been unsure of the meaning of *arhwate*, another hapax legomenon, and consequently substituted a phrase which heightened the alliteration and rhyme in his final lines.

53 *Brunebirig*. Consensus: *Bruneberi*.

## 19. GEOFFREY GAIMAR, *ESTOIRE DES ENGLEIS*

Adapted by Michael Livingston, from Gaimar, *Estorie*, ed. Hardy and Martin, 1.147–148, 2.113. Trans. Michael Livingston.

*Manuscripts*: **D**: Durham Cathedral, MS C.iv.27; **H**: London, Herald's College, MS Arundel XIV; **L**: Lincoln Cathedral, MS A 4/12; **R**: London, British Library, MS Royal 13 A.xxi, fols. 133r–33v [base text].

About Geoffrey Gaimar, whose *Estoire des Engleis* is perhaps the oldest surviving history in French, little is known beyond his sole extant work. In Dalton's concise summary, Gaimar "was possibly a secular clerk acquainted with life in court circles, who may have begun writing in Hampshire and finished in Lincolnshire, and who wrote for Constance, wife of Ralf of Fitz Gilbert" ("Date," p. 23). His *Estoire* is largely a translation of the *ASC* up to the year 959, using a now-lost copy that might well have been the archetype from which Version

E derives (Short, "Gaimar's Epilogue," p. 331; see Item 15 in this volume), and it holds a significant place in the movement of these historical accounts into the hands of first the Anglo-Norman chroniclers writing in the wake of William the Conqueror and second the later Middle English chroniclers.

Short argued that the *Estoire* was written between the years 1136 and 1137 ("Gaimar's Epilogue," pp. 336–40), but Dalton has more recently argued that this specificity is impossible to maintain. He tentatively suggests that the narrowest range of dates possible for the text's composition is instead 1141–50 ("Date," p. 38).

3515 *Adelstan*. So R, H. D, L: *Edelstan*.

3516 *tresk'el*. So R, L. D: *tresqual*; H: *el*.

3517 *Daneis*. Athelstan's battle with the Danes was in 927.

3518 *Gudfrid*. So R, H. D: *Gaufrit*; L: *Guafrit*.

3519 *asembla*. So R, D, L. H: *semblad*.

*mult*. So R, D, L. H omits.

3519–20 *empire . . . navire*. So R, H. D, L transpose. Regardless of the order of presentation, it is interesting that Gaimar takes care to note that Athelstan's northern campaign in 933 had both land and sea components, a detail that can be traced back to the *ASC*.

3521 *Dreit en Escoce*. So R, H. D: *A dreit Escoce*; L: *a Escoce dreit*.

3522 *preia*. So R, D, L. H: *proia*.

3523 *un an*. By misstating that only one year passed between the events, Gaimar (or his source) creates a direct relationship between Athelstan's raid on Scotland in 933 and the battle at Brunanburh in 937. Gaimar's relative dating between Brunanburh and Athelstan's death — three years, since the king dies on 27 October 940 — is correct.

*mains*. So R. D: *meis*; H, L: *meins*.

3524 *Bruneswerce*. So R. D, L: *Burneweste*; H: *Brunewerthe*.

3525 *les Escoz*. So R, D, L. H: *Escoteis*.

*Combreis*. So R, H. D, L: *les Cumbreis*.

3526 *Gawaleis*. So R. D: *Galwains*; H: *Galewarz*; L: *Galwaneis*. There is no evidence that the Welsh were present at Brunanburh. It appears, rather, that Gaimar has collapsed Athelstan's success against the Welsh into the Great Battle. As with Athelstan's campaign against Scotland, the events of the English king's reign are combined into the momentous event of the battle.

*Picteis*. So R. D, H, L: *Pecteis*.

3527 *en*. So R, D, L. H omits.

*furent*. So R, D, L. H: *erent*.

*tant*. So R, D. H: *tanz*; L: *tant tant*.

3528 *crei*. So R, D, L. H: *Jeo croi*.

*parlé*. So R, H. D, L: *parole*.

*en*. So R, H, D. L omits.

3529 *il*. So R, L. D, H omit.

3530 *ne*[1]. So R, L. D, H omit.

*altres*. So R. D: *autre*; H: *autres*; L: *altre*.

3531 *donc*. So R, D, L. H omits.

3532 *Eadmund*. So R. H: *Eadmon*; D, L: *Edmund*.

## 20. Symeon of Durham, *Historia regum*

Ed. Paul Cavill. Trans. Scott Thompson Smith.

*Manuscript*: Cambridge, Corpus Christi College, MS 139, fols. 75v and 84v.

The unique manuscript (s. xii[2]), a collection of mostly historical works relating to the north of England, was edited by Arnold in 1885 for the Rolls Series and variants from this edition are noted below.

The manuscript is 300 x 215 mm, written in two columns with wide margins, with predominantly red and green rubricated paragraph capitals. The first passage, a summary, begins at fol. 75v, in the middle of the first column. The second passage, taken by Symeon almost verbatim from John of Worcester's *Chronicon*, begins at the middle of column 1 of fol. 84v. The vellum of this page is rather poor quality.

1–2 *regemque Onlafum cum dc. et xv. nauibus*. In agreement with Item 13, above.

4 *dccccxxxvi*[i]. MS: The last *i* is superscript, probably added after the passage was first written to correct the date.

5 *ostium*. MS: *hostium*.

7 *Brunanburh*. Unusually, the place-name begins with a capital.

7–8 *uesperum tracto*. MS: There is an erasure of some three letters after *uesperum*.

10 *infusum*. MS: The *in-* is lighter in color, possibly an incomplete erasure. Arnold (2.125) reads *fusum* (as do John of Worcester manuscripts).

## 21. *CHRONICLE OF RAMSEY*

Ed. Paul Cavill. Trans. Scott Thompson Smith.

*Manuscript*: Oxford, Bodleian Library, MS Rawlinson B. 333, fol. 2r.

Written in England (s. xiii/xiv), the manuscript is 345 x 235 mm and composite. The *Chronicon* is written throughout in two columns with rubrics and rubricated paragraph capitals. Section numbers are neatly written in the margin in a later hand. The present extract, section 7, begins on fol. 2r, col. 2.

The edition of Macray for the Rolls Series takes its text from a later manuscript (s. xiv[1]), and substantive variants from that edition are noted below.

3 *uirum sanctum*. Though unnamed here, the "holy man" in Athelstan's company in other sources is Oda. See, e.g., Item 11.

*belli*. MS: *bellum*.

4–8 *Igitur hostibus . . . importauit*. The syntax of this sentence is difficult, with two ablative absolutes (*hostibus . . . inuadentibus* and *facta . . . congressione*) followed by two *dum* clauses (meaning "while" or "when") before the subject of the sentence appears (*ensis*) with the finite verb (*importauit*) in final position. The direct object *incrementum* has two attached genitives (*audacie* and *formidinis*) in parallel phrases. The translation offered here separates the text into two sentences.

7 *audacie*. Classical Latin *ae* regularly appears as *e* in medieval orthography. See also *diuine* and *regie uictorie* in line 10.

8–9 *immissus est ensis*. Macray: *missus est*.

9–10 *et de eis inopinata celeritate triumphatum*. *Triumphatum* (from *triumphare*) functions as an impersonal verb with an understood *est*. Literally, "and there was triumph over them with surprising swiftness."

11 MS: fol. 2v, col. 1 begins after *uictorie*.

*thesauris*. MS: *tesauris*.

## 22. *CHRONICLE OF MELROSE*

Adapted by Ulrike Hogg, from *Chronicle of Melrose*, ed. Broun and Harrison. Trans. Ulrike Hogg.

*Manuscript*: British Library, MS Cotton Faustina B. IX, fol. 7v.

Written in the Cistercian Abbey of Melrose in the Scottish Borders, this work was first begun in 1173–74. In the annalistic style typical of Cistercian historiography, it gives a retrospective account of history up to this point, starting with the birth of Christ, and was then sporadically updated until the late thirteenth century. It is a valuable contemporary source for Scottish history of that period; for earlier events such as the Battle of Brunanburh, which were far beyond living memory, the writers naturally relied on, and adapted, earlier records.

## 23. GWYNFARDD BRYCHEINIOG, *CANU Y DEWI*

Ed. and trans. John K. Bollard.

*Manuscripts*: **H**: National Library of Wales MS 6680B (*The Hendregadredd Manuscript*), fol. 79v [base text]; **R**: Jesus College, Oxford, MS 111 (*The Red Book of Hergest*), col. 1187.

For more information on this item, see pp. 264–65.

53 *Deu ychen Dewi*. Oxen as both animals and metaphor appear several times in Rhygyfarch's eleventh-century *Life of St. David* (e.g., chapters 12 and 35 ["Rhygyfarch's 'Life' of St. David," ed. Sharpe and Davies, pp. 118–19, 130–33]), though not in reference to the bell of Glascwm.

*ardderchawc*. A rare early instance of *dd* = [ð]. R: *arderchawc*.

54 *gar*. H, R: *garu*. For sound metrical reasons, Owen emends to *gar*, from *car* (Modern Welsh *câr*) [dear one, companion], but notes that the verbnoun *caru* may be used adjectivally to mean "dear" and that adjectives can be used as nouns (Gwynfardd Brycheiniog, "Gwaith," ed. Owen, p. 466). In his diplomatic typescript, Evans prints *garn* (*Poetry in the Red Book*, ed. Evans, col. 1187.20). This reading has been accepted by *Geiriadur Prifysgol Cymru* (s.v. *carn* [hoof]) and others, and interpreted as a synecdoche *pars pro toto*: "Two oxen . . . two hooved [ones] who would go yoked together." However, examination of the manuscript reveals that the correct reading is *garu*, for the final letter is open-topped. On the same manuscript page, *n* is closed at the top 146 times and partially open only once; *u* is open 70 times and only partly turned toward closed in three instances. For additional analysis of this scribe's differentiation between *u* and *n*, see Bollard, "Gliui / Glini."

*gydpreinyawc*. R: *gyt breinawc*.

56 *y Lasgwm*. H: ~~*y lassann*~~ *y las- / gwm*.

*Lasgwm*. < Glasgwm, now Glascwm, a village in Powys (formerly Radnorshire). The present St. David's Church was built in the thirteenth century, on the site of an earlier enclosure. Glascwm was one of twelve monasteries founded by St. David (see J. James, *Rhigyfarch's Life of St. David*, ch. 13, pp. 8, 33).

*urtassawc* [dignified, noble]. R: *urdassawt*. The adjective is here used nominally, "noble ones." The oxen deliver three fine gifts, though here we only learn what one of them is — Dewi's bell, *Bangu*.

57 *Edewid*. H: ~~*Edewiti*~~ *Edewid*.

*Bangu*. The name of St. David's bell. Gerald of Wales writes of it in his *Journey Through Wales*: "In the church at Glascwm, in Elfael, there is a handbell which has most miraculous powers. It is supposed to have belonged to Saint David and it is called a 'bangu'. In an attempt to liberate him, a certain woman took this handbell to her husband, who was chained up in the castle of Rhaiadr Gwy, in Gwrthrynion, which castle Rhys ap Gruffydd had built in our time. The keepers of the castle not only refused to set the man free, but they even seized the bell. That same night God took vengeance on them, for the whole town was burned down, except the wall on which the handbell hung" (trans. Thorpe, p. 79).

*gadwynawc*. R: *garwynnawc*.

58 *Urycheinyawc*. R: *urecheinawc*.

59 *arnam ny ry bytwn*. R: *arnam ni ry bydwn*. At twelve syllables rather than the usual nine, the line is too long and perhaps corrupt. Owen suggests the line is best understood if we interpret the verb *bytwn* as consuetudinal (habitual) 1 pl. and *ny* (R: *ni*) not as a negative particle, but as the 1 pl. affixed pronoun reinforcing *arnam*, which is the 1 pl. form of the preposition *ar* [on], and then deleting the syntactically unnecessary *arnam-ny*, yielding a nine-syllable line with the sense "When need comes, we shall be fearful" (see Gwynfardd Brycheiniog, "Gwaith," p. 466). The implication of the following lines is that such fears will be assuaged with the help of God and St. David.

*ofnawc*. R: *ofynawc*.

60 *gormes*. Meaning "oppression by an alien race or conqueror, tyranny, violence, . . . intrusion, attack, invasion" (*Geiriadur Prifysgol Cymru*, s.v. *gormes*).

*kedeirn*. R: *ketyrn*; orthographic variants of the plural of *cadarn* [strong], used nominally [strong ones, mighty ones]. Compare *Ynys y Kedeirn* [The Island of the Mighty], used throughout the Second Branch of *The Mabinogi* as a name for Britain.

*Cad Dybrunawc*. H: *cad / dybrunawc*; R: *ketyrn cattybrunawc*. Possibly a reference to the Battle of Brunanburh, and perhaps related to the reading *kattybrudawt* in *Glaswawt Taliessin* (see Item 5.28). It is generally accepted that the first element is *cad* [battle]. If we accept the reading of H, we may have /-d/ + /ð-/, yielding in modern orthography an underlying *Cad Ddybrunawg* (Gwynfardd Brycheiniog, "Gwaith," p. 450). (As a feminine noun, *cad* causes the lenition of a following /d/ to /ð/ in a proper name.) Owen renders the phrase in Modern Welsh as *Brwydr Dybrunog* [the Battle of Dybrunog] (p. 457). However, in Welsh the combination of the sounds /d/ + /d/ becomes /t/ through the process known as provection, giving us the reading in the *Red Book*. The prefix *dy-* may be either an intensifying prefix in nouns and verbs or a negative prefix. (The latter is not likely here.) The Middle Welsh suffix *-awc*, Modern Welsh *-og*, is a common adjectival ending, as in *cadwynawc* [chained] (line 57), from *cadwyn* [chain], and *ofnawc* [fearful] (line 59), from *ofn* [fear]; it can also be a nominal agentive ending, as in *marchawc/marchog* [rider, knight], from *march* [horse]. This leaves us with *-brun-*, which, absent another suitable etymon, has tentatively been equated with the *Brun(e)* of *Annales Cambriae* (Item 6.1) and *Brut y Tywysogion* (Item 34.2). Lloyd-Jones indicates his uncertainty about the word with the query "? *a.* neu *ep.*" [? *adjective* or *personal name*] and simply draws attention to the phrase *coch kattybrudawt* in *Glaswawt Taliessin* (Lloyd-Jones, *Geirfa*, s.v. *dybrunawc*). In his entry for *cat* [battle], he again cites these forms and queries a connection with the readings in *Brut y Tywysogion* and *Annales Cambriae* (s.v. *cat*). An early alternative etymology which is no more than speculation is implied in J. Davies' *Antiquae Linguae* of 1632, which glosses *Dybrunawg & Dybrynawg* as "meritorious," perhaps assuming *prynu* [to buy, redeem] as the underlying root. Though unsubstantiated from elsewhere, this would give us a sense of something like "before the oppression of the mighty ones of meritorious battle"; such a reading would itself require further explanation and identification.

Why there should be a reference to the Battle of Brunanburh in a twelfth-century Welsh poem to St. David remains a mystery. Even if the battle had become in Wales a standard of comparison for a terrible conflict (and there is no clear evidence for this), its appearance in the present poem is striking, especially in that it would seem to be doing little more than providing specificity to an otherwise general statement about God and the saint.

62 *yd alwnn*. H, R: *yd gallwnn*. First person pl. of *galw* [to call], not *gallu* [to be able]. In MW *-ll-* occurs occasionally for [l].

*vodawc*. R: *uodawt. AmeN*. In spite of the *Amen* in R, this is only the end of the *awdl* or stanza, not of the poem.

## 24. ROGER OF HOWDEN, *CHRONICLE*

*Manuscript*: London, British Library, MS Royal 14.C.2.

This manuscript is edited by William Stubbs in the Rolls Series. Roger quotes John of Worcester verbatim, adding only *regem quoque Cumbrorum* [as well as the king of the Cumbrians] to the account of those who fled to the ships from the battle.

## 25. *EGIL'S SAGA*

Adapted by A. Keith Kelly, from *Egils saga*, ed. Nordal. Trans. A. Keith Kelly.

*Egils saga Skalla-Grímssonar* is one of the best-known, and widely considered best-written, sagas in the in Old Norse corpus. The tale spans some 150 years from the unification of Norway under the tyrannical Harald Fair-hair to the conversion of Iceland to Christianity around the year 1000. The first one-third of the narrative follows the lives of the grandfather and father of the titular character, Egil, while the remainder focuses on the life of Egil himself. Egil is a rough, unsightly and violent Viking-poet whose wit, dark moods and unyielding principles embroil him in a number of events significant to both Iceland and

England. Four middle chapters of the saga provide a detailed account of the "Battle of Vin-heath," which is the Battle of Brunanburh. *Egil's Saga* was composed in Iceland in the second quarter of the thirteenth century and attributed by most scholars to the great Icelandic historian Snorri Sturluson, who was himself a descendent of Egil. The text survives in a number of manuscripts and fragments dating from the mid-thirteenth century onward.

The Old Norse text presented in this volume is based upon the 1933 edition by Sigurður Nordal. The chapter headings and paragraph breaks, which are not in the Nordal text, are used to benefit the reader of the translated text and follow the patterns in Sveinbjorn Thordarson's electronic edition. Where Nordal had a penchant for using semi-colons, full stops have been employed in accordance with modern English writing conventions.

1 *Óláfr Skotakonungr*. Anlaf as the king of Scotland is first introduced in the previous chapter of *Egil's Saga*, where he is described as "Óláfr the Red," the son of a Scottish father and a Danish mother, with descent from Ragnar Lodbrok. The saga-writer thus appears to mistakenly combine the historical identities of Anlaf (king of the Dublin Hiberno-Norse who indeed had Ragnar among his ancestors) and Constantine (king of Scotland). Smyth has attempted to gloss over this discrepancy by observing that Anlaf's claim upon York, in addition to his presumed rule over Hiberno-Norse colonies in the Scottish isle, put him "a short step" from being called king of the Scots (*Scandinavian York and Dublin* 2.77–78). He likewise places much weight on the authority of John of Worcester's claims that Anlaf was Constantine's son-in-law, and his description of Anlaf as "king of the Irish and of many other islands" (Item 16).

*Egil's Saga* presents the campaign described in this and the subsequent chapters as following close upon Athelstan's coronation and before the death of Harald Fair-hair of Norway, a date range (925–934) that hardly matches Brunanburh (937). The identification with Brunanburh has nevertheless been widely accepted for a variety of reasons: sagas are notoriously loose regarding timelines, and there is simply no other historical moment outside the Brunanburh campaign that remotely matches the stakes and the events described in the saga.

4–5 *Goðrekr jarl . . . Álfgeirr*. Godric and Alfgar are the two earls of Northumbria under King Athelstan. They are unmentioned in the other sources for the battle.

6 *Fekk Álfgeirr þá enga viðstǫðu*. There is an oddity in the Old Norse text here, as it literally reads, "Got Alfgar then no resistance." Because Alfgar is in the nominative form the text indicates that he is the one who did not receive resistance, when in fact he is the one who offered no resistance to Anlaf. Nordal notes in his edition that *Álfgeirr* should read *Óláfr*, suggesting that a scribal error has occurred (p. 130).

12–13 *lagt undir sik*. The Norse is a reflexive statement that means literally to "put under himself."

14 *Hringr . . . Aðils*. The two brothers, Hring and Adils, are most often identified as Cumbrian earls who join with Anlaf after his routing of the forces of the Northumbrian earls, Godric and Alfgar. In the decade preceding the Battle of Brunanburh Cumbria had been settled widely by Vikings, specifically those with ties to

Norway and Ireland (particularly the Hiberno-Norse in Dublin, of which Anlaf is one) so it would make sense that they would betray Athelstan and join their kinsmen. In this respect, Hring and Adils "may well derive," as Smyth points out, "from a genuine tradition which was originally aware of the role played by Strathclyde in the events of 937" (*Scandinavian York and Dublin* 2.74).

However, it is also quite possible that the Adils of *Egil's Saga* is in fact Idwal, the Welsh king of Gwynedd. Chapter 51 of *Egil's Saga* identifies Adils and Hring as two brothers from "Bretland" who were tributary kings under Athelstan:

> Fyrir Bretlandi réðu brœðr tveir, Hringr ok Aðils, ok váru skattgildir undir Aðalstein konung, ok fylgði þat, þá er þeir váru í her með konungi, at þeir ok þeira lið skyldi vera í brjósti í fylking fyrir merkjum konungs. Váru þeir brœðr inir mestu hermenn ok eigi allungir menn. (Ed. Nordal, p. 129)
>
> [Bretland was ruled by two brothers, Hring and Adils, and they were tributaries under King Athelstan. And they had the honor when they were with the king in battle, that they should be in the front lines of the array with the king's standard. These brothers were great warriors but they were not young men.]

Wales is typically referred to as "Bretland" in Old Norse sources, though that term could potentially be used to describe Cumbria as well because each is a land of the Britons. Some scholars would say that by Bretland the Norse simply mean Wales and those regions that are populated predominantly by Celtic peoples.

However, there are other reasons beyond the word *Bretland* to believe that Adils might be the Welsh king Idwal rather than a Cumbrian earl, at least within the frame of the saga. Idwal was indeed subjugated by Athelstan in 926, and he was forced to fight for the English king in Scotland. He did have a brother, though his name was not Hring, and the two of them fought against King Edmund in 942, five years after Brunanburh. Both Idwal and his brother were slain in that battle. Coincidentally, the enemy of Edmund at that time was another Anlaf/Olaf, namely Óláfr Tryggvason. As at Brunanburh, the English defeated the Viking-Celtic forces in the north. The similarity of these two battles may have caused the saga writer to conflate some of the principal figures.

It would have made logical sense for Idwal to have been at Brunanburh, though there is no evidence that the Welsh were involved at all, and Idwal clearly did not die in the battle. One might surmise, however, that since Athelstan had used the Welsh, and Idwal specifically, to fight against the Scots years before, that he would intend to use them again. They are, however, notoriously absent from the battle on the English side. Thus within the framework of the saga, it seems clear that Adils is the Welsh king, Idwal. Whether Idwal was involved in the historical Battle of Brunanburh, however, is another question.

26 *Þórólf . . . Egil.* Thorolf and Egil, the titular character in the saga, are both sons of Skalla-Grímr, a successful farmer and Viking who had fled Norway to settle in Iceland during the reign of King Harald Fair-hair. Thorolf is the older of the two brothers.

31–38 Examples of such skaldic poetry are found throughout *Egil's Saga*, as the titular character is considered to be quite a *skáld*, the Old Norse word for "poet." Skaldic poetry, particularly in *Egil's Saga*, is often occasional in nature and speaks directly to the events or persons in the saga narrative. The eight-line construction is the most common form for skaldic verse and is the form employed by Egil. The meter, and particularly the syntax, of skaldic verse can be quite complex as it is often an opportunity for the poet to demonstrate wit and subtlety. Fittingly, Egil's skaldic utterances are often rather scathing or even belligerent in tone, though they are also quite complex and exhibit the wit and intelligence of their author.

40 *hasla . . . vǫll*. The Old Norse here simply means to mark out a ground with hazel wands. I have elaborated slightly upon this in translation for the sake of the reader by providing an explanation that this indicates that a battle will be fought in this designated area. This process of "hazelling" a field for a pitched battle seems to be related to the marking of ground for single combat. According to this custom, which is called *holmganga*, literally an "island-going," two men fight a duel on an island or islet. On the island, or perhaps when no island was nearby, the space for the combat was marked out with a large cloak or piece of cloth, the corners being staked down with hazel wands. The two combatants fought according to prescribed rules within this "hazelled" area. This marking out of official ground with hazel rods was also used at times for designating spaces for important gatherings. In *Egil's Saga* the concept of the designated space for single combat is expanded significantly to mark out an entire battlefield. By using this terminology the saga writer likens this battle to a duel, emphasizing not only the winner-take-all importance of the clash, but the fact that it was Athelstan versus Anlaf. For more information on single combat and the *holmganga*, see Ashdown, "Single Combat."

*Vínheiði við Vínuskóga*. The exact locations for Vínheiði and Vínuskóga have not been satisfactorily determined, though there can be no doubt that the Battle of Vínheiði and the Battle of Brunanburh are one and the same. *Heiði* is simply a heath or field, and *skógr* is forest. The first element in the words, *Vín* or *Vínu*, could be connected to the river that runs through the geography in the saga, as some have suggested. For a consideration of these names in the effort to determine the location of the battle, see Paul Cavill's essay in this volume, p. 336.

67–71 I have elected to preserve the present tense form of Athelstan's message to Anlaf. For more information on tense shifts in Old Norse saga, see note to 92 below.

72–73 The Old Norse here reads simply "ok ætlaði at at ríða" [and intended to ride out]. The assumption is that Anlaf intended to ride out with his army into battle. Thus the ruse that Athelstan's messengers employ effectively delays his attack, which was eminent.

92 The Old Norse text here reads *biðja*, which is "ask" in the present tense, making a literal translation"the messengers ask for a respite of three days." This shift in tense from the preterit to the present is quite common in saga literature,

particularly when referring to speech, even indirectly. As a side note, it is also relatively common for oral story transmission in Modern English. For the purposes of this translation, however, such instances of tense shift will be regularized to follow modern English conventions, and the preterit tense will be used. The exception to this rule will be when the text provides the words recorded directly as the speaker had given them; see note to lines 67–71, above.

108–09 The details here would suggest that the two towns, one to the north of the heath and the other to the south, are approximately half a night's ride from each other. Details of this nature, that suggest locations and distance, have often been used in an effort to locate the Battle of Brunanburh, but their reliability is questionable for a variety of reasons. For further discussion of this see Cavill's essay in this volume and McDougall, "Discretion and Deceit."

114 The saga writer at this point specifies that there is a fortress south of the battlefield. As I read it, this is quite a bit south of the site (confirmed by the beginning of chapter 54 and its implication that Athelstan decides to make a second camp closer to the battlefield); indeed, it would seem that it is around eight hours on horseback. Bromborough to Chester is roughly thirteen miles as the crow flies, suggesting that the fortified town could be Chester. If we read the saga as an accurate source for geographical information this gives weight to the Bromborough theory for the battle site.

122 Interestingly, the word at this point in the text is *ódjarfari*, which, by adding the prefix *ó-* [un-] to *djarfr* [bold], literally translates to "unbold." This is not an uncommon way of forming antonyms in Old Norse and creates a sense of understatement or even humor for the reader of saga literature in English. This is not unlike similar features found in Old English poetry.

131 The text here names only the men under Thorolf's command, but most understand this to mean the forces being commanded by Thorolf and Egil jointly. Given the description of the armaments of both men that immediately follows, as well as the fact that the standard that they raise is said to be theirs (plural), this is a safe and likely accurate assumption.

142 The word *norrœnir* is used here and literally means Norse, or Norwegian. However, another manuscript reads *útlendir* which would mean, much more broadly, outlander or foreigner. This variance points to the multinational nature of the forces in play in this battle and also suggests the presence of mercenaries from numerous foreign lands. This multinationalism, on both sides of the battlefield, is common for this period in history, and while the Battle of Brunanburh may well be a battle that kept England "English" it was by no means simply the English versus "foreign" invaders.

157 The precise location of *Jarlsnes* [lit. Earlsnes; Earl's Promontory] is not known, though it is named in *Orkneyinga Saga* (ch. 72), as well, and there undoubtedly means a location in or very near Wales that is raided from the Isle of Man. Moffat thus suggested the location *Tir Iarll* [Earl's Land, near modern Monknash] on the Bristol Channel, largely due to place-name familiarity and its proximity to the Isle of Lundy, which may be the fortified "Lund" to which the

raiders in *Orkneyinga Saga* retreat after leaving Jarlsnes ("Norse Place-Names," pp. 101–02). The word *iarll* first appears in Welsh in the thirteenth century, however, and the name *Tir Iarll* is first attested in the *Red Book of Hergest* (1382–1410); these place-names are thus too late to be of certain use here. Tudsbery calls a location near the medieval port of Ness on the Dee coast of the Wirral "more likely" (*Brunanburh*, p. 7), and such an identification might give weight to those who place the battle in the west of England (such as Bromborough), as Alfgar would have in all likelihood chosen the most expedient route to a port from which he could sail to France. While it is tempting to see some measure of its distance from the battle site in the fact that Alfgar has to ride "day and night" to get to Jarlsnes, at best the detail can only be seen to indicate that he rode without stopping (in which case, a location closer to the battle site would be preferable to one farther away). For a separate argument in favor of Ness as a destination for elements of Anlaf's army fleeing the battle, see Harding's essay in this volume, pp. 358–62.

219 This advance against the Scottish king's *opna skjǫldu* [open shields] is a descriptive way to describe a flank assault in this context. As both armies would have employed walls of interlocking shields facing to the front, any attack on the side would be against the open side of the shield wall.

257 The exact type of poem is a *drápa*, which is a heroic poem typically praising an individual. It contains a refrain in the middle section of the poem.

259 This is probably Ælla, king of Northumbria, d. 867. Little factual information is known regarding the familial connection between Ælla and Athelstan, and there may be none since Ælla, as a Northumbrian king, likely had few ties to Athelstan, a West Saxon. Ælla figures prominently in *Ragnarssona þáttr* [*The Tale of Ragnar's Sons*], in which he executes the Viking king, Ragnar Lodbrok, by having him put into a pit of vipers. The saga writer may simply be connecting Athelstan to a prior English king who achieved a great victory over a Viking invader. Given Anlaf's descent from Ragnar, it seems an appropriate connection to make.

265–66 Old Norse skaldic poetry is notoriously difficult to translate, and even in the original language it is often cryptic or laden with multiple meanings. Old Norse kennings present a particular challenge. The last two lines of Egil's *drápa* to Athelstan are a perfect example of this. The way I have translated these two lines — "this I swear, to the breaker / of the wave of fire, king of men" — is slightly unconventional compared to what other translators have done, though in truth there is little agreement on the translation of this verse. *Hyrr*, genitive form *hyrjar*, means "fire" and is often a kenning for gold; it is thus associated with kings who give out rings and gold. Other translators have read it in this way, applying *hyrjar* to Athelstan in terms of his role as ring-giver. But some translations do not deal with the word *hrannbrjótr* at all. The word means "wave-breaker" and is in the nominative case. A "wave-breaker" would be expected as a kenning for a longship, or perhaps a Viking sea captain, and its attribution to Athelstan in that way is ambiguous. A wave-breaker, however, could also be a rock or shoreline upon which the waves break. Thus one possible interpretation is that *hyrjar* in the genitive case is meant to be connected with wave-breaker, suggesting that Athelstan is that upon which the wave of fire broke. Viewing the kenning in this way, Anlaf and the foreign invaders could be seen as the wave of fire that threatened to wash over England. Athelstan was thus the rock upon which that fiery wave broke. The fact that England is an island and the invaders came from the sea makes such a reading all the more poetic.

## 26. ROGER WENDOVER, *FLORES HISTORIARUM*

*Manuscript*: Manchester, Chetham MS 6712.

The text is edited by Henry Richards Luard in the Rolls Series (1.495–96). The account of the battle, with very minor variants, is taken from John of Worcester; the chapter title, *Ut rex Ethelstanus multos hostes prostraverit* [Where King Athelstan struck down a great enemy], is added (as it is in Matthew Paris).

## 27. MATTHEW PARIS, *CHRONICA MAJORA*

*Manuscript*: Cambridge, Corpus Christi College, MS 26, 16.

The text is edited by Henry Richards Luard in the Rolls Series (1.451). The account of the battle is taken almost verbatim from John of Worcester. The title, *Ut rex Ethelstanus multos hostes prostraverit* [Where King Athelstan struck down a great enemy], is added.

## 28. *LIVERE DE REIS DE ENGLETERRE*

Ed. and trans. Michael Livingston.

*Manuscripts*: **A**: Cambridge, Trinity College, MS R.14.7, fol. 167r [base text]; **Z**: Rome, Vatican, MS Barberini Lat. 3528, fols. 7v–8r.

There is some tradition in assigning authorship of this work to Peter of Ickham, the scant evidence of which is outlined by Glover in his early edition of the text (pp. ix–xiv). This issue, like the text itself, is too little studied. The source for its information about Athelstan and Brunanburh, at least, can be said with some confidence to be traceable to William of Malmesbury (Item 17), though as the notes below will show, some historical coherence has been lost in its line of transmission.

Both versions of the work have been separately edited, the A-text by Glover and the Z-text by Foltys. The text presented here ignores orthographical variants between the two versions.

2 *regna xvi. anz*. Though there is some uncertainty about identifying the exact beginning of Athelstan's reign, at best it lasted fifteen years and most probably

fourteen. A scribal error of minim confusion somewhere in the tradition behind both manuscripts has likely changed *xiv* to *xvi*.

7 Athelstan had no issue known to history; at some point the transmission of this text has apparently garbled the facts of the marriage of Athelstan's sister (not daughter) to the Northumbrian king Sihtric (Anlaf's grandfather) in 926.

*a*. So Z, Glover. A: *a la*.

10 *al*. So A, Z. Glover: *a*.

18 *fei*. So Glover. A: *fei*, with *des* inserted after. Z: *fey des il*.

## 29. BARTHOLOMEW OF COTTON, *HISTORIA ANGLICANA*

Adapted by Paul Cavill, from Bartholomew, *Historia*, ed. Luard, p. 22. Trans. Scott Thompson Smith.

*Manuscript*: London, British Library, MS Cotton Nero C.v.

1 *DCCCCXLV*. Luard: "MS. DCCCXLV."

## 30. *ANNALS OF WINCHESTER*

Adapted by Michael Livingston, from *Annales monastici*, ed. Luard, 2.10. Trans. Scott Thompson Smith.

*Manuscript*: London, British Library, MS Cotton Domitian A.xiii.

According to tradition, the *Annals of Winchester* was written by Richard of Devizes, a monk of St. Swithun's; this is likely to be true, and if so the work was perhaps composed in the last years of the twelfth century (Appleby, "Richard"). Regardless of his identity, the annalist utilized a number of sources to create his *Annals*, including local records and William of Malmesbury (Riall, "New Castles," pp. 117–18). It is almost surely from Malmesbury's summation of Brunanburh (17.pr31–33) that the *Annals* acquired its brief one-line account of the here-unnamed battle.

Though somewhat tangential to Brunanburh itself, it is interesting to observe that for its short account of Athelstan's reign (s.a. 924), the *Annals of Winchester* makes note also of the safe condition of England in the king's time: "Iste tantam pacem teneri fecit in Anglia, quod torques aureus si exponeretur in compito, citius ibi putresceret quam furto tolleretur" [He maintained such peace in England that if a ring of gold had been left at a cross-roads, it would have more quickly rotted away than been taken by a thief]. In Malmesbury, this "hanging of gold" tale appears instead during the reign of Alfred (see Rouse, "Peace of the Roads," pp. 125–26). A similar observation about the peace in Athelstan's time, though not mentioning the hanging of gold rings, is made in Æthelweard's *Chronicle* (Item 7.6–7).

### 31. JOHN OF OXNEAD, *CHRONICLE*

Adapted by Paul Cavill, from John of Oxnead, *Chronica*, ed. Ellis, pp. 5–6. Trans. Scott Thompson Smith.

*Manuscript*: London, British Library, MS Cotton Nero D.II.

The account of the battle here is an abbreviation (and garbling) of Henry of Huntingdon. Ellis notes (p. 6n3):

> This passage has been unintelligibly abridged. In Cotton it runs thus:— Anno Domini dccccxlv et regni sui iiij. commisit prælium maximum apud Brunesberich contra Anlaf, regem Hiberniæ, qui venit in auxilium Scotorum et Dacorum conversantium in Anglia . . . in quo bello v. reges occuberunt . . . ducesque vii. regis Anlavi absque, etc.

4 *Quinque reges . . . duces septem*. Compare to Henry of Huntingdon, lines 31–32.

5–7 *Non fuit bellum . . . regna susceperunt*. Compare to Henry of Huntingdon, lines 46–49. John simply omits *trans mare latum* and *Britones*, changes *huc* to *hic*, and inverts the word order of *Saxones et Angli*.

### 32. ROBERT OF GLOUCESTER, *METRICAL CHRONICLE*

Adapted by Michael Livingston, from Robert, *Metrical Chronicle*, ed. Wright, 1.400–09. Trans. Michael Livingston.

*Manuscripts*: **A**: London, British Library, MS Cotton Caligula A.xi, fols. 84v–85v [base text] [ca. 1325]; **B**: London, British Library, MS Harley 201; **C**: London, British Library, MS Additional 19677.

Robert of Gloucester's *Metrical Chronicle* was exceedingly popular in the fourteenth and fifteenth centuries. Some sixteen medieval manuscripts of the work survive, generally recognized as falling into two recensions. The earlier recension is provided here (see notes to lines 5581 and 5583–85 for differences).

Robert utilized many sources in composing his work, but this particular portion of his narrative is indebted in the main to William of Malmesbury and, in some details, Henry of Huntingdon.

Minor orthographic variants between the texts are ignored in these notes; for a more complete accounting of such differences, see Wright's edition.

5491 *vourtene*. So A, B, and C. Some MSS of the later recension of Robert's work read *fiftene*.

5493 St. Dunstan's birth in the first year of Athelstan's reign is a detail found in few of the sources. It is included, however, in Version A of the *ASC* (s.a. 925 [924]), from which Robert may have taken it. On an argument that Dunstan was actually born much earlier, in 909, see Ramsay, *St Dunstan*, pp. 3–5.

5505 *Analaf*. So B, C. A: *Analf*.

5508 *Analaf*. So B, C. A: *Analf*.

*god*. The readings in B (*gode*) and C (*goude*), as well as those in the later recension (*good*) make clear that the chronicle is not challenging the tradition of Anlaf's heathenism.

5522 *pavilon*. So B, C. A: *pauilons*.

5528 *the*. So B, C. A omits.

5545 *him nom*. So B, C. A: *him he nom*, with the *he* inserted above the line by a later hand.

5550 *Brymesbury*. So A, B. C: *Bremesbury*. Some manuscripts of the later recension read *Brunesburi(e)*. The scribes here conflate Brunanburh with the *burh* constructed by Æthelflæd in 909–10, as recorded in the Mercian Register (*ASC* C 910 *Bremes byrig*, D 909 *Bremes burh*). For an example of confusion in the opposite direction in manuscripts of Bartholomew of Cotton, see Cavill's essay in this volume, pp. 331–32.

5561 *in*. So B, C. A: *bi*.

5568–71 The tribute imposed on Wales by Athelstan first finds record in William of Malmesbury (*GR* 2.6), where the yearly amounts given are 20 pounds of gold, 300 pounds of silver, 25,000 oxen, and as many hounds and hawks as the English king desires. Robert's rendition has reduced both the silver (to 30 pounds) and oxen (to 20,000), both no doubt attributable to variances in his manuscript sources.

5568 *hom hym*. So C. A: *hom*; B: *hem hym*.

5581 The later recension of Robert's text inserts 34 lines on the marriage of Athelstan's sister to Hugh of France and the elaborate gifts given to the king on the occasion. Text is provided in Wright 2.831–32.

5583–85 The later recension of Robert's text replaces these lines with a re-ordered summary of Athelstan's reign. Text is provided in Wright 2.832.

## 33. *ANNALS OF WAVERLEY*

Adapted by Paul Cavill, from *Annales monastici*, ed. Luard, 2.164. Trans. Scott Thompson Smith.

*Manuscript*: London, British Library, MS Harley 651.

The account of the battle here is dependent on Henry of Huntingdon, though extremely abbreviated.

2 *maximum praelium apud Bruneberi*. Compare Henry of Huntingdon, *prelium ad Brunebirih, preliorum maximum* (lines 12–13).

### 34. *BRUT Y TYWYSOGION*

Ed. and trans. John K. Bollard.

*Manuscripts*: **M**: National Library of Wales, Mostyn MS 116, fol. 144r [base text]; **R**: Jesus College, Oxford, MS 111 (*The Red Book of Hergest*), fol. 59r, col. 234.

The text is taken from National Library of Wales, Mostyn MS 116, written in the second half of the fourteenth century. The only variants in Jesus College, Oxford, MS 111 (*The Red Book of Hergest*), written not long after 1382, are trivial orthographic ones. Corrected dates have been supplied in the translation. For more information about this item, see Bollard and Haycock's essay, pp. 265–66.

1 *Gruffud ab Ywein*. R: *Gruffud ap Owein*. Gruffudd ab Owain was a king in the district of Gower in South Wales (Bartrum, *Welsh Classical Dictionary*, p. 297).

1–2 *y gan wyr Keredigyawn* [by the men of Ceredigion]. The equivalent of this phrase does not appear in *Annales Cambriae*.

2 *Hennyrth*. The forms of this name in *Annales Cambriae* (*Himeid*, *Hewed*, *Hiveid*) and *Brenhinedd y Saesson* (*Hymeith*) indicate that this should be emended to a form such as Hemeyd or Hemeyth, i.e., Hyfaidd in modern orthography. The name, which means "bold," was fairly common during the early medieval period. Hyfaidd and presumably Meurig were the sons of Clydog ap Cadell, the brother of Hywel Dda, who shared the rule of Seisyllwg with Clydog, before the latter was slain in 920 by his brother, Meurig ap Cadell (Bartrum, *Welsh Classical Dictionary*, pp. 371, 478).

2–3 *y vrawt* [his brother]. This occurs in neither *Annales Cambriae* nor *Brenhinedd y Saesson*.

### 35. *BRENHINEDD Y SAESSON*

Ed. and trans. John K. Bollard.

*Manuscripts*: **C**: British Library, MS Cotton Cleopatra B.v, fol. 116 [base text]; **B**: National Library of Wales, MS 7006 (*The Black Book of Basingwerk*, in the hand of Gutun Owain, fl. 1460–1500), fols. 209a–210a.

Simple orthographic textual variants are not shown. For more information about this item, see Bollard and Haycock's essay, pp. 266–67.

Title — Welsh *Sais*, plural *Saeson*, originally meant "Saxon" and is so translated in earlier contexts in this book. However, as the Anglo-Saxon kingdoms coalesced into England, *Sais/Saeson* became the standard Welsh word for "Englishman/ Englishmen" and "the English." This is the most likely sense in the title *Brenhinedd y Saesson*, a fourteenth-century compilation of Welsh and English chronicle materials, as well as in the short chronicle of English kings, *Brut y Saesson*; hence the translations "Kings of the English" and "Chronicle of the English."

1 — *Edward vrenhin*. B: *Edwart vrenhin Lloegr* [Edward, king of England].

4 — *rodes*. B: *dodes* [he gave].

6 — *ieirll* [earls, pl.]. B: *iarll* [earl, sg.]. The singular form of a noun is normal after numerals in Welsh; plural forms appear in Middle Welsh not infrequently, especially in translated texts.

*ac ev lluoed*. B: *a'i lluoedd oll* [and all their hosts].

*a ystyngawd*. B: *a ddarostyngodd* [he subdued, subjected, humiliated].

7 — *megys y talawd brenhin Nortwei ydaw*. B: *val y talasai vrenin Norwae* [as the king of Norway had paid].

7–8 — The tribute imposed on Wales by Athelstan first finds record in William of Malmesbury (*GR* 2.6), where the yearly amounts given are 20 pounds of gold, 300 pounds of silver, 25,000 oxen, and as many hounds and hawks as the English king desires. These numbers shift through the sources (see, e.g., Items 32. 5568–71, and 36.9–10). Those given here are remarkably accurate to William's accounting, aside from the considerable reduction of the oxen to a "mere" 5000.

9–19 — The story of the marriage of Eadhild to Hugh, duke (not king) of France, is not included in the *Annals of Winchester*. It does appear in William of Malmesbury's *De gestis regum Anglorum*, but the details are sufficiently different in the present text to indicate that Malmesbury is not the direct source (see Item 17). The tradition of the gifts to Athelstan can be traced back by inference to a late tenth-century poem quoted and summarized by William; see L. Loomis, "Holy Relics," and "Athelstan Gift Story."

9 — *yd oed*. B: *yr*.

*Hilde*. B: *Hilda*.

10 — *Boloyn*. B: *Bolwyn*.

*a Baudewine* [and Baldwin]. In accord with all other versions of this episode, the text should read *vab Baudewine* [the son of Baldwin].

11 — *brenhin Lloegyr*. B: *brenin Lloegr a Chymry* [king of England and Wales]. Jones failed to note this provocative addition in his edition of *Brenhinedd y Saesson*, p. 30.

11–12 — *nyt amgen try chant emmys*. B: *nyd amgen no chant emys* [none other than a hundred steeds].

12 — *amheraudyr*. B: *amerawdr Ruvain* [emperor of Rome].

13 *kethreu* [nails, spikes]. B: *hoelion* [nails].

14 *yn gaeyedic*. B: *a honno yn gaiedic* [and that set (lit. 'enclosed')].

15 *gynt* [long ago]. B omits.

*a choron Seyn Moris* [and the crown of St. Maurice]. The Welsh text is apparently in error here; other sources identify the *vexillum*, *gunfanun*, or *baner* [standard, banner] of St. Maurice, many of them adding that this was the banner the saint carried into battle against the Saracens.

*y diodefaut Crist* [on which Christ suffered]. B omits.

16 *ar benn* [on the head of]. B: *am benn* [about the head of].

17 *gwyrthuaur* [precious]. B omits.

18 *ef a'y derbynnws*. B: *ef a'i dderbyniodd* [he received them]. The common Middle Welsh 3 sg. preterite ending *-wys*, *-ws* was gradually displaced in the late medieval period by -(*i*)*awd*, Modern Welsh -(*i*)*odd*, and survives as *-ws* only in the dialects of southeastern Wales; compare *gynhelijs*/*gynhaliodd* in note to line 20 below.

*ac [a] anvones*. C: *ac anvones*; B: *ac a anvones*.

19 *yn y damvnaw* [wishing for her]. B: *yn i cheisiaw* [seeking her].

*ys*. B: *yr ys*.

20 *Ac ef a gynhelijs yr ynys yn gyn gadarnhet pei*. B: *Ac a gynhaliodd y gyfraith kynn gadarned ped* [And he upheld the law so strongly that if].

*ar fford* [on the road (lit. 'on a road')]. B: *ar y ffordd* [on the road].

This tradition of the safe condition of England under Athelstan is also recorded in the *Annals of Winchester* (*Annales monastici*, ed. Luard, 2.10). Other sources record this tradition in Alfred's reign, as for example in *Brut y Saesson*: "Ef a wnaeth kyfreitheu y Saesson, ac ef a beris y gymeint o hedwch yn y deyrnas, a pheri crogi modrwyeu ar hyt yr heolyd ar plassoed, ac nyt oed neb a lauassei eu kymryt" [He made the laws of the English, and he brought about great peace in the realm, and he had rings hung along the roads and the open spaces, and there was no one who would dare to take them] (*Red Book of Hergest*, fol. 249ra; my translation). Similarly we find in *Le Livere de Reis de Engleterre*: "e fit tant de pes en Engletere par les leis ki il establi ke si homme eust veu or hu argent gisir en le chimin nul ne leust en porte" [And he (Alfred) caused such peace in England through the laws which he established, that if any man had seen gold or silver lying on the road, no one would have taken it away] (*Livere de Reis*, ed. Glover, pp. 56–57). William of Malmesbury has a more explicit version in his account of Alfred: "By this regulation he diffused such peace throughout the country, that he ordered golden bracelets, which might mock the eager desires of the passengers while no one durst take them away, to be hung up on the public causeways, where the roads crossed each other" (*Chronicle of the Kings of England*, trans. Giles, p. 118).

20–21 *na lauassey neb y dwyn y lledrat*. B: *ni lyvassai neb i dywyn oddyno yn lladradaidd* [no one would dare take it from there surreptitiously].

24 *Howel Da vab Cadell*. B: *Howel Dda ap Kadell ap Rodri Mawr* [Hywel Dda son of Cadell son of Rhodri the Great].

25 *y gan wyr Keredigyawn*. B: *gann wyr Karedigion*. This phrase does not occur in *Annales Cambriae*.

26 *Brune*. B: *y Brynnev*.

27 *Hymeith*. B: *Kyfnerth*. See the note on *Hennyrth* in the notes to the corresponding passage in *Brut y Tywysogion* (Item 34.4).

**36. PETER OF LANGTOFT, *CHRONICLE***

Adapted by Michael Livingston, from Pierre de Langtoft, *Chronicle*, ed. Wright, 1.322–33. Trans. Michael Livingston.

*Manuscript*: London, British Library, MS Cotton Julius A.v.

The Augustinian monk Peter of Langtoft (d. 1305) occupies a centrally important role in the literary history of Athelstan and his battles: it is in Langtoft's Anglo-Norman chronicle that we first find the accretion into the English king's reign of a second campaign by Anlaf following his defeat at Brunanburh (lines 74–84). This later invasion (lines 85–107) sees Anlaf arrive at the head of a Danish army rather than a northern alliance, and he invades from Sandwich, eventually cornering Athelstan at Winchester. Saving England from complete seizure by the Danes is the hero Guy of Warwick, newly arrived from foreign lands in the guise of a pilgrim; Guy agrees to fight the Danish giant Colbrand, a single combat to determine the fate of all. His victory at last puts an end to Anlaf's predations.

This tale of a second invasion is based on two primary sources. The first is the historical incursion of another "Anlaf," King Óláfr Tryggvason of Norway, in 994. Óláfr Tryggvason's adversary was King Æthelred II — Athelstan had been dead for more than half a century — and it was decided not by single combat but by Æthelred's decision to pay an enormous tribute to the king of Norway, as described in various versions of the *ASC* and the many chronicles that followed it. Langtoft's second primary source is the Anglo-Norman romance *Gui de Warewic*, probably written sometime between 1205 and 1215, which outlines the basic legend of the hero's life.

We can only guess at the reasons for Langtoft's decision to bring these two traditions together as a continuation of the events at Brunanburh in the reign of Athelstan, but we can be sure of its impact: the Guy of Warwick material was a rousing success in England, and the second invasion was a part of Athelstan's "history" for centuries. In the competition of narratives, it was Guy's heroism that was more apt to be repeated, often to the complete omission of the historical events at Brunanburh.

Only deviations from the base manuscript are provided here. For a full accounting of the manuscripts, see the edition by Wright.

9–10 The tribute imposed on Wales by Athelstan first finds record in William of Malmesbury (*GR* 2.6), where the yearly amounts given are 20 pounds of gold, 300 pounds of silver, 25,000 oxen, and as many hounds and hawks as the English king desires. These numbers shift through the sources (see, e.g., Item 32.5568–71, and 35.7–8), as they do here, where Wales must provide 24 pounds of gold, 300 pounds of silver, and 10,000 oxen.

12 *fors*. So Wright. MS: *For*.

33 *en*. So Wright. MS omits.

40 *en*. So Wright. MS omits.

43–44 *se mist le ray de Loundres devers Abendoun; / où messagers ly venent du riche ray Karloun*. The manuscript appears garbled here, recording *U messagers ly venent devers Abendoun, / Se mist le ray de Loundres al riche ray Karloun*. Wright notes the difficulty without emending his text. I have followed other manuscripts in transposing elements of the lines.

56–58 This passage contains several difficulties, beginning with the location intended by Langtoft's *Scaloun* (line 58). Robert Mannyng of Brunne, who translates this text into Middle English, uses the form *Askalone* here (Item 40.648), presumably identifying *Scaloun* with Ascalon (modern Ashqelon), where on 12 August 1099 a relic of the Cross was carried (though not won) at the head of the Christian army in the last major engagement of the First Crusade (Asbridge, *First Crusade*, pp. 322–26; Baldwin, *History of the Crusades*, 1.340–41). Mannyng's identification is questionable, however. Aside from the fact that Constantine the Great had died 750 years before that battle, the relic at Ascalon was already in Christian hands, having been rediscovered in Jerusalem five days earlier by Arnulf of Choques, the newly appointed patriarch of Jerusalem, who also carried it in the battle. In addition, the Fatimid leader at Ascalon was Al-Afdal Shahanshah, whose name bears not even a passing resemblance to *Maudans* (line 58). If Ascalon indeed lies behind *Scaloun*, it may be that Langtoft (or his source) conflated the battle of Ascalon with the surrender of the Cross by the Persians in 627 to Emperor Heraclius, who had surrounded the Sassanid capital of Ctesiphon. After the Muslim conquest of Mesopotamia, Ctesiphon and Seleucia, on the opposite bank of the Tigris, began to be called in Arabic *Al-Mada'in* [The Cities] or Madain/Madayn, and this could well be the origin of Langtoft's sultan *Maudans*. It is worth noting in this regard that, because of this recovery of the Cross from the Persians, Heraclius is often paired with Constantine's mother Helena, both in literature and art, a fact that may have led Mannyng, in translating these lines, to refer to Heraclius indirectly as Helena's son (see Item 40.646–48).

77 *d. cc. et xv. nefs*. An extra hundred ships appear to have entered the record at some unknown point; the original tradition (beginning with Symeon of Durham, Item 13.3, 20.2) counted the fleet as 615 ships.

90 *Colebrand*. The name means "coal-sword." For more on the figure, see note to Item 37.2805, below.

97 *tut*. So Wright. MS omits.

105 *Guy de Warwik, sun livre*. I.e., the Anglo-Norman *Gui de Warewic*; an English version of this source is given as Item 37, below.

## 37. *STANZAIC GUY OF WARWICK*

Ed. and trans. Michael Livingston.

*Manuscript*: Edinburgh, National Library of Scotland, Advocates' MS 19.2.1 (the Auchinleck manuscript), fols. 162v–165v.

The figure of Guy of Warwick dominates the late medieval landscape like few other legends outside of the Arthurian mythos. From his relatively simple beginning in the Anglo-Norman *Gui de Warewic*, which was written between 1205 and 1215 (C. Harding, "Dating *Gui*"), Guy exploded into the popular consciousness of the subsequent centuries as his story was widely (and wildly) read. Thus, when Peter of Langtoft (Item 36, above) combined in the reign of Athelstan two separate martial traditions — that of the king's great victory at Battle of Brunanburh and that of the single-handed rescue of England by Guy of Warwick — he further pushed Brunanburh toward an obscurity that had perhaps been threatening since the Norman Conquest. Indeed, perhaps because of the intervention of that conquest, with its political, social, and (perhaps more than all else) linguistic changes, it was easy for the new tale, rooted in the vernacular, to replace the old tale.

Presented here is just one of the many Guy of Warwick texts that propagated this fresh and exciting version of the great threat to England in Athelstan's reign. Here Guy's story — complete with its one-on-one combat between a giant and a larger-than-life action hero who prayed often to God, conducted himself with every knightly virtue, and had slain Saracens and dragons alike — has wholly overtaken the historical story of a pitched battle in which England's levy at terrible cost defeated the kingdom's old enemies. Despite its popularity, therefore, the tale is a significant marker in the "forgetting" of Brunanburh.

A thorough edition of the whole of *Stanzaic Guy of Warwick* was recently completed by Wiggins, whose extensive glossing has been utilized in the construction of this translation (*Stanzaic Guy*, pp. 21, 102–18), and whose notes (pp. 127–29, 148–51, and 155) are included in an adapted form here by kind permission of Medieval Institute Publications.

1–24 As the Middle English redactor selected a tranche of material from midway through his source *Gui de Warewic*, a certain amount of editorial shaping was necessary at various narrative junctures. Here, at the opening of the romance, the conventional laudatory description of the protagonist has been extended to include a recapitulation that summarizes events from the earlier part of Guy's life. These first two stanzas are not included in *Gui de Warewic* but were added by the Middle English redactor in order to orient the narrative and to signal, in the traditional manner, the opening of a new romance.

1–3 *God graunt hem heven-blis to mede / that herken to mi romaunce rede / al of a gentil knight*. As is typical of romance, an oral storytelling context is imagined. This opening stanza contains a number of traditional elements: a prayer for the audience, a statement of subject, and praise for the hero. The narrator's call to an audience to "listen" to his romance being "read" aloud is suggestive of the affiliations of romance with both orality and literacy in terms of origins, composition, and transmission. The opinions of commentators vary as to the relative extent to which orality and literacy should each be regarded as influential.

12–13 *Of Warwike wise and wight. / Wight he was for sothe to say*. The repetition of *wight* links the end of one stanza and the start of the next. This use of repetition has an obvious structural function and can be compared with certain forms of "catenation" in Anglo-Norman *chansons de geste*, where they are accounted for as memorial aids for the oral reciter. Similar structural repetitions appear elsewhere in the *Stanzaic Guy of Warwick*. For example, Guy's parting speech to Felice begins with his address to her as "Leve leman" and this is echoed as "Leman" four more times during the speech, each at the start or mid-point of a stanza (ed. Wiggins, lines 337, 349, 361, 373, 379).

22–24 *For his love ich understond / He slough a dragoun in Northhumberlond / Ful fer in the north cuntré*. The dragon-slaying episode from Guy's youth is recounted in other versions of the romance and is the concluding episode of the couplet *Guy of Warwick* (*Romance*, ed. Zupitza, lines 7141–7306). The episode is also referred to in *Bevis of Hampton*, where the narrator includes Guy in a list of great heroes of romance: "And Gy a Warwik, ich understonde, / Slough a dragoun in North Homberlonde" (ed. Herzman, Drake, and Salisbury, lines 2607–08). The reference suggests this was a particularly well-known episode, though the similarity of phrasing with the *Stanzaic Guy* may imply that one of these references was based upon the other.

2794 *At Winchester*. Winchester was a town of some importance between the tenth and twelfth centuries. Second in size after London, it shared the developing functions of a national capital. The association fostered with Guy of Warwick was apparently motivated by the popularity of the legend and an awareness of the prestige to be gained from a local connection. The account by Gerard of Cornwall (fl. 1350?) seems to have been particularly important in this respect. It presents a highly localized and selective version of the legend that focuses entirely on Guy's battle with Colbrond. Gerard names "Hyde Mede" near Winchester as the location for the battle and mentions that Colbrond's axe can still be seen in Winchester Cathedral (this axe is reported to have been held in the treasury of St. Swithun's Priory until the Dissolution). The rubric identifying Gerard states that his book was kept on a writing table close to the high altar of St. Stephen's Cathedral in Winchester. The account goes on to describe the hospice in Winchester, where Guy is alleged to have spent the night and which, it says, is located "250 paces in a northerly direction, where a new monastic building has now been built." Another association was suggested by Thomas Warton in the eighteenth century. He claimed to have seen a wall painting in the north transept of Winchester Cathedral when he was a boy which illustrated the fight between Guy and Colbrond. For a full discussion of these artifacts, see Richmond, *Legend*, pp. 70, 97–106.

2803 *hem*. MS: *him*.

2805 *Colbrond*. The Sussex Lay Subsidy Rolls (1296–1332) and the Rolls of Knight's Fees in Kent (1254) both record the surname "Colebrond," which is glossed as "firebrand" by the *MED* (col, n.2, 4[c]). The choice of this name, however, which can also be glossed "black sword," clearly has significance in terms of race and religious imagery; compare lines 2816, 3060, 3066, and 3079.

2814 *toun*. MS: altered from *doun*.

2816 *out of Aufrike*. Colbrond's African origin is a detail not found in Langtoft's *Chronicle*. It may be that the detail was added due to his name; see note to line 2805, above.

2822 *Inglond*. MS: *Inglong*.

2833 *is Herhaud*. MS: *iherhaud*.

2867 *and*. MS: 7 7.

2878 *Stil*. MS: *Til*.

2923 *about prime*. Prime is the first canonical hour. That is, it is the monastic office or prayer service to be sung or recited at the first hour of the day, 6 a.m. (though the term can refer to the period between 6 and 9 a.m. when the next office begins). The sense here is "first thing in the morning."

2951 *þe*. Inserted above the line in the manuscript.

2968 *God*. MS: followed by a second, erased *god*.

2974 *To the king of Danmark he sent than*. In the manuscript each stanza is headed by a blue and red paraph sign with the exception of this stanza which has two paraphs. The second appears at this the tenth line and it may be intended to provide a visual marker to signal the beginning of Guy's final, climactic battle.

2984 *cercle*. MS: *cecle*. The metal band encircling the helmet.

2986–88 *In the frunt stode a charbukel ston / as bright as ani sonne it schon / that glemes under schawe*. Medieval lapidaries record the various virtues and special powers that precious stones were commonly believed to possess. This included the belief that certain stones shone with their own light, which would emanate even in dark places. References to such stones are not unusual in romance; for example, the magnificent cup in *Floris and Blancheflour* is surmounted by a carbuncle stone said to provide sufficient light for a butler to pour wine even in the darkest cellar (ed. Sands, lines 171–75).

2991 *bihold*. MS: *bhold*.

2997 *targe listed*. A light shield (usually small and round in shape); here described as either edged or banded with strips of gold.

2998–99 *portreyd with thre kinges corn / that present God when He was born*. The offering of the Three Kings is an especially appropriate image for Guy to carry at this point in the text. As Dyas, *Pilgrimage*, p. 131, has observed, the journey of the Three Kings from the East to see the infant Christ "made them ideal role models for pilgrims." An image of kings, figures of the highest social rank, is also appropriate for Guy as the "king's champion."

3013–17 *rered Lazeroun . . . / and halp Daniel fram the lyoun*. The miracle in which Christ raised Lazarus from the dead appears in the New Testament (John 11), whereas Susanna and Daniel are both Old Testament figures: Susanna was rescued from the Jewish elders (Vulgate, Daniel 13) and Daniel was miraculously saved from the lions' den (Daniel 6:16–22). They are all examples of the kind of miraculous deliverance that Guy himself requires as he is about to enter a desperate situation. References to any of these biblical figures is rare in Middle English romance, though Dalrymple, *Language and Piety*, pp. 133–35, records that prayers to Lazarus and Daniel appear in *The Song of Roland* and the French *Romance of Horn*. A parallel also occurs in *Bevis of Hampton* at the moment when Bevis, finding himself in a similarly desperate situation to Guy, offers a prayer which refers to Lazarus: "Lord, that rerede the Lazaroun, / Dilivre me fro this fend dragoun!" (ed. Herzman, Drake, and Salisbury, lines 2839–40).

3027–29 *after the relikes thai sende, / the corporas and the Messe gere. / On the halidom thai gun swere*. The *Messe gere* refers to the Eucharistic vestments and articles used for the swearing of oaths. These included the missal (the book containing the order of service for the Mass), the chalice (to hold the communion wine), the paten (to hold the host or bread wafer), and the corporal cloth or altar cloth on which all the Eucharistic elements were placed during consecration and with which they were subsequently covered. All of the *Messe gere* is sacred as it is essential to the re-enactment of Christ's death during the Mass, the principal Christian liturgical rite. The *halidom* can refer to either the sacred relics themselves or to a box containing sacred relics.

3031 *ywis*. MS: inserted above *furst* to maintain column width.

3061 *mailes*. The small metal rings or plates linked together in a mesh to make chain armor.

3064 *splentes of stiel*. Rod-like plates of steel.

3068 *splentes*. MS: *spentes*.

3074 *bacinet*. "A hemispherical helmet, without a visor, worn under the fighting helmet" (*MED*).

3088 *axes*. MS: *axs*.

*gisarmes*. "A long-shafted battle ax or halberd with a knife-like point rising from the blade" (*MED*).

3094 *wicked hert*. Here "heart" refers to character or disposition. Compare, for example, to Chaucer's *Troilus and Criseyde* 3.736, where Pandarus calls Troilus a "wrecched mouses hert."

3095 *aferd*. MS: *d* altered from *t*.

3115 *arsoun*. The pommel (the front of the saddle).

3137 *charbukel ston*. See the note to lines 2986–88.

3194–96 *al sone he gan him turn tho . . . / ther his axes stode bi hemselve*. This episode parallels Guy's request to Amorant for a drink of water (ed. Wiggins, lines 1429–52 and 1513–24). In both cases, Guy appeals to his opponent's honor and sense of fair play, then, when he is denied, makes a dash for the item requested.

3199 *Colbrond*. MS: *Colbron*.

3208 *dint*. MS: preceded by erased *de*.

3213 *wounde*. MS: *o* altered from *a*.

3222 *gan*. MS: omitted.

3236 *Te Deum laudamus thai gun sing*. The *Te Deum* is a hymn of praise (*Te Deum laudamus* being the opening words of this Latin hymn) sung during the night offices, especially matins, and on special occasions of thanksgiving. The "terminal" position of this hymn in the romance prompts Richmond to suggest that its choice "appropriately suggests that Guy's story is near conclusion" (*Popularity*, p. 186).

3280 *mi*. MS: *þi mi*.

3299 *half*. MS: *In half*.

3301 *Gii*. MS: added above (possibly in a later hand).

## 38. *ANONYMOUS SHORT ENGLISH METRICAL CHRONICLE*

Ed. and trans. Michael Livingston.

*Manuscript*: Edinburgh, National Library of Scotland, Advocates' MS 19.2.1 (the Auchinleck manuscript), fols. 312v–313v.

There are seven manuscripts of the *Anonymous Short English Metrical Chronicle*, representing three redactions of the text. The version presented here is the most popular version, the C-redaction, as it appears in the famed Auchinleck manuscript, copied in the 1330s. The primary edition of Auchinleck is now *Auchinleck*, ed. Burnley and Wiggins (BW, below). For redaction variants, see the edition by Zettl (pp. 22–26).

1579 *here*. So MS. BW: *her*.

1583 The paragraph break, unrecorded by BW, is marked by a two-line rubricated initial.

1584 Line 1559 (*Ne wiser in al þing*) follows this line in the manuscript, written at the bottom of the manuscript column (fol. 312vb) and marked for insertion by *a* and *b* markers.

1595 *to*. So BW. MS omits.

1612 *Baldwine of Coloine*. Baldwin's place of origin varies in the sources dependent upon the political landscape at the time. Here an earl of Cologne, he is the count of Flanders in Item 35.10 and of Burgundy in 36.46.

1667 *Colbrond*. So BW. MS: *colbrod*.

1668 *Gii*. So MS. BW: *Gy*.

## 39. Ranulf Higden, *Polychronicon*

The text is edited from Cambridge, University Library, MS Ii. 2. 24 (s. xv$^{in}$), by Churchill Babington and Joseph Rawson Lumby in the Rolls Series. The account of the battle and the circumstances surrounding it (6.436–40) initially follows John of Worcester, but then blends in William of Malmesbury's account of Anlaf's singing and Athelstan's sword. Variants in the spelling of the place-name are recorded in the manuscripts, namely *Brumford* and *Brunfort*.

The death of Oda (ed. Babington and Lumby, 7.2) also leads to mention of Athelstan's friendship and the sword: "Nec multo post clericaliter attonsus Wyltoniensis præsul effectus est, regem Adelstanum amicum sibi fecerat, potissime per elapsum gladii amissi in regiam uaginam" [Not long after he was tonsured a priest and made bishop at Wilton (*recte* Ramsbury), he made King Athelstan his friend, mainly on account of the lost sword's return to the royal scabbard].

## 40. Robert Mannyng of Brunne, *Chronicle*

Adapted by John K. Bollard, from Mannyng, *Chronicle*, ed. Sullens, pp. 503–07. Trans. John K. Bollard.

*Manuscripts*: **P**: London, Inner Temple Library, MS Petyt 511, vol. 7 [1375–1400] [base text]; **L**: London, Lambeth Palace Library, MS Lambeth 131 [1425–50].

Robert Mannyng of Brunne, one of the relatively few medieval English poets whose names are known to us, translated two surviving works into Middle English verse for the benefit of those who knew no French or Latin. In his prologue to *Handlyng Synne*, he names himself as "Roberd of Brunne" and says that he lived for fifteen years in the Gilbertine priory of Sempringham, where he began translating that work from the Anglo-Norman *Manuel des Pechiez* in the year 1303 [lines 61–76]. He also identifies himself at the beginning of the *Chronicle*:

> Lordynges þat be now here,
> if ye will listene & lere
> alle þe story of Inglande
> als Robert Mannyng wryten it fand. (lines 1.1–4)

> [Gentlemen who are now here, / if you will, listen and learn / all the story of England / as Robert Mannyng found it written.]

He writes even more explicitly a bit later: "Of Brune I am if any me blame, / Robert Mannyng is my name" (lines 1.135–36). While Mannyng is usually regarded as coming from Bourne in Lincolnshire, some scholars believe the Brunne in question to be Nunburnholme or Nunburnham in Yorkshire, midway between York and Beverley, which was recorded as Brunne in 1280 (see "Mannyng, Robert" in *Oxford Dictionary of National Biography*). (Were his hometown thought to be the *Brun-* of Brunanburh, one might expect, or at least have hoped, that Robert would have been more explicit regarding the location of the battle if he knew of any relevant local traditions, but of course his silence tells us nothing.)

That Mannyng may have been educated in Cambridge around the turn of the fourteenth century is suggested by his account in the *Chronicle* of the feast in which Alexander, the brother of Robert Bruce, king of Scots, celebrated receiving his Master of Arts degree, a celebration at which Mannyng states he was present: "& he sauh alle þe gest þat wrote & mad þis ryme" [And he who wrote and made this rhyme saw all the festivity] (line 2.8234). In 1327 a certain "Sir Robert de Brunne in [of?] Lincoln, Chaplain" was named as the administrator of the will of Avice de Crosseby, a parishioner of St. Cuthbert's in Lincoln (Seaton, "Robert Mannyng," p. 77). Other late thirteenth-century documents naming "Robert of Brunne" are known, but it is unclear whether any of these — or indeed Avice de Crosseby's administrator — is our poet (Mannyng, *Chronicle*, ed. Sullens, pp. 17–19). Mannyng says that he completed the *Chronicle* on the Ides of May, 1338 (lines 2.8386–87). Nothing is known of him after this date.

Mannyng's *Chronicle* is written in two parts; the first ends, as does Geoffrey of Monmouth's *Historia* and other works based on it, with the year 689, and it is written in rhyming four-stress couplets. The second part is written in a longer six-stress line and ends in the early fourteenth century when Mannyng runs out of history to write. The *Chronicle* is taken from numerous sources. Mannyng sets out to translate Peter of Langtoft's Anglo-Norman chronicle (Item 36 in this volume), but, especially in the first part, he also draws directly on some of the sources that Langtoft would also have used. In his prologue he gives a brief summary of early English historiography, as it were, naming "Dares þe Freson of Troie" [Dares Phrygius, line 1.145], "Geffrey Arthure of Minume" [Geoffrey of Monmouth, line 1.163], "Mayster Wace" (line 1.177), and "Pers of Langtoft, a chanon" (line 1.188). He also drew on other sources, including Bede, Henry of Huntingdon, William of Malmesbury, and possibly John (formerly Florence) of Worcester. The second part of the *Chronicle*, from which the present extract is drawn, follows Langtoft more closely, though he mutes Langtoft's virulent anti-Scottish partisanship, especially in the later portions.

Reading Mannyng's clear and lively account of British history, we are moved to agree when he says, "And gude it is for many thynges / for to here þe dedis of kynges, / whilk were foles & whilk were wyse, / & whilk of þam couth mast quantyse" [And it is good for many reasons to hear the deeds of kings — which ones were fools and which ones were wise, and which of them had the most intelligence] (lines 1.15–17).

Only significant or clarifying variants from the later Lambeth manuscript (L) are given in these notes; for other variants, see the edition by Sullens. Line numbers are those of Part Two of the *Chronicle*; in the notes and discussion references to lines not in the passage included herein are distinguished by part; e.g., 1.123 and 2.123.

592 *him*. A synecdoche identifying the king with the land.

596 *fyve hundreth kie ilk yere*. L: *fyue thousand kyn by yere*.

597 *Silver . . . not*. L: *But he nolde of Southwalys take*.

*ferthing noke*. *MED*: "a piece or segment of a farthing, least bit"; compare Modern English *nook* [corner], perhaps from Old Norse. The phrase also occurs in Mannyng's *Handlyng Synne*, line 5812: "Wyþheld he nat a ferþyng noke."

599–604 This passage draws ultimately on the *ASC* entry for 926, recording Athelstan's lordship over Hywel Dda, king of West Wales, i.e., Dyfed (*Owald, a werreoure*); Constantine, king of Scotland; and Owain ap Hywel ap Rhys, king of Glywysing and Gwent, the father of Morgan the Old (*Onwer, kyng of Wentland*). For more on these figures, see also Bollard and Haycock's essay, pp. 256–57.

603 *thorgh Godes grace*. The qualifier is not found in Langtoft.

*so with tham fore*. L: *so wente hem byfore*.

607 *wiknes*. L: *yuel* [evil].

611–12 *he wild take no mede . . . wikkednes*. I.e., Athelstan would accept no payment in compensation for the crime from his brother or those connected with him, but rather insisted on executing him.

617–22 Around 714, John, bishop of Hexham and bishop of York, who had earlier ordained Bede as both deacon and priest, built and retired to a monastery near the town of Beverley in Yorkshire, and he died there on 7 May 721. A cult venerating him grew up rapidly, and he was canonized as St. John of Beverley in 1037. The church of Beverley Minster, where his relics were interred owed its importance largely to the popularity of his gravesite as a destination for pilgrims (see "John of Beverley" in *Oxford Dictionary of National Biography*). A charter (S 451) dated 925 CE, but better understood as referencing sometime in the period 927–935, records Athelstan's grant of privileges to the church of Beverley. Some historians suggest this might be a spurious charter from the fourteenth century. In any case, the tradition grew up that Athelstan visited there sometime before the Battle of Brunanburh.

618 *fertre*. *MED*: "a reliquary, a shrine holding the relics of a saint."

620 *franchise ond fe*. These are legal terms denoting (a) *franchise*: a grant of special privileges such as the right to hold land exempt from taxes and/or to exercise jurisdiction over the courts, etc., and (b) *fee*: the holding of land in perpetual tenure.

625 *holdes*. L: *yit haldes al*.

627 *did full stress*. L: *put him tyl distresse*.

631 *selcouth*. L: *wonder*.

632 *elne*. An ell is a unit of measure equal to approximately 45 inches. L adds: *Þey seyn yit at Dunbarre þat Athelston so smot / An elne dep y þe ston many men hit wot* [They still say at Dunbar that Athelstan so smote an ell deep in the stone that many men know it].

633 *the feast of our Lady, the Assumpcion*. August 15.

636 *com the erl of*. P: *com þe of*; L: *Cam þe Erl of*.

640 *Morice bar in*. P: *Morice in*; L: *Morice bar in*.

646–48 Mannyng's source, Langtoft, presents here a mélange of references touching on the history and lore of the True Cross (line 646). *Saynt Helen* (line 647) is undoubtedly St. Helena, the mother of Constantine I, who is named in her place in Langtoft, and who is widely revered in tradition as the finder of the Cross in the early fourth century. See note to Item 36.56–58.

649 L: *Þan blewe þey faste trompe boþe loude & schrille* [Then they vigorously blew trumpets, both loud and shrill].

654 *to . . . Ilde*. L: *to yonge Hilde*.

656 L: *of fetoures so fair in erthe was ther non ywrought* [There was none on earth made so fair of feature].

663 *In*. The capital is omitted in P.

674 *that . . . fled*. L: *& þe fewe þat fledde wyþ þe lyf* [and the few who fled with their lives].

680 *ond com unto*. L: *ffor he cam vntil* [for he came to].

682 L: *Of wham we haue herd telle his name was Colibrant*.

684 *yeld the lond*. L: *fighte for þe lond*.

693 *palmere*. Originally a term for a pilgrim, especially one who wore two crossed palms to signify a pilgrimage to the Holy Land, *palmer(e)* came to mean "a crusader."

695 *if he wild*. L: *yif þou wilt*.

696 *thei suld*. L: *þou schalt*.

701 *affraies*. L: *frayes*. Sullens prints the clear manuscript reading, *affaies*, a form otherwise unknown. The emendation to *affraies* [assaults, attacks] (see *MED*, s.v. *affrai*) is based on the variant reading in L. There is, however, a possibility that the scribe misread *assaies* in his original, turning two long s's into f's; such a reading would parallel Mannyng's similar summations of the reigns of Henry II at 2.3477 — "Whan he had regned here & felt of fele assaies Foure & tuenty yere . . . he died" [When he had reigned here and experienced many trials for twenty-four years . . . he died] — and Edward I at 2.8348 — "Four & tuenty yere, auht monethes & fiue daies / noblie regned he here bi profe & gode assaies" [Twenty-four years, eight months and five days he reigned here, by fortune and good tests (of character)]; see *MED*, s.v. *assai* 2(a): "A testing of character or personal traits . . . ; trial, ordeal."

709 *god*. This may be the adjective "good" or the noun "God." However we understand the line, the syntax and word order are awkward or unusual. If we take *god* as "God," the passage would translate something like "The year of God [=*anno domini*] when he died, men say, was 940," which gives a reading closer

to that of L: *When he deide þe date of crist was writen redely* [When he died, the date of Christ was accurately written]. It may be, however, that the scribe of L's clearer construction, with its somewhat curious reference to the written date, is an attempt to rationalize a difficult line in his exemplum. Whichever reading is preferred, the *(god) men* can be understood to be the historians Mannyng is drawing on.

## 41. *Scottish Chronicle* (alias *Pictish Chronicle*)

Adapted by Paul Cavill, from Anderson, "Scottish Pieces," p. 251. Trans. Scott Thompson Smith.

*Manuscript*: Paris, Bibliothèque Nationale, MS Latin 4126, fol. 29r.

The unique manuscript is a miscellany (s. xiv$^{med}$), the relevant part of which was probably compiled by Robert of Poppleton in Yorkshire. For full manuscript details, see M. Anderson's article.

1 *Duinbrunde*. Anderson's note: "What I have represented as *un* consists of four quite ambiguous minims" ("Scottish Pieces," p. 251).

*in xxx.iiij. eius anno*. As Constantine's predecessor died in 900, the chronicle here dates the battle to 934, evidently confusing it with Athelstan's northern expedition of that year. See Campbell, *Battle of Brunanburh*, p. 47n3.

## 42. John of Fordun, *Chronica gentis Scotorum*

[See Item 49, and notes.]

## 43. *Eulogium historiarum*

Adapted by Paul Cavill, from *Eulogium historiarum*, ed. Hayden, 2.166 and 3.10. Trans. Scott Thompson Smith.

*Manuscript*: Cambridge, Trinity College, MS R. 7. 2.

*Eulogium historiarum* contains two passages on Brunanburh. The first passage (from book 4, col. 175; ed. Hayden 2.166) substantially derives from the account of John of Worcester; it is followed by an account of the miracle of Athelstan's sword attributed to Oda (as in Eadmer). The second passage (from book 5, col. 84; ed. Hayden 3.10), included here, mainly draws upon William of Malmesbury's *GR* but also includes material additional to that source.

1 *anno regni sui xii*. This date is accurate if reckoned from Athelstan's consecration in 925.

4 *ceciderunt autem ibi duo nepotes regis Athelstani, scilicet, Elwyn et Athelwyn*. William of Malmesbury states that Athelstan had Ælfwine and Æthelwyn, "quos in bello contra Analauum amiserat" [whom he had lost in battle against Anlaf], buried at Malmesbury (*GR* 2.135).

5–6 *Angelum de caelo . . . dedisse*. Indirect statement following *dicunt*.

6 *incontinenti regi*. The adjective *incontinens* generally means 'immoderate' or 'intemperate,' in which case the attributive would seem critical of Athelstan. The adjective might also be construed to mean that the king was simply unable to hold onto his sword in the fight.

7 *adhuc Malmesburiae inter sacras reliquas*. Reminiscent of William of Malmesbury's statement in *GR* that the miraculous sword from the battle is still preserved "in thesauro regum" (lines 28–29). William also states that Athelstan entrusted treasures and holy relics (including a bejeweled crown made of gold and pieces of the Cross) to Malmesbury (*GR* 2.135).

## 44. *BRUT Y SAESSON*

Ed. and trans. John K. Bollard.

*Manuscripts*: **R**: Jesus College, Oxford, MS 111 (*The Red Book of Hergest*), fols. 249r–249v, cols. 1001.35–1002.30 [base text]; **P32**: National Library of Wales, Peniarth MS 32 (*Y Llyfr Teg*), p. 252.8–11 [1404]; **P19**: National Library of Wales, Peniarth MS 19, fols. 153v–154r [ca. 1400–10].

For more information about this item, see Bollard and Haycock's essay, pp. 267–68.

1 *Gwedy*. P32: *A gwedy* [And after].

*gawssoedit*. P19: *gawssodit*.

2 *orderchyat*. P32: *orderchat*; from *gorderchyat* (Modern Welsh *gordderchiad*) [concubinage, adultery]. William of Malmesbury recounts the tale of Athelstan's illegitimate birth as he learned it from "old ballads" (*Chronicle of the Kings of England*, trans. Giles, p. 139).

*dewr a doeth oed*. P32: *deor a doyth oeed*. Elsewhere P32 regularly writes *oed oeet* for the usual *oed oet*.

4 *Nordhwmbyrlont*. P19: *Northwmbyrlwnt*. In February 925 Athelstan's sister married Sihtric at Tamworth (*ASC*, s.a. 925).

5 *darestyngawd*. P19: *darostyngawd*.

6 *Ffreinc*. P19: *freingk*.

7 *Ysgottyeit*. P19: *yscottyeit*.

8 *Ysgotlont*. P19: *yscotlont*.

10 *drach eu kefyn*. P19: *drachefyn*. In R the *h* has been inserted superscript after the *c* in an early hand, though perhaps not the main scribe's.

12 *Damchwein*. The word has several possible meanings: "accident, mishap; rare event, chance."

*y oes ef*. P19: *y oes*.

12–13 *nys anrydedawd*. P19: *nys anrydedei* [he would not honor it].

14 *dyrchafawd*. P19: *drychafawd*.

*Ysgotlont*. P19: *yscotlond*.

Athelstan's role in the baptism of Constantine's son is recorded by William of Malmesbury: "The barbarians had no idea of resistance, but without delay coming to a place called Dacor, they surrendered themselves and their kingdoms to the sovereign of England. Out of regard to this treaty, the king himself stood for the son of Constantine, who was ordered to be baptized, at the sacred font" (*Chronicle of the Kings of England*, trans. Giles, p. 133).

16 *Ef a vynnassei . . . y dallu ef*. P19: *Ef a dyvynnassei rei atta6 ac Elret o Winsestyr yn dywyssa6c arnadunt a'r Elret h6nn6 a'e dalla6d ef*. P19's version, "He had summoned some to him, with Elfred of Winchester as leader over them, and that Elfred he blinded," or possibly ". . . and that Elfred blinded him," seems to be the work of a scribe trying to clarify a confusing or faulty exemplar. William of Malmesbury quotes the first person account by Athelstan (surviving in charter S 415): "Be it known to the sages of our kingdom, that I have not unjustly seized the lands aforesaid, or dedicated plunder to God; but that I have received them, as the English nobility, and even John, the pope of the church of Rome himself, have judged fitting on the death of Elfred. He was the jealous rival both of my happiness and life, and consented to the wickedness of my enemies, who, on my father's decease, had not God in his mercy delivered me, wished to put out my eyes in the city of Winchester: wherefore, on the discovery of their infernal contrivances, he was sent to the church of Rome to defend himself by oath before pope John. This he did at the altar of St. Peter; but at the very instant he had sworn, he fell down before it, and was carried by his servants to the English School, where he died the third night after" (*Chronicle of the Kings of England*, trans. Giles, pp. 137–38). The identity of Elfred is uncertain, but William of Malmesbury later says of him: "Elfred alone, a man of uncommon insolence, disdaining to be governed by a sovereign whom he had not voluntarily chosen, secretly opposed with his party to the very utmost" (*Chronicle of the Kings of England*, trans. Giles, p. 139).

17 *dalpwyt*. P19: *delit*. These are variant forms of the preterite impersonal, "was caught."

*wrth . . . pab*. P19: *att y pab wrth y amdiffyn* [to the pope for his defense].

*drwy* [through, by means of, because of]. Something seems to be missing after *drwy*. A phrase such as *drwy tyngu llw* [by swearing an oath] would accord with the following sentence.

*ger bronn y pab* [before the pope]. A *y* was inserted superscript between the *e* and the *r* of *ger*, probably to match the orthography of *geyr bronn* in the next sentence; both spellings are common, though the three additional instances in R are all *geyr*. This insertion is in a different (later?) hand and with a different, smaller pen, than the correction on line 10 above.

19 *odyno* [from there]. Supplied from P19.

20–21 *A'r Edylstan . . . Malmesburi*. P32: *ac vn vlwydyn ar bymthec y gwledychawd ac yMalmmesberi y cladwyt* [And sixteen years he ruled and in Malmesbury he was buried]. P19: *Malmesbri*.

### 45. RICHARD OF CIRENCESTER, *SPECULUM HISTORIALE*

The text is edited by John E. B. Mayor in the Rolls Series. The substance of the account of the battle (2.64) derives, via Roger of Wendover and Matthew Paris, from John of Worcester. The only significant variant is a mis-spelling of the place-name, *Brunkerih*.

### 46. PSEUDO-INGULF, *CHRONICLE OF CROWLAND*

Adapted by Paul Cavill, from *Rerum Anglicarum scriptorum veterum*, ed. Fulman and Gale, pp. 29, 37. Trans. Scott Thompson Smith.

No manuscript of this history survives; several once existed, one at the monastery of Crowland in Lincolnshire and another in the Cottonian collection, but the first disappeared sometime during the century after the Dissolution of the Monasteries and the second was burnt in the fire of 1731. The first editor, Sir Henry Savile, published the work in his *Rerum Anglicarum scriptores post Bedam praecipui* (1596); it was later edited from a version by Thomas Gale in Fulman's *Rerum Anglicarum scriptorum veterum* (1684), and the following excerpts are taken from this edition.

The main source for the account of the battle is William of Malmesbury, though the chronicler elaborates it with the story of Turketel's exploits. The chronicle also conflates the battle of 934 and Athelstan's offering of his dagger to St. John of Beverley (a tradition shared with Ranulf Higden and the *Eulogium historiarum*) with the Battle of Brunanburh.

16–17 *uel uincendi diffidentia, uel solita gentis suae uersutia*. Two ablatives of cause explain Anlaf's decision to make a surprise attack at night.

18 *peremptoque*. Fulman: *peremtoque*.

23 *promptus*. Fulman: *promtus*.

*tota*. Fulman: *nota*.

27–28 *cessantibus cito ferentariis armis, pede pes, et cuspide cuspis, umboque umbone pellebatur*. An ablative absolute followed by a string of nominative singular nouns, each attached to the passive verb *pellebatur* and each accompanied by its own ablative form (in example of polyptoton) functioning as an ablative of means.

31 *assumptis*. Fulman: *assumtis*.

32 *Wicciorum*. Presumably the Hwiccans (see *BEASE*, s.v. "Hwicce").

32–34 *qui spectata fortitudine . . . viribus robustissimus*. A long relative clause modifying *Singino* (line 32).

34 *praeuius ipse*. The sentence returns to its subject, Turketlus (lines 30–31).

39 *Regem*. I.e., Constantine.

*dejecit, dejectumque*. A case of polyptoton.

39–41 This sentence employs polysyndeton, or a succession of clauses connected by conjunctions (dejectum*que* . . . *et* Scoti . . . *et* plures . . . præcipue*que*), perhaps in a chiastic pattern.

43–44 *cum Singrinus centurio gladio confodit eum*. A temporal *cum* clause with an indicative verb.

45–46 *morte Constantini.* Like William of Malmesbury (*GR* 2.131), the Crowland chronicle includes Constantine among those killed at the battle.

50 *licit*. Fulman: *licete*.

### 47. *PROSE BRUT*

Adapted by John K. Bollard, from *Brut*, ed. Brie, 1.112. Trans. John K. Bollard.

*Manuscript*: Oxford, Bodleian Library, MS Rawlinson B.171.

This extract from the anonymous chronicle known as the *Prose Brut*, or *The Chronicle of England*, is taken from the edition prepared from the late fourteenth- or early fifteenth-century Bodleian Library MS Rawlinson B.171 by Brie. The Middle English *Prose Brut* is a translation of an Anglo-Norman text compiled from a wide variety of sources around the end of the thirteenth century and extended into the early fourteenth. The English version, produced in the second half of the fourteenth century, became one of the most popular late medieval and early modern texts, surviving in over 180 manuscripts — more than any other work, including the works of Chaucer, with the exception of the Wycliffite translations of the Bible. (Anglo-Norman and Latin versions increase the number of manuscripts to more than 250.) Its popularity is also attested by the fact that the *Brut* was first printed by William Caxton in 1480 and in twelve more editions by Wynkyn de Worde and others during the next fifty years, while the manuscript tradition reaches even into the mid-seventeenth century. Thus, this short passage on Athelstan's reign was for a long time one of the most widespread sources of information about him. Though the Battle of Brunanburh is not explicitly named, it is identifiable by the approximate date three years before Athelstan's death, and its reputation as a great victory clearly survives in this spare account.

Before 1 *Athelstone*. So Brie. MS: *Atheltone*.

4–7 This unnamed campaign appears to be Brunanburh. Interestingly, Anlaf's great pan-Irish Sea alliance is here reduced to an invasion of Scots from the area of Strathclyde. In an ironic twist, the historical equivalent to this portion of Anlaf's great army would have been the relatively small contingent led by Owain, whose presence is more often ignored than remembered in the majority of sources.

7 The statement that Athelstan's reign lasted *xxv* years is mistaken: he ruled from 924 or 925 to 939; it is likely that a scribal error has introduced an *x* to what was originally written as *xv* years.

### 48. *BOOK OF HYDE*

The text is edited by Edward Edwards from London, British Library, MS Lansdowne 717 (s. xv[in]). The account of the battle (pp. 123–24) follows Higden's *Polychronicon*, though material from the Guy of Warwick romance is inserted earlier. The place-name is given in the form *Brunfort*. *The Book of Hyde* also mentions a brother of Athelstan's otherwise unknown to English tradition, one Elfredus born of the same mother, Ecgwynn (*ex nobili fœmina*). Edward the Elder reportedly loved Elfredus before all others (*præ cæteris paternali amore*) and intended him to succeed, but Elfredus died before his father (ed. Edwards, p. 113).

### 49. WALTER BOWER, *SCOTICHRONICON*

Selected by Ulrike Hogg, from Bower, *Scotichronicon*, ed. and trans. Watt, 2.330–33 and 340–45.

The works of Fordun and Bower have been closely linked for centuries. John of Fordun (died in or after 1363), a priest probably from Perthshire, wrote his *Chronica gentis Scotorum* in order to recover the historical record lost during the Wars of Independence, travelling widely to collect source material. His account, which goes up to the year 1153, circulated for some eighty years until Walter Bower (1385–1449), abbot of the Augustinian monastery on the island of Inchcolm in the Firth of Forth, was asked to transcribe and continue his work. Between 1441 and 1445, Bower expanded Fordun's original work from five to sixteen books, inserting passages of his own, which he was careful to distinguish from Fordun's text, and taking the record up to the year 1437. His work is one of the most significant Latin documents of Scottish medieval literature and valuable for its record of contemporary history and attitudes. It survives in a number of manuscripts, including his own working copy; Fordun's, however, only exists in later copies. While Bower's work has recently been edited and translated under the editorship of Watt (1987–98), the task of editing Fordun's work on its own was last tackled by W. F. Skene in 1871, and in the light of more recent research this edition can no longer be considered reliable.

The account of the Battle of Brunanburh — where Bower's text closely follows Fordun's — is therefore presented here only through the text of Bower's *Scotichronicon*, with text and translation taken from the edition cited above.

Before 1 In Skene's edition of Fordun's work the chapter headings are not always taken from the same manuscript source and therefore occasionally different, but not significantly so. Fordun's chapter 4.21, for example, is headed as follows: "De successione Constantini regis, filii Heth alipedis, et quod Cumbriae dominium dedit Eugenio filio, etc." [Of the succession of King Constantine, son of Aed Wing-Foot, and how he gave the rule of Cumbria to his son Eochaid, etc.].

31 Bower leaves out Fordun's two final sentences of the chapter which relate continental affairs, and adds other continental matters here. His next two chapters equally bear no relation to Scottish affairs. He then begins chapter 24 with the last two sentences of Fordun's chapter 21.

46–47 The chronology here is somewhat mistaken. Guthfrith did, in fact, attempt to maintain control of Northumbria after Sihtric's death, but he was Sihtric's brother or cousin, not his son. His failure ultimately led to the Brunanburh campaign led by his son (not Sihtric's), Anlaf, which took place after Guthfrith's death. The confusion is no doubt due to the fact that Sihtric himself had a son, Anlaf, who also took part in the history of the north. See Introduction, p.12n36.

Before 60 Chapter heading in Fordun: "De damnis per hoc bellum Scotorum gentibus illatis, et de obitu Constantini, etc." [Of the damages inflicted upon the Scottish people in this battle, and of the death of Constantine, etc.].

72–75 This verse does not appear in Fordun.

86–92 Bower here adds some indignant comments about the inclusion of old wives' tales in serious histories.

92 Fordun's chapter ends here.

## 50. *ANNALS OF ULSTER*

Adapted by Paul Cavill, from *Annals of Ulster*, ed. Mac Airt and Mac Niocaill, pp. 384–86. Trans. Scott Thompson Smith.

*Manuscript*: Dublin, Trinity College, MS 1282 (H.1.8).

The manuscript is written (at this point) in the late fifteenth-century hand of Ruaidhrí Ó Luinín (Mac Airt and Mac Niocaill, pp. viii–ix).

2–4 The sentences relating the respective outcomes for "the Northmen" and "the Saxons" show some notable repetitions in structure and vocabulary: "many thousands" of the northern forces *ceciderunt* while a "multitude" of Saxons also *cecidit*; after relating the number of the fallen in both cases, the annal describes the outcome for each king, and each of these descriptions is introduced by an adversative conjunction (*sed* and *autem*) to show opposition (i.e. countless numbers of soldiers died *but* both kings survived).

## 51. HECTOR BOECE, *HISTORIAE*

Ed. and trans. Ulrike Hogg.

Educated at the University of Paris, Hector Boece (c. 1465–1536), first principal of Aberdeen University, was also Scotland's first humanist historian. His *Scotorum historiae,* in seventeen books, is an account of the Scottish people from their earliest origins to the year 1438. Boece's epic narrative follows the ideals of classical historiography and incorporates a strong message that combines ideals of ancient virtue with advice to princes. It was translated several times into Scots, most notably in the very free version of Boece's contemporary John Bellenden, but a modern, exact translation is still outstanding. Although Boece's work is fanciful and unreliable when judged by modern historical standards, his achievement lies in introducing new sources, points of view, and historiographical angles. In his account of the Battle of Brunanburh he takes the opportunity to emphasize once again his concerns about virtue, kingship, and the disastrous consequences of monarchal incompetence. The tragic outcome for the Scots, who in Boece's version had only entered into the conflict in order to support their allies, found a parallel in the very recent, equally devastating, Battle of Flodden (1513) that would not have been lost on Boece's Scottish audience.

The text here is based on Boece's first edition (SH), published in Paris in 1527.

4 *fetialem*. SH: *faecialem*.

7 *fetialem*. SH: *faecialem*.

32 *Beatrice*. The name of Edward's daughter by Egwina, who was married to Sihtric, is uncertain. Most sources name her Edith.

44 *iniuriam, Eduardus*. SH: *iniuriam. Eduardus*.

47 *extinctum*. SH: *exinctum*.

52 On the genealogical confusion of Anlaf and his family, see note to Item 49.46–47, above.

83 *omnia, nullum*. SH: *omnia: nullum*.

115 *regendum, nam*. SH: *regendum. Nam*.

## 52. *ANNALS OF CLONMACNOISE*

Adapted by Michael Livingston, from Mageoghagan, *Annals*, ed. Murphy, pp. 150–51. Trans. Michael Livingston.

*Manuscript*: London, British Library, MS Additional 4817.

Among the many sources for the Battle of Brunanburh gathered in this volume, perhaps none manages to be as simultaneously frustrating and tantalizing as the *Annals of Clonmacnoise*. It is clearly a source of a very early date, perhaps even among the earliest available to us, yet we know hardly anything of its existence prior to 1627, when Conell Mageoghagan translated its text from a now-lost Irish Gaelic manuscript of uncertain origin into Early Modern English. Without the original annals themselves, we cannot know how much Mageoghagan altered the information in the course of his translation, though it is generally assumed from his often tortured wording that he did little or no conscious alteration to its contents and was (as he claimed) dutifully trying to preserve a text containing a "genuine tradition" (Smyth, *Scandinavian York and Dublin*, 2.39; compare Campbell, *Battle of Brunanburh*, pp. 55–57). The manuscript copy of Mageoghagan's own translation was also subsequently lost, though its text has survived in several copies, including that presented here. It has been traditionally assumed that Mageoghagan's lost Irish Gaelic manuscript source had come from the important monastery at Clonmacnoise, for which reason it is so named, though even this basic fact is uncertain.

Adding to our difficulties in grappling with this text is Mageoghagan's syntax, which can be tremendously hard to parse. In this present extract, are Sihtfrith and Audgisl (line 6) the two sons of Sihtric, or are these four different men? Are Iloa and Deck two men or one (line 9)? The information contained in this source is largely unique and clearly essential to our comprehension of who took part in the campaign that culminated at Brunanburh, yet our understanding of it leaves much to be desired.

1 *931*. So MS. The dates in Mageoghagan's text are regularly off by a number of years. Athelstan's death, for instance, an event in 940, is related by the chronicler under the year 933 (ed. Murphy, p. 151).

*Loghrie*. Though Dún Laoghaire, on the coast south of Dublin, does merit mention in the Irish sources, the location meant here is undoubtedly Lough Ree, the great lake on the Shannon north of Clonmacnoise. It was here that Anlaf Guthfrithson solidified his position in Ireland by defeating the rival Norse king of Limerick, Anlaf Cenncairech, before sailing for the confrontation at Brunanburh. The arrival described here, therefore, is of Cenncairech and the other prisoners; the strong implication is that they were forced to accompany Anlaf in his fight. See note to line 6, below.

4 *othlyn*. The location intended by the chronicler is uncertain — in part due to the possibility that Mageoghagan has inadvertently corrupted the Irish Gaelic form — though the subsequent description is undoubtedly Brunanburh. Various identifications have been offered, from Getling (Skene, *Celtic Scotland*, p. 359) to the boundary of Cheshire, called the Lyne or Lyme (Higham, "Context," p. 152n66). The latter would fit well with what we now suspect about the location of Brunanburh (see Cavill's essay in this volume, pp. 346–47; on the possible Latin origin of the name, see Coates, "Lyme," p. 48).

5 *Normans*. That there were many men of Normandy at Brunanburh would be a fact nowhere else recorded — though it is perhaps worth note that Alfgar, one of the leaders fleeing the battle in *Egil's Saga*, was half-French, and it is to Normandy that he ultimately sails after his defeat (Item 25.157–58). It is likely that the original Annals made clear that the Normans here are, in fact, Northmen (from which "Norman" derives). Given the separate listing of Danes in this passage, it is within the realm of possibility that the term is meant to refer to

Constantine's forces, though it could just as well be the men answering to Anlaf from Man, the Hebrides, or even further north.

6 *Sithfrey and Oísle ye 2 sones of Sithrick Galey*. It is assumed that two individuals are recorded here, not four, and that the Sihtric mentioned is Anlaf's grandfather, who in the Irish sources is often termed either Sihtric *Caoch* [blind or one-eyed] or, as here, Sihtric *Gaill* [foreigner]; compare *Cogadh Gaedhel*, ed. and trans. Todd, pp. 34–35. While there is no other record of two sons of Sihtric named Sihtfrith and Audgisl (or anything similar), it is "quite possible" that their early deaths are to blame for their lack of additional trace (Smyth, *Scandinavian York and Dublin*, 2.39). Downham accepts their reality and relationship in constructing her useful genealogy of the grandsons of Ívarr (*Viking Kings*, p. 19).

*Awley ffroit*. I have followed Smyth (*Scandinavian York and Dublin* 2.39) in taking this to represent Norse *Óláfr Fífl* [Anlaf the Fool]. The name was common enough among the Hiberno-Norse that there is no reason to connect this with any particular Óláfr known to history on such scant evidence. A speculation could be made, however, that he is to be identified with Anlaf Cenncairech, the rival Norse king of Dublin captured by Anlaf on Lough Ree in 937 and presumably forced to accompany him to Brunanburh. There is no record of him after this date.

6–7 *Moylemorrey the sonn of Cosse Warce*. Moylemorrey is very likely a rendition of Gaelic *Máel-Muire*, meaning "Servant of Mary" and indicating (along with the Moyle Isa named in line 7) not only that Anlaf's army contained a significant Gaelic component but also that it was not as pagan as it is described in many of the later sources; as Downham notes in another context, "the heathenism of the Dublin-vikings has been rather overplayed" (*Viking Kings*, p. 34). Of this particular man nothing else is known, though his father Cosse Warce could be identified with Cosair Crolian (Mac Firbis, *On the Formorians*, ed. Bugge, pp. 2, 8), recorded as "Cossar, Crouantyne" in the *Annals*' entry for 830 among the "Great & valiant Captaines" of the Danes (Mageoghagan, *Annals*, ed. Murphy, p. 133). The same man might well be identified with Cossa-Nara, who seized Waterford and plundered Munster in 915 (*Cogadh Gaedhel*, ed. and trans. Todd, pp. 26–27). Interestingly, a son of Anlaf Sihtricson is later named Máel-Muire (d. 1021).

7 *Moyle Isa*. Very likely this is a rendering of Gaelic *Máel-Ísu*, meaning "Servant of Jesus." See previous note. Nothing more is known of him.

*Gebeachan king of the Islands*. About Gibhleachán, a sub-king of the Hiberno-Norse ruling the Hebrides and, perhaps, the Isle of Man, little else is known. His name, like those of Moylemorrey and Moyle Isa (lines 6–7), appears to be Gaelic.

7–8 *Ceallagh prince of Scottland*. Though other sources note the death of Constantine's son at Brunanburh, this is the only place that his name (Modern Irish *Kelly*) is recorded.

8 *Awley mcGodfrey*. I.e., Anlaf Guthfrithson.

9 *Arick m<sup>c</sup>Brith*. Smyth suspects this to be a representation of Norse *Hárekr Bárdarsson*, who might also be identified with the unnamed "'son of Bárdr' who sacked Kilclief near the mouth of Strangford Lough in the same year as the battle of *Brunanburh* was fought" (*Scandinavian York and Dublin* 2.39). See Downham, *Viking Kings*, p. 263.

*Iloa, Deck*. It is possible that the two names are one. See Downham, *Viking Kings*, p. 257. Campbell suggests that this would thus be meant to represent Norse *Illugi Digri*, a common Norse name combined with the epithet "the Stout" (*Battle of Brunanburh*, p. 57). It is presumably only a coincidence that the legendary character Illugi in *Illuga saga Gríðarfóstra* [*Saga of Illugi, Grid's Foster Son*] is similarly described as "stout" and answers to a king named Hring, the same name as one of the leaders present at Brunanburh according to *Egil's Saga* (see note to Item 25.14). In the saga, Illugi wins great riches from a cave; Iloa Deck, whomever he was, might well have accompanied Anlaf in the plundering of the wealthy burial mounds at Knowth in 935 reported by the *Annals of Ulster*. Interestingly, an earlier plundering of the caves at Knowth in 863 occurred at the hands of a different generation of men named Anlaf, Imar, and Audgisl.

*Imar, the king of Denmarks owen son*. Like many of the other names listed here, Ívarr is too common to pinpoint. Campbell suggests an association with Limerick, but there is no convincing reason to think this is so (*Battle of Brunanburh*, p. 57). The seemingly grand title is, as Smyth points out, "rather meaningless . . . in later Irish records" (*Scandinavian York and Dublin* 2.39–40), perhaps representing as little as the fact of a royal bloodline. Downham speculates that he might be the son of Anlaf, but she does not accept this as firm enough to include in her genealogy (*Viking Kings*, p. 259).

## 53. *ANNALS OF THE FOUR MASTERS*

Adapted by Michael Livingston, from *Annála Rioghachta Eireann*, ed. and trans. O'Donovan, 2.640–41.

Like the *Annals of Clonmacnoise* (Item 52), the *Annals of the Four Masters* is a text much complicated by its textual history. Under the title *Annals of the Kingdom of Ireland*, it was written between the years 1632 and 1636 by Mícheál Ó Cléirigh and three assistants, who collectively became known in English as the "Four Masters," a name subsequently attached to their work. In formation, the *Annals of the Four Masters* is a compilation of sources intended to present Irish history up to the seventeenth century. For much of the medieval period (until the twelfth century), the Four Masters relied on monastic materials that have almost entirely disappeared and for which their work is now the sole surviving record. The *Annals* are thus of profound importance for understanding the events in medieval Ireland.

1 *938*. Like most medieval chronicles, the *Annals* are misdated, such that the year 938 instead indicates events that occurred in 940. Obviously, the entry has been entered in the wrong place.

2 *mac Sitric*. Downham speaks for the majority when she notes that the record here has "confused" Anlaf Guthfrithson with Anlaf Sihtricson (*Viking Kings*, p. 244). While this is entirely possible, we cannot discount the chance that both Anlafs took part in the Battle of Brunanburh. See Introduction, p. 12n36.

# Essays on the Sources

John K. Bollard, with Marged Haycock

# The Welsh Sources Pertaining to the Battle

There are no records of a Welsh contingent at the Battle of Brunanburh, against Athelstan or with him. The Battle of Brunanburh was, understandably, of sufficient interest to the Anglo-Saxon chroniclers to warrant its entry in celebratory verse, and it became a key event in the subsequent glorification and romanticization of Athelstan. But in Welsh contexts it figures as neither a glorious victory nor a lamentable defeat. Other encounters serve both those functions in Welsh tradition. Nevertheless, the Battle of Brunanburh is relevant to one and (possibly) referenced in two other Welsh poems, and it is clearly listed, if tantalizingly briefly, in various Welsh chronicles.

In any assessment of the place of Brunanburh in British history, these Welsh materials take on more significance than their seemingly peripheral status might suggest. The prophetic poem *Armes Prydein Vawr*, in particular, may have been written shortly before, or not long after, the battle in 937. The evidence is reviewed below, but even before weighing it we can surmise that any poem addressing mid-tenth-century political relations between the Welsh and the Saxons will have some bearing on our understanding of the significance of the battle itself. At the heart of the matter is the question of date. If *Armes Prydein Vawr* was written before the Battle of Brunanburh, it tells us much, albeit indirectly, about Welsh relations with all their neighbors at the time and something about the conditions leading up to the battle. If it was written after the battle, it raises questions about the shifting balance among those living in and/or laying claim to the British Isles. In either case, it teaches us something about the early medieval conception of a region in which several different peoples came into proximity and much also about power and its all too frequent concomitant — conflict.

Two Welsh poems, one from the twelfth century and the other possibly as early as the tenth, are intriguing because each has a textual crux very similar to the other, a crux that may — or may not — be a reference to the Battle of Brunanburh. If Brunanburh is intended in these poems, the implications are significant for the reputation of that battle as a typological moment not only in English history, but in the Welsh historical memory as well. An argument, too, might be made that the Welsh chronicles, with their bare mention of the battle of *Brun* but no indication of who fought there, might indicate an assumption of familiarity with the event, although the early date and the terseness of *Annales Cambriae*, upon which these chronicles draw, weigh against such an interpretation.

## *Armes Prydein Vawr [The Great Prophecy of Britain]*

John K. Bollard

The Welsh poem known as *Armes Prydein Vawr* (Item 1 in this volume; hereafter *Armes Prydein*) contains no direct reference to the Battle of Brunanburh, nor does it specifically name any of the political figures involved. Nevertheless, a careful reading shows that this, perhaps the oldest surviving Welsh prophecy, can best be understood in the context of that battle and that the poem in turn furthers our understanding of the conditions leading up to it. Indeed, it was the implications of this poem that gave rise to the idea for the present book.

*The Book of Taliesin*

*Armes Prydein* is preserved on fols. 6r–8v of National Library of Wales Peniarth MS 2, known at least since the seventeenth century as *Llyfr Taliesin* (*The Book of Taliesin*), one of the most famous, important, and intriguing medieval Welsh manuscripts. *The Book of Taliesin* was written in the first half of the fourteenth century and contains some sixty-one poems.[1] However, the contents of the manuscript are generally older than the fourteenth century, and the dating of many of the poems is problematic or inconclusive. A dozen poems are now generally considered to have been composed by the sixth-century poet Taliesin, though not with absolute certainty.[2]

Over time, legends grew up around Taliesin, especially the belief that he had full knowledge of the past, present, and future, and like other early poets (e.g., Myrddin/Merlin and Virgil), he became known as a prophet.[3] The *Book of Taliesin* contains numerous poems that are explicitly or implicitly attributed to this legendary "Taliesin," that are written in what Marged Haycock terms "the Taliesin voice," or that are in a style which might have been assumed to be his. These include poems of wisdom derived from Welsh tradition and Latin learning, poems alluding to Welsh myth and legend, including several with important early Arthurian references, and, most notably for our present purposes, eleven prophecies. In her recent edition of the *Legendary Poems from the Book of Taliesin*, Haycock outlines some important and intriguing evidence regarding some of the poetry in this "layered anthology."[4] Most unexpected and exciting, perhaps, is her analysis showing striking correspondences between a number of Taliesin poems and the poetry of Llywarch ap Llywelyn, Prydydd y Moch (fl. ca. 1174/75–ca. 1220):

> Speculation aside, I would conclude with the generalisation that many of the poems edited here agree in language and diction with those by the known twelfth- and thirteenth-century poets, especially Prydydd y Moch. There are few signs of a significantly more archaic layer of composition. In the present state of knowledge, however, it would be rash to dismiss the well-entrenched opinion that some of the material has a pre-twelfth-century origin.[5]

Though they need not apply to all the prophetic poems in the manuscript, of which *Armes Prydein* is the longest and perhaps the earliest, these comments do suggest that our con-

---

[1] For the complete text, see *Book of Taliesin*, ed. Evans. For descriptions of the manuscript, see Haycock, "*Llyfr Taliesin*"; *Legendary Poems*, ed. Haycock, pp. 1–9, 558–59; and Huws, *Medieval Welsh Manuscripts*, pp. 77–79.

[2] For the historical Taliesin and his poetry, see *Poems of Taliesin*, ed. Williams, and the articles on Taliesin by Charles-Edwards and by Williams.

[3] On the legendary Taliesin, see *Legendary Poems*, ed. Haycock, especially pp. 9–21, *Poems of Taliesin*, ed. Williams, pp. xv–xxvi, and *Ystoria Taliesin*, ed. Ford, which contains an excellent introduction to accompany his Welsh edition of Elis Gruffydd's sixteenth-century tale of Taliesin, translated in *Mabinogi*, pp. 159–81. See also Williams, *Chwedl Taliesin*.

[4] *Legendary Poems*, ed. Haycock, p. 9.

[5] *Legendary Poems*, ed. Haycock, p. 36. Numerous articles by Haycock provide further invaluable insight into the poetry in *The Book of Taliesin*; in addition to *Legendary Poems*, see especially "Taliesin's Questions" and "*Preiddeu Annwn* and the Figure of Taliesin."

ception of the development and role of the legendary Taliesin needs careful study and considerable revision. It seems at present safe to say that the prophetic poems were attracted to Taliesin because of their style, tone, subject matter, and vocabulary.

*The Nature of Prophecy*

Perhaps earlier but certainly from the tenth century on, prophetic poetry became increasingly popular in Wales. The Welsh translation of a late-twelfth-century Latin biography of Gruffydd ap Cynan (ca. 1055–1137), ruler of Gwynedd in north Wales, testifies to a belief in prophecy and prophetic poetry among the aristocracy and even among ecclesiastics.[6] In this biography a passage from a prophetic poem attributed to Myrddin (who also appears in *Armes Prydein*, line 17) is interpreted as a reference to Gruffydd.[7] At a later period we find the following triad in a fourteenth-century Welsh law text: "Three officers who serve the king at his session: a judge and a foot-holder and a chief poet, that is a chaired bard who knows what is coming in the future from the poetry of Taliesin."[8]

Prophecy is a problematic and enigmatic genre at best, but it is perhaps safe to say that there are three basic types: (a) "true" prophecy expressing something about expectations, hopes, or fears for the future; (b) ex post facto prophecy referencing events that have already occurred, while purporting to have been written prior to those events; and (c) "rhetorical" prophecy, designed to impress with its language but having little or no real world reference. These three types are not mutually exclusive; a text may contain elements of each. Indeed, recognition of events named in the ex post facto style serves to strengthen a reader's confidence in statements of the "truly prophetic" sort. All three types may also sound very similar, especially if their references are sufficiently metaphorical, vague, allusive, or elusive as to be applicable, according to the beliefs or whims of the reader, to any number of events.

The language of prophecy is often intentionally obscure.[9] It may sound obscure because the poet does not know precisely or clearly what the future holds or simply because opaque but resonant language can impress a listener even if it contains little, if any, substantive underlying meaning, as in type (c) rhetorical prophecy. This type might be illustrated with numerous examples of high-sounding, though ultimately inexplicable, passages culled from the Prophecies of Merlin incorporated into Geoffrey of Monmouth's *Historia regum Britanniae*; two should suffice: "The island will lie sodden with the tears of the night-time, and everyone will be encouraged to try to do everything," and "An ass shall call to itself a long-bearded Goat and then will change shapes with it. As a result the Mountain Bull will lose its temper: it will summon the Wolf and then transfix the Ass and the Goat with its horn."[10]

---

[6] It has recently been demonstrated by Russell that a late sixteenth-century Latin version of the life is not a translation from the Welsh, as had been thought, but rather a copy of the twelfth-century original; see *Vita Griffini filii Conani*, ed. Russell.

[7] "Ef a'e daroganvs Merdin ef ynni val hynn . . ." [Myrddin prophesied of him for us thus . . .] (*Historia Gruffud vab Kenan*, ed. Evans, 5.22). For a translation of the poem and its context, see Bollard, "Myrddin," pp. 14–15.

[8] A. Owen, *Ancient Laws*, 2.586 (my translation).

[9] To say nothing of the practical difficulties of interpreting the forms and subtleties of a language at a remove of a thousand years or more.

[10] *History of the Kings of Britain*, trans. Thorpe, pp. 174, 180; *Historia Regum Brittanniae*, ed. Hammer, 7.85–87, 7.108–10.

Thus, the purpose of, or impulse behind, prophecy is varied. It may be designed simply to entertain or dazzle the reader (as might be argued for the two passages quoted from Geoffrey above) or to impress the reader or listener with the poet's wisdom or rhetorical skills. More often, and perhaps at its most effective, prophetic poetry is exhortatory, either instilling fear in, or providing hope and encouragement to, its audience.[11]

*The Date of* Armes Prydein

*Armes Prydein* is couched throughout in prophetic language, and thus it must be determined which of the above types of prophecy it might contain, or what combination thereof. Even a cursory reading suggests that it is not to any great extent "rhetorical" prophecy of the indeterminate sort quoted above from Geoffrey. Naturally, the poem is couched in the present/future tense,[12] and though its statements for the most part are general and non-specific, they seem not to be simply fanciful. Thus we must ask, to what extent can they be read as "true" prophecy, expressing a real, specific hope for the future, or, alternatively, what might be ex post facto reference to past or current events? *Armes Prydein* is, on the whole, more coherent in language, form, and structure, and has a more focused and sustained discourse, than most of the other surviving Welsh prophecies. Our first task in dating the poem, then, is to identify, if we can, any events and historical, political, or social conditions that accord with what we read in the text. The evidence for establishing an approximate date and context may be summarized as follows:[13]

1. The English are consistently named as the enemy, with twelve references to *Saesson* (Saxons, the English), one to *Seis* (Saxon, Englishman), two to the *Iwys* (West Saxons [see point 3, below]), and one to the men of *Lloegyr*.[14] There is no hint of the Normans or of the consequences of 1066 as felt in Wales. The dominance of the Normans would certainly have been recognized by 1070 when William Fitz Osbern occupied Gwent in southeast Wales, or by 1073–74 when, according to *Brut y Tywysogion*, "the French ravaged Ceredigion and Dyfed. . . . Then for the second time the French ravaged Ceredigion."[15] By 1081 the Norman presence was felt throughout South Wales; as one version of the chronicle states, "Then William the Bastard, prince

[11] "Generally this last is most important — & perhaps the prophetic mode was also developed as a matrix to contain bits and pieces of historical 'tradition' (perhaps only vaguely known)" (Haycock, personal communication).

[12] There is no formal future tense in Welsh. The present tense is generally used to express the future, made clear by context.

[13] A relationship between *Armes Prydein* and the Battle of Brunanburh was first articulated by Williams beginning in the early twentieth century. Much of the following discussion draws on and reviews his research and reasoning, set out in *Armes Prydein*, ed. Williams, which has been translated and augmented by Bromwich, now the standard edition of the poem. See also Williams, *Lectures*, pp. 52–54. Another influential study of the date of *Armes Prydein* is Dumville's "Brittany and 'Armes Prydein,'" which comes to somewhat different conclusions than the date proposed by Williams.

[14] On *Saesson*, *Seis*, see the notes to lines 26 and 96. *Lloegr* is the modern Welsh term for "England," but in the early Middle Ages it generally designates the approximate region of Anglo-Saxon Mercia; see the note to Item 1.109.

[15] *Brut y Tywysogion*, ed. and trans. Jones (1955), p. 29.

of the Saxons and the French and the Britons, came on a pilgrimage to Menevia to offer prayers."[16] This suggests strongly, though not definitively, that *Armes Prydein* predates the Norman Conquest.[17]

2. *Gwyr Dulyn* [the men of Dublin] (line 9) or *gynhon Dulyn* [the foreigners (or less likely, heathens) of Dublin] (line 131) are distinguished from the *Gwydyl* (*Iwerdon*) [the Goidels or Irish (of Ireland)] (lines 10, 130). Dublin was captured and fortified by Norsemen between 837 and 842 and was in turn taken by Danes in 852. Some time after this, therefore, the Scandinavians of Dublin would be identified as distinct from the Irish. This is evidenced in an entry for the second decade of the tenth century in the Welsh chronicles, "And Ireland and Anglesey were ravaged by the folk of Dublin."[18] Our poem, then, must be later than 852, or 837 at the very earliest.[19]

3. Archaic place names suggest a period earlier rather than later in the 842–1066 range. The poet refers to the men of Wessex as *Iwys/Iwis* (lines 108, 181). This form corresponds to Asser's *Geguuis*, and to the *Annales Cambriae* entry for 900: "Albrit rex giuoys moritur" [Alfred king of the Iwys dies].[20] An earlier reference in Bede's *Ecclesiastical History* suggests that the name was even then archaic or obsolete among the English (though it clearly survived longer among the Welsh): "gens occidentalium Saxonum qui antiquitus Geuissae vocabantur" [people of the West Saxons, who long ago were called *Gewissae*].[21] Other than the Welsh chronicle entries, derived ultimately from *Annales Cambriae*, an early list of Anglo-Saxon peoples (Angles, the Iwys, the men of Lloegr, and those of Kent), and its appearances in the *Book of Taliesin* (in *Armes Prydein* and in the prophetic poem *Ymarwar Lludd Bychan*), the term *Iwys* appears only twice in the twelfth century: once in Gwalchmai's elegy for Madog ap Maredudd, the ruler of Powys who died in 1160, and in a poem about St. David by Gwynfardd Brycheiniog (fl. ca. 1180) naming the regions of the British Isles and the continent from which saints were drawn to David and hence referencing much earlier history.[22]

---

[16] *Brut y Tywysogion*, ed. and trans. Jones (1955), s.a. 1081, p. 31; Lloyd, *History*, pp. 393–94. "Menevia" (Welsh *Mynyw*) is an early name for the area around the cathedral city of St. Davids on the western tip of Dyfed.

[17] There is, of course, a possibility that such prophetic poetry was written at a later period to be intentionally archaic. If this were the case, however, one might expect less historical consistency than we see in this poem.

[18] *Brut y Tywysogion*, ed. and trans. Jones (1955), s.a. 918, p. 11.

[19] Dumville suggests that on these grounds we might perhaps rule out the years 902 through 917, when the Vikings were driven out of Dublin, though they might still have been known as "Dubliners" during that period ("Brittany and 'Armes Prydein,'" p. 145). This latter point might also be argued from the date of the Welsh chronicle entry for 918.

[20] The medial -*g*- in Asser's *Geguuis* and in *Gleguising* (see note to *Armes Prydein*, line 1) shows the influence of Old Welsh orthography. See Asser, *Life of King Alfred*, ed. Stevenson, pp. 2, 66; *Nennius: British History*, ed. and trans. Morris, p. 90.

[21] Bede, *Ecclesiastical History*, 3.7.

[22] See the citations listed in *Geiriadur Prifysgol Cymru*, s.v. *Iwys*. For a proposed reference to the Battle of Brunanburh in Gwynfardd's poem to St. David, see Item 23 in this volume.

The form *Glywyssy[n]g* (line 99) designates an early kingdom in south Wales. In the mid-twelfth-century *Book of Llandaf* (*Liber Landavensis*), copies of charters ranging from ca. 625 to ca. 862 mention (in an earlier orthography) several kings of *Gleuissicg*.[23] This name also appears in the ninth-century *Historia Brittonum*, in *Annales Cambriae*, and in Asser's *Life of Alfred*.[24] Morgan Hen [Morgan "the Old"] ruled Glywysing from ca. 930 until his death in 974 at the age of about eighty-five.[25] He is in all likelihood the Morgan from whom the kingdom subsequently took the name Morgannwg, perhaps during the latter part his rule, certainly after it.[26] *Glywysing* occurs rarely in later medieval Welsh sources. It occurs in a poem of Gwilym Ryfel to Dafydd ab Owain Gwynedd written ca. 1175, but in a context that looks back to Owain's family origins.[27] Indeed, the scribal variants of the name under the year 865 in the manuscripts of the Peniarth 20 version of *Brut y Tywysogion* suggest that *Glywysing* had become unfamiliar in the later Middle Ages.[28] While we cannot completely rule out a late date on this place name evidence, the relative scarcity of these names in the twelfth century suggests that we might expect an earlier date for *Armes Prydein*.

4. The poet calls for an alliance with the men of Dublin. Though Wales may have suffered less than some other countries or regions at the hands of the Vikings, there *were* frequent Viking raids along the Welsh coast. While the Welsh and Irish chronicles and other sources certainly did not record every such attack, they did record major events, and it is reasonable to assume that *Armes Prydein* would most likely have been composed during a period in which the antagonism between the Welsh and the Scandinavians was at an ebb.

   The late ninth century records considerable Viking activity, but after 918, when "Ireland and Anglesey were ravaged by the folk of Dublin" as noted above, the Welsh

[23] See *Book of Llan Dâv*, ed. Evans, pp. 156, 157, 190–91, 195, 204a, 204b, 206, 209, 212, 214, and 230. For the dates, see the charters bearing these same page numbers in Chapter 3 of W. Davies, *Llandaff Charters*. For a discussion of the manuscript itself, see "Making of *Liber Landavensis*" in Huws, *Medieval Welsh Manuscripts*, pp. 123–57.

[24] In *Historia Brittonum*, ch. 41, Glywysing is named as the country in which the boy Ambrosius (=Myrddin, Merlin) is found (*Nennius: British History*, ed. and trans. Morris, pp. 30, 70). *Annales Cambriae*, s.a. 864, reads: "Duta vastavit Gliuisigng" ["Duda laid waste to Glywysing"] (*Nennius: British History*, ed. and trans. Morris, pp. 48, 89). Asser names Hywel ap Rhys as "rex Gleguising" (*Life of King Alfred*, ed. Stevenson, p. 66).

[25] Morgan is signatory to a charter of Athelstan for the year 934 (S407), and his death in 974 is recorded in the Welsh chronicles; see *Brut y Tywysogion*, ed. and trans. Jones (1955), p. 15.

[26] Bartrum, *Welsh Classical Dictionary*, pp. 485–86. In the *Book of Llandaf*, the eighth-century king Morgan ab Athrwys is named both *rex morcannhuc* and *rex gleuissic* (*Book of Llan Dâv*, ed. Evans, pp. 143, 156), giving rise to the possibility that he is the eponymous figure after whom Morgannwg was named, but the distribution through time of the names Glywysing and Morgannwg suggests that Morgan Hen is the more likely candidate to have lent his name to the land and that the designation of the earlier Morgan as "Rex Morgannwg" was retroactive.

[27] See Llywelyn Fardd I, et al., *Gwaith*, 28.45.

[28] Most of the manuscripts, including Peniarth 20 (ca. 1330), read *gly[n]nyssic*; MS C (1587) reads *eglwyssec* (*Brut y Tywysogion*, ed. Jones [1941], p. 5). The annal for this year derives ultimately from that in *Annales Cambriae*.

chronicles list no such attacks until 954. Indeed, in 928 Hywel Dda, king of Dyfed, traveled to Rome. Whatever his reasons for the pilgrimage, this would seem to indicate that he considered his rule relatively safe from both internal and external threat.

After about the year 950 there is scarcely a stretch of more than five years in which some instance of Viking attack on some part of Wales is not recorded in the chronicles. For instance, between the years 971 and 988 Godfrey Haraldson and his brother Mark carried out a series of extensive raids. In 987 Godfrey ravaged Anglesey, leaving a thousand dead and taking two thousand slaves. In the words of the historian J. E. Lloyd, "The Welsh of the age of Maredudd ab Owain had no more persistent or pitiless foe than Godfrey Haraldson."[29] The second half of the tenth century, therefore, is an unlikely period for a Welshman to be recommending a Viking alliance. Furthermore, as Peter Hunter Blair notes, "The expulsion and subsequent death of Eric Bloodaxe [in 954] marked the end of the Scandinavian attempt to establish an independent kingdom based upon Dublin and York."[30] This, in conjunction with Edmund's ravaging of Strathclyde in 945 and giving the rule over to Malcolm, king of Scots, makes a Viking-Strathclyde-Scot alliance like that defeated at Brunanburh less and less likely as time passes.[31]

Thus, we might narrow our range of likely dates to the thirty-six-year stretch 918–54. Can we be any more precise? Further telling indications can be teased out of both the poem's vocabulary and its content.

5. Mention is twice made (lines 18, 100) to the agents of a *mechtëyrn* coming to collect taxes from the Welsh. *Mechdeyrn* (to use the modern spelling) is used sparingly in Middle Welsh and has the basic sense of "great king" or "high king." It is a compound of the prefix *mech-*, from the root **megh-*, cognate with Latin *magnus* [great, mighty, important], plus the base *teyrn* [king, sovereign, lord]. The connotations of the early instances of *mechdeyrn* are remarkably favorable, as in two other poems in *The Book of Taliesin*. One refers to "dy haeled a'th drugared, vechteyrn byt" [thy generosity and thy mercy, Great King of the world], i.e., God.[32] In *Canu y Cwrw* (*The Song of the Ale*), the poet declares that no one before Judgment Day will be able to do the littlest thing "heb gyfoeth Mechtëyrn" [without the power of the Great King].[33] That God is also meant here is evidenced by the echo in the poem's last lines, "Ny digonir nebawt / heb gyfoeth y Trindawt" [Nothing is done without the power of the Trinity].[34] Another reference to God occurs in a poem in the *Red Book of Hergest*: "Mechdeyrn kaeroed na cheryd vi" [Great King of Protection (lit. 'fortresses'), do not rebuke me].[35] Secular

[29] Lloyd, *History*, p. 352.

[30] Blair, *Anglo-Saxon England*, p. 89.

[31] For a full account, see Downham, *Viking Kings*, especially ch. 3: "England: From the Battle of *Brunanburh* to the Danish Conquest, 937–1013."

[32] Haycock, *Blodeugerdd Barddas*, p. 83.

[33] *Legendary Poems*, ed. Haycock, p. 362.

[34] *Legendary Poems*, ed. Haycock, p. 363.

[35] *Poetry in the Red Book*, ed. Evans, col. 1149.24.

uses of the word are not uncommon, generally in praise of a Welsh ruler, but there is also a reference in the Welsh Triads to "Aneiryn Gwavtryd Mechdeyrn Beird" [Aneirin of Flowing Verse, Prince of Poets].[36]

For our present purposes, perhaps the most immediately revealing instance of *mechdeyrn* occurs in a passage in the Welsh Laws enumerating the causes of and payment for the *sarhaed* [insult or injury, as well as the payment for the same] of the king of Aberffraw, i.e., the king of Gwynedd:

> O deruyd y ur o wlat arall e sarhau, teyr a thry ugeyn punt yu y sarhaet (a henny yu e uechteyrn delyet enteu e urenhyn Llundeyn pan gymero y tyr y ganthau; ac amen henne heuyt ny dele dym byth y ganthau namen kun a hebogeu a meyrch).[37]

> [If it happens that a man from another country does sarhaed to him, his sarhaed is three score and three pounds; and that is his own sovereign tribute (*mechteyrn delyet*) to the king of London when he receives his land from him; and save for that he is never entitled to anything from him save dogs and hawks and horses.][38]

Though London was gaining in prominence in the mid-tenth century, it did not function as a royal capital at least until the reign of Aethelred the Redeless, which began in 978. While this passage was written at a late enough period to recognize the suzerainty of the Anglo-Saxon kings, the reference to the king of London in this context undoubtedly evokes an earlier tradition of British (i.e., Welsh) rule over the entire island before the rise of the Anglo-Saxons and perhaps harks back to Roman administrative rule, which was relocated to London sometime after 60 CE. Thus, *mechdeyrn* denotes the highest royal status and evokes a past golden age of Brythonic independence.

But why use a term with such positive connotations to describe the enemy ruler? There is a discernible note of irony in the second *awdl* or stanza of *Armes Prydein*, which states, for example, that though no one will pay, the agents will collect their "taxes" in the form of death in battle. Williams suggests that this irony extends as well to the use of *mechdeyrn*.[39] Both instances in *Armes Prydein* make reference to the English king. The most likely candidate for such a title, especially if it is sarcastic in tone, is Athelstan, king of Wessex (i.e., of the *Iwys*) and of Mercia (*Lloegyr*[?], line

---

[36] *Geiriadur Prifysgol Cymru*, s.v. *mechdeyrn*, includes citations referring to Madog ap Maredudd (d. 1160), Owain Cyfeiliog (d. 1197), and Llywelyn ap Iorwerth (d. 1240). For the reference to Aneirin, see *Trioedd*, ed. and trans. Bromwich, Triad 33. Unless it contains a simple scribal error, the fourteenth-century version of this triad (33W) in the *White Book of Rhydderch* suggests that the word may have been unfamiliar to the scribe or a predecessor, for it reads "Aneirin Gvavt ryd merch teyrnbeird 'Aneirin of Flowing Verse daughter of Teyrnbeirdd'" (*Trioedd*, ed. and trans. Bromwich, pp. 70–72). Of the five sixth-century poets from the North of Britain named in *Historia Brittonum* 62, Aneirin, author of the sixth-century elegiac poem *The Gododdin*, and Taliesin are the only two whose works have survived. Even Taliesin's epithet, *pen beird* [chief of poets], is trumped by that of Aneirin's *mechdeyrn beirdd* [high-king of poets].

[37] *Llyfr Iorwerth*, ed. Wiliam, p. 73.

[38] *Hywel Dda: The Law*, trans. Jenkins, p. 154.

[39] *Armes Prydein*, ed. Williams, pp. xvii–xviii.

109 and see note), who came to power in 924 and died in 939. Athelstan was very fond of titles. Coins minted during his reign bear the inscription "ÆĐELSTAN REX TO[tius] BR[itanniae]" [Athelstan king of all Britain]. He is more extravagantly titled in many charters, where we find him described as "monarchus," "imperator," and "basileus."[40] In a charter of the 920s or early 930s, he is named "Angelsaxonum Denorumque gloriosissimus rex" [the most glorious king of the Anglo-Saxons and Danes],[41] and in a grant to Byrhthelm, dated 850 (which should be corrected to 939 or 940, after the Battle of Brunanburh), he is styled "rex Angulsexna and Norþhymbra imperator . paganorum gubernator Brittanorumque propugnator" [King of the Anglo-Saxons and emperor of the Northumbrians, ruler of the Pagans, and defender of the Britons (i.e., the Welsh and/or the people of Strathclyde)].[42] In most of the charters witnessed by Welsh rulers he is styled "Æðelstanus rex Anglorum per omnipatrantis dexteram totius Britanniæ regni solio sublimatus" [Æthelstan, king of the English, raised by the right hand of the Almighty to the throne of the whole kingdom of Britain].[43] Williams asks rhetorically, "What wonder that the poet should use the term *mechteyrn* in reference to such a ruler?"[44]

But connotation and irony can be difficult to pin down or interpret, especially after so many centuries. Thus, while it may be less likely, given the context, let us assume for a moment that *mechtëyrn* could be used here without sarcasm. In such a case it would simply mean "high king," a designation adopted to acknowledge Athelstan's position of power, while simultaneously reminding the audience of former British/Welsh rule over all Britain. In this context we might note the use of Latin *subregulus* [under-king], identifying the Welsh rulers who were signatory to ten of Athelstan's charters.[45] Thus, with or without an accompanying sneer, the best candidate for the intended referent of *mechdeyrn* remains Athelstan, though we must recognize the possibility that it could refer to one of his successors who occasionally used similar titles — though none did so as regularly or with such grandiloquence.

6. Following his father's death in 924 or 925, Athelstan became the first to assume power formally over both Wessex and Mercia, and he instituted a series of councils

---

[40] Texts of the Anglo-Saxon charters may be accessed online at http://www.anglo-saxons.net/hwaet/ (accessed 24 June 2010).

[41] Winchester, Winchester College Muniment 12092, S 1417 (*Charters of the New Minster*, ed. Miller, pp. 49–51 [no. 9]). See also Stenton, *Anglo-Saxon England*, p. 348n2: "The most interesting of Athelstan's styles — Angelsaxonum Denorumque gloriosissimus rex — occurs in a private document written in the New Minster at Winchester (C.S.648). The inclusion of the Danes in Athelstan's kingdom is noteworthy in a record composed in southern England, and the style is one of the earliest pieces of evidence which exist for the use of the compound Angelsaxones."

[42] *Charters of Burton*, ed. Sawyer, pp. 7–8 (no. 4).

[43] S 413, S 416, S 417, S 418a, S 407, S 425, S 434, S 435, and S 436. S 407 reads ". . . per omnipotentis dextram, quae Christus est. . . ." All of these predate the Battle of Brunanburh; S 434, S 435, and S 436 are dated 21 December 937, but are more likely to pertain to 935, if they are not altogether spurious.

[44] *Armes Prydein*, ed. Williams, p. xvii.

[45] On the *subreguli*, see below.

that were larger than those of his predecessors and that included a higher proportion of lay nobility.[46] The poet refers to the connection between Wessex and Mercia and apparently to Athelstan's expanded councils in lines 107–10:

> Dysgogan awen — dydaw y dyd
> pan dyffo Iwys y vn gwssyl,
> vn cor, vn gyghor, a Lloegyr lloscit,
> yr gobeith anneiraw ar yn prydaw luyd.
>
> [Inspiration prophecies — the day will come
> when the men of Wessex will come to one council,
> one song, one counsel, with the Mercian arsonists,
> hoping to bring shame upon our handsome hosts.]

7. About 926 or 927 Athelstan summoned the most important of the Welsh rulers to Hereford, and, if we can take William of Malmesbury at his word, he exacted from them a staggering annual tribute, accepting the general implication of William of Malmesbury's account, even if we are skeptical of his exact figures: twenty pounds in gold, three hundred in silver, twenty-five thousand cattle, and as many hounds and hawks as he wished.[47] This brings to mind the *tretheu*, the taxes or tribute, of which the poet complains repeatedly (lines 21, 72, 84, 86, and 123), with increasing vehemence, though such a complaint might have been voiced after the imposition of heavy taxes at any time. Especially in the light of the stress on suffering as in line 104, David Dumville suggests that we must regard these councils and the imposition of heavy taxes as fairly recent past events.[48]

At this council Athelstan also defined the boundary of Wales as along the river Wye. While the precise history of the border area, especially in the south, is obscure indeed, a strong argument can be made that the lower Wye had been the de facto border since at least the reign of Offa in the eighth century, though the Severn may have remained the traditional boundary in Welsh thought. The region was certainly contested periodically. The poet may be objecting to a perceived loss of Welsh territory, or he may simply be using the new officially designated border as a symbol of Welsh-Saxon enmity; in either case his response in lines 58–60 is uncompromising:

> ac am Gwy — geir kyfyrgeir y am peurllyn,
> a lluman adaw, agarw discyn,
> a mal bwyt balaon Saesson syrthyn.
>
> [and on the Wye — shout against shout upon the shining water,
> and dropping of banners, fierce attacking,
> and Saxons will fall as food for wild beasts.]

[46] On these councils, see Stenton, *Anglo-Saxon England*, p. 347, and Blair, *Anglo-Saxon England*, pp. 220–21.

[47] William of Malmesbury, *GR*, 1.148. There is a notable similarity between the tribute in kind enumerated by William and that listed in the Welsh law of *sarhaed* to the king of Aberffraw quoted above in point 5.

[48] Dumville, "Brittany and 'Armes Prydein,'" p. 146.

It is also possible that the council held at Cirencester in December 935, attended by Hywel Dda, Idwal Foel, and Morgan ab Owain, underlies the poet's identification of the English agents as *Meiryon Kaer Geri* [agents of Cirencester] (line 69), though it may simply be that Cirencester was the usual staging place for collecting Welsh tribute.[49]

8. In the very first *awdl* the poet envisions a grand alliance among the Cymry, the Scandinavian Dubliners, the Irish of Ireland, the Isle of Man (or possibly Anglesey), and Scotland, the Cornish, and the men of Strathclyde. Before the Battle of Brunanburh, of course, there must have been a period during which preparations for an alliance were being made. It would be odd indeed if the Welsh were left out of such extensive planning, and *Armes Prydein* might thus be read as part of an internal campaign to convince the Welsh to join an alliance against Athelstan. Williams argues that it is scarcely credible "that any Welshman would have had the heart to compose 'The Prophecy of Britain'" after the defeat of the armies of Anlaf Guthfrithson, king of Dublin, Constantine, king of Scotland, and Owain, king of Strathclyde, at Brunanburh in 937 and the consequent consolidation of Athelstan's power, often cited as marking the beginning of an English nation.[50]

   Dumville was the first to question seriously Williams' assumption of a pre-937 date, asking, "How could the prospect of such a coalition come to be the stuff of credible prophecy?" Of the conclusion that no Welshman after 937 would have the heart to compose such a poem, he suggests that "this makes no allowance for the resilience of the medieval warrior-politician, for the rapid shifts in fortune which could and did occur, as in the winter of 939/40 . . . [which] undid what Æthelstan seemed to have achieved at Brunanburh." Side-stepping Williams' crushing defeat and loss of heart hypothesis for a pre-Brunanburh date, Dumville suggests a broader range of dates: "Rather we should consider *ca* 935 x *ca* 950 to be more realistic, and it is difficult to say that an extension to *ca* 960 or even *ca* 980 would be absolutely out of the question."[51]

   Accepting most of Dumville's arguments, Andrew Breeze identifies the *ar Lego* (line 106) as Leicester and concludes from this that the poem should be dated to the summer of 940, after Athelstan's successor Edmund made significant concessions there to Anlaf Guthfrithson.[52] In a review of the historical events of the tenth century, Helen Fulton accepts a date-range of 920–55, slightly broader than Dumville's. Questioning the function of prophetic poetry as it is often conceived, she proposes a setting for the poem after the death of Hywel Dda in 950:

> The poem can hardly be meant literally as a call to arms. . . . Instead, it can be read as a conventional response to a major political event, using the format of prophecy

---

[49] See Dumville, "Brittany and 'Armes Prydein,'" p. 146.

[50] *Armes Prydein*, ed. Williams, p. xxiv.

[51] Dumville, "Brittany and 'Armes Prydein,'" pp. 147–51.

[52] Breeze, "*Armes Prydein*, Hywel Dda, and Edmund," pp. 216–17. For the etymologically simpler suggestion that *Lego* is Caerleon, see the note to line 106.

> to promote a renewed sense of grievance against the English following the death of Hywel and the treacherous English slaying of Cadwgan ab Owain of Glywysing in 949. . . .
>
> The function of the poem, then, could be occasional, formally marking the end of Hywel's long period of leadership in Wales with a dramatised vision of chaos and bloodshed whose only purpose must be to ensure Welsh liberty from English oppression.[53]

In assessing all of these theories of dating, it is important to keep in mind, as Brynley F. Roberts states with reference to *The Mabinogi* but in terms that are apposite here, "It is dangerous to argue from text to specific historical events."[54] All of the suggested date ranges proposed to date are based on subjective arguments. It is perhaps best for us to withhold final judgment until further evidence arises. We can, however, be reasonably confident that *Armes Prydein* can be placed in the mid-tenth century. Whether it was composed prior or subsequent to the Battle of Brunanburh, there can be little doubt that the political events and alliances that resulted in the battle and subsequent events are equally pertinent to the composition of this intriguing Welsh poem. Let us turn, then, to the historical context to see how it illuminates the poem and vice versa.

*The Poet, Purpose, and Provenance of* Armes Prydein

Determining the context of *Armes Prydein* is difficult not only because the poem is anonymous and undated. In the early tenth century Wales was not a unified country or region, though a long-standing, and perhaps increasing, awareness of a Welsh cultural unity was manifest, especially in response to the continuing Anglo-Saxon and Scandinavian incursions which had begun in earlier centuries. This awareness is exemplified in the term *Cymry* [the Welsh], literally "[those who are] of the same region" (see the note to line 9).[55] Before, during, and after the tenth century, Wales was divided into various distinct kingdoms or realms whose number, fortunes, and boundaries shifted over time. The most important of these were Gwynedd in the northwest, Powys in the northeast, Seisyllwg and Dyfed (combined under Hywel Dda into Deheubarth) in the southwest, and Brycheiniog, Glywysing, and Gwent in the southeast.

Hywell ap Cadell ap Rhodri Mawr, later known as Hywel Dda [Hywel "the Good"], succeeded through marriage — and perhaps more than a little intrigue — to the rule of Dyfed in 905/06 and on the death of his brother Clydog in 920 to all of Seisyllwg, on his way to becoming the most powerful Welsh ruler before his death in 950. After 916 Gwynedd was ruled by Hywel's cousin Idwal Foel [Idwal "the Bald"] ab Anarawd ap Rhodri Mawr until his death in 942, and Glywysing and Gwent were ruled by Owain ap Hywel ap Rhys until he died in 930. Morgan ab Owain (later known as Morgan Hen) succeeded to the rule of Glywysing and extended his rule over Gwent to the east in 942, though losing some western territory to Dyfed. Claims to the rule of Gwent in the early tenth century are somewhat unclear, but it may be that the name "Wurgeat" which appears on two of Athelstan's charters (S 400, S 417) represents Gwriad (ap Brochwel?), the father of Nowy (who may have assumed the rule

---

[53] Fulton, "Tenth-Century Wales and *Armes Prydein*," p. 16.

[54] Roberts, "Where?" p. 63.

[55] Pryce, "British or Welsh?" examines the medieval terminology used to refer to the Welsh.

of Gwent as early as 942 when Cadell ab Arthfael of Gwent was poisoned). These are the principal names which inhabit the historical complexities to be taken into account when reading *Armes Prydein*. Relations among these men shifted over time, as undoubtedly did their individual and joint interactions with the Anglo-Saxon rulers across a contested border.

Received opinion, originally propounded by Williams, has long been that the poem was written by a poet, probably a monk, from Dyfed who was disaffected with the accommodating *realpolitik* policies of Hywel Dda toward the kings of Wessex.[56] This is based on the references to St. David and on the assumption that no court poet within Hywel's realm would sing in blatant opposition to the policies of his king and patron. The belief that Hywel Dda was a willing ally of the Anglo-Saxons is based, in turn, on J. E. Lloyd's brief summary of Hywel's career and on his appearance as a witness on a number of Athelstan's charters between 928 and 937.[57] Lloyd understood Hywel to be an admirer of Alfred the Great, and he surmised that Hywel's journey to Rome in 928 or 929 was in imitation of the pilgrimage that Alfred took with his father in 855.[58]

However, though we can only conjecture the reasons for Hywel's journey to Rome,[59] we can more confidently surmise that, as with Alfred, it would have brought him into close contact with at least some members of the late Carolingian dynasty, giving him a broader view of the ideals and practice of tenth-century kingship, and, more to the point, that he must have felt that his own rule in Dyfed was sufficiently secure to make such a journey in the first place. Whatever its background, this security was undoubtedly colored by and perhaps even a consequence of Hywel's relations with Athelstan. His name on the witness list of a possibly spurious charter (S 400) implies that Hywel, along with Idwal and Gwriad, was with Athelstan in Exeter on Easter, 16 April 928, which must have been just prior to Hywel's journey to Rome.[60] This meeting took place during Athelstan's campaign to push the Cornish frontier back to the river Tamar. The preceding year, following Idwal's failed resistance campaign in 926–27, Hywel and Owain ap Hywel ap Rhys, along with the other major Welsh kings, had submitted, however reluctantly, to Athelstan in the meeting at Hereford discussed above and in which the Welsh border was similarly defined as the Wye.[61] While the strong terms of the Hereford settlement certainly

---

[56] See Williams, *Lectures*, pp. 52–54; *Armes Prydein*, trans. Bromwich, pp. xxiv–xxvi.

[57] Lloyd, *History*, pp. 333–43. The number depends on the reliability of the charters; some are probably and others certainly later forgeries. Only two of these charters, from 931 and 935, have survived in original tenth-century copies. Though the specifics of the later copies may fall under suspicion, the names in the witness lists are likely to have been drawn from authentic sources. One of three charters dated 16 December 937 is certainly spurious, and the other two may be as well. Thus it would be unwise to draw any conclusions from the appearance of Hywel's name so close to the Battle of Brunanburh. Loyn, "Wales and England," suggests that the year should be 935.

[58] "There is good reason to think that he made Alfred, in whose reign he was doubtless born, his model and exemplar. . . . The remarkable feature of the years which followed Hywel's return [from Rome] is his close association with the English court" (Lloyd, *History*, pp. 334–35).

[59] Kirby suggests "an act of self-assertion and penance" ("Hywel Dda: Anglophil?" p. 4), but does not speculate further on what he would be asserting or what that penance might be for. Are we to assume that it is penance for earlier opposition to Athelstan? If so, this would put the lie to the notion of an Anglophilic Hywel; if not, then the motivation for the pilgrimage remains obscure.

[60] Hywel next appears on charter S 413, dated 20 June 931.

[61] Hywel had also submitted to Edward, Athelstan's father, in 918.

would not win Athelstan the love and lasting loyalty of the Welsh leaders, they do demonstrate the degree of power he was able to exert over them. For the next ten years, Athelstan seems to have been keeping the Welsh kings on a short leash. Between 928 and 937 Hywel, Morgan, Idwal, and Owain (possibly Owain of Strathclyde, if not Owain of Glywysing) appear as signatories to Athelstan's charters at numerous locations in what can now be called England. They are usually identified as *subreguli* [underkings], a term that must have carried considerable sting.[62]

Prior to Brunanburh Athelstan made a foray into Scotland in 934. Though the details of this incursion are not known, on 28 May 934, Hywel, Idwal, Tewdwr, and probably Morgan signed a charter (S 435) in Winchester and on 7 June 930 (= 934), Hywel, Morgan, and Idwal witnessed another (S 407) to the north in Nottingham. This has been interpreted as indicating that these Welsh princes accompanied (or had been compelled to accompany) Athelstan on this expedition, though there is no direct evidence that they did.[63] On 13 September 934 at Buckingham a grant of land (S 426) was signed by Constantine, signaling his acquiescence to Athelstan, temporary though that proved to be. However long he was in England and in some measure of concord with the king, we can confidently surmise that Constantine was soon discussing an anti-English coalition with Strathclyde, the Irish, and the Dublin Scandinavians. Whether any Welsh — either kings or subjects disaffected with conciliatory Welsh policies toward the English — were included in the conversation has not been documented, but it is difficult to believe that they were not. The English version of a charter (S 427) from Frome, 16 December 934, names "ÆÐELSTAN Ongolsaxna cyning and brytenwalda ealles þyses iglandæs" [Athelstan, king of the Anglo-Saxons and high king of all this island] and is witnessed by "Huwal Vndercyning" — a clear indication of Athelstan's assumption of overlordship. However much the title of underking might have stung Hywel, a ruler with aspirations as high as Athelstan's, at least within Wales, there can be little doubt that a certain, if indeterminate, percentage of his subjects and other Welsh would be displeased.

In any case, *Armes Prydein* may not have been written by a direct subject of Hywel at all. From the numerous religious references in the poem, Williams concludes that the poet must have been a monk, but invocations and references to God are common to many early poems about which no such assertion need be made.[64] Nor need the five times that Dewi (St. David) is mentioned imply that the poet is from Dyfed, for churches dedicated to Dewi reach from St. Davids in the extreme west of Dyfed as far east as the Wye, Athelstan's proposed eastern border of Wales, especially along the routes of the Roman roads across South Wales.[65]

The geographic focus of the poem is not limited to or even predominately concerned with Dyfed. Specific geographic references within Wales are few in the poem, and they do

[62] "Such a man [as Hywel] is not likely to have embraced with enthusiasm the title of *subregulus* by which he was so styled at the West Saxon court. His visits there must have been an indignity and a humiliation for one bent rather on personal self-aggrandisement within Wales" (Kirby, "Hywel Dda: Anglophil?" p. 7). Charter S 433, dated 937, includes "Howel regulus" as a sole Welsh name, but it is in all likelihood an eleventh-century forgery.

[63] Kirby, "Hywel Dda: Anglophil?" p. 5; Fulton, "Tenth-Century Wales and *Armes Prydein*," p. 11.

[64] *Armes Prydein*, ed. Williams, pp. xxiv–xxvi.

[65] Rees, *Historical Atlas*, plate 25b. In "Geography of the Cult of St David," H. James restricts her discussion to the extensive medieval diocese of St. Davids, noting that "it is of course necessary to point out that there are dedications to St. David and his close associates in south-east Wales and south-western Britain not covered at all in this analysis" (p. 81).

suggest a southern provenance. It is noteworthy that Dyfed is named twice (lines 99, 173) and Glywysing, to the east of Dyfed, once (line 99). The river Wye is also in the south, marking the eastern boundary of Gwent, and the poet's prophecy of a battle fought on its banks seems particularly heartfelt, if not downright fierce (lines 54–68).[66]

Aber Peryddon, that is the mouth or confluence of the Peryddon, is mentioned twice (lines 18, 71). Identification of the Peryddon is not certain, but it would seem to be the same as the *fluvium Perironis* or *Peryronis* of Geoffrey of Monmouth's *Historia*.[67] In the Welsh translations of Geoffrey this is rendered as *Auon Perydon* (i.e., Afon Peryddon in modern orthography).[68] A note amongst the charters in the *Book of Llandaf* records the return ca. 970 of certain territories by King Morgan to Gwgawn, the bishop of Llandaf. The boundaries of one of these parcels are traced, in part, "Along the Catlan, as far as Aber Periron, along the Catlan as far as the Monnow."[69] The location has been identified as probably the area of Rockfield, just northwest of the town of Monmouth. This is certainly within the region of particular interest to the *Armes Prydein* poet, as well as to Geoffrey in a later century. It is also telling that the passage in Geoffrey's text that includes the *fluvium Perironis* also mentions Cynan and Cadwaladr, as well as an alliance with Scotland. Indeed, this passage may reflect some knowledge of *Armes Prydein* itself, as a similar passage in Geoffrey's *Vita Merlini* almost certainly does.[70]

The manuscript reading *gelli kaer* (line 197) makes better sense if emended to *Keli kaer* [Heavenly Fortress]. However, the manuscript reading may have been influenced by (or misunderstood as) the place-name Gelli-gaer, two of which are found within the bounds of Glywysing; the best known is a town in the east with the remains of a Roman fort (*caer*) nearby, and the other, less likely, location survives as the name of a farm in the west near the border with Dyfed.[71]

The area of most detailed focus in the poem, therefore, is Glywysing, Gwent, and the Wye valley. It is perhaps there that we might expect to find our poet. Who then might the poet be? The closest we can get to a direct statement is line 23: "It is a high-born man who says this," which may or may not refer to the poet himself. While it is possible that he was a monk or cleric, the quality of the verse is excellent and it seems likely that he would have been a trained bard, perhaps occupying a position as *bardd teulu* [household bard, more literally "poet of the household troops"] or *pencerdd* [chief poet] in a court of Glywysing or Gwent. The *bardd teulu* is listed as one of the traditional twenty-four officers of the court in the Laws of Hywel Dda, and the *pencerdd* is included among the "additional officers"; though his status appears to have been more elevated than that of the *bardd teulu*, his connection to a specific court was perhaps

---

[66] The Wye as an eastern boundary is implied in the note ca. 970 in the *Book of Llandaf* discussed in the next paragraph. There the rule of Morgan Hen is described as extending from the mouth of the Wye to the mouth of the Tywi, incorporating the region of Gwent in the east. The rule of Gwent was often in contention, and both the eastern and western boundaries of Morgan's territory may be wishful thinking or exaggeration, reflecting the greatest extent in each direction of the varying fortunes of the realm over several generations.

[67] Ed. Hammer, 7.108–09; trans. Thorpe, p. 175. The form *Peridonis* is recorded by Morris in his *Celtic Remains* (1757); see *Brut Dingestow*, ed. Richards, p. 254n107.14.

[68] See, for example, *Brut y Brenhinedd*, ed. Parry, p. 128, and *Brut Dingestow*, ed. Richards, p. 107.

[69] *Book of Llan Dâv*, ed. Evans, pp. 241, 379. For the date, see Davies, *Llandaff Charters*, p. 125.

[70] *Armes Prydein*, ed. Williams, pp. xxxi–xxxii.

[71] See the note to line 197.

not as immediate or clearly defined. The *pencerdd* is defined as a winner of the chair in a poetic competition — still a coveted prize in Wales — and is recognized as the head of the bardic order within a certain region.[72] As Dafydd Jenkins notes, "The bards certainly formed an independent order, older than the 'state' organisation with which the Laws of Court are primarily concerned."[73] (Bardic training, of course, does not necessarily preclude a clerical vocation.)[74]

The loyalties and affections of the Welsh princes toward Athelstan and the *Saeson* in general were undoubtedly conditioned more by the exigencies of an imbalance of power and the recognition of the juggernaut of Anglo-Saxon military and bureaucratic might than by unalloyed friendship and admiration. The summoning of Welsh kings to Athelstan's court was not simply an invitation for friends to attend an extended banquet. Such meetings were bound to have been scenes of considerable diplomatic negotiation and tension, as well as demonstrations of Athelstan's superior might and growing authority. Thus, there is no necessity to assume that the poet was composing "underground," as it were, as part of an opposition movement discontented with a growing fondness for Anglo-Saxon ways amongst their leaders.

In this context it is worth noting one of the stated obligations of the *bardd teulu*:

> He is entitled to a cow or an ox from the booty which the bodyguard [*teulu*] takes in a strange country, after the King has had his third; and it is right for him, when they share out the booty, to sing *The Sovereignty of Britain* to them.[75]

Though the text has not survived, *Unbeiniaeth Prydein* [*Sovereignty* (or *Monarchy/Lordship*) *of Britain*] was almost certainly a poem about the ancient right of the Britons (i.e., the Welsh) to rule over the entire island. On the one hand, the surviving texts of these laws are later than the rule of Hywel Dda himself; on the other hand, the laws often reflect earlier custom and tradition. This reference, in any case, demonstrates that the presence in court of a poet combining long-held and fresh grievances in his verse may have been neither unlikely nor unwelcome.

Thus while the location for the composition of *Armes Prydein* is not known for certain, rather than being the court of Hywel, it is perhaps more likely to have been that of Owain ap Hywel ap Rhys before 930 or his son Morgan after 930 in Glywysing (and possibly Gwent), or that of one of the rulers of Gwent, perhaps Gwriad, who might not have ruled Gwent during the period in question, but may have had a claim to it (hence his appearance in the English charters cited above).

The poet's call for cooperation among the peoples of the British Isles and Brittany is an impressive one and it must have struck a chord in the hearts of many Welsh who heard it — if many did. His explicit references to the coming of the Anglo-Saxons to Britain

---

[72] See *Hywel Dda: The Law*, trans. Jenkins, pp. 20, 38, and the notes on these passages.

[73] *Hywel Dda: The Law*, trans. Jenkins, p. 371.

[74] Haycock documents repeatedly the clerical and popular religious learning (and boasting) imbedded in many of poems in *The Book of Taliesin*, and she points out that "the Taliesin voice" frequently offers challenges "to other poets and other supposedly learned groups, such as monks and clerics" (*Legendary Poems*, ed. Haycock, p. 11).

[75] *Hywel Dda: The Law*, trans. Jenkins, p. 20. Some of the law texts state that this poem was sung before going into battle, and Jenkins points out that "to sing it at the sharing of the spoils of a raid was evidently a vestigial practice" (p. 227).

clearly indicate a familiarity with the traditional history of Britain, perhaps even a specific knowledge of the *Historia Brittonum*. The author makes powerful use of this tradition in expressing his feelings and political leanings, explicitly referencing the stories of Vortigern (*Gwrtheyrn*, lines 27, 137), Hengist and Horsa (line 32), and perhaps the Night of the Long Knives (line 34) and the reference to four hundred and four years (line 146).[76] We do not know why the Welsh are not recorded as participating in the Battle of Brunanburh (on either side), and, even if he did indeed write the poem before that day in 937, it is perhaps fruitless to speculate whether the outcome might have been different if the poet of *Armes Prydein* had been heeded.

*A Note on the Poetic Structure of* Armes Prydein

As was the general practice in early medieval insular manuscripts, the poetry in the *Book of Taliesin* is written with run-on lines, like prose, rather than verse line by verse line as in the later medieval and modern convention. However, most of the verse lines of *Armes Prydein* are indicated in the manuscript by the use of a *punctus* (a period or full stop). To illustrate the complex and sophisticated poetics of *Armes Prydein*, the first *awdl* or stanza is reprinted below and marked to highlight its metrical features. Because of the complexity and irregularity of Middle Welsh orthography, it has been respelled according to Modern Welsh spelling conventions in order to make the rhymes, assonances, and other metrical features more apparent.

Note the following Modern Welsh spelling principles and pronunciation features: Welsh *dd* = *th*ese; *f* = *v*; *ff* and *ph* = *f*; *ll* = /ɬ/ (a voiceless *l*); *u* = /ɨ:, ʉ/ (i.e., a high front or back vowel, similar to the vowels of b*i*d and b*ea*t); *w* = a semiconsonant as in *w*ith (e.g., *gwedy*, *gwyr*) or a vowel as in b*oo*k, r*oo*f (e.g., *wrth* [by, line 62], *cwd* [where, line 112]); *y* = prett*y* in final syllables and *a*bove in other syllables; *y* = b*i*d or b*ea*d in most monosyllables, but *a*bove in *y, yn, yng, ym*.

The remaining vowels are pronounced much as in other European languages. Diphthongs are pronounced more or less as combinations of vowels. Phrases connected by initial consonant mutation are spoken as a unit, not as distinct words:

line 4 ym mhob = *ymhob /əm'hɔ:b/
line 5 yn nhrydar = *ynhrydar /ən'hrədɑr/
line 6 yng ngofud = *yngofud /əŋ'ɔ:vi:d/
line 15 yng nghyntedd = *ynghyntedd /əŋ'hən-teð/

End rhyme is indicated below in **boldface**, internal rhyme in *italics*, and alliteration and consonantal correspondence by underlining.

[76] It is striking that the Anglo-Saxon poet *of The Battle of Brunanburh* (Item 4 in this volume) alludes to a written version of that same tradition, perhaps that recorded in the *ASC* entry for 449 CE (version A): "In their days Hengest and Horsa, invited by Vortigern, king of the Britons, sought out Britain in the landing-place which is named Ebba's Creek, at first to help the Britons, but later they fought against them. The king ordered them to fight against the Picts, and they did so and had victory wheresoever they came. They then sent to Angeln and ordered them to send more help, and tell them of the worthlessness of the Britons and of the excellence of the land. They then sent them more help. These men came from three tribes of Germany: from the Old Saxons, from the Angles, from the Jutes" (trans. Stanton, p. 12).

Dyogan awen — dyofrys**yn**;
maran*edd* a meuf*edd*(or meu*edd*) a h*edd* genh**yn**,
a phenn*aeth* ehe*laeth* a ffr*aeth* unb**yn**,
a gwedy dy*hedd*, an*hedd* ym mhob meh**yn**.
Gwyr gwychr yn nhryd*ar*, Casn*ar* ddeng**yn**,
esg*ud* yng ngof*ud*, ryhyd ddiff**yn**,
gwaethlwyr hyd Gaer Wair gwasgarawd allm**yn**.
Gwnahawnt gorfoledd gwedy gweh**yn**
a ch*ym*od C*ym*ry a gwyr Dul**yn**.
Gwyddyl Iwerdd*on*, M*on*, a Phryd**yn**,
Cornyw a Chlud*wys* eu cynn*wys* genh**yn**.
Atbor*ion* fydd Bryth*on* pan ddy*or*f**yn**.
Pell dyoganh*er* ams*er* dybydd**yn**,
teÿrn*edd* a bonh*edd* eu goresg**yn**,
gwyr Gogl*edd* yng nghynt*edd* yn eu cylch**yn**;
ym mherf*edd* eu rhagw*edd* y disgynn**yn**.

An *awdl* may be defined at this period as a variable number of lines with a single end rhyme (with occasional exceptions). The end rhyme in *Armes Prydein* is marked by a fairly high incidence of Irish rhyme (so-called because it is a regular feature of early Irish verse), in which the vowels match but consonants may vary within certain classes; thus, the following sets rhyme: *lawer : gwragedd* (lines 36–37); *gynt : Glywysing : mechdeyrn : ebryn* (lines 98–101); *cusulwyr : cusul : Dofydd* (lines 161, 165, 166). Also, line 151, ending in *diwair*, does not carry the end rhyme *-ydd*, but it does match the internal rhymes of *Prydain firain* in line 152. There is one example of *proest* (half-rhyme), in which *daear* (line 29) rhymes with *aber* (line 30).

The poem is composed in lines of a type known as *Cyhydedd Naw Ban*, with a syllable count of nine (46%), ten (43%), eleven (6%), twelve (2%), or eight (1%), with a caesura usually after the fifth (53%) or sixth (34%) syllable, and with two accentual stresses in each half of the line. This is a formal type of line used in the *Book of Taliesin* particularly for eulogy, elegy, and prophecy.[77] The high incidence of alliteration, consonance, assonance, and internal rhyme throughout the poem prefigures the later development of *cynghanedd* (consonantal and vowel correspondence) in Welsh poetry, but the system had not become as rigorous or formalized as it was in the fourteenth century and later.

## *GLASWAWT TALIESSIN [TALIESIN'S VERDANT SONG]*
Marged Haycock

*Glaswawt Taliessin* (Item 5 in this volume) is one of eleven prophetic poems in the fourteenth-century *Book of Taliesin* (Aberystwyth, National Library of Wales, MS Peniarth 2), a collection that displays many facets of Taliesin's repertoire as an omnicompetent poet and sage including religious and scriptural verse, arcane learning, native tradition and prophecy.[78] For the most part the poems are tacitly attributed to this legendary figure who appears to have been developed from a historical poet whose name is mentioned in the ninth-

[77] See Haycock, "Metrical Models," pp. 169–71. On the syllable in early Welsh poetry, see also Griffen, *Phonetic Regularity*, especially Chapter 5, "Epenthesis and Mesotomy."

[78] For details, see *Legendary Poems*, ed. Haycock.

century *Historia Brittonum* (ch. 56) along with four others who "were renowned in British poetry" in the second half of the sixth century; indeed, the manuscript contains what are thought to be versions of the historical Taliesin's praise-poems.

The attribution of prophetic verse to Taliesin — and to the figure of Myrddin — is a medieval commonplace, and the explicit attribution in the title confirms that the voice in the present poem was imagined to be that of the inspired legendary Taliesin claiming foresight of political and social upheaval, and of foreign incursions, stout defenders and fierce battles that were possibly quite far in the past by the time the poem was composed. Such post-eventum discourse is a staple of the medieval Welsh prophetic tradition. The *glaswawt* of the poem title (possibly abstracted from line 34) is a compound of *glas* [blue, green, grey, pale; fresh, verdant] and *gwawt* which, despite its etymological connections with words for inspiration and prophecy (compare Irish *fáth* and Latin *vates*), is a very common generalized term for a poem or poetry, especially praise-poetry; note, however, that another *Book of Taliesin* prophecy is entitled *Gwawt Lud y Mawr* [*The Great Song Concerning Lludd*]. *Gwawt* is very frequently compounded, as in *gwenwawt, bardwawt, gwawtryd*, etc. *Geiriadur Prifysgol Cymru*'s interpretation of the meaning of *glaswawt* as "vigorous song" is likely; possible, too, is "verdant" or "fresh."

The poem is assigned a "worth" of 24 points, a value also accorded to two short legend poems in the manuscript; other pieces are reckoned at 90, or at 300, the value given to three of the long poems (*gorchanau*) appended to Aneirin's *Gododdin.* No other prophecies are given such values. The *Gododdin* rubric copied in the mid-thirteenth century implies that these "worths" were, or were imagined to have been, operational in poetic contests where the recital of older verse as well as the composition of new items may have been adjudicated.[79]

*Glaswawt Taliessin* is concerned with events in Gwynedd in North Wales — its greatest rivers, the Menai and Conwy are named in lines 7 and 8, along with its highest fastness of Snowdonia (*Eryri*, line 16) in the north-west. The mention of "a man of steel / from the line of Anarawd" (lines 25–26) suggested to Ifor Williams that the poem is to be dated later than 916 when Anarawd son of Rhodri Mawr of Gwynedd, styled *rex Brittonum* in the annals, died.[80] But despite Williams' tentative suggestion that the poem *might* belong to the 916–46 generation,[81] this is far from certain, especially since poets continued to make references to Anarawd and to his lineage as paragons of martial prowess well into the twelfth century (see notes on lines 25–26). Similarly, while mentions of Conwy and Eryri may well allude to the events around 881 when ealdorman Æthelred of Mercia was conclusively defeated by the men of Gwynedd (see note on line 8), they do not necessarily demonstrate that the poem was composed soon afterwards. The patently late *Cyfoesi* prophecy (cast as a dialogue between Myrddin and his sister Gwenddydd, which is no earlier than the twelfth century), for instance, recalls Anarawd's action in the "Wednesday battle" on the Conway: "Ar lann Konwy, kymwy duw Merchyr; / etmyckawr y deuawt: / arbennic anian Anarawt" [On Conwy shore, affliction on a Wednesday; / his custom will be honored, / Anarawd of excellent nature].[82] The stylistic

[79] Discussed in *Legendary Poems*, ed. Haycock, pp. 257–58.

[80] Williams, *Chwedl Taliesin*, p. 23.

[81] See Williams, *Chwedl Taliesin*, p. 23, and *Poems of Taliesin*, p. xxvi.

[82] *Poetry in the Red Book*, ed. Evans, p. 579.4–6; trans. Bollard, "Myrddin," p. 36 (emending MS *dauawt* [tongue] to *deuawt* [custom]).

evidence of *Glaswawt Taliessin* does not rule out a dating later than the tenth century; indeed, some of the poems's prophetic topoi, such as the advent of the three fleets and the proliferation of incest, are seen in twelfth- and thirteenth-century material. Nor is the lexicon conclusive, since much of its diction and some collocations (such as *durawt/Anarawt*, or *ysgwyt/ yscawn* as in the *Gododdin*) are found in later verse. In short, the 916–46 dating suggested as a possibility by Williams, and confidently followed by others, remains uncertain; consequently the poem's status as a early source for a potential reference to the virtually contemporary Battle of Brunanburh in 937 (discussed in notes to line 28) should be viewed with some caution.[83]

The text has been partially translated by Williams; and the drift of a number of lines summarized by Margaret Enid Griffiths, who notes the absence of any reference to the Normans.[84] A diplomatic text appears in Evans' *Book of Taliesin*, and a fully annotated edition is forthcoming in Haycock's *Prophecies from the Book of Taliesin*.[85] Here, the notes are confined to explaining the references to places and people and the emendations made to the text, and to laying out in detail the competing interpretations of the crucial *kattybrudawt* in line 28 by which the Brunanburh reference stands or falls.

## GWYNFARDD BRYCHEINIOG'S *CANU Y DEWI [SONG TO ST. DAVID]*
John K. Bollard

There is an uncertain but possible reference to the Battle of Brunanburh in *Canu y Dewi* [*Song to St. David*], by Gwynfardd Brycheiniog (Item 23 in this volume), composed around 1170–80. St. David died around 589, and was buried at Mynyw (Menevia / Tyddewi / St. Davids) in western Dyfed. Churches dedicated to him were established throughout southwest Wales, in southeast Wales (especially in the Brecknock region), and further afield in Anglo-Saxon England, Cornwall, and Brittany. A dominant theme of the religious history of twelfth-century Wales was the hope of establishing the primacy of St. David over the other saints of Wales, and elsewhere, with the ultimate goal of getting the cathedral church of St. Davids recognized as an archiepiscopate equal in status to Canterbury and York. Gwynfardd's 296-line poem fits within this history as it references many of the events and miracles in the life of St. David, though Morfydd Owen demonstrates that it shows a closer affinity to the famous church of Llanddewibrefi than to Mynyw, and she postulates that it "could have been intended for an audience assembled at Llanddewibrefi for a feast day possibly at which the Lord Rhys [1132–97, Lord of Deheubarth] was present."[86]

The present excerpt comprises lines 53–62, beginning with a reference to Dewi's oxen bringing his bell to the church at Glascwm as a gift. These six lines are included here simply

---

[83] Among other scholars following Williams' dating, see Breeze, "Welsh Tradition," p. 480, and Downham, *Viking Kings*, p. 214.

[84] Williams, *Chwedl Taliesin*, pp. 22–23 (lines 7–12, 17, 25–28), and M. Griffiths, *Early Vaticination in Welsh*, pp. 120–21.

[85] *Book of Taliesin*, ed. Evans, 30.24–31.20; title 30.23.

[86] M. Owen,"Prolegomena," p. 61. Owen prints the poem with a translation in "Prolegomena"; a full edition is in Gwynfardd Brycheiniog, "Gwaith," ed. Owen, pp. 435–91, and Lewis' *Hen Gerddi Crefyddol*, pp. 43–52. The texts are also printed in *Llawysgrif Hendregadredd*, ed. Morris-Jones et al., pp. 197–206, and *Poetry in the Red Book*, ed. Evans, cols. 1186–92.

to give some context for the four lines following, which end a thirty-one line *awdl* or stanza rhyming in *-awc*. While the manuscript readings are clear, the meaning of line 8, "Rac gormes kedeirn Cad Dybrunawc," is not entirely certain. The crux of the matter lies in the forms (H) *cad dybrunawc* and (R) *cattybrunawc*, discussed in the note to line 60.

This passage from *Canu y Dewi* cannot be fully appreciated without reference to the form *kattybrudawt* which appears in line 28 of *Glaswawt Taliessin* [*Taliesin's Verdant Song*], edited and discussed herein by Haycock. The fact remains that the relationship of these readings to one another is difficult to explain fully, and at present the safest course is perhaps to suspend judgement while noting the various possibilities. There are also some rather large questions remaining about the function of a reference to Brunanburh in the context of Gwynfardd Brycheiniog's poem to St. David. The poem is neither narrative in structure nor historical in intent, at least insofar as it might relate to events in the tenth century, rather than the sixth or the twelfth. Lines 59–62 are either an expression of the Christian idea that when we have cause to fear we can call upon God and St. David for aid, or, if we reject Owen's reading of line 59, that we need not fear because we have their support. If there is indeed a reference to Brunanburh here, then that battle must have become a standard measure of fierce battle having resonance in Wales two hundred and forty years after the fact. If so, then it is striking that there is no similar reference elsewhere in Welsh tradition, not to mention the fact that, for the Welsh, the Battle of Brunanburh was neither a great defeat nor a notable victory, at least not directly.[87]

## THREE WELSH CHRONICLES
John K. Bollard

*Brut y Tywysogion [The Chronicle of the Princes]*

Toward the end of the thirteenth century, probably at the Cistercian abbey of Strata Florida in mid-Wales, a Latin chronicle of Welsh history was compiled covering the years ca. 680, picking up from the end of Geoffrey of Monmouth's *Historia regum Britanniae*, to 1282, the year in which Llywelyn ap Gruffudd, the last prince of Wales, was slain. This Latin chronicle is no longer extant, but fortunately it was translated into Welsh and survives in three versions. Two of these versions were given the title *Brut y Tywysogion* [*The Chronicle of the Princes*] by the late fourteenth century (Item 34 in this volume), and, while not identical, they are relatively close in content.[88] The most complete is the version in National Library of Wales Peniarth MS 20, written ca. 1330 at Valle Crucis abbey in northeast Wales.[89] Unfortunately a leaf is missing

[87] There are other battles that fulfill these roles in Welsh tradition, most notably, in the literary tradition, the battle of Catraeth in Aneirin's *Gododdin* and the battles of Baddon and Camlan in Welsh Arthurian tradition. The Welsh chronicles, too, are replete with historically documented victories and defeats that might serve this function as well.

[88] Critical editions and translations have been published by Jones: a 1941 diplomatic edition of the Welsh text; a 1952 translation of the preceding, with notes; and a 1955 edition with Welsh text, translation, and notes. Dumville, who has begun publishing a variorum edition of all three versions, has come to doubt Jones' theory of three separate translations from the original Latin (*Brenhinoedd y Saeson*, pp. vi–vii).

[89] On the date and location, see Huws, *Medieval Welsh Manuscripts*, p. 47.

for the years 900–50. This lacuna is replicated without notice in the remaining thirteen manuscripts of this version, demonstrating their ultimate dependence on Peniarth 20. Numerous errors in transcription show that Peniarth 20 is a copy of an earlier Welsh text, which demonstrates a fairly early demand for the chronicle in the vernacular. The earliest manuscript of the so-called *Red Book of Hergest* version is found in Peniarth MS 18, written in the mid-fourteenth century at or not far from Strata Florida by one of the best early Welsh vernacular scribes, who identifies himself elsewhere as "the Anchorite of Llanddewibrefi." Unfortunately this manuscript is also fragmentary, and the chronicle begins in the middle of the entry for 1089. The earlier entries can be supplied from National Library of Wales Mostyn MS 116, written in the second half of the fourteenth century, and from the *Red Book of Hergest* itself, which is the earliest complete text of this version, though its readings are often faulty.

The precise sources of the lost Latin text cannot be known for certain, of course, but the surviving texts of *Brut y Tywysogion* from the beginning through the tenth century show a close relationship to the *Annales Cambriae* (Item 6 in this volume). The *Brut*, however, is not a series of annals; rather it is written as running prose and only the decennial dates are given explicitly. The entire entry for the 930s is included herein to show the context in which the notice of the battle of Brun [= Brunanburh] appears. That some additional source other than the known text of *Annales Cambriae* was available to the compiler is indicated by two bits of information for the years 934 ("by the men of Ceredigion") and 938 ("his brother") not included in the *Annales*.

*Brenhinedd y Saesson [The Kings of the English]*

The third version of the Welsh chronicle is known as *Brenhinedd y Saesson* [*The Kings of the English*] (Item 35 in this volume).[90] The earliest copy, in British Library, MS Cotton Cleopatra B.v, written in the first half of the fourteenth century at Valle Crucis abbey, begins in 683 but ends incomplete in the midst of the entry for 1198.[91] In National Library of Wales MS 7006, *The Black Book of Basingwerk*, written by the poet Gutun Owain (fl. 1460–1500), the text continues the account through the year 1461.[92] From its beginning to the year 1097, *Brenhinedd y Saesson* is a composite text, combining a record of Welsh events, closely related to the *Annales Cambriae*, with a narrative (rather than concise annalistic) record of English events, many of which are derived ultimately, though probably not directly, from the *Annales de Wintonia* [*Annals of Winchester*], attributed to Richard of Devizes (Item 30). That a chronicle of English history has been folded into the text of the Welsh chronicle can be seen in the passage reproduced here in the duplicated notices of both the Battle of Brunanburh and the death of Athelstan.

[90] Some confusion has been caused by the fact that a manuscript copy made by Iolo Morganwg in 1800 is given the incorrect title *Brut y Saeson*, as is the version printed in both editions (1801–07, 1870) of the Myfyrian Archaiology (Morris-Jones et al., *Myfyrian Archaiology*, pp. 652–84). An extract from the proper *Brut y Saeson* relevant to our present purposes is discussed in this volume.

[91] On the date and location, see Huws, *Medieval Welsh Manuscripts*, p. 53.

[92] Regarding this manuscript, Huws remarks, "The evidence for a Basingwerk provenance seems sound but Valle Crucis is a likelier place of origin" (*Medieval Welsh Manuscripts*, p. 190n). National Library of Wales MS 7006 can be viewed at http://www.llgc.org.uk/index.php?id=126 (accessed 24 June 2010).

Some passages in *Brenhinedd y Saesson* are not paralled in either *Annales Cambriae* or the *Annals of Winchester*. Among these is the account of the gifts brought to Athelstan upon bestowing his sister on Hugh the Great, duke of the Franks and count of Paris, the father of Hugh Capet. The story of Athelstan's Gifts first appears in William of Malmesbury's history, and he has taken it from a tenth-century Latin panegyric on the life of Athelstan that he partially quotes from and partially summarizes.[93] The precise contents of this poem cannot, therefore, be known confidently in detail. The Welsh version of the gift story contains some details not in William's account but found in others, for example in versions of *Le Livere de Reis de Engleterre* (Item 28 in this volume), and the *Anonymous Short English Metrical Chronicle* in the famous Auchinleck manuscript in the National Library of Scotland (Item 38).[94] No attempt is made here to identify the source or nearest analogues to this Welsh version of the tale, for that is a study beyond the purview of this book.

*Brut y Saesson [The Chronicle of the English]*

*Brut y Saesson* (Item 44 in this volume) is a Welsh version of a short chronicle or rather a narratized catalogue of English rulers.[95] (It should not be confused with *Brenhinedd y Saesson*, which is given the title *Brut y Saeson* in both a manuscript copy of 1800 and in early print editions.) The source or sources of this work have not yet been identified, but "it is almost certainly a translation of another Latin chronicle composed as a continuation of the *Historia Regum Britanniae*."[96] Like so many other chronicles, *Brut y Saesson* begins with a link to the end of Geoffrey of Monmouth's *Historia* through a reference to Cadwaladr and this is followed by a somewhat garbled list of the seven major English kingdoms (the Anglo-Saxon heptarchy). However, the explicit chronology begins in 850 and extends to the reign of Richard II. The fact that the account of Richard II mentions the Peasants' Revolt of 1381, earthquakes in 1382, and floods the following year, but ends with no mention of the crises of Richard's reign in 1387–88 and 1397–99, nor of his abdication in 1399, nor his death in 1400, suggests that the chronicler was writing in the mid 1380s. The *Red Book of Hergest* itself has been dated to a fairly short period soon after 1382, and thus *Brut y Saesson* must have been considered a very up-to-date account when it was translated into Welsh and copied into the three surviving manuscripts.[97]

---

[93] See L. Loomis, "Holy Relics," pp. 437–39, and "Athelstan Gift Story," pp. 521–22.

[94] For editions outside this volume, see *Le Livere de Reis*, ed. Glover, *Anonymous Short English Metrical Chronicle,* ed. Zettl, and *Riming Chronicle*, ed. Carroll and Tuve. The Gift Story is on fol. 313r, lines 1599–1662.

[95] The present text has been edited from the excellent, high-resolution digital photographs of the *Red Book of Hergest* available on the Early Manuscripts at Oxford University website at http://image.ox.ac.uk/ (accessed 24 June 2010) and from transcriptions of the complete texts of *Brut y Saesson* in the *Red Book of Hergest*, Peniarth MS 19, and Peniarth MS 32 (*Y Llyfr Teg*) available on the "Rhyddiaith Gymraeg / Welsh Prose 1350–1425" website created by Peter Wynn Thomas, D. Mark Smith, and Diana Luft, 2007; http://www.rhyddiaithganoloesol.caerdydd.ac.uk/ (accessed 24 June 2010). The Peniarth 32 version is greatly truncated, comprising only the first two sentences and the last sentence of this extract. A diplomatic edition of the *Red Book* text was published in *Text of the Bruts from the Red Book*, ed. Rhys and Evans, pp. 385–403.

[96] *Brenhinedd y Saesson*, ed. and trans. Jones, p. 25.

[97] Huws, *Medieval Welsh Manuscripts*, p. 82.

The three copies of *Brut y Saesson* are closely related, for the same scribal hand appears in each of the manuscripts, though not necessarily in this text.[98] Because there is no available edited version of the full text, fairly complete variants and notes have been given for the passage included here.

[98] See Huws, *Medieval Welsh Manuscripts*, p. 60.

SCOTT THOMPSON SMITH

# *PRELIORUM MAXIMUM*: THE LATIN TRADITION

In the year 937 King Athelstan and his brother Edmund led English forces against a northern coalition at a place known as Brunanburh, winning a victory there that would be famously commemorated in a poem entered in the *ASC*. This introduction of verse into an environment of annalistic prose marks a startling shift in style, one which lends the English victory an even greater presence within the *ASC*. This essay surveys a number of Latin texts written throughout the medieval period in order to consider how such works might contribute to our understanding of the vernacular poem's creation and reception. Does the Latin literature surviving from Athelstan's time suggest an intellectual culture that might have produced or valued such an poem in English? How does the prominence of the poem within the *ASC* translate in later Latin histories and chronicles interested in the Anglo-Saxon past? Might later Latin texts contain otherwise lost traces of stories or legends that had accumulated around the battle through its famed reputation? The answers to such questions must often remain tentative, but the queries themselves can enrich our appreciation of the ways in which poetic art transformed a historical event into legend.[1]

## THE TENTH CENTURY

Although meagerly represented in the *ASC*, the reign of King Athelstan (r. 924–39) was a time of significant political and cultural achievement. Athelstan extended his political power far into the west and north of England and he cultivated connections with a number of continental rulers.[2] Athelstan's reign also saw conspicuous accomplishments in learning as evidenced by a substantial number of surviving Latin texts, including some occasional poems and a group of stylistically ambitious charters.[3] Traces of other works now lost suggest a much larger corpus of Latin writing from Athelstan's time: William of Malmesbury, for example, mentions a long Latin poem composed in Athelstan's time while a Glastonbury library catalogue lists the item "bella Etheltani regis."[4] Such a substantial production and circulation of Latin texts indicates a court culture interested in royal panegyric, and such a literary climate surely would have been receptive to similar productions in the vernacular.

---

[1] For other discussions of Brunanburh in Latin texts, see Campbell, *Battle of Brunanburh*, pp. 147–60, and Lendinara, "Battle of Brunanburh."

[2] Stenton, *Anglo-Saxon England*, pp. 339–57.

[3] See Robinson, *Times of St Dunstan*, pp. 25–80, and Gretsch, *Intellectual Foundations*, pp. 332–41. For the charters of the draftsman known only as "Athelstan A," see Bullough, "Educational Tradition in England," pp. 469–73, Keynes, "King Athelstan's Books," pp. 156–57, and Lapidge, "Schools, Learning and Literature," pp. 20–21.

[4] See Lapidge, "Some Latin Poems," pp. 62–71 and 61n6.

Two pieces of occasional Latin verse survive from the time of Athelstan. *Carta dirige gressus* (Item 2 in this volume), probably the earlier of the two poems, survives in two manuscripts.[5] A partial version of the poem was copied in a late-tenth-century hand into Durham, Cathedral Library, MS A.ii.17 (Gneuss 220), an early-eighth-century gospel book of Northumbrian provenance, while a longer version of the poem survives in the eleventh-century London, British Library, MS Cotton Nero A.ii (Gneuss 342).[6] The poem is unfortunately corrupt in both versions, but Michael Lapidge has reconstructed the poem on the evidence of meter and rhyme.[7] Historical figures and events named in the poem also suggest a precise date for its composition. The Sihtric named in the poem was a Scandinavian king of York who allied with Athelstan and married his sister in January of 926. Since Sihtric is "defuncto" in line 13, the poem must have been written sometime after his death in 927. Athelstan campaigned in the north after Sihtric's death and thereafter received the submission of Constantine II (r. 900–43) and other northern kings.[8] Lapidge suggests that the poem served as a report back to the royal household in Winchester of Athelstan's success in the north, which would indicate a date of composition sometime soon after July 927.[9] After showing his strength across all of Britain ("per totum Bryttanium," Item 2.16), the poem tells us, Athelstan now rules over a complete kingdom ("perfecta Saxonia," 2.10). Produced early in Athelstan's reign, *Carta dirige gressus* provides an example of celebratory verse commemorating the king's territorial authority and military success.

A second poem in honor of Athelstan (*Rex pius Athelstan*, Item 3 in this volume) survives in London, British Library, MS Cotton Tiberius A.ii, a gospel book produced on the continent sometime in the late ninth or early tenth century but later donated by Athelstan to Christ Church, Canterbury.[10] The manuscript may have come to England sometime after the marriage of Otto I (r. 936–73) to Athelstan's half-sister in late 929 or early 930. A prose dedication and the poem were both copied onto a single leaf (fol. 15) by different scribes, the prose dedication being written in Anglo-Saxon Square minuscule and the verse in Caroline minuscule (most likely by a continental scribe).[11] Both prose and verse specifically celebrate

[5] Lapidge, "Some Latin Poems," pp. 83–93. Stevenson established that a Carolingian poem addressed to Charlemagne ("Carta, Christo comite") was the model for the Athelstan poem ("Latin Poem"). For the earlier poem, see *Poetae Latini Aevi Carolini*, ed. Dümmler, no. 4 at pp. 399–400.

[6] A prayer appealing to God for victory over one's enemies appears immediately after *Carta dirige gressus* in MS Cotton Nero A.ii. Citing such precedents as David's defeat of Goliath and the drowning of the Egyptians in the Red Sea, the prayer also appears in the eleventh-century prayer-book British Library, MS Cotton Galba A.xiv (Gneuss 333) where it is followed by an English translation (see Item 10 here). The prayer has been linked tentatively to Athelstan but such a connection has never been verified. See Robinson, *Times of St Dunstan*, p. 68, and Lapidge, "Some Latin Poems," p. 84n111. The prayer is printed in *Pre-Conquest English Prayer-Book*, ed. Muir, no. 6 at p. 21, no. 11 at p. 29, and no. 12 at p. 30.

[7] Lapidge, "Some Latin Poems," p. 98.

[8] *ASC* D records the alliance and marriage s.a. 925. Sihtric's death, Athelstan's northern campaign, and the subsequent submission of all the kings on the island all appear s.a. 926. See *ASC*, ed. Cubbin, p. 41, Stenton, *Anglo-Saxon England*, pp. 339–40, and Lapidge, "Some Latin Poems," pp. 90–92.

[9] Lapidge, "Some Latin Poems," pp. 91–92.

[10] Gneuss 362. See Keynes, "King Athelstan's Books," pp. 147–53.

[11] The prose dedication is printed in *Cartularium Saxonicum*, ed. Birch, 2.417–18, no. 711. The dedication names Athelstan "Anglorum basyleos et curagulus totius Bryttanni" [ruler of the English and leader of all Britain].

Athelstan's donation of the gospel-book, but the poem also lauds Athelstan's military might: God has elevated Athelstan "ut ualeat reges Rex ipse feroces / Vincere bellipotens, Colla superba terens" [so that this king himself, strong in war, / might conquer defiant kings, treading upon their arrogant necks (Item 3.5–6)]. If this is an allusion to Athelstan's victory at Brunanburh, as it seems to be, it would narrow the date of the poem's composition to sometime between 937 and Athelstan's death in 939.[12] *Carta dirige gressus* and *Rex pius Athelstan* both honor the king on notable occasions; these poems also more specifically praise the king's military triumphs and territorial control. The two poems may be the remnants of an active tradition of royal panegyric in Latin — such verse would have provided a suitable analogue (and possible inspiration) for the contemporary production of similar verse in English.[13]

Latin texts produced in the later tenth century testify to the enduring and far-ranging reputation of Brunanburh. The battle is recorded, for example, in the A-manuscript of the *Annales Cambriae* (Item 6 in this volume), a group of Welsh chronicles which may have been initiated at Mynyw in Dyfed in the very early ninth century.[14] Of uncertain provenance, the A-manuscript was written sometime in the second half of the tenth century.[15] The mention of Brunanburh in this manuscript may testify to the battle's fame, but difficulties in determining the chronicle's various sources complicate the question.[16] At any rate, the battle was deemed worthy of inclusion in a group of annals primarily dedicated to obituary notices of royal figures and bishops with only occasional mention of major battles.[17]

Other Latin texts of the later tenth century attest not only to the battle's fame but also to the abiding influence of the *ASC* poem in establishing the event as the pinnacle of Athelstan's kingship. Æthelweard, a leading ealdorman from 973–98 and a patron of Ælfric, translated the *ASC* into Latin sometime around 980, employing a style reminiscent of the hermeneutic Latin fashionable in the later tenth century.[18] Æthelweard compresses Athelstan's reign into the single event of Brunanburh, and like the *ASC*, establishes it as the defining moment of Athelstan's political career. Æthelweard describes the conflict as a massive battle ("pugna immanis," Item 7.3) waged against barbarian forces ("barbaros," 7.3), and he also names the location of the battle ("in loco Brunandune," 7.3–4). Æthelweard furthermore states that the English victory brought peace to the entire realm ("undique pax, omniumque foecundia

---

[12] Lapidge, "Some Latin Poems," p. 97n158. This line might also be a reference to the submissions of 927 recorded in the *ASC*, but not if the manuscript had traveled to England after the marriage between Otto and Edith in 929/30. The poem also contains several characteristics of the hermeneutic Latin which would make it an early example of that style. For the hermeneutic style, see Lapidge, "Hermeneutic Style."

[13] For an argument that the tenth-century *ASC* verse was influenced by contemporary Norse skaldic poetry, see Townend, "Pre-Cnut Praise-Poetry."

[14] *Annales Cambriae*, ed. and trans. Dumville, pp. v–xv. See also Hughes, "Welsh Latin Chronicles."

[15] The manuscript was probably in southern England during the first half of the twelfth century (*Annales Cambriae*, ed. and trans. Dumville, p. vii).

[16] *Annales Cambriae*, ed. and trans. Dumville, pp. ix–x.

[17] MS A of the *Annales Cambriae* also mentions the battles of *Dinmeir* (s.a. 906), Dinas Newydd (s.a. 921), and Carno (s.a. 951).

[18] See Sharpe, *Handlist*, no. 67, and *BEASE*, s.v. "Æthelweard." For Æthelweard's style, see Æthelweard, *Chronicle*, ed. Campbell, pp. xlv–lv, Lutz, "Æthelweard's *Chronicon*," and Winterbottom, "Style of Æthelweard."

rerum," 7.7) in a rhetorical flourish reminiscent of Bede's idealization of King Edwin's (d. 633) reign as a time of peace and plenty.[19] Æthelweard also describes the battle's great reputation among the *uulgus* [the common people], suggesting that Athelstan's triumph at Brunanburh enjoyed an abiding place in the popular imagination.

Æthelweard's description of the Scots and Picts bending their necks in submission (Item 7.6) recalls similar language in *Rex pius Athelstan*, but both texts may have drawn upon biblical precedent for the image.[20] While Æthelweard does provide some rhetorical color to his account, his writing makes no clear attempt to follow (or even acknowledge) the form or diction of the *ASC* poem (Item 4 in this volume). Æthelweard does, however, notably provide Latin verse in honor of both King Edgar's coronation in 973 and his death in 975. Both of these events are also commemorated by poetry in the *ASC*, and Æthelweard's language approximates the content of the *ASC* poems at several points, indicating that he was working from those texts as a base.[21] That Æthelweard gave such attention to Edgar seems understandable — he was writing in the years soon after Edgar's death, a time when monastic writers actively celebrated Edgar's reign as a golden age recently passed.[22] In contrast, Æthelweard's presentation of Brunanburh does not follow the model of the celebratory verse he found in his source. His account focuses as much on the battle's after-effects as it does on the battle itself, suggesting (perhaps) that Athelstan's victory at Brunanburh had already become somewhat distant legendary material by the late tenth century.

Brunanburh also appears briefly in the *Vita S. Ethelwoldi* (Item 8 in this volume), a text written by Wulfstan, monk and precentor at Winchester, soon after the translation of Æthelwold's remains in 996.[23] Wulfstan used the *ASC* to establish chronology in the work, and while he does not name the location of the battle, he does date it to four years before Athelstan's death.[24] Lapidge and Winterbottom suggest that the final four lines of the *ASC* poem may have inspired Wulfstan's description of Athelstan as a king "uictoriosissimum" (Item 8.1), while the hexameter cadence of "strage peremit" (8.2) might be a poetic ornamentation in response to the vernacular verse.[25] The fondness for superlative language in Wulfstan's account also recalls Æthelweard's own statement that Brunanburh was commonly known as "bellum . . . magnum" [the great war (Item 7.4)]. This enduring reputation of Brunanburh, coupled with the prominent example of the *ASC* poem itself, might have informed Wulfstan's own presentation of the event as he wrote at the end of the tenth century. Similar language underscores the magnitude and fame of the battle in later chronicles such

---

[19] Bede, *Ecclesiastical History*, ed. Colgrave and Mynors, p. 192 (2.16). Ælfric would later present the reign of Edgar (r. 959–975) in a similar fashion in his "Life of St Swithun" (Lapidge, *Cult of St Swithun*, p. 606).

[20] See the Introduction to this volume, pp. 22–23, and Vulgate Psalm 109:1: "Dixit Dominus Domino meo sede a dextris meis donec ponam inimicos tuos scabillum pedum tuorum" [The Lord said to my Lord, "Sit thou at my right hand: Until I make thy enemies thy footstool"]. See also Matthew 22:44, Acts 2:34–35, Hebrews 1:13, and Hebrews 10:12–13.

[21] For comparison of the vernacular poetry against the Latin verses, see J. Carroll, "*Engla Waldend*."

[22] See Salvador-Bello, "Edgar Panegyrics."

[23] See Sharpe, *Handlist*, no. 2229, and Wulfstan, *Life*, ed. Lapidge and Winterbottom, pp. xiii–xvi.

[24] This dating agrees with the Parker Chronicle, the oldest surviving manuscript (A) of the *ASC* (Wulfstan, *Life*, ed. Lapidge and Winterbottom, pp. cviii and 17n6).

[25] Wulfstan, *Life*, ed. Lapidge and Winterbottom, pp. 17n6 and 17n7.

as the *ASC* manuscript written at Canterbury in both Latin and Old English (*ASC* F, Item 12 in this volume), further indicating that Athelstan's northern victory quickly became fertile ground for stylistic and narrative embellishment.[26]

THE LATE-ELEVENTH AND TWELFTH CENTURIES

During the great proliferation of historical writing in Latin in twelfth-century England, some authors grafted legendary material onto the matter of Brunanburh while others elaborated upon its more factual details. These influential contributions extended the historical afterlife of Brunanburh by providing a core of material which would be exploited to various degrees by later writers in a long process which resulted in a largely fossilized historical record of the battle. After the Norman Conquest, we see substantial additions to the story of Brunanburh. The sources for this new material remain unknown, but post-Conquest writers must have drawn upon surviving stories and traditions both secular and sacred, oral and written. One of the most significant developments transforms the battle into a setting for miracles and holy men in a clear departure from the *ASC* poem's own interest in dynastic and military triumphalism.

The Canterbury hagiographer Eadmer (ca. 1060–ca. 1128) is best known for his *Vita S Anselmi* and *Historia novorum in Anglia* and his attention in those texts to contemporary persons and events, but his earlier works also include several lives of English saints. His *Vita Odonis* (Item 11 in this volume), composed sometime in the late eleventh century, remarkably places its saintly protagonist by Athelstan's side at Brunanburh and furthermore assigns him an instrumental role in the English victory.[27] Oda's presence at the battle has no known precedent in earlier sources. After Athelstan's sword shatters in the fight, Oda rushes to the king's side and calls upon him not to despair as his sword rests unbroken in its sheath. Oda further rallies the king by predicting an English victory before sunset, recalling Joshua's victory at Gabaon

[26] "Hic factum est illud magnum et famosum bellum in Brunanbyri cum rex Æðestanus et frater eius Eadmundus pugnauerunt contra Anelaf et Auxiliante Christo uictoriam ceperunt et occiderunt .v. reges et .vii. comites de sociis Anelafi" (*ASC*, MS F, ed. Baker, pp. 79–80) [In this year was waged that great and famous war at *Brunanbyri* when King Athelstan and his brother Edmund fought against Anlaf and, with the help of Christ, took the victory and killed five kings and seven earls among the confederates of Anlaf]. The annal originally read, "Hic factum est illud magnum et famosum bellum in Brunanbyri cum rex Æðestanus pugnauit contra Anelaf et auxiliante Christo victoriam cepit" before it received additions from later scribes. *ASC* MS F, written soon after 1100, used a lost Winchester chronicle as one of its Latin sources. This chronicle is partially preserved in three later chronicles, one of which (London, British Library, MS Cotton Nero A.viii) corresponds closely with the text of *ASC* MS F: "Hoc anno factum est illud magnum et famosum bellum in Bruningafeld, cum rex Aethelstan contra Anlaf pugnavit et, auxiliante Christo, victoriam suscepit" (Liebermann, *Ungedruckte anglo-normannische Geschichtsquellen*, p. 68). See also *ASC*, MS F, ed. Baker, pp. xlvi–xlix. Similarly, a forged charter (S 439) in the twelfth-century cartulary of the Old Minster at Winchester mentions the famed battle in its dating clause: "annum quo bellum celebre in Bruningafelda factum fuit" (*Cartularium Saxonicum*, ed. Birch, 2.420, no. 713) [the year in which a celebrated war was made at Bruningafelda].

[27] For Oda, see *BEASE*, s.v. "Oda." For his tenure as archbishop of Canterbury (941–958), see Brooks, *Early History*, pp. 222–27. See also Smyth, *Scandinavian York and Dublin*, 2.102–03. For Eadmer, see Sharpe, *Handlist*, no. 247, Gransden, *HWE* 1, 129–42, and Eadmer, *Lives and Miracles*, ed. and trans. Turner and Muir, pp. xiii–xxxv.

when God "made the sun stand still until all of Joshua's enemies were slain."[28] Like the *ASC*, Eadmer makes Brunanburh the centerpiece of Athelstan's reign (it is the only event included aside from Athelstan's succession and death) but Eadmer's addition of Oda's miracle significantly introduces the idea of divine intervention in favor of the English.[29]

Eadmer used this same material again in his *Vita Oswaldi* (Item 14 in this volume), written sometime soon before 1116.[30] Eadmer devotes two chapters to Oda in the *Vita Oswaldi* in order to demonstrate the excellence of Oswald's family (Oswald was Oda's nephew): the first chapter recounts the miracle at Brunanburh while the second surveys other highlights from Oda's life, including two additional miracles. In this second account of Brunanburh, Eadmer condenses the story and enhances certain dramatic details. Athelstan's sword breaks late in the day just as the sun begins to set, for example, while the restored blade is described as "fulgidum, fortem et insignem" [shining, strong, and glorious]. These particulars, entirely absent in the *Vita Odonis*, draw attention to the impressive appearance of the sword and the swiftness of the English victory. Oda's miracle at Brunanburh demonstrates his own sanctity and by extension distinguishes Oswald's lineage, but Eadmer's strategic revisions in the *Vita Oswaldi* also testify to the strong appeal the story must have held for both author and audience in the early twelfth century. It seems to have been a tale worth retelling.

William of Malmesbury (ca. 1090–ca. 1143) also added a significant amount of material with no known sources to his various accounts of the battle. His *Gesta regum Anglorum* (*GR*) and *Gesta pontificum Anglorum* (*GP*) both contain accounts of Brunanburh.[31] *GR* contains the more extensive material, treating the battle twice in its second book: chapter 131 provides an overview of Athelstan's political career, culminating in a long account of the battle; chapters 132–40 draw on various sources to survey his entire reign once again (Item 17 in this volume).[32] William's first story of Brunanburh at first glance resembles that found in Eadmer — both stories feature the miraculous recovery of the king's sword, for example, and William notably singles out Eadmer as a praiseworthy source in his prologue to *GR*. Yet the two versions differ in nearly every other detail. William furthermore seems to have used a source (or sources) other than the *ASC* poem — he states that Constantine died at the battle, for example — and many of his narrative details are unique. The story of Anlaf disguising himself as a minstrel in order to spy upon the English, for example, has no precedent in surviving texts, although it does recall (perhaps suspiciously) William's own story earlier in *GR* (2.121) of Alfred posing as a *mimus* [entertainer] in order to spy upon the Danes.[33] The

---

[28] Eadmer, *Lives and Miracles*, ed. and trans. Turner and Muir, p. 14n21.

[29] A forged charter dated to 938 (S 443) in the Old Minster, Winchester cartulary likewise ascribes the English victory at Brunanburh to heavenly aid. The charter's dating clause reads in part, "anno ab incarnatione domini nostri Jhesu Christi . dccccxxxviii . in quo anno bellum factum est in loco qui bruninga feld dicitur ubi Anglis victoria data est de caelo" (*Cartularium Saxonicum*, ed. Birch, 2.437, no. 727) [in the year 938 from the Incarnation of our lord Jesus Christ, in which there was war in the place called *bruninga feld* where victory was granted to the English from heaven]. This evidence suggests a tradition of miraculous elements at Brunanburh. See also note 26 above.

[30] Eadmer, *Lives and Miracles*, ed. and trans. Turner and Muir, pp. cvi–cvii.

[31] The earliest version of each work was completed ca.1125. See Sharpe, *Handlist*, no. 2114, Gransden, *HWE* 1, pp. 166–85, and R. Thomson, *William of Malmesbury*.

[32] William of Malmesbury, *GR*, ed. and trans. Mynors, et al., 1.206–29.

[33] William of Malmesbury, *GR*, ed. and trans. Mynors, et al., 1.182–85.

knowledge Alfred gains through his subterfuge allows him to mount a sudden attack that ends in a decisive victory for the English. The Anlaf story differs notably in its outcome. The Norse leader gains admission to Athelstan's tent but he is dismissed with his pay before the war council begins, and his subsequent nocturnal raid ends in his defeat.

Other unique elements in *GR* include the death of a bishop unlucky enough to pitch his tent in the spot vacated by Athelstan just prior to Anlaf's raid,[34] as well as the king's prayer to St. Aldhelm during the battle. In William's version, the king's blade does not shatter in the fight, but is simply dropped or lost. William also attributes the miracle to St. Aldhelm with no mention of Oda. In his *GP*, however, William provides additional information on Brunanburh, some of it contradictory: at one point he attributes the miracle of the divinely-restored sword to Oda (1.14.3–4); he later states that Bishop Theodred of London assisted Oda in praying for the miracle, with the qualification that this was a story told by the *ciues* of London (2.73.16); and finally he attributes the miracle to Athelstan's prayer to St. Aldhelm with no mention of either bishop (5.246.2).[35] Such variability may indicate inconsistency in the broad view, but the common factor of the recovered sword in all cases suggests some tradition centered on that miraculous event. Other material in *GR* further suggests some tradition of an exceptional sword owned by Athelstan: King Alfred provided a young Athelstan with "ense Saxonico cum uagina aurea" (2.133) [a Saxon sword with a gilded scabbard], while Hugh the Great, count of Paris (William calls him *rex Francorum*), gifted him with the sword of Constantine the Great in an embassy seeking Athelstan's fourth sister in marriage (2.135).[36] The differences between Eadmer and William, and the differences within William himself, indicate the ready availability of such a tradition in a variety of forms.

Brunanburh appears once again in *GR* (2.135) when William introduces the verse of a poet from whom "omnia haec excerpsimus" [I have taken all this].[37] The nature of William's source here, which he calls a "uolumine uetusto" [ancient book] written during Athlestan's lifetime in an inflated style of which he clearly disapproves (2.132),[38] has occasioned some controversy, but it seems clear from stylistic evidence that the verse William cites did not come from that lost tenth-century work.[39] Indeed it may be the case that William reworked his source in order to render it in a style more acceptable to his own tastes.[40] William includes two portions from the poem: the first excerpt (2.133) praises Athelstan in general

[34] William names the hapless victim as Bishop Wærstan in *GP* 2.80.4 (ed. and trans. Winterbottom, 1.280–81).

[35] William of Malmesbury, *GP*, ed. and trans. Winterbottom, 1.26–27, 228–31, and 592–95. William presents Athelstan in a less than flattering light when he states in *GP* 1.26 that Athelstan was surprised by Anlaf's night attack due to heedlessness ("ipsa securitate incautior").

[36] See William of Malmesbury, *GR*, ed. and trans. Mynors, et al., 1.210–11 and 218–19.

[37] William of Malmesbury, *GR*, ed. and trans. Mynors, et al., 1.220–23.

[38] William faults the style of his source but he also excuses it as "consuetudo illius temporis" [the custom of its time] and hopes that a more plain style might better reveal Athelstan's merit. William of Malmesbury, *GR*, ed. and trans. Mynors, et al., 1.210–11.

[39] See Lapidge, "Some Latin Poems," pp. 62–71, and William of Malmesbury, *GR*, ed. and trans. Mynors, et al., 2.116–18.

[40] William does show a flair for invention elsewhere in *GR*. See Winterbottom, "*Gesta regum*," p. 172. The varying status of line 27 ("Hic strepitus mouit") in different manuscripts also suggests that William may have been revising a pre-existing poem (*GR*, ed. and trans. Mynors, et al., 2.125–26).

terms, celebrating his accomplishments in learning and war; and the second (2.135) focuses upon a "bello contra Analauum" [war against Anlaf] that must be the battle at Brunanburh (although the poem does not name the location). This second poem makes no mention of the recovered sword from *GR* 2.131, and curiously enough, it shows Athelstan as somewhat sluggish in his defense of the realm against a ravaging enemy. As a result, the tone in this poem seems more critical than the exuberant praise found in the earlier verse (2.133). Although the poem names Anlaf as the enemy leader, it mentions neither a surprise attack at night nor the miraculous recovery of the king's sword. William here seems to have drawn upon an entirely different tradition from that informing his earlier story (*GR* 2.131). The sensational and miraculous events evident in that first account were probably derived from the same popular traditions that informed Eadmer's own presentation of the battle.

Other twelfth-century writers elaborated their accounts of the battle without including the more legendary materials found in Eadmer and William of Malmesbury. Henry, archdeacon of Huntingdon (ca. 1088–ca. 1160), completed the first version of his *Historia Anglorum* ca.1133 and continued to revise the work until sometime soon after 1154, the year in which his narrative ends.[41] In addition to established written sources, Henry drew upon unknown sources and traditions (such as the famous story of King Cnut and the waves) and also included many of his own poems in the work, creating a kind of historical *prosimetrum*. Henry's account of Brunanburh (Item 18 in this volume) is most remarkable for its ambitious Latin translation of the Old English poem. Henry states that English writers commemorated the battle with a poetry which uses strange ("extraneis," Item 18.15–16) words and figures; a careful translation, he hopes, will allow the *grauitas* of those people and their past deeds to emerge through the *grauitas* of their language. Henry's translation has been maligned by modern scholars for its occasional blunders,[42] but such errors should not eclipse the significance of the attempt. Most of Henry's mistakes are minor, especially if we consider the challenges he would have faced when dealing with an archaic poetry (such as frequent apposition and *hapax legomena*). Henry recognized this first appearance of poetry in the *ASC*, for example, despite the fact that manuscript layout in the *ASC* does not distinguish between prose and verse.[43] He alone made the effort to represent that significant shift through the deliberate and extended use of rhythm, stress, and alliteration in his translation of the vernacular source. Henry's stylistic efforts in Latin at the very least preserved an approximation of the ornamentation and amplification he recognized and valued in his vernacular source.[44] Many writers later drew upon *Historia Anglorum* heavily for their own accounts of Brunanburh, incorporating portions from the poem as well as repeating Henry's description of the battle as "maximum preliorum" [the greatest of battles (Item 18.51)].

---

[41] Henry, Archdeacon of Huntingdon, *Historia Anglorum*, ed. and trans. Greenway. See Sharpe, *Handlist*, no. 461, and Gransden, *HWE* 1, pp. 193–201.

[42] Campbell, for example, acidly dismisses Henry's translation as "atrocious" (*Brunanburh*, p. 148).

[43] For manuscript layout and pointing of the *ASC* poems, see O'Brien O'Keeffe, *Visible Song*, pp. 108–37. On the version(s) of the *ASC* used by Henry, see Henry, *Historia Anglorum*, ed. and trans. Greenway, pp. xci–xcviii.

[44] For Henry's translation, see Rigg, "Henry of Huntingdon's Metrical Experiments." Rigg argues that Henry "was trying, within the limits of a close verbal rendering, to reproduce the spirit of the poem by means of an imitation of native English verse" (p. 66).

The *Chronicon* of John of Worcester (Item 16 in this volume) was probably begun sometime before 1095 and completed by the early 1140s.[45] Once attributed to Florence of Worcester, the chronicle more accurately was a work of compilation with many contributing hands. Scholars now assign a crucial role in the compilation to John, and the principal manuscript (Oxford, Corpus Christi College MS 157), completed in the early 1140s, contains additions and corrections made in his own hand.[46] Written in an annalistic format, the Worcester chronicle draws upon a number of sources, with the *ASC* being the primary source for pre-Conquest events.[47] John largely based his account of Brunanburh upon what he found in the *ASC*, extrapolating only the most essential details. The Worcester chronicle, however, introduces several innovations into its account of the battle: it designates Anlaf as a "rex paganus"; names Constantine as Anlaf's father-in-law ("socer"); claims that Anlaf was urged on by Constantine; and perhaps most significantly, states that Anlaf entered the Humber River with his fleet before Athelstan met him in battle. None of these details appear in the various versions of the *ASC*, and since they all appear in a single sentence just before material clearly drawn from the *ASC*, it seems likely that they were drawn from some other lost source.[48] The Worcester chronicle circulated widely and its extra details would be repeated by many later authors and compilers.[49] John of Worcester's chronicle, along with the works of William of Malmesbury and Henry of Huntingdon, profoundly influenced (and in many ways determined) the transmission of the story of Brunanburh in later Latin texts.

In addition to these influential southern productions, the community at Durham produced several important historical works in the early twelfth century. This northern material includes two works with accounts of Brunanburh, both of which are attributed to or associated with Symeon of Durham: the *Libellus de exordio atque procursu istius hoc est Dunhelmensis ecclesie* and the compilation *Historia regum*. The *Libellus de exordio* (Item 13 in this volume), written sometime between 1104 and 1115,[50] provides a history of the churches at Lindisfarne, Chester-le-Street, and Durham up to 1096, with a clear interest throughout in the abiding power of St. Cuthbert. Not surprisingly then, the *Libellus de exordio* account of Brun-

[45] John of Worcester, *Chronicle*, ed. Darlington and McGurk, pp. xvii–lix.

[46] See Sharpe, *Handlist*, no. 984; and Gransden, *HWE* 1, pp. 143–48. For a description of the manuscripts, see John of Worcester, *Chronicle*, ed. Darlington and McGurk, pp. xvii–xviii. See also Simon Keynes' review of the Darlington and McGurk edition in *Speculum* 72 (1997), pp. 177–79.

[47] For the pre-Conquest sources, see Darlington and McGurk, "'Chronicon ex Chronicis.'" John may also have used Symeon of Durham's *Libellus de exordio atque procursu istius hoc est Dunhelmensis ecclesie* (ed. and trans. Rollason, pp. lxxvi–lxxvii), although John's account lacks the extra details found in that work (such as place-names and the number of ships). See also Brett, "John of Worcester," pp. 119–22.

[48] Lendinara has suggested that the information about the Humber may have been John's own creative addition: "The Humber was the natural line of division between the Scots and the rest of England and, in my opinion, John of Worcester was simply transferring the motif of the crossing of the Humber (frequent in Wace and other writers) to the momentous battle of Brunanburh" ("Brunanburh," p. 206). Smyth, on the other hand, has argued for "a sound historical and geographical basis" for John's statement about the Humber (*Scandinavian York and Dublin*, 2.44). See Cavill's essay, pp. 337–38.

[49] Copies of the Worcester chronicle up to the end of 1130 were sent to Abingdon, Bury St. Edmunds, Peterborough, and Gloucester soon after 1130 (Gransden, *HWE* 1, p. 148).

[50] Symeon, *Libellus de exordio*, ed. and trans. Rollason, pp. xlii–xliv. See also Sharpe, *Handlist*, no. 1625; Gransden, *HWE* 1, 114–21, and Rollason, ed., *Symeon of Durham*.

anburh links Athelstan's success in the battle directly to his trust in Cuthbert's protection. The *Libellus de exordio* significantly names the site of the battle (even providing alternative place-names) and correctly dates it to 937. It also provides the additional detail that Anlaf commanded 615 ships, and it names the king of the Cumbrians as one of Anlaf's confederates; these pieces of information would in turn find their way into many later Latin texts.

The *Historia regum*, a northern miscellany of historical materials once attributed to Symeon of Durham (Item 20 in this volume), survives in a single manuscript (Cambridge, Corpus Christi College MS 139) written ca. 1170. Peter Hunter Blair divided the contents of the *Historia regum* into nine sections: (1) the Kentish legends; (2) the early Northumbrian kings; (3) material taken mainly from Bede; (4) a chronicle from 732 to 802; (5) a chronicle from 849 to 887, taken mainly from Asser;[51] (6) a chronicle from 888 to 957; (7) selections from William of Malmesbury; (8) a chronicle from 848 to 1118, taken mainly from John of Worcester; and (9) a chronicle from 1119 to 1129.[52] Although rubrics at the beginning and end of the work name Symeon as its author, he was probably responsible only for the chronicle from 1119 to 1129 (section 9) and some northern material added to the chronicle from 848 to 1118 (section 8). Brunanburh appears twice in the *Historia regum*: in section 6, the chronicle from 888 to 957; and in section 8, the chronicle from 848 to 1118. The former section gives a brief annal for 937 which includes the detail of Anlaf's 615 ships, the place-name Wendun, and the participation of the king of the Cumbrians (all in common with Symeon's *Libellus de exordio*). The annals throughout this sixth section differ greatly in style and content from preceding material and they may have been culled from various sources with various local interests.[53] The account of Brunanburh in section eight, however, was taken entirely from an early version of John of Worcester's chronicle. Indeed this entire section of the *Historia regum* derives largely from that Worcester chronicle with some added northern material.[54] While more expansive than the annals found in section six, this second account of Brunanburh says nothing about either the number of Anlaf's ships or the involvement of the Cumbrian king; it also provides the place-name Brunanburh rather than the Wendun given in section six. The two apparently independent accounts in the *Historia regum*, then, based upon different source material, do not add new content to the Latin tradition of Brunanburh.

Another twelfth-century chronicle, the *Chronicon Ramesiensis*, simply conflates material from William of Malmesbury in its account of Brunanburh (Item 21 in this volume). The Ramsey chronicle survives in two fourteenth-century manuscripts but was probably composed sometime around 1170.[55] The chronicle relates the loss the king's sword and its restoration after Oda's prayer, and it further notes that the sword remains in the royal treasury to the present day.[56] In its previous chapter, the Ramsey chronicle also quotes two lines from

[51] The first five sections can be attributed to Byrthferth of Ramsey (ca. 970–ca. 1020). Lapidge, "Byrhtferth of Ramsey." See also Byrhtferth of Ramsey, *Lives*, ed. and trans. Lapidge, pp. xxxix–xlii.

[52] Blair, "Some Observations," p. 76.

[53] Blair, "Some Observations," pp. 105–06.

[54] Blair, "Some Observations," pp. 107–111. See also Brett, "John of Worcester," pp. 119–121.

[55] Eadmer, *Lives and Miracles*, ed. and trans. Turner and Muir, pp. cxii–cxvi. See also Gransden, *HWE* 1, pp. 269–86.

[56] *Chronicon Abbatiae Rameseiensis*, ed. Macray, pp. 15–16.

William of Malmesbury's poem on Athelstan (*GR* 2.133).[57] The Ramsey chronicle does not name the site or date of the battle, however, and its account focuses largely upon Oda. In the process, the historical event of Brunanburh becomes a backdrop for staging Oda's sanctity.[58] The manuscript rubric introducing the episode makes this emphasis especially clear: "Miraculum quod per eundem Sanctum Odonem Dominus operatus est" [A miracle that the Lord worked through Saint Oda].[59] The twelfth-century texts surveyed here established a core of material absent from surviving Anglo-Saxon sources, and this new content would provide the foundation for later treatments of Brunanburh in Latin texts.

## THE THIRTEENTH AND FOURTEENTH CENTURIES

Chroniclers of the thirteenth and fourteenth centuries primarily compiled material from older authorities in their treatment of events before the Norman Conquest. As a result, many of these later medieval texts simply repeat material wholesale from earlier texts in their accounts of early events. The chronicle of Roger of Howden (d. 1201), for example (Item 24 in this volume), contains an account of Brunanburh derived ultimately from John of Worcester,[60] as does the universal history, *Flores historiarum* (Item 26), compiled by the St. Albans monk Roger Wendover (d. 1236).[61] Matthew Paris (d. 1259), also a monk at St. Albans, later incorporated Roger Wendover into his own *Chronica maiora* (Item 27), a history from the creation to 1259, for his account of events up to 1234/35.[62] Richard of Cirencester's (d. 1401) *Speculum historiale*, a late fourteenth-century text covering events from 447 to 1066 (Item 45), in turn combined material drawn from William of Malmesbury, Roger of Wendover, and Matthew Paris.[63] These chronicles all repeat content, often verbatim, from William of Malmesbury and John of Worcester, and while they may contribute no new material to the afterlife of Brunanburh, they do maintain its presence in Latin historical writing.

[57] The Ramsey chronicle cites lines 3–4 of the poem: "Magnus Æthelstanus patriæ decus, orbita recti, / Illustris probitas de vero nescia flecti" (*Chronicon Abbatiae Rameseiensis*, ed. Macray, p. 14).

[58] Lendinara, "Brunanburh," p. 206.

[59] *Chronicon Abbatiae Rameseiensis*, ed. Macray, p. 15.

[60] Sharpe, *Handlist*, no. 1571. See Roger of Howden, *Chronica Magistri*, ed. Stubbs, 1.54–55. Compiled in the last years of the twelfth century, the chronicle mainly drew upon the *Historia post Obitum Bedae* (a mid-twelfth century text extracted from the *Historia Regum* and Henry of Huntingdon) for events before 1148. See also Gransden, *HWE* 1, pp. 225–30, and Frank Barlow, "Roger of Howden."

[61] Roger's text contains some minor variations on John Worcester. It omits some information (Constantine is not Anlaf's "socero suo" [father-in-law], for example) and adds other material (observing that the West Saxons "cum glorioso triumpho ad propria remearunt" [returned to their own people in glorious triumph]). See Roger Wendover, *Chronica*, ed. Coxe, 1.392. See also Sharpe, *Handlist*, no. 1596, Gransden, *HWE* 1, pp. 359–60, and Galbraith, *Roger Wendover and Matthew Paris*.

[62] Matthew Paris, *Chronica majora*, ed. Luard, 1.451. Matthew began work on the *Chronica* ca. 1240. See Sharpe, *Handlist*, no. 1043, Gransden, *HWE* 1, pp. 356–79, Vaughn, *Matthew Paris*, and Taylor, *English Historical Literature*, pp. 59–77.

[63] Sharpe, *Handlist*, no. 1302; Richard of Cirencester, *Speculum historiale*, ed. Mayor, 2.64. The chronicle includes William's two verses on Athelstan in full (3.13) as well as Hugh's gift to Athelstan of the sword of Constantine the Great (2.66–73).

Some chroniclers also notably drew upon Henry of Huntingdon in their presentation of the event. Bartholomew of Cotton (d. 1321/22), a monk at Norwich, began writing his *Historia Anglicana* ca. 1292 (Item 29 in this volume), using an earlier chronicle written at Norwich for events up to 1290.[64] Bartholomew's sources include Geoffrey of Monmouth, William of Malmesbury, Roger of Howden, and Matthew Paris, but his account of Brunanburh primarily relies upon Henry of Huntingdon. He echoes Henry, for example, by describing the battle as "proelium maximum apud Brunesberich" (Item 29.1–2).[65] The *Chronica* attributed to John of Oxnead (d. 1293), a monk at St. Benet, Hulme (Item 31 in this volume), likewise condenses material culled from Henry of Huntingdon, quoting the final lines of Henry's poem nearly verbatim in its account of Brunanburh.[66] Finally, the *Annals of Waverley*, compiled in the early thirteenth century, borrow language from Henry ("maximum praelium apud Bruneberi," Item 33.2) either directly or through an intermediary source.[67] Despite their lack of additions or elaboration, these texts all maintain Brunanburh's privileged place in this historical record as the defining event of Athelstan's reign.

Some chroniclers did make some adjustments to earlier sources, however, and in some cases introduced what appears to be new information on the battle. Ranulf Higden's (d. 1364) sprawling universal history the *Polychronicon* (completed ca. 1327–52) conflates material from John of Worcester and William of Malmesbury for its account of Brunanburh (Item 39 in this volume).[68] Higden imposes some control over disparate material, however, by establishing an order of events at the battle which attempts to resolve the incongruities he found in William: according to Higden, Athelstan first prayed to St. Aldhelm and *then* found his sword returned through Oda's prayers. Athelstan loses his sword in the rush of battle, "sed inclamato Deo et sancto Aldelmo, ad preces Odonis archiepiscopi, qui tunc cum rege erat, gladium vaginæ relapsum invenit"[69] [but calling out to God and Saint Aldhelm, he found the sword returned to its sheath through the prayers of Archbishop Oda, who was with the king at that time]. Higden also emphasizes that Athelstan's victory was a gift from God, thereby reaffirming the trope of divine intervention at the battle.[70]

---

[64] Gransden, *HWE* 1, pp. 444–48.

[65] See Sharpe, *Handlist*, no. 145. Bartholomew of Cotton, *Historia Anglicana*, ed. Luard, p. 22.

[66] Sharpe, *Handlist*, no. 832. The chronicle survives in a single manuscript (British Library, MS Cotton Nero D.ii) dated to the early fourteenth century and it ends in an incomplete entry for 1293 (ed. Ellis, pp. 5–6). See also Granden, *HWE* 1, pp. 402–03.

[67] *Waverley Annals*, ed. Luard, 2.164.

[68] For the *Polychronicon* in general, see Taylor, *Universal Chronicle*. See Sharpe, *Handlist*, no. 1264; Gransden, *HWE* 2, pp. 43–57; and Taylor, *English Historical Literature*, pp. 95–103. Higden includes the first four lines of the poem on Athelstan from William's *GR* (2.133). Higden also used part of a Scottish chronicle as one of his sources. These annals survive in the fourteenth-century Poppleton manuscript (Paris, Bibliothèque Nationale, MS Latin 4126), a miscellany of historical materials (M. Anderson, "Scottish Pieces," p. 250n127). The Scottish chronicle records the death of King Constantine's son after the battle but mistakenly dates it to 934 (the date of Athelstan's first northern campaign).

[69] *Polychronicon*, ed. Babington and Lumby, 6.438.

[70] "quo Dei dono rex tunc fretus, hostes per totam auroram et diem sequentem fugavit" (*Polychronicon*, ed. Babington and Lumbry, 6.438) [wherefore the king, trusting in God's gift, routed the enemy throughout the morning and the following day].

The *Eulogium historiarum*, a compilation written at Malmesbury ca. 1367 and heavily indebted to the *Polychronicon*, mentions Athelstan's success at Brunanburh on two occasions (Item 43 in this volume). The first account begins with material derived from John of Worcester and concludes with a truncated reference to the miracle of the recovered sword attributed to Oda (4.175). The second account appears among material largely derived from William of Malmesbury's *GR*,[71] but it also contains additional information (5.84): the battle was fought "apud Donelew in Wilthschire"[72] [at Dunlow in Wiltshire];[73] the recovered sword was given to Athelstan by an angel sent from heaven; and Athelstan was accustomed to wearing a holy cross around his neck in battle (this cross, furthermore, is still venerated among the holy relics of Malmesbury).[74] These additional details are at slight odds with the first account's attribution of the miracle to Oda, but their presence demonstrates how Brunanburh's status as a legendary battle from the Anglo-Saxon past invited narrative elaboration in later Latin texts.

## LATE FOURTEENTH AND FIFTEENTH CENTURIES

The accumulation of fabulous elements around the story of Brunanburh becomes especially evident in the *Historia Croylandensis* (*Chronicle of Crowland*), a notorious forgery created in the late-fourteenth or fifteenth century (Item 46 in this volume). The Crowland chronicle was intended in part to confirm monastic claims to lands and privileges, and it consequently includes copies of several spurious charters as touchstones in its narrative of the monastery's history.[75] An anonymous compiler wrote the work under the name of Ingulf (d. 1109), an abbot at Crowland in the late eleventh century, and the first part of the chronicle covers events from the monastery's foundation in the early eighth century up to 1089. The chronicle gives two accounts of Brunanburh: the first conflates the battle in 937 with Athelstan's northern campaign in 934 and Æthelstan's offering of his dagger to St. John of Beverley; the second and much longer account offers one of the more fantastic additions to the Brunanburh tradition in its story of Turketul (d. 975?), a nobleman in the service of West Saxon kings and later abbot at Crowland.

In its celebration of Turketul as an early hero in the abbey's history, the Crowland chronicle offers a detailed narrative of his remarkable career. Turketul served as chancellor

---

[71] *Eulogium historiarum*, ed. Haydon, 3.iv–v. Haydon argues that the *gesta Britonum* named in 5.84 is William of Malmesbury's *Gesta Regum*. The *Eulogium* shortly thereafter quotes from William by name in its account of King Edgar (5.88). See also Gransden, *HWE* 2, pp. 101–05.

[72] *Eulogium historiarum*, ed. Haydon, 3.10.

[73] See Cavill's essay in this volume, p. 339n43.

[74] "Gesta autem Britonum dicunt Angelum de caelo missum gladium suum de manu sua lapsum incontinenti regi dedisse. Sancta autem crux quod circa collum sum in bellis gestabat adhuc Malmesburiae inter sacras reliquias, ut decet, venerator" (*Eulogium historiarum*, ed. Haydon, 3.10–11) [The deeds of the Britons moreover say that an angel sent from heaven gave the intemperate king the sword that had fallen from his hand. A holy cross that he wore around his neck in war also is still venerated (as it should be) among the holy relics of Malmesbury].

[75] See Sharpe, *Handlist*, no. 538, Gransden, *HWE* 2, pp. 400 and 490–92, Roffe, "Historia Croylandensis," and *Rerum Anglicarum scriptorum veterum*, ed. Fulman and Gale, pp. 1–107. See also *Ingulph's Chronicle*, trans. Riley.

to King Eadred before entering the monastic life, and during a mission for the king, he meets the diminished brethren at the ruined Crowland. Inspired by their sanctity, he pleads with the king to restore Crowland and vows to become a monk there himself. The king reluctantly honors this request and Turketul is later appointed abbot of the monastery. The chronicle then presents a sprawling charter (dated to 948) which records the king's conveyance and confirmation of the monastery's substantial properties and privileges.[76] The chronicle at this point pauses to give additional back-story for Turketul, telling of his noble birth and of his chastity and humility as a youth.[77] As chancellor to Athelstan, Turketul also accompanied the king to the fight against Anlaf's coalition at Brunford in Northumbria where he led a force of Londoners and Mercians against the invaders. The chronicle's long account of the battle initially draws upon William of Malmesbury's *GR* — it includes Anlaf's surprise night-attack, for example, and the death of the unfortunate bishop — but it then turns to its own story of Turketul's heroic prowess at the battle. Turketul's fantastic exploits at Brunford seem to be a story of pure invention grafted onto the existing source material.[78] While the Crowland chronicle does not tell of miracles or divine intervention, it does appropriate the battle as an opportunity to laud a local hero. Brunanburh becomes an occasion for story rather than a contextualized historical event.

A similar creative expansion appears in the *Liber monasterii de Hyda* (Item 48 in this volume), a chronicle-cartulary written in the mid-fifteenth century at Winchester which covers the years 445–1023.[79] Beginning with King Æthelwulf (r. 839–58), the chronicle is organized by reign of individual kings with charter materials copied into the end of each chapter. The author compiled his chronicle from various sources (some entirely spurious): the section on Athelstan has material largely derived from Higden's *Polychronicon* but also contains a lengthy story of Guy of Warwick inserted just prior to its account of Brunanburh.[80] The leaders of a Danish invasion offer Athelstan three choices: surrender the kingdom, become an under-king subservient to the Danes, or settle the matter in single combat. Athelstan selects the final option. Guy fights as the English champion and defeats the Danish giant Colbrand in the melee. As in the *Historia Croylandensis*, the legendary status of Brunanburh attracts other legends in this late Winchester chronicle, in this case incorporat-

---

[76] S 538. The charter is a post-Conquest compilation of material derived from the Domesday Book (Roffe, "Historia Croylandensis," p. 104).

[77] The Crowland Chronicle claims that Turketul was the eldest son of Æthelweard, brother of Edward the Elder. Although he says nothing about Turketul, William of Malmesbury does note that two of Æthelweard's sons, Ælfwine and Æthelwine, were killed "in bello contra Analauum" [in battle against Anlaf] (*GR*, ed. and trans. Mynors et al., 1.220–21).

[78] The Old English poem does mention separate forces of West Saxons and Mercians at the battle. Was the Crowland chronicler simply inserting his own hero into an existing story or might he have been drawing upon existing traditions and stories surrounding the battle?

[79] The work has been attributed to Thomas Rudborne (d. after 1450), a monk at Winchester. See Sharpe, *Handlist*, no. 1822; and Gransden, *HWE* 2, pp. 391–92 and 395n30.

[80] *Book of Hyde*, ed. Edwards, pp. 118–23. At the end of the episode the chronicler states that, "Istud extractum est ex scriptis Gyrardi Cornubiensis, in libro *De Gestis Regum Westsaxonum*" (ed. Edwards, p. 123) [That was extracted from the writings of Gerard of Cornwall, in the book *Deeds of the West-Saxon Kings*]. See also Lendinara, "Brunanburh," pp. 224–26.

ing the popular story of Guy of Warwick.[81] By the fifteenth century, Brunanburh had become an antiquarian matter fully open to elaboration and invention.

In contrast to the Crowland chronicle and the *Liber monasterii de Hyda*, the account of Brunanburh in the *Annals of Ulster* (Item 50), compiled in the late fifteenth century with annals written in both Irish and Latin, might seem relatively subdued.[82] Its annal for 937, however, describes the battle in evocative language, noting both its immensity ("ingens") and intensity ("lacrimable atque horribile," Item 50.1) as well as the staggering number of casualties on both sides (although the annal does not name the battle's location).[83] This presentation of the battle preserves in miniature the English poem's contrast between Athelstan's triumph and Anlaf's retreat with only a few survivors, but here the triumphal note is muted by the statement of heavy losses among the English. The *Annals of Ulster* presents the battle in a critical voice, neither commemorating victory nor lamenting defeat. Indeed the closing statement that Athelstan "magna uictoria ditatus est" [was enriched by the great victory (Item 50.4)] seems poised somewhere between censure and celebration.

## CONCLUSION

This survey of Latin texts dealing with the story of Brunanburh testifies in many ways to the success of the Old English poem as panegyric verse. For centuries the Latin historical tradition in England would repeat and preserve the *Anglo-Saxon Chronicle*'s celebration of the battle as the most memorable moment in Athelstan's reign. The battle's great reputation is already apparent in Latin texts of the later tenth century, and the various elaborations among the Anglo-Norman historians further suggest that a lively tradition of story had grown up around Brunanburh. This tradition became largely fixed after the twelfth century, although several writers would make small but significant adjustments through instances of emphasis, addition and omission. By the fifteenth century, however, Brunanburh had become a distant legend, attenuated perhaps through a long process of retelling but still an appropriate antiquarian matter for the introduction of new stories.

---

[81] For the legend of Guy of Warwick, see Cooper, "Romance after 1400," pp. 704–06, and Richmond, *Legend*.

[82] Attention to English events is not unprecedented in these annals, but is most frequently contained to obituary notices of English royal figures. The death of Æthelflæd, "Lady of the Mercians" ("famosissima regina Saxonum" [most renowned queen of the Saxons]), for example, appears s.a. 918 while King Athelstan's death appears s.a. 939. Smyth suggested that the "earliest account of the battle may well be that in the *Annals of Ulster*, which is unusually long and includes details which by comparison even with other Irish entries is very extensive" (*Scandinavian York and Dublin*, 2.36). In Smyth's opinion, then, the entry preserved in the *Annals of Ulster* is a contemporary account perhaps written even before the *ASC* poem.

[83] *Annals of Ulster*, ed. and trans. Mac Airt and Mac Niocaill, p. 384. See also Dumville, "Latin and Irish," and "On Editing and Translating Medieval Irish Chronicles."

THOMAS A. BREDEHOFT

# *THE BATTLE OF BRUNANBURH* IN OLD ENGLISH STUDIES

The Old English poem now known as *The Battle of Brunanburh* survives only as an anonymous, untitled annal within the lengthy and complex series of historical compilations we now know collectively as the *Anglo-Saxon Chronicle*. Its place within the *ASC*, like its place within the tradition of Old English verse, has long been a matter of debate, just as the place of the battle itself has long seemed uncertain. And while this present essay probably cannot lay to rest the questions under debate in relation to *Brunanburh* as a literary object, it will attempt to articulate some of them, as well as some of my own positions on those questions. Importantly, though, a surprisingly broad range of questions are centralized in an investigation of *Brunanburh*'s place within Old English studies; alongside *The Battle of Maldon* and *Beowulf*, *Brunanburh* bears the brunt of great deal of our thinking about the Anglo-Saxon literary world. If the Old English poetic tradition is a world of heroes and a heroic code, these three poems stand at the very heart of that tradition.

*Brunanburh*, of course, is the only one of the three to be preserved in multiple copies, and its earliest manuscripts seem clearly to predate those of *Beowulf* and *Maldon*: in terms of manuscript age and distribution, *Brunanburh* has a greater claim to have been influential and widespread during the Anglo-Saxon period than either of these other two poems. Yet *Brunanburh* is far shorter than *Beowulf* or *Maldon*, and the mode of its narration is different: here the reader will not find heroic posturing and speechifying or elaborate descriptions of battle or weaponry. If we find the poem moving, it is on other grounds than the vigor of its action or the appeal of its heroes as characters. Yet it remains one of the most widely read of Old English poems, not only for its frequent placement in anthologies and Old English textbooks, but as a poem in its own right, and as translated by Tennyson. A recent upsurge in interest in the *ASC* and in Anglo-Saxon nation-building has likewise increased attention to the poem, and it seems worth the effort to attempt a broad view of the place of the Old English poem in relation to its chief contexts: in the *ASC*, in the tradition of Old English poetry, and in the minds of modern critics.

## THE PLACE OF *BRUNANBURH* IN *THE ANGLO-SAXON CHRONICLE*

In his 1938 edition of *The Battle of Brunanburh*, Alistair Campbell printed the name "Æþelstan" as the poem's first word, passing over "Her," an editorial choice also followed in one of the two editions of the poem in the present volume.[1] Campbell offers the following explanation in his note to line 1:

[1] See Item 4b in this volume. To the contrary, both Item 4a in this volume and Elliot van Kirk Dobbie's edition of the poem in volume 6 of the Anglo-Saxon Poetic Records include "Her" within the lineation (*Anglo-Saxon Minor Poems*, p. 16).

> The word *her* is omitted in the critical text, as it is not a part of the poem. . . . It is metrically unnecessary, and would not appear in the original copy, unless the poem were specially written for the *Chronicle*.[2]

Campbell's commentary, of course, leaves the door open for the possibility that the poem was written specifically for the *ASC*, but his claim that the word "Her" is not a part of the poem remains. The metrical argument about "Her" being unnecessary, I think it is safe to say, is a tendentious one: Campbell elsewhere tries to insist on the poem's close adherence to classical Old English metrical forms, despite at least some evidence (to be discussed below) that such adherence may be overstated and overstressed. Indeed, in the late tenth-century witness from *ASC* version B (the basis of Item 4b in this volume), the final word of verse 1a is written as "cing," a monosyllable, which makes "Her" metrically necessary, since otherwise the verse is too short by a full syllable. Even in the A-text (from Cambridge, Corpus Christi College, MS 173; often termed the "Parker" text), it is possible that the disyllabic spelling "cyning" represents an orthographic habit, rather than phonological reality, especially as the same scribe of the Parker text has spelled the word "cing" in his first line of writing (annal 924). A strong case can be made that the scribe of B, one of the two earliest known readers of *Brunanburh*, saw "Her" as metrically necessary — if the scribe of B understood the poem's meter at all.[3]

The question of *Brunanburh*'s place within the *ASC* is important because modern readers have sometimes wished to imagine a place for *Brunanburh* outside the pages of the *ASC*. Whatever level of importance we attach to Fred C. Robinson's suggestion that we always take into account Old English poetry's "most immediate" manuscript context,[4] *Brunanburh*'s status as a "*Chronicle* poem" rests largely on whether or not we imagine it was written for the *ASC* itself or for another purpose entirely. If the latter, we understand the poem's placement in the *ASC* as part of a later, perhaps less interesting, poetic afterlife. Whether it was metrically justified or not, Campbell's editorial decision to eliminate the word "Her" from his edition effectively served to dissociate the poem from the *ASC*, opening the door for modern readers to imagine that it may have functioned first as a courtly praise poem and even that it may have circulated orally; editions like that found in the Anglo-Saxon Poetic Records (ASPR), which also excise *Brunanburh* from its *ASC* context (even while keeping "Her"), also implicitly make room for readings of the poem for which the *ASC* context is downplayed.[5] I suspect that modern readers' efforts to see meaningful parallels between *Brunanburh* and Old Norse verse likewise ultimately derive from a reading strategy that imagines that *Brunanburh*'s original context was oral and courtly, as opposed to the literate and presumably monastic or ecclesiastical context implied by the poem's survival in the *ASC*.[6]

The notion that *Brunanburh* may have circulated orally might appear to receive some paleographic support from its record in the A version, where it appears as part of the stint

---

[2] Campbell, *Battle of Brunanburh*, p. 96.

[3] For an argument both advancing a new prosody and supposing that the B-scribe understood the resulting meter of the present poem best, see Robert P. Creed's essay in this volume, pp. 295–304.

[4] Robinson, "Old English Literature in Its Most Immediate Context."

[5] *Anglo-Saxon Minor Poems*, ed. Dobbie, pp. 16–20. On *Brunanburh* as a "praise poem," see, for example, Townend, "Pre-Cnut Praise Poetry."

[6] See Niles, "Skaldic Technique in *Brunanburh*," and Zacher, "Multilingualism."

of Bately's Scribe 3 (fols. 26r–27v), covering annals 924 to 955; if these annals were all entered at the same time (as they appear to have been), the earliest date for their entry would seem to be 955 or shortly thereafter.[7] In its earliest surviving appearance in the *ASC*, then, the poem was not recorded until at least eighteen years after the events it describes; the record in manuscript B dates from after about 977. But the gap in time between the battle itself and the record of the poem in the *ASC* need not prove that the poem existed before 955; nothing in the poem, I think, marks it as especially close in time to the events described, and it may well take a retropective viewpoint. Donald Scragg's recent essay suggests a date of composition in the 950s and ties the authorship of *Brunanburh* to the authorship of the 942 *ASC* poem *Capture of the Five Boroughs*; certainly the frequency of annals opening "Her Eadweard [or Æþelstan or Edmund] cyning" may mark virtually all of Parker Scribe 3's annals as a coherent block (see annals 924A, 937A, 940A, 942A, 944A, 945A, 946A).[8] Indeed, noticing this pattern strongly suggests that the opening verses of *Brunanburh* and *Capture* (including "Her") fit almost too perfectly within the pattern set by Parker Scribe 3's annals to justify reading them as poems not written for the *ASC*.

In terms of *Brunanburh*'s content, a strong case can also be made for suspecting that it was specifically written for the *ASC*. As I have suggested elsewhere, *Brunanburh* fulfills the poetic potential implied in the Common Stock of the *ASC* by the use of alliterating genealogies, and *Brunanburh*'s closing lines, invoking both the *adventus Saxonum* and the value of books as a source of historical authority, makes the *ASC* itself the most relevant context for the poem.[9] Renée Trilling's recent work takes the context of the *ASC* as a given for *Brunanburh*, and Trilling also notes contextual similarities to annals of Edward the Elder; her reading seems to my mind compelling.[10]

Whether or not we see *Brunanburh* as originally composed for the *ASC*, it is abundantly clear that the presence of *Brunanburh* in the *ASC* seems to have reshaped the nature of Anglo-Saxon vernacular historiography. With no true poems appearing before the 937 annal, *Brunanburh* set the stage for the increasing presence of poetry within the *ASC* pages that continued right through the rest of the tenth century and all of the eleventh. The full extent of the *ASC* poem tradition may not yet have been fully recognized, but the ASPR prints poems from annals 942, 973, 975, 1036, and 1065. The 1036 poem clearly employs late Old English forms, rather than *Brunanburh*'s classical meter, and similar late Old English poetic forms are also widely understood as appearing in annals 975, 979, 1011, 1067, 1086, and 1103. In a recent essay, I have proposed that previously unidentified poetic material also appears in annal 1003, and there may yet be more such passages to be discovered.[11] Importantly, these late Old English poetic passages are most commonly preserved in versions C, D, and E, although one of these versions, E, does not include *Brunanburh* itself. In that sense, *Brunanburh*'s influence seems to have extended far beyond its most local habitations in the A, B, C, and D versions of the *ASC*.

---

[7] *Anglo-Saxon Chronicle*, ed. Bately.

[8] Scragg, "Reading of *Brunanburh*."

[9] Bredehoft, *Textual Histories*, pp. 100–02.

[10] Trilling, *Aesthetics of Nostalgia*, pp. 194–99.

[11] Bredehoft, "OE *yðhengest*."

The fact that the E version lacks the poem, however, brings us to one further point about *The Battle of Brunanburh*'s place in the *ASC*. Appearing in full in versions A, B, C, and D (and in the now-lost G), *Brunanburh* is replaced by brief summaries in E and F. Certainly the scribe of F had access to the poem, as he clearly had access to version A. And indeed, the bilingual annal 938F seems to borrow details directly from the poem, although the Latin version describes the battle as "magnum et famosum bellum," a detail seemingly not derived directly from either the poem or the exemplar of version E, which reads only "Her Æðelstan cyning lædde fyrde to Brunanbyrig" ("In this year Athelstan the king led the levy to Brunanburh"). It is striking that E does not record Athelstan's victory, although its wording closely parallels the wording of F as far as it goes. Likewise, while F's interlinear additions "ond Edmund his broðer" and "ond þar slogon .v. cingas ond .vii. eorlas" clearly echo passages of the poem (lines 2–3, 28–30), the original portion of F's text does mention Anlaf, unlike the record in E. The textual history of the E and F annals (and the E and F manuscripts more generally) is complex and difficult to reconstruct, but it seems likely indeed that the ancestor of E read more fully than E does here, and that the interlinear additions to F were added after consultation with version A. My point, however, is simply that the immediate ancestor of E seems not to have had the poem, though the shared EF text may ultimately derive from an even earlier radical abbreviation of the poem. Elsewhere (975E, 1067E) it may be the case that the E tradition has demonstrably abbreviated or excised poetic passages: at least one *ASC* scribe or compiler may have had an active antipathy towards some of the *ASC* poems, possibly including *Brunanburh*. Our appreciation for the poem may not reflect the taste or opinions of all this poem's Anglo-Saxon readers.

Reading *Brunanburh* in the context of the *ASC*, then, raises a crucial series of questions for how we read the poem's record of history as well as its own textual history. Readers who wish to place *Brunanburh* — as a poem — close in time to the events it relates will probably argue against the notion that the poem was written for the *ASC*. But, in my view, the contextual and codicological evidence for a date in the 950s makes the stronger argument, although it naturally makes the poem more retrospective in its outlook and less close in time to the battle itself. And as the next section will suggest, *Brunanburh*'s place within the tradition of Old English verse may actually urge us towards a similar conclusion.

## *BRUNANBURH*'S PLACE IN THE OLD ENGLISH VERSE TRADITION

*The Battle of Brunanburh* is a great rarity within the Old English verse tradition: it is a fairly substantial poem for which the date of composition can be placed within a quite precise span of time: between the date of the battle itself in 937 and the poem's first appearance in the Parker Chronicle around 955 or 960. As such *Brunanburh* (and to a lesser extent, the other canonical tenth-century *ASC* poems) occupies a very important position in our understanding of tenth-century developments in Old English verse. If *Brunanburh* can be taken as typical of its time, it gives us a pivot point on which to balance virtually the whole literary history of classical Old English verse.

Perhaps, then, it is not surprising that students of Old English meter have so often stressed how closely *Brunanburh* hews to the metrical standards of Old English verse as understood most fully from *Beowulf*. Campbell's 1938 assessment, for example, suggests that

> The poem is remarkably 'correct' in metre: that is to say, its half-verses are constructed with regard to the limitations, and bound together by alliteration with regard to the laws, which are also found in the earlier Old English poetry.[12]

Such a position is seconded by Julie Townsend in a 1996 essay in relation to all of the *ASC*'s classical Old English verse: "it is as 'correct' as the most highly regarded poems of the period, including *Beowulf*."[13] Even so, I hope to trace here just how troublesome such claims are, and how much *Brunanburh* and a small handful of contextually and codicologically related poems stand out as unique within the Old English verse tradition. And as we shall see, while *Brunanburh* is fairly classical in meter, it is not exclusively so; more importantly, its classicism needs to be understood in relation to the contemporary (and flourishing) tradition of less classical late Old English verse.

Most troubling for those who wish to see *Brunanburh*'s meter as highly conventional and correct is the fact that, in *Brunanburh*, *g*-alliteration appears to be highly unusual. Specifically, palatal and velar *g* do not appear to alliterate in *Brunanburh*, as Table 1 suggests. Two verses (lines 18a and 44a) do seem to indicate co-alliteration of the two sounds, but as I have argued recently, both verses show unique parallels in *Andreas* (*Andreas* lines 1143a, "garum agetan," and 1330a, "gingran æt guðe").[14] As such, both verses are unlikely to represent true widespread formulas and can probably be best understood as direct borrowings from *Andreas*, and thus they may not be typical of the *Brunanburh*-poet's own compositional practice.[15] Treating palatal and velar *g* as distinct alliterators, it must be noted, is very unusual indeed in Old English verse, and it is impossible, I think, to see it as highly traditional. The B-version of verse 18a, it should be noted, offers an alternate version of the ACD verse that preserves the two distinct *g*s as separate alliterators; here the B-scribe apparently makes a change towards a less-traditional form of alliteration, but in the direction of internal consistency within the poem.

**Table 1: *G*-alliteration in *Brunanburh***

| | |
|---|---|
| line 15 | glad ofer grundas, godes candel beorht, |
| 18 | garum forgrunden, guman norðerne, |
| | (ACD: garum ageted) |
| 44 | geongne æt guþe. Gylpan ne þorfte |
| 50 | garmittinge, gumena gemotes |
| 64 | grædigne guþhafoc and þæt græge deor |

If Table 1 were all the evidence available on the question, it would not be sufficient to make the case on its own. But while all the evidence is impossible to repeat here, I argue that *Brunanburh* shares a number of unusual metrical peculiarities with the other three tenth-century classical *ASC* poems and with *The Menologium*; all five poems, I suggest, belong to a small and closely localized tradition, marked not only by their unusual treatment of

[12] Campbell, *Battle of Brunanburh*, p. 16.

[13] J. Townsend, "Metre of the *Chronicle*-verse," p. 157.

[14] Bredehoft, *Authors, Audiences, and Old English Verse*, pp. 123–24.

[15] Bredehoft, *Authors, Audiences, and Old English Verse*, pp. 121–22.

*g*-alliteration, but by a spectrum of other shared features as well.[16] All five poems, it seems likely, were composed between the 950s and the 970s, and possibly at the same location.

Among the shared features of this larger goup of poems to which *Brunanburh* belongs is a tolerance for a small number of late Old English verse forms. At least two verses in *Brunanburh* appear to be plainly unmetrical from a classical perspective: verse 64a, "grædigne guþhafoc," and verse 3b, "ealdorlangne tir." The first Campbell accepts with virtually no discussion, while Bliss offers a variety of choices, mostly unsatisfactory, and J. Townsend echoes Bliss.[17] Fulk's "rule of the coda" strongly suggests that the verse is Type D, but with an exceptionally heavy first foot that most metricists would identify as unmetrical.[18] Non-parasiting (which understands the "-or" in "ealdor" as non-syllabic) is generally assumed for verse 3b (Bliss, J. Townsend, Fulk), but Fulk identifies exactly two examples of non-parasiting in poems after 900: in the current example and in *Maldon*, verse 130b, which I believe is not relevant, as it is ambiguous in scansion (Fulk scans it as type E, but type D is probably correct).[19] In short, while Fulk accepts *Brunanburh*, line 3a as a late example of a non-parasite vowel, there seems no reason to do so, unless we are committed in advance to a view of *Brunanburh* as closely following traditional metrical rules. Note also that the metrical argument about the non-necessity of "Her" in *Brunanburh*, line 1a depends on an assumption that the verse is classically structured: there is zero metrical difficulty in "Her Æþelstan cyning" from a late Old English metrical perspective, and the desire to remove "Her" from the text may be intimately related to a desire to see the verse forms as thoroughly classical. But it seems fairest overall to suggest rather that *Brunanburh* allows a handful of verses of questionable classical metricality as well as non-traditional *g*-alliteration. But all of *Brunanburh*'s questionably metrical verses are understandable within the late Old English verse tradition, which was clearly contemporary with *Brunanburh*.

One should note, of course, that verse 3a, "ealdorlangne tir," would be extremely hard to understand as an orally generated formulaic archaism, an old form preserved and transmitted to the *Brunanburh*-poet through an oral-formulaic tradition. Not only is there no surviving evidence that the verse in question is formulaic, but (as I noted above) all the other surviving poetry from the late ninth to the tenth centuries shows that the parasite vowels were always assumed, rather than suppressed: all of the other evidence suggests that the tradition itself had changed by this time. Yet scansions that see it as featuring a non-parasited vowel (Campbell, Bliss, J. Townsend, Fulk) necessarily take it as just such a remarkable survival. Likewise, the treatment of *g*-alliteration does not seem to have an oral origin, especially as co-alliteration of the two *g*s seems to have been typical in the late Old English tradition of the *Metrical Psalms* and other poems, just as it was in the classical tradition at large. Of course, the suggestion that *Brunanburh* borrows the two counter-example verses from *Andreas* fits in well with an understanding of the poem as composed in a literate environment, rather than an oral-formulaic one, and in *Authors, Audiences, and Old English Verse*,

---

[16] Bredehoft, *Authors, Audiences, and Old English Verse*, pp. 113–30. In this section of *Authors, Audiences*, I suggest that we may be able to localize the composition of these poems to Winchester, and I hypothesize an attribution of them to Æthelwold or a member of his school.

[17] Campbell, *Battle of Brunanburh*, p. 28, Bliss, *Metre of Beowulf*, p. 101, J. Townsend, "Metre of the *Chronicle*-verse," p. 150.

[18] Fulk, *History of Old English Meter*, p. 201.

[19] Fulk, *History of Old English Meter*, pp. 82–83.

I present more extensive evidence that *Brunanburh* relies heavily on access to written exemplars, rather than oral tradition.[20] That conclusion also dovetails nicely with a reading that sees the poem as having been prepared for the *ASC* itself, rather than circulating orally before being recorded in writing.

The nature of *Brunanburh*'s poetic conservatism, then, its close but not perfect adherence to traditional metrical standards, seems very unlikely to reflect an ongoing and current tenth-century tradition of oral-formulaic composition. Instead, *Brunanburh*'s place within Old English poetry must be seen in the context of the simultaneous (and seemingly much more prominent) developing tradition of late Old English verse, as seen in *The Metrical Psalms*, *Judgment Day II*, and similar poems which were also being written in the middle of the tenth century. *Brunanburh*, like *Maldon* and the other canonical *ASC* poems, seems best understood as partaking of a willful and intentional archaic and heroic perspective, imperfectly but impressively mobilizing the meter and diction of the classical tradition of Old English verse for its purposes. But the full impact of that choice must be assessed in conjunction with the poetic path not taken, the contemporary mode of late Old English verse: *Brunanburh* is not only quite like much of the older poetry, it is also very unlike much of the poetry of its own time. And in the ways in which it departs even from the classical tradition, we must see *Brunanburh* as not merely a tenth-century exemplification of the classical ideal, but as an intentionally archaizing production. Its content may be roughly contemporary, and its alliteration on *g* may be innovative, but as a poem it is also strikingly old-fashioned.

In that sense, the retrospective orientation of *Brunanburh* as a poem is exemplified both in its probable date of composition in the 950s and in its very poetic form, which embodies a certain nostalgia for both a heroic past and a tradition of heroic poetry. *The Battle of Brunanburh*'s place within the tradition of Old English poetry is, I think, ultimately inseparable from its content, as the poem itself works to insist that the heroic Germanic tradition was still alive and well in the persons of Athelstan and Edmund, although both kings were probably dead when the poem was written. And the poem likewise asserts that the old tradition of heroic verse is also alive and well. But on both sides of the equation we have nostalgia at work, and the propaganda value of the claims very probably outweighs their truth value.

## *BRUNANBURH* IN CONTEMPORARY ANGLO-SAXON STUDIES

To an extent, my comments in this section must echo comments made above: *Brunanburh* is a mirror in which many sorts of critical notions and ideas about Anglo-Saxon literature find themselves reflected. But it seems to me that *Brunanburh*'s place within the "big picture" of contemporary Anglo-Saxon studies can be understood primarily by reference to one or both of the following broad generalizations. As will be clear, I have reservations about both generalizations, but it seems useful to articulate how *Brunaburh* fits into these schematic literary conceptualizations because what is at stake in our understanding of *Brunanburh*, as it turns out, is surprisingly central to what is at stake in Anglo-Saxon literary studies more broadly.

[20] Bredehoft, *Authors, Audiences, and Old English Verse*, pp. 116–26.

1. *Anglo-Saxon poetry is heroic, oral, and formally stable across the whole period, from the beginnings to 1066.*

This perspective is remarkably strong and alive in Old English studies, though some recent work has begun to take seriously the notion that a number of poems were written late in the period that do not fit the heroic, Sieversian metrics paradigm (see, for example, Trilling). Thomas Cable has made the mainstream claim explicit: "From the composition of *Cædmon's Hymn* around 680 until the death of Edward the Confessor and the ensuing Conquest, the Anglo-Saxon verse form was transmitted in a highly regulated, technically precise, essentially monolithic continuous tradition."[21] The chief (indeed, almost the only) tenth- and eleventh-century examples of this tradition are the *ASC* poems and *Maldon*, and the span of time between *Maldon* (after 991) and *The Death of Edward* (after 1065) is apparently not too great for Cable's imagined tradition to continue being transmitted. Even more than *Brunanburh*, *The Death of Edward* is a remarkable exercise in archaizing versification, but I do not believe it can bear the weight of certifying the "monolithic" and enduring nature of the tradition, especially when *Brunanburh* itself seems to employ non-traditional alliteration.

But it is certainly the case that *Brunanburh* is taken by many Anglo-Saxonists as a crucial indicator of poetic and heroic continuity, even to the point of suggesting it indicates a living tradition of oral composition. Further, claims of the highly traditional meter of *Brunanburh* (as by Campbell, Bliss, and J. Townsend) explicitly understand *Brunanburh* as exemplifying formal continuity or stasis. Yet the evidence for the stability of the tradition across the tenth and eleventh centuries is distressingly small: *Maldon*, *Brunanburh*, and all the other relevant *ASC* poems total only 503 lines of poetry, which is easily outweighed by the amount of verse in *Judgment Day II* and *Instructions for Christians*. If my dating of *The Menologium* to the 970s is correct, that adds another three hundred lines or so to the tally of tenth-century classical verse, but these totals are still vastly outweighed by *The Metrical Psalms*, which are over 5000 lines long in themselves. In short, the relatively conservative meter of *Brunanburh* (alongside that of *Maldon* and the other classical *ASC* poems) has been used to stress the uniformity of the Old English poetic tradition, even in the face of a far greater amount of contemporary poetry that operates on a less classical basis. My point, of course, is not that *Brunanburh*'s conservatism is unimportant — I firmly believe it is — but rather that that very conservatism takes on a different tenor when we recognize more fully and consciously how closely it sits alongside the flourishing of a more innovative, more prolific, and less conservative tradition.

2. *The Anglo-Saxon Chronicle is a record, document, or work of propaganda regarding Anglo-Saxon nation-building.*

This perspective has gained prominence in recent years, perhaps because it has the virtue of matching contemporary critical interest in topics such as the nature of the nation and of nationalism in areas outside of Anglo-Saxon England. From this viewpoint, however, *Brunanburh* is generally invoked as articulating clearly the role of heroic traditions and lordship as structuring or defining that act of nation-building.[22] The passages indicating

---

[21] Cable, *English Alliterative Tradition*, pp. 55–56.

[22] See Thormann, "*Anglo-Saxon Chronicle* Poems," and Bredehoft, *Textual Histories*.

collaboration between West-Saxons and Mercians and the whole force of the poem as a statement of a kind of national unification are obviously brought to the fore in readings of this sort. Readings that find significant parallels from Old Norse tend to cluster here, identifying Athelstan's court as a multi-lingual and multi-ethnic gathering place; such readings, of course, appear to implicitly or explicitly take the poem as contemporary, rather than retrospective.[23]

Notably, of course, the question of whether or not *Brunanburh* was written specifically for the *ASC* or not becomes a central question when considering how the *ASC*'s investment in nation-building does or does not match the poem's. Is the vision of nation-building that we might see in the poem more consistent with a poem from the 930s, when Athelstan himself was still alive, or does it suit more precisely a date in the 950s, when Athelstan and Edmund both are dead and gone? Perhaps the poem suits even better a moment when Edmund's son (and Athelstan's nephew) Eadwig has taken the throne in 955? The latter possibility, of course, meshes very well indeed with the textual history of *Brunanburh*, entered into the Parker Chronicle in or shortly after 955, in a manuscript usually associated with Winchester in the mid-tenth century. Or are the two possibilities perhaps both viable simultaneously, with the poem in circulation outside the *ASC* first, and then entered into the *ASC* as a part of a block of annals in or after 955? Did Athelstan himself see his work as nation-building, or did such a perspective only come later? The difficulty of answering such questions persuasively, perhaps, reminds us that having a relatively precise date of composition for this poem does not really ease the problems of interpretation after all. To interpret *Brunanburh* effectively, we must attend to metrical, codicological, aesthetic, linguistic, tradition-oriented, historical, and literary concerns. *Brunanburh* is, for almost all its readers, a test case for our commitment to historical understanding.

In these final comments, it is probably fair to say I have engaged in my own share of tendentious commentary. But I hope to have been explicit in my own positions: *Brunanburh*'s relation to the hypothesis of a stable and enduring tradition of versification (to say nothing of oral composition) is far from plain, and even the existence of that tradition may be in doubt as far as the tenth and eleventh centuries are concerned, as intentional and nostalgic archaism may account for the poems in question as well or better than the hypothesized existence of a continued living tradition. Likewise, I am skeptical of readings that remove *Brunanburh* from its textual and codicological roots: to do so seems to me to engage in speculation, rather than criticism. All of the Anglo-Saxon readers we can be certain of seem to have encountered the poem in the *ASC*; without hard evidence that it also circulated outside of the *ASC* and prior to the 950s, we should probably read the 950s *ASC* as its most meaningful original context.

But I also wish to emphasize that my skepticism, of course, does no harm to the poem at all, which still has all the virtues that generations of readers have seen in it. My skepticism concerns the critical fashion of seeing this poem as evidence for continuity of a heroic poetic tradition that — in all its earlier manifestations — features and centralizes speech-making and actual sword-play. My skepticism concerns the habit of seeing this poem's meter as highly traditional, when it may follow unique and innovative alliteration patterns as well as

[23] See, for example, see Niles, "Skaldic Technique in *Brunanburh*," Zacher, "Multilingualism," and Townend, "Pre-Cnut Praise Poetry."

tolerating late Old English metrical forms. *Brunanburh*, I firmly believe, has not yet yielded up all its secrets, but we will hardly be ready to hear what it has to tell us if we hold too dearly to our familiar habits and fashions regarding the poem and its place within the tradition.

ROBERT P. CREED

# *THE BATTLE OF BRUNANBURH* AS A POEM

The poem that modern scholars call *The Battle of Brunanburh* is one of the most frequently read texts in the corpus of Old English literature. As such, the work has a fascinating and complex critical history, a brief summary of which is provided elsewhere in this volume.[1] The present essay is focused on a far more particular but no less vital matter: through an examination of the poem's physical presentation in the manuscripts and its prosodic presentation as an oral text, I aim to provide a way to read the text in the most literal sense possible.

## READING THE POEM IN THE MANUSCRIPTS

The poem that modern scholars call *The Battle of Brunanburh* survives in four of the manuscripts that contain the *Anglo-Saxon Chronicle*. Since most Old English poems survive in a single, often damaged manuscript, as *Beowulf* does, for example, it is unusual for modern scholars to have access to the thinking of four different Anglo-Saxons about a particular poem.

Anglo-Saxon scribes were usually monks who had been trained to write down what they saw in a manuscript given to them to copy. If, however, more than one copy of a particular text was needed, a reader would read the text to a group of scribes each of whom copied, as well as he could, what he heard. Later, each scribe would usually reread and correct what he had written. Each of the scribes who took down the poem about Brunanburh made corrections. But even with careful proofreading, Anglo-Saxon scribes, like modern writers and editors, sometimes made mistakes. We know little about the circumstances in which the various manuscripts of the *ASC* were produced. Much of what we do know was summed up by two scholars of the nineteenth century, Charles Plummer and John Earle, whose work was reviewed, edited, and republished in two volumes by Dorothy Whitelock in 1952.[2]

Before discussing the four manuscripts that contain the poem, I list them below, using the modern designation for each manuscript of the *ASC* that has survived.[3]

• *A text: Parker Version*
Cambridge, Corpus Christi College, MS 173; tenth century.

This manuscript is often referred to as "The Parker Manuscript" because the sixteenth-century Anglican archbishop Matthew Parker had it in his possession before he bequeathed it to Corpus Christi College of the University of Cambridge.

---

[1] See the essay by Thomas A. Bredehoft in this volume, pp. 285–94.

[2] The poem as it was recorded by the A-scribe appears on pp. 106, 108, and 110 of their edition.

[3] A facsimile of the A text has been published in Flower and Smith, eds., *Parker Chronicle and Laws*. Photographs of B, C, and D can be found in Robinson and Stanley, eds., *Old English Verse Texts* (hereafter "Robinson and Stanley").

• *B text*
London, British Library, MS Cotton Tiberius A.vi; ca. 1000.

• *C text*
London, British Library, MS Cotton Tiberius B.i; ca. 1050.

• *D text*
London, British Library, MS Cotton Tiberius B.iv; ca. 1050–1100.

• *E text: Peterborough Version*
Oxford, Bodleian Library, MS Laud Misc. 636; ca. 1121.

There are only the date and seven words, with no poem, at the entry for the year of the battle, 937. For the full text, see Item 15 in this volume.

• *F text: Canterbury Version*
London, British Library, MS Cotton Domitian A.viii; ca. 1100.

For the full text, see Item 12 in this volume.

The text of the poem that I have chosen to reproduce for this volume (Item 4b) is essentially that of the B text, with variant readings supplied in the notes from A, C, and D. In this regard, the text offered for the reader differs considerably from the excellent composite text put together by the great scholar Elliott van Kirk Dobbie, who based his 1942 edition of the text on A — our oldest copy of the *ASC* — supplying variant readings from the other three manuscripts.[4] The other standard edition frequently consulted by scholars is Alistair Campbell's *Battle of Brunanburh* (1938). Besides offering a critical text of the poem, Campbell also provides a diplomatic text, in which he lists every variant reading of every line in a manner easy to follow. He also provides detailed — and at times persuasive — notes and a full glossary, as well as a lengthy introduction and six appendices. Campbell, like Dobbie, based his text on the work of the A-scribe; the same is true of Item 4a in this volume.

That the A text has been the standard edition is, on the one hand, quite understandable. We think it is the oldest copy of the *ASC* by some decades. Likewise, the A-scribe's handwriting is beautiful and clear, and his work has survived essentially undamaged. On the other hand, the A-scribe seems to have been sometimes puzzled when it came to copying or taking down poetry composed in the vernacular. For example, in line 13 the A text reads *secgas hwate*; while this is a legitimate phrase that can be translated as "the men [were] brave," the words clearly lose the double alliteration of *secga swate* [(with) men's blood], found in all the other versions. Even more, "secgas hwate" is something of a non-sequitur following "feld dænnede" in line 12: "the field grew slippery (or dark), / the men were brave." The A text gives us five more places like this, places where we wonder what the scribe might have been thinking about. For example, in line 56 he writes *hira land* where the others have the alliterating *Iraland* (B) or *Yraland* (C, D). Is his *weealles* at line 72 a simple inattentive error, or is there something more complex underlying it? B, C, and D all give us the familiar *wealas*, the source of the Modern English word *Welsh*.

---

[4] *Anglo-Saxon Minor Poems*, ed. Dobbie, pp. 16–20; Dobbie discusses the poem on pp. xxxvi–xl in the Introduction and on pp. 146–49 of the Notes.

The C-scribe, who writes well and whose work has also survived undamaged, at two places has problems with the meter. In the middle of lines 20 and 31 he adds the "and" sign, thus changing the meter. Finally, in some ways the work of the D-scribe is the most beautiful of all, complete with an ornamental "G" at line 53. But what he gives us as the rest of this line is gibberish: "Gewiton him þa norðmen dæggled ongarum" or "dæg gled on garum." Whatever the last two/four words might mean, they do not alliterate.

In our search for an editorial base text, we are left, then, with the B-scribe, who may have been a bit careless with spelling and whose work has not survived undamaged, but who seems to have had a better ear for poetry than any of the other scribes. Once we get beyond B's spelling of King Athelstan's name (which may not be a mistake at all), the damage to the name of the battlefield (for which he was not responsible), and his misspelling of *-linda* in line 6, we can make out what is clearly a well-composed poem. To make B's version of the poem perhaps even better, I have added *oð* from A, C, and D at line 16 and deleted the *-r* from *her* in line 40, following both A and D. But even without these changes, the lines of the B-scribe's copy always make good meter and pretty good sense, and they always alliterate properly. It can be argued that, like Dobbie and Campbell, I have produced a composite text by adding two words to the text written down by the B-scribe. That is true, but the B-scribe left us much less to do in order to achieve a good text than did the other scribes.

*The "Pointing" of the Manuscripts*

Since Anglo-Saxon scribes had to use their resources as efficiently as possible, or because the tradition of writing a poem line by line had not yet developed in vernacular Britain, they did not set out the poems they recorded as modern editors do. Scribes simply wrote as much of the running text as they could fit onto each manuscript line, beginning at the left margin and writing all the way across the page to the right margin. They often included two lines of a poem — or parts of two or three lines — on a single manuscript line.

When they were writing down a poem, scribes sometimes "punctuated" the manuscript lines with "points" — period-like dots — some on the line, some slightly above it. They placed most of the points between two successive lines of the poem — "poetic lines" — or between the two halflines of a particular poetic line. Modern editors do not print the Anglo-Saxon scribes' points. Instead, they print each poetic line as a separate line of text, as in the modern convention for poetry, deleting the final point. They replace those points that occur in the middle of a poetic line with a space usually about three letters wide. When one of the points occurs at a sentence-boundary, modern editors replace it with a period. At some other places where scribal points occur, editors replace them with commas, colons, or semicolons. But at many places editors, feeling that no punctuation is required for the sense, simply delete the point.

Modern scholars rarely mention manuscript pointing, feeling — correctly — that such formatting, along with modern punctuation, makes such mention unnecessary. But occasionally a scholar, especially one who studies versification (a "metrist" or "prosodist"), notes that the pointing of the scribes was an important guide for the nineteenth-century editors who figured out the lines and halflines of most of the poems that have come down to us. Scribal pointing probably played some role in the work of the early editors, but, as I have demonstrated elsewhere, understanding or sensing how the poets used alliteration played the major role.[5]

[5] Creed, *Reconstructing the Rhythm*, pp. 49–53 (note that all occurrences of "formative(s)" on p. 50 should be changed to "superlative marker(s)").

To show the importance of alliteration in locating the lines of the poem and at the same time to demonstrate the secondary visual role pointing played in that process, here are two lines from the B-scribe's manuscript (Cotton Tiberius A.vi, fol. 32r, lines 16–17):

> ʒrædiʒneʒuþhavoc⁊þʒrægedeor.ƿulfonƿealde.neƿearð
> ƿælmare.onþyseʒlande.æfreʒyta.folcesafylled befo

Anglo-Saxon scribes did not leave a space between each successive word. Still, it is possible to make out about three and three-quarter lines of the poem in these two manuscript lines. The beginning of line 16 in the manuscript matches the beginning of line 64 of the poem. The end of line 17 in the manuscript falls in the middle of the word *beforan* in the second half of line 67. It appears thus in this volume (Item 4.64–67):

> grædigne guþhafoc     and þæt græge deor,
> wulf on wealde.     Ne wearð wæl mare
> on þys eglande     æfre gyta
> folces afylled     befo[ran þyssum]

There are five points in these manuscript lines: (1) between *deor* and *wulf*, (2) between *wealde* and *ne*, (3) between *mare* and *on*, (4) between *eglande* and *æfre*, and (5) between *gyta* and *folces*. Using these lines from the B-scribe's manuscript, I make three observations about scribes' points. First, *every* point that appears in these two manuscript lines, in the lines of the four manuscripts under discussion, and in other manuscripts containing poetry, occurs at a word-boundary; that is, every point falls between two complete words. Second, three of the points in manuscript lines 16 and 17 do what most of the scribal points do in manuscripts containing poetry: they guide the reader through the lines of the poem by indicating the end of one line of poetry and the beginning of the next. These are the points between *deor* and *wulf*, between *mare* and *on*, and between *gyta* and *folces*. Third, each of the remaining two points in these two manuscript lines, like many of the scribes' points, occurs at an another important place within its poetic line. These are the points between *wealde* and *ne*, and between *eglande* and *æfre*.

Here, then, is how I would describe the function of the three points in the passage from the B-text that occur between two whole lines of poetry: such points occur either at the first alliterating syllable of the line or at a non-alliterating syllable of a word or prefix that is associated by sense and/or by syntax with the first alliterating syllable. In the lines above, the point between *deor* and *wulf* occurs at the first alliterating syllable, *wulf*, which begins a new line of poetry, line 65. The last point, between *gyta* and *folces*, occurs at the first alliterating syllable, *folc-*, of line 67 of the poem. These points can serve to remind us that most — about 60% — of the lines of an Anglo-Saxon poem begin with the first alliterating syllable of the line.

The B-scribe used a point, then, to flag the beginning of line 65 of the poem, the line that runs — to quote the scribe — *.wulf on wealde.ne wearð wæl mare*. But, since the scribe could not fit all of this line of the poem on manuscript line 16, he ended the manuscript line with *wearð* and continued poetic line 65 on manuscript line 17, placing a point after *mare*. Then the scribe continued the manuscript line with *on þys eglande*.

The point before *on* does not occur before the first alliterating syllable of the new line but before a preposition, a "little word" that, preposed to a noun, cannot be stressed. I would characterize the function of this point as a flag that tells us to look ahead, to see whether there is a noun, a "big" word that is stressed and therefore can alliterate, to which the preposition is preposed. And there is: *eglande*. The point before *on*, then, occurs at a word that is associated with, but is not itself, the first alliterating syllable of the line.

Thus, the scribes sometimes used points to mark the beginning of a new poetic line. These points remind the reader that the poet built every line around the alliteration of important words. Even a reader who knew how the poetry works might have been grateful for this guidance, but no speaker of Old English really needed the points. He or she knew that alliteration, not formatting on the page, builds poetic lines. Accordingly, most scribes who set down or copied poems did not bother to use points very often.

There are still two points in the quotation above to be considered. I begin with the last point in manuscript line 16, the one between *wealde* and *ne*. When we set out the poem in modern format, that point occurs in the middle of line 65. Like the preposition *on*, the negative particle *ne* is unstressed and cannot alliterate. This point, then, indicates that the reader should look ahead for an important word that will *complete* the alliteration of the line. A point that occurs in the middle of the line marks either the *last* alliterating syllable itself or a non-alliterating word or words or even a non-alliterating syllable that is associated with the last alliterating syllable. Since the negative particle *ne* cannot alliterate, and the verb *wearð* rarely alliterates, the reader looks ahead to the noun *wæl*.

The scribes' pointing, then, is directly related to the poet's use of alliteration. The scribes are not telling the reader something that he or she cannot find out without the help of the points. Some scholars have claimed, however, that it is the points that identify the "verses" that the poets composed. I would turn that around: it is our understanding of the process of composing, in which alliteration governs the lines and halflines of the poem, that allows us to identify a prosodically significant point from one that is randomly placed, like the D-scribe's point *after* "hord" in line 10 of the poem.

Let us turn briefly now to the way in which each of the four scribes of the surviving manuscripts of this poem distributed the points in his manuscript. As noted earlier, the A-scribe is the easiest to deal with: he used points to mark all but two of the larger prosodic divisions of the poem, the lines and halflines. The B-, C-, and D-scribes were not so meticulous in their use of pointing. The C-scribe appears to have placed a point between forty-nine lines and a point at the midpoint of thirty-three lines. The D-scribe is the most erratic. He placed a point between forty-seven lines, at the midpoint of nine lines, and elsewhere — that is, *within* a halfline — four times.

The B-scribe's pointing is most interesting. He placed a point between two whole poetic lines sixty-two times. But he placed a point at the midpoint of only fourteen lines. Was he telling us that the whole line of a poem is harder to keep track of, and therefore offering us all this help? Or was the B-scribe telling us that the lines of a poem matter more than the halflines? It is difficult to know for certain.

*The "Accents" of the A and B texts*

If the pointing of the manuscripts presents us with questions of scribal intent, the same is no doubt true of the "accenting" in the manuscripts. The A-scribe, for instance, placed a forward slash or accent-like mark, sometimes with a short hook at the top, above twenty-six words in his copy of the poem. These marks are not so-called bars of suspension, like the three bars on folio 26r, line 5, the first of which, "hī," indicates that the word is not *hi* but *him*. The bars of suspension are always flat, even though some end in a small flourish. Instead, the marks listed below slant up into the space between the lines. The mark is always a slash with or without the hook at the top.

These marks occur over the following syllables or words in the A text, identified by the line number of the printed text of the poem: *eac* (2), *tir* (3), possibly over *ecȝum* (4), *hamas* (10), *secȝas* (13), *up* (13), *tid* (14), *eac* (19), *piȝ* (20), *forð* (20), *eac* (30), *on* (36), *eac* (37), *har* (39), *on* (41, 43, 49, 51, 54), possibly at end of the line after *land* (59), *oc* (64), *on* (65, 66), possibly over *ecȝum* (68), and *bec* (68).

Sixteen of these marks occur over stressed words like *eac*, but not one of the *on*'s the scribe marked can be given stress in its context. Six of the eight marked *on*'s occur at the beginning of a halfline; two do not (lines 51 and 65). More tellingly, perhaps, none of the *on*'s through line 35 are marked, but from line 36 to 66 eight are marked and only one (line 38) is not.

Like the A-scribe, the B-scribe marked *eac* in line 2. Then, because of a stain on folio 31v, it becomes hard to tell whether there are any over-line markings for the next twenty-nine lines. The visible marks are as follows: *rim* (31), *þorfte* (39), possibly over the *rm* of *garmittinge* (50), *mot* (50), *þad* (61), and *bec* (68). If the marks listed are what they seem to be, then the B-scribe, unlike the A-scribe, placed every one of them over a stressed syllable, usually a syllable that bears intermediate stress in its line.

The editor's job is to make the reader aware of these markings, even though he, the editor, may, like me, not know what to make of them. They are, after all, there in the manuscript; the scribe made them, just as he penned the letters that we can read. The marks do not seem to be random. They meant something to the scribe and his readers. I leave it to the interested reader to try to figure out what they might mean.

## *THE BATTLE OF BRUNANBURH* AS A POEM

*The Battle of Brunanburh* is composed in the Old English poetic tradition that includes *Beowulf*.[6] The poetic line with which Anglo-Saxon poets worked — and which may have been

---

[6] A more detailed version of this work will appear elsewhere (Creed, "Meter of 'The Battle of Brunanburh'"). In brief, my account of the meter of the poem is based on two rather different kinds of activity. On the one hand, I have examined both the sources, in this case the poem as it appears in the four manuscripts, and also what others have had to say about the poem. And I have applied to the text of the poem, particularly the B-text, what I have learned from the study of the prosody of *Beowulf* as it survives in its unique manuscript, British Library, MS Cotton Vitellius A.xv. In 1990, I published an account of the results of a study of about 13% of the manuscript text of *Beowulf* (*Reconstructing*). A newer study based on an analysis of all of the 12,500 surviving measures of *Beowulf* is in progress. Thus, the account that follows is based not only on the 293 measures of *Brunanburh* but on a study of approximately one-tenth of the surviving corpus of Old English poetry. I have been guided by the works of Sievers ("Rhythmik des germanischen Alliterationsverses") and Pope (*Rhythm of Beowulf*), though my results differ significantly from theirs, and from those of many other studies that have appeared during the last century and a half (see, e.g., Stockwell and Minkova, "Prosody"). The other kind of activity is performance. I have not been content to put together a prosody of a poem without trying to perform the poem according to that prosody. My colleague and accompanist, John Bollard, and I perform *Brunanburh* according to the prosody discussed here, and we have similarly performed every line of *Beowulf* in preparation for a recording of the entire poem in Old English. In the late 1970s, I wrote a two-act (two-hour) version of *Beowulf* for National Public Radio, in which I performed all of the passages of *Beowulf* based on what I had learned from more than a decade of studies of Old English meter. A two-CD set of the recording of the 1978 radio performance has just become available.

identified in part through the manuscript pointing already discussed — consists of four isochronous measures, two or three of which begin with the same sound ("alliterate"), and each of which reiterates, with varying numbers and arrangements of stressed and unstressed syllables, the same simple rhythm: heavy downbeat/light upbeat.[7]

The components of the Old English poetic measure are few. The number of syllables in a measure is limited, ranging from one to six. Each syllable is stressed or unstressed, long or short. In three types of measures, a syllable is replaced by a rest.[8] The patterns made by different numbers of long and short, stressed and unstressed, syllables and rests produce a finite set of measure types and subtypes. It is the combination of measures of varying shapes and weights that produces the enormous variety of the Old English poetic lines.

There are two broad categories of measure in Old English poetry: "major class" measures and "introductory" measures.[9] Major class measures begin with a stressed syllable of a major class word — in Old English, a noun, verb, adjective, or adverb — that takes the downbeat. Introductory measures which lack an initial stressed syllable begin with a stress taken by a rest or by a note on the accompanying instrument that supplies or augments the downbeat. An introductory measure can only occur as the first or the third measure of the line, while a major class measure can occur at any position.

While the principles of Old English composition are simple, prosodic analysis can be daunting: there are seven measure types made up of fifty-one theoretically possible subtypes. The *Brunanburh*-poet used twenty-eight subtypes, the *Beowulf*-poet forty-six.[10] Sorting the measures of the lines of an Old English poem into these types and subtypes makes it possible to take precise and systematic account of the variations in the expression of the rhythm available to the poet. But it is not my purpose here to offer such an account. Rather, I aim to acquaint the reader with the basic framework of the lines of *Brunanburh* in order to make it possible to for the reader to hear the poem as a poem. The remainder of this section describes the process of analyzing the measures of a few lines according to the approach just described.

## A BRIEF TUTORIAL ON A NEW APPROACH TO THE METER OF OLD ENGLISH POETRY

Here is the first line of the *Battle of Brunanburh* as printed in this volume (Item 4.1):

Æþelstan cing,    eorla drihten

Line 1 consists of four words, all of them nouns. Modern editors usually leave a space between the second and third words, the "midline space" that divides the lines into two

[7] There is one five-measure line in this poem, line 53, which accounts for the odd number (293) of measures. Here are the five measures: "| (/) Ge|witan him þa | Norþmenn | nægled|cnearrum."

[8] I had constructed a grid that indicates exactly where rests occur in the lines of Old English poems before I discovered that linguists like Selkirk (*Phonology and Syntax*) and Hogg and McCully (*Metrical Phonology*) provide support for such ideas. I first came across the idea of the halfline-initial rest in Pope's *Rhythm of Beowulf*.

[9] I have taken the term "major class word" from linguistic studies such as Hogg and McCully, *Metrical Phonology*.

[10] The one outlier measure in *Brunanburh* is at line 16: "* æþele gesceaft," where the poet took four syllables on the downbeat. There are only nineteen outliers in the 12,500 measures of *Beowulf*.

"halflines." The first halfline of a line of Old English poetry always ends with a word-boundary and frequently, as it does here, with a phrase-boundary. The first alliterating syllable defines the first halfline; the last alliterating syllable defines the second halfline.

Line 1 is headed by the stressed syllable that begins the king's name, "Æþ." The second halfline is headed by a stressed syllable that begins with the diphthong "eo." Since in Old English poetic tradition all initial vowels and diphthongs alliterate with each other, these syllables alliterate. The alliteration of line 1 is "vocalic" (*V*); the alliteration of line 2 is *B*, line 4 *S*, and so on.

Since eleven lines of *Brunanburh*, beginning with line 1, consist of exactly four major class words, the first syllable of which is stressed, it is easy to mark the beginning of each measure of these lines with a solid bar, |:

| Æþelstan | cing,     | eorla | drihten[11]

Locating the measures of other kinds of line takes a little practice. The next easiest kind of line to divide into its measures is one that consists of four major class words plus one or two little words that occur between the major class words. Lines 10 and 24 are good examples:

| hord and | hamas.     | Hettend | crungon (line 10)

| mecum | mylenscearpum.     | Myrce ne | wyrndon (line 24)

Note that the bar of the second and fourth measures of a line is always placed before the main syllable of a major class word or compound ("mylen-scearpum"), never before an unstressed particle like "ne" when it occurs in the middle of the halfline. In the three lines analyzed so far, the first and third measures also begin with a major class word. When a major class word heads a halfline, it usually establishes or completes the alliteration. In the lines analyzed, "Æþelstan/eorla," "hord/Hettend," and "mecum/Myrce" establish and complete the alliteration. About sixty percent of the halflines of any Old English poem — and sixty-six percent of those in *The Battle of Brunanburh* — begin similarly with an alliterating syllable.

If, on the other hand, either halfline begins with a little word like "and," or with an unstressed syllable — or even with a stressed syllable that does not alliterate in the line — the reader should follow two steps. Step 1: locate and place a bar before the first alliterating syllable in the halfline. Step 2: place a bar before the first syllable of the halfline. The second halfline of line 2 and the first halfline of line 5 provide good examples of such halflines; so do both halflines of line 8.

*Step 1*:
| beorna beaggifa,     and his | broþor eac (line 2)

embe | Brunanburh.     | Bordweall clufon (line 5)

fram | cneomagum,     þæt hie æt | campe oft (line 8)

[11] The other such lines are 3, 6, 12, 18, 23, 25, 31, 33, 59, and 72.

*Step 2*:
| beorna beaggifa, | and his | broþor eac (line 2)

| embe | Brunanburh. | Bordweall clufan (line 5)

| fram | cneomagum, | þæt hie æt | campe oft (line 8)

The reader should note that we have placed a bar before the *first* and the *last* alliterating syllable in every line.[12] These syllables often head the halfline, as they do in every halfline of lines 1, 10, and 24. When the first alliterating syllable does not head the halfline, it is important to locate the alliterating syllable before placing a bar before the syllable that heads the halfline. If, at this point, there is no bar *inside* the halfline, as is the case with 2a and 3b, the reader should then place a bar before the stressed syllable of the next major class word or compound in the measure, as we will do when we complete Step 3.

There is a third step for halflines that do not begin with an alliterating syllable. Step 3: indicate that the halfline begins with a rest that takes the downbeat. I place a forward slash in parentheses, (/), to indicate a halfline-initial rest:

*Step 3*:
| beorna | beaggifa, | (/) and his | broþor eac (line 2)

| (/) embe | Brunanburh. | Bordweall | clufan (line 5)

| (/) fram | cneomagum, | (/) þæt hie æt | campe oft (line 8)

The reader can now locate the beginning of the four measures of every line of the poem.

When the reader does so, he or she will note the variety of ways with which the *Brunanburh*-poet filled the measures. The range is from a single unstressed syllable "ge-" that fills the first measure of line 4 and line 53, to the four syllables with which he filled the fourth measure of line 7, "æþele wæs," and the second measure of line 24, "mylenscearpum." In line 4, the halfline-initial rest supplies the downbeat, the syllable "ge" the upbeat. That situation is reversed in certain major class measures like "cing" at line 1, "clufan" at line 5, or "homera" at line 6. In measures that contain only a monosyllabic word like "cing," a disyllabic word that begins with a short stressed syllable like "clufan," or a trisyllabic word that begins with a short stressed syllable and continues with another short syllable as "homera" does at line 6, the upbeat is taken by a rest that replaces the syllable that ends many measures. I illustrate this "light" or upbeat rest using an "x" in parentheses, (x):

| Æþelstan | cing (x), | eorla | drihten (line 1)

| (/) embe | Brunanburh. | Bordweall | clufan (x),
| heowan | heaðolinda | homera (x) | lafum (lines 5–6)

---

[12] The middle alliterating syllable of three marks the beginning of a measure whenever the line begins with the first alliterating syllable. When the first halfline does not begin with the first alliterating syllable and two alliterating syllables occur in the first halfline, as at line 17, the second (of three) alliterating syllables does not usually head a measure. For example, I divide the first halfline of line 22 into only two measures: "| (/) on | last legdon."

The *Brunanburh*-poet used only twenty-one different kinds of major measures and seven different kinds of introductory measures. The twenty-one different kinds of major measures can be sorted into five types; the seven different kinds of introductory measures can be sorted into two types. These seven types and their subtypes take account of every possible kind of variation that occurs in the measures: in the number of syllables, in the placement of the stressed and unstressed syllables, and in the length of the stressed syllables. The prosody sketched here is thus the most systematic, the most complete, but also the simplest account of the meter of an Old English poem. And it makes it possible to take account of every detail of the astonishingly varied lines of *Brunanburh* and *Beowulf* — and probably of any surviving Old English poem.[13]

[13] I am very grateful to the staff of the Robert Frost Library of Amherst College, particularly to Susan Sheridan, for generously making the Robinson and Stanley volume not only available to me, but also for providing me with many excellent photographic copies of the relevant pages.

A. KEITH KELLY

# TRUTH AND A GOOD STORY: *EGIL'S SAGA* AND BRUNANBURH

Arguments about the historicity of the Icelandic sagas range from claims that they should be assumed to be historically accurate unless proven otherwise to assertions that they should be viewed as fictional narratives that may contain occasional references to real people, places, and events when suitable to the story, but that are nevertheless unreliable as historic evidence. This short essay is not the place to stake my allegiance to either side of this debate — nor would I wish or be able to choose a side, the reasons for which are to follow — but I will offer the reader who may be unfamiliar with Old Norse saga an introduction to some of the key elements of saga literature that will not only address these issues of historicity but will draw attention to aspects of literary aesthetics as well: two narrative elements that are inextricably interwoven in Old Norse literature. I thus hope to provide something of a critical framework for placing *Egil's Saga* within the scope of the broader Brunanburh discussion put forth in this volume.

In his introduction to the 1933 edition of *Egil's Saga* — still the standard edition — Sigurður Nordal expressed his belief in the value of the Icelandic family sagas as sources of historical truth.[1] Such a position, that the sagas are best taken generally at face value as a kind of elaborate literary off-shoot of chronicle narratives, is rooted in a long-standing tradition. In the preface to his own edition of 1856, for instance, Einar Thordarson writes:

> The Saga agrees well with other Icelandic Sagas, and may be reckoned as one of the most truthful; but when it is considered that it was kept in men's memory for a very long time — the events happening before the year 1000, and the story not being put into writing till near the end of the twelfth century — naturally every syllable of it will not be true. Neither in this, however, nor in any of the best Icelandic Sagas do the writers thereof deliberately assert untruth or mean to exaggerate.[2]

This belief that sagas such as Egil's were innocent until proven guilty was by no means universally accepted, however, as other scholars had begun to cast serious doubt upon the credibility of the saga material.[3] It is probably no surprise that this debate has often centered upon the account in *Egil's Saga* of the battle of Vínheiðr (see Item 25 in this volume), which has long been understood to represent the important historical battle more commonly known by its Old English name, Brunanburh.

[1] *Egil's Saga*, ed. Sigurður Nordal, pp. xliii–xlvi.

[2] Quoted in translation in *Egil's Saga*, trans. W. C. Green, p. viii.

[3] See the introduction to Finnur Jónsson's edition, pp. lix–xci, in which the editor casts doubts upon the accuracy of *Egil's Saga* concerning events outside of Iceland and Norway, and remarks upon the inaccurate chronology of some sequences in the text.

The account of the battle is quite detailed in *Egil's Saga*, more so in fact than in any other source. It begins with Anlaf, whom the saga writer names as king of the Scots, invading Northumbria with a great army. He defeats the resisting forces of the Northumbrian earls, Alfgar and Godric, and in doing so rallies more men to his side, including the two brothers, Hring and Adils, who are earls and who have their own significant following. Upon hearing of this, King Athelstan goes south to gather his host with the intention of returning to the north to face Anlaf. Meanwhile, Egil and his brother Thorolf, both of whom are Icelanders, are placed in command of the forces that will stay behind and delay Anlaf. To accomplish this purpose messengers are sent to Anlaf with a challenge to battle in one week's time on a predetermined field. This site is described as follows: "in the place chosen for the battle the heath was level and on one side a river flowed and on the other was a great forest" (25.53–54). The saga-writer declares that the narrowest point between the forest and the river is still very wide. It is in fact there that Egil and Thorolf set up their camp, spanning the distance with many tents. This, however, is a ruse meant to make Anlaf believe that Athelstan's entire army is already encamped. They accomplish this by pitching far more tents than are needed, leaving every third tent empty, and placing but few men in the others. Additionally, they order all their men to move about at the front of the camp (the side facing the enemy lines) to give the impression of even greater numbers. Anlaf agrees to the terms of the battle and moves to a fortified town north of the field, which is named in the saga Vínheiðr. In order to allow Athlestan the time necessary to gather his army and return to the north, Egil and Thorolf, on the day the battle is to be fought, propose a peace settlement to Anlaf. The negotiations are drawn out for three days, by which time Athelstan has arrived in full force and made camp in a fortified town to the south of Vínheiðr. Anlaf, realizing that he has been duped, sends a strike force under the command of the earls Adils and Hring to attack in the night, but this attempt to destroy the Viking mercenary forces of Thorolf and Egil is thwarted. The two brothers and their men fight valiantly, and Hring is slain and Adils is forced to retreat. When morning comes, Athelstan arrives on the battlefield with his full army, as does Anlaf. A pitched battle ensues in which Thorolf is slain by Adils, who makes a surprise attack out of the forest. Egil responds by charging Adils' ranks, breaking them and slaying his brother's killer. Anlaf's ranks are broken and Athelstan achieves the victory.

The arguments about the historicity of this account have typically centered around such issues as place-names, the participants in the battle and their identities, the geographical features of the battle site, the series of events and strategies employed, and the connections between *Egil's Saga* and other source material. In the same year that Nordal brought out his edition of the saga, for instance, L. M. Hollander published an article on the Vínheiðr battle section of *Egil's Saga*, drawing comparisons between it and scenes from other saga material, particularly *Hervarar's Saga*, seeing in the commonalities a literary rather than a historical background.[4] Several years following, Alistair Campbell's edition of *The Battle of Brunanburh* raised further doubts as to the veracity of the account of the battle in *Egil's Saga*.[5] Through more than a century of these debates *Egil's Saga* has been portrayed as both one of the most historically accurate of all Icelandic sagas (Nordal felt this quite passionately) and one of the most literary — Egil is a fascinating and colorful character and some of the episodes in the saga strike many readers as very good fiction indeed. The intersection of many important historic events and personages with the celebrated deeds of a character like Egil, who is

[4] Hollander, "Battle of the Vin-Heath."

[5] Campbell, *Battle of Brunanburh*, pp. 62–80.

himself a figure of historical record, often spurs our desire to seek the "truth" of the story, yet at the same time this narrative characteristic makes it exceedingly difficult to unravel truth from fiction. The presence of a great deal of allusive (and elusive) skaldic poetry, which some scholars feel preserves original meaning more accurately than prose due to the nature of social memory and oral transmission, further complicates the debate, as does the undeniable fact that the saga was composed, at least in its surviving written form, some three centuries after the events that it relates, and that much of its preservation relies on memory and oral tradition, or possibly upon written documents that no longer exist.[6] While one could hardly be faulted for surrendering to a simple *nescio* in light of these compounded complexities (as Campbell suggested in regards to identifying the battle-site),[7] the issue of historicity remains an essential determinant in how we utilize the saga materials, especially when it comes to our attempts to access the truth of the events at an already hazily seen event such as Brunanburh.

Fittingly, perhaps no aspect of *Egil's Saga* unites this dynamic interface of historical and literary merits than the compelling the figure of Egil himself. Son of Skalla-Grímr, son of Kveld-Úlfr, Egil is a man of documented historical existence who lived ca. 910–990. His life, and that of many of his kinfolk, is well-attested in the *Landnámabók*, the book of the settling of Iceland. Surrounding him in both history and fiction are other well-known historical figures, such as King Harald Fair-hair of Norway, his son, Erik Bloodaxe; and of course King Athelstan of England, for whom he supposedly fights at Brunanburh. In his saga — which is variously placed somewhere on the spectrum between biography and romance — Egil is drawn with exceptional richness. He is remarkably strong and gifted as a warrior, just and principled in his role as a farmer and an Icelandic leader, and is recognized as a highly talented poet. Yet Egil is also stubborn and vengeful, full of pride, and prone to brutality when provoked. The physical descriptions given to the character at times border upon the grotesque — with his great strength and hardiness comes a heavy, beetled brow, huge shoulders, a bent back, and practically a pelt of unruly dark hair. A reader of the saga will immediately appreciate the literary complexity of the character, both in his form, his actions, and his psychology. At the same time, many critics see in the complexities that make him anything but a straight-forward heroic protagonist evidence of a very real accuracy at work. As W. C. Green suggests, the fact "that the bad points in Egil's character are not screened is surely one proof of the truthfulness of the Saga-writer; a mere eulogist would have blazoned forth all his hero's noble exploits, but veiled the other side, and hardly would anyone inventing a fictitious character have put such dark blots in it."[8] Whether Green is right, or the saga-writer was simply a very creative and gifted writer with a penchant for anti-heroes, one cannot readily determine. Similarly, Jesse L. Byock uses the descriptive evidence from *Egil's Saga* to explore the possibility that the historical Egil suffered from Paget's disease, a condition that results in dramatic bone growth, particularly in the skull. Like many who delve into the sagas as evidence for fact, Byock questioned if it was possible, or

[6] For general discussions on Icelandic saga see Liestol, *Origin of the Icelandic Family Sagas*, and Robert Kellogg's introduction to *Sagas of the Icelanders*, ed. Thorsson. For information on *Egil's Saga* in particular, see Sigurður Nordal's complete introduction to his edition and Gwyn Jones' introduction to his translation. See also the website of The Northvegr Foundation <www.northvegr.org> for a wealth of online information and texts of saga literature.

[7] Campbell, *Battle of Brunanburh*, p. 80.

[8] *Egil's Saga*, trans. Green, p. vi.

even important, to answer the question of whether or not Egil's descriptions were accurate and possibly due to a provable disease: "I pondered this question at the beginning of my research and considered it again when I realized that the enigma of Egil lies at a nexus of medical science, history, archaeology and literary analysis."[9] While it may be debatable as to whether or not Egil suffered from Paget's disease — and as Byock suggests the truth would lie in the discovery of his actual bones — it is certain that the man, both real and imagined, commands the interest of many.

One of the many reasons that *Egil's Saga* is such a beguiling work of fiction, and an intriguing source of history, is the fact that Egil is not the only character who captures the interest of readers. From his brother Thorolf, who is as handsome and charismatic as Egil is unsightly and blunt, to figures of undeniable historical significance, like King Anlaf and King Athelstan, the saga forms a mosaic of compelling people. There is a tendency among scholars to want to either draw connections between these characters and fact in an effort to support the veracity of the saga, or to point out the discrepancies in order to achieve the reverse goal. Thus a figure like Anlaf, who was certainly at the Battle of Brunanburh, and who, as a leader of the Hiberno-Norse from Dublin could have very well enticed such figures as Hring and Adils (possibly two Cumbrian earls of Hiberno-Norse descent, or two Welsh princes with no love for Athelstan) to join in his efforts to destroy the Saxons, fascinates those who wish to talk about the socio-political significance of the event. However, the saga clearly refers to Anlaf as the king of Scotland (Item 25.1), which he certainly was not — that position was held by Constantine for a considerably long time. For some critics, it is clear that the saga-writer has conflated Anlaf and Constantine into one character, a point that for very obvious reasons would raise questions about the reliability of the text as a source for historical truth. Other critics have endeavored to reveal valid explanations that Anlaf would rightly be termed a king of Scotland.[10]

Questions of reliability cut straight to the heart of the purported evidence in *Egil's Saga* for determining information about the site of the Battle of Brunanburh. In *Egil's Saga* the battle is said to take place at Vínheiði and Vínuskóga, Vin-heath and Vin-wood, tantalizing as place-names but hardly identifiable as sites on their own account: heaths and woods were far from rare in tenth-century England. So the name of the site in the saga provides only scant evidence for the researcher seeking out the "real" Brunanburh.[11] The topographical features provided by the text — a heath, a forest, a river, and fortified towns to both the north and the south — are even more enticing to the would-be identifier, particularly given the fact that *Egil's Saga* offers yet more intriguing details like suggestions of distances and differences in elevation. For instance, the saga offers readers a location, a heath, that "ought to be level and large enough for armies to draw up in battle array" (25.52–53). Though exact sizes of medieval armies are hard to determine, particularly in such a "dark" time as the tenth century, several sources in addition to *Egil's Saga* suggest that Brunanburh was quite a large conflict, involving a significant number of combatants.[12] Thus we have a large

[9] Byock, "Egil's Bones," p. 82.

[10] Bjarni Einarsson makes an argument, based in part upon William of Malmesbury, that the saga-writer conflated Anlaf and Constantine and that this should not discount the historical veracity of the text (*Litterære forudsætninger*, pp. 240–41). See note to Item 25.1 in this volume.

[11] For more information on place-names, see Cavill's essay in this volume.

[12] The *Anglo-Saxon Chronicle* and the *Annals of Ulster* independently corroborate the degree of heavy casualties suffered by both sides, reinforcing that this was a large-scale tenth-century conflict.

open field that is level. On one side, the saga tells us, flows a river and on the other is a forest. The span between these two geographical features at its narrowest point, where Egil and Thorolf make their camp, ought to be wide enough to accommodate a large tenth-century army, but not more: "But where the distance was least between the forest and the river, and that was a very long way, there King Athelstan's men had pitched camp; their tents stood in all the space between the forest and the river" (25.55–56). Even taking into consideration issues such as deforestation of England, this sort of detail does offer a convincing degree of specificity. Further indication of the nature of the heath is offered by the fact that "King Anlaf's men pitched their tents north of the hazel rods and there the ground had a slight downward slope" (25.62–63). To the north of the heath, less than a day's march, lies a fortified town where Anlaf makes his headquarters; to the south lies another, where Athelstan makes his. Such evidence has led many a scholar to believe that the site can be pin-pointed in large part by following the "directions" it provides. Thus W. S. Angus, writing in 1937, went so far as to assert that the topographical details provided in *Egil's Saga* are the single most valuable historical clues for determining the battle-site.[13] Following the same line of reasoning, A. H. Burne in 1952 contended that "where the saga makes statements of a topographical nature for which there can be no motives for falsification I accept their essential accuracy, though allowing that slight exaggeration and errors of detail may well be present."[14] Such assumptions cannot be dismissed as entirely old-fashioned, as more recent authors such as Michael Wood (1980) and Alfred P. Smyth (1984) have essentially come to the same positive conclusion about relying on *Egil's Saga* to locate Brunanburh.

For those scholars who seek to use *Egil's Saga* to locate the battle the question of motive seems to hold significant weight: if there is no motive for falsification, then there is little reason to suspect that the details given by the saga-writer are not true.[15] Here, too, however, things are from simple, for there is in fact a very real motivation for fictionalizing such elements in a saga: the writer's aim to create a good story. The site, as described by the saga-writer, conveniently allows for the tactics that unfold during the course of the battle narrative. The river and the forest create a "tunnel-vision" effect for Anlaf's men, making possible the ruse that Egil and Thorolf employ to convince them that they command a greater force than they in fact do. The forest in particular allows Adils to ambush Thorolf and bring about his death in the final battle. A great hero like Thorolf could be killed no other way than through subterfuge, after all. So these elements may simply be crafted as part of the story. After all, if the saga-writer made such fundamental mistakes as calling Anlaf the king of Scotland — perhaps to make it a better story — can it not be assumed he would likewise invent terrain to make for a better battle? Such are the arguments that critics have offered in their efforts to discount *Egil's Saga* as a credible source for locating Brunanburh. However, there are, as the present volume clearly demonstrates, many sources on the Battle of Brunanburh, and *Egil's Saga* need not, and ought not, function in a vacuum. Comparisons between the description of Brunanburh in other sources, such as *The Chronicle of Crowland* and William of Malmesbury's later writings on the matter do allow for the possibility that

[13] Angus, "Battlefield," pp. 291–93.

[14] Burne, *Battlefields*, p. 52.

[15] For more detailed investigations of the arguments pertaining to the location of the Vínheiðr battle in *Egil's Saga*, see both Ian McDougall, "Discretion and Deceit," and Magnús Fjalldal, "Farmer in the Court of King Athelstan."

the same battle is being described.[16] The fact that *Egil's Saga* is much more detailed, in keeping with the features of the genre, need not mean that the details are there simply for the purposes of crafting a compelling narrative.

On balance, our natural either/or perspective on saga literature — either it is fiction or it is fact — appears to be woefully limited and short-sighted. Sagas are neither purely history nor purely fiction; they are both, and indissolubly so. Without the historic elements the Icelandic family sagas would not be what they are, but would be more like the eddic material that is clearly mythic or legendary. Even so, without the fictional elements the same sagas would be episodic, fractured, incohesive, and, in a word, boring. The origin of saga is oral, and thus as much as it was intended to entertain it was intended to inform. Saga literature is not just spontaneous creative art, it is a product of social memory and serves a distinct role in the Icelandic culture. As is evidenced by the considerable amount of history in the corpus of Icelandic family saga, a real connection with the past was essential to the saga-writer, and to those who received and enjoyed saga literature. Byock, in "Social Memory and the Sagas," points out that "the process created in the sagas is a pastiche that satisfied the needs of a thirteenth-century audience without letting their story-telling or literature (why quibble about such terms) evolve into pure fiction."[17] In this way the saga is as much a product of the present (the time of its telling) as it is of the past it incorporates, a fact that in itself does not deny or disprove the veracity of the past it presents. Like so many artistic endeavors that enmesh themselves in the history of their own creators and audiences, sagas engage with a remembered past to serve the present. Because of this desire to tap the power of the past — one that is often preserved in memory or oral tradition more than in verifiable documentation — the saga-writer is much more likely to employ history rather than create it. Of course this is the history as it is remembered, not necessarily as it happened; since social memory is organic in nature, it is subject to interpretation and reinterpretation, and of course exaggeration. Historical elements within the social consciousness need not be factual in order to be accepted as true.

In considering the connection between fact and fiction in the art of Icelandic saga-writing, and its reception, one might do well to consider Panofsky's famous principle of disjunction.[18] Panofsky argued that the medieval mind perceived history in a way that is noticeably different from our own perception of it, that it was not detached from its representations — though I would argue that the difference is found more in the arena of intellectual scholarship than on the practical level of human societal memory and its functions. Similar to a number of theoretical approaches born in the 1960s, Panofsky argued that the recipient of artistic expression participated in judgments regarding truth and thus value, separate from any historical fact or lack thereof. These judgments were based as much, or more, upon the perceived relevance of the truth to the present. To grossly over-simplify the matter, what is perceived as true *is* true. Thus in such genres as epic, saga, and *chanson de geste*, history must be participatory in literature in order for the recipient to feel that it has value and relevance. Panofsky's idea of first-phase epic, a term he used to describe material similar to *Egil's Saga*, suggests that the veracity of past events, or people, is closely related to the ideas and perceptions of the time period producing the story. As Stephen Nichols elegantly points out,

[16] See Smyth, *Scandinavian York and Dublin*, 2.74–75.

[17] Byock, "Social Memory," p. 301.

[18] For a fuller understanding of the principle, see Panofsky, *Renaissance and Renascences*.

> First-phase epic thus stands in a highly ambiguous relationship to the past events it seeks to record. In one sense, the authority of the events derives from their status as accomplished fact, of their being true and irreversible. But in another sense the value of these past events — as the words of the mass or Panofsky's principle of disjunction showed — lay in their quality as immanence, as a real force in present existence. The language of this phase must reflect this complexity; of necessity, it exercises a dual function. While exalting the wonder and authority of the past, it must yet cast these events in accord with the perspective of the present and in a language calculated to seize the imagination of the audience.[19]

The saga-writer uses language in order to create a world that borrows as much authority from the past as possible, thereby augmenting the "truth" of his work with the power of history, while at the same time making it as real for the audience as he can, based upon their expectations, associations, and experiences. Thus in Icelandic saga we discover names of people, sequences of events, and even remarkably specific descriptions of locales and topography because these are the elements that result in instant participation and recognition among the saga audience. One need only read a handful of Icelandic sagas to realize that some of the most important features of the genre are long genealogical lists. *Egil's Saga* itself, for example, begins, "There was a man named Ulf, the son of Bjalfi and Hallbera, the daughter of Ulf the Fearless. She was the sister of Hallbjorn Half-troll from Hrafnista, the father of Ketil Haeng."[20] Of equal importance are place-names that are incredibly specific to events that occurred there — in *Hrafnkell's Saga* a man leaves behind a goat when he moves away from his farmstead, and a landslide kills that goat, giving the place the name *Geitdalr* [Goat-dale] from that time forth. Of no less significance are topographical features that create a rich setting and become palpable to readers — in *Njal's Saga* it is the presence of a river and a ford with a boulder in it that allows the drifting corpse of a man to become trapped there. Whether or not the saga-writers use these features because they are historically true, because they convey realism, or only because they further the exigencies of the story is difficult to answer in many cases. One might argue that such things are so insignificant to the fictional narrative that it is unlikely that they would be invented — who would think up such trivialities? — but conversely one might point out that such details are far too insignificant to have survived accurately throughout the centuries that separate the events described and the composition of the sagas.[21]

There are features of *Egil's Saga* that transcend the genre of Icelandic saga, however, and some of these features oblige investigation if we hope to establish a context for reading truth in *Egil's Saga* as it pertains to Brunanburh. In 1933 Hollander illuminated the many

[19] Nichols, "Spirit of Truth," p. 373. Nichols' article provides an in-depth consideration of Panofsky's principles and their application to medieval narratives.

[20] *Egil's Saga*, trans. Scudder, p. 8.

[21] It is worth noting that the inclusion of these at times seemingly "insignificant details" has been a feature of Icelandic prose, and arguably of northern story-telling, from its beginnings through the present. Many a "Swedish grandmother's" stories begin with a genealogy reminiscent of a phone book. One might also suggest that the precursor to the modern novel can best be found in Icelandic saga, where attention to detail, character psychology, and elements of realism mark pivotal features of the genre. The differences between a thirteenth-century Icelandic saga and a work of modern Icelandic prose — say for instance Nobel-prize-winning author Halldor Laxness's novel *Independent People* — are in large part simply due to temporal setting, not style. In fact, in the novel, which is a richly dense example of natural realism, Laxness deliberately draws many allusions to the saga tradition and makes clear the connections to the past that is deeply rooted in Icelandic social memory.

folk-tale features of the Vínheiðr episode, and others have followed suit, noting the persistent presence of pairings, the law of threes, sham armies, prolonged negotiations used as a stalling tactic, and the central role of a topography that allows for the exercising of certain military maneuvers and stratagems. Many of the characters in the battle occur in pairs, either in allegiance with or opposition to one another. Egil and Thorolf are brothers, as are Hring and Adils. The Northumbrian earls Godrek and Alfgar form yet another pairing. Geographically there is the river and the wood, the town to the north and its sister to the south. Each king forms his army into two battalions for the final battle. In opposition to one another we find the English and the Scots (Hiberno-Norse), Athelstan and Anlaf, Thorolf and Hring, Egil and Adils. The delaying ruse that the English propose — arguably at the suggestion of Egil and his brother — is countered by Adil's sneak attack from the forest that results in the death of Thorolf. And following the common folk-motif of the law of threes, there are three requests for peace negotiations and the result is three days of delay that essentially determines the outcome of the battle.

The folk-motif elements of the stratagem employed to allow Athelstan sufficient time to raise an army, all the while leading Anlaf to believe that the English force is greater than it is at the time, are worth particular attention here, as they are central to the Vínheiðr episode. Indeed, many of the details that are interwoven in this rather complex charade are precisely the points of evidence that scholars have used to argue both for and against the historicity of the account of the battle. As the saga presents it, the ruse involves two elements: one, convincing Anlaf that Athelstan is already on the field of battle with a considerable army, and two, assuring that he delays his assault for long enough that Athelstan can actually be there in force. Both of these devices are readily recognizable folk-tale motifs. According to Stith Thompson's *Motif-index*, folk-tale type K2368 deals with the device of deceiving an enemy into believing that a larger force is present, and type K548 addresses the ruse of making attackers believe a fortified place is defended by many when only a few are actually present.[22] Likewise, in Inger M. Boberg's *Motif-index of Early Icelandic Literature*, type K2369.7 governs shammed discussions of peace while getting reinforcements.[23] Neither of these ploys is at all uncommon in literature and date back well into ancient times; they even appear elsewhere within the specific context of the sagas. Hollander points out that in *Hervarar's Saga* the attacking Hun army is stalled through the use of prolonged negotiations and the "hazelling" of a battle-site, just as it is in *Egil's Saga*.[24] All of this certainly does not mean that these ruses are nothing more than recurring folk-motifs, as they are indeed effective strategies and have been employed successfully both in historical accounts as well as in literary works. However, when such recognizable literary patterns are apparent in a work, particularly in such number, a careful critic would be wise to take note and take such factors into consideration when seeking to gauge the historical reliability of such a source. At the same time, according to Panofsky's theories regarding first-phase epic, the authority of the past is irreversible and borrowing long-accepted, and successful strategies from history is clearly a means of emulating authority.

[22] Thompson, *Motif-index of Folk-literature*, 4.496, 313, cited by McDougall, "Discretion and Deceit."

[23] Boberg, *Motif-index of Early Icelandic Literature*, p. 187, cited by McDougall, "Discretion and Deceit."

[24] Hollander, "Battle of the Vin-heath," pp. 38–39. See also *Hervarar saga*, ed. Guðni Jónsson and Gabriel Turville-Petre, p. 63.

*Egil's Saga* is undeniably a well-crafted, detailed and compelling narrative. Such is the great achievement of the saga-writer, and the major source of the problem for scholars who attempt to rely on its account in pursuit of history. Numerous critics have observed the essential presence of objectivity and realism in Icelandic saga, and the fact that "even apparently inconsequential details in saga-narrative tend to reveal themselves ultimately as crucial story-elements."[25] The Vínheiðr episode in particular is rich with narrative detail as well as narrative action and, as Fjalldal points out quite accurately, it is of great importance to the saga as a whole, being the climax of the hero's life, the high point of his career as a leader and a warrior.[26] Because of this the scene is rightfully staged in descriptive language, with special attention paid to the details of the topography, the movements of the troops, and the cleverness of their leaders. *Egil's Saga* is not the story of Brunanburh, nor of Athelstan or the English; it is the tale of Egil. It is Egil and his brother Thorolf who thwart the night attack made by Hring and Adils; Egil and Thorolf who take primary command of Athelstan's forces, even though they are but late come into his service and are Northmen more like those against whom they are fighting than the Saxon English; it is Egil who achieves ultimate victory for Athelstan, and is richly rewarded for it. In fact, the saga-writer is careful to keep the English king well in the background, taking little role in the battle himself. So the presence of ruses, strategies, bold attacks, ambushes from the forest, vengeance and victory are not necessarily there as common romantic motifs plucked from a cauldron of folklore, as Hollander implies.[27] They are in fact integral to the creation of the battle episode, to make it believable and real to the reader or listener who seeks, as Panofsky suggests, to participate in the truth of the event. The saga-writer succeeds in transporting his audience into the episode through the use of these details, and each of them would very well strike the audience as authentic for the very reason that they are a part of social memory, be that memory a product of literary motifs or history. It is "true" that a successful Viking leader employs ruses to get the better of his enemies, that he strategically uses the land to his advantage in a battle, that like Thorolf he can only be defeated when out-maneuvered in his own game — bested by a more clever strategy. The details provided in the Vínheiðr episode allow the saga-writer to craft a very real battle according to the expectations and desires, even the collected social memory, of his audience. Or, perhaps, those details seem so very real because they are in fact historically accurate; they make sense because they are probable; they are remembered even in their precision because they are the most important components around which the episode unfolded. Like Caldbec Hill at Hastings, or Little Round Top and Pickett's charge at Gettysburg, these details are essential; without Vínheiðr and Vínuskógr, without the towns to the north and the south, there would have been no battle, at least not as it plays out in the saga. One could say that the best fiction mirrors truth, making it seem real; one might also assert that perhaps truth sometimes emulates fiction.

If we return now to the original issue and the question of how *Egil's Saga* can or ought to be used in an attempt to better understand the Battle of Brunanburh, it is admittedly certain that we have not really arrived at an answer at all. It is clear that the saga is not to be taken as an authentic record of history; there are simply too many red flags in the way to do that. Conversely, it is certainly more than simply a creative invention full of nothing more than fictions woven together for the purpose of telling a good story. Byock puts it

[25] McDougall, "Discretion and Deceit," p. 13.

[26] Fjalldal, "Farmer in the Court of Athelstan," p. 30.

[27] Hollander, "Battle of the Vin-heath," p. 38.

quite elegantly and succinctly when he states that "Icelandic prose story telling was a form of ethnographic expression that allowed authorial creativity while retaining its roots in historic tradition. . . . Like many sagas, [*Egil's Saga*] is a well-developed animation of the past, relying on a good deal of social memory."[28] So what do we do with the material then? We can accept that the fact and fiction are inextricably woven together and do nothing, or we can attempt to unravel the individual threads of truth from the skein of fiction. The first option leaves us with a vacuum, and of course those are abhorred, but the latter demands that certain judgments be made and theories proposed, theories that will instantly be subjected to criticism. A work like the present volume, one would hope, will allow scholars to make more informed decisions on the matter, and to derive even more enjoyment from the detective work of wrestling truth out of the past. Regardless of the outcome, the search itself will make for a good story.

[28] Byock, "Social Memory," pp. 303, 314.

ROBERT ROUSE

# ROMANCING THE PAST: THE MIDDLE ENGLISH TRADITION

For a post-conquest Latin historiographer such as William of Malmesbury, the Battle of Brunanburh occupied an important place in the received history of England, and was therefore recorded and embellished as a significant episode in his narrative of England's formation as a discrete kingdom. Given this initial importance of Brunanburh in post-conquest historiography, it is curious that accounts of the battle play no lasting role in the vernacular narratives of England's past that begin to appear during the fourteenth century. Patrizia Lendinara goes as far as commenting that:

> The battle of Brunanburh did not feature either in the Middle English romances of the so-called Matter of England or the French chronicles, which do not mention the battle but, in their account of the reign of Athelstan, dwell on more personal and courtly details.[1]

While Lendinara perhaps goes too far in such an assessment,[2] the accounts of England's past that appear in Middle English romance and chronicle during the fourteenth century point towards the disappearance of the Battle of Brunanburh from the stage of celebrated national history, presenting a fascinating study in the processes of the transformation of cultural memory and history. This chapter will examine the rise of a competing romance narrative tradition to Brunanburh that — for some few hundred years — elides the battle from popular accounts of Athelstan's reign, and establishes an alternative account of the Anglo-Saxon past within English history: the romance legend of Guy of Warwick and his defeat of the Danes at the behest of Athelstan.

*The Chronicle of Robert of Gloucester (ca. 1320)*

However, before we examine the disappearance of Brunanburh from the national consciousness, we need to acknowledge that this was not an uncontested process. For the early-fourteenth-century chronicler Robert of Gloucester, whose *Chronicle* presented a history of England from its legendary founding by Brut, great-grandson of Aeneas, through to the year 1270, Brunanburh remained an important episode. Drawing primarily upon William of Malmesbury, Robert's version of the battle (Item 32 in this volume), located in *Brymesbury* (line 5550),[3] includes those interpolations introduced by William such as the tale of Anlaf sneaking into Athelstan's camp disguised as a harper, the ironic punishment of the tardy bishop, and the miraculous appearance of Athelstan's sword.

---

[1] Lendinara, "Battle of Brunanburh," p. 201.

[2] Peter of Langtoft's insular Anglo-Norman chronicle, for example, does provide an account of the battle "A Bruneburge sur Humbre." See Item 36 in this volume.

[3] On *Brymesbury*, see Cavill's essay in this volume, p. 332.

*The Chronicle of Robert Mannyng of Brunne (ca. 1338)*

While Robert of Gloucester broadly follows the course of history charted by William of Malmesbury, there was, at the same time as he was writing, the competing romance narrative of Guy of Warwick and his defeat of the Danes[4] during Athelstan's reign was steadily growing in popularity. In the *Chronicle* of Robert Mannyng of Brunne, a translation and enlargement of first Wace's *Brut* and then Pierre de Langtoft's insular Anglo-French chronicle, we find an early example of the integration of this episode into Middle English popular history (see Item 40 in this volume). The second portion of Mannyng's *Chronicle*, which covers insular history from the death of Cadwaladr to the end of Edward III's reign, is drawn from Pierre de Langtoft, and it is in this section of the text that we find the account of Athelstan's conflict with Anlaf that incorporates the romance narrative of Guy into chronicle history.

The process by which Guy enters chronicle history is a curious one, and begins not as one of replacement, but of accretion. Mannyng, following Langtoft, and well aware of the conventional medieval accounts of Athelstan's reign that placed the decisive battle with Anlaf at Brunanburh, relates:

> In the yere after that Ilde wedded was,
> Constantyn of Scotlond did yit more trispas.
> He brought the Kyng Anlaf, aryved up in Humbere,
> seven hundreth schippes ond fiftene, so fele were the numbere.
> Athelstan herd say of ther mykelle oste;
> he ond Edmunde, his brother, dight tham to that coste.
> At Brunesburgh on Humber thei gan tham assaile;
> fro morn unto even lasted that bataile.
> At the last, to ther schippes the kyng gan tham chace,
> alle away thei fled, that was of Godes grace,
> bot the most partie algate was slayn;
> that with the life fled, I trowe thei were fulle fayn.
> Whan the Kyng Anlaf sauh his folk lorn,
> he fled unto Danmark ther there he was born. (Item 40.663–76)

However, this account of Athelstan's defeat of Anlaf's invading army was not the only one that was available to Mannyng's source. In the Guy narrative, Guy saves England from Anlaf's invading Danish army by defeating the giant Colbrond in single combat at Winchester. In the light of this popular competing historical narrative, Langtoft was faced with the decision of which account to believe. Langtoft, in an apparent attempt to integrate these two competing accounts into his chronicle, seems to have solved this problem by simply adding a second invasion. Mannyng's version describes the additional episode thus:

> At the Pask after, he ryved in the south
> at a haven of Sandwich in the portis mouth.
> Whan he was aryved, the folk was affray
> ond com unto Wynchestre ther the kyng lay.
> He brouht with him a develle, a hogge geant;
> wele haf ye herd telle, he hight Colibrant.

---

[4] The Danes here act as an externalising simplification of Anlaf's multi-ethnic force.

Anlaf sent messengers unto Athelstan
ond bad him yeld the lond or fynd another man
to fight with Colibrant that was his champion.
Who felle to haf the lond, on tham it suld be done.
Athelstan tok a day, a parlement did make,
if any ageyn Colibrant the bataile durst take.
He fond no man that durst, for non had myght
with Colibrant alone in bataile to fight.
Than praied Athelstan to Criste ond sore wepe,
ond God sent him tokenyng on nyght as he slepe
that he suld fynd a palmere orly at morn
at the south gate, alone as he was born,
ond if he wild praie him for Jhesu Cristes love,
he wild do the bataile ond thei suld be above.
That was Guy of Werwik as the boke sais;
ther he slouh Colibrant with hache Daneis.
Anlaf turned agayn (I trowe him was wo),
he ond alle his to schippe gan thei go. (Item 40.677–700)

A second invasion led by Anlaf has no known precedent in either the chronicle or romance traditions, and it seems that Langtoft invented it in order to incorporate what he viewed as two equally valid historical narratives. However, despite Mannyng's use of Langtoft's invented second invasion, the dual-invasion narrative does not seem to have found wide favor. Later chroniclers either use the Brunanburh tradition or the Guy narrative, but rarely both.

*The Stanzaic Guy of Warwick (ca. 1300)*

So where does this second narrative come from, and why does it come to replace Brunanburh in popular English history and romance from the fourteenth century? Guy of Warwick is a figure who in many ways transcends his own genre, moving from romance to hagiography, wisdom literature to chronicle.[5] First appearing in the early thirteenth-century Anglo-Norman romance *Gui de Warewic* (ca. 1200–1220),[6] the romance of Guy was translated into Middle English in both couplet and stanzaic forms by the beginning of the fourteenth century. The couplet romance relates Guy's early life, his pursuit of chivalric glory, his wooing of his paramour Felice, and his defense of Constantinople from the invading Saracens. The *Stanzaic Guy of Warwick* (Item 37 in this volume) continues Guy's narrative, covering his disavowal of the secular life and his wandering as a pilgrim in the lands of the East. Nearing the end of the romance, and of his life, Guy returns home to find Athelstan's England in a perilous state. Enquiring as to where Athestan is, he is informed that the king has retreated in disarray to Winchester:

For Sir Anlaf the king of Danmark
with a nost store and stark
into Inglond is come

[5] The many and varied faces of Guy of Warwick are surveyed in Wiggins and Field, eds., *Guy of Warwick*.

[6] The standard edition is *Gui de Warewic*, ed. Ewert. On the continued use of the Guy narrative in histories see Cooper, "Romance after 1400," pp. 704–05.

with fiften thousend knightes of pris,
alle this lond thai stroyen, ywis,
and mani a toun han nome.
A geaunt he hath brought with him
out of Aufrike stout and grim,
Colbrond hat that gome.
For him is al Inglond forlore
bot Godes help be bifore
that socour sende hem some.

To the king he hath sent his sond
forto yeld him al Inglond
and gif him trowage outright
yif he no wil nought finde a baroun,
a geaunt other a champioun,
ogain Colbrond to fight,
and therof thai han taken a day.
Ac our king non finde may
erl, baroun, no knight,
no squier, no serjaunt non
ogain the geaunt dar gon
so grim he is of sight. (Item 37.2809–32)

Anlaf's invasion is here orientalized in typical fourteenth-century fashion. The invading Danish *other* is constructed in terms more suited to the Saracen enemies that Guy has battled for the majority of his romance. Colbrond, a "geaunt . . . out of Aufrike" (lines 2815–16), embodies this national threat in terms appreciable to an audience familiar with the perfidious Saracen monsters of crusade romance. Furthermore, we find the conflict with the now-Saracen Danes transformed into a romance single-combat, a national *judicium Dei* through which the right to rule England will be established.

Fortunately for Athelstan and England, Guy's return from his extended pilgrimage comes at an opportune time, as he has not been able to find a willing champion to face Colbrond. Unaware of Guy's return, the king laments the lack of English knights prepared to face the giant:

"Allas," seyd the king, "that Y was born.
Al mi joie it is forlorn,
wel wo is me olive.
Now in al mi lond nis no knight
ogains a geant to hold fight
mine hert wil breken on five.
Allas of Warwike Sir Gii
Y no hadde geven thee half mi lond frely
to hold withouten strive;
wele were me than bifalle.
Ac certes now the Danis men alle
to sorwe thai schul me drive." (Item 37.2881–92)

That night, Athelstan is visited by an angel, who reveals that a champion will be found the next day, if the king seeks him at the south gate to the city. Following this heavenly advice,

Athelstan goes to the gate the next day and encounters Guy, who is disguised as an anonymous pilgrim, and beseeches him to aid the national cause:

> "Pilgrim," quath the king, "par charité,
> yif it be thi wil understond to me,
> Y schal schewe thee al our nede:
> the king of Danmark with gret wrong
> thurth a geaunt that is so strong
> wil strou al our thede." (Item 37.2935–40)

Guy, initially unwilling to take up arms once more, is eventually convinced by Athelstan's pleas, and — in a striking moment of synthesis of national and religious devotion — agrees:

> Sir Gii tok up the king anon
> and bad the lordinges everichon
> thai schuld up stond,
> and seyd, "For God in Trinité
> and forto make Inglond fre
> the batayle Y nim on hond." (Item 37.2965–70)

The single combat that follows sees Guy, in typical romance come-back fashion, defeat the monstrous Colbrond, striking off the giant's head with his own Danish axe:

> and Guy gave him a blow to the neck
> as he bent down for the blade
> that his head from the body he smote
> and into the earth half a foot
> thurth grace of Godes sond.
> Ded he feld the glotoun thare.
> The Denis with sorwe and care
> thai dight hem out of lond. (Item 37.3221–28)

In the construction of English history represented in the Guy of Warwick tradition, Guy's fight replaces Athelstan's historical victory over Anlaf and the Scottish King Constantine at Brunanburh in 937. In a manner perhaps analogous to the translation of a saint's relics, the fight is re-situated from the north of England to Winchester, thereby appropriating for Winchester what was one of England's most treasured national triumphs.[7] The romance of *Guy of Warwick* established an alternative historical tradition to the Battle of Brunanburh, and — for a number of centuries — displaced it within the popular English historical imagination.

## THE POPULARITY OF THE GUY AND COLBROND NARRATIVE

The lasting impact of the Guy and Colbrond legend can be seen in the account of Winchester found in the *Itinerary* of John Leland, the early sixteenth-century antiquarian and scholar. During the period from 1539 to 1545 Leland undertook a grand tour of England

---

[7] For a full analysis of the importance of the *Guy of Warwick* narrative to the urban identity of late-medieval Winchester, see Rouse, *Idea of Anglo-Saxon England*, ch. 6.

at the behest of Henry VIII. Leland was under instructions to visit the libraries of the newly dissolved monasteries, and to judge what should be saved.[8] Leland's record of his journey was later published in his *Itinerary*. Written around 1544, this account provides us with what is arguably the last medieval description of much of England. Leland was of course undertaking a survey of England as part of that great act of cultural vandalism, the Dissolution of the Monasteries, and his description, as David Lawton has noted, constructs the "medieval" while at the same time participating in its destruction. Leland's account, standing as it does at the end of the medieval period, while acting as an agent of its end, represents a crystallized late-medieval image of England. As part of Leland's visit Winchester, he describes Hyde Abbey:[9]

> On the south side of Hyde Abbay betwixt it and the waulle is a medow caullid Denmark, wher the fame is that Guido Erle of Warwik killid great Colebrande the Dane *singulari certamine*.[10]

It is clear that by the time of Leland's visit, the Guy and Colbrond episode operated as an established and influential signifier of Winchester's past. An important element of Winchester's urban geography, the meadow of *Denmark* (or *Denemarche*) functions as a tangible memorial to this most famous of Guy's exploits.

The meadow of Denemarche was not, however, the only urban signifier of Winchester's role in the Guy narrative. Walking through Winchester, Leland would have had encountered a variety of spatial markers signifying the legend. In the accounts of the Winchester City Chamberlains we find a record from 1455/56 naming part of the city wall as *Colebrondis Hede*.[11] This section of the wall seems likely to have been that part of the North wall that overlooked Denemarche. The anonymous *History and Antiquities of Winchester* records that even in 1773 there was still visible a representation of the combat carved on a stone in the city wall known as "Colbrond's Chair."[12] The memorial upon the wall above the field functions as both a site of urban memory and as place from which to view the memorialized site itself. Also preserved within Winchester were physical mementos of the combat. One such, the "Danish" axe with which Guy decapitated Colbrond, was preserved within the treasury of St. Swithun's priory until the Dissolution.[13] Celebrated as a relic by St. Swithun's, this artefact would have been available for the urban wayfarer to see, and further attests to the importance of the narrative to both the Priory and to Winchester as whole. Like most relics, the authenticity and location of Guy's weapons and armor were contested, with the debate

---

[8] And by extension, as Lawton observes, Leland judges what should be condemned to destruction ("Surveying Subject," p. 33). Simpson offers a fine discussion of Leland's role in construction of the Middle Ages in his "Ageism."

[9] Hyde Abbey was a prime target of Henry VIII's acquisitions program.

[10] *Itinerary*, ed. Smith, p. 272.

[11] Winchester City Archives, 38/BX/CR 1–6, s.a. 1455–6, cited in Keene, *Survey of Medieval Winchester*, p. 947.

[12] *History and Antiquities of Winchester*, 2.15–20. See also Milner, *History Civil and Ecclesiastical*, 1.144–48 and 2.210 (2.221 in second ed.), cited in Keene, *Survey of Medieval Winchester*, p. 947.

[13] In like manner to Arthur's transformation of the Green Knight's axe into a memorial in *Sir Gawain and the Green Knight*, the monks of St. Swithun's preserved Colbrond's axe "to telle þe wonder" of Sir Guy's victory (*Sir Gawain and the Green Knight*, ed. Tolkien and Gordon, p. 10, lines 477–80).

regarding the location of Guy's armor and sword becoming a particular concern of some later Guy narratives, an issue to which I shall return later in the chapter.

In addition to the site and armaments of the battle, Winchester's "densely marked" urban terrain also contained secondary signifiers, created by the community to display the importance of the Guy legend to the institutional and civic pride of the city. One such secondary signifier was a wall painting depicting the battle that once graced the inner wall of Winchester Cathedral. Thomas Warton observed in the eighteenth century that the battle was depicted in a "rude painting against the walls of the northern transept of the cathedral," although he did not estimate its age.[14] The presence of a visual memorial to the battle within the Cathedral itself constructs an important and influential urban sign, which, if it existed in the sixteenth century, would no doubt have been witnessed by Leland.

As well as by place-names, memorials, relics, and paintings, the episode was also remembered through performance of the narrative itself. Nancy Bradbury provides an account of a performance of a version of the Guy and Colbrond episode in the introduction to her valuable study *Writing Aloud*: "From a rare record of a storytelling performance in fourteenth-century England, we learn that one Herbert, called a *joculator*, performed in 1338 two narrative entertainments in the hall of the Winchester Cathedral priory, St. Swithun. The occasion was a visit of the bishop, Adam de Orleton, to his prior, Alexander de Herriard, and the entertainments specified were a song (*canticum*) of Colbrond and a tale (*gestum*) of Queen Emma vindicated by ordeal of fire."[15] That this part of the Guy narrative was considered to be suitable entertainment for the visit of a bishop is high praise indeed, and suggests that the process of memorializing the battle was one that was held in high regard by the monks of St. Swithun's.

*The Anonymous Short English Metrical Chronicle (Auchinleck manuscript version)*

That the Guy and Colbrond episode was influential beyond Winchester is evident from Langtoft's and Mannyng's use of the narrative, and other chronicles followed suit in preferring the romance version of history. The *Anonymous Short English Metrical Chronicle*, found following the Guy romances in the Auchinleck manuscript (Item 38 in this volume), is one such chronicle that entirely elides Brunanburh in favor of the romance narrative. While much of the *Anonymous Short English Metrical Chronicle*'s account of Athelstan's reign concerns his wealth and control over England and the surrounding territories, the narrative ends with the Guy and Colbrond battle. Thorlac Turville-Petre describes this account of English history as a text in which "romance-fiction and historical fact are inextricably intertwined."[16] His suggestion that this text acts as both a structural and thematic backbone through which the romances of the Auchinleck manuscript can be understood seems compelling.[17] Reading the Auchinleck "historical" romances within the context of the *Anonymous Short English Metrical Chronicle* and of the manuscript as a whole, the romances can be seen

---

[14] Warton, *History of English Poetry*, ed. Hazlitt, 2.97n1, cited in Bradbury, *Writing Aloud*, p. 2.

[15] Bradbury, *Writing Aloud*, pp. 1–2.

[16] Turville-Petre, *England the Nation*, p. 111.

[17] Turville-Petre, *England the Nation*, p. 112. A parallel case of the use of a chronicle text to coordinate the historicizing of a number of romances within a manuscript can be seen in the example of MS Bibliothèque Nationale fonds français 1450, which interpolates Chrétien de Troyes' five Arthurian romances into Wace's *Brut* (Gaunt, "Romance and Other Genres," p. 50).

as episodes within an extensive and unified retelling of the whole of English history. As part of its summation of English history, the *Anonymous Short English Metrical Chronicle* makes use of Guy's fight with Colbrond in its rapid abridgment of the Anglo-Saxon period. Again placing the combat in Athelstan's reign, the chronicle provides the bare bones of what was evidently a well-known "historical" event:

> In Athelstonis time, ich understond,
> was Gii of Warwike in Inglond
> ond for Athelston he dede a bateyle
> with a geaunt gret, saunfaile.
> The geaunt hiht Colbrond,
> Gii him slouh with his hond.
> At Winchester the bataile was don. (Item 38.1663–69)

There is nothing too surprising here — a chronicle making use of the narrative authorised by Mannyng's *Chronicle*. It is not so much the text, but rather its manuscript context, that is of interest. Turville-Petre argues that the Guy and Colbrond interpolation in the Auchinleck manuscript version of the *Anonymous Short English Metrical Chronicle*, which differs from other versions of the *Short Metrical Chronicle*, is an indication of the historical importance placed upon Guy within the manuscript as a whole.[18] Guy's centrality to the Auchinleck manuscript — the "handbook of the nation" — is made clear by the presence of his eponymous romance, the romance of his son Reinbroun, and the curious *Speculum de Guy of Warwicke*.[19] This last text, a piece of doctrinal instruction delivered to Guy by his spiritual advisor Alcuin, seems to spring from an episode in the romance when Guy seeks out the holy man for advice on how best to live his life. This short passage in the romance is expanded in this text into a treatise on how to live the life of a good Christian in the world. The Auchinleck manuscript brings together historical, romance, and personal salvation narratives in the person of Guy. Considered as a whole, the manuscript stands as an example of the textual and intellectual co-positioning of history and romance.

In the prominence that the Auchinleck manuscript gives to Guy of Warwick, it seems that it is not just interested in replacing Brunanburh with the Colbrond fight, but also in replacing Athelstan with Guy himself. The Athelstan of the Guy romances, far from being the celebrated warrior-king of *The Battle of Brunanburh* (Item 4 in this volume), is presented as an impotent monarch reliant upon God and Guy for the salvation of his kingdom. While much of this can, one suggests, be put down to the generic demands of romance, in which the narrative is more concerned with the reputation of the protagonist than of his king, one can perhaps also read in the competition between the Brunanburh and Colbrond versions of history a changing sense of the value of the Anglo-Saxon past in post-conquest England. For twelfth-century chroniclers such as William of Malmesbury, recounting the Anglo-Saxon past was of great importance in establishing links between the new French-speaking aristocracy and the land which they had conquered. By the fourteenth century, it seems, such concerns were less pressing, and other — more fanciful — versions of the past could be told.

[18] Turville-Petre, *England the Nation*, p. 116.

[19] Turville-Petre, *England the Nation*, pp. 112 and 116.

*The Popular Romance Athelston (ca. 1400?)*

The lack of interest in the historical reign of Athelstan and in the Battle of Brunanburh perhaps reaches its apogee in the late fourteenth-century romance *Athelston*. Although we might expect — from its title — that the romance might engage with the historical Athelstan, instead we find yet another elision of his historical legacy. In this romance the eponymous king is transformed into a tyrant figure through the treacherous advice of Wymound, the earl of Dover. On Wymound's counsel, he imprisons Egeland, the earl of Stane, his pregnant wife Edith, and their two sons, and declares that they will be executed for their treason. Athelston is then subjected to advice regarding the limits of royal justice, first from the queen and then from the archbishop, who both assert the prisoners' right to trial by their peers. The king violently objects to these entreaties, first with mortal consequences for his own unborn heir, whom he kills when he kicks his wife while in a rage, and secondly for the country, which the archbishop places under interdict. The archbishop's interdict finally brings Athelston to his senses, and transforms him from tyrant to good king as he falls in line with the demands of both the Church and the Baronage. The implementation of justice is then transferred to the Church, and Egeland and his family are exculpated by undergoing a *judicium Dei* in the form of an ordeal by fire. The treacherous Wymound is discovered and punished through the same ordeal and the narrative concludes with the naming of Egeland's newly born son St. Edmound as Athelston's heir.

Resonant with parallels to such historical conflicts between kings and the Church as the Henry II and Thomas Becket affair, the construction within *Athelston* of tyrannical kingship has attracted much critical attention.[20] Elizabeth Ashman Rowe has argued that *Athelston* represents a significant shift in the depiction of kingship in the romances: "The confidence in human institutions of justice demonstrated in earlier English romances (e.g., *Havelok the Dane*, *Bevis of Hamtoun*, *Guy of Warwick*, and *Fulk Fitz Warin*) had evidently broken down by the second half of the fourteenth century, for the figure of the king, once depicted as true to his coronation oath to uphold the law, has now become a tyrant who both swallows and speaks lies with equal ease."[21]

In *Athelston* we find the culmination of the elision of Brunanburh from the popular historical record. A romance that has at its heart a late-medieval concern with the limitations of royal power has no place for a victorious nation-building warrior-king, and the name Athelstan becomes merely a historical marker of a past time. Through the historical romances of the fourteenth century, Brunanburh is replaced by competing narrative traditions, and it is left for the historians of later centuries to rediscover the importance of Athelstan's glorious victory of 937 CE.

[20] Another relevant dispute was that which occurred between King John and Pope Innocent III, resulting in a papal interdict on England and the excommunication of the monarch (Cheney, "King John and the Papal Interdict").

[21] Rowe, "Female Body Politic," p. 79.

# Essays on the Battle

PAUL CAVILL

# THE PLACE-NAME DEBATE

The location of the Battle of Brunanburh is a problem that has fascinated historians, literary scholars and toponymists alike, many of whom have expressed strong views on the subject. These views tend to divide between those who think that the location cannot be identified and that the attempt should probably not be made, and those who see this lack of certainty as an opportunity to explore possible sites selected on the basis of a wide variety of criteria. Among the former, significant voices are those of Alistair Campbell and Dorothy Whitelock; among the latter are the voices of Alfred P. Smyth, Michael Wood, and Cyril Hart (all of these discussed below), but many earlier and later voices could be added on both sides.

The evidence relating to the question of the battle's location is extraordinarily diverse. Some assessment has to be made of this diverse range: the relative reliability of the source texts; the spellings and variants and meanings of the elements and names in the sources; other indications of location given in the sources; the validity of scholarly assumptions about, and accounts of, the place and the battle.

This volume presents as fully as possible the range of evidence relating to the battle, bringing the latest scholarship to bear. What this essay aims to add is a perspective using, in addition to paleographical and textual evidence, recent developments in toponymical research. One of the controlling factors in discussing the location of the battle must be the fact that the place-names in the sources refer to places; that the kind of terms used define, often very precisely, the topographical and other features of the place; and the corollary is that names of places tell us something significant about the places themselves.

In this essay, therefore, I will begin by discussing the sources briefly (section 1; see earlier essays for more detail), setting out as objectively as possible the evidence relating to the names given for the site of the battle (section 2). This involves linguistic and, where relevant, topographical analysis of the elements (section 3). As the essay progresses, I will discuss the various locational interpretations of ancient (section 4) and modern scholars (section 5), and it will become clear that I think the evidence points in a particular direction for the site. I will ultimately propose that, while an element of doubt remains, the site of Brunanburh can with reasonable confidence be located in the light of all the evidence available (section 6).

## 1. THE SOURCES

The original source of many of the traditions can be traced. The *Anglo-Saxon Chronicle* versions supply the earliest accounts of the battle, and clearly the Old English poem extant in four copies derives ultimately from a single original. Some of the texts depend on sources not extant but of a type that can be identified: Henry of Huntingdon used a version of the *ASC* related to version E, but also other versions, which show closer correspondence with version C.[1] Later accounts show writers like Bartholomew of Cotton and John of Oxnead copying their information from Henry of Huntingdon, and Symeon of Durham (directly) and, for example, Richard of Cirencester (indirectly) copying some of theirs from John of Worcester.[2]

The ultimate source of some of the variant traditions is uncertain: for example, Æthelweard reports the battle as taking place "in loco Brunandune," and it is impossible to say whether that represents a genuine tradition or whether he garbled the name or made it up: that Symeon of Durham has an apparently independent tradition which includes a name with *-dun*, "We(o)ndun," may be thought to reinforce the credibility of Æthelweard's report.

Some extant texts may have used sources now lost. As the evidence now stands, the source of the tradition that the invading forces came into the Humber is John of Worcester: the passage in Symeon of Durham's *Historia regum* copies directly from John (this strand of tradition is labeled *c* below). But Symeon has his own independent traditions: the *Historia regum*, in a passage separate from that borrowed from John, reports that the battle took place at "Wendun" and that the invaders had 615 ships (this is labeled *a* below); those same traditions are found in Symeon's *Libellus de exordio*, but there the variant names "Et Brunnanwerc uel Brunnanbyrig" are also given (this particular tradition is labeled *b* below). We cannot be sure whether John or Symeon made up the details that are peculiar to their works or knew traditions, oral or written, that recorded them, though further analysis may make some conclusions possible here. It may be, for example, that Geoffrey Gaimar knew his near-contemporary Symeon's *Libellus de exordio* since he gives a name for the battle that apparently represents "Brunanwerc" (see further the discussion in section 3.5 below);[3] but since all the manuscripts of Gaimar spell the name, however garbled, with a single *-n-*, it is possible that Gaimar knew the source used by Symeon for this particular detail and the *-nn-* forms are Symeon's variant spellings.

There is no very strong reason to believe that these particular details were available in, and used from, other sources than Symeon and John in the later tradition. For example, Pierre de Langtoft writes of 715 (sic) ships at "Bruneburge sur Humbre," thus apparently conflating and garbling material borrowed from Symeon, and by Symeon from John.[4] It would certainly be unwise to claim that Langtoft had any other immediate source for his information at this point than Symeon. Langtoft or an intermediate source added an extra *C* to the "DC et XV" ships of Symeon, just as William of Malmesbury or an intermediate source read the number of dead *comites* as XII instead of the VII *eorlas* of the vernacular tradition. Interestingly both of these errors indicate that the tradition here is most likely being passed on by document, not by word of mouth, since the numbers indicate graphical confusion.

The Irish, Welsh, and Norse sources appear to be independent of the English, Anglo-Norman, and Anglo-Latin sources; and in turn, the Irish, Welsh, and Norse sources appear to be independent of each other. These sources provide the tersest notice of the battle in the *Annales Cambriae*, and one of the most extensive and imaginative accounts of it in *Egil's Saga*. Though it is difficult to be sure, the medieval Welsh sources seem to recognize an English place or person, *Brun(e)*, which gives no difficulties of interpretation in the spread

---

[1] Henry, Archdeacon of Huntingdon, *Historia Anglorum*, ed. and trans. Greenway, p. xci.

[2] For the texts mentioned in this essay, see the collected accounts in this volume.

[3] See Gaimar, *Estoire*, ed. Bell, p. lii, where the date of composition is given as 1135–40, and Symeon, *Libellus de exordio*, ed. and trans. Rollason, p. xlii, where it is shown that it was written by 1115.

[4] *Chronicle*, ed. Wright, 1.330.

of name-spellings.[5] The *Scottish Chronicle*'s *Duinbrunde* appears also to make independent reference to an unproblematical *-brun-* name. On the other hand, *Egil's Saga* gives a welter of topographical information about the site of the battle, and references to woods, hills, and streams abound. Scholars have made much of this, but it is unlikely to be more than imaginative reconstruction. However, the place-names *Vínheiðr* and *Vínuskógi*, because they are more likely to be preserved in tradition (and thus possibly become the basis of imaginative reconstruction), merit detailed treatment (see 3.9, below). The same applies to the name *Othlyn*(*n*) found in the *Annals of Clonmacnoise*.

Thus, while the relationships between texts can be complex, there are some clear lines of descent and some clear indications of independence. In discussing the sources it will be a useful shorthand to refer by way of (for example) "John of Worcester" to "the tradition found first extant in John of Worcester, and for which no other source is known or can plausibly be reconstructed."

## 2. EARLY SPELLINGS OF THE NAME *BRUNANBURH* AND ALTERNATIVE NAMES FOR THE SITE

| | |
|---|---|
| *Anglo-Saxon Chronicle*, MS A | *Bru*$^{n}$*nanburh* |
| *Anglo-Saxon Chronicle*, MS B | *Brunanburh* |
| *Anglo-Saxon Chronicle*, MS C | *Brunnanburh* |
| *Anglo-Saxon Chronicle*, MS D | *Brunanburh* |
| *Anglo-Saxon Chronicle*, MS E | *Brunanbyrig* |
| *Anglo-Saxon Chronicle*, MS F | *Brunanbyri* |
| *Anglo-Saxon Chronicle*, MS O[3] | *Brunanburh* |
| Æthelweard | *Brunandune* |
| Symeon of Durham (*a*), *Libellus de exordio* and *Historia regum* | *Weondune*, *Wendune* |
| Symeon of Durham (*b*), *Libellus de exordio* | *Et Brunnanwerc uel Brunnanbyrig* |
| William of Malmesbury | *Brunefeld*, *Bruneford* |
| John of Worcester | *Brunanburh* |
| Henry of Huntingdon | *Brunebirih* |
| Geoffrey Gaimar | *Bruneswerce*, *Brunewerche*, *Burneweste* (x2) |
| Twelfth-century charters | *Bruningafeld* |
| Scottish traditions | *Bruningafeld*, *Brouningfeld* |

[5] See further the essay by Bollard and Haycock in this volume, and Items 5.28, 23.60, and notes.

| | |
|---|---|
| *Scottish Chronicle* | *Duinbrunde* |
| Welsh chronicles and traditions | *Brun(e), Cad Tybrunawc [?]* |
| *Annales Cambriae* | *Brune* |
| *Annals of Clonmacnoise* | *Plaines of othlynn, othlyn* |
| *Egil's Saga* | *Vínheiðr* |

Derivative accounts

(1) from John of Worcester

| | |
|---|---|
| Symeon of Durham (*c*), *Historia regum* | *Brunanburh* |
| Richard of Cirencester | *Brunkerih* |
| *Eulogium historiarum* | *Brunanburge* |

(2) from Henry of Huntingdon

| | |
|---|---|
| Bartholomew of Cotton | *Brunesberich* |
| John of Oxnead | *Brunesberich* |
| *Annals of Waverley* | *Bruneberi* |

(3) from William of Malmesbury

| | |
|---|---|
| Ranulf Higden | *Brumford, Brunfort* |
| *Book of Hyde* | *Brunfort* |

(4) from Symeon of Durham

| | |
|---|---|
| *Chronicle of Melrose* | *Brunanburch* |
| Pierre de Langtoft | *Bruneburge, Brunesburgh, Bronneburgh* |

This list (see above for the sources and manuscripts) differs in several respects from that given by Campbell: it is fuller, and the manuscript spellings have been more widely collected.[6] An account needs to be given of the various elements in these different place-name forms: the most common first element, *bruna* or *brune*; the most common second element *burh*; *dun*; the first element in *we(o)-*; *weorc*; *feld* and *ford*; *-inga-*. Other names relating to the location of the battle include *Othlynn* and *Vínheiðr*, recorded respectively in the *Annals of Clonmacnoise* and

[6] *Battle of Brunanburh*, p. 60. The main differences are: *ASC*, MS B, where Campbell reads *Brunnanburh* (but see note to Item 4.5 in this volume); Henry of Huntingdon, where Campbell has *Bruneburh*, *Brunesburh* (see further Appendix, below); and Campbell's "Pictish Chronicle" (following Skene) is now called *Scottish Chronicle* (see Smith's essay in this volume, p. 280n68).

*Egil's Saga*. And two further place-names are mentioned in the Old English poem not as the site of the battle but as the departure point and destination of some of the defeated Norsemen: *Dingesmere* and variants (line 54), and *Difelin* and variants (line 55). While the name *Difelin* [Dublin] is uncontroversial, some discussion of the others is needed. But first, it may be suggested that while there is a variety in the name-forms and elements, there is sufficient consistency, not solely related to borrowing, for the accounts to be plausibly conceived of as referring to the same place and its general area.

## 3. DISCUSSION OF THE ELEMENTS

### *3.1 Bruna* or *brune*

Some recognizable form of this element appears in all the names except Symeon's *We(o)ndune*, *Othlynn* in the Clonmacnoise *Annals*, and *Vínheiðr* in *Egil's Saga*.

In the vast majority of cases, the first element appears as an Old English weak noun, with oblique (here genitive) singular inflection *-an*. In one manuscript of Henry of Huntingdon (see appendix), and in traditions derived from Henry, namely Bartholomew of Cotton and John of Oxnead, there is evidence of a Middle English secondary genitive *-s-*; this spelling also appears in the Anglo-Norman traditions of one manuscript of Gaimar and one of Langtoft. In distinctively northern sources, namely Symeon and Langtoft, and in the *ASC* MS C and in an addition/correction to the *ASC* MS A, the element appears with *-nn-*.

This element might be thought to represent Old English *Bruna*, a weak masculine personal name; Old English *brune*, a weak feminine river-name meaning "dark, brown, shining (one)"; or a metathesized version of the Old English weak masculine noun *burna* [a stream]. Formally, the majority of spellings could fit equally well with the first two Old English elements.[7] The Scandinavian noun *brunnr* [a stream] (genitive singular *brunns*) might have influenced the northern forms with *-nn-* and those with the genitive *-s-*; or, as these two variants do not coincide (there are no *-nns-* spellings), these spellings may be expedients used by scribes to make sense of an unrecognized element; or they could be without significance.[8] The Old English noun *burna* [stream] could be represented, but metathesized and unmetathesized spellings are usually present in the series of name-forms, and if this were *burna*, the only unmetathesized spelling available is in the garbled Gaimar forms, *Burneweste*.

The spellings with *-e-* for the inflectional *-an-* (William of Malmesbury, Henry of Huntingdon, Gaimar, Waverley, and Langtoft) represent the Middle English reduction of unstressed weak inflections to schwa [ə]. Those forms without an interconsonantal vowel (Higden and the *Book of Hyde*) represent the further reduction of the unstressed inflection to zero. The *-s-* genitive forms generally may be seen as hypercorrection, the substitution of the Middle English generic genitive for a recognized weak Old English genitive on the part of one or two scribes within the tradition.

---

[7] Burnley, increasingly discussed on the Web as a candidate site for the battle, most probably has as its first element the strong noun or adjective *brun*: early spellings include *Brunlaia* 1124, *Brunleya* 1155–58, *Brunley* 1154, *Bronley* 1258 (Ekwall, *Place-Names of Lancashire*, p. 83). These might possibly indicate very early loss of the weak inflection, but the consistent appearance of the strong form in the early records makes this unlikely. The spellings with medial *-e-* begin with *Bruneley* 1311. Ekwall suggests that *Brun* "may be O.E. *burna* 'stream' . . . [or] the adj. *brūn* 'brown'," or be influenced by *brom* [broom].

[8] See further Cavill, "Site," pp. 304–05.

The strong masculine personal name *Brun* is well evidenced in sources from Anglo-Saxon England, but the element *brunan-* is clearly declined weak. Searle lists several men called *Brun*, two men called *Bruna*, and a considerable number with *Brun-* as the first element of the name (*Brunfrith*, *Brungar*, *Brunheard*, *Brunhelm*, etc.).[9] Compound names with *Brun-* would become *Bruna* in shortened, hypocoristic, form. And while the genitive inflection in the specific of place-names may be used in relation to animate or inanimate subjects, it is most often used to denote association with or ownership by a person.

*3.2 burh*

The origin of the predominant second element of the battle place-name in the sources is Old English *burh* [a fortification]. Versions A, B, C, and D of the *ASC*, the manuscripts including the Old English poem, have the *Brunanburh* form of the name, since the preposition *ymbe* in the poem, line 5, takes the accusative. Other sources have the dative (*-byrig* and variants), following other prepositions including OE *to* and Latin *apud*. *ASC* manuscripts E and F, Symeon of Durham's own tradition (*b*), and Henry of Huntingdon and those following him, use dative forms. However, after the end of the Anglo-Saxon period, it is difficult to be sure whether forms have inflectional endings or are simple appellatives: spellings such as *Bruneberi* or *Bruneburge* may simply be fossilized variants of an uninflected name.

The *Scottish Chronicle* form of the name, *Duinbrunde*, apparently reflects a Gaelic tradition: as Campbell noted, "*dun* in Gaelic place-names is equivalent to *burh*."[10] This form, in a clearly non-English source, together with the fact that *Brunanburh* and variants appears in Old English prose accounts, discredits recent interpretations suggesting that the *burh* element might not have been the name of the original site of the battle, but made up and inserted in the poem for metrical reasons. Kevin Halloran supposed the *burh* element to have been introduced as "a variant of the real place-name that was poetically more satisfying" and a "poetic paraphrase of the *werc(e)* original"[11]; and Hart that it was "added to make up the metre and alliteration."[12] The additional fact that it is the *Brun-* syllable that satisfies the requirements of the meter here vitiates this argument.

The type of fortification referred to by the element *burh* in place-names ranges from that of the Iron Age hillfort, which tends to be a near-permanent landscape feature, to mainly wooden or earthen and hence often temporary and barely traceable Anglo-Saxon fortifications. The former names may be represented by Burrough on the Hill in Leicestershire, the site of a hillfort. A program of fortification of the latter type at strategic places was undertaken by Edward the Elder and Æthelflæd in the first half of the tenth century. It is probably no more than a casual error that a *burh* constructed by Æthelflæd, *Bremesbyrig*, recorded in the *ASC* in 910 in the annals from the source known as the Mercian Register, is

[9] Searle, *Onomasticon*, pp. 117–18.

[10] *Battle of Brunanburh*, p. 61n1. See also Cavill, "Site," p. 313, where the parallel of Edinburgh's Gaelic name *Dunedin* is offered in illustration.

[11] "Brunanburh Campaign," p. 146, and repeated, "Identity," p. 248n3. There are, by my calculations, 33 lines of the poem which lack double alliteration in the first half-line, and approximately 15,000 in the rest of Old English poetry. It remains a fact of Old English prosody that only one alliterating stress in the first half-line is required for the meter.

[12] *Danelaw*, p. 520.

identified as *Bruneberich* by Bartholomew of Cotton.[13] It is noteworthy that the fortification might not have outlived its immediate usefulness, but that the non-hillfort sites themselves tend to be important places, close to major roads, boundaries, or coasts.

*3.3 dun*

The element *dun* appears in Æthelweard's *Chronicle*, *Brunandun*, and in Symeon of Durham's own tradition (*a*), *We(o)ndun*. These traditions are independent.

The element, while common in early English nomenclature, has a specialized meaning and a restricted distribution. Margaret Gelling and Ann Cole note that the element "is consistently used in settlement-names for a low hill with a fairly level and fairly extensive summit which provided a good settlement-site in open country"; typically the element refers to "hills of 200ft–500ft."[14] Names with *dun* cluster in the south Midlands and Essex; there are examples further north both west and east of the Pennines, but none north of the Ribble in Lancashire and the north-west.[15] Isolated examples of *dun* in Scotland are found in the eastern counties and conform to the low hill pattern, as shown by Stella Pratt.[16] It should be stressed that Gelling's and Cole's studies relate to early settlement-names: they have not collected and dealt with late-recorded minor names. But the early settlement-names clearly indicate the main aspects of the meaning of the name element and its distribution in English place-names. These criteria have implications for the location of the battle if we are to take Æthelweard and Symeon's traditions seriously.

*3.4 we(o)-*

The first element of Symeon's *We(o)ndun* was suggested by Campbell to be a scribal error for **Weordun*, with the first element being the name of the river Wear in County Durham.[17] A. Hugh Smith reads it as an oblique case of **weoh* [holy], used in relation to heathen rites.[18]

Sites with heathen names have been examined most fully by Gelling, and her conclusion, that "the evidence for an adjective **weoh* [holy] in English place-names is not sufficiently strong for it to be regarded as established," was endorsed by Carole Hough.[19] The distribution of heathen names, predominantly in the central and eastern parts of England, was the most important factor leading these scholars, and Campbell, to dismiss the possibility that Symeon's *We(o)ndun* might refer to a "holy hill."[20] It is, however, worth noting that the *dun* element and feature provides us with a significant number of heathen names: with

---

[13] Luard, in his edition of Bartholomew's work (p. 21), suggests Brentford (!) as the place.

[14] *Landscape*, pp. 164–65.

[15] Gelling, *Place-Names*, pp. 155–58.

[16] "Summer Landscapes," p. 100.

[17] *Battle of Brunanburh*, p. 62n2. Campbell's statement that the confusion might be due the "great similarity of *n* and *r* in O.E. MSS" is also open to doubt. While in certain insular scripts at this time, such as that of *ASC* A, there are similarities between *n* and *r*, the long descender of *r* generally distinguishes it clearly from the short descender of the *n*. In other scripts, such as the Carolingian minuscule, the two letters are even more distinct.

[18] *Elements* 2.254.

[19] "Further Thoughts," p. 102, and "Some Ghost Entries," pp. 28–29, respectively.

[20] See, e.g., Campbell, *Battle of Brunanburh*, p. 73n2.

*hearg* [a heathen shrine], Harrowden in Bedfordshire and Northamptonshire and possibly Harrowdown in Essex; and with *weoh, wih* [a heathen shrine], Weedon in Berkshire, and Weedon Bec and Weedon Lois in Northamptonshire.[21]

Whatever the uncertainties relating to this "heathen" interpretation in relation to Symeon's *We(o)ndun*, I am not aware that any serious alternative has been proposed other than Campbell's **Weordun*. Some further evidence is offered below (section 6.5) that may serve to address the problem of distribution.

*3.5 weorc*

This element appears in the alternative names for the battle given by Symeon in his *Libellus de exordio*, *Et Brunnanwerc uel Brunnanbyrig*, and in the forms in manuscripts of Gaimar. Two of the latter have the spelling *Burneweste*, which is generally thought to be a scribal error for some form of *Brunewerc*, a reasonable conclusion given the spellings *Bruneswerce* and *Brunewerche* in the other two manuscripts. It is noted above that Gaimar might have known Symeon or his source for this particular name.

The element *(ge)weorc* refers in place-names to a building or structure, usually defensive in nature, and thus it has much in common with *burh*. Symeon's collocation of the two forms *Et Brunnanwerc uel Brunnanbyrig* led John Dodgson to conclude that "the *-werc(e)* forms are no more than a paraphrase of *Brunanburh*" (*PN Ch* 4.238).[22]

*3.6 feld* and *ford*

The element *feld* is found in most manuscripts of William of Malmesbury in the form *Brunefeld*, and in non-contemporary charters and the Scottish traditions as *Bruningafeld*, later *Brounyngfeld*. The Old English poem has the phrase *feld dennade* in line 12 and the noun *wælfeld* in line 51. There is no reason to suppose that the use of the simplex and compound nouns in the Old English poem is related to the *-feld* place-names in the later traditions; it is, rather, an intriguing coincidence.

An alternative form found in some manuscripts of William of Malmesbury and later writers using his material, is *ford*. The variant *-frord* is taken to be a scribal error. In Higden and the *Book of Hyde*, *-fort* is a variant of *ford*. It seems probable that the apparently distinct *ford* element is a misreading of *feld*: this form appears only in one family of related manuscripts, and no early source makes reference to a river-crossing in the account of the battle. There remains a possibility that the first element of *Brunanburh* is a river name (see above), though a river does not feature in the early accounts of the battle, and in *Egil's Saga* the place-name *Vínheiðr* has a river name as its first element (see below).

In late Old English the element *feld* developed the sense that gives us the modern word *field*, namely "an enclosed piece of land, usually arable." But in early and settlement-names it means "open land." Gelling and Cole write:

---

[21] See the discussion of these names in Gelling, "Further Thoughts."

[22] Halloran, "Identity," pp. 249–51, dismisses this notion (p. 251) and suggests instead that in Symeon's phrase "apud Wendune, quod alio nomine Et Brunnanwerc uel Brunnanbyrig appellatur" [at Wendun which is called by another name Et Brunnanwerc or Brunnanbyrig] two distinct features are discriminated and the *burh* element is "changed" to *werc*. The point of Symeon's phrase, however, is that he regarded the names as synonymous, hence the use of *alio nomine* [by another name] for the two variants.

> The word is used in literary texts to describe unencumbered ground, which might be land without trees as opposed to forest, level ground as opposed to hills, or land without buildings. In many references there is a contrast between *feld* and areas which are difficult of access or passage. The contrast most often recorded is that with woodland, but contrast with hills is also well evidenced, and . . . *feld* might be contrasted with marsh as well as woodland and hills.[23]

Gelling and Cole note that not all *feld* names refer to settlement-sites, but "include sites of battles and synods."[24] In these cases, the unencumbered and accessible nature of the ground was what made the site suitable for the purpose of military or ecclesiastical encounter: though there might be other landscape features in the vicinity, the pitched battle was initially sited on open land.

*3.7 -inga-*

The charter forms and Scottish traditions with spellings like *Bruningafeld* reinforce the notion that the first element of *Brunanburh* is most likely to be a personal name *Bruna* or a river name *brune*. The element *-inga-* is clearly present, though it is later reduced to *-ing-* in Bower, for example. This is the genitive of a group name, in this case the *Bruningas*. There are two types of *-ingas* names according to Smith: those which refer to an individual and those which refer to a geographical feature.[25] Those of the former type are ancient names, the latter more chronologically spread. If *Bruna* is the masculine personal name, the *Bruningas* might then be "the followers or descendants of *Bruna*, *Bruna*'s people"; if the element is *brune*, a river-name, the *Bruningas* might then be "dwellers by the river *Brune*." Gelling and Cole list nine places (and two further probable ones) with the generic element *feld* combined with a personal name + *-inga-* as against one place with a name combining *feld* with a topographical element + *-inga-*.[26] An example of the personal name type is Benefield in Northamptonshire, recorded as *Beringafeld* [open land of Bera's people] in c. 970; the only example of the topographical name type is Waldingfield in Suffolk, recorded as *Wealdingafeld* [open land of the forest dwellers] in c. 995.

*3.8 othlynn*

This name occurs only in the *Annals of Clonmacnoise*, a source only known in a modern English translation and thus quite possibly corrupt: "the Danes . . . gave battle to the Saxons on the plaines of othlynn." Campbell dismissed a range of suggestions as to the derivation of this name in unequivocal terms, and suggested that the name represented *Lothlinn*: "If the initial consonant of *lothlinn* had been lost at some point in the transmission of the *Annals*, the form *othlynn* would be explained. The *Annals of Clonmacnoise* possibly used *Lothlinn* vaguely of almost any place beyond the seas east of Ireland."[27] In a recent article, Colmán Etchingham has reviewed the evidence for the location of *Laithla(i)nn* and has concluded that it was most likely part of Norway.[28] This adds to the difficulty of a lost consonant in the proposed identifi-

---

23 *Landscape*, pp. 269–70.

24 *Landscape*, p. 272.

25 *Elements* 1.300 (5).

26 *Landscape*, p. 276.

27 *Battle of Brunanburh*, p. 65.

28 "Location," p. 27.

cation of *othlynn*. A brilliant suggestion was made by Nicholas Higham that this might be Old English *oð Lynne* [up to the Lyme (Lyne)], with the preposition *oð* [as far as, up to] and a regional name ultimately of Celtic origin.[29] This is discussed further below in section 6.4.

*3.9 Vínheiðr*

This is the name of the place of the battle in the Icelandic *Egil's Saga*. The second element, *heiðr*, occasionally replaces Old English *hæð* [heath, uncultivated open land] in north-country names.[30] In Icelandic, *heiðr* is "chiefly used of a *low barren heath* or *fell*."[31] There is significant semantic overlap between *heiðr*, *hæð*, and *feld*, and little problem therefore in accepting that the second element of the Icelandic name might imaginably refer to the same kind of terrain as the English names containing the element *feld*.

The first element of *Vínheiðr* is (according to the pattern of names given by the saga-writer) the river name *Vína*, and the saga also identifies a wood, *Vínuskógi*. This river name *Vína* is also that of the Russian river Dvina, where Egil and his brother Thorolf fought and raided. Campbell believed that the saga conflated accounts of two battles, one in Bjarmaland near the Dvina, where he believed Thorolf was killed, and the other at *Vínheiðr*; later tradition confused the two, he thought, locating Thorolf's death in England.[32] This suggestion, and Campbell's associated rejection of the possibility that Symeon's *Wendun* and the saga's *Vínheiðr* might be related, are effectively rebutted by Matthew Townend. Townend points out that before the saga was composed, a twelfth-century Icelandic poem, the *Íslendingadrápa* by Haukr Valdísarson, recorded Thorolf's death in Athelstan's battle.[33] He goes on to argue that though the assimilation of Symeon's *Wen-* to *Vína* is problematic, it is not inconceivable. So far as this name is concerned, then, the Icelandic saga might have preserved a tradition which at some removes relates to the Battle of Brunanburh.

*3.10 Dingesmere*

*Dingesmere* appears in the A and C versions of the *ASC* at line 54 of the poem, with variants *Dyngesmere* in B, *Dynigesmere* in D, and *Dinnesmere* in O:

Gewitan him þa Norþmen    nægledcnearrum,
dreorig daraða laf,    on Dingesmere
ofer deop wæter    Difelin secan,
eft Ira land,    æwiscmode.[34]

Old English scribes and modern scholars have struggled to make sense of this, as may be deduced from the variant forms in the early documents and the explanations, or lack of them, in the later literature. I have discussed the modern interpretations of the name at length,[35] but

[29] "Context," p.152n66.

[30] Smith, *Elements*, 1.242, s.v. *heiðr*.

[31] Cleasby, Vigfusson, and Craigie, *Dictionary*, p. 247.

[32] *Battle of Brunanburh*, pp. 74–78.

[33] *Skaldic Verse*, pp. 88–93.

[34] Campbell, *Battle of Brunanburh*, p. 94, lines 53–56; compare Item 4a.53–56 in this volume.

[35] Cavill, Harding, and Jesch, "Revisiting," and Cavill, "Coming Back."

to summarize, explanations invoking *dynge* [noise or storm] and poetic *mere* [sea] seem to me to be strained both on the basis of logic (what sea is not "noisy" or "stormy"?) and on the basis of usage (*mere* in poetical compounds means "sea" by metaphorical extension, explained by the first element; the base meaning is "pool"). It should also be noted that the online Toronto *Corpus* and *Dictionary of Old English* does not recognize the existence of a word **dyng(e)* "noise, dashing or storm" in Old English. I argue instead that *Dingesmere* is, as it most naturally presents itself to be, a place-name, the place of the departure of the Norsemen, who sailed thence to arrive at *Dyflen/Difelin*, Dublin, in lines 53–56 of the Old English poem.

*Mere* occurs very commonly in place-names with a genitive singular specific. It means "pond, lake, pool, wetland," and refers to a landscape feature, not a maritime one, though it may occur in coastal situations. The first element of *Dingesmere*, I suggest, is Old Norse *þing* [meeting, assembly], there being a wide range of names, particularly in Norse territory in England and Gaelic-influenced Norse territory in Scotland, where *þing* is realized as *ding-* in compound place-names.[36] I suggest, then, that *Dingesmere* is "wetland of the assembly," a site named to identify both a feature near where a Norse Thing met, and to warn travelers to it of potential danger.

This survey of the extant place-name spellings and toponymical elements used in the sources for names relating to the Battle of Brunanburh and its area reveals an internal consistency in the names and their meanings. Within reasonable limits, the aberrations and variations in the spellings can be explained by the vagaries of textual transmission; the topographical features denoted by the elements in the names broadly tally in sources which are not obviously textually related, and across languages; the main types seem to be meaningful and not random, and once again occur in apparently unrelated sources; and even where a name like *We(o)dun* occurs only in Symeon, the second element of the name is found in another source. It is clear that not all the scribes fully understood the meaning of the place-names they recorded, but that makes it less likely that they egregiously created names themselves rather than attempted to record what they saw or heard. The overall pattern of consistency, then, yields a certain amount of critical evidence that needs to be considered in locating the battle.

The principal name of the site had an Old English weak noun for the first element, most likely the male personal name *Bruna* or a feminine river name *Brune*. There was an area occupied by people who characterized their social group by reference to their relationship to *Bruna* or the river *Brune* (this is the import of *-inga-*). The elements *burh* and *weorc* indicate that the principal site, probably that of a settlement, was fortified. In the vicinity was a rounded hill of low elevation (*dun*), and an expanse of open uncultivated land (*feld*, *heiðr*) on which the fighting began. There was a site of heathen significance (referred to in **weoh*), possibly a river ford (*ford*) or a wood (*skógr*) somewhere in the vicinity, and a boundary or region called Lyme or Lyne at some further distance; in addition there was probably a wetland feature in the area, close to a navigable river or the sea.

## 4. JOHN OF WORCESTER AND THE HUMBER ENTRY

There are some strong elements in the tradition that apparently have little or no bearing on the site of the battle. Among these we might include the hagiographical stories of the

[36] Cavill, "Coming Back," pp. 31–35.

loss of or damage to Athelstan's sword and its miraculous restoration, and William of Malmesbury's and others' use of the king-disguised-as-an-entertainer topos. But other elements may have significant bearing on the site of the battle, and the most important of these is John of Worcester's statement that the invading forces came via the Humber.

Darlington and McGurk observe that "The description of Olaf's dominion and the statements that he was Constantine's son-in-law, that he was incited by the Scottish king, and that the fleet sailed up the Humber are peculiar to J[ohn of] W[orcester] and are not in *ASC*."[37] It is to be noted that this information forms the opening to John's entry, and the remaining details in the account following are essentially a summary of the Old English poem as it appears in the *ASC*.

In one respect, however, John misreads or adjusts the information given in the poem, namely in reporting that Athelstan and Edmund "reges Anlafum et Constantinum ad naues fugere compellentes" [forced kings Anlaf and Constantine to flee to the ships]. In the Old English poem, it is Anlaf who is forced to flee to a ship, followed at some remove of time or place by the rest of the surviving Norsemen;[38] and Constantine escapes north, presumably by land (the usual meaning of *fleam*).[39] Later, in 941, John reports that the Northumbrians chose Anlaf, "rex Nordmannorum" [king of the Norsemen], as their king. This was Anlaf Sihtricsson, but John does not distinguish this Anlaf from Anlaf Guthfrithsson who was at Brunanburh. Anlaf Guthfrithsson is called "Norðmanna bregu" [chief of the Norsemen] in the Old English poem at line 33, perhaps giving rise to John's confusion.[40] These two passages, with their conflation and misreading of information in the *ASC*, associate Anlaf with Northumbria. It would be logical for John, with these associations in mind, to assume that if Constantine and Anlaf were northern confederates, then the likeliest waterway for their entry and escape would be the Humber.

As the most significant northern English river and boundary, and as a place of entry for invading forces, the Humber figures numerous times in the *ASC* and other authorities.[41] One of the series of battles around the time of the Norman Conquest, as reported by John using a version of the *ASC* related to C, was when Harald Hardrada's force "in ostio Tine fluminis intrauerunt" [landed at the mouth of the Tyne] and was joined by Tostig's forces:

> Ad quem comes Tostius . . . sua cum classe uenit, et citato cursu ostium Humbre fluminis intrauerunt, et sic aduersus cursum Vse fluminis nauigantes, in loco quo Richale dicitur applicuerunt.

[37] John of Worcester, *Chronicle*, 2.393n9.

[38] Lines 32–36 of the Old English poem, detailing Anlaf's flight, strikingly use singular verbs; *litle weorode* [with a small company] (line 34b) is similar to *mæte we(o)rode*, which in *The Dream of the Rood* lines 69 and 124 means "alone."

[39] The abundant examples refer to land-based flight: Vercelli Homily 19 neatly illustrates the distinction between land and sea flight: "He [Ionas] þeah on fleame wæs, oð he to sæ becwom, & him þær scip gebohte" [Jonah fled, instead, until he reached the sea, where he took passage] (*Vercelli Homilies*, ed. Scragg, line 115).

[40] William of Malmesbury, *GR* 2.131.4, also confuses the two Anlafs.

[41] Higham, "Context," p. 144n6, and Lendinara, "Battle of Brunanburh," p. 206.

[Earl Tostig joined him with a fleet . . . and on a swift course they entered the mouth of the River Humber; sailing thus up the River Ouse, they landed at a place called Ricall.][42]

Darlington and McGurk note that "The approach through the Humber and the landing-place are not mentioned in *ASC*."[43] In this case the Humber entry is accurate, but the almost formulaic addition of the details to the *ASC* record, closely parallel to those John records for Brunanburh, reveals a habit of mind; in the preceding passage John even confuses Harald Harfagri with Harald Hardrada, much as he confuses the two Anlafs.

No earlier or independent tradition mentions the Humber in relation to the Battle of Brunanburh, but many of the traditions show a knowledge of that important waterway. John misunderstands the Old English poem, confuses personnel, and regards the Humber as the point of entry typically used by northern forces. All these factors make it reasonable to doubt that John has the only accurate tradition about Brunanburh and that all the others omitted such a useful detail.

## 5. THE LOCATION OF THE BATTLE IN RECENT DISCUSSION

There is a tendency among scholars discussing the battle and its location either to call the place-name evidence "speculation" or actually to treat it as such. The caution of early scholars such as Alistair Campbell and Dorothy Whitelock was expressed in a context where onomastic study was developing, and a good deal of relevant material was not available. Taking that caution as the scholarly consensus, more recent investigators have selected sites for the battle on the basis of partial or superficial similarity of names, political or social conditions, or resemblance of sites to adventitious detail in narrative sources. No one has taken very seriously the idea from *Guy of Warwick* (Item 37) that the battle (transmuted into single combat between Guy and Colbrond)[44] took place just outside Winchester; nor the specific location of the battle in *Eulogium historiarum* (Item 43) at *Donelew in Wilthschire* [Dunlow in Wiltshire].[45] And indeed while accurate history, together with political and social conditions, might well rule out certain sites such as these, superficial similarity of names and reliance on late narrative sources is not a strong basis on which to construct a theory of where the battle might have taken place.

At its most extreme, this results in populist writers such as Cockburn, *Brunanburh and its Period*, in 1931 and Hill, *Age of Athelstan*, in 2004 assembling an assortment of names, mostly beginning with *B-*, which might by some prestidigitation be made to match details in the sources. Serious recent claims have also been made for Burnswark (Dumfriesshire), Brinsworth (Yorkshire), Bromswold (Bedfordshire, Northamptonshire, Huntingdonshire,

---

[42] John of Worcester, *Chronicle*, 2.602–03.

[43] John of Worcester, *Chronicle*, 2.602n5.

[44] See also Lendinara, "Battle of Brunanburh," and Rouse, *Idea of Anglo-Saxon England*, pp. 57–62.

[45] This place can be identified as the meeting-place of Dunlow hundred, now preserved in the name Dunley, in Littleton Drew, Wiltshire, approximately halfway between Chipping Sodbury and Chippenham. Early forms recorded for the name, which appears to be compounded of a personal name *Dun* and *hlaw* or its mutated form *hlæw* [mound, tumulus], include *Denelau* 1086 Domesday Book, *Dunelewe* 1268 Assize Rolls, *Donlowe* 1476 Patent Rolls. See Gover, Mawer, and Stenton, *Place-Names of Wiltshire*, pp. 75–76, and O. S. Anderson, *English Hundred-names*, 2.156. Why the *Eulogium* identifies this place as the site of the Battle of Brunanburh is a matter for speculation.

and Cambridgeshire), and Bourne (Lincolnshire). All these display a partial or superficial similarity of name to the Old English *Brunanburh*; all but the first of these rely on John of Worcester's tradition of the Humber entry for the invading fleet. Against these stands Bromborough on the Wirral (Cheshire), the only site suggested for the battle where the name actually derives from Old English *Brunanburh*. I have elsewhere examined some of the arguments put forward in support of Burnswark, Brinsworth, Bromswold, and Bourne, but some summary comments are appropriate here.[46]

*5.1 Burnswark*

Burnswark near Dumfries is an Iron Age hillfort reaching 920 feet above sea level. The name is recorded from 1542 in the spelling *Burnyswarke* and variants.[47] The second element is late Middle English/Scots *wark*, deriving from Old English *weorc*. Thus there is a similarity with Symeon's *Brunnanwerc* and Gaimar's *Bruneswerce*, with which, Kevin Halloran maintains, "there is no doubt that early forms of the place-name Burnswark would fit."[48] Apart from the fact that currently there are no known spellings of the place-name Burnswark within 600 years of the battle, there is no philological "fit" in the forms. Only the garbled Gaimar spellings *Burneweste* give any evidence that *Brunanburh* might have had a metathesized *burn-* form in any tradition. Indeed, the best explanation for the first element of the Dumfries name is *burn* [a spring, a stream], in possessive and/or plural form: there are numerous springs and streams around the hill and numerous *burn* names. None of the recorded spellings for Burnswark suggest that it originally had a weak Old English noun in the first element.

Another argument put forward by Halloran in favor of identifying Burnswark with *Brunanburh* is that the *dun* referred to in Æthelweard's *Brunandun* and Symeon's *Wendun* associates the battle site with "a prominent hill."[49] Gelling's and Cole's examinations of the early settlement-names containing *dun*, however, as mentioned above (section 3.3), show that *dun*s are not necessarily "prominent" and rarely reach higher than 500 feet, that *dun* is not used "to describe great prehistoric hill-forts," and that *dun* names are significantly lacking in the north-west of England and south-west Scotland.[50] There is thus very good reason to doubt the identification of *Brunandun* or *We(o)ndun* with Burnswark.

One further shred of evidence is to be found in the Old English poem. Following the mention of the name *Brunanburh*, the poet claims that it was natural for Athelstan and his brother to defend their land, treasures and homes (lines 7b–10a). The verb used here is *ealgian* [to defend], and though Henry of Huntingdon garbles some of the Old English verse, he has here, accurately, "defenderent patrie" [they should defend their native land]. The implication is that Brunanburh was English, was part of the English king's patrimony in a way that the Solway region never was at this time, nor Northumbria, and even in a way that east Mercia was not when Edmund overran it in 942 capturing the Five Boroughs. Although one might take William of Malmesbury's observation that Anlaf and his forces

[46] For a fuller discussion, see Cavill, "Site."

[47] Neilson, "Brunanburh and Burnswork," p. 49.

[48] "Brunanburh Campaign," p. 144.

[49] "Brunanburh Campaign," pp. 144, 147.

[50] *Landscape*, pp. 164–65.

"multum in Angliam processerat" [had advanced far into England] with a pinch of salt (since he is the only one to make such a statement and it most likely refers to the raiding that preceded the battle), the general consensus of the sources is that the battle was fought on English soil, and that the Scots and Cumbrians were not on home territory.

*5.2 Brinsworth*

The argument for Brinsworth has been advanced by Michael Wood.[51] The strength of his argument is that Brinsworth is in an area of south Yorkshire close to important lines of communication and several fortified places with *burh* names. There is a hill nearby, White Hill reaching 230 feet, and suggested by Wood to be Symeon's *Wendun* on the basis that the northern part of it, Canklow, has Iron Age and Roman remains which include a temple podium. This suggests confusion, on the part of the tradition, of Old English *wiht* [river bend] in the name White Hill, with *wih* [holy].[52] And Brinsworth, first recorded as *Brynesford*, might be confused with *Bruneford* in William of Malmesbury (though Wood does not argue for this).

Despite introducing place-name evidence of this kind, Wood essentially dismisses it:

> The evidence of the place-name is not decisive: what the Norman scribe wrote down [for the name Brinsworth] in the later eleventh century implies a *Brȳni*, not a *Bruna* or a *Brune* as in *Brunanburh*. This does not allow us to be definite about the name the site bore in 937. Indeed the uncertainty over *Brunanburh* has always been compounded by the multiplicity of names for the site which arose as early as the tenth century, suggesting that the real location was soon forgotten in the south of England. It is the strategic significance of *Brynesford* which forces our attention upon it.[53]

To the central assertion of this passage, Ray Page responded, "it is also clear that, whatever the name was in the tenth century, it is unlikely it was *Brunanburh*": so whatever the uncertainties about Brunanburh, and whatever the significance of *Brynesford*, no source links the two places.[54] And in terms of the strategic importance of the site, Nicholas Higham and Sarah Foot have separately argued with just as much evidence and conviction for the strategic and political significance of west Mercia at this time.[55]

The point is, perhaps, that arguing for a series of name confusions can only be an expedient when all other suggestions fail to give a reasonable interpretation of the evidence; and despite the variety of names, as has already been observed, there is a remarkable level of consistency in the attestation of the grammatically weak first element in the name Brunanburh.[56]

---

[51] "Brunanburh Revisited" and *In Search of England*, pp. 206–14.

[52] "Brunanburh Revisited," p. 212. There is a significant difference, however, between the proposition that *wiht* in place-names may develop into "white," as illustrated by Wood ("Brunanburh Revisited," p. 217n74, which is demonstrable), and the proposition that **wih* was confused with *wiht* and gave rise to White Hill in this particular example (for which there is no evidence at all).

[53] "Brunanburh Revisited," pp. 211–12.

[54] "Tale," p. 345n4.

[55] See Higham, "Context," and Foot, "Where English Becomes British."

[56] Contradicted in this proposal by the persistent *-s* genitive in Brinsworth spellings, also noted by Page, "Tale," pp. 344–45.

*5.3 Bromswold*

This was an area of ancient woodland along the borders of Northamptonshire and Huntingdonshire, and Alfred Smyth argues that the name, first recorded as *Bruneswald*, is consistent with *Brunanburh* and its variants, placing particular emphasis on the Rolls Series edition of Henry of Huntingdon which attests a form *Brunesburh*.[57] In my earlier article, I doubted that this spelling was in any sense standard,[58] and in fact my research has shown since (1) that it does not occur in the manuscript (London, British Library MS Arundel 48), but is a reconstructed form for *Brunesburi(t)h*;[59] and (2) that these spellings with *-s-* are idiosyncratic and do not accord with the spellings in any other of the main manuscript traditions of Henry of Huntingdon; indeed a manuscript which was apparently copied from the same exemplar as Arundel 48 consistently has *Brunebur(i)h* spellings.[60] The spellings of Bromswold are thus not consistent with the grammatically weak first element of Brunanburh.

Only one of the names recorded as near the battle site refers to a wood, namely *Egil's Saga*'s *Vínuskógi*. It has been argued that *Egil's Saga* is a tissue of conventional story elements, and this might be thought to throw some doubt on the validity of the wood name; and not even in this source is the battle fought in the wood.[61] The Old English poem has a reference to "wulf on wealde" [the wolf of/from/in the wood] in line 65a, but the reference to the wolf here is doubly conventional: the creature is persistently associated with woodland in Old English poetry[62] and the particular context of the reference in the poem is the "beasts of battle typescene," where the wolf, raven, and eagle pick the bones of the slain on the battlefield.[63] At most, the evidence might suggest that there was a wood in the vicinity of the battle site; it offers no support for the notion that the battle was fought in a predominantly wooded area such as Bromswold was. In Fox's words, "where the element [*wald*] occurs in names first recorded before about 1200 . . . we can be sure that a woodland context of some kind is implied."[64]

In my earlier article, I pointed out some of the topographical difficulties associated with *Bruneswald* as the battle's location.[65] Gelling and Cole's study of early settlement-names, quoted above (section 3.6), has shown that *feld* is used in names to distinguish open land from forest or hill. And upon examination, there is no evidence of early names with *feld* in the Bromswold area; the same is true of *dun* and *weorc* names; and while there are good numbers of *burh* names along the Watling Street Roman road in particular, there are none in the Bromswold region.

---

[57] Smyth, *Scandinavian York and Dublin*, pp. 51–52.

[58] Cavill, "Site," p. 309.

[59] This fact is acknowledged by the editor, Arnold, p. 160n1.

[60] Henry of Huntingdon, *Historia Anglorum*, ed. Greenway, p. cxviii; see the Appendix, below.

[61] McDougall, "Discretion and Deceit." See, more recently, Kelly's essay in this volume.

[62] The phrase "wulf on w(e)alde" occurs also in *Elene* (line 28a) and *Judith* (line 206a). In *Elene* again (line 113a), the wolf is termed "holtes gehleða" [companion of the wood], in *Maxims II* (line 18b), "wulf sceal on bearowe" [the wolf belongs in the wood], and in *Wulf and Eadwacer* (line 16b), the wolf carries off its prey "to wuda" (all references are to editions in Krapp and Dobbie's *Anglo-Saxon Poetic Records*).

[63] Griffith, "Convention and Originality," pp. 197–99, lists eight examples.

[64] "People of the Wolds," p. 81.

[65] "Site," pp. 317–18.

*5.4 Bourne*

Hart pointed out that there was more than one medieval *Bruneswald*, and one of them, spelt *Brun(n)eswold*, *Brouneswelḍ* in thirteenth-century sources, covered "the whole of the high clay-lands of the Isle of Ely,"[66] and the other, *Waldis de Brun(n)e* and *Burneweld* in the thirteenth and fifteenth centuries respectively, along the border of Cambridgeshire into Huntingdonshire. It is, as Hart acknowledges, a little difficult to assess what the first element of these compounds might be, but he dismisses the idea that it could be a personal name *Brun*, as there are too many *Bruneswald* areas for them all to be named after the same man, or men with the same name. He suggests instead that the West Saxon who wrote the poem might have been unfamiliar with "either the local topography or the Old Norse elements in dialects within the Danelaw"; that the name might actually be a simplex and the Old English poem might have added *burh* "to make up the metre and alliteration"; and that the simplex element might be Scandinavian *brunnr* [a spring], which in the dative plural gives name to Bourn in Cambridgeshire and Bourne in Lincolnshire. Hart settles on the latter of these as the site of the battle.[67]

Since independent sources, including prose Old English and Celtic ones, refer to the site as *Brunanburh* or *Duinbrunde* (an accurate translation), since *burh* adds nothing essential to the alliteration and meter of the poem, and since *brunnr* is not inflected as *brunan*, this string of supposition breaks down. Moreover, some of the topographical objections mentioned above in relation to Bromswold also apply here. Bourne in Lincolnshire is on flat, low-lying land, with no *dun* feature in the locality; there are *feld* names in the area, but they are predominantly later than the enclosing of land in the late Anglo-Saxon period, that is, they are "fields" rather than "open land."

Any support for the Bourne or Bourn *Bruneswald* location from the spelling *Bruneswerce* in one Gaimar manuscript may be considered weaker for the fact that Gaimar knew very well where *Bruneswald* or *Bruneswalt* was: the name is given at lines 5548 and 5574 of his poem.[68] Gaimar records at length the story of Hereward's campaigns and skirmishes in the area. He does not, however, relate or confuse *Brunanburh* and *Bruneswald*. Indeed, the story of Hereward told by Gaimar shows that the *Bruneswald* region offered refuge for outlaws conducting guerilla warfare: it was not a place for pitched battles.

Many another site has been proposed for the battle. Those above have been discussed in some detail because they are the ones most prominent in recent literature, and have been proposed by scholars with a detailed knowledge of the context of the battle. Some of the weaknesses of these arguments have been exposed, however: they dismiss the name as it appears in the sources or fail to account for the grammar; they make false assumptions about the topography implied by the name elements; they do not embrace the range of evidence relating to the place in the sources; and they do not always assess the relative value of sources such as John of Worcester or Gaimar. If we cannot ultimately be certain where the battle took place, we can at least weigh up the merits of these suggestions and point out why and in what particulars they do not fit the evidence.

---

[66] See Hart, *Danelaw*, p. 518, and Reaney, *Place-Names of Cambridgeshire*, p. 54.

[67] Hart, *Danelaw*, pp. 520–22.

[68] Gaimar, *Estoire*, ed. Bell.

## 6. BROMBOROUGH

The remaining generally-accepted possibility for the site of the battle is Bromborough on the Wirral. There is now no doubt that this modern name derives from an Old English *Brunanburh*, and when Campbell and Whitelock were initially writing about the uncertainties of the name, the comprehensive survey of the names of Cheshire (in which county Bromborough appears) had not yet been published. The etymology of the name was supposed by Ekwall to be "*burh* where broom grows" as late as 1960, despite Smith's evidence that it derived from *Brunanburh*.[69]

There is now *a priori* good reason to consider Bromborough as the site. But this fact has either been disregarded or minimized in the search for alternatives. There has been a good deal of scholarly reticence about making sweeping claims: Dodgson concurred with Campbell that "the identity of place-name does not prove that this *Brunanburh* in Wirral is the same as that near which the battle took place."[70] However, the failure of any of the alternatives to provide anything remotely like the consistent range of spellings of *Brunanburh* in the sources, or to fit spellings of the alternative sites to the fundamental grammar of, and topography indicated by, the elements, makes a re-examination of the claims of Bromborough necessary. So the evidence relating to this location needs to be reviewed, to see whether it can be reconciled with the basic philological, sociological, and topographical information provided by the sources.

### *6.1 From the name Brunanburh to Bromborough*

The processes by which *Brunanburh* changes to *Bromborough* were summarized by Niles and are here illustrated from the spellings recorded by John Dodgson.[71] Dodgson believed that Bromborough was the site of the battle of 937, but with proper caution he refrained from giving the various spellings of *Brunanburh* as the earliest forms of the modern name. It should be noted that the changes outlined by Niles are not necessarily sequential in the spelling record, but represent trends in pronunciation and orthography before the standardization of spelling in the modern era. The dates given are those of the original document:

· loss of nasal after unstressed syllable → *Bruneburgh* (1153)
· syncope of unstressed vowel → *Brunburg* (1100–35)
· assimilation of *-n-* to the following bilabial *-b-* → *Brumburg'* (1153)
· lowering of *-u-* to *-o-* → *Brombur'* (1153–59)
· parasite vowel appears in second element → *Bromboreh* (c. 1200), *Bromborough* (1277)

One might also note within the series of spellings for *Bromborough* many of the minor variants in the series of spellings for *Brunanburh*: thus we find the second element spelled *-burch-*, *burg(h)*, *-burth*.

### *6.2 Bruna* or *Brune* and the *Bruningas*

Dodgson notes that "there is evidence which suggests that before 1086 Bromborough was the capital of an extensive tract of country" (*PN Ch* 4.239). Its name indicates that it was

[69] See Ekwall, *Dictionary*, s.n., and Smith, "Site of the Battle," pp. 58–59.

[70] "Background," p. 249.

[71] Niles, "Skaldic Technique," p. 364n2; Dodgson, *PN Ch*, 4.237–38.

fortified, and it may be surmised that this fortification dated from the earliest settlement since the land at any point of Anglo-Saxon history was threatened to south and north by the Celts of Wales and Cumbria, and in the tenth century particularly by the Irish and Norse from the west. Dodgson reports that local tradition holds that the original fortification was at Court House, which had an early earthwork enclosing nine acres of land, and was later used as a stronghold by the abbots of St. Werburgh's monastery in Chester (*PN Ch* 4.241).

Two other names, presumably of originally different places, but later merged, contain the same first element as *Brunanburh*, *Bruna*, or *Brune*, namely Brimstage and Brimston. Brimston is now lost; Brimstage is three miles west of Bromborough, equidistant from the Dee and Mersey shores in the middle of the Wirral peninsula. The second elements of the names are respectively *stæþ* [river-bank, landing-place], and *stan* [stone], probably a boundary marker. Dodgson gives *Bruna*, the masculine personal name, as the first element in all these names (*PN Ch* 4.234–36). Though the stream (on which Brimstage stands) might seem to make the alternative river-name *Brune* plausible as the first element, it is hardly a significant landscape feature, and thus the name of a leading settler may be more likely. What Dodgson apparently missed was the significance of these names and the ancient territory they mark out. So far as we can tell, this area was never known locally by a clan- or tribe-name in *-inga-* or *-ingas*; indeed such names are rare, possibly altogether absent, in Cheshire, and in Mercia as a whole.[72] This reinforces the possibility that what the *Bruninga-* spellings from the twelfth-century charters and Scottish sources reflect is a non-local administrative and onomastic convenience, a way of referring to a territory containing *Bruna-* named settlements that borrows or imitates naming convention elsewhere. In Norfolk, for example, Happisburgh [*Hæp's fortification] (*Hapesburch* 1086 Domesday Book) is in the region of Happing [area of land belonging to *Hæp's people] (*Hapinga* 1086 Domesday Book). Happing was named as a hundred in the twelfth century as it became an administrative land-unit.[73] The uncultivated area surrounding Bromborough, Brimstage, and Brimston might then have been known for non-local convenience as Bruningafeld [open land of the Bruningas].[74]

*6.3 The topographical elements*

Much of the Wirral peninsula consists of low hilly land of the type referred to by the element *dun*. An area which retains *dun* in the name is Haddon [heath hill] (*hæð* + *dun*, *PN Ch* 4.213) between Burton and Ness about six miles south-west of Bromborough; Dodgson surmises that Dunstan Farm might also contain the *dun* element (*PN Ch* 4.212). Neither of these names is recorded early. The closest expanses of *dun* land in extant names are Weathertons in Little Neston and the lost, but identical, *Wethredoun* in Willaston [sheep hill] (*weðer* + *dun*, *PN Ch* 4.227, 234): these are four and three miles distant from Bromborough respectively, and though they are (clearly) not originally settlement-names, *Wethredoun* is recorded from 1309. However, the toponymy of the Wirral was influenced by particularly Scandinavian settlers and it is possible that some English names were replaced; certainly as *Wethredoun* shows, some were lost; and the more general and later term *hyll* is common in the area.

[72] Dodgson, *PN Ch* 5.1.249–50; see further Ekwall, *English Place-Names in -ING*, p. 98.

[73] Sandred et al., *Place-Names of Norfolk*, 2.84, 92–93.

[74] If, with due regard to the obscurities and difficulties of the text, we accept the translation given above of *Glaswawt Taliessin*, Item 5.28, we have another non-local reference, from early Welsh tradition, to "Brun's region."

The battle initially took place on an expanse of open uncultivated land of which the terms *feld* in Old English and *heiðr* in Old Norse were used. The crucial term here is *feld*, which is used in several sources, but the significance of *heiðr* (used in a single, and unreliable, source) and the cognate Old English *hæð* is that they refer to broadly the same type of land and vegetation as *feld*. Along much of the coast of the Wirral can be found a string of Heathfield and Heath Field and other heath names, too many to specify, and while (as noted above) *feld* began to change its meaning at the end of the Anglo-Saxon period, Old Norse *heiðr* and Old English *hæð* retained their core sense of "heath, uncultivated land." Haddon, the area of *dun* land mentioned above, also contains the element *hæð*. In Bromborough, Far, Higher, and Lower Heath still exist as names, found earliest in the documentary record as *le heth* in 1412 (*PN Ch* 4.243).

One of the more common field-names in the rural parishes of the Wirral is Hay or Hey, from Old English *(ge)hæg* [enclosure], which denotes the taking-in of common land, and implies the existence of large areas of such land before enclosure. The *feld* names in Bromborough include some early and interesting examples. New Field is recorded as *le New(e)feld* from 1412 and may imply the existence of an old *feld*, or be named in contrast to Oldfield across the Wirral at Heswall. *Lathegestfeld* 1412 and *Ranesfeld* 1265–91 appear to preserve Norse names: *Lathegest* is probably in origin a Norse personal name (*PN Ch* 4.244); *Ranesfeld* may preserve the Norse name *Hrafn* or the English *Hraefn* or *hræfn* [raven] (*PN Ch* 4.245). It is impossible to be sure whether these early names refer to tracts of originally open land, but overall, the names chime with the modern topography to suggest that much of the central part of the Wirral was land of this type.

Two of the remaining topographical features referred to in the various names for the area of the battle, namely a (possible) *ford* and a wood, *skógr*, also appear in the names of Bromborough. The Marfords is Old English *(ge)mære* + *ford* [boundary ford], between Bromborough and Poulton in Bebington parish, the name first recorded in 1406. Bromborough Wood is recorded from 1347 (*PN Ch* 4.242), and there are later names Oak Wood, Shore Wood, Slack Wood, and Woodlands in the parish. There are similar patches of woodland throughout the central area of Wirral, and the names indicate that there were larger areas of woodland in the north and west of the peninsula.

*6.4 Othlynn* and *Dingesmere*

These two are apparently place-names, one in Irish annals and perhaps garbled, the other in the Old English poem. The possibility that *othlynn* in the *Annals of Clonmacnoise* referred to the region called The Lyme or Lyne was suggested by Nicholas Higham,[75] and the suggestion that *Dingesmere* in the Old English poem referred to the wetland at Heswall was made by Cavill, Harding, and Jesch, "Revisiting *Dingesmere*," later augmented in Cavill, "Coming Back." The first of these names refers to the general area where the battle took place; the second, an area from which the surviving Norsemen embarked for the return to Dublin.

The Lyme is an upland area (over 400 feet) which forms the eastern and south-eastern boundary of Cheshire, but stretches north into Lancashire, and runs through Staffordshire and Shropshire. The place-names which make reference to the feature include Audlem and Burslem, Ashton under Lyne, Newbold, Moreton, Laughton, Norton, and Betton all under Lime, Newcastle under Lyme, and Whitmore under Lyme.[76] At its closest, The Lyme is about

[75] "Context," p. 152n66.

[76] Gelling, *West Midlands*, p. 64, fig. 32.

twenty-five miles east from Bromborough. From an Irish perspective, any battle between the Irish Sea coast and the uplands of north-central England might be described as taking place "on the plaines of othlynn," because the significant boundaries were the sea and the upland ridge of The Lyme. Richard Coates suggests that the name itself might ultimately derive from Latin *limen* [threshold], or *limes* [boundary].[77] The Lyme might have had two particular features of interest to the writer of the annals: it was wooded, thus providing cover for fugitives; and it was an ancient territorial boundary at the limits of the Mercian and later palatine power of Chester (*PN Ch* 1.4).

It is clear from the sources that the defeated forces from Ireland were unable to return immediately to their ships and escape: the day-long pursuit detailed in the Old English poem suggests that the coalition forces were cut off from any simple escape route, possibly with the exception of Anlaf who apparently made good his escape alone or with a small company (see above). Fugitives from the battle fleeing west and north-west might intend to take refuge among the potentially more sympathetic Scandinavian settlements of Thingwall, West Kirby, Meols, or in the woods and marshes of those parts of the peninsula.

Four miles directly west of Bromborough is Thingwall, named from the meeting-place of the *thing*, the local moot of the Scandinavian settlers (*þing-völlr, PN Ch* 4.273). Two miles further west is the expanse of Dawpool Bank and the river Dee. In medieval times the course of the Dee varied: it sometimes flowed closer to the north Wales coast, sometimes closer to Wirral, and Ranulf Higden records the tradition that the closer side to the flow of the river would have the disadvantage in war.[78] The river was canalized in 1737 to stabilize its course, but there is still a vast area of mud and sandbank along the littoral. The *mere* element in Old English usually means "pool, lake," but Ann Cole identified a different sense, "wetland," which has been augmented by Mattias Jacobsson, as "land liable to flood."[79] This sense may be found in coastal features subject to periodic or tidal flooding such as Mersea Island in Essex and Cuckmere Haven near Eastbourne in East Sussex.[80]

The west coast of Wirral is commanded by the low hills of Thingwall, Pensby, and Heswall, and the suggestion is that *Dingesmere* in the Old English poem refers to "the wetland of the *thing*." Evidence to support John Dodgson's proposal that it is a "poetic and figurative invention of a name for the Irish Sea" is in the nature of the case lacking, whereas supporting evidence for the kind of name-formation suggested here is plentiful.[81] There may well be a contrast intended by the Old English poet between the embarkation point *on Dingesmere* — far from ideal, even for shallow-draft Viking warships — and the relative safety of the river and sea, sailing *ofer deop wæter* [over deep water] to Dublin.[82]

---

[77] "Lyme," p. 48.

[78] Harding, "Locations and Legends," p. 120.

[79] "Distribution and Use of *mere*," and *Wells, Meres, and Pools*, p. 218, respectively.

[80] See further Gelling and Cole, *Landscape*, pp. 21–27.

[81] See Cavill, "Coming Back," pp. 36–37, and Jacobsson, *Wells, Meres, and Pools*, p. 216.

[82] The assumption made by Halloran ("Brunanburh Campaign," p. 146n84, and, repeated, "Identity," p. 253n24) that the place of embarkation for Anlaf and the Northmen was the same is not justified by the poem. Not only does it deal with the two episodes separately (lines 32a–36 for Anlaf, lines 53–56 for the Northmen), but the persistent singulars of the first episode contrast strikingly with the plurals of the second. Thus the fact that Anlaf puts out "on flot" and "on fealene flod" [on the water . . . on the yellowy-brown sea] very likely has no relevance to the departure of the other Norsemen.

*6.5 We(o)ndun*

One of the significant hesitations that scholars have had, as outlined above (section 3.4), was that if the first element of this name is the adjective **weoh* [holy], the evidence is lacking for heathen sites as far west in England as Bromborough. While this may be a problem of evidence and distribution, it is not one of possibility. With topographical names we can say that some features do not exist in certain areas, but even if evidence were lacking of heathen names in certain areas, heathen practices and sites plausibly existed at one time. In other words, the issue of distribution here would be by no means as conclusive as it is in names relating to topographical features.

However, two separate pieces of evidence have been brought forward to suggest that there were names relating to heathen practice in the Wirral. Prudence Vipond, in "*Harrow* Fields," discussed the Harrow names along the boundary of Heswall and Thurstaston. She disputed Dodgson's etymology (Old English *herra* + *hoh* or Old Norse *hærri* + *haugr*, both meaning "higher hill") on the grounds that these fields are on the gentle slope down towards the Dee. She argued that as elsewhere these refer to a heathen site, Old English *hearg*. In a postscript to Vipond's article ("Paganism and Christianity"), Margaret Gelling accepted the evidence, suggesting that Landican probably commemorates a Welsh missionary saint, Tegan, who worked among the heathen here.

The second piece of evidence was Richard Coates' discussion, "Further Snippet," of an earlier name for Rice Wood in Bromborough, *Welondrys* 1357, which he interprets as *Weland*, a Middle English form of an inflected Old English **weon land* [sacred land], with the addition of the specifier *hris* [scrub].

David Wilson has suggested that a *hearg* site "occupied a prominent position on high land and was a communal place of worship for a specific group of people," as against the *weoh* which was "a small wayside shrine."[83] It is interesting to note that the Harrow names of Heswall are at the foot of a steep hill, leveling out towards Pensby and Thingwall. The Rice Wood site is, as Coates observes, just over half a mile from the Court House, the earthworks which may be those of the *burh* of *Brunanburh*;[84] and it is even closer to the modern A41 road which follows an ancient non-Roman routeway; it is also on gently rising land. Thus in names of the Wirral, there is not only evidence of heathen sites, but also evidence that the particular elements *hearg* and **weoh* were used in a similar fashion to those in the rest of the country.

7. CONCLUSION

In the nature of the case, it is not possible to map in precise detail the progress of the battle and its aftermath, despite the best efforts of commentators. In the discussion above I have tried to take seriously and present carefully the evidence provided by the names used in the medieval sources. What I think has been established is that Bromborough on the Wirral and its area fits the philological, topographical, and sociological descriptors given in the names; and it fits these descriptors in a way that none of the other proposed sites do.

[83] "Pagan Saxon Worship Sites," pp. 181, 182.

[84] "Further Snippet," p. 289.

## APPENDIX ON HENRY OF HUNTINGDON'S BRUNANBURH SPELLINGS

In the table below, I give the spellings of *Brunanburh* in manuscripts of Henry of Huntingdon's *Historia Anglorum*. There are three references to the place of this name in Henry's history: the first is in Book 5.18, the general introduction to the battle and the poem translation that follows; the second is in Book 5.19, Henry's translation of the Old English poem; and the third, in Book 5.32, Henry's summary of the reigns of the West Saxon kings. Early copies of manuscripts representing each of the six versions have been consulted as follows:

Version 1: Edinburgh, National Library of Scotland, Advocates' MS 33.5.4
Version 2: Aberystwyth, National Library of Wales, Peniarth MS 382
Version 3: Cambridge, Corpus Christi College, MS 280
Version 4: London, Lambeth Palace Library, MS 327
Version 5: London, Lambeth Palace Library, MS 118
Version 6: Edinburgh, National Library of Scotland, Advocates' MS 33.5.2

In addition, the readings of London, British Library, MS Arundel 48 (the text edited by Arnold), and Oxford, Bodleian Library, MS Laud Misc. 564, copied from the same exemplar as Arundel 48 (Greenway's δ, *Henry of Huntingdon*, p. cxviii), have been included. Arundel 48 is a text of version 5, but as will be clear from the spellings listed below, the *brunes*- forms are unique to this scribe.

| **Version** | **Book 5.18** | **Book 5.19** | **Book 5.32** |
|---|---|---|---|
| 1 | brunebirih | brunebirih | brunebirig |
| 2 | brunebiri | brunebiri | Brunebiri |
| 3 | brunebirih | brunebirih | brunebrig |
| 4 | brinebirih[85] | brunebirih | brunebiri |
| 5 | bruneburih | brunebirih | bruneburith |
| 6 | bruneburih | brunebirih | brunebirih |
| Arundel 48 | brunesburith | brunesburih | brunesburith |
| Laud Misc. 564 | bruneburih | bruneburih | bruneburh[86] |

This evidence clearly demonstrates that the -*s*- genitive is idiosyncratic to the scribe of Arundel 48 and not organic to the *Historia Anglorum* tradition as a whole. This reinforces the point made earlier that the earliest sources represent the first element of *Brunanburh* as originally an Old English weak noun. Interestingly, it appears to be from the idiosyncratic tradition of Arundel 48 that the source(s) of Bartholomew of Cotton and John of Oxnead descend.

[85] A minim in the first syllable is missing.

[86] With -*i*- (-*burih*) underdotted for excision.

STEPHEN HARDING

# WIRRAL: FOLKLORE AND LOCATIONS

Earlier chapters have examined the possible locations within Britain for the Battle of Brunanburh and have shown that it might have taken place in the Wirral peninsula in north-west England. If this is correct then it is possible to make suggestions as to where the battle may have taken place and the possible escape route of Anlaf's men. But this is a rather hazardous enterprise because the earliest sources give little indication of place beyond names: the contemporary (or near-contemporary) Old English poem provides only a few clues, but these, together with knowledge of the current and former topography of the area and surrounding coastline, and knowledge of how the local Scandinavian and English populations were distributed in tenth-century Wirral, enable some suggestions to be made. First, though, this essay examines the local folklore to see if any reliable evidence may be found as to the location of the battle from antiquarian traditions of the Wirral.

## 1. LOCAL FOLKLORE: BROMBOROUGH COURT HOUSE AND WARGRAVES

Two places on Wirral have been associated in local antiquarian lore with the battle and both are within the (modern) township of Bromborough itself. These traditions are interesting in themselves and are worth investigating; but they generally tell us more about the antiquarian enthusiasm of the writers than the location of the battle.

The first of these is at what was formerly a set of fields near the banks of the River Mersey referred to in a 1731 map as *Wargraves* and in the 1839 Tithe Apportionment as *Wergreaves*. Because of its unusual name, local folklore has associated this place with the battle. Reflecting this folk-etymology, a well-known local Victorian clergyman, the Reverend Edward Dyer Green, later echoed by the local historian Phillip Sulley,[1] made the suggestion that the elements were ME *werre* [war] and *graef* [a grave, a digging] (an etymology at first accepted by Dodgson).[2] Thomas Helsby also records Green as reporting that

> A large tract of land near the sea shore at Bromborough has long been known by the name of Wargraves. This fact, and that of the recent discovery (June 1877) of a large number of skeletons near the coast of the Dee, a few miles further off, with other circumstances, combine to prove that this parish was the unquestionable site of Athelstan's famous victory over the Danes and their allies in 937.[3]

[1] Sulley, *Hundred of Wirral*, pp. 213–16.

[2] Dodgson, "Background," p. 303n7, rpt. in Cavill, Harding, and Jesch, *Wirral and Its Viking Heritage*, p. 61n7.

[3] See Ormerod, *History of the County*, p. 427n1.

Dodgson later more plausibly suggested the second element to be OE *græfe* [a wood] and the first to be ME *werre* or ON *verri* [worse, the less valuable], and concluded that the name is not evidence for a battle (*PN Ch* 4.242). Today Wargraves is an industrial area off the A41 trunk road and on the 1831 Bryant map of Wirral (the relevant part of which is shown in Figure 1) — which, besides the tithe maps, provides one of the last maps of the area before heavy urbanization — it corresponds approximately to the area between Rice Wood and Bromborough Mills.

Secondly and more recently, 1.5 km (1 mile) further north along the A41 (New Chester Road) at Bromborough Pool, the formerly highly ditched/moated nine-acre site of what used to be (until 1969) the Bromborough Court House and Court House Farm, has been associated with the battle, possibly as the site of the *burh* or stronghold. The site is located on the south bank of the River Dibbin just near its entry into the River Mersey. The earliest attestation of the name is 1412 *le Courteway* [the way to the court] (see *PN Ch* 4.241). The site was the manor house of the abbots of St Werburgh's in Chester and is described in 1819 — not long before the Bryant and Tithe maps were produced — as follows: "occupying an

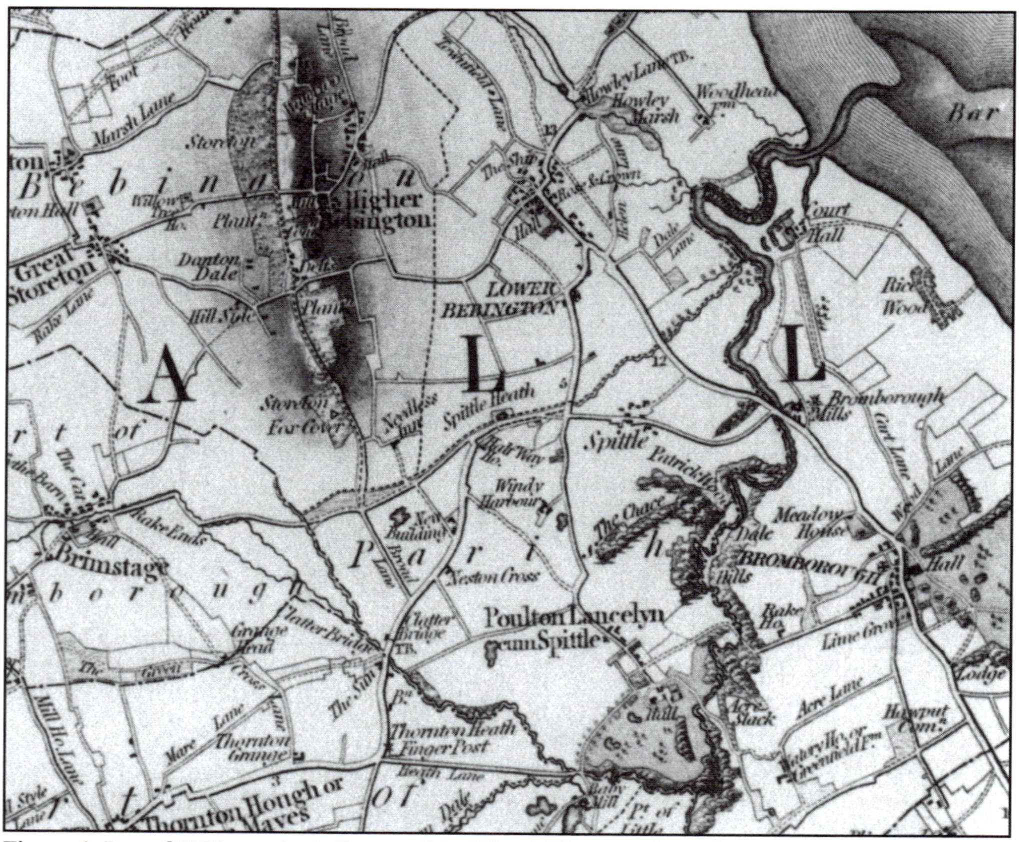


**Figure 1**. Part of 1831 map by A. Bryant of the Wirral. The map shows the ridge of high ground (now Mount Road) in the Storeton/Bebington area running up to Tranmere Pool and Oxton. Bebington Heath and Storeton woods can be seen as well as "Court Hall" near the mouth of the Dibbin and Poulton Hall to the bottom of the map and Brimstage Hall to the left. Courtesy of Chester & Cheshire Archives & Local Studies.

extremely strong position at the neck of land, accessible only from the south, to the east it is defended by the estuary, on the other sides by precipitous banks descending to an inlet which forms a channel between this parish and Bebington" (*PN Ch* 4.241).

The unlikelihood of the name Wargraves having anything to do with "war" does not preclude the possibility that the Court House could have been sited on the ancient fortified site of Brunanburh. The occupation of some such site commanding the river by Athelstan's forces would have denied the defeated forces the means of a quick escape to ships arriving via the Mersey and could have forced the day-long retreat mentioned in the Old English poem.

*Mount Road Ridge, Bebington, Storeton, Brimstage, and Heathland*

In the early decades of the twentieth century local historians were fostering the belief that the battle had taken place around what is now Bebington Heath, 2.4 km (1.5 miles) south-west from Bromborough Court House, and (if that was where the *burh* was sited) still very much *ymbe Brunanburh*. Bebington Heath is adjacent to the Norse townships of Storeton to the west and Tranmere to the north: on the Bryant map (Figure 1) its position is centered around the first of the large L letters. Just over 1000 years later World War II American soldiers were using the same heathland for battle practice. Today part of it is common land and part of it is the site of Brackenwood Golf Course sloping eastwards to the ridge of high ground of Prospect Hill and Storeton Hill. Mount Road — the township boundary — now runs along the ridge. The ridge is now partially wooded and although some of this is due to seventeenth- and eighteenth-century fir plantations it is not unimaginable this might have been the case in medieval times. Sir John Stanley, knight of the Garter (1453–1519) was resident at Storeton Hall (top left corner of Figure 1) and Master Forester of Wirral.[4]

One early twentieth-century local historian, Godfrey Mathews, made the suggestion that the ridge would have made an ideal defensive position for Anlaf's army, as recalled by Anne Anderson, and that it was from this ridge between Spital and Higher Bebington that the battle was fought.[5] Another, Francis W. T. Tudsbery, a student at Oxford and colleague of the Icelandic antiquarian Eiríkur Magnússon, in his 1907 book, *Brunanburh AD 937*, argued that the bulk of the fighting took place on the *western* side of this ridge between Brimstage and Storeton which was also, he says, heathland.[6]

Although a lot of the evidence presented by these historians is based on unreliable sources, for example *Egil's Saga*, this is an intriguing argument. The topography of the area can be gauged from the Bryant map of Wirral in 1831 and one can see that, regardless of which side of the ridge the bulk of the fighting might have taken place, the heathland around Mount Road makes a plausible site for a battle. From here it is 8 km (5 miles) as the crow flies to the Dee estuary at Heswall or Ness, and 13 km (8 miles) to the medieval seaport of Meols. Anlaf's raiders escaping from the Saxons might have headed in these directions (Figure 2).

*The Lancelyn Greens and Poulton Hall*

Although the Reverend Dyer Green may have been building on an earlier tradition with his learned suggestion concerning Wargraves — only shown by later scholarly analysis to be unlikely — this cannot be said for some other interesting pieces of Victorian folklore sur-

---

4 See, for example, E. Wilson, "*Sir Gawain and the Green Knight* and the Stanley Family."

5 See A. Anderson, *Story of Bromborough*, p.18.

6 For discussion and citations, see Wawn, "Vikings and Victorians."

rounding the battle. Although these stories are based on fantasy rather than fact, they nonetheless demonstrate the wish of the locals to appropriate the significant battle for the area and its history: they are also interesting in a study of the imaginative and sociological impact of local history on residents.[7] The first piece of Victorian tradition concerns the roadway leading down from Mount Road to Storeton Hall known as Red Hill Road (the road running below "Danton Dale" on Figure 1), which was so named from "the blood that once ran down it." In reality the Red Hill refers to the red sandstone: Storeton Hill is part of one of two ridges of sandstone running through Wirral. The other ridge of red sandstone runs along the western side of the peninsula, and at Thurstaston Common is an impressive outcrop known as "Thor's stone." It has been impossible to trace this name before the Victorian period and it appears to have been introduced by the prominent Liverpool antiquarian Sir James A. Picton on the mistaken assumption that the place-name Thurstaston derived from Thor's stone[8]: the origin of Thurstaston was shown by Dodgson and others to derive from the personal name Thorsteinn with *tun*. Nonetheless Picton's association of the place with the Norse god was quickly echoed by others, culminating in Hilda Gamlin's suggestion in *Twixt Mersey and Dee* that "the stone was probably raised by the Danes to commemorate the great battle of Brunanburh."[9] Not only does the folklore have the Danes fighting at Brunanburh — and celebrating a victory — but also has King Alfred fighting, too: King's Road on the Bebington side of Mount Road was once believed to have been named after King Alfred, who was thought in this tradition to have fought at Brunanburh. Although locals now accept this could not possibly be true, another piece of folklore was that King's Road had not been improved since King Alfred's time — this is considered true!

**Figure 2**: Escape routes to the coast. Top line: through the *carrs* and *holms* to Meols. Dark line: to Heswall. Third line: to Ness. Adapted from 18th-century map of Moll (ca. 1724).

One final piece of folklore which is worthy of more serious consideration concerns the Lancelyn Green family, residents at Poulton Hall (2 km south of Bebington Heath) since 1093. The late Roger Lancelyn Green was a well-known author and his many books included *The Saga of Asgard: Retold from the Old Norse Poems and Tales* (Puffin, 1960) reprinted in 1994 as *Myths of the Norsemen* (Puffin Classics, 1994). He was well-

[7] For evidence of widespread interest in Brunanburh among the Victorians, see Joanne Parker's essay in this volume, pp. 385–407, and Wawn, *Vikings and Victorians*.

[8] Picton, "Great Stone of Thor," pp. 364–65.

[9] Gamlin, *Twixt Mersey and Dee*.

versed in all things Viking. In memory of him the family commissioned the *Brunanburgh Viking*, a bronze sculpture which was unveiled in April 2004 and stands high in the gardens of the hall. The family believe the grounds were once the site of Bruna's stronghold or *burh*, with some stones from it remaining not far from the present building.[10]

The parish/township map of Wirral shown in Figure 3 has changed little over hundreds of years. Although Poulton is now in the parish of Bebington, it lies between the two modern townships of Bromborough and Brimstage which make up Bromborough parish: right in the middle of the territory anciently bearing Bruna's name. Poulton as a name may not have existed in 937 CE (it is not recorded before 1260). The commanding position of Poulton Hall, flanked by the River Dibbin and overlooking the Norse settlements at Raby and Storeton, would have made this location an ideal position for a boundary or border stronghold and a good alternative to Bromborough Court House as a possible location of Bruna's *burh*. As Ormerod reports,

> Poulton Hall and the ground adjacent are situated above the most romantic part of the valley, sheltered with respectable timber and commanding a delightful prospect of the Clwydian mountains. The former hall stood at short distance from the present one, on a knoll, overhanging the dale below, and within the area of the ancient castle of the Lancelyns, the site of which is still indicated by the slight traces of earthworks, and was remarkably strong, defended by the dale in front, and on the two sides by deep ravines issuing from it. At the early period of its erection its strength and difficulty of access was materially increased by a large pool or mere, then formed by the tide below, which seems to have given its name to the township, and to the contiguous tracts of meadow ground called the Marfords. The effects of waves are still visible in the worn face of the rocks, at the upper end of the valley.[11]

*Folklore Conclusions*

This brief review of the local traditions reveals a great deal of interest in the battle and the possibility that it might have taken place locally. None of the supposed connections between the names and local features made by enthusiastic antiquarians can be historically verified, but nevertheless the traditions show a serious and creative interaction between the literary sources and the Wirral topography. It remains a question worth asking: how does the local evidence chime with arguments that the battle was fought on the Wirral?

## 2. WIRRAL AS A POSSIBLE LOCATION FOR THE BATTLE

*The Old English poem*

The tenth-century poem (Item 4 in this volume) tells us the following geographical information:

1. Line 5: the battle took place *ymbe Brunanburh* [around Brunanburh];
2. Line 21: the retreating raiders were chased by troops of West Saxons *ondlongne dæg* [for the entire day] (though it may be this is a poeticism meaning "for a long time");
3. Line 54: the fleeing raiders from Dublin escaped from a place on or near the coast called *Dingesmere* and sailed to Dublin.

---

[10] Mrs. June Lancelyn Green, personal communication.

[11] *History of the County*, p. 440.

This information indicates that the battle took place somewhere around Brunanburh but at some distance from the point of escape; it took Anlaf's men an entire day of evading hostile forces to get to *Dingesmere*. If, as has been argued in other chapters, *Brunanburh* is Bromborough and *Dingesmere* is "the wetland by the Thing" (the meeting-place denoted by the name Thingwall), then the battle ranged from east to west across the Wirral. The escape-route for the repelled raiding army was one that might have been used by sea-travelers trading with the Wirral or visiting the Thing.

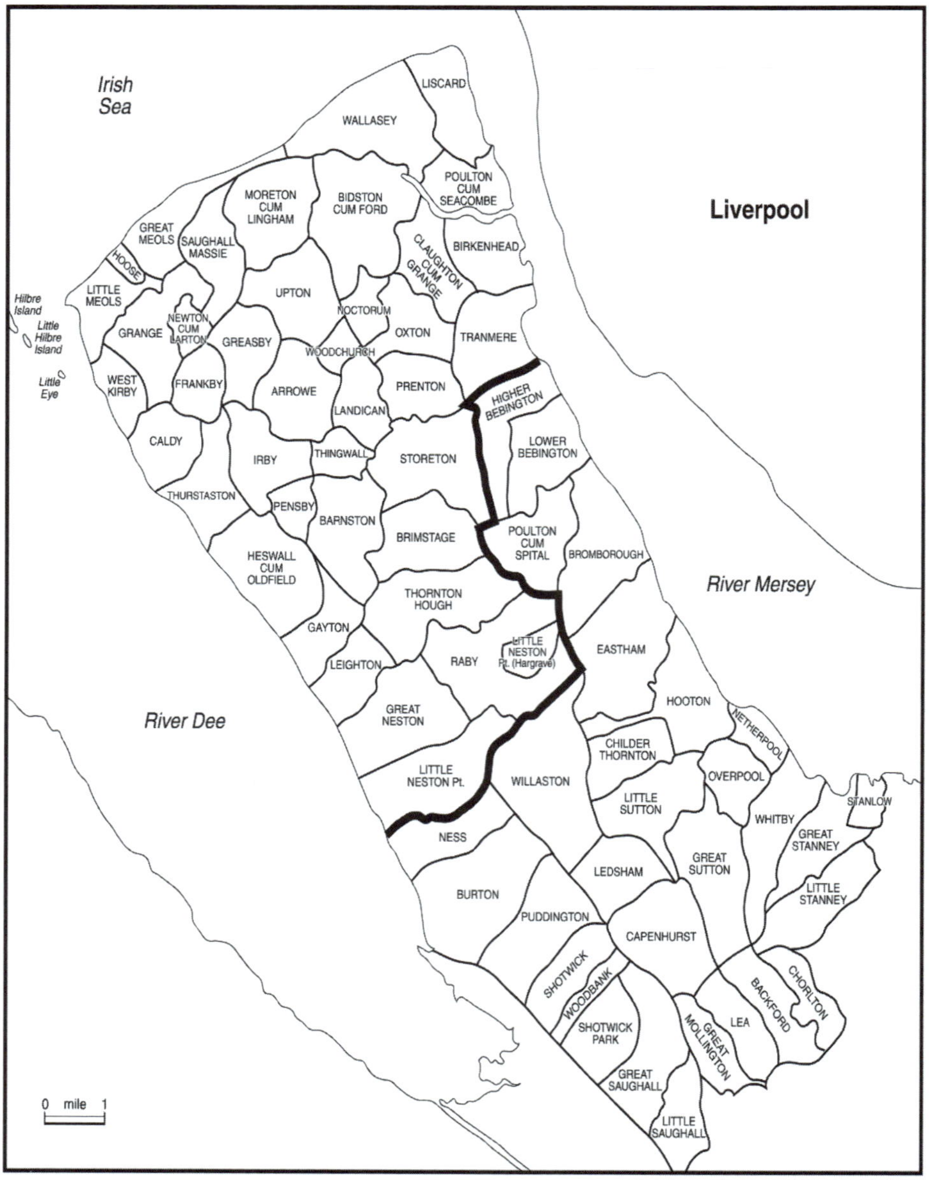


**Figure 3**: Wirral parish/township map (19th century). The bold line demarks the approximate boundary of the tenth-century Norse enclave, based on baronial manor holdings and place-names. Courtesy of Chester & Cheshire Archives & Local Studies.

*Tenth-century Wirral*

By the time of the Battle of Brunanburh, a linguistically Scandinavian population had been established in the north and west of the Wirral peninsula, and the existence of its Thing at Thingwall — one of only two surviving Thingwall place-names in England — attests to the Scandinavians being the dominant population. Although there may have been some degree of integration, the English-speaking communities were concentrated to the south of the peninsula. Within the conjectured Norse area there are some English-named places like Moreton, Upton, Bidston, and (just outside) Poulton: these could have been in existence by the time the Norsemen arrived although there is no clear evidence to support this (the earliest of these, Upton, is first recorded in Domesday Book, 1086); they could equally have been established after the Scandinavian settlement period.

Norse Wirral is blessed with many fine examples of Viking Age stonework and treasure; the most outstanding examples include the magnificent hogback grave marker at St. Bridget's Church, West Kirby (recently beautifully restored by the Merseyside Conservation Centre), and another smaller hogback from Bidston, identified in 2004. Other examples include a large number of Viking artifacts discovered in low tides off the old Viking port of Meols. Although the majority of the finds were made in the nineteenth century they have only recently been cataloged and include coins, Hiberno-Norse pins, brooches, a drinking horn, and what appear to be weapons from a possible pagan burial.[12] Evidence was presented at a recent public meeting of the remains of an elliptically shaped Viking house at Irby.[13] Amongst other impressive evidence of the Viking settlements are artifacts at the Church of St. Mary and St. Helen at Neston. There are seven fragments belonging to at least three Hiberno-Norse crosses, with fascinating imagery including the touching scene of a Viking couple embracing.[14] A silver ingot attributed to the Viking period was discovered not far away in Ness.[15]

This wealth of archaeological evidence has been supported by modern genetic research tools. Recent y-chromosomal DNA analysis of men from old Wirral families (i.e., those possessing surnames extant in the area prior to the industrial revolution) has shown, in common with neighboring West Lancashire, substantial Norse ancestry with a prevalence for example of the haplogroup R1a, common in Norway but relatively rare in other parts of Western Europe.[16]

Ness and Neston probably mark the southern extremity of the original Norse enclave, and it is possible to assess the initial boundary of the settlements from the distribution of Scandinavian place-names and the topography. The neighboring settlement of Raby (ON *rá-byr*) means "boundary settlement." On the English side of the posited boundary is the Old English place-name Hargrave [grey wood], with Old English *hār* [grey] used in a specialized sense meaning "boundary."[17] From Raby the boundary appears to have run north-eastwards along the River Dibbin and the ridge of high ground separating Bebington from Storeton (ON *stórr*

[12] See D. Griffiths, Philpott, and Egan, *Meols*, pp. 58–76.

[13] Philpott and Adams, *Irby, Wirral*.

[14] R. White, "Viking Period Sculpture," pp. 45–58.

[15] Bean, "Silver Ingot."

[16] Bowden, et al., "Excavating Past Population Structures," pp. 301–09; see also Harding and Jobling, "Looking for Vikings," pp. 22–25.

[17] A. Smith, *English Place-Name Elements*, 1.234.

[big], presumably with ON *tún* [farm]), up to Tranmere (ON *trani-melr* [crane sandbank]). This division (Figure 3) also corresponds to the boundary of major baronial holdings in Domesday Book which, according to Dodgson, "represents a Norman adaptation of an administrative pattern that already existed when the Norman earls took over the shire. It looks as though the Norse enclave in Wirral was so politically distinctive that it justified a special feudal administration,"[18] an administration that survived in relict form as the "Hundred of Caldy" until 1819.[19] Along the boundary there is evidence from early field-names of a certain degree of assimilation or communication between the originally distinct communities. In the township of Storeton, for example, there is an old name (last recorded 1330) *le Gremotehalland*, where the first element is the Old Norse compound *griða-mót* [place of a meeting under a truce], which may reflect a mechanism for the resolution of disputes (*PN Ch* 4.256).

There is evidence for the notion that in 937 there was an originally Scandinavian community to the west and north of the boundary shown in Figure 3, and a primarily English community to the east and south. In assigning battle lines for Anlaf's men it would therefore make sense to place them with their backs to this Scandinavian community (for the reason that there might be some element of sympathy between the marauders and the originally Scandinavian settlers), and vice versa for Athelstan's forces. This, together with the three points identified from the poem above, may help us in the attempt to locate the battlefield and *Dingesmere*.

*Thingwall, Dingesmere, and Heswall*

Placing Anlaf's (and Constantine's) forces with their backs to the enclave would therefore be consistent with the local tradition considered above that the battle had taken place at or near Bebington Heath (or on the other side of the ridge near Storeton and Brimstage). In the battle, however, the tenth-century poem tells us the surviving marauders were put to flight. So for where on the coast would Anlaf's forces head? The solution offered in 2004 to the Dingesmere mystery allows us to make some informed suggestions.[20] It is a distinct possibility that the fleeing forces were prevented from reaching their own vessels which *might* originally have been moored as far away as the River Ribble as hypothesized by Nicholas J. Higham: the escaping forces would have attempted to head for any part of the coast likely to have seaworthy vessels, or where their own vessels manned by a skeleton crew could have hurried, to effect an escape (Figure 2).[21]

**Figure 4**: View of Cross Hill, possible site in Thingwall of the Thing. Photo: Stephen Harding.

[18] Dodgson, "Background of Brunanburh," p. 312; rpt. in Cavill, Harding, and Jesch, *Wirral and Its Viking Heritage*, p. 66.

[19] Ormerod, *History of the County*, 2.518.

[20] See Cavill, Harding, and Jesch, "Revisiting Dingesmere."

[21] Higham, "Context of Brunanburh," p. 153.

One such place was the coastal water used by travelers to the Wirral from Wales and elsewhere. The Dee bank of the Wirral, as suggested in a 2004 paper, could be named *Dingesmere* as in the Old English poem, from the Norse assembly (*þing*) of Thingwall, and the wetland or tidal marshland that lines the coast (OE *mere* [pool or wetland]).[22] But where was this Dingesmere? The nearest accessible point (that is to say not involving negotiation of a cliff) on the coast to Cross Hill (believed to be the site of the Thing at Thingwall, Figure 4) is at Heswall Point (Bryant map, Figure 5) not far from the former, now lost, settlement at Warmby. Figure 6 shows the scene from there today. Based on the present-day topography of Wirral, this would appear to be a good candidate for the escaping forces after Brunanburh after they had dodged their way to the coast in search of anything seaworthy: today the area is marshland and, depending on the tide, vessels can reach the estuary only by a channel through it. Moving along the coast northwards the marshland has disappeared before Thurstaston. Moving the other way along the Dee coastline to the south is the ancient ferry at Gayton — connected to Thingwall via an old track: this is another candidate as a coastal entry point for visitors to the Thing. Still further down the coast there are other ancient ports at Parkgate and Neston which may also have been coastal targets for the fleeing raiders. Tudsbery has also suggested the promontory at Ness, another entry point used by medieval mariners.[23] Wherever the main entry point for the Thing was, the whole stretch of the Dee coast from Ness to Heswall Point could have been known by the locals and sailors as *Dingesmere*.

Some caution is necessary here as we know the topography of the Dee river and coastline was different at the time of the battle. Large changes are known to have occurred in the nineteenth century through silting and coloni-

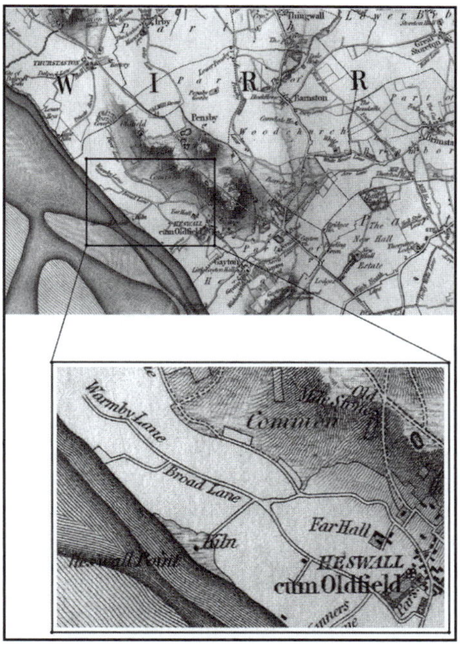

**Figure 5**: Part of Bryant map showing Bebington, Thingwall, and Heswall in 1831. Storeton and Brimstage are at the right, Cross Hill and Thingwall can be seen at the top, with the area around Heswall Point highlighted. Courtesy of Chester & Cheshire Archives & Local Studies.

**Figure 6**: Heswall Point today, now known as Sheldrakes after the nearby restaurant of the same name. Photo: Stephen Harding.

[22] Cavill, Harding, and Jesch, "Revisiting Dingesmere," pp. 25–38.

[23] Tudsbery, *Brunanburh*, p. 30.

zation with Spartina grass brought in by ships from America, rapidly colonizing the coastline from Heswall down to Chester.[24] The once-thriving seaports of Parkgate and Neston and the old ferry between Gayton and Holywell in north Wales all ceased to operate. However it is possible to gauge from earlier records that areas of difficult navigation along the Dee coast may well have existed in medieval times: this has already been alluded to in Paul Cavill's chapter in this volume. In John Trevisa's translation of the *Polychronicon* of Ranulf Higden, for example, he notes the folklore which had arisen in relation to the Dee:

> Below the city of Chester runs the River Dee, which now separates England and Wales. The river often leaves the established channel, and changes the places shallow enough for fording every month, as the local people tell. Whichever side the water draws closer to, either England or Wales, that side will have the disadvantage in war and be overthrown in that year, and the men of the other side will have the advantage and will get the better of them. When the water changes its course in this fashion, it presages these events.[25]

"The river often leaves the established channel" implies that the medieval Dee had large amounts of silt and mud around it even then. The larger-scale Bryant map (Figure 7) shows the distribution of channels and less navigable waters in 1831: this is before the Spartina colonizations, which would have required existing marshland and silt to gain a hold.

It is therefore not unreasonable to suppose that along the Wirral side of the Dee estuary in 937 there were significant areas of wetland or marshland. This was the mere of the Thing — *Dingesmere* as suggested in 2004.[26] The location of *Dingesmere* on the Dee coast is also *at least* consistent with the activities of King Edgar some forty years after the battle. John of Worcester, a twelfth-century historian, reports how in 973 Edgar took a party of Celtic kings in a boat along the Dee in Chester:

> Edgar, the peaceable king of the English, was blessed, crowned with the utmost honour and glory, and anointed king in the thirtieth year at Pentecost, 11 May, in the first indiction, by the blessed bishops Dunstant and Oswald, and by the other bishops of the whole of England in the city of Bath. Then, after an interval, he sailed round the north coast of Wales and came to the city of Chester. Eight underkings, namely Kenneth, king of the Scots, Malcolm, king of the Cumbrians, Maccus, king of many islands, and five others, Dufnal, Siferth, Hywel, Iacob, and Iuchil, went to meet him, as he had commanded, and swore that they would be loyal to, and co-operate with, him by land and sea. With them, on a certain day, he boarded a skiff; having set them to the oars, and having taken the helm himself, he skilfully steered it through the course of the Dee, and with a crowd of ealdormen and nobles following in a similar boat, sailed from the palace to the monastery of St John the Baptist, where when he had prayed, he returned with the same pomp to the palace. As he was entering it he is reported to have declared to his nobles at length that each of his successors would be able to boast that he was king of the English, and would enjoy the pomp of such honour with so many kings at his command.[27]

Edgar was *probably* re-enacting Athelstan's taking submission from the Celtic kings at Eamont Bridge, Westmorland, in 926, reinforced by military power at Brunanburh in 937:

[24] Freethy and Freethy, *Discovering Cheshire*, p. 33.

[25] Text taken from Sisam, ed., *Fourteenth Century Verse and Prose*, with translation by Cavill.

[26] Cavill, Harding, and Jesch, "Revisiting Dingesmere."

[27] John of Worcester, *Chronicle*, ed. Darlington and McGurk, pp. 423–25.

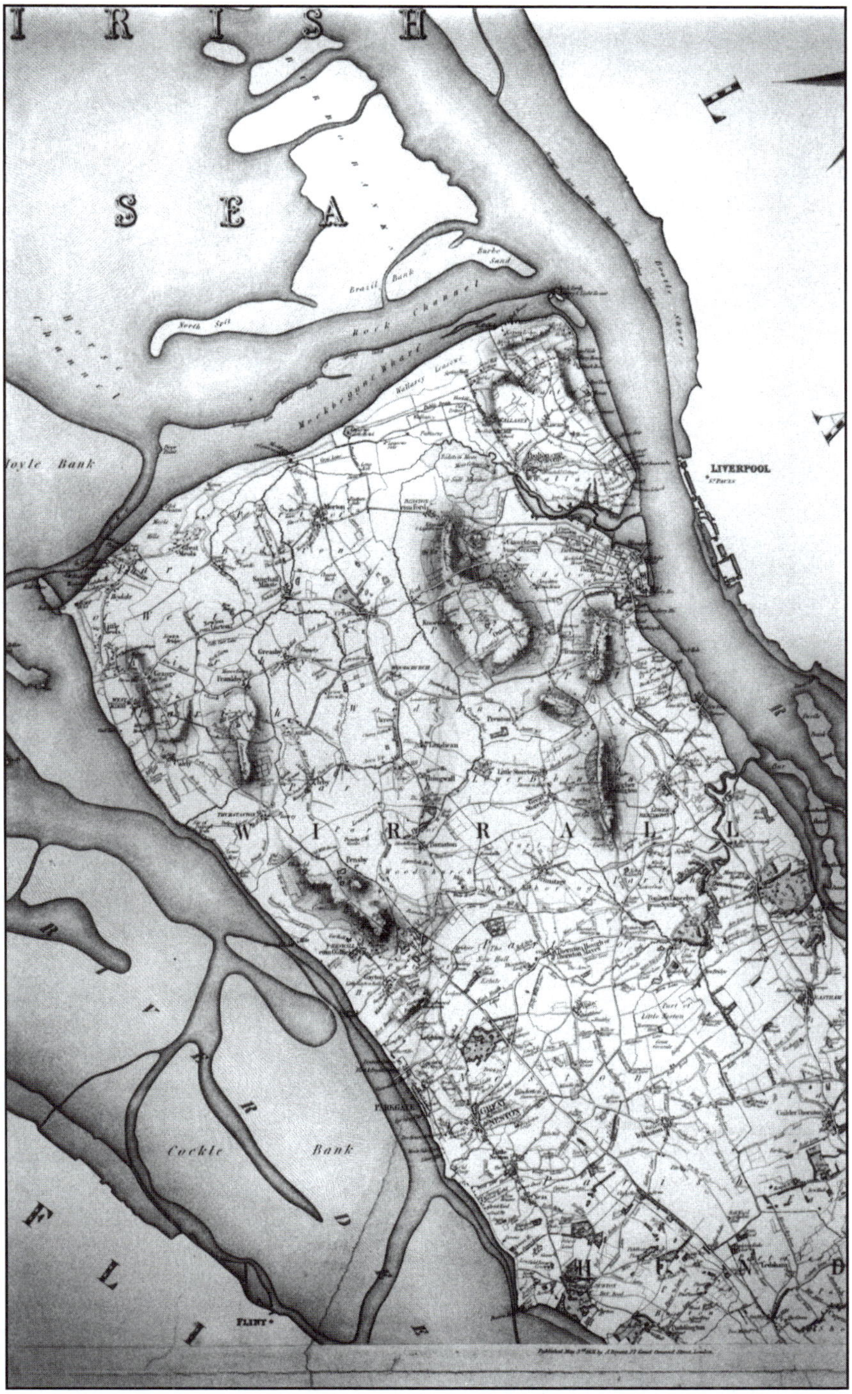


**Figure 7**: Larger-scale Bryant map showing the channels of the River Dee in 1831. Courtesy of Chester & Cheshire Archives & Local Studies. Dingesmere, suggested by Cavill, Harding, and Jesch to be the Thing's wetland or marsh, is believed to correspond to the shallow channel from Heswall down to Ness.

he was asserting his authority over the kings and waterways of those areas which most recently had fomented rebellion against the English crown. The trip along the Dee at Chester would then have been refreshing Celtic memories of what happened a short distance downstream 46 years previously (see further Cavill's "Note," below).

*The Wirral carrs and holms: Meols*

There is another candidate location for *Dingesmere*. There are fifty-one ancient field- or track-names in Wirral with the element *carr*, ultimately from the ON *kjarr* [marsh, or brushwood]. There are a further twenty-four names containing the element *holm*, ultimately from ON *holmr* [an island or useable area in a marsh], a notable example being Lingham (*lyngholmr*) at SJ252910.[28] All the carrs, and all but four of the holms lie between Bebington and Meols in the flood plains of the Rivers Birket and Fender (Figure 8). Parts of north Wirral have been subject to inundation throughout the centuries, and this was so until the twentieth-century construction of sea defenses. This flooding has led to the modern local tradition that the famous story of King Canute trying to repulse the sea actually might have taken place here.[29] The early part of the nineteenth century saw the erection of a "Canute chair," which survived until 1950.[30] An alternative to a coastal *Dingesmere* on the Dee (since a wetland is only rarely coastal) might therefore be flooded marshland around the Fender and Birket, between Thingwall and the north Wirral coast: Anlaf's men might be trying to get to Meols, the ancient Roman seaport revived by Wirral's Scandinavian community. This would be consistent with the suggestion that here the fleeing raiders would expect to find vessels to escape in, even if they were not their own.[31]

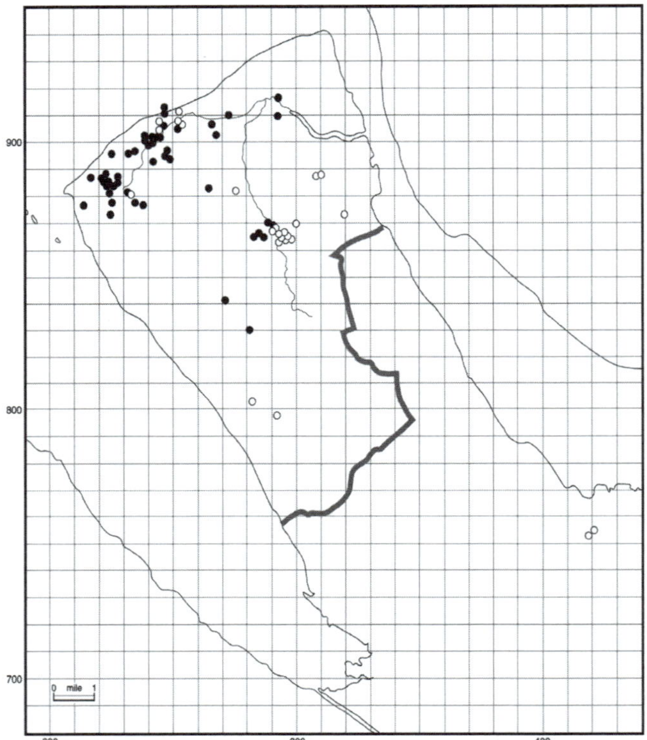


**Figure 8**: Distribution map of field/track names in *carr* (filled circles) and *holm* (open circles). Courtesy of the English Place-Name Society.

[28] Harding, "Wirral Carrs and Holms," pp. 46–49.

[29] Cavill, Harding, and Jesch, *Wirral and Its Viking Heritage*, pp. 120–22.

[30] Ormerod, *History of the County*, p. 473n1.

[31] Higham, "Context," p. 155.

## CONCLUSION

In summary, on the premise that Brunanburh in the contemporary Old English poem is the same place as the modern Bromborough, and with the recent identification of Dingesmere in the poem with the "the wetland or marshland of the Thing," we can make informed suggestions as to possible sites for the battle and the place of escape for the marauding forces. Bearing in mind the large scale of the conflict and the likelihood the fighting would have taken place over a wide area, two possible sites for the battle — or at least the main part of the fighting — have emerged: Wargraves and Bebington Heath. Two coastal locations for Dingesmere have also been considered: Heswall Point and Meols. Two possible sites for Bruna's fortress have also been discussed: the former Bromborough Court House, where the River Dibbin joins the Mersey, and Poulton Hall, positioned between the two Bruna townships in modern Bromborough parish of Bromborough and Brimstage. Other possible sites for any of these cannot be ruled out, but as yet no evidence for alternatives has been advanced. Narrowing down of the possibilities in this way may also help the field archaeologist although the chances of finding significant remains would appear to be remote. Tudsbery reported the discovery of many bones of unknown age in Storeton Hall garden, Brimstage Hall and moat, and bones and arrow-heads in Lower Bebington Church around 1870: these may be significant, but we have no modern analysis of the evidence.[32]

Finally, in January 2005 a group of ten hardy enthusiasts, including two contributors to this book and several members of the re-enactment society (the Wirhalh Skip Felag, dressed in contemporary clothing), retraced a possible route of retreat of the Dublin raiders. The 12 km (7.5 mile) route started at Poulton Hall, through Bebington Heath and then up Storeton Hill (possibly near Anlaf's base), through the woods onto Red Hill Road, past the historic Storeton Hall (ancient home of the Stanley family). From there they cut though the woods connecting Storeton with Thingwall. Emerging from the woods, passing Cross Hill, the possible Scandinavian Thing site, they passed the Barnston *gil* (ON dip or ravine), to refreshment at the Fox and Hounds in Barnston. This was then followed by a field hike to Heswall Slack (ON *slakki* [cutting]), and down to Heswall Point (now known as Sheldrakes), and finally, after a six-hour trek, past Sheldrakes restaurant to the wetland/marshland of *Dingesmere*. They fought no desperate rearguard action against enemies, and there was no need for escape to Dublin, but at a comfortable pace the walk took a whole day. As they retired to the local hostelry,

> the sun, up
> in the morningtide, that splendid light,
> glided over the ground — God's bright candle! —
> . . . the eternal Lord's noble creature
> sank to its seat. (Item 4.13–17)[33]

---

[32] Tudsbery, *Brunanburh*, pp. 22–23.

[33] The author thanks Dr. Paul Cavill, Professor Judith Jesch, Dr. David Griffiths, and Dr. Rob Philpott for helpful comments, and also Mr. Allan Alsbury, author of *Fir Bob Land* (Birkenhead: Countyvise Limited, 1999), and Mrs. June Lancelyn Green concerning some aspects of folklore. The views expressed are those of the author.

A NOTE ON THE DEE-ROWING OF EDGAR IN 973
Paul Cavill

Two articles have recently been published on this episode. David E. Thornton ("Edgar and the Eight Kings") argues the John of Worcester misunderstood Ælfric's phrase about the submission of the "eight" kings of Britain to Edgar, "hi ealle gebugon to Eadgares wissunge" [they all submitted to Edgar's rule].[34] According to Thornton, John took the naval situation as the backdrop and interpreted *gebugon* as something like "bent (at the oars)" and *Eadgares wissunge* as "Edgar's steering (at the tiller)." At any rate, this notion of the Dee-rowing appears to be John's invention, and in view of John's weaknesses in understanding Old English evident from his distortion of the poem on Brunanburh, this is entirely plausible as the source of the episode.

The second article, by Julia Barrow ("Chester's Earliest Regatta?"), gives important parallels from European sources for peace meetings and submissions taking place in neutral territory such as on rivers or bridges. However, Barrow's argument that this was a companionable affair, more of a regatta than a submission, depends on the supposition that in the *Anglo-Saxon Chronicle* phrase "ealle wið hine getreowsodon þæt hi woldon efenwyrhtan beon on sæ [ond] on lande" [they all pledged to him that they would be helpers/fellow workers by sea and on land],[35] the words "wið hine" "leave open the possibility that all seven swore the same oath" and that "they were making a treaty as equals rather than acknowledging the overlordship of Edgar."[36] This is not the case: *getreowsian* [to pledge oneself] takes the preposition *wið* plus the accusative (here *hine*, i.e., Edgar) to indicate the person to whom submission is made.[37] The same phrase is used of the Northumbrian submission to Eadred at Tanshelf in 947, and there can be no disguising the savagery of Eadred's retribution the following year when the oaths and pledges were not kept.[38]

This broadens the context of Brunanburh. The *ASC*, version D, locates important tenth-century political maneuverings of the English kings in relation to the Celtic kings in the north-west: the 926 submission at Eamont Bridge (near Penrith) and Edgar's taking submission in 973 at Chester, either side of the Brunanburh encounter, all three (if the argument made elsewhere in this volume is accepted) in the north-west. Barrow has helpfully indicated that the peaceful meetings have a ritual function and the place is significant. Perhaps the 973 submission was not as explicitly humiliating as John of Worcester's rowing episode would make it, but the Dee was not merely a convenient site for the day's events: it was, within living memory, the place where the Celtic and Norse forces *were* humiliated at Brunanburh and therefore a timely reminder of the consequences of rebellion.

---

[34] Text and translation from Lapidge, *Cult of St Swithun*, pp. 606–07.

[35] See s.a. 972 for 973, *Anglo-Saxon Chronicle* [MS D], ed. Cubbin, p. 46.

[36] Barrow, "Chester's Earliest Regatta?" pp. 89, 92–93.

[37] Bosworth and Toller, *Anglo-Saxon Dictionary*: *Supplement*, *sub verbum*.

[38] *Anglo-Saxon Chronicle* [MS D], ed. Cubbin, p. 44.

Richard Coates

# The Sociolinguistic Context of Brunanburh

The systematic reader of this book will already know that there has been debate over many decades about where the Battle of Brunanburh, commemorated in poetry in the *Anglo-Saxon Chronicle* (Item 4 in this volume) and mentioned briefly in other many other sources, actually took place. Paul Cavill and Stephen Harding have shown in their essays, to my mind convincingly, that the only serious candidate for the battle-site is Bromborough in Wirral (see also the works cited in footnote 10 below). My purpose here is to take that identification for granted, to explore the evidence revealed, chiefly in place-names, for the linguistic history of this area, and to relate that evidence to the battle, its background, and its consequences.

The north-western part of Wirral, formerly in the county of Cheshire, now in the metropolitan county of Merseyside, has one of the most complex linguistic histories in England. The purpose of this work is to disentangle it, refine what is known, and comment on the sociolinguistic status enjoyed by the relevant languages, especially at the time of the battle in the early tenth century and subsequently. The evidence to be assessed comes from place-names, an Irish chronicle and, to a lesser extent, local dialect.

The oldest layer of place-naming identified by John McNeal Dodgson (in *PN Ch*) is Proto-Welsh. It will be shown that some of the evidence previously claimed in support of this view is really, however, early Middle Irish. The second layer is Old English, which is relatively uncontentious, but its relation to Scandinavian naming needs to be discussed. It will be shown that some names claimed as Old English are in fact equally, or more, likely to be Scandinavian, at least in some sense. The third layer is represented by a simultaneous deposit of Old Scandinavian and Middle Irish, which can be understood as the result of a documented invasion and controlled landtaking by Vikings in the first decade of the tenth century. An assessment will be made of what sociolinguistic conditions permitted the exercise of the naming function in two different languages, when, in the light of later dialect developments, it is clear that Scandinavian must have been the language of everyday activity, or perhaps even the local lingua franca; Scandinavian usage was clearly intense.

It has been claimed by Gillian Fellows-Jensen that the Irish and Norse evidence permits the view that the Viking invasion contained an element from the Isle of Man.[1] This claim will be assessed briefly. The significance of names apparently referring to Danes and Franks or Frenchmen will also be assessed.

## Academic Sources of Evidence

Firstly, we need to consider the place-name evidence. The groundwork is presented in Dodgson's *PN Ch*, and in some preparatory studies published mostly in advance of the first

[1] See, e.g., Fellows-Jensen, "Anthroponymical Specifics" and "Scandinavian Settlement."

volume of this work.[2] The multi-volume work contains all the essential material, and where a claim about linguistic forms serving as evidence is made in this paper without chapter and verse, the spellings are to be found at the appropriate place in it (mainly volume 4, published in 1972). Despite his subtle use of the material, I do not agree with all his conclusions. I shall also refer frequently to the work of Fellows-Jensen on Scandinavian personal and place-names and their distribution and significance in the islands.[3]

*Wirral Place-Names Testifying to a Welsh Presence*

The oldest identifiable layer of place-naming in Wirral is Welsh. There is a thin scattering of names of Brittonic or Welsh origin over the whole of Cheshire (with a concentration near to the current boundary with Wales). There ought therefore to be nothing special to say about Wirral, since what goes for Wirral goes in principle for the rest of the county too. I shall pay attention to those in Wirral only because several of them are not certain to be what they have been claimed to be, and an alternative view of those will have repercussions for a proper understanding of the tenth-century situation. So let us deal with them first. They are shown on Map 1, but for some mysterious reason the best candidate name, which I shall discuss immediately, is absent from the original version of the map; the crudity of my calligraphy draws attention to it.

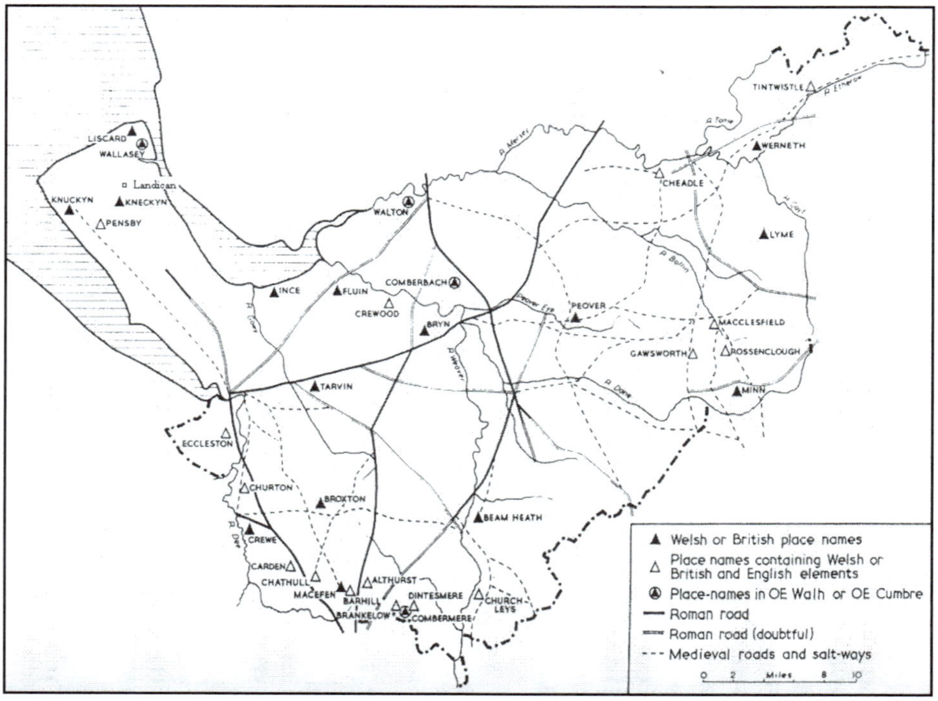


**Map 1**. Welsh place-names in Cheshire. Reprinted courtesy of the Historic Society of Lancashire and Cheshire.

---

[2] Dodgson, "Background," "Old-Irish Placename," "English Arrival," and "Welsh Element."

[3] The evidence relating to major place-names in Wirral is also conveniently presented, with some updating, in Cavill, Harding, and Jesch, eds., *Wirral and Its Viking Heritage*.

The only ancient Welsh place-name securely identified in Wirral is that of the township of Landican in Woodchurch parish. Current scholarship takes it to consist of Proto-Welsh (PrW) **lann* [church-site], with a personal name spellable as *Tecan*, i.e. /te'gan/, which may or may not be a saint's name (*PN Ch* 4.266–67). Names in such constructions usually are, but no such saint is known, and place-names like this in Wales occasionally contain the name of a private person. Dodgson, following Melville Richards (apparently private correspondence), rejected an older alternative view that it commemorated one Dagan, a seventh-century saint-bishop of Ennereilly, Wicklow, Ireland, since the <g> in this name represents a voiced velar fricative, and no Welsh borrowing of it at any historic period would be likely to yield a plosive in the modern name.[4]

Dodgson analyzes the first element of the hybrid name *Pensby* as being PrW *penn* [head; used in names for hills]; Pensby would therefore be a Scandinavian name meaning "farmstead at the place called (by the English using its original Welsh name) *Penn*" (*PN Ch* 4.271). This seems quite possible. It therefore contains a Welsh name which is now lost in its original application — no hill called *Penn* (the word never actually *meant* "hill") exists in Wirral at present. A similar case may be that of Carnsdale in Barnston, Woodchurch parish, with PrW *carn* [cairn] as the first element of an essentially Scandinavian name, but this is less secure.[5] Also doubtful is the identification of the first element of the field-name *Wirloons* in Frankby (Caldy parish) with Welsh *gwern* [alder(-swamp)] on the strength of a form of 1454 *the Werne Londes*; the same document has *Werle* (*PN Ch* 4.286). This element may however be found elsewhere in Cheshire.

There is a further English-language name which indicates the presence of Welsh people, namely *Wallasey*, whose earlier name, for which a typical spelling is *Waley*, reveals that it probably meant "island of the Welsh." This might imply that it became a refuge for Welsh people driven out of mainland Wirral by the original English colonization, and separated from mainland Wirral by the ancestor of the watercourse now known as The Fender; or it might mean that the incoming Angles never got as far as colonizing this remote and detached corner. The modern name *Wallasey* is a pleonastic expansion of the original, amounting to "Waley's *ey*" [Waley's island] (*PN Ch* 4.323–34). Or, less redundantly, if the name *Waley* had become attached to an inhabited site rather than to the island itself, then the new island name is "island of the site called *Waley*."

*Prenton*, a township of Woodchurch, is taken by Dodgson to contain the historically-attested nickname *Præn* belonging to an eighth-century Kentish earl who was mutilated on the orders of Cœnwulf, king of Mercia (*PN Ch* 4.272). It would not necessarily refer to that earl himself, of course. This suggestion poses a problem, because one would expect **Prenston* with a genitive suffix on the first element, in line with the overwhelmingly dominant pattern of such names; the form *Prestune* found in *Domesday Book* suggests confusion with the frequent name *Preston* rather than a garble of **Prenes-tūn* as Dodgson claims. A thirteenth-

[4] I defended, wrongly as I now think, the older view in the conference paper ("Sociolinguistics of North-western Wirral") which was a precursor to this chapter. The only purpose in mentioning this fact is that my earlier opinion was cited by Cavill, Harding, and Jesch (*Wirral and Its Viking Heritage*, p. 137, under *Landican*), with a reference to the paper as forthcoming. But it was never published in that form after all. That said, the Wirral place-name *Saughall* (*PN Ch* 4.321–22) is pronounced with /g/ for a historic fricative, but this seems to be a late spelling-pronunciation.

[5] Fellows-Jensen, *Scandinavian Settlements*, p. 367.

century spelling in *Premp-* found in a surname may suggest something entirely different and uncertain. It is the *lectio difficilior*, but it is also unique in the medieval record and I avoid discussion of it here.[6] With due allowance made for this, one might suspect the first element of *Prenton* to be the ancestor of Welsh *pren* [tree, wood].

It is not known how long any distinctive Welsh presence survived. There are at least two other names containing a Welsh personal name in the south-west of Wirral, but they are likely to be very much later, even modern. There was a *Granowes Fielde* in 1592 in Burton-in-Wirral, Shotwick Park, analysed by Dodgson as commemorating a man whose Welsh name was *Gronw/ Goronwy*, and a late thirteenth century *Iagowesmedwe* in Great Meols, from *Iago* (*PN Ch* 5.2.367). In Woodbank township in Shotwick lay land held by Adam *le Waleys* [the Welshman] in 1284.[7]

The site of the Battle of Brunanburh itself seems to have had a Welsh name, *Tybrunawc*, probably a purely literary and rather artificial rendering of the English name, something like "*Brun*-ious house."[8]

Also in Wirral were the names *Kne(c)kyn* and *Knukyn*, lost places respectively in Caldy and Irby townships. Dodgson analyses these as descending from Welsh *cnycyn* [little hill] (this is printed in error as *cyncyn*; *PN Ch* 5.2.293). The Celtic root of this word is **knokk-* meaning "boss, knuckle" or the like. Welsh *cnwc* appears to be a copying from fairly recent Irish (Modern Irish pron. /knuk/), and *cnycyn* is therefore a modern derivative. There is no strong phonological reason why the Wirral names cannot be for Irish *cnoicín*, and the significance of this will be explored later. *Knockeen* is a frequent Irish place-name. Although in Manx the *-an* suffix is generally preferred and the corresponding word in later Manx is *crongan*, George Broderick accepts that the Manx place-name *Knockean* may be a form corresponding to the Irish one cited, and fossilized in English prior to the change of [n] → [r] in certain environments which characterizes other Manx names.[9]

A case has been made that *Liscard* is also Welsh, but the claim is demonstrably false and I shall return to it below. I believe that it too is Irish in origin.

The ground has now been cleared, and there will be no further reference to Welsh-language activity in Wirral.

*Wirral Place-Names Testifying to an English Presence*

In common with the situation in most of the rest of England, any other Welsh names which might have existed have been obliterated by an overlay of English ones, such as *Saughall*, *Leighton*, *Woodchurch*, *Heswall*, *Bebington*, and *Bromborough*. No further attention will be paid to unambiguously English names, except to note that Bromborough is almost certainly *Brunanburh*, for reasons spelt out in this book in abundance.[10]

---

[6] For full analysis of some similar spellings in <mp> for names with probable historic /n/ in Lincolnshire, see Coates, "Reflections," under *Panton* and *Ponton*.

[7] *PN Ch* 5.2.364. I cannot tell what is meant on the map at *PN Ch* 5.2.356 by a symbol in Wirral indicating an "English place-name with a Welsh alternative."

[8] Breeze, "Welsh Tradition"; see Haycock, p. 181 in this volume, and Bollard, p. 206n60.

[9] Broderick, *Placenames of the Isle of Man*, 3.138, 7.132–33. Names with *cronkyn* are alluded to by the indexes to Broderick's books, embedded in discussion of the many *cronk* names.

[10] Other candidates are identified in Campbell, *Battle of Brunanburh*, pp. 57–80, for instance, but, following Dodgson, "Background of Brunanburh," opinion has hardened in favor of Bromborough, for a range of reasons; see Higham, "Context of *Brunanburh*" (against Wood, "Brunanburh Re-

*Wirral Place-Names Testifying to a Scandinavian Presence*

The particular interest in Wirral, and the main point of this chapter, resides in a layer of post-English names. Several are clearly Scandinavian in their entirety.[11] These names include *Meols* in West Kirby [sandhills], *Raby* in Neston [boundary farmstead, on whose significance see below], two instances of *Kir(k)by* [church farmstead or churchtown], the lost *Hesby* in Bidston [ash farmstead], *Tranmere* in Bebington [crane sandhills], the lost *Routheholm* [red marsh-island] in Wallasey,[12] *Lingdale* [heather valley] in Oxton, Woodchurch; and probably the following containing a Scandinavian personal name: *Arno* [Arni's burial-mound] in Oxton; and finally *Irby*, about which, again, more will be said later. These are sufficient to guarantee that Scandinavian was a language of everyday activity, including name-bestowal, at some stage in the history of Wirral. A preliminary analysis of these names by Dodgson is represented on Map 2, and an updated one on Map 3, but what it represents will not survive unscathed.

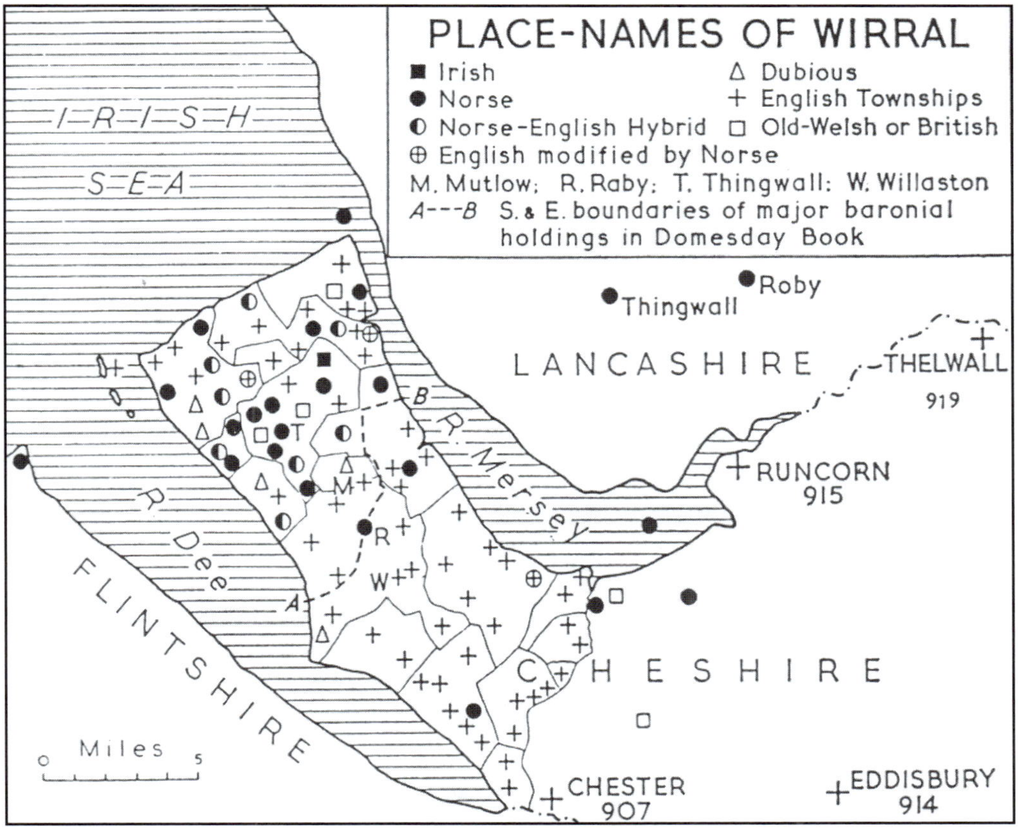


**Map 2**. Place-names of Wirral. From Dodgson, "Background of Brunanburh"; reprinted courtesy the Viking Society for Northern Research.

visited"); Cavill, Harding, and Jesch, *Wirral and Its Viking Heritage*; and Coates, "Further Snippet."

[11] See Dodgson, *PN Ch*, *s.nn.*, and the Scandinavian background is thoroughly rehearsed by Fellows-Jensen, "Scandinavians in Cheshire," and Jesch, "Scandinavian Wirral."

[12] Gelling, "Scandinavian Settlement," p. 192.

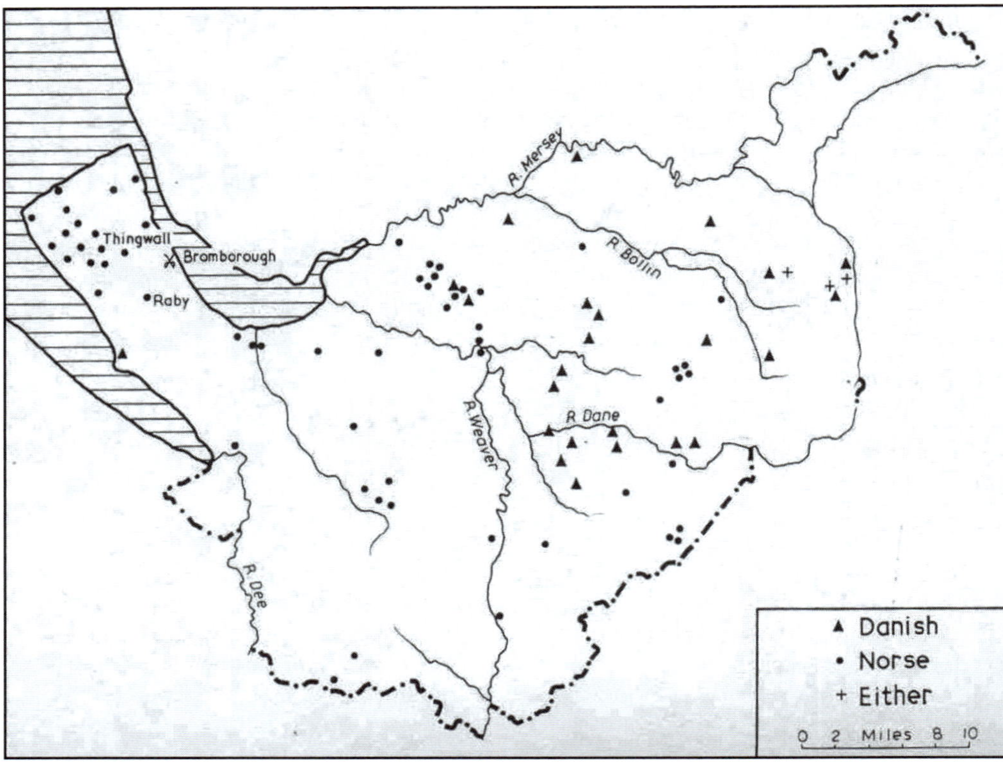


**Map 3**. Scandinavian-influenced place-names in Cheshire. Courtesy the Historic Society of Lancashire and Cheshire.

There are also some names on which, as a type, the history of scholarship has had a distorting effect. These are names which may be of English origin, but which are claimed to have undergone Scandinavianization; the tendency has been for such names to have been presumed to be originally English even where the evidence is at best ambiguous. For instance, this has been claimed for *Gayton* in Heswall [goat farm], on the presumption that the second element is OE *tūn* [farm] and the first Scandinavian *geit* [goat], presumably replacing OE *gāt*. This needs some commentary. There was of course an Old English word *tūn* meaning "farm," and it is the commonest of all English place-name elements. But there was an ON word *tún* of the same phonological form and with a compatible range of meanings. (I shall write *tun* without a diacritic where it is desirable not to prejudice the reader into viewing the word in question as either Old English or Scandinavian.) It has generally been argued, for instance by A. Hugh Smith, that names with a Scandinavian first element and *tun* as the second are "hybrids," on two sorts of grounds:[13]

1. that the documentary record for some of these names shows the replacement of Scandinavian *bý* by *tun* long after Scandinavian had ceased to be spoken in the relevant

[13] *English Place-Name Elements* 2.192–93. The concept "hybrid" is problematic, even incoherent, but this is not the place for a critique. See Cox, "Questioning."

area. It is therefore argued that the active replacing element must be the Old or Middle English word, not the Scandinavian one. Furthermore, *tún* is exceptionally rare as a place-name element in the East-Scandinavian speaking regions of Denmark and South Sweden (Scania) from which Scandinavian settlers in the Danelaw are generally assumed to have come, and some simplex names of the form *Tune* may be new coinings in the wake of administrative reorganization at the end of the first millennium.[14]

2. that, more crucially for our purposes here, Scandinavianization of specifiers is also found. Given that the number of *tun* names in the island of Britain with Scandinavian first elements is small, it has been argued that one should assume that these Scandinavian elements replace corresponding native English ones — this would mean for example that the place called *Stainton* [stone farm] in the West Riding of Yorkshire originated in a form which would give Modern English *Stanton* if it had not passed through the mouths of Scandinavian-speakers in around the ninth century.

To recap: it is therefore claimed that apparently hybrid names in *tun* fall into two types; those where a Scandinavian generic element is replaced by an English one, and those where an English name receives a Scandinavianized specifier. The standard view as I have just presented it does not amount to a watertight position, but it is not a priori unreasonable, and we can allow it for the sake of argument insofar as it applies to the Danelaw. It is bolstered by the existence of so-called *Toton*-"hybrids" (formerly misleadingly known as *Grimston*-"hybrids"), which have a Scandinavian personal name as their first element and what is believed to be OE *tūn* as their second. However, the problem looks different from the perspective of early Cheshire. Cheshire was not part of the Danelaw, and we need to know what sort of Scandinavians could have been responsible for namegiving in Wirral.

The township of Storeton in Bebington has a name transparently including Scandinavian *stór-* [big, no English alternative comes to mind] and the word *tun*, so we need quite powerful arguments to stop us believing that it is not a purely Scandinavian name meaning "big farm."[15] We have seen that such a name is unlikely to be Danish, and the likelihood diminishes still further in the light of evidence to be presented below. But if it were Norwegian rather than Danish, we would not need to believe in an English reformation of some older name like **Storebý*. West-Scandinavian place-names in *tún* do in fact exist, for instance the saga-period *Túnir* and *Túnsberg* in Norway and *Túngarðr* in Iceland.[16] On the modern map, there are names with *tun* as a second element in both Norway and Iceland; note *Fortun* in the fylke or county of Sogn og Fjordane in Norway and *Ártún* high in Geitadal in eastern Iceland.[17] *Sigtúnir*

[14] Fellows-Jensen, "To Divide the Danes," p. 45, citing T. Andersson, "*Tuna*-problem," and Hyenstrand, *Centralbygd – Randbygd*, p. 103. There are special problems concerning the dating and significance of Swedish names with the special additionally-suffixed form *-tuna*; see also Holmberg, *De Svenska* Tuna-*namnen*.

[15] Smith, despite his enthusiasm for hybrids, in effect acknowledges the latter fact (*English Place-Name Elements* 2.193).

[16] Notably with *tún* always as specifier; for early names in Norway, see Rygh, *Norske*, p. 82.

[17] Rygh (*Norske*, pp. 81–82) claims that *tun* as a second element is confusable with *tó* "Græsplet." Lárusson, "Ísland," pp. 66–68) claims that all the tiny places named with such names in Iceland are post-Viking.

in Sweden was outside Scania. It is generally conceded that *tún* is not found as an element in the Scandinavian toponymy of the Western and Northern Isles. W. F. H. Nicolaisen notes that the several Orkney names in modern *-ton* (for instance *Herston*, South Ronaldsay) are derived from Scand. *stǫðum*, the dative plural form of *stað-* [place, dwelling].[18] Scottish mainland and island names such as *Plockton* (Wester Ross), *Milton* (Applecross, Wester Ross), *Kirkton* (Lochalsh, Wester Ross) and *Middleton* (Tiree) are probably Scots.[19]

But evidence that would be most impressive, if it were credible, has been offered that we find some such names in the Isle of Man. The old name for Peel was *Hólmtún*, according to J. J. Kneen, a clearly Scandinavian creation involving the word *holmr/holmi* [island], referring to St. Patrick's Isle, and *tún*.[20] Kneen appears to say that there is an ancient record of the name in this form; I have not however discovered it, and it is not mentioned by Broderick.[21] Kneen also cites a form from a bull of Pope Gregory IX dating from 1231, *Holme Towen* (correctly "le Holme towne"), though the form as cited appears to be later. If these could be taken at face value, they represent the clearest possible evidence for *tún* being in everyday use in an environment where one of the languages is known to have been Scandinavian — that is, long before English was a significant force in local namegiving. However, the oldest attestation of the name offered by Broderick is of 1417, after the arrival of English interest in Man in 1405.[22] If this new face value does not deceive, the older name of Peel is Middle English rather than Scandinavian. This name is an important element in assessing whether *tun* names in Wirral are (a) translated from or amended from English, or (b) Scandinavian, taking into account further historical evidence that I shall discuss a little later.

Other names in *tún* were identified in Man by Kneen: *Glayton* in Kirk Christ Rushen[23] and *Brystone* in Kirk Christ Lezayre, but Broderick rejects the identification.[24] C. J. S. Marstrander suggested that *Milntown* in Kirk Christ Lezayre was for Scand. *mylnu-tún*, but Broderick believes that it is English, with parallels in English toponymy in Ireland.[25] Marstrander rejected the detail of Kneen's etymologies but accepted that Glayton and Brystone were probably names in *tún*.[26] Broderick's general notes, however, suggest that he believes *tún* is

[18] Nicolaisen, *Scottish Place-Names*, p. 116.

[19] No attention is drawn to any names in *tun* in the Western Isles by Cox in his work on "hybridity" ("Questioning" and "*Allt Loch Dhaile Beaga*").

[20] Kneen, *Place-Names of the Isle of Man*, p. 404. Kneen's form is suspicious, and it is surely his etymology for the later name rather than a documented form; the entry for Peel is garbled. Hólmtún is not mentioned in Moore, "Bull of Pope Gregory IX."

[21] Broderick, *Placenames of the Isle of Man* 1.298 and 7.147.

[22] Broderick, *Placenames of the Isle of Man* 1.298.

[23] Kneen, *Place-Names of the Isle of Man*, p. 37; this appears certain, though the first element is doubtful — Broderick's ongoing work does not yet cover this parish.

[24] Kneen, *Place-Names of the Isle of Man*, p. 508; Broderick, *Placenames of the Isle of Man*, 3.378 rejects this in favor of a bungling of English *Dry Stone*, the earliest form in the record being exactly that. See also Broderick, *Dictionary*, p. 182.

[25] Marstrander, "Det Norske Landnåm på Man," p. 254; Broderick, *Placenames of the Isle of Man*, 3.435–36.

[26] Marstrander, "Det Norske Landnåm på Man," pp. 117–18, 245.

absent from Manx toponymy, and therefore, for caution's sake, we shall not build on the apparent evidence just discussed.[27]

If the presumption in the Danelaw is that names in *tun* with Scandinavian first elements are or may be English renamings of Scandinavian-named places, then I submit that, irrespective of the evidence from Man, the opposite presumption should at least be entertained in Wirral: that such names are Scandinavian inventions. This allows Storeton, where we started this part of the discussion, and Claughton, Larton and Gayton, with indisputably Scandinavian first elements, to be Scandinavian names, and pushes the possibility that Barnston in Woodchurch was farmed not by an English Beornwulf but by a Scandinavian Bjǫrnulf;[28] likewise that Thurstaston was named for a Scandinavian Þorsteinn, not an Englishman bearing a fashionable Scandinavian name.[29] These two names are therefore not necessarily *Toton*-hybrids (see above). It is possible to tilt the balance too far in the opposite direction, though; we must acknowledge that Bebington, Moreton, and Upton are clearly English names in the middle of all this Scandinavian debris, and may have been there when Scandinavian arrived. Some cases will remain in principle undecidable, for example Neston, Oxton, and Thornton, for which phonologically indistinguishable English and Scandinavian etymologies could be provided.

The fact that English names could indeed by influenced by Scandinavian speech is illustrated by *Birkenhead*, for which an obsolete variant *Birket* existed. Birkenhead is Old English [birch head(land)], but the /k/ betrays Scandinavian influence; Birket shows this also, and additionally has a generic descending from Scand. **havuð*, later *hǫfuð* [head], rather than English *hēafod*, if the earliest attestation is taken at face value (*PN Ch* 4.313–14). The modern form of *Tranmere* shows obscuration of its Scandinavian etymology in *mel-* [dune] or **mal(u)-* [pebbly beach] in favor of a (late) suggestion of OE *mere* [pond]. Some names also show Scand. *bý-* [farm] replacing the English element *byrig* [(at the) fort] during the historic, post-1066, record; these are *Greasby* in West Kirby, earlier OE *Græfesbyrig*, *Whitby* divided between Eastham and Stoke parishes, earlier apparently OE *Hwitbyrig*, and perhaps in parallel fashion *Irby* in Woodchurch, but I am less confident about that, and generally a little skeptical about the apparent existence of so many (evidently minor) fortified sites in a small area; the one undoubted fortification-name, *Bromborough*, shows no sign of such Scandinavianization. All this suggests on balance that the partial replacement or transformation of English names did indeed take place, and warns us of the risk of overemphasizing Scandinavian name-creation in the region.

Perhaps the scenario which most adequately accommodates all the facts presented above is as follows. *Tún* was probably not a place-name element in the earliest West Scandinavian. But it was a lexical word with the meaning "farmyard." When the Scandinavians arrived, they found such pre-existing English place-names as *Poulton* (x2), *Leighton*, and *Hooton*, which would have been semi-transparent to them. They either copied OE *tūn* as a place-name forming element, or copied it as a lexical word and applied it themselves on the Old English model in their own place-names such as *Claughton*, *Larton*, *Storeton*, and *Gayton*. This obviates the need to believe in either re-anglicization of such hypothetical names as **Storebý* or

[27] *Santon* is undoubtedly for the saint's name *San(c)tan* (Kneen, *Place-Names of the Isle of Man*, p. 133).

[28] On this personal name, compare Fellows-Jensen, *Scandinavian Personal Names*, pp. 55–56.

[29] Although this particular place-name admittedly shows traces of anglicization in some attestations; see *PN Ch* 4.279–80.

English copying of Scandinavian lexical words that do not show up in modern dialect vocabulary. The key names can be regarded as showing English substrate (or adstrate) influence on Scandinavian; recall that this area was administratively Scandinavian and their language was the probable lingua franca.[30] There is no reason to believe that influence between English and Scandinavian was unidirectional, nor that it was the same over the whole country.

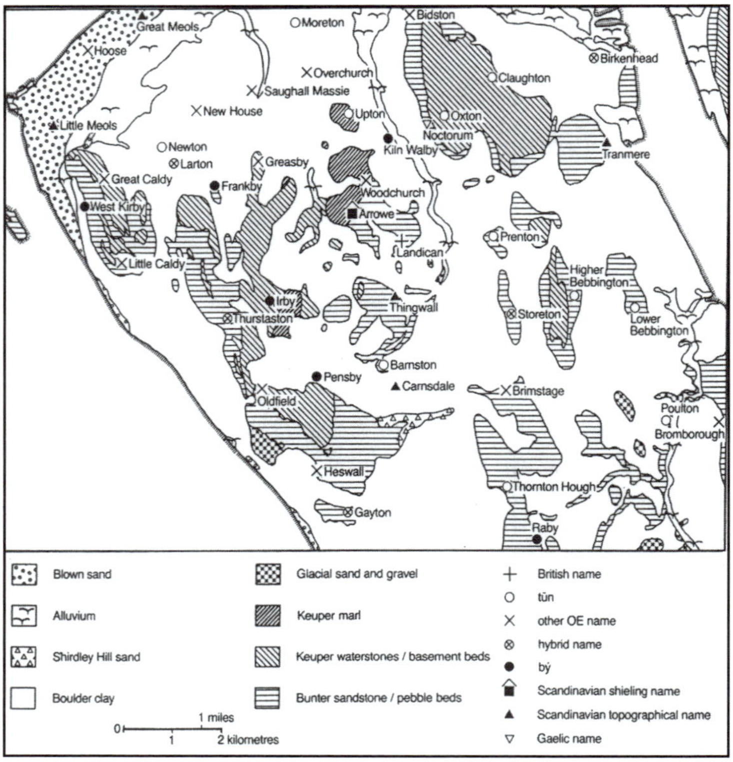


**Map 4**. Geology of the Wirral. From Fellows-Jensen, *Scandinavian Settlements*, map 22; reprinted courtesy C. A. Reitzels forlag.

There are events in the historical record which allow us to be more confident than we might otherwise be that significant Norwegian input into place-naming in Wirral occurred, and we can be much more precise about the date at which such names are likely to have been formed. There is an Irish source preserved in a late copy in the royal library in Brussels, entitled *Three Fragments of Irish Annals*.[31] The third fragment informs us that a party of Scandinavians under the effective leadership of Ingimund arrived in Wirral in 902. They came in the aftermath of the death of King Alfred three years previously, perhaps expecting

[30] This suggestion is at variance with the proposal in the ancestor of this chapter, as originally delivered at a conference in 1998, that *tun* in these names was indeed the Scandinavian word ("Sociolinguistics of North-western Wirral"). I have concluded that the evidence for onomastic *tún* in Norse is harder to sustain than I first thought.

[31] Wainwright, "Ingimund's Invasion"; first published in 1860 by O'Donovan.

easy pickings, and were granted permission to settle. After a few years, they became discontented with the land that they had been granted, which can be presumed to have been less productive than other land in Wirral. Map 4 shows the probably Scandinavian names *Larton* and *Pensby* on the inhospitable Boulder Clay, and by the edge of it are *Raby* and *Tranmere*. *Irby* is also on the claylands. But there is no clear relation between the language in which some name was formed and the geology of its location. Some English names are on the bad lands too: *Moreton* (as its name suggests), and *Poulton* (by Bromborough); but the dates of their coining are unknown. Perhaps the currently apparent situation reflects some redistribution amounting to a practical consequence of Ingimund's agitation. Margaret Gelling speculates that the original land-grant was nearer to Chester and that the present situation indeed shows the effect of Scandinavian movement into an "English" area.[32]

Armed with their grievance, the settlers attacked the English in their administrative center of Chester. But some of them were eventually bottled up in the old city by the forces of Æthelflæd, Alfred's daughter, and then slaughtered. Their fellows, if we are to believe the Irish account, tried to mine their way into the city, but were deterred by having boiling ale poured on them, followed by a cascade of hives full of disgruntled bees. They fled, at least temporarily. The *Fragment* breaks off here, and we do not know what happened after that from any historical source.

The *Fragment*, most interestingly, gives us details of the ethnic composition of the party that I have been referring to as Scandinavian. This party had been thrown out of Ireland in 901 ("alias 902") according to the *Annals of Ulster* and had fought battles in North Wales in 902 under "Igmunt" according to the *Annales Cambriae* and the *Brut y Tywysogion*.[33] We know that it contained Norsemen and Danes, since Ingimund, the most malcontent of Æthelflæd's grantees, persuaded "the leaders of the Norsemen and Danes" to embark on the painful adventure that I have just described. This distinction was crucial, and fatal. We are told that the party also contained many Irishmen, described in a marginal note as *dalta* [fosterlings]. Æthelflæd appealed to their Christian sensibilities against the pagan Northmen. In a classic, if crude, divide-and-rule maneuver, she persuaded them to lure the Danes in the mixed party into a trap where they were killed. If there was a strategically subtle reason for this about-turn by the Irish, we are not told; the *Fragment* just says that they were "less friends to [the Danes] than to the Northmen."[34]

We can infer from this that the settlers were ethnic Danes, Norsemen and Irish, and that they had at first enjoyed more or less equal status with each other as small farmers. Dodgson assembled evidence that the area they collectively controlled from 902 amounted to a separate fiefdom (*PN Ch* 5.2.255–57); place-names surviving to today reveal that it had a *Thingwall* or parliament-field (**Þing-wall(u)-*), and a *Raby*, or farm at a boundary (*rá*).[35]

The feudal arrangements of the Norman period confirm that north-west Wirral had a separate status, and that Raby was indeed at the boundary of this fiefdom. The boundary is shown by the bold solid line on Map 5. It does not follow that the whole of this area was devoid

---

[32] Gelling, *West Midlands*, p. 134.

[33] See Phillimore, "Annales Cambriae," p. 167; Breeze, "Welsh Tradition."

[34] Citation for *Fragment*.

[35] These names are paralleled, the latter as *Roby*, in south-west Lancashire, as has long been noted (see Wainwright, "Scandinavians in Lancashire").

of English farmers, but the Northerners appear to have held sway, at least for a time.[36] For this fiefdom to have become established suggests that the unpleasant business under the walls of Chester was a temporary setback, and that they were neither absolutely defeated, nor dispersed into a condition where they were indistinguishable from the English. In the longer run, it is believed that merger of the English and Norse communities did indeed take place, a view required by the fact that the English language survived as the dominant one, and accepted a largish Scandinavian lexical tribute into the dialect of Cheshire (recorded especially, though not annotated as such, by Robert Holland's *Glossary of Words*).

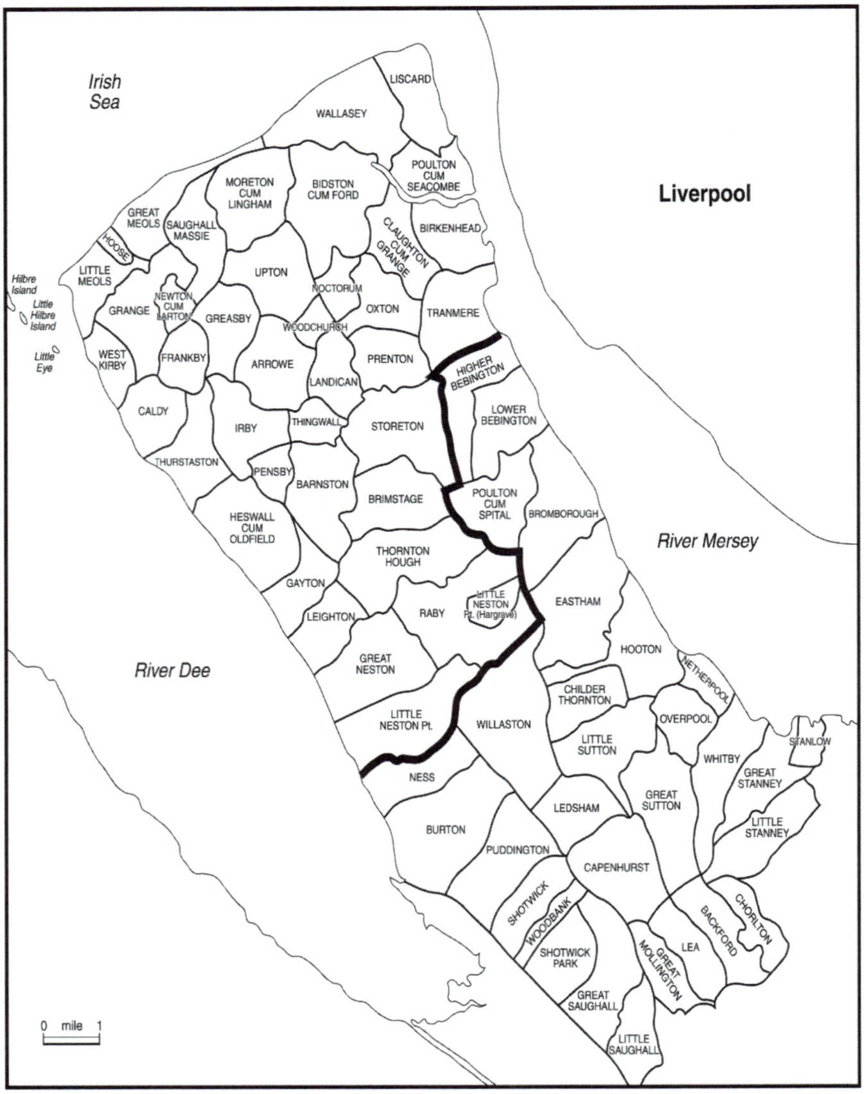


**Map 5**. Wirral parish/township map (19th century). Courtesy of Chester & Cheshire Archives & Local Studies.

[36] Compare Gelling, *West Midlands*, pp. 132–34, and "Scandinavian Settlement."

If a (partly-)Norse fiefdom existed, as the record appears to make certain, we should have even fewer qualms about interpreting the names in the region, or at least some of them, as Norse. There is no pressing reason to believe that Storeton and Claughton have been anglicized by having an English element *tūn* inserted into them, as we have seen.

The concept of a Norse place which can be identified on linguistic grounds receives some support from considering some of the other place-names of the area. One place was recognized as a Danish place: *Denhall*, either OE *Dena-wælle/a* [Danes' spring] or Scand. **Dana-wall(u)-* [Danes' grassy field/paddock] (*PN Ch* 4.220). The lack of others reminds us what happened to the Danes at the hands of the Irish. Dodgson speculates that *Lach Dennis* by Chester was that Lach which was held by a person called, or by the people called, in Old English *denisc* and in (Anglo-)Norman French *daneis* [Danish] (*PN Ch* 2.286).

*Wirral Place-Names Testifying to an Irish Presence*

Other places we can identify as Irish places. It has long been believed that *Noctorum* in Woodchurch is a fully Irish name, late Old Irish *cnocc tírim* or *tirim* [dry hillock].[37] This in itself tends strongly to confirm the general veracity of the *Three fragments* account discussed earlier. An Irish name here is no surprise. But a mere one would be disappointing. I believe others can be identified. I mentioned above that *Liscard* has been thought to be a Welsh survival, meaning "hall of the rock," as if Modern Welsh *llys y garreg*, though the form of the second word, the article, is not so much Welsh as Cumbric */in/, as witnessed by such spellings as the thirteenth-century *Lisenecark*; Welsh lost the form with /n/ early on and it survives only in such fossilized expressions as *yn awr* [now (lit. "the hour")]. However, there are three phonological problems with this solution, and I have proposed that the meaning suggested by Dodgson, "hall of the rock," is correct, but that the name is Irish, as if *lios na carraige* (to use the modern spelling).[38] This solution solves three phonological difficulties at a stroke (the form of the article, the /k/ rather than /g/ at the beginning of the final element, and the elision of the vowel of a final syllable stressed in Old Welsh), as well as the problem of accommodating a Cumbric name so far south, and it ties the name into a known cultural context.

Other place-name evidence suggests the Irish contingent in a slightly more shadowy way. There is a Scandinavian parish-name *Irby*, on the face of it meaning "Irishman's/-men's farm." The face of it may be candid; but sometimes the word *Íri* was applied either as a descriptive term or as a by-name to a Norseman who had settled and traded at Dublin or one of the other east-coast Norse colonies in Ireland.[39] There is a place-name *Arrowe*, a township of Woodchurch, which could be a Brittonic river-name of a known type, but is much more likely to be a Scandinavian word meaning "shieling, summer pasture"; if so, it testifies to the practice of seasonally-shifting stock-raising here. More specifically, it may derive from *ǽrgi*, which is Scandinavian for "halfway house shieling," but this is copied from Old or Middle Irish *áirge*.[40] Fellows-Jensen has argued that the word is always Scandinavian in early place-names in Britain outside the Scottish islands, and is inclined to dismiss the

[37] Dodgson, "Old-Irish Placename."

[38] Coates, "Liscard and Irish Names," contra Dodgson, *PN Ch*, 4.324.

[39] Compare Fellows-Jensen, *Scandinavian Settlements*, p. 16.

[40] Compare Fellows-Jensen, "Gaelic-Scandinavian Loanword," pp. 24–25, comparing the form and meaning of the Manx *eary* and the meaning of the Norwegian *heimseter*.

idea that the Wirral place-name is Irish.[41] Finally, we can revisit the two lost names *Kneckyn* and *Knuckyn*. Whilst Dodgson claims them for Welsh *cnycyn* [hillock], they may well be for Irish **cnoicín* in the same sense, not a recorded form, but entirely regularly formed with the diminutive suffix *-ín*; that would fit with the known context in which other minor names arose in Wirral. Let us note that the secure Irish names are all topographical and refer to elevated land (rather than, say, its occupational status — there are no analogues of *Dundonald* or *Ballygowan*). The *carraig* [rock] in the name of Liscard doubtless refers to the hill which was a prominent landmark overlooking the Mersey estuary before urbanization, or to one of the more local possibilities mentioned by Dodgson (*PN Ch* 4.325–26). *Noctorum* contains the word *cnocc* [hillock], and the two lost names may contain a diminutive of this. *Áirge* in its original application would by its nature denote upland. Collectively, these seem to suggest a local Irish onomastic pattern, distinct from English or Scandinavian in being exclusively topographical.

We can take it as certain, then, that West Scandinavian and Irish were in use as languages of name-bestowal in tenth-century West Wirral.

## SOCIOLINGUISTIC CONSIDERATIONS

Let us conclude with some sociolinguistic considerations, especially on relations between Norse and Irish, and with some rather bitty reflections on particular details, namely a point of Scandinavian dialect phonology and a Manx connection. Let us consider each language of the tenth-century situation in turn.

### *English*

English can be assumed to be the general background noise in the region, eventually becoming dominant because of the centralization of political power in southern England and through the failure of Danish to achieve sociopolitical pre-eminence during the Scandinavian kingships of the eleventh century. Scandinavian-speaking communities shift at unknown dates to English, which itself absorbs substantial amounts of vocabulary into both standard and non-standard lects, along with some grammatical words and inflectional morphology. There is a consequential impact on English phonotactics. All this is very well known, and does not require extensive discussion.[42]

On the face of it this is a classic shift from a language of narrower to a language of wider currency. It is often claimed that the close similarity of the two languages facilitated adstrate influences; this would entail a fluid common core vocabulary, with the perceived divergences being interpretable as ethnic markers, these being lost in due course wherever they were perceived as non-English equivalents, i.e., as marked cipherings of English expressions.[43] In that sense, the process of de-Scandinavianization would be as closely akin to standardization as to language shift. Scandinavian would have lacked any conscious maintenance as an ethnic variety. It appears, however, that English may locally have been non-dominant in the tenth century, and the shift to English will have followed a period when the perceived status of the

---

[41] Fellows-Jensen, "Gaelic-Scandinavian Loanword," p. 22, and "Common Gaelic *áirge*," p. 70.

[42] See, for instance, Baugh and Cable, *History of the English Language*, pp. 93–105; Crystal, *Stories of English*, pp. 65–77, 82–85.

[43] As argued in Coates, "Survival."

two languages was reversed and when Scandinavian was actually dominant, with English serving as the language of ethnic marking.

*Irish*

The situation of Irish in Wirral is very interesting to speculate upon. The political and social basis of Ingimund's invasion in 902 appears to require that the Irish in the party also spoke Scandinavian, since they had thrown in their lot with the Norse (and more doubtfully the Danes) as fosterlings. Everyone in the party appears to have had a modest aspiration: to farm in comfort. It is hard to imagine that these warriors with cows and ploughs employed a class of professional interpreters. Scandinavian was the language of the numerical majority, and for the Irish it must have been a second language learned as a community necessity. It must, after all, have been the language of the assembly known as the Thing, and of the fiefdom identified by Dodgson. The scattered Irish personal names found in place-names throughout central and eastern Cheshire (that is, not in Wirral) can perhaps be taken to be evidence for persons speaking Scandinavian rather than Irish, and embedded in Scandinavian-speaking networks. No Irish words have been identified in the dialect of Cheshire and few indeed have been suggested among the general Scandinavian words copied in the English of the north.[44]

But the place-name evidence precludes the simple assumption that the invasion was, in effect, linguistically Scandinavian. The use of Irish must have been an indicator of ethnicity, and possibly also of Christianity, the Scandinavians still being pagan as noted earlier; the English were able to trade on this to achieve the Irish betrayal of the Danes at the walls of Chester. Irish was used in place-name bestowal for the settlements at Noctorum and Liscard, but for none at parish level. It appears to have supplied words for small hills which may have been treated as names.[45] What is significant in assessing the relationship between Irish and Scandinavian is that these names stuck — that is, they outlasted both of the invasion languages. This appears to suggest that although the names represent the internal view of the settlements — the view of the inhabitants — they were used by Scandinavian speakers, as well as ultimately by English-speakers, as the proper names of the relevant places. It may be that *Irby* [Irishman's farm] also had an Irish name which was superseded by the present name which appears to indicate an external, Norse, view of the settlement. That the external perception was usually dominant is strikingly confirmed by the fact that Christian churches in Wirral dating from before the invasion — more likely to interest Christians, one might have thought — are referred to by a term of the language of the pagan invaders, **kirkju-bý-*, and not by an Irish word such as the ancestor of *domhnach* or *eaglais*. Bestowal of novel names in Irish evidently however had some legitimacy in the wider community, which does not suggest a classic modern relation of dominance and inferiority between the two languages. It was simply an ethnicity indicator. The extinction of Irish is likely to have had to do with lack of a distinct territorial base, small numbers of speakers, exogamy, loss of contact with Irish communities as opposed to Irish Sea trading communities, and perhaps restriction to domestic business, without the presumption that this latter condition marked

[44] Though Andrew Breeze has a series of recent notes identifying over 20, mainly in Scots; we should notice one in nearby Lancashire: Old/Middle English *beltancu* ("Irish *Beltaine*").

[45] But note the definite article in *The Kneckyn* in Caldy (1454) may suggest that the word was copied into English and applied as an English term.

it as inferior and therefore ripe for abandonment — in short, a selection including some of the classic weaknesses suggested by Ronald Wardhaugh.[46]

Irish has left no local traces in the dialect, suggesting that English speakers never heard it, or could not understand it if they did.

*Scandinavian*

Using place-name evidence in order to make judgements about the language in which places were named, English or Scandinavian, is fraught with problems. An apparently Scandinavian name is not irrefutable evidence for Scandinavian settlement and language. An instructive name in this respect is the field called *Routlothefeld* in Farndon, 15 km south of Chester. It appears to be from Scand. *rauð-* [red] and *laut* [hollow, dingle]; but if that is its real source, then we must assume that these words had passed into the general vocabulary of Cheshire folk speaking English and been compounded for use in this name, because the area around Farndon offers no other evidence, linguistic or historical, for occupation by Scandinavians.

It is also clear from Dodgson's analysis that elements of Scandinavian origin appearing in place-names are not restricted to the most obvious deeply Scandinavianized areas of the county: *carr, bosk,* and *intack* are widespread in the North Country; *flat* is actually rare in Wirral despite the appropriateness of some of the topography for its usage; and *scale* [temporary hut] is absent (*PN Ch* 5.2.230–47).

Some eighty-two Scandinavian place-name elements are identified by Dodgson in the place-name forming vocabulary of Cheshire, many not specifically topographical terms, for instance *kringla* [circle], *skamm-* [short], and *útar-* [outer, further] (*PN Ch* 5.1.255, 339, 376, respectively). Some of these recur and appear restricted to Wirral and adjacent areas, for instance *bý-* [farmstead], *deil-* [share], *rein* [boundary strip],[47] and *brekka* [slope], as well as the problematic *klint* [steep bank, rock outcrop] (*PN Ch* 5.1.124, 157, 318, 113, 254, respectively). Coupled with the historical evidence we have seen, these are indisputable evidence for the nature of the language used locally in Wirral. The general dialect vocabulary collected by Holland is less certain in this regard. His evidence is hard to tie down to specific areas, and in many cases Cheshire words of Scandinavian origin appear in not especially Scandinavian areas of the county. By the time Holland made his collection, there was a general northern vocabulary with a Scandinavian stamp on it, for instance *pace-egg* [Easter egg], *muck* [filth], and *stang* [pole]. These may be local, but may equally have spread from other Scandinavianized districts. This applies even to topographical vocabulary: we find *carrs* near Cheadle and *gate* [road into a moss] on the north side of Lindow Moss.[48] Some of Holland's words are however specific to Wirral and adjacent districts, and can be presumed to have been first applied there, for instance *reean* [furrow between two butts in a field], which continues the place-name element *rein* noted by Dodgson (*PN Ch* 5.1.318).

Even the field-name in Liscard, *Golacre*, recorded as early as 1398 as *le Goliacr'*, cannot be assumed to have been bestowed by Scandinavians, although it consists of Norse words meaning "merry" and "field" (*PN Ch* 4.328); the former is known to have been copied into Middle English (see *golik*, in *OED*), and the latter is indistinguishable from the Middle English reflex of the corresponding Old English word. There is, however, sparse but clear

[46] Wardhaugh, *Languages in Competition*, p. 3.

[47] But on its significance see also Gelling, "Scandinavian Settlement," pp. 188–89.

[48] Holland, *Glossary of Words*, pp. 57, 139.

evidence of local Scandinavian impact on English; *Middlefield* in Caldy, West Kirby, shows signs of being influenced by the Scandinavian word *međal* in the same sense; *Afnames* [detached portions of land, intakes] in Childer Thornton shows Scandinavian phonology; sandbanks appear to have been known by the Scandinavian term *mel-*; *bý-* is found only in Wirral and adjacent hundreds along the Mersey.[49]

These things suggest what history confirms: that Scandinavian was temporarily a locally dominant language, given what is known about directions of linguistic influence and political-cultural prestige, and this is what licenses my conclusion about the lexical copying involved in such names as *Storeton*. But our final word about Scandinavian involves a consideration of a dialect feature distinguishing Danish and Norse, evidence for which here is paradoxical. We have seen that Scandinavian in Wirral is likely to have been predominantly Norse, though we know that there were Danes in the invading party, some of whom were massacred at Chester, but who were commemorated in toponymy at *Denhall* (see above). West and East Scandinavian are distinguished by the complete assimilation of a nasal consonant to a following voiceless plosive (as in *drekka* [to drink]) in the western, or Norse, dialect. This took place in between the seventh and ninth centuries.[50] It is exemplified, by its presence or absence, in two key words of local toponymy:

| | | |
|---|---|---|
| "bank" | *brekka* | *brink* (giving English *brink*) |
| "steep bank, rock outcrop" | *klett-* | *klint* |

All these forms except *klett-* are found in Wirral. What can this mean? Traces of *brekka* are found only in north-western areas of Cheshire (in Wirral hundred, for instance *Cambrick* in Liscard, Wallasey); and in northern parts of Bucklow and Eddisbury hundreds close to the Mersey,[51] suggesting possible spread from the focal area further west and therefore confirming the presence of Norse in a relatively self-contained area, if not confined to the original Norse fiefdom.[52] *Brink* is found early further east and south, and it then spreads to be found in relatively late names in Wirral presumably as a general English word, historically copied from Danish.[53]

Problematically, *klint* is found in field-names only in four Wirral parishes[54]; but in three such instances the name is *The Clints* (or a translation-equivalent), suggesting by the article and the inflection that this too is a late introduction into Wirral as an English word copied from Danish and spreading westward.[55] It is also seen in what is probably a fully-English name *Clinton (Hill)* in Over Alderley in the east of Cheshire (*PN Ch* 1.100). In favor of this

[49] Norse field-name types hereabouts are extensively discussed by Wainwright ("Field-names").

[50] Haugen, *Scandinavian Languages*, p. 155, citing Moberg, *Nordiska Nasalassimilationerna*; note that this isogloss is not an absolutely firm diagnostic of the West/East distinction.

[51] On the dubious exception of *Limeric* in Moston, Warmingham, see *PN Ch* 2.260.

[52] *PN Ch* 1.70; 2.44, 179, 260; and 3.251.

[53] It has been suggested that a cognate English word **brince* existed, and that it is this which occurs in place-names, in particular of course in non-scandinavianized areas, for instance *Brinkburn* (Northumberland; see also O. Anderson, *English Hundred-names*, p. 133; Arngart's Review of Dodgson, p. 576). Dodgson (*PN Ch* 5.1.115) appears to sit on the fence. Note that *bank* is also a copy of a Danish word, and it appears in the Wirral parish-name *Woodbank* as an English term.

[54] *PN Ch* 4.182, 196, 242, 243, and 334.

[55] For illustrated discussion of this word, see Harding, "Locations and Legends," pp. 116–18.

idea also is the fact that the four Wirral parishes alluded to are not all in the Norse fiefdom identified above.

An alternative to this account is that the Scandinavian of this area showed variability for the assimilation process, and that both variants were taken up into local usage. This is out of the question chronologically, if it is true that assimilation took place before the tenth century.[56] Dodgson nevertheless entertains this possibility, as does Fellows-Jensen;[57] if there was such variation, it must have arisen from the juxtaposition of differentiated West and East Scandinavian in the new context of Wirral. However, even if Dodgson's view were admissible chronologically, the history that we have been examining makes it improbable that in the specific context of Cheshire in the early tenth century a variant signaling Danish ethnicity should be preferred. From the early eleventh century, when Danish political ascendancy developed in England in general, preference for Danish forms is more credible. This therefore meshes with the account above to reinforce the idea that the unassimilated forms are in fact general English words, first copied from Eastern Scandinavian but spreading as English words.

In the light of this, we must examine the Wirral place-name *Frankby*. If this is a Scandinavian name, as appears necessarily to be the case, it is non-Norse, because it shows unassimilated <*-nk-*>, unless — dubiously as we have seen — sociolinguistic conditions allowed for the stabilization of a clearly Danish phonological variant of a name. Fellows-Jensen observes that the personal name *Franki* is known to have been in use in its unassimilated form (runic *FRĄKA*) in the Isle of Man; it appears on Odd's Cross (Kirk Braddan), datable to the turn of the millennium.[58] This is impossible to square with Moberg's date for assimilation (700–somewhat after 800) unless we reckon with conservative usage among the inscribers of runic inscriptions — a timelag of a good hundred years.[59] Fellows-Jensen argues further that Frankby may have therefore gained its name from a Manx Viking. We can accept that Irish names (like *Noctorum*) could have been left formally unaltered by Scandinavian-speakers, but not a Scandinavian name with a feature serving as a strong ethnic indicator where speakers of a competing lect of the same language were numerically and politically dominant. It would have been expedient for Danes to downplay any cultural differences between themselves and the local Norse, perhaps even in speech by convergent phonological shifting; and in any case, as with Irby, the external perception, as well as numerical dominance, is likely to have dictated which form of the name had general validity. That perception would have been in favor of Norse, and *Frakka bý* → *Frackby* is expected, just as the word for "slope" locally gains *brekka* as its final stable form. All sociolinguistic considerations lead us to expect the name to have developed as **Frackby*. The fact that the place is called *Frankby* therefore remains a problem.

Dodgson cuts the knot by suggesting rather that *Frankby* testifies to the presence of an eleventh-century Frenchman (with a serf), *unus Francigena cum i serviente*, in Little Caldy manor, of which Frankby can be assumed to be have been a part, a possibility which Fellows-Jensen does not deny.[60] Dodgson's account avoids the difficulty with both the phonology and the sociolinguistics. It also requires a belief in *-by* as a living place-name element in the

[56] Haugen, *Scandinavian Languages*, p. 155.

[57] *PN Ch* 4.287 and "Anthroponymical Specifics," respectively.

[58] Fellows-Jensen, "Anthroponymical Specifics," pp. 49–51.

[59] Moberg, *Nordiska Nasalassimilationerna*, pp. 183–205.

[60] *PN Ch* 4.288; Fellows-Jensen, *Scandinavian Settlements*, pp. 31, 372.

1080s (not necessarily as a Norse word of course; it could have been copied into English). That is not a problem, because of the existence of *Kiln Walby* in Overchurch parish, which contains a place-name or surname *Gildewalle* and is therefore (possibly in the case of a place-name, certainly in the case of a surname) medieval (*PN Ch* 4.305). It was certainly a living element in northern Cumberland at this period.

## TAILPIECE: A MANX CONNECTION?

The discussion about Frankby makes it desirable to consider together the alleged evidence for a Manx strain in the linguistic history of Wirral.

1. The probable presence of Old Irish *áirge* in *Arrowe* suggests that Scandinavian namers were aware of this element in use among Gaelic speakers, which requires contact to have been made in the Western Isles or Man. It does not follow that transhumance economy was itself practiced in Wirral; the word may have been applied in a bleached sense "area of poorer-quality land only of economic value as summer pasture" → "poorer-quality land." Arrowe is at the edge of an isolated patch of the Keuper Marl, and an area in the township was divided into pasture-lands at the time of the Tithe Award in 1846.[61]

2. It is probable that some *-tun* names are Scandinavian, in the qualified sense of including a copy of an English word, as argued above. If there are names in *-tún* in the Isle of Man, that would reinforce the claims of the Wirral *tuns* to be Scandinavian, because it would guarantee the use of the element among Irish Sea Vikings. As we have seen, some scepticism is desirable about Manx *túns* and about apparent instances of the element in names of the Northern Isles and the west coast of Scotland.

3. The name of Frankby is subject to an interpretation which bypasses Scandinavian dialect phonology completely; this name is not necessarily evidence for Norse personal-naming at all.

The above three points have to do with Scandinavian. The fourth is about Irish:

4. If the lost names derived by me from Gaelic *cnoicín* are correctly analyzed, they are evidence for a dialect of Gaelic which uses *-ín* as a diminutive suffix. The evidence for this is, as we have seen, better in Irish than in Manx, though the *cronkyn*-names may testify to its use in Man.

On the basis of this, we should probably conclude that the evidence is too weak and ambiguous to support fully the view that the settlers in Wirral contained a component which had experienced the Isle of Man, though it cannot be ruled out that there was one.[62]

---

[61] Wainwright, "Field-names."

[62] My thanks to the Centre for Manx Studies, Douglas, for its hospitality during the conference at which an early version of this paper was delivered in 1998; also to Andrew Hamer, Jennifer Kewley Draskau, and Rhisiart Hincks for comments on the paper as delivered.

Joanne Parker

# Brunanburh and the Victorian Imagination

## Rediscovery and Translation

In his 1799 *History of the Anglo-Saxons*, Sharon Turner pondered:

> Our old chroniclers vary on this subject: some denominate Alfred the first monarcha [sic]; some give it to Athelstan. The truth seems to be, that Alfred was the first monarch of the Anglo-Saxons, but Athelstan was the first monarch of England.[1]

Turner's history was hugely influential, as the first extended attempt to reclaim the Saxons as worthy ancestors and founding fathers — and to dispel the negative, Norman-derived images of them as ruthless invaders and barbarians that had biased British authors against Anglo-Saxon subjects from the twelfth to the eighteenth century. As Turner stated in the introduction to the third edition of the text, when he began work on the history, "the subject of the Anglo-Saxon antiquities had been nearly forgotten by the British public."[2] By 1836, the book had run to six editions, and had helped to inspire editions of *Beowulf* and the *Anglo-Saxon Chronicle*, as well as another seminal history of the Saxon period by Francis Palgrave.[3] Further editions of Old English texts followed, as did other histories of the Saxons.[4] The phenomenon now known and studied as Victorian "Anglo-Saxonism" had begun.

This interest formed one of the most pervasive aspects of a broader fascination with the medieval period in the nineteenth century, which has recently attracted much critical analysis. Victorian "medievalism" has been related in general terms to the rapid industrialization, increasing secularism, and burgeoning nationalism of nineteenth-century Britain.[5] In the case of Anglo-Saxonism, it is also necessary to take into account the Napoleonic Wars and subsequent relations with France; Chartism (whose proponents looked back to earlier theories of a Norman Yoke); the development of the study of philology, which demonstrated that the English language was essentially Teutonic; and the presence on the British throne of a series of Germanic monarchs.[6]

---

[1] Turner, *History of the Anglo-Saxons*, p. 351.

[2] Turner, *History of the Anglo-Saxons*, third ed., (1820), p. i.

[3] Palgrave, *History of England, vol I.*

[4] Such as Giles' accessible *Six Old English Chronicles*, and Freeman's monumental *History of the Norman Conquest*.

[5] See Chandler, *Dream of Order*, pp. 158–82, 184–230; Morris, *Image of the Middle Ages*, pp. 103–25, 134–43; and Dellheim, *Face of the Past*, pp. 6 and 39.

[6] See Frantzen and Niles, *Anglo-Saxonism*; Simmons, *Reversing*; and Melman, "Claiming."

In the period between the publication of Turner's history and the outbreak of the Great War, these influences combined to create a cultural climate in which "Anglo-Saxon" became almost synonymous with "English" (particularly in discussions of national character, achievements, or institutions); in which artwork and statuary were commissioned to commemorate the Anglo-Saxon period (not least for the new Houses of Parliament); and in which Queen Victoria, with her hitherto frowned-upon Germanic heritage, was celebrated for having in her veins "the blood of Cerdic of Wessex, the fierce Teutonic chief, out of whose dignity English kingship grew."[7] As part of this new enthusiasm, popular literature on Saxon subjects also emerged, using as its source material (with varying degrees of laxity) the recently available histories and translations from Old English. Today, the best-remembered products of this vogue are perhaps Charles Kingsley's *Hereward the Wake* and Edward Bulwer-Lytton's *Harold;* but besides these, numerous novels, plays, poems, children's books, and popular histories were produced — not least, several substantial rewritings of the Battle of Brunanburh, and the events surrounding it.

Of the twenty-plus Saxon monarchs who reigned over Southern England between the establishment of the heptarchy by Offa and the defeat of Harold at Hastings, Athelstan attracted a marked level of interest during the nineteenth and early twentieth centuries. Indeed, perhaps only Harold himself and Alfred were more enthusiastically rewritten by authors. Harold's seeming relevance to contemporary Anglo-French politics, and the uniquely rich visual source available for his life in the form of the Bayeux Tapestry, made him an obvious choice of subject for Victorian authors. A unique source similarly furnished rich details about the life and character of Alfred — Asser's ninth-century biography of the king — while the coincidence that Alfred had lived precisely a thousand years before the Victorians (thus furnishing them with a series of significant anniversaries) also seems to have added substantially to the literary interest in him during the nineteenth century. This interest extended to the publication of around seven novels, the production of over twenty works of art, and the penning of numerous plays, essays, and poems, which hailed him as "the highest type of Englishman" and "the greatest of English kings."[8] Indeed, by 1852, the popular historian J. A. Froude could claim that Alfred's life was "the favourite story in English nurseries."[9]

Athelstan did not enjoy such pervasive adoration in the nineteenth century — despite Turner's assertion that while Alfred may have been the first monarch of the Anglo-Saxons, it was Athelstan who was "the first monarch of England" and despite the glory of his victory at Brunanburh, which could easily be claimed equal in national significance to Alfred's at Ethandune. In his 1869 *Old English History* for children, Edward Freeman drew attention to this inequity, musing:

> Altogether there are perhaps as many stories about Æthelstan as there are about either Alfred or Edgar, but they do not seem to have been so famous in later times, or to be so well known now.[10]

---

[7] Quoted in Lilly, "British Monarchy," p. 859.

[8] Quoted in Lilly, "British Monarchy," p. 859.

[9] Froude, "King Alfred," p. 82.

[10] Freeman, *Old English History*, p. 149.

If Athelstan was overshadowed by Alfred in the nineteenth century, however, on the other hand a portion of the fame he did enjoy seems to have been borrowed from the earlier king. Athelstan's birth is referred to near the conclusion of several Alfredian texts, suggestively presenting him to would-be imitators as a likely subject for a sequel, while those nineteenth-century writers who celebrated him and his victory at Brunanburh often invoked the figure of Alfred.[11] In George Darley's 1841 play, *Ethelstan, or, The Battle of Brunanburh*, when the Danish king Olaf (here "Anlaf") enters Athelstan's camp disguised as a minstrel, the song he performs tells of Alfred's disguised visit to the Viking king Guthrum's camp, sixty years earlier,[12] while the anonymous 1862 *Athelstan: A Poem* is peppered with allusions to Alfred, both in the text itself and in its copious notes. Here, Athelstan is hailed as "son of the son of Alfred great and wise," and described as hunting the foe "who had pursued of old / His grandsire through the bogs of Somerset." Its author evidently viewed Alfred himself as a rather over-worked subject, averring that "the interest in [his] story is positively damaged by injudicious repetition."[13] Despite this, though, there is clearly good cause to view the nineteenth-century literary interest in Brunanburh in part as an off-shoot of that century's fascination with Athelstan's fêted grandfather.

## TRANSLATIONS OF THE SOURCES

The disparity in attention that Alfred and Athelstan received from Victorian authors was probably due in large part to the eleventh- and twelfth-century apocryphal narratives about each king which were handed down to the nineteenth century. The chief sources of these were Simeon of Durham and William of Malmesbury. Simeon of Durham, in his *History of Saint Cuthbert*, related how that saint had appeared to King Alfred while the monarch was in hiding from Danish invaders, instructing him to engage again with the Danes, and promising him a great victory. William of Malmesbury reiterated and elaborated the tale, adding that Cuthbert had appeared while Alfred's men were away ice-fishing, and had accurately predicted, as a token of the truth of his prophecies, that they would return with a huge catch. William also added several other stories to Alfred's biography: that he had been forced into hiding from the Danes because his neighbors refused to unite against them; that he had created such public order that golden bracelets could be safely left hanging from trees; that he was a great warrior who had also translated most of the Roman authors; and that disguised as an entertainer, he had secretly entered the tent of the Danish king to learn something of his enemies' battle plans.

The *History of Saint Cuthbert* was published in 1732, while William of Malmesbury's *History of the Kings of England* was printed as early as 1596 by Sir Henry Savile, and was published in an English translation in 1815. Both texts were therefore available by the nineteenth century, and their narratives about Alfred were enthusiastically taken up and rewritten by Victorian authors, in works that celebrated the ninth-century king. The narratives which Simeon of Durham and William of Malmesbury related of Athelstan, however, were of a rather different order. The first and most serious claim made by both Simeon and William was that Athelstan

---

[11] See the accounts of Athelstan's birth in, for instance, Austin, *England's Darling*, p. 93; Pollard, *Hero King*, p. 409.

[12] Darley, *Ethelstan*, p. 69.

[13] *Athelstan: A Poem*, p. 222.

had murdered his brother Edwin. According to Simeon, in the year 933, "King Ethelstan ordered his brother Edwin to be drowned in the sea."[14] William offers more detail, explaining that Edwin was accused of treachery by Athelstan's cup-bearer:

> Edwin though imploring both personally and by messengers the confidence of his brother, and though invalidating the accusation by an oath, was nevertheless driven into exile. . . . He was compelled to go on board a vessel with a single attendant, without a rower, without even an oar, and the bark was crazy with age. Fortune laboured for a long time to restore the innocent youth to land; but when at length, far out at sea, the sails could not endure the violence of the wind, the young man, delicate and weary of life under such circumstances, put an end to his existence by a voluntary plunge into the water.[15]

Later, we are told:

> Ethelstan, when his anger cooled and his mind became calm, shuddered at the deed; and submitting to a seven years' penance, he inflicted severe vengeance on the accuser of his brother.[16]

These assertions seem to have been based on the Peterborough Manuscript of the *ASC*, which uniquely claims that in 933 "the aetheling Edwin drowned at sea."[17]

William insisted that "These circumstances of Edwin's death, though extremely probable, I the less venture to affirm for truth, on account of the extraordinary affection he manifested towards the rest of his brothers."[18] Despite this disclaimer, though, his tale was reiterated in several other chronicles, including those traditionally attributed to Henry of Huntingdon, Roger of Howden, Matthew of Westminster, and John Brompton.

The fourteenth-century text traditionally designated as by John Brompton was first published in 1752, and the thirteenth-century *Flores Historiarum* attributed to Matthew of Westminster was printed by Archbishop Matthew Parker in 1567. Henry of Huntingdon's *Historia Anglorum* and the annals of Roger of Howden were both first printed, with William of Malmesbury's text, in 1596. Several English translations of these chronicles were then published during the course of the nineteenth century. More significantly, however, in terms of considering the production of unscholarly Victorian novels, plays or poems — or even the works of amateur historians — the chronicles were also all consulted by Turner, and their claims incorporated into his *History of the Anglo-Saxons*.[19] Turner seems to have been strangely reluctant to recount the tale of Athelstan's fratricide. It is only in the very last paragraph of his chapter on Athelstan (as if included as an afterthought) that we are told:

---

[14] *Church Historians*, trans. Stevenson, 3.3.502.

[15] *Church Historians*, trans. Stevenson, 3.1.123.

[16] *Church Historians*, trans. Stevenson, 3.1.123.

[17] See *ASC*, trans. Swanton, p. 107.

[18] *Church Historians*, trans. Stevenson, 3.1.124.

[19] The local historian Thomas Holderness, for instance, in his 1888 attempt to identify the site of Brunanburh, cites Turner as his main source.

> The memory of Athelstan is stained with the murder of his brother. For seven years, Athelstan mourned his death with a penitence which could neither compensate nor obliterate the crime.[20]

Turner's chapter on Athelstan also opened, however, by recounting another story which William of Malmesbury had contributed to Athelstan's reception history: that his mother had been a shepherdess, and his birth therefore illegitimate.[21] This claim was also restated in Brompton and Matthew of Westminster, so like the tale of Athelstan's fratricide it was readily available by the nineteenth century. Neither story was figured to make him a widely appealing character in an age whose dominant discourses were committed to endorsing the family unit, celebrating British law and order, and trumpeting the moral rectitude of the "typical" man of the race. Where Alfred could be hailed in the nineteenth century as "the most perfect character in history" and "the best type of Englishman," his grandson Athelstan must have seemed, in that shadow, to have made a poor moral exemplar or embodiment of national virtues.[22]

Turner did include in his history a more appealing story about Athelstan from William of Malmesbury: his account of how the Danish king Olaf (here, and often subsequently, Anlaf) disguised himself as a minstrel to sneak into the Saxon camp. On leaving Athelstan's camp, the Dane:

> received the recompense of his song; but disdaining to take it away, he hid it beneath him in the earth. This circumstance was remarked by a person who had formerly served under him, and immediately related to Ethelstan [sic]. The king blaming him extremely for not having detected his enemy as he stood before them, received this answer, "The same oath which I have lately sworn to you, O king, I formerly made to Analaf [sic]: and had you seen me violate it towards him, you might have expected that I would have been guilty of similar perfidy towards yourself."[23]

The story hardly contributed to a more positive image of Athelstan himself. It does seem to have increased the popularity of the king's biography among Victorian rewriters though, featuring in most accounts of Brunanburh. This was perhaps partly because of its striking similarity to the story of King Alfred's disguised visit to the camp of the Danish Guthrum, but the strong moral message that it conveyed was also surely attractive.

More important than the minstrel story for securing Athelstan's popularity with nineteenth- and twentieth-century rewriters, however, were two earlier accounts of the Battle of Brunanburh. The account of the conflict included in *Egil's Saga* was first published in 1786 as part of James Johnstone's *Antiquitates Celto-Scandicae* and thence paraphrased at length by Turner. This added to Athelstan's own dubious biography a colorful cast of "Viking" characters, which appealed to the Victorian and early-twentieth-century enthusiasm for Northern antiquity.

The second significant source was of course that verse account of the battle included in all but two manuscripts of the *Anglo-Saxon Chronicle*. Like Asser's *Life of King Alfred* and the

---

[20] Turner, *History of the Anglo-Saxons*, p. 364.

[21] See *Church Historians*, trans. Stevenson, 3.1.122.

[22] Freeman, *History of the Norman Conquest*, p. 51; Conan Doyle, quoted in Bowker, *King Alfred Millenary*, p. 118.

[23] *Church Historians*, trans. Stevenson, 3.1.114.

depictions of Harold on the Bayeux Tapestry, this seems to have set Athelstan apart, endowing his biography with the sort of life and color that appealed to a nation which had recently been exposed to the joys of publicly-exhibited historical painting. In 1841, the author George Darley proclaimed: "the Saxon Ode on Brunanburh Battle has always moved my heart more than a trumpet" — alluding to Sir Philip Sidney's remark on the ballad of *Chevy Chase*.[24]

Part of the nineteenth-century popularity of the song seems to have originated from the fact that it was widely thought to have originally been oral. In 1774, Thomas Warton, in the dissertation "Of the Origin of Romantic Fiction in Europe" (forming part of his influential *History of English Poetry*) speculated that it represented "extemporaneous effusions" from a "glowing bard," and had been suited to the rhythms of the harp.[25] Turner, likewise, imagined that it had been "so popular" as a song that it had then been inserted by general demand into the *ASC*.[26] In his 1874 *Short History of the English People*, John Richard Green described the poem as having been originally a "warsong."[27] And in his 1879 *Development of English Literature*, "Brother Azarius" (the Irish educator Patrick Francis Mullany) asserted:

> The poem must have been the war-lyric of that day . . . the alliteration, the constant repetition of the same expression in short lines for sake of emphasis — all remind one of the hammering sound of swords that must have gone to make this war-play. It is a chaunt that in its day must have been soul-stirring.[28]

The poem thus provided the sort of close link with the past that was also satisfied in nineteenth-century Britain by the pursuit of historical tourism and the rediscovery of folk tradition.

The Brunanburh poem was not universally admired by nineteenth-century commentators. The historian Edward A. Freeman complained in his 1869 *Old English History* that it contained "nothing like a story or legend, nothing, if you strip it of its poetic language, beyond a few plain facts which the writer might have put into three or four lines of prose."[29] And in his preface to Warton's *History of English Poetry*, Henry Sweet averred (following the lead of Henry of Huntingdon, who had complained about the "extraneous words and uncommon figures" in the poem): "There is a perceptible tendency to bombast and overcharging with epithets, while the finest passages have rather the character of reminiscences from the common poetical tradition than of original invention." Nevertheless, he conceded that "as a whole it is a noble poem, and stands alone in our literature."[30] This assertion that the Brunanburh poem "stood alone" raises another factor that fed into the popularity of the text in the nineteenth century: namely, the position that it was considered to hold in the early history of English poetry and, more broadly, in English cultural history. This status was first acknowledged by its inclusion in George Hickes' 1703 *Thesaurus*, a landmark study of

---

[24] Darley, *Ethelstan*, p. vi.

[25] Warton, *History of English Poetry*, 1.lii.

[26] Turner, *History of the Anglo-Saxons*, p. 350. For discussion, see Bredehoft's essay in this volume.

[27] Green, *Short History of the English People*, p. xxx.

[28] Azarias, quoted in Langley-Crow, *Maldon and Brunanburh*, p. xxxi.

[29] Freeman, *History of the Norman Conquest*, p. 158.

[30] Warton, *History of English Poetry*, 1.xxx.

Old English literature. Following its appearance there — and as interest in early English literature became more general — it was selected for inclusion in many anthologies of English literature, such as Warton's history (where it was translated literally into prose), Ellis' 1801 *Specimens of the Early English Poets*, and E. Guest's 1838 *History of English Rhythms*. In addition, it was also reproduced in popular histories like Charles Knight's 1856 illustrated *Popular History of England* (later published as the *School History of England*) where it was published not only as an historical source for the battle, but also as a literary artifact in its own right.

Much of the appetite for rediscovering early native heritage in the nineteenth and late eighteenth century was fuelled by the publication in 1765 of Thomas Percy's immensely popular *Reliques of Ancient English Poetry*. Although ballads were being collected and published at the start of the seventeenth century, it was not until Percy claimed that his anthology shed an informative light on "the progress of popular opinions" and "the peculiar manners and customs of former ages" that ballads and early verse really began to be valued both as a reflection of, and a crucial influence upon, "the formation of the national character" — a feeling still present in Azarius' 1879 assertion that the Brunanburh poem contained a "sentiment akin to . . . national feeling."[31]

Percy also collected and translated Old Norse poetry as part of his interest in the early stages of British culture and in 1763, two years before the publication of the *Reliques*, he published a pamphlet, *Five Pieces of Runic Poetry*, which contained his English-language translations of, among other works, "The Dying Ode of Regner Lodbrog" and "The Ransome of Egill the Scald." In planning the edition, Percy also came across "The Battle of Brunanburh." Noticing similarities with the Old Norse verse, he wrote of it to the Welsh translator Evan Evans in 1762:

> If you compare it with the Runic Ode of Regner Lodbrog, you will see a remarkable affinity between them: some of the phrases and imagery being common to both; as the play of arms &c, &c.[32]

Two Old English editions of the poem were then available (one in Hickes' *Thesaurus*, and another in Edmund Gibson's 1692 edition of the *ASC*) but rather than simply translate direct from these, Percy seems to have enlisted the help of a neighbor, Edward Lye, to first produce a literal Latin version of the text. He then seems to have attempted his own free English translation using both this and an Old English version.[33] The project was, he stated, "a slight attempt of my own to see if I could throw a little spirit into a literal, interlinear version."[34] Percy apparently completed a translation to his satisfaction, for he sent it to Evan Evans, and planned to include it in *Five Runic Pieces*. For some reason, however, he ultimately decided against its inclusion. Later, he considered appending it to his translation of Mallet's *Northern Antiquities* — but this scheme never came to fruition either.

Percy's *Brunanburh* translation was never published. Indeed, the full work no longer exists. All that survives of it are two fragmentary versions in his notebook. The first is in verse, consisting of 44 half-lines in total. A taste of it may be gained from the opening section:

---

31 Percy, *Reliques*, 1.ix; Walford's 1880 "Preface" to Percy, *Reliques*, 1.18.

32 Percy, *Correspondence*, ed. Lewis, p. 32.

33 Percy, *Old Norse*, ed. Ross, pp. 267–68.

34 Percy, *Five Pieces of Runic Poetry*, p. 268.

King Athelstan
Lord of valiant chiefs
He that giveth gold-chains to his nobles
Together with his brother
Edmund Etheling
A Prince descended of an ancient race
Smote in war
With the edges of the sword
Near to Brunanburh.[35]

This translation ends with the death of Constantine's kinsmen and friends, but three short sections from the original are also missing before that — whether for aesthetic reasons or because they had posed difficulties to Percy is unclear. The first elision is the first reference to the Scots; the second, the lines referring to the Saxon cavalry or mounted troops; and the third, the tally of dead jarls, seamen and Scots who died in the battle besides the five kings.

Percy's second attempt at translating the Brunanburh poem is in three prose paragraphs and is far shorter, ending with the rising of the sun after the first day of battle. This version has a far more expansive style:

King Athelstan, Lord of the Warriours, he that giveth
Chains to his nobles, and prince Edmund his brother
A prince descended from an ancient race: struck
In war with the Edges of the sword near Brunan:
burh.[36]

It is not possible to know which of Percy's versions was ever finished — though since he refers to it as a poem it was presumably the former. It is also difficult to say how the reception history of the battle of Brunanburh might have differed had the full translation ever been published. It is possible that the poem might have engendered a welter of other versions and rewritings. However, *Five Runic Pieces* was never widely popular: copies of its first edition were still being advertised a dozen years after publication, and even *Northern Antiquities* was far from a best-seller.[37]

The Brunanburh poem did find a literary translator to refashion it around a century later, however. In 1880, Alfred, Lord Tennyson's verse translation "The Battle of Brunanburh" was published as part of his collection *Ballads and Other Poems*. It had originally been requested by James Knowles in 1877, for the founding issue of the periodical *The Nineteenth Century* — a notion almost certainly inspired by the publication of a prose translation of the work by Tennyson's son, Hallam, a year earlier in the *Contemporary Review* (which Knowles had formerly edited).[38] Hallam's work had clearly interested the elder Tennyson, who referred twice to "that old song of Brunanburh" in his 1876 play *Harold*, and it later served as the basis for his own reworking of the poem — he professed, "I have more or less availed myself

[35] Percy, *Old Norse*, ed. Ross, p. 270.

[36] Percy, *Old Norse*, ed. Ross, p. 273 (original lineation).

[37] Groom, Review.

[38] A. Tennyson, *Poems*, ed. Ricks, p. 18.

of my son's prose translation."[39] What Tennyson importantly added to Hallam's version, however, was an attempt to emulate the alliteration and rhythms of the original — for which purpose he seems to have also consulted the Old English text published in Guest's *History of English Rhythms*.[40] Writing of his translation, Tennyson stated, "In rendering this Old English war-song into modern language and alliterative rhythm I have made free use of the dactylic beat. I suppose that the original was chanted to a slow, swinging recitative."[41] Hallam, too, noted his father's interest in what he viewed as the oral or phonic dimension of the original, recalling: "My father liked the rush of the alliterative verse, as giving something of the old English war-song."[42]

Tennyson's verse translation was much admired. In Hallam's memoir of his father he quotes a letter from Edward Fitzgerald — the translator of *The Rubaiyat of Omar Khayyam* — which requests that he "tell [Tennyson] that . . . when I saw his version of your 'Battle of Brunanburh,' I said to myself, and afterwards to others, 'There's the way to render Aeschylus's Chorus at last!'"[43] The Tennyson version of the Brunanburh poem freely adapts the original in several places — Constantine is not "The grey haired warrior / old crafty one" in his version, but "Traitor and trickster / And spurner of treaties" (lines 79–80). In general, however, it is a close translation. Perhaps what Tennyson lent to the poem above all, besides returning to it its alliteration and rhythms for those unable to read Old English, was simply his name — which instantly raised the profile of the battle of Brunanburh in popular culture. His version of the poem not only appeared in *Ballads and Other Poems*, it was also anthologized in several popular works — such as Arthur Compton Auchmuty's 1882 *Poems of English Heroism*, where it appeared alongside patriotic effusions like Campbell's "Ye Mariners of England," Wordsworth's "To the Men of Kent," extracts from Shakespeare's *Henry V*, and several other Tennyson poems including "The Charge of the Light Brigade." In the wake of the publication of this and similar anthologies, the 1880s and early 1890s saw a significant number of new editions and translations of the Old English Brunanburh poem, including several in periodicals such as *Poet Lore*, *Modern Language Notes*, and the *American Journal of Philology*, while the periodical press also saw a rash of articles on the subject, including a series of comments in *Athenaeum* and *Antiquary*. While Tennyson may have been the most influential and best known of nineteenth-century poets to have shown interest in Athelstan and the battle of Brunanburh, he was by no means the first. Nor, perhaps, is his "Battle of Brunanburh," although accomplished, the most interesting verse on the subject.

## TWO VICTORIAN DRAMATISTS

Four decades before the appearance of Tennyson's "Battle of Brunanburh," the first verse drama based on Athelstan's life was published. The author of the 1841 *Ethelstan, or, The Battle of Brunanburh* was George Darley, a long-time contributor to the *London Magazine*,

[39] H. Tennyson, *Memoir*, 2.255.

[40] A. Tennyson, *Poems*, ed. Ricks, p. 18. The copy of this text at Lincoln contains Hallam's annotations.

[41] A. Tennyson, *Poems*, ed. Ricks, p. 18.

[42] H. Tennyson, *Memoir*, 2.255.

[43] H. Tennyson, *Memoir*, 2.272.

reviewer for *Athenaeum*, and friend of the Romantic essayist Charles Lamb and the poet John Clare. This was Darley's second historical drama — his first, written on Thomas Becket the previous year, had been unsuccessful. Darley's biographer for the *Dictionary of National Biography* suggests that as a writer he was "wilfully self-effacing," producing works that would enjoy a "deliberately restricted dissemination."[44] This arguably goes some way towards explaining his choice of Brunanburh as a subject at that period. In the preface to the play, he describes it as "out of the present taste."[45] However, Darley also seems to have been motivated in his writing by a desire to educate, his most commercially successful works being a series of mathematical textbooks. The Preface to *Ethelstan* continues in a vein that echoes the agenda of Turner:

> I have sought to portray [the Saxons] in one of its best representatives — steady-hearted, high-souled, strong of will and of mind, yet soft through his affections. Strange prejudice! That the proverbial valour of a nation which has won the title of war-smiths should have been rated beneath the Norman from a single ill-judged trial; ignorant prejudice, moreover, that the same nation is pronounced blockish and unimaginative, despite its wonderful poems still before us.[46]

Darley was not simply interested in Brunanburh for its Saxon characters, however; like many other authors writing in the wake of Percy's *Northern Antiquities* he was fascinated by Vikings, and was also therefore attracted by the Danish figures involved in the episode, relating that:

> Anlaf's picturesque retinue — the sea-kings or prince-pirates of Scandinavia — gave occasion to sketch that people also, from whom we, as part Danish have derived, perhaps, much of our enterprising character, as well as the daring and wild sublimity which distinguishes our poetic genius.[47]

Born and raised in Dublin, but by then an inhabitant of England for twenty-five years, Darley perhaps had personal reasons for hailing the mixed, part Danish origins of the modern British. He was also writing less than half a century after the Act of Union with Ireland. Unsurprisingly, then, his play is striking in its fascination with characters who must come to terms with divided loyalties. The sentinel from William of Malmesbury's tale of Anlaf's visit to Athelstan's camp here plays a prominent role, telling Athelstan (in noble pentameters):

> The oath I've ta'en to thee I took to Anlaf
> When he was king of Dane-law; had I now
> Betray'd him, I might do as much by thee![48]

In this play Fergus, son of the Scottish king Constantine (and taken as a hostage by the Saxons, according to Florence of Worcester), is also Athelstan's foster-son. He too, therefore,

---

44 Dingley, "Darley."

45 Darley, *Ethelstan*, p. v.

46 Darley, *Ethelstan*, p. vi.

47 Darley, *Ethelstan*, p. vi.

48 Darley, *Ethelstan*, p. 72.

must decide to which king his loyalty is due (he chooses his biological father, but dies bewailing this decision). Likewise, Athelstan has a captured Danish princess as his bondmaiden, who betrays him, but then sacrifices her own life to save his on the battlefield at Brunanburh. The play ends, in the wake of that battle, in a celebration of union. Athelstan magnanimously returns Scotland to Constantine, exclaiming "How more glorious far / To make a king than be a king!" and proclaims (as "Picts, Gaels and Cambrians" submit to his overlordship), "I am full king of England now, and lose / The conqueror in the father, over all!"[49] Strikingly, this vague reference to "Gaels" is the closest the play comes to depicting Darley's Irish homeland as in any way involved in the Battle of Brunanburh.

Darley's play may be classed among the historical fiction that became such a dominant genre during the Victorian period. However, as an author he has been described as "representative of a transitional phase" between the Romantic and early Victorian periods, and *Ethelstan* shows little of the meticulous historical accuracy that characterizes the most developed nineteenth-century historical novels.[50] On the contrary, it shares many of the features of the earlier Gothic novel. It opens by moonlight in the cloisters of St. John's church in Beverley, with Athelstan beside a tomb and a recumbent statue. Here the Gothic is combined with the historical: there is much evidence to suggest that Athelstan had a close affiliation with St. John's (although S 451, a grant of privileges from him to the church is thought to be a fourteenth-century forgery). On the other hand, there is no basis for the play's claim that the king's hair turned dramatically white overnight; that he was unknowingly and tragically in love with the widow of his brother Edwin (put to sea according to William of Malmesbury); that she was coincidentally also the daughter of Alfred (a traitor whom Athelstan sent to Rome, again according to William of Malmesbury); or that she poisoned Athelstan's sister Edgitha in revenge for these two deaths.[51]

Darley's *Ethelstan*, then, while it might have set out to educate against biased views of the Saxons, did not worry itself inordinately about a historically accurate education. Its more specific ambition seems to have been to develop and dramatize William of Malmesbury's defense of Athelstan in his *History of the Kings of England*. In William's chronicle, Athelstan's own words are reportedly recorded:

> Be it known to the sages of our kingdom, that I have not unjustly seized the lands aforesaid, or dedicated plunder to God; but that I have received them, as the English nobility, and even John, the pope of the church of Rome himself, have judged fitting, on the death of Elfred. He, the jealous rival both of my happiness and life . . . wished to put out my eyes in the city of Winchester . . . he was sent to the church of Rome to defend himself by oath before pope John. This he did at the altar of St Peter; but at the very instant he had sworn, he fell down before it, and was carried by his servants to the English school, where he died the third night after.[52]

In Darley's play, Athelstan's treatment of Alfred is further vindicated, as the murder of Edgitha by Alfred's daughter is presented as evidence of the father's guilt. Athelstan's sister

[49] Darley, *Ethelstan*, pp. 94–95.

[50] Dingley, "Darley."

[51] For William of Malmesbury's claims, see *Church Historians*, trans. Stevenson, 3.1.121, 123.

[52] *Church Historians*, trans. Stevenson, 3.1.121.

advises him: "doth not the basilisk beget the basilisk," retrospectively condoning the king's decision to send Alfred overseas on a journey from which he was not to return.[53]

In its interest in clearing Athelstan's reputation, Darley's play differs dramatically from a second Brunanburh drama, published just six years later. Printed only by subscription, *Athelstan: A Tragedy* was the work of Edmund H. White, a guard on the Great Western Railway. Little more is known of White, beyond the fact that *Athelstan* seems to have been his first published work, and that a decade after its publication he appears to have become blind. Quite why White began his brief literary career with the story of Athelstan's life remains a mystery. No light is shed on the matter in the book's preface, which confesses the lowly status of its author — "a man born and reared in humble circumstances" — and conventionally apologizes for his attempts to "thrust himself forward upon the notice of the public."[54]

However, where Darley's fascination with Athelstan was rooted in the king's historical and political significance, for White the Saxon king's interest seems to have been primarily as a character in a domestic tragedy which had been hitherto unexploited for its potential dramatic appeal. His play's main focus is not the Battle of Brunanburh (though that forms its climax) but rather the claim in the Worcester manuscript of the *ASC* (version D) that in 925 Athelstan gave his sister in marriage to Sihtric, the Danish king of Northumbria. This story, as with many others, was disseminated by Sharon Turner, who stated in his history that "Sigtryg" deserved "the character of a barbarian, both in mind and nation. Athelstan, however, signalised the first years of his government by committing one of his sisters to his affection."[55] The tale, recounted either here or elsewhere, seems to have chimed a chord of indignation in White. In his play, Editha begs Athelstan not to marry her to the Dane, and weeps at the outrage of being "offer'd to the highest bidder . . . like the daughter of a vulgar serf."[56] Athelstan is unmoved. Far from wishing to raise Athelstan's reputation, White's play condemns him as a cold, heartless figure. Indeed, its hero is not the king, but rather one of his retainers, "Essex," who is in love with the princess. It is he, for instance, who recognizes Anlaf when he visits Athelstan's camp in disguise (an incident here spun out to five full pages). Moreover, in White's play, the Danish king does not flee from the battlefield of Brunanburh — instead he is dispatched by Essex.

In essence, White took a minor element of Athelstan's biography and from it wove a pseudo-Shakespearean Anglo-Saxon tragedy. The shadow of the Bard is never far away: in the county names of Athelstan's retainers (not just Essex, but also the faithful servant "Kent"); in Essex's dramatic soliloquies in which he importunes the gods to "look down upon this sublunary sphere"; or in the ending, in which Athelstan repents his actions and Essex and Editha, Romeo and Juliet-like in death, are interred in one tomb.

The many differences between the two Athelstan plays are intriguing. Some may perhaps be attributed to the differing class and national affiliations of the two authors. Where Darley, a man of independent means, made Athelstan his hero, the working-man White chose a more humble retainer as his champion. Likewise, where the Irish-born Darley cele-

---

[53] Darley, *Ethelstan*, p. 53.

[54] White, *Athelstan*, p. v.

[55] Turner, *History of the Anglo-Saxons*, p. 341.

[56] White, *Athelstan*, p. 15. Editha is probably not the right sister. In his translation of *ASC*, Swanton (p. 104) suggests that Edith was married to the German Otto.

brated both Danes and Saxons, in the work of the English White the Danes are incendiary figures, given to treachery and incest, and the Saxon period is made as "English" as possible: personal names are anglicized, and Brunanburh becomes the more familiar Brunbury. Part of these differences also doubtless reflect different intended readerships. What they demonstrate more broadly, however, is the unfixed and malleable significance of Athelstan, and the Saxon period generally, as subjects for the author at this period.

## ATHELSTAN AND THE EPIC POEM

Brunanburh's versatility as a subject meant that it was celebrated in writing of several different genres. However, the existence of the highly respected poem commemorating the battle in the *ASC* seems to have dissuaded many would-be versifiers from producing their own Brunanburh poems in the nineteenth century. Figures like Martin Farquhar Tupper, arch-Alfredianist and editor of the short-lived *Anglo-Saxon Magazine*, who commemorated numerous historical figures and events in his poetry, might have been expected to have turned their questionable talents to Athelstan and Brunanburh — and yet did not. Again, the dubious morality of certain aspects of Athelstan's life might have contributed to this unexpected reticence — but it seems likely that the quality of the extant poem was a greater source of discouragement.

A small handful of the Victorian period's "historical poets" were not dissuaded from the task, however. Chief amongst these was the (perhaps rightly) anonymous figure who in 1862 produced the 265-page *Athelstan: A Poem*. Where White's play presents Athelstan in rather a dim light, as a cold and unsympathetic figure, this work is an unmitigated attack on the king's character. Here, Athelstan's "foul play" towards his cousin Alfred "cannot be doubted." Alfred is assassinated in Rome which, we are told, "has always been ready to oblige such princes as have displayed an inclination to enrich its treasury."[57] The king is also accused of ascending the throne "by means the most unscrupulous." While the author concedes that there is no actual proof that he made away with the eldest of his legitimate brothers," he avers that Athelstan's subsequent behavior "seems to justify the worst suspicions" (p. 9). This "subsequent behaviour" includes the death of Edwin at sea, which in this play is entirely Athelstan's responsibility, while the cupbearer is a mere stooge, unjustly allotted a "share of the king's criminality" (p. 73). Indeed, after the cupbearer has been unfairly executed, the poet imagines how:

> . . . the wife of Eldred
> Went silent to her widow'd bed; her children
> Cried for their father's kiss, but found it not.
> Time sped, and still "How great is Athelstan!"
> Cried all men. (p. 98)

Athelstan is also guilty here of cynically allowing the bishop of Sherborne to be killed in his place, after Anlaf has entered the Saxon camp.

Brunanburh, in this poem, seems to mark an important turning point. The battle brings out the best in several characters: Athelstan's sister Eadgitha, for instance, who begins the poem with a desire to take the veil, is spurred on to public responsibility, deciding on the field

[57] *Athelstan: A Poem*, p. 4.

of battle, "King Edward was my sire, and Alfred his! / Here will I stay. Here may I be of use" (p. 179). The most marked development is in Athelstan's character, however. Brunanburh, to some extent, vindicates Athelstan. He fights like "a fierce angel . . . With more than mortal warrant to avenge / The outrage upon England's majesty" and afterwards has gained wisdom, refusing to invade France and Burgundy because "Tis not alone by armed force of hands / That a whole country can be brought to yield" (pp. 222, 232). The battle also marks, however, the start of his repentance for the crimes that in this play secured him the throne. A full thirty pages are given over to Athelstan's years of penance and the poet seems to take unmitigated delight in detailing the agonies of the king's "uneasy mind," describing how

> A fever'd body may be soothed by art
> But what medicament can cool the mind
> That blows its own consuming fire within? (p. 246)

Athelstan is allowed no comfort on his deathbed, and the poet offers him little hope of forgiveness in an afterlife. Although the king confesses, his words are drowned out by horns and battle-trumpets, and after his death exorcists sprinkle holy dew "to damp the ardour of approaching hell" (pp. 260, 263).

The main object of *Athelstan: A Poem*, then, seems to be to make of Athelstan an object lesson in morality. Much of the reason for this may lie in the politics of the work's author. The poem's main source is cited as James Augustus St. John's *History of the Four Conquests of England*. One of several notes directing the reader to this work states:

> It will be immediately perceived that, in my theory of Athelstan's character, I agree with Mr St John, who . . . has given a totally new interpretation of this period of our annals.[58]

St. John was a known and active radical, whose first novel was entitled *Liberty, or, The Rights of Nations*. He also contributed to both *Sherwin's Weekly Political Register* and the *Republican*, and from 1820 to 1822 acted as the editor of the *Patriot*. His views on kingship are perhaps best summed up by his opinion on Athelstan's treatment of the alleged traitor Alfred, which he considered "in the highest degree harsh and arbitrary, since if Elfred had committed an offence against the laws of England, by the laws of England and his peers should he have been tried."[59]

Two other reasons seem to have contributed to the dim view of Athelstan presented in the epic poem. The first was the anti-Catholicism of the anonymous poet, who describes the monks of Beverley as skilled in the art of subsisting "in affluence upon the credulity and folly of their contemporaries" and terms vanity "a curious plant / That grows in cloisters."[60] This feeling appears to have led to a distrust of the monastic chroniclers of Athelstan's life as either corrupt or inept, and following from that, to the supposition that their works disguise or omit many faults in the king. Thus Matthew of Westminster is dismissed as "confused and rambling," while William of Malmesbury is categorized as a "florid and flattering monk" (pp. 90, 15).

---

[58] *Athelstan: A Poem*, p. 9.

[59] St. John, *History*, p. 332.

[60] *Athelstan: A Poem*, pp. 180, 64.

The final factor which perhaps contributed to the poem's depiction of Athelstan was its author's admiration for the king's enemies. Like Darley, the anonymous poet seems to have been a keen Viking enthusiast. Guthforth and Anlaf, the sons of the Northumbrian Sihtric, thus emerge as the poem's true heroes. The former's life is described as "a poem in itself," which imparts "a flush and a glow to the early history of England." He is given the space to sing a long ballad about his fortunes, and when Athelstan defeats him in battle we are told: "of two combatants the losing one / May be the braver" (p. 42). Anlaf, his brother, emerges as a figure in tune with nature. The winds "seem'd leagued" with his hopes, and he is happiest at sea where "the strong arm settles our supremacy / Good honest blows — and not the drivelling skill / Of cravens, which men call diplomacy" (pp. 122, 127). Most strikingly, perhaps, we are told that "had the justice of those times been regulated by poetical justice," Anlaf would have successfully snatched the crown (p. 192). Constrained by historical fact, however, the best the anonymous poet could do was to give him a domestic happy ending with his true love — while Athelstan is left ruing his own bachelorhood.

Besides the 1862 epic poem, two shorter poems were also produced on the subject of Athelstan in the nineteenth century, which take a rather different approach to the king. The earliest was Thomas Dibdin's "Athelstan," published in 1813 as part of his *Metrical History of England*. It opens by referring to the king's "doubtful birthright" — one reason perhaps why many similar metrical histories from this period skip so briefly over Edward and Athelstan. Dibdin, however, defends the king, asserting that "he made [the crown] his own." The poem then goes on to further vindicate Athelstan's right to the throne by recounting the story of Alfred's failed rebellion and subsequent trip to Rome where, when trying to profess his innocence, "The oath he took, of most tremendous size / Stuck in his throat."[61] This is biographically fascinating in light of the fact that Dibdin's own illegitimacy was a matter of common knowledge, and suggests that Athelstan had the potential to be a hero for the marginal and disenfranchised at the time. More generally interestingly, however, the poem also claims that:

> Athelstan made a useful rule;
> Three voyages for merchants should acquire
> The rank and place of gentleman, or squire;
> Had all the squires we daily see
> So earn'd the right of their assumed degree,
> Lord! what a travell'd nation we shou'd be![62]

Such pithy social criticism is typical of Dibdin's politics in the *Metrical History*. He was, after all, a poet who had to struggle throughout his life for any rank in society. In the section on Alfred, for instance, that king is enthusiastically celebrated for his supposedly democratic politics. Alfred was commonly employed for such political ends in the nineteenth century, however, whereas this reference appears intriguingly to be the sole use of Athelstan for such a purpose, and a use entirely opposite to the presentation of the king in *Athelstan: A Poem*.

One other poem was written about Athelstan in the nineteenth century — excluding the many translations of the Brunanburh poem itself. John Hookham Frere's "Metrical Version of an Ode on Athelstan's Victory" could perhaps be described most kindly as falling some-

---

[61] Dibdin, *Metrical History*, p. 75.

[62] Dibdin, *Metrical History*, p. 77.

where betwixt translation and original composition. Composed in pseudo-Middle English, its opening stanza gives a fair representation of the full 66 lines:

The mightiest of alle manne,
Was the gude kinge Athelstan,
Alle his knytis to hir medis
Weren riche and ryal wedis.
Edmond his brother, was a Knyt
Comelich, brave, and fair to syht.[63]

Besides this work, Athelstan and Brunanburh also received treatment in two poetic works by John Herman Merivale. Merivale's 1844 *Chronicle of the Kings of England* relates only briefly:

. . . tho' basely born,
Wise *Athelstan*, defends the crown he ought not to have worn,
The Britons, Danes, and Scots, at Brunanburgh confounds,
And restless Cornishmen confines within the Tamar's bounds.[64]

In another of Merivale's works of the same year, however — *Devon's Poly-Olbion* — the king receives a fuller treatment. Nearly fifty lines of the long poem are allotted to Athelstan's victory at Brunanburh, which Merivale claims took place in Devon, just outside of Axminster. The poem mixes detail from the *ASC* with a good dose of muscular patriotism:

Five kings and eight stout earls lie slain;
Nor stone is raised, nor mound, to tell
They bravely fought, or nobly fell.
But they who for their country bled,
For them their country's tears are shed.
. . .
Such honours grateful England owes,
And such be ever duly paid
To her loved patriot's peaceful shade.[65]

## LOCATING BRUNANBURH

Merivale was born and lived in Exeter. He therefore had obvious reasons for wishing to claim that one of the most significant battles of English history had taken place on his own doorstep. He did not, however, either in the poem itself or in any notes to it, attempt in any way to justify his claim, or provide evidence to support it. This rather debonair approach was to become superseded as the century progressed and as the location of the battle became a matter of regular debate and dispute among local historians and antiquarians, and rival claims were scrupulously substantiated with topographical, philological, and folkloric evidence.

Some speculation about the whereabouts of Brunanburh seems to have developed during the course of the seventeenth century, inspired by the lack of any details about the

[63] Frere, "Metrical Version," p. 38.

[64] Merivale, *Chronicle*, pp. 310–11.

[65] Merivale, *Devon's Poly-Olbion*, p. 117.

location in the *Anglo-Saxon Chronicle*, and by the plethora of different names for the battlefield used by later medieval chroniclers. William Camden (following Ingulph) mentions the battle in his chapter on "North-Humberland," in the late sixteenth-century editions of *Britannia*. In a note to the 1695 English translation of the text, however, Camden's editor Edmund Gibson disputes this location, concluding: "one may probably conjecture, that Brunanburh . . . must have been somewhere nearer the Humber."[66]

It was with the increasing numbers of local historical groups in the nineteenth century, however, that interest in Brunanburh's location really grew. This growth of interest also probably owed much to the gradual mapping of Britain by the Ordnance Survey — a fact testified to by the number of to-scale maps which were published as appendices to articles on the question. A one-inch-to-the-mile map of "The Site of the Battle of Brunanburh" accompanied Charles Spilman Todd's 1875 article, "The Battle of Brunanburh: Its Cause, History and Site," for instance. Published as a thirty-page pamphlet, the piece was first presented as a lecture for the Hull Literary and Philosophical Society. It concludes that Brunanburh was fought in "the neighbourhood of little Weighton, in the East Riding of the County of York," using the evidence of human remains found on the site, its proximity to the Humber, and the names of the surrounding woods, villages and tumuli, which it claims are "derived from incidents of the battle." Todd refers to many other nineteenth-century authors and lecturers who had forwarded competing theories: to (among others) T. T. Wilkinson, who chose Burnley in Lancashire as the site; Mr. Hesleden, who told the Winchester Archaeological Association that it was Barrow-on-Humber; and the editors of *Knight's Pictorial History of England*, who favored "Burn in the South of Lincolnshire."[67] His own theory was clearly motivated by local pride. His pamphlet is dedicated to the chairman of the Hull, Barnsley, and West-Riding Junction Railway and Dock Company, and asserts in its preface:

> We may congratulate ourselves, Sir, that the energy and courage of the races which fought at Brunanburh survive in the people in whose veins their blood is blended; and still more that these great qualities are exerted in such peaceful victories over opposition and difficulty as that which you and your colleagues have won in your successful effort to obtain for our town the new railway and dock.[68]

Local pride also seems to have motivated Thomas Holderness who, writing thirteen years later in Driffield, asserted that Brunanburh had been fought at "Kirkburn, near Driffield" and that Anlaf, after landing, must have traveled through Driffield. "Although we have no documentary evidence that such was the fact," he admitted, "we may fairly presume that Driffield was, at that time, a place of considerable interest."[69] Holderness cites an even broader range of rival claims "varying from Dumfriesshire in Scotland to Axminster on the south coast; and from Flamborough Head, on the east coast of Yorkshire, to Cheshire on the west coast."[70] His own claim, like Todd's, was based on the evidence of place-names, the discovery of burial grounds, and the geography of the land. He also, however, seems to have

---

[66] E. Gibson, *Camden's Britannia*, p. 1097.

[67] Todd, "Battle of Brunanburh," p. 11.

[68] Todd, "Battle of Brunanburh," p. vi.

[69] Holderness, *Battle of Brunanburh*, p. 16.

[70] Holderness, *Battle of Brunanburh*, p. 3.

interviewed a number of elderly local residents in the hope of discovering oral traditions of the oldest possible vintage. "In October of last year," he relates, for instance, "I was agreeably surprised by being informed by Mr Johnson of Southburn, a trustworthy but uneducated man, that an old man named Harrison, now dead, had informed him, many years ago, that a battle was fought here. I will give his statement in his own words, 'Yis, there was a battle there. Battleb'n was thick o'battle, an when Danes was bet they went up ti Ga'tan. They we' campt at Gat'an an Elmswell.'"[71]

The fashion for interviewing elderly yokels, surveying potential sites, and claiming Brunanburh for one's local area continued into the early twentieth century. In 1904, Alfred Hunt, vicar of Welton near Lincoln, announced in lectures to the British Association, the Lincolnshire Architectural and Archaeological Society, and the Spalding Gentlemen's Society that Brunanburh had taken place at Thornton Curtis in North Lincolnshire.[72] In 1907, Francis W. T. Tudsbery produced a forty-page pamphlet claiming that the battle was fought at "Bromborough on the Mersey."[73] And in 1913, in the *Yorkshire Archaeological Journal*, the folklorist Sabine Baring-Gould assured readers that the site of Brunanburh had been "the broad dreary flat by Boroughbridge," near York.[74] These are just a few of the disquisitions published on the subject in the early decades of the twentieth century. More interestingly, however, the new century also brought forth a fresh genre of Brunanburh writing: the children's adventure novel.

## CHILDREN'S LITERATURE

The Battle of Brunanburh was first presented to juvenile audiences early in the nineteenth century, when it was featured in a number of broad children's histories. The earliest of these to include the battle seems to have been *Little Arthur's History of England* by Lady Maria Callcott. Callcott, as might be expected of a respectable lady author of the period, tidied away some of the more questionable traditional aspects of Athelstan's biography for her young readers. She left no relatives dying in mysterious circumstances and in her text, Athelstan is not illegitimate but rather "Edward's eldest son."[75] In place of these stories, however, there is a wealth of domestic detail. Athelstan's hall, we are told, had "no carpets . . . only wooden benches and high stools," and was without a chimney, having only "a hole in the roof." Callcott also seems to have been familiar — at least at second-hand — with *Egil's Saga*. She relates:

> Once I was reading a very old book, and I found something in it about this Athelstane that I will tell you. A king of the Danes and three other kings, who all lived in very cold, poor countries, agreed that they would come to England, which was a much better country than their own . . . but Athelstane soon heard of their coming, and called his soldiers together, and went to meet these kings at a place called Brunanburh, and fought with them, and conquered them, and took some of them prisoner. One of the prisoners was called Egil, and

---

[71] Holderness, *Battle of Brunanburh*, p. 33.

[72] Hunt, "Brunanberh: A. D. 937," p. 1.

[73] Tudsbery, *Brunanburh*, p. 3.

[74] Baring-Gould, "Battle of Brunanburh," p. 29.

[75] Callcott, *Little Arthur's History*, p. 31.

> he told the man who wrote the old book I mentioned to you, that King Athelstane behaved very kindly to all the people after the battle.[76]

It is frustratingly unclear precisely what Callcott might have read. Her references to an "old book" may just be attempts to forge a sense of authenticity, and she may simply have read Turner's history or a similar paraphrase of the saga. Certainly there is sufficient confusion in her account to indicate that she did not read *Egil's Saga* herself: Egil fights not for but against Athelstan and is later referred to as a king, and although Callcott relates how Athelstane sat by the fire with the Danes with "a very long and broad sword . . . laid across his knees," there is no mention of the death of Egil's brother Thorolf or of his reaction to it.[77]

On the other hand, however, it is difficult to determine how much of Callcott's inaccuracy is accidental and how much deliberate. Certainly, her vague account of "three other kings" from "very cold, poor countries" seems suspiciously like a deliberate omission of both the British origin of Athelstan's enemies and any political grounds for their disquiet — perhaps in order to avoid alarming her young readers about the stability of their own country. British internal politics are similarly confused in Charles Dickens' brief account of Brunanburh in his 1852 *Child's History of England,* in which "the turbulent people of Wales" are reduced to Athelstan's overlordship before Brunanburh, and obliged to pay "a tribute in money, and in cattle, and to send him their best hawks and hounds." No detail is given of the battle itself, but it is confidently justified on the grounds that in its wake, Athelstan's "lords and ladies . . . had leisure to become polite and agreeable."[78]

Both *A Child's History of England* and *Little Arthur's History* were widely read. Each went through around fifteen editions in the nineteenth century, and Callcott's history went through a further ten editions in the twentieth century, while Dickens' history was published more than twenty times between 1900 and 2000. Almost equally influential as a juvenile history was Edward Freeman's *Old English History*. First published in 1869, it went through a subsequent nine reprints between then and 1900. Freeman allotted thirteen pages of his history to Athelstan and Brunanburh. His approach to the subject was very different from that of both Callcott and Dickens, however. Where the earlier historians omitted any stories which cast Athelstan in a poor light, Freeman included them all — not for the purpose of making of Athelstan's life a moral tale of sin and repentance, but rather for the didactic aim of teaching his young readers how to "distinguish between truth and falsehood, and to know how much more trustworthy one writer is than another."[79] Thus he incorporated all of the stories from William of Malmesbury's chronicle, but warned his readers that "we cannot trust William's stories as we can trust the history in the Chronicle."[80] Unlike the author of *Athelstan: A Poem,* Freeman is not aggressively hostile towards the Norman chronicler. Rather, he suggests that William of Malmesbury did not invent tales but took them "most likely out of some ballad."[81]

[76] Callcott, *Little Arthur's History*, p. 32.

[77] Callcott, *Little Arthur's History*, p. 33.

[78] Dickens, *Child's History*, p. 25.

[79] Freeman, *Old English History*, p. 162.

[80] Freeman, *Old English History*, p. 149.

[81] Freeman, *Old English History*, p. 150.

Freeman's measured method of judging sources for the Battle of Brunanburh against each other perhaps influenced the first Athelstan novel to be written for children. Charles Whistler's *Dragon Osmund: A Story of Athelstan and of Brunanburh,* published in 1914, professed to be based on two accounts of the Battle of Brunanburh, "concerned with two different leaders": *Egil's Saga* (Item 25 in this volume) and the mid-fifteenth-century *History of Ingulph* (now known more accurately as the *History of Crowland*; Item 46).[82] The latter source focuses mainly on the heroism of Turketul, who is claimed to be Athelstan's Lord Chancellor. Whistler, then, chose one source for Brunanburh with a Saxon focus, and one with a Danish perspective. This approach is characteristic of all of his work as an author. *Dragon Osmund* was the thirteenth historical novel that Whistler produced for children; his earliest, *A Thane of Wessex*, was published in 1896. Like the Brunanburh novel, each of his former works is set in the period between the arrival of the Saxons in England and the Norman Conquest. Although the series is chronological, the individual books are usually separated by three or four generations. One theme pervades them all, however: the question of Britain's mixed national heritage and the challenges overcome throughout the country's history to achieve a union between those peoples.

It is hardly surprising, then, that Brunanburh — involving so many nations, and complete with William of Malmesbury's tale of the sentinel's divided loyalties — should have attracted Whistler's attention as a subject. In his version of the minstrel story, however, Athelstan does not blame the sentinel for protecting the disguised Anlaf. Rather, the king sees through the Dane's disguise himself, but chooses not to act:

> "Thanes, thanes," said Athelstan laughing. "Did he not learn that trick from Alfred my grandsire? How could I blame him? And, by Alfred himself, the man is a brave man, and a good singer."[83]

Throughout Whistler's work, martial values are vigorously promoted, and *Dragon Osmund* is a text in which bravery and comradeship are held in high esteem. Much is made of the story of Egil's attachment to his brother Thorolf, for instance, and when Athelstan presents a gold ring to Egil for his efforts in the battle "it was hard to say which was the more honoured by that gift — the man who gave or the man who received" (p. 301).

Indeed, if Whistler was interested in union he was also, like Darley before him, particularly partial to the Vikings. This predilection is evident in the titles of some of his other works: *King Olaf's Kinsman* (1897), *King Alfred's Viking* (1899), *Havelock the Dane* (1900), and *A Son of Odin* (1914). In *Dragon Osmund*, most of the first twelve books of the novel, set in the three years preceding Brunanburh, follow the adventures of Osmund, Edwin's apocryphal Saxon foster-brother, who is adopted by the Viking Thorfin after he has escaped drowning alongside Edwin. Whereas in earlier works, figures who divide their loyalties like this are made to return finally to the Saxon side, in Whistler's novel, Osmund is allowed to retain his "joint-nationality." Although he fights for Athelstan, he ends the novel by proclaiming himself to have both a "Saxon father" and a "Norse sea father" (p. 309). Norse mythology figures prominently: the night before the battle "men say that all night long they heard the wild hunt of Odin pass over the two camps" (p. 245). The Viking physique is also admired:

---

[82] Whistler, *Dragon Osmund*, p. 2.

[83] Whistler, *Dragon Osmund*, p. 249.

Olaf is "tall, fair-haired and very handsome" (p. 247). And Egil — rather than Athelstan himself — is allotted the glory of having ensured victory at Brunanburh. He kills Constantine's son "and that was the turning point of Brunanburh fight" (p. 292).

It is tempting to consider Whistler's resolution of national differences in *Dragon Osmund* in the context of the political events of 1914. In particular, the novel's distinction between the manliness of the Danes and the treacherousness of Frisians might give pause for thought. Throughout the book, Frisians are figures to distrust, and Athelstan's cupbearer, the conniving Orgar who plots Edwin's death, is also made a Frisian. The novel ends not with the celebrations after Brunanburh, but with his symbol-laden death by hanging from an oak tree.

Orgar raises the question of *Dragon Osmund*'s other main interest, which is — like Darley — to clear Athelstan's name. Here, when Edwin is put to sea in a leaking boat it is emphatically without Athelstan's knowledge. When Athelstan learns of the crime from the hero Osmund, he asks: "Do you — did he — blame me for that setting adrift — if it was that?" Osmund reassures him "There is no blame to you, my king, from me — nor was there from him," and Athelstan is able to fight at Brunanburh "with a light heart" (pp. 273–74). Clear anxiety about his reputation remains within the text, however, suggesting a marked sympathy for public figures on the part of the author. Near the end of the narrative, Athelstan realizes: "Always there will be folk who are glad to hear and to speak evil of the king, and they will see to it that it shall ever be said that Edwin was set afloat thus by me, or by my contrivance. It will be hard to prove that so it was not, as I can see plainly" (p. 330).

Whistler's admiration for both Athelstan and the Danes, and his interest in mixed ancestry were also features of the next adventure story to be written around the Battle of Brunanburh. Captain W. H. Milligan's *Helgi the High-Born: A Story of the Days of Athelstan* was serialized in *The Boy's Own Paper* in 1925. Again, the hero has divided loyalties. Born a Saxon, he is raised by Norsemen after his mother is taken hostage and then dies. Milligan's narrative shows little of the historical research of Whistler's text, however. Helgi returns to Britain as Athelstan is "busy mustering his army, on the eve of the greatest struggle from which the Saxon fyrds had ever emerged victoriously."[84] And he defeats the enemies who have usurped his Saxon birthright (as ealdorman of Acmanceaster) in a domestic triumph that occurs concurrently with Athelstan's own victory. However, we do not see the Battle of Brunanburh itself, because Helgi is seized and held captive onboard a ship while that conflict is taking place. In this text, then, Brunanburh really serves only as a back-drop to a domestic-drama-cum-Freudian-adoption-fantasy.

## ANGLO-SAXONS IN THE TWENTIETH-CENTURY

*Helgi the High-Born* was published as popular interest in Anglo-Saxon subjects was dwindling. This was part of a general slump in the popularity of historical literature in the early twentieth century, in favor of mythical or legendary narratives which allowed authors greater imaginative freedom and imposed "the minimum demand for historical accuracy."[85] More specifically, however, Anglo-Saxon subjects also lost much of their appeal for popular audiences around the turn of the century as the theory of the Norman yoke was superseded by the view that Norman blood had contributed positive qualities to the composite English character,

[84] Milligan, *Helgi*, p. 687.

[85] Doel, Doel, and Lloyd, *Worlds of Arthur*, p. 168.

thus negating one of the prime reasons for glorifying both Saxons and Danes: the desire to trace English institutions back to a pre-Norman era.[86] This shift was also compounded in the aftermath of the First and Second World Wars by a growing consciousness that a close and probably influential relationship had existed between the nineteenth century's theories of Saxon superiority and the twentieth century's active fascism.[87] For several decades afterwards, subjects that might be viewed as loosely "Germanic" were out of fashion in Britain.

The beginnings of this development are perhaps reflected in Milligan's lack of focus on the Battle of Brunanburh itself. His poem does end, however, with a Norse warrior circling his sword above his head and reciting a panegyric in verse on the subject of the conflict:

> Down the ages men will listen
> Saga-men recite the tale
> Of brave Athelstan, the victor
> In the strife nigh Annan's Vale.

He continues with further verses, now in sprung rhythm:

> O'er the broad billow red Anlaf sailed eager,
> But swifter fled back o'er the Bath of the Swan
> From Caithness to Cantyre flocked Alba's bold heroes,
> Now stark, cold and silent, the war-men of Conn.[88]

As pseudo-Old English, inspired by the existence of the Brunanburh poem in the *ASC*, the verses themselves may be laughably inept. What Milligan's concluding poem demonstrates, however, is the continuing charm which the Brunanburh poem exerted over writers — even as Anglo-Saxon subjects fell from favor, and even among the least likely writers; in this case the unscholarly author of popular adventure stories for young boys.

Only one notable literary work on the subject of the Battle of Brunanburh was published after Milligan's story, and that, too, was inspired by the Old English poem, and written by a seemingly unlikely author. In 1975, the short poem "Brunanburh, 937 A.D." by the Argentinean author Jorge Luis Borges was published as part of his anthology *La Rosa Profunda* [*The Unending Rose*]. Two years later, on the 1040th anniversary of the battle, an English translation of the poem by Alastair Reed appeared in *The New Yorker*. The poem is in the first person, narrated by a Saxon warrior who has fought in the battle:

> Nobody at your side.
> Last night I killed a man in battle.
> He was lively and tall, from the pure stock of Anlaf.
> The sword pierced his chest, a little to the left.
> He rolled on the ground and was a thing,
> a thing for crows.
> You will wait for him in vain, woman I've never known.

---

[86] See, for instance, C. Gibson, "Some Characteristics of the Normans," p. 507. On this change in attitude, see Simmons, *Reversing*, p. 198.

[87] See Simmons, *Reversing*, p. 202.

[88] Milligan, *Helgi*, p. 757.

> The ships fleeing over the yellow sea
> will not return him.
> At the hour of dawn,
> your hand will look for his in dreams.
> Your bed is cold.
> Last night I killed a man in Brunanburh.[89]

Borges' crows on the battlefield evoke the spirit of the Brunanburh poem in the *ASC*. There is, however, little sense of being "exultant in war" from his speaker, and the emphasis is not upon impersonal, national victory, but on personal tragedy.

"Brunanburh, 937 A.D." presents the battle for a late-twentieth-century audience, fully familiar with the horrors of warfare from decades of front-line journalism. It is also a poem aimed at an audience schooled in bottom-up rather than top-down history, and thus as interested in the fate of the individual man as in the fortunes of monarchs. Finally, "Brunanburh, 937 A.D." can be read as a post-colonial work, written by a South American poet whose paternal grandmother was English, and printed (in *The New Yorker*) for a North American audience whose ancestors were predominantly European. In his 1977 lecture "Blindness" Borges said of the Old English language: "I am returning to the language my ancestors spoke fifty generations ago. . . . It is not the first time I speak it; when I had other names this was the language I spoke."[90] And in a poem on the same subject, "Embarking on the Study of Anglo-Saxon Grammar," he wrote of the Old English language which "I used in the days of Northumbria and Mercia" and looked to the Anglo-Saxon past for "some other self."[91] Likewise, "Brunanburh, 937 A.D." is a dream of origins, but one that expresses both a yearning for connection with one's ancestry and also the horror of that past.

Borges' poem demonstrates the continuing relevance which the Battle of Brunanburh and Athelstan can have in modern culture. However, no other works on the battle or the king followed in the wake of "Brunanburh 937 A.D." What, then, might be their future, in the twenty-first century? In recent years, Anglo-Saxon subjects have seen some revival of popular interest, with a trilogy of novels about King Alfred published by the historical novelist Bernard Cornwell.[92] The way, then, may be open for new works on Athelstan and Brunanburh. In this context, it is interesting to consider the genesis of Borges' Brunanburh poem. Borges began to learn Anglo-Saxon while suffering from increasing blindness. In the lecture "Blindness," he recounted: "I thought: I have lost the visible world, but now I am going to recover another; the world of my distant ancestors."[93] Perhaps, then, in a future time of crisis, loss, or uncertainty on a national scale, culture may once again look back for comfort to the lost world of Athelstan and the Battle of Brunanburh.

---

[89] Borges, "Brunanburh," trans. Reid, lines 1–13.

[90] Borges, "Blindness," p. 478.

[91] Borges, "Embarking," p. 129.

[92] Cornwell, *Last Kingdom* (2004), *Pale Horseman* (2006), and *Lords of the North* (2007).

[93] Borges, "Blindness," p. 478.

## MICHAEL LIVINGSTON
## BIBLIOGRAPHY FOR THE VOLUME


Ælfric of Eynsham. *The Old English Version of the Heptateuch*. Ed. S. J. Crawford. EETS o.s. 160. London: Oxford University Press, 1922.

Æthelweard. *The Chronicle of Æthelweard*. Ed. and trans. Alistair Campbell. London: Nelson, 1962.

Ainarsson, Bjarni. *Litterære forudsætninger for Egil's Saga*. Reykjavík: Stofnun Arna Magnússonar, 1975.

Anderson, Anne. *The Story of Bromborough*. Brombrough: Bromborough Library, 1964.

Anderson, Marjorie O. "Scottish Pieces from the Poppleton MS." In *Kings and Kingship in Early Scotland*. Edinburgh: Scottish Academic Press, 1973. Pp. 235–60.

Anderson (later Arngart), Olof S. *The English Hundred-names*. 3 vols. Lund: Ohlsson, 1934.

Andersson, T. "*Tuna*-problem." *Namn och Bygd* 46 (1968), 88–124.

Aneirin. *Y Gododdin*. Ed. and trans. A. O. H. Jarman. Llandysul: Gomer Press, 1988.

*The Anglo-Saxon Chronicle*. In *The Parker Chronicle and Laws (Corpus Christi College, Cambridge, MS. 173), a Facsimile*. Ed. Robin Flower and Hugh Smith. EETS o.s. 208. London: Oxford University Press, 1941.

———. In *Two of the Saxon Chronicles Parallel*. Ed. Charles Plummer and John Earle. Rev. Dorothy Whitelock. Oxford: Clarendon Press, 1952.

———. In *The Peterborough Chronicle (The Bodleian Manuscript Laud Misc. 636)*. Ed. Dorothy Whitelock. Early English Manuscripts in Facsimile 4. Copenhagen: Rosenkilde and Bagger, 1954.

———. In *The Anglo-Saxon Chronicle: A Collaborative Edition*. Vol. 3: MS A. Ed. J. M. Bately. Cambridge: D. S. Brewer, 1986.

———. In *The Anglo-Saxon Chronicle: A Collaborative Edition*. Vol. 4: MS B. Ed. Simon Taylor. Cambridge: D. S. Brewer, 1983.

———. In *The Anglo-Saxon Chronicle: A Collaborative Edition*. Vol. 6: MS D. Ed. G. P. Cubbin. Cambridge: D. S. Brewer, 1996.

———. In *The Anglo-Saxon Chronicle*. Trans. and ed. Michael Swanton. New York: Routledge, 1998.

———. In *The Anglo-Saxon Chronicle*. Trans. Michael Swanton. London: Phoenix, 2000.

———. In *The Anglo-Saxon Chronicle: A Collaborative Edition*. Vol. 8: MS F. Ed. Peter S. Baker. Cambridge: D.S. Brewer, 2000.

*Anglo-Saxon Minor Poems*. Ed. Elliott van Kirk Dobbie. Anglo-Saxon Poetic Records 6. New York: Columbia University Press, 1942.

Angus, W. S. "The Battlefield of Brunanburh." *Antiquity* 11.43 (1937), 283–93.

*Annála Rioghachta Eireann: Annals of the Kingdom of Ireland by the Four Masters, from the earliest period to the year 1616*. 7 vols. Ed. and trans. John O'Donovan. Dublin: Royal Irish Academy, 1848–51.

*Annales Cambriae*. Ed. John Williams ab Ithel. Rolls Series 20. London: Longman, Green, Longman, and Roberts, 1860.

———. Ed. and trans. David Dumville. In *Annales Cambriae, A.D. 682–954: Texts A–C in Parallel*. Cambridge: Department of Anglo-Saxon, Norse and Celtic, 2002.

*Annales monastici*. Ed. Henry Richards Luard. 5 vols. Rolls Series 36. London: Longman, Green, Longman, Roberts, and Green, 1864–69.

*The Annals of Ulster*. Ed. and trans. Séan Mac Airt and Gearóid Mac Niocaill. Dublin: Institute for Advanced Studies, 1983.

*An Anonymous Short English Metrical Chronicle*. Ed. Ewald Zettl. EETS o.s. 196. London: Oxford University Press, 1935.

Appleby, J. T. "Richard of Devizes and the Annals of Winchester." *Bulletin of the Institute for Historical Research* 36 (1963), 70–77.

*Armes Prydein Vawr*. Ed. Ifor Williams. In *Armes Prydein o Lyfr Taliesin*. Cardiff: University of Wales Press, 1964.

———. Trans. Rachel Bromwich. In *Armes Prydein: The Prophecy of Britain from the Book of Taliesin*. Dublin: Dublin Institute for Advanced Studies, 1972. [Based on *Armes Prydein*, ed. Williams.]

Arngart (previously Anderson), O. Review of Dodgson, *The Place-Names of Cheshire Parts I and II*. *Studia Neophilologica* 43 (1971), 571–78.

Asbridge, Thomas. *The First Crusade: A New History*. Oxford: Oxford University Press, 2004.

Ashdown, Margaret. "The Single Combat in Certain Cycles of English and Scandinavian Tradition and Romance." *Modern Language Review* 17 (1922), 113–30.

Asser. *Life of King Alfred*. Ed. William Henry Stevenson. Whitefish, MT: Kessinger Publishing, 1904, 2006.

*Athelstan: A Poem*. London: Moxon, 1862.

*Auchinleck Manuscript Project*. Ed. David Burnley and Alison Wiggins. Edinburgh: National Library of Scotland, 2003. <http://www.nls.uk/auchinleck/>

Austin, Alfred. *England's Darling*. London: Macmillan, 1896.

Bailey, Maggie. "Ælfwynn, Second Lady of the Mercians." In Higham and Hill. Pp. 112–27.

Baldwin, Marshall W. *A History of the Crusades*. Vol. 1: The First Hundred Years. Madison: Univ. of Wisconsin Press, 1969.

Baring-Gould, Sabine. "The Battle of Brunanburh." *Yorkshire Archaeological Journal* 22 (1913), 16–29.

Barlow, Frank. "Roger of Howden." *EHR* 65 (1950), 352–60.

Barrow, Julia. "Chester's Earliest Regatta? Edgar's Dee-rowing Revisited." *Early Medieval Europe* 10 (2001), 81–93.

Bartholomew of Cotton. *Historia Anglicana*. Ed. Henry Richards Luard. Rolls Series 16. London: Longman, Green, Longman, and Roberts, 1859.

Bartrum, Peter C. *A Welsh Classical Dictionary*. Aberystwyth: National Library of Wales, 1993.

Baugh, Albert C., and Thomas Cable. *A History of the English Language*. Fifth ed. London: Routledge, 2002.

Bean, Simon C. "Silver Ingot from Ness, Wirral." In Cavill, Harding, and Jesch, 2000. Pp. 17–18.

Beavan, Murray L. R. "King Edmund I and the Danes of York." *English Historical Review* 33 (1918), 1–9.

Bede. *Ecclesiastical History of the English People*. Ed. Bertram Colgrave and R. A. B. Mynors. Oxford: Clarendon Press, 1969.

*Bevis of Hampton*. See *Four Romances of England*.

Blair, Peter Hunter. "Some Observations on the 'Historia Regum' Attributed to Symeon of Durham." In *Celt and Saxon: Studies in the Early British Border*. Ed. Nora K. Chadwick. Cambridge: Cambridge University Press, 1963. Pp. 63–118.

———. *Anglo-Saxon England*. Cambridge: Cambridge University Press, 1977.

Bliss, A. J. *The Metre of Beowulf*. Second ed. Oxford: Blackwell, 1962.

Blunt, C. E. "The Coinage of Athelstan, 924–939." *British Numismatic Journal* 42 (1974), 35–159.

Boberg, Inger M. *Motif-index of Early Icelandic Literature*. Bibliotheca Arnamagnaeana 27. Copenhagen: Munksgaard, 1966.

Bobrycki, Shane. "Æthelstan, 'King of All Britain': Royal and Imperial Ideology in Tenth-Century England." Unpublished thesis. Williams College, 2007.

Boece, Hector. *Scotorum historiae a prima gentis origine, cum aliarum & rerum & gentium illustratione non vulgari: praemissa epistola nuncupatoria, tabellisque amplissimis, & non poenitenda Isagoge quae ab huius tergo explicabuntur diffusius*. Paris: J. Badius Ascensius, 1527.

Bollard, John K. "Myrddin in Early Welsh Tradition." In *The Romance of Merlin*. Ed. Peter Goodrich. New York: Garland, 1990. Pp. 13–54.

———. "Arthur in the Early Welsh Tradition." In *The Romance of Arthur*. Ed. James J. Wilhelm. New York: Garland, 1994. Pp. 13–25.

———. "Gliui / Glini." *Studia Celtica* 41 (2007), 232–34.

*The Book of Hyde*. Ed. Edward Edwards. In *Liber monasterii de Hyda*. Rolls Series 45. London: Longmans, Green, Reader, and Dyer, 1866.

*The Book of Llan Dâv*. Ed. J. Gwenogvryn Evans. In *The Text of the Book of Llan Dâv*. Oxford: Evans, 1893; reprinted, Aberystwyth: National Library of Wales, 1979.

*The Book of Taliesin*. Ed. J. Gwenogvryn Evans. In *Facsimile & Text of the Book of Taliesin*. Llanbedrog: Evans, 1910 [1916].

Borges, Jorge Luis. "Brunanburh, 937 A.D." In *La Rosa Profunda*. Buenos Aires: Emece, 1975.

———. "Brunanburh, 937 A.D." Trans. Alastair Reed. *The New Yorker* (18 April 1977), p. 42.

———. "Blindness." In *Jorge Luis Borges, The Total Library: Non-fiction 1922–1986*. Ed. Eliot Weinberger. Harmondsworth: Penguin Books, 1999. Pp. 473–83.

———. "Embarking on the Study of Anglo-Saxon Grammar." In *Jorge Luis Borges: Selected Poems*. Harmondsworth: Penguin, 2000. P. 129.

Bosworth, Joseph, and T. Northcote Toller, eds. *An Anglo-Saxon Dictionary*. London: Oxford University Press, 1898; rpt. 1973.

———. *An Anglo-Saxon Dictionary: Supplement*, with rev. and enlarged addenda by Alistair Campbell. London: Oxford University Press, 1921; rpt. 1980.

Bowden, Georgina R., Patricia Balaresque, Turi E. King, Ziff Hansen, Andrew C. Lee, Giles Pergl-Wilson, Emma Hurley, Abigail Jones, Stephen J. Roberts, Patrick Waite, Judith Jesch, Neil Bradman, Mark G. Thomas, Stephen E. Harding, and Mark A. Jobling. "Excavating Past Population Structures by Surname-based Sampling: The Genetic Legacy of the Vikings in Northwest England." *Molecular Biology and Evolution* 25 (2008), 301–09.

Bower, Walter. *Scotichronicon*. Ed. D. E. R. Watt. 9 vols. Edinburgh: Mercat Press, 1987–98.

Bowker, Alfred. *The King Alfred Millenary: A Record of the Proceedings of the National Commemoration*. London: Macmillan, 1902.

Bradbury, Nancy Mason. *Writing Aloud: Storytelling in Late Medieval England*. Urbana: Illinois University Press, 1998.

Bredehoft, Thomas A. *Textual Histories: Readings in The Anglo-Saxon Chronicle*. Toronto: University of Toronto Press, 2001.

———. "OE *yðhengest* and an Unrecognized Passage of Old English Verse." *Notes and Queries* ns 45.2 (June 2007), 120–22.

———. *Authors, Audiences, and Old English Verse*. Toronto: University of Toronto Press, 2009.

Breeze, Andrew. "Irish *Beltaine* 'May Day' and *Beltancu*, a Cattle-rent in Pre-Norman Lancashire." *Éigse* 29 (1996), 59–63.

———. "*Armes Prydein*, Hywel Dda, and Edmund of Wessex." *Études celtique* 33 (1997), 209–22.

———. "The Battle of Brunanburh and Welsh Tradition." *Neophilologus* 83 (1999), 479–82.

*Brenhinedd y Saesson or The Kings of the Saxons*. Ed. and trans. Thomas Jones. Cardiff: University of Wales Press, 1971.

———. Ed. and trans. David N. Dumville. In *Brenhinoedd y Saeson, 'The Kings of the English', A.D. 682–954: Texts P, R, S in Parallel*. University of Aberdeen: Department of History, 2005.

Brett, Martin. "John of Worcester and his Contemporaries." In *The Writing of History in the Middle Ages: Essays Presented to Richard William Southern*. Ed. R. H. C. Davis and J. M. Wallace-Hadrill. Oxford: Clarendon Press, 1981. Pp. 101–26.

Broderick, George. *The Placenames of the Isle of Man*. 7 vols. Tübingen: Niemeyer, 1994–2005.

———. *A Dictionary of Manx Place-Names*. Nottingham: English Place-Name Society, 2006.

Brooks, Nicholas. *The Early History of the Church of Canterbury: Christ Church from 597 to 1066*. Leicester: Leicester University Press, 1984.

*Brut y Brenhinedd: Cotton Cleopatra Version*. Ed. and trans. John J. Parry. Cambridge, MA: Medieval Academy of America, 1937.

*The Brut or The Chronicles of England*. Ed. Friedrich W. D. Brie. 2 vols. EETS o.s. 131, 136. London: K. Paul, Trench, Trübner & Co., 1906–08.

*Brut Dingestow*. Ed. Melville Richards. Cardiff: University of Wales Press, 1942, 1974.

*Brut y Saesson*. In *The Text of the Bruts from the Red Book of Hergest*. Pp. 385–403.

*Brut y Tywysogion*. Ed. John Rhys and J. Gwenogvryn Evans. In *The Text of the Bruts from the Red Book of Hergest*. Pp. 257–384.

———. Ed. Thomas Jones. In *Brut y Tywysogion: Peniarth MS. 20*. Cardiff: University of Wales Press, 1941.

———. Trans. Thomas Jones. In *Brut y Tywysogyon or The Chronicle of the Princes, Peniarth MS. 20 Version*. Cardiff: University of Wales Press, 1952.

———. Ed. and trans. Thomas Jones. In *Brut y Tywysogyon or The Chronicle of the Princes: Red Book of Hergest Version*. Cardiff: University of Wales Press, 1955.

Bullough, D. A. "The Educational Tradition in England from Alfred to Ælfric: Teaching *Utriusque Linguae*." La scuola nell'Occidente latino dell'alto medioevo. *Settimane di studio del Centro italiano di studi sull'alto medioevo* 19 (1972), 453–94.

Burne, A. H. *More Battlefields in England*. London: Methuen, 1952.

Byock, Jesse L. "Egil's Bones." *Scientific America* 272.1 (1995), 82–87.

———. "Social Memory and the Sagas: The Case of *Egil's saga*." *Scandinavian Studies* 76 (2004), 299–316.

Byrhtferth of Ramsey. *The Lives of St. Oswald and St. Ecgwine*. Ed. Michael Lapidge. Oxford: Oxford University Press, 2009.

Cable, Thomas. *The English Alliterative Tradition*. Philadelphia: University of Pennsylvania Press, 1991.

Callcott, Maria, Lady. *Little Arthur's History of England*. 2 vols. London: Murray, 1835.

Campbell, Alistair. *The Battle of Brunanburh*. London: William Heinemann, 1938.

———. *Old English Grammar*. Oxford: Oxford University Press, 1959.

Carroll, Jayne. "*Engla Waldend, Rex Admirabilis*: Poetic Representations of King Edgar." *Review of English Studies* 58 (2007), 113–32.

Carroll, M. C., and R. Tuve. "Two Manuscripts of the Middle English *Anonymous Riming Chronicle*." *PMLA* 46 (1931), 115–54.

*Cartularium Saxonicum: A Collection of Charters Relating to Anglo-Saxon History*. Ed. Walter de Gray Birch. 3 vols. London: Whiting, 1885–93.

Cavill, Paul. *Vikings: Fear and Faith in Anglo-Saxon England*. London: Harper and Collins, 2001.

———. "Coming Back to *Dingesmere*." In *Language Contact in the Place-Names of Britain and Ireland*. Ed. Paul Cavill and George Broderick. Nottingham: English Place-Name Society, 2007. Pp. 27–41.

———. "The Site of the Battle of *Brunanburh*: Manuscripts and Maps, Grammar and Geography." In *A Commodity of Good Names: Essays in Honour of Margaret Gelling*. Ed. Oliver J. Padel and David N. Parsons. Stamford: Shaun Tyas, 2008. Pp. 303–19.

———. "*Eorodcistum* in *The Battle of Brunanburh*." *Leeds Studies in English*, n.s. 39 (2008), 1–15.

Cavill, Paul, Stephen E. Harding, and Judith Jesch. "Revisiting *Dingesmere*." *Journal of the English Place-Name Society* 36 (2003/04), 25–38.

———, eds. *Wirral and Its Viking Heritage*. Nottingham: English Place-Name Society, 2000.

Chandler, Alice. *A Dream of Order: The Medieval Ideal in Nineteenth-Century English Literature*. Lincoln: University of Nebraska Press, 1979.

Charles-Edwards, T. M. "Wales and Mercia 613–918." In *Mercia: An Anglo-Saxon Kingdom in Europe*. Ed. Michelle P. Brown and Carol A. Farr. London: Leicester University Press, 2001. Pp. 89–105.

———. "Taliesin." In *The Oxford Dictionary of National Biography*. Oxford: Oxford University Press, 2004.

*Charters of Burton Abbey*. Ed. P. H. Sawyer. Anglo-Saxon Charters 2. Oxford: Oxford University Press, 1979.

*Charters of the New Minster, Winchester*. Ed. Sean Miller. Anglo-Saxon Charters 9. Oxford: Oxford University Press, 2001.

Chaucer, Geoffrey. *The Riverside Chaucer*. Third ed. Ed. Larry D. Benson. Boston: Houghton Mifflin, 1987.

Cheney, C. R. "King John and the Papal Interdict." *Bulletin of the John Rylands Library* 31 (1948), 295–317.

*The Chronicle of Melrose Abbey: A Stratigraphic Edition*. Ed. Dauvit Broun and Julian Harrison. Scottish History Society, Sixth Series. 1 vol. so far. Woodbridge: Boydell Press, 2007.

*Chronicon Abbatiae Rameseiensis*. Ed. W. Dunn Macray. Rolls Series 83. London: Longman & Co., 1886.

*The Church Historians of England*. Trans. Joseph Stevenson. 5 vols. London: Seeleys, 1853–58.

Cleasby, Richard, Gudbrand Vigfusson, and William A. Craigie, eds. *An Icelandic Dictionary*. Second ed. Oxford: Clarendon Press, 1957.

Coates, Richard. "Survival of Ciphered Forms of Language." *Grazer linguistische Studien* 9 (1979), 24–31.

———. "A Further Snippet of Evidence for *Brunanburh* = Bromborough." *Notes and Queries* 243 (1998), 288–89.

———. "Liscard and Irish Names in Northern Wirral." *Journal of the English Place-Name Society* 30 (1998), 23–26. Rpt. with minor changes in Coates and Breeze, 2000. Pp. 260–62.

———. "The Sociolinguistics of North-western Wirral in the Tenth Century." Conference paper at "Centred on Mann: Issues in Sociolinguistic Theory and Method." Centre for Manx Studies, Douglas, Isle of Man, 1998.

———. "The Lyme." *Journal of the English Place-Name Society* 36 (2004), 39–50.

———. "Reflections on Some Lincolnshire Major Place-Names, Part 2: Ness Hundred to Yarborough." *Journal of the English Place-Name Society* 41 (2009), 57–102.

Coates, Richard, and Andrew Breeze. *Celtic Voices, English Places*. Stamford: Shaun Tyas, 2000.

Cockburn, John Henry. *The Battle of Brunanburh and its Period Elucidated by Place-Names*. London: Sir W. C. Leng & Co., 1931.

*Cogadh Gaedhel re Gallaibh: The War of the Gaedhil with the Gaill*. Ed. and trans. James Henthorn Todd. Rolls Series 48. London: Longmans, Green, Reader, and Dyer, 1867.

Cole, Ann. "The Distribution and Use of *mere* as a Generic in Place-Names." *Journal of the English Place-Name Society* 24 (1992/93), 38–50.

Collingwood, William Gershon, with Frederick York Powell. *Scandinavian Britain*. London: Society for Promoting Christian Knowledge, 1908.

Cooper, Helen. "Romance after 1400." In *The Cambridge History of Medieval English Literature*. Ed. David Wallace. Cambridge: Cambridge University Press, 1999. Pp. 690–719.

Cornwell, Bernard. *The Last Kingdom*. London: Harper Collins, 2004.

———. *The Pale Horseman*. London: Harper Collins, 2006.

———. *The Lords of the North*. London: Harper Collins, 2007.

Cox, Richard A. V. "Questioning the Value and Validity of the Term 'Hybrid' in Hebridean Place-Name Study." *Nomina* 12 (1988–89), 1–9.

———. "*Allt Loch Dhaile Beaga*: Place-Name Study in the West of Scotland." *Nomina* 14 (1990–91), 83–96.

Crawford, Barbara E., ed. *Scandinavian Settlement in Northern Britain: Thirteen Studies of Place-Names in their Historical Context*. London: Routledge, 1995.

Creed, Robert Payson. *Reconstructing the Rhythm of Beowulf*. Columbia: University of Missouri Press, 1990.

———. "The Meter of 'The Battle of Brunanburh': Sievers, Pope, and Beyond." In *Vox Germanica: Essays in Germanic Culture in Honor of James E. Cathey*. Ed. Stephen Harris and Michael Moynihan. Forthcoming.

Cronenwett, Philip Nathaniel. "Basileos Anglorum: A Study of the Life and Reign of King Athelstan of England, 924–939." Ph.D. Dissertation. University of Massachusetts, 1975.

Crystal, David. *The Stories of English*. London: Allen Lane, 2004.

Cynddelw Brydydd Mawr. *Gwaith Cynddelw Brydydd Mawr*. Ed. Nerys Ann Jones and Ann Parry Owen. Cyfres Beirdd y Tywysogion 4. Gen ed. R. Geraint Gruffydd. Cardiff: University of Wales Press, 1995.

Dalrymple, Roger. *Language and Piety in Middle English Romance*. Cambridge: D. S. Brewer, 2000.

Dalton, Paul. "The Date of Geoffrey Gaimar's *Estoire des Engleis*, the Connections of his Patrons, and the Politics of Stephen's Reign." *Chaucer Review* 42 (2007), 23–47.

Darley, George. *Ethelstan, or, The Battle of Brunanburh: A Dramatic Chronicle in Five Acts*. London: E. Moxon, 1841.

Darlington, R. R., and P. McGurk. "The 'Chronicon ex Chronicis' of 'Florence' of Worcester and its Use of Sources for English History before 1066." *Anglo-Norman Studies* 5 (1982), 185–96.

Davidson, Michael R. "The (Non)submission of the Northern Kings in 920." In Higham and Hill. Pp. 200–11.

Davies, John. *Antiquae Linguae Britannicae et Linguae Latinae: Dictionarium Duplex, 1632*. Menston: Scolar Press, 1968.

Davies, Wendy. *The Llandaff Charters*. Aberystwyth: National Library of Wales, 1979.

Dellheim, Charles. *The Face of the Past: the Preservation of the Medieval Inheritance in Victorian England*. Cambridge: Cambridge University Press, 1982.

Dibdin, Thomas. *A Metrical History of England*. London: J. Hartnell, 1813.

Dickens, Charles. *A Child's History of England*. London: Chapman, 1853. Rpt. 1910.

*Dictionary of Old English Corpus in Electronic Form*. Ed. Angus Cameron, Ashley Crandell Amos, Sharon Butler, and Antonette diPaolo Healey. Toronto: Dictionary of Old English, 1981. <http://tapor.library.utoronto.ca/doecorpus/>

*Dictionary of Old English in Electronic Form, A–G*. Ed. Angus Cameron, Ashley Crandell Amos, and Antonette diPaolo Healey. Toronto: Dictionary of Old English, 2003. <http://tapor.library.utoronto.ca/doe>

Dingley, Robert. "Darley, George (1795–1846)." *Oxford Dictionary of National Biography*. Oxford: Oxford University Press, 2004.

Dodgson, John McNeal. "The Background of Brunanburh." *Saga-Book of the Viking Society* 14 (1957), 303–16. Rpt. in Dodgson, *Place-Names of Cheshire*, 5.2.249–61. Also rpt. in Cavill, Harding, and Jesch, *Wirral and Its Viking Heritage*, pp. 60–69.

———. "An Old-Irish Placename in Cheshire." *Dinnseanchas* 1 (1964), 24.

———. "The English Arrival in Cheshire." *Transactions of the Historic Society of Lancashire and Cheshire* 119 (1967), 1–37. Rpt. in Dodgson, *Place-Names of Cheshire*, 5.2.262–307.

———. "The Welsh Element in the Field-names of Cheshire." *Beiträge zur Namenforschung* (New Series), Sup. 23 (1985), 154–64. Rpt. in Dodgson, *Place-Names of Cheshire*, 5.2.354–70.

———. *The Place-Names of Cheshire*. 5 parts in 7 vols. English Place-Name Society 44–48, 54, and 74. Cambridge: Cambridge University Press and Nottingham: English Place-Name Society, 1970–97. [*PN Ch.*]

Doel, Fran, Geoff Doel, and T. G. Lloyd. *Worlds of Arthur: King Arthur in History, Legend and Culture*. Stroud: Tempus, 1998.

Douglasson, Hrolf. *Wirral Vikings: The Wider Context*. Birkenhead: Countyvise, 2005.

Downham, Clare. *Viking Kings of Britain and Ireland: The Dynasty of Ivarr to A.D. 1014*. Edinburgh: Dunedin Academic Press, 2007.

———. "'Hiberno-Norwegians' and 'Anglo-Danes': Anachronistic Ethnicities and Viking-Age England." *Medieval Scandinavia* 19 (2009), 139–69.

Dumville, David N. "The Ætheling: A Study in Anglo-Saxon Constitutional History." *Anglo-Saxon England* 8 (1979), 1–13.

———. "Latin and Irish in the *Annals of Ulster*, A.D. 431–1050." In *Ireland in Early Mediaeval Europe: Studies in Memory of Kathleen Hughes*. Ed. Dorothy Whitelock, Rosamond McKitterick, and David Dumville. Cambridge: Cambridge University Press, 1982. Pp. 320–41.

———. "Brittany and 'Armes Prydein Vawr.'" *Études celtique* 20 (1983), 145–59.

———. "On Editing and Translating Medieval Irish Chronicles: The *Annals* of Ulster." *Cambridge Medieval Celtic Studies* 10 (1985), 67–86.

———. *Wessex and England from Alfred to Edgar: Six Essays in Political, Cultural and Ecclesiastical Revival*. Woodbridge: Boydell Press, 1992.

Duncan, A. A. M. *The Kingship of the Scots, 842–1292: Succession and Independence*. Edinburgh: Edinburgh University Press, 2002.
Dyas, Dee. *Pilgrimage in Medieval English Literature, 700–1500*. Woodbridge: D. S. Brewer, 2001.
Eadmer of Canterbury. *Lives and Miracles of Saints Oda, Dunstan, and Oswald*. Ed. and trans. Andrew J. Turner and Bernard J. Muir. Oxford Medieval Texts. Oxford: Clarendon Press, 2006.
*Egil's Saga*. Ed. Finnur Jónsson. In *Egils saga Skallagrímssonar tilligemed Egils större kvad*. Copenhagen: Møller & Thomsen, 1886–88.
———. Trans. W. C. Green. In *The Story of Egil Skallagrimsson*. London: E. Stock, 1893.
———. Ed. Sigurður Nordal. In *Egils saga Skalla-Grímssonar*. Reykjavík: Íslenzk fornrit, 1933.
———. Trans. Gwyn Jones. New York: Penguin Classics, 1977.
———. Trans. Bernard Scudder. In *Sagas of the Icelanders*. Ed. Thorsson. Pp. 3–184.
———. Ed. Sveinbjorn Thordarson. In *Icelandic Saga Database*. <http://www.sagadb.org/egils_saga.on>. Accessed 24 June 2010.
Einarsson, Bjarni. *Litterære forudsætninger for Egils saga*. Reykjavík: Stofnun Árna Magnússonar, 1975.
Ekwall, Eilert. *The Place-Names of Lancashire*. Manchester: Chetham Society, 1922.
———. *The Concise Oxford Dictionary of English Place-Names*. Fourth edition. Oxford: Oxford University Press, 1960.
———. *English Place-Names in -ING*. Second ed. Lund: C.W.K. Gleerup, 1962.
Ellis, George, ed. *Specimens of the Early English Poets*. 3 vols. London: W. Bulmer, 1801.
Etchingham, Colmán. "The Location of Historical *Laithlinn / Lochla(i)nn*: Scotland or Scandinavia?" In *Proceedings of the Seventh Symposium of Societas Celtologica Nordica*. Ed M. Ó Flaithearta. Stockholm: Acta Universitatis Upsaliensis, 2007. Pp. 11–31.
———. "Viking-age Gwynedd and Ireland: Political Relations." In *Ireland and Wales in the Middle Ages*. Ed. K. Jankulak and J. M. Wooding. Dublin: Four Courts Press, 2007. Pp. 149–67.
*Eulogium Historiarum sive Temporis*. Ed. Frank Scott Haydon. 3 vols. Rolls Series 9. London: Longman, Brown, Green, Longmans, and Roberts, 1858–63.
Evans, J. Wyn, and Jonathan M. Wooding, eds. *Saint David of Wales: Cult, Church and Nation*. Woodbridge: Boydell and Brewer, 2007.
Evans, D. Simon. *A Grammar of Middle Welsh*. Dublin: Institute for Advanced Studies, 1964.
Fell, Christine, ed. *The Viking Age in the Isle of Man: Select Papers from the Ninth Viking Congress, Isle of Man 1981*. London: Viking Society for Northern Research, 1983.
Fellows-Jensen, Gillian. *Scandinavian Personal Names in Lincolnshire and Yorkshire*. Copenhagen: Akademisk forlag, 1968.
———. "A Gaelic-Scandinavian Loanword in English Place-Names." *Journal of the English Place-Name Society* 10 (1977/78), 18–25.
———. "Common Gaelic *áirge*, Old Scandinavian *ǽrgi* or *erg*?" *Nomina* 4 (1980), 67–74.
———. "Anthroponymical Specifics in Place-Names in *bý* in the British Isles." *Studia Anthroponymica Scandinavica* 1 (1983), 45–60.
———. "Scandinavian Settlement in the Isle of Man and North-West England: The Place-Name Evidence." In Fell, 1983. Pp. 37–52.
———. *Scandinavian Settlements in the North-West*. Copenhagen: C. A. Reitzels forlag, 1985.
———. "To Divide the Danes from the Norwegians: On Scandinavian Settlement in the British Isles." *Nomina* 11 (1987), 35–60.
———. "Scandinavians in Cheshire: A Reassessment of the Onomastic Evidence." In Rumble and Mills, 1997. Pp. 77–92.
Finberg, H. P. R., ed. *Scandinavian England*. Chichester: Phillimore, 1975.
Fjalldal, Magnús. "A Farmer in the Court of King Athelstan; Historical and Literary Considerations in the Vínheiðr Episode of *Egils Saga*." *English Studies* 77 (1996), 15–31.
*Flores historiarum*. Ed. Henry Richards Luard. 3 vols. Rolls Series 95. London: Eyre and Spottiswoode, 1890.
*Floris and Blancheflour*. In *Middle English Verse Romances*. Ed. Donald B. Sands. Exeter: Exeter University Press, 1966.

Foot, Sarah. "The Making of *Anglecynn*: English Identity Before the Norman Conquest." *Transactions of the Royal Historical Society*, Sixth Series, 6 (1996), 25–49.
———. "Remembering, Forgetting, and Inventing: Attitudes to the Past in England After the First Viking Age." *Transactions of the Royal Historical Society*, Sixth Series, 9 (1999), 185–200.
———. "Where English Becomes British: Rethinking Contexts for *Brunanburh*." In *Myth, Rulership, Church and Charters: Essays in Honour of Nicholas Brooks*. Ed. Julia Barrow and Andrew Wareham. Aldershot: Ashgate, 2008. Pp. 127–44.
*Four Romances of England: King Horn, Havelok the Dane, Bevis of Hampton, Athelston*. Ed. Ronald B. Herzman, Graham Drake, and Eve Salibury. Kalamazoo, MI: Medieval Institute Publications, 1999.
Fox, Harold S. A. "The People of the Wolds in English Settlement History." In *The Rural Settlements of Medieval England: Studies Dedicated to Maurice Beresford and John Hurst*. Ed. Michael Aston, David Austin and Christopher Dyer. Oxford: Blackwell, 1989. Pp. 77–101.
Frantzen, Allen J., and John D. Niles, eds. *Anglo-Saxonism and the Construction of Social Identity*. Gainesville: University Press of Florida, 1997.
Freeman, Edward A. *The History of the Norman Conquest of England: Its Causes and Results*. Oxford: Clarendon Press, 1867.
———. *Old English History*. Second ed. London: Macmillan, 1895 [1871]. Rpt. many times.
Freethy, Ron, and Marlene Freethy. *Discovering Cheshire*. Edinburgh: John Donald, 1997.
Frere, John Hookham. "Metrical Version of an Ode on Athelstan's Victory." In *The Works of John Hookham Frere in Verse and Prose*. London: Pickering, 1872. Pp. 38–39.
Froude, J. A. "King Alfred." *Fraser's Magazine for Town and Country* 45 (1852), 82.
Fulk, R. D. *A History of Old English Meter*. Philadelphia: University of Pennsylvania Press, 1992.
Fulton, Helen. "Tenth-Century Wales and *Armes Prydein*." *Transactions of the Honourable Society of Cymmrodorion* n.s. 7 (2001), 5–18.
Gaimar, Geoffrey. *The Anglo-Norman Metrical Chronicle of Geoffrey Gaimar*. Ed. Thomas Wright. Publications of the Caxton Society 9. London: Caxton Society, 1850.
———. *Lestorie des Engles*. Ed. and trans. Thomas Duffus Hardy and Charles Trice Martin. 2 vols. Rolls Series 91. London: Eyre and Spottiswoode, 1888–89.
———. *L'Estoire des Engleis*. Ed. Alexander Bell. Anglo-Norman Texts 14–16. Oxford: Blackwell, 1960.
Galbraith, V. H. *Roger Wendover and Matthew Paris*. Glasgow: Glasgow University Publication, 1970.
Gamlin, Hilda. *Twixt Mersey and Dee*. Liverpool: Marples, 1897.
Gaunt, Simon. "Romance and Other Genres." In *The Cambridge Companion to Medieval Romance*. Ed. Roberta L. Krueger. Cambridge: Cambridge University Press, 2000. Pp. 45–59.
*Geiriadur Prifysgol Cymru, A Dictionary of the Welsh Language*. Cardiff: University of Wales Press, 1950–2002.
Gelling, Margaret. "Further Thoughts on Pagan Place-Names." Rpt. in *Place-Name Evidence for the Anglo-Saxon Invasion and Scandinavian Settlements*. Ed. Kenneth Cameron. Nottingham: English Place-Name Society, 1987. Pp. 99–114. [First published 1973.]
———. *Place-Names in the Landscape*. London: Dent, 1984.
———. *The West Midlands in the Early Middle Ages*. Studies in the Early History of Britain. Leicester: Leicester University Press, 1992.
———. "Paganism and Christianity in Wirral?" *Journal of the English Place-Name Society* 25 (1992–93), 11.
———. "Scandinavian Settlement in Cheshire: The Evidence of Place-Names." In Crawford, 1995. Pp. 187–94.
Gelling, Margaret, and Ann Cole. *The Landscape of Place-Names*. Stamford: Shaun Tyas, 2000.
Geoffrey of Monmouth. *Historia Regum Britanniae: A Variant Version Edited from Manuscripts*. Ed. Jacob Hammer. Cambridge, MA: Mediaeval Academy of America, 1951.
———. *The History of the Kings of Britain*. Trans. Lewis Thorpe. Harmondsworth: Penguin, 1966.
Gerald of Wales. *The Journey through Wales and The Description of Wales*. Trans. Lewis Thorpe. Harmondsworth: Penguin, 1978.
Gibson, Charles. "Some Characteristics of the Normans." *Catholic World* 65 (1897), 506–13.

Gibson, Edmund, ed. "Battle of Brunanburh." In *Camden's Britannia, Newly Translated into English.* London: A. Swalle, 1695.
Giles, J. A. *Six Old English Chronicles*. London: G. Bell and Sons, 1878; rpt. London: Henry G. Bohn, 1848.
Gneuss, Helmut. *Handlist of Anglo-Saxon Manuscripts: A List of Manuscripts and Manuscript Fragments Written or Owned in England up to 1100*. Medieval and Renaissance Texts and Studies 241. Tempe: Arizona Center for Medieval and Renaissance Studies, 2001. [Gneuss.]
Gover, J. E. B., Allen Mawer, and F. M. Stenton. *The Place-Names of Wiltshire.* English Place-Name Society. Cambridge: Cambridge University Press, 1939.
Gransden, Antonia. *Historical Writing in England c. 550 to c. 1307*. Ithaca: Cornell University Press, 1974. [*HWE* 1.]
———. *Historical Writing in England ii c. 1307 to the Early Sixteenth Century*. London: Routledge and Kegan Paul, 1982. [*HWE* 2.]
Green, John Richard. *A Short History of the English People*. London: Macmillan, 1874.
Gretsch, Mechthild. *The Intellectual Foundations of the English Benedictine Reform*. Cambridge: Cambridge University Press, 1999.
Griffen, Toby D. *Phonetic Regularity in Welsh Poetry*. Lampeter: Mellen, 2004.
Griffith, Mark S. "Convention and Originality in the Old English 'Beasts of Battle' Typescene." *Anglo-Saxon England* 22 (1993), 179–99.
Griffiths, David, Robert A. Philpott, and Geoff Egan. *Meols: The Archaeology of the North Wirral Coast.* Oxford: Oxford University School of Archaeology, 2007.
Griffiths, Margaret Enid. *Early Vaticination in Welsh with English Parallels*. Cardiff: University of Wales Press, 1937.
Groom, Nick. Review of *The Old Norse Poetic Translations of Thomas Percy: A New Edition and Commentary*, edited by Margaret Clunies Ross. *Review of English Studies* 55 (2004), 467–69.
Guest, Edwin. *A History of English Rhythms*. 2 vols. London: William Pickering, 1838.
*Gui de Warewic: roman du XIII siècle*. Ed. Alfred Ewert. 2 vols. Les Classiques Français du Moyen Age 74–75. Paris: E. Champion, 1933.
Gwynfardd Brycheiniog. "Gwaith Gwynfardd Brycheiniog." Ed. Morfydd E. Owen. In Llywelyn Fardd, et al., *Gwaith Llywelyn Fardd I ac Eraill*. Pp. 417–78.
Halloran, Kevin. "The Brunanburh Campaign: A Reappraisal." *Scottish Historical Review* 84 (2005), 133–48.
———. "The Identity of *Etbrunnawerc*." *Scottish Historical Review* 89 (2010), 248–53.
Hamp, Eric. "*Lloegr*: The Welsh Name for England." *Cambridge Medieval Celtic Studies* 4 (1982), 83–85.
Harding, Carol E. "Dating *Gui de Warewic*: A Re-evaluation." *Notes and Queries* 56 (2009), 333–35.
Harding, Stephen E. "Locations and Legends." In Cavill, Harding, and Jesch, 2000. Pp. 100–24.
———. *Viking Mersey: Scandinavian Wirral, West Lancashire and Chester*. Birkenhead: Countyvise, 2002.
———. *Ingimund's Saga: Norwegian Wirral*. Second ed. Birkenhead: Countyvise, 2006.
———. "The Wirral Carrs and Holms." *Journal of the English Place-Name Society* 39 (2007), 45–57.
Harding, Stephen E., and Mark A. Jobling. "Looking for Vikings in North-West England." *British Archaeology* (Nov/Dec, 2008), 22–25.
Hart, Cyril. *The Danelaw*. London: Hambledon Press, 1992.
Haugen, Einar. *The Scandinavian Languages*. London: Faber & Faber, 1976.
Haycock, Marged. "*Preiddeu Annwn* and the Figure of Taliesin." *Studia Celtica* 18/19 (1983–84), 52–78.
———. "*Llyfr Taliesin*." *National Library of Wales Journal* 25 (1987–88), 357–86.
———. "Metrical Models for the Poems in the Book of Taliesin." In *Early Welsh Poetry: Studies in the Book of Aneirin*. Ed. Brynley F. Roberts. Aberystwyth: National Library of Wales, 1988. Pp. 155–77.
———. *Blodeugerdd Barddas o Canu Crefyddol Cynnar*. [Swansea]: Barddas Publications, 1994.
———. "Taliesin's Questions." *Cambrian Medieval Celtic Studies* 33 (1997), 19–79.
Henry, archdeacon of Huntingdon. *Historia Anglorum*. Ed. Thomas Arnold. In *Henrici Archidiaconi Huntendunensis Historia Anglorum*. Rolls Series 74. London: Longman and Co., 1879.

———. *Historia Anglorum: The History of the English People*. Ed. and trans. Diana Greenway. Oxford Medieval Texts. Oxford: Clarendon Press, 1996.

*Hervarar saga ok Heiðrekr*. Ed. Guðni Jónsson and Gabriel Turville-Petre. London: Viking Society for Northern Research, 1956.

Higden, Ranulf. *Polychronicon Ranulphi Higden Monachi Cestrensis*. Ed. Churchill Babington and Joseph Rawson Lumby. 9 vols. Rolls Series 41. London: Longman & Co, 1865–86.

Higham, Nicholas J. "The Context of *Brunanburh*." In Rumble and Mills, 1997. Pp. 144–56.

Higham, N. J., and D. H. Hill, eds. *Edward the Elder: 899–924*. London: Routledge, 2001.

Hill, Paul. *The Age of Athelstan: Britain's Forgotten History*. Stroud: Tempus, 2004.

*Historia Brittonum*. See *Nennius*.

*Historia Gruffud vab Kenan*. Ed. D. Simon Evans. Cardiff: University of Wales Press, 1977.

*The History and Antiquities of Winchester*. 2 vols. Winton: J. Wilkes, 1773.

Hogg, Richard, and C. B. McCully. *Metrical Phonology: A Coursebook*. Cambridge: Cambridge University Press, 1987.

Holderness, Thomas. *The Battle of Brunanburh: An Attempt to Identify the Site*. Driffield: T. Holderness, 1888.

Holland, Robert. *A Glossary of Words Used in the County of Chester*. London: English Dialect Society, 1884.

Hollander, L. M. "The Battle of the Vin-Heath and the Battle of the Huns." *Journal of English and Germanic Philology* 32 (1933), 33–43.

Holmberg, K. A. *De Svenska* Tuna-*namnen*. Stockholm: Acta Academiae Regiae Gustavi Adolphi 45. Studier till en svensk ortnamnsatlas utgivna av Jöran Sahlgren 12. Uppsala dissertation, 1969.

Hough, Carole. "Some Ghost Entries in Smith's *English Place-Name Elements*." *Nomina* 17 (1994), 19–30.

Hughes, Kathleen. "The Welsh Latin Chronicles: *Annales Cambriae* and Related Texts." *Proceedings of the British Academy* 59 (1973), 233–58.

Hunt, Alfred. *Brunanberh: A.D. 937: Identification of this Battle Site in North Lincolnshire*. Lincoln: privately printed, 1905. [Paper read in 1904.]

Huws, Daniel. *Medieval Welsh Manuscripts*. Cardiff: University of Wales Press and the National Library of Wales, 2000.

Hyenstrand, Åke. *Centralbygd – Randbygd*. Studies in North-European Archaeology 5. Stockholm: Almqvist & Wiksell, Acta Universitatis Stockholmiensis, 1974.

*Hywel Dda: The Law*. Trans. Dafydd Jenkins. Llandysul: Gomer Press, 1986.

Ingulf. *Chronicle of Croyland*. Ed. William Fulman. In *Rerum Anglicarum scriptorum veterum*. 2 vols. Oxford, 1684.

———. Trans. Henry T. Riley. In *Ingulph's Chronicle of the Abbey of Croyland with Continuations by Peter of Blois and Anonymous Writers*. London: H. G. Bohn, 1854.

Iolo Goch. *Iolo Goch: Poems*. Ed. and trans. Dafydd Johnston. Llandysul: Gomer Press, 1993.

Isaac, Graham R. "'Armes Prydain Fawr' and St. David." In Evans and Wooding, 2007. Pp. 161–81.

Jackson, Kenneth H. *Language and History in Early Britain*. Edinburgh: Edinburgh University Press, 1953.

Jacobsson, Mattias. *Wells, Meres, and Pools: Hydronymic Terms in the Anglo-Saxon Landscape*. Uppsala: Acta Universitatis Uppsaliensis, 1997.

James, Heather. "The Geography of the Cult of St David: A Study of Dedication Patterns in the Medieval Diocese." In Evans and Wooding, 2007. Pp. 41–83.

James, J. W. *Rhigyfarch's Life of St. David*. Cardiff: University of Wales Press, 1967.

Jarman, A. O. H. "The Welsh Myrddin Poems." In Loomis, 1959. Pp. 20–30.

———. *The Legend of Merlin*. Cardiff: University of Wales Press, 1960.

Jesch, Judith. "Scandinavian Wirral, From Scandinavia to the Wirral." In Cavill, Harding, and Jesch, 2000. Pp. 1–16.

John of Oxnead. *Chronica*. Ed. Henry Ellis. Rolls Series 13. London: Longman, Brown, Green, Longmans, and Roberts, 1859.

John of Worcester. *The Chronicle of John of Worcester*. Ed. R. R. Darlington and P. McGurk. Trans. Jennifer Bray and P. McGurk. 3 vols. Oxford Medieval Texts. Oxford: Clarendon Press, 1995–98.

John, Eric. "The Age of Edgar." In *The Anglo-Saxons*. Ed. James Campbell, Eric John, and Patrick Wormald. Ithaca: Cornell University Press, 1982. Pp. 160–89.

Jury, Louise. "For the Cradle of English Civilisation, Go to the Wirral." *The Independent* (First Edition, 8 December 2004), A.15.

Keene, Derek. *Survey of Medieval Winchester*. Oxford: Clarendon, 1985.

Ker, Neil R. *Catalogue of Manuscripts Containing Anglo-Saxon*. Oxford: Clarendon Press, 1957.

Keynes, Simon. "King Athelstan's Books." In *Learning and Literature in Anglo-Saxon England: Studies Presented to Peter Clemoes on the Occasion of his Sixty-Fifth Birthday*. Ed. Michael Lapidge and Helmut Gneuss. Cambridge: Cambridge University Press, 1985. Pp. 143–201.

———. "King Alfred and the Mercians." In *Kings, Currency and Alliances: History and Coinage of Southern England in the Ninth Century*. Ed. Mark S. Blackburn and David N. Dumville. Woodbridge: Boydell Press, 1998. Pp. 1–46.

Kirby, D. P. "Hywel Dda: Anglophil?" *Welsh Historical Review* 8 (1976), 1–13.

Kneen, J. J. *The Place-Names of the Isle of Man, with their Origin and History*. Douglas: Yn Cheshaght Ghailckagh, 1925–28. [Originally printed as six fascicles, continuously paginated. Rpt. 1973.]

Knight, Charles. *The Popular History of England*. 8 vols. London: Bradbury and Evans, 1856. [Rpt. as *School History of England*, 1865.]

Koch, John T. "Marwnad Cunedda a diwedd y Brydain Rufeinig." In *Yr Hen Iaith: Studies in Early Welsh before 1500*. Ed. Paul Russell. Aberystwyth: Celtic Studies Publications, 2003. Pp. 171–97.

Krapp, George Philip, and Elliot van Kirk Dobbie, eds. *The Anglo-Saxon Poetic Records: A Collective Edition*. 6 vols. New York: Columbia University Press, 1931–42.

Langley-Crow, Charles. *Maldon and Brunanburh: Two Old English Songs of Battle*. Boston: Ginn, 1897.

Lapidge, Michael. "The Hermeneutic Style in Tenth-Century Anglo-Latin Literature." *Anglo-Saxon England* 4 (1975), 67–111.

———. *Anglo-Latin Literature 900–1066*. London: Hambledon Press, 1993.

———. "Byrhtferth of Ramsey and the Early Sections of the *Historia Regum* attributed to Simeon of Durham." *Anglo-Saxon England* 10 (1982), 97–122. Rpt. in Lapidge, 1993. Pp. 317–42.

———. "Schools, Learning and Literature in Tenth-Century England." In Lapidge, 1993. Pp. 1–48.

———. "Some Latin Poems as Evidence for the Reign of Athelstan." *Anglo-Saxon England* 9 (1981), 61–98. Rpt. in Lapidge, 1993. Pp. 49–86.

———. *The Cult of St Swithun*. Winchester Studies 4.2. Oxford: Clarendon Press, 2003.

Lapidge, Michael, John Blair, Simon Keynes, and Donald Scragg, eds. *The Blackwell Encyclopaedia of Anglo-Saxon England*. Oxford: Blackwell, 1999. [*BEASE*.]

Lárusson, Ó. "Ísland." In *Stedsnavn*. Ed. Magnus Bernhard Olsen. Nordisk Kultur 5. Stockholm: A. Bonnier, 1939.

Lawton, David. "The Surveying Subject and the 'Whole World' of Belief: Three Case Studies." In *New Medieval Literatures* 4. Ed. Wendy Scase, Rita Copeland, and David Lawton. Oxford: Oxford University Press, 2001. Pp. 9–37.

*Legendary Poems from the Book of Taliesin*. Ed. Marged Haycock. Aberystwyth: CMCS Publications, 2007.

Leland, John. *The Itinerary of John Leland*. Ed. Lucy Toulmin Smith. London: Bell, 1907.

Lendinara, Patrizia. "The Battle of Brunanburh in Later Histories and Romances." *Anglia* 117 (1999), 201–35.

Lewis, Henry. *Hen Gerddi Crefyddol*. Cardiff: University of Wales Press, 1931. Rpt. 1974.

———, and Holger Pedersen. *A Concise Comparative Celtic Grammar*. Göttingen: Vandenhoeck and Ruprecht, 1937.

*Liber Eliensis*. Ed. Ernest Oscar Blake. Camden Third Series, vol. 92. London: Butler and Tanner, 1962.

———. Trans. Janet Fairweather. Woodbridge: Boydell, 2005.

Liebermann, Felix, ed. *Ungedruckte anglo-normannische Geschichtsquellen*. Strassburg: K. J. Trübner, 1879.

Liestol, Knut. *The Origin of the Icelandic Family Sagas*. Cambridge, MA: Harvard University Press, 1930.

Lilly, W. S. "British Monarchy and Modern Democracy." *The Nineteenth Century* 41 (1897), 853–64.

*Livere de Reis de Engleterre*. Ed. and trans. John Glover. In *Le Livere de Reis de Britannie e Le Livere de Reis de Engleterre*. London: Longmans, Green, Reader, and Dyer, 1865.

———. Ed. Christian Foltys. In "Kritische Ausgabe der anglonormannischen Chroniken: *Brutus, Li Rei de Engleterre, Le Livere de Reis de Engleterre*." Ph.D. Dissertation. University of Berlin, 1962.

*Llawysgrif Hendregadredd*. Ed. John Morris-Jones and Thomas Parry-Williams. Cardiff: University of Wales Press, 1933. Rpt. 1971.

Lloyd, John Edward. *A History of Wales: From the Earliest Times to the Edwardian Conquest*. London: Longmans, 1911. [Rpt. many times.]

Lloyd-Jones, J. *Geirfa Barddoniaeth Gynnar Gymraeg*. Cardiff: University of Wales Press, 1931–63.

*Llyfr Du Caerfyrddin*. Ed. A. O. H. Jarman. Cardiff: University of Wales Press, 1982.

*Llyfr Iorwerth: A Critical Text of the Venedotian Code of Medieval Welsh Law*. Ed. Aled Rhys Wiliam. Cardiff: University of Wales Press, 1960.

Llywelyn Fardd I et al. *Gwaith Llywelyn Fardd I ac Eraill o Feirdd y Ddegddegfed Ganrif*. Ed. Morfydd E. Owen et al. Cyfres Beirdd y Tywysogion 2. Gen ed. R. Geraint Gruffydd. Cardiff: University of Wales Press, 1994.

Loomis, Laura Hibbard. *Medieval Romance in England*. London: Oxford University Press, 1924. Rpt. New York: Burt Franklin, 1960.

———. "The Holy Relics of Charlemagne and King Athelstan." *Speculum* 25 (1950), 437–56.

———. "The Athelstan Gift Story: Its Influence on English Chronicles and Carolingian Romances." *PMLA* 67 (1952), 521–37.

Loomis, R. S., ed. *Arthurian Literature in the Middle Ages*. Oxford: Oxford University Press, 1959.

Loyn, H. R. "Wales and England in the Tenth Century: The Context of the Athelstan Charters." *Welsh History Review* 10 (1980–81), 283–301.

Lutz, Angelika. "Æthelweard's *Chronicon* and Old English Poetry." *Anglo-Saxon England* 29 (2000), 177–214.

*The Mabinogi*. Trans. Patrick K. Ford. In *The Mabinogi and Other Medieval Welsh Tales*. Berkeley: University of California Press, 1977. Pp. 35–109.

———. Trans. John K. Bollard. Llandysul: Gomer Press, 2006.

Mac Firbis, Duald. *On the Fomorians and the Norsemen*. Ed. and trans. Alexander Bugge. Christiania: J. Chr. Gundersens Bogtrykkeri, 1905.

Mageoghagan, Conell. *Annals of Clonmacnoise*. Ed. Denis Murphy. Dublin: University Press of Dublin, 1896.

Mannyng, Robert, of Brunne. *The Chronicle*. Ed. Idele Sullens. Binghamton, NY: Medieval and Renaissance Texts and Studies, 1996.

———. *Handlyng Synne*. Ed. Idelle Sullens. Binghamton, NY: Medieval and Renaissance Texts and Studies, 1983.

Marstrander, C. J. S. "Det Norske Landnåm på Man." *Norsk Tidsskrift for Sprogvidenskab* 6 (1932), 40–386.

Matthew Paris. *Chronica majora*. 7 vols. Ed. Henry Richards Luard. Rolls Series 57. London: Longman & Co., 1872–84.

McCarthy, Daniel P. "The Original Compilation of the Annals of Ulster." *Studia Celtica* 38 (2004), 77–84.

McClure, Judith. "Bede's Old Testament Kings." In Wormald, Bullough, and Collins, 1983. Pp. 76–98.

McDougall, Ian. "Discretion and Deceit: A Re-Examination of a Military Stratagem in *Egils Saga*." In *The Middle Ages in the North-West*. Ed. Tom Scott and Pat Starkey. Oxford: Leopard's Head Press, 1995. Pp. 109–42.

McKenna, Catherine, ed. and trans. *The Medieval Welsh Religious Lyric*. Belmont, MA: Ford & Bailie, 1991.

Meilyr Brydydd et al. *Gwaith Meilyr Brydydd a'i Ddisgynyddion*. Ed. J. E. Caerwyn Williams et al. Cyfres Beirdd y Tywysogion 1. Gen ed. R. Geraint Gruffydd. Cardiff: University of Wales Press, 1994.

Melman, Billie. "Claiming the Nation's Past: The Invention of an Anglo-Saxon Tradition." *Journal of Contemporary History* 26 (1991), 575–95.

Merivale, John Herman. *A Chronicle of the Kings of England, from the Invasion of Julius Caesar to the Revolution of 1688: Tenth Century*. In *Poems Original and Translated*. London: William Pickering, 1844. Pp. 310–11.

———. *Devon's Poly-Olbion*. In *Poems Original and Translated*. London: William Pickering, 1844. Pp. 108–28.

Miller, Sean, ed. *Charters of the New Minster, Winchester*. Anglo-Saxon Charters 9. Oxford: Oxford University Press, 2001.

Milligan, Captain W. H. *Helgi the High-Born: A Story of the Days of Athelstan*. Serialized in *The Boy's Own Paper* 47.6 (March 1925)–47.11 (August 1925).

Milner, John. *The History Civil and Ecclesiastical, and Survey of the Antiquities, of Winchester*. 2 vols. Winchester: J. Robbins, 1798.

Moberg, Lennart. *Om de Nordiska Nasalassimilationerna mp > pp, nt > tt, nk > kk med Särskild Hänsyn till Svenskan*. Språgliga Serien 1. Uppsala: Uppsala University, 1944.

Moffat, Alexander G. "Norse Place-Names in Gower (Glamorganshire)." *Saga-book of the Viking Club* 2 (1898), 95–117.

Moore, A. W. "Bull of Pope Gregory IX to the Bishop of Sodor, 30 July 1231." *English Historical Review* 5.17 (1890), 101–07.

Morris, Kevin L. *The Image of the Middle Ages in Romantic and Victorian Literature*. London: Croom Helm, 1984.

Morris-Jones, John. *A Welsh Grammar*. Oxford: Oxford University Press, 1913.

Morris-Jones, Owen (Myfyr), Edward Williams (Iolo Morganwg), and William Owen Pughe (Idrison), eds. *The Myfyrian Archaiology of Wales*. Second ed. Denbigh: Thomas Gee, 1870.

Neilson, George. "Brunanburh and Burnswark." *Scottish Historical Review* 7 (1909), 37–39.

Nelson, Janet L. "The Earliest Surviving Royal *ordo*: Some Liturgical and Historical Aspects." In *Authority and Power: Studies on Medieval Law and Government*. Ed. Brian Tierney and Peter Linehan. Cambridge: Cambridge University Press, 1980. Pp. 29–48.

———. "Eadgifu (d. in or after 951)." *Oxford Dictionary of National Biography* 17 (2004), 526–27.

*Nennius: British History and the Welsh Annals*. Ed. and trans. John Morris. London: Phillimore, 1980.

Nichols, Jr., Stephen G. "The Spirit of Truth: Epic Modes in Medieval Literature." *New Literary History* 1.3 (1970), 365–86.

Nicolaisen, W. F. H. *Scottish Place-Names: Their Structure and Significance*. Second ed. Edinburgh: John Donald, 2001.

Niles, John D. "Skaldic Technique in *Brunanburh*." *Scandinavian Studies* 59 (1987), 356–66.

Ó Cróinín, Dáibhí. *Early Medieval Ireland 400–1200*. Longman History of Ireland. London: Longman, 1995.

O'Donovan, John, ed. *Annals of Ireland, Three Fragments*. Dublin: Irish Archaeological and Celtic Society, 1860.

O'Keeffe, Katherine O'Brien. *Visible Song: Transitional Literacy in Old English Verse*. Cambridge: Cambridge University Press, 1990.

Ormerod, George. *History of the County Palatine and City of Cheshire*. Second ed., rev. by Thomas Helsby. London: G. Routledge, 1882.

Owen, Aneurin. *Ancient Laws and Institutes of Wales*. [London]: Commissioners on the Public Records, 1841.

Owen, Morfydd E. "Prolegomena to a Study of the Historical Context of Gwynfardd Brycheiniog's Poem to Dewi." *Studia Celtica* 26/27 (1991–92), 51–79.

Page, Raymond I. "A Tale of Two Cities." *Peritia* 1 (1982), 335–51.

Palgrave, Francis. *History of England, vol I: Anglo-Saxon Period*. London: John Murray, 1831.

Panofsky, Erwin. *Renaissance and Renascences in Western Art*. Stockholm: Almqvist & Wiksell, 1960.

Parry, John J., and Robert A. Caldwell. "Geoffrey of Monmouth." In Loomis, 1959. Pp. 70–93.

Percy, Thomas. *Five Pieces of Runic Poetry: Translated from the Islandic Language*. London: R. and J. Dodsley, 1763.

———. *Reliques of Ancient English Poetry: Consisting of Old Heroic Ballads, Songs, and Other Pieces of our Earlier Poets*. 3 vols. London: J. Dodsley, 1765.
———. *The Correspondence of Thomas Percy and Evan Evans*. Ed. Aneirin Lewis. Baton Rouge: Louisiana State University Press, 1957.
———. *The Old Norse Poetic Translations of Thomas Percy*. Ed. Margaret Clunies Ross. Turnhout: Brepols, 2001.
Peter of Ickham. See *Le Livere de Reis de Britannie e Le Livere de Reis de Engleterre*.
Phillimore, Egerton. "The Annales Cambriae and Old-Welsh Genealogies from Harleian MS. 3859." *Y Cymmrodor* 9 (1888), 141–83.
Philpott, Robert A., and Mark H. Adams. *Irby, Wirral: Excavations on a Late Prehistoric, Romano-British and Medieval Site, 1987–96*. Liverpool: National Museums Liverpool, 2009.
Picton, James A. "The Great Stone of Thor." *Notes and Queries* Fifth Series 8 (1877), 364–65.
Pierre de Langtoft. *The Chronicle of Pierre de Langtoft*. Ed. Thomas Wright. 2 vols. Rolls Series 47. London: Longman, 1866.
*The Poems of Taliesin*. Ed. Ifor Williams. Trans. J. E. Caerwyn Williams. Dublin: Dublin Institute for Advanced Studies, 1968.
*Poetae Latini Aevi Carolini*. Ed. Ernst Dümmler. 4 vols. MGH I. Berlin: Weidmann, 1881.
*The Poetry in the Red Book of Hergest*. Ed. J. Gwenogvryn Evans. Llanbedrog: Evans, 1911.
Pollard, Eliza F. *A Hero King: A Romance of the Days of Alfred the Great*. London: Partridge, 1898.
Pope, John Collins. *The Rhythm of Beowulf*. New Haven: Yale University Press, 1942.
Pratt, Stella. "Summer Landscapes: Investigating Scottish Topographical Place-Names." *Nomina* 28 (2005), 93–114.
*A Pre-Conquest English Prayer-Book: BL MSS Cotton Galba A.xiv and Nero A.ii (ff. 3–13)*. Ed. Bernard James Muir. Henry Bradshaw Society 103. Woodbridge: Boydell, 1988.
Prescott, Andrew. "'Kinge Athelston That Was a Worthy Kinge of England': Anglo-Saxon Myths of the Freemasons." In *The Power of Words: Anglo-Saxon Studies Presented to Donald G. Scragg on his Seventieth Birthday*. Ed. Hugh Magennis and Jonathan Wilcox. Morgantown: University of West Virginia Press, 2006. Pp. 397–434.
*Prophecies from the Book of Taliesin*. Ed. and trans. Marged Haycock. Aberystwyth: CMCS Press. Forthcoming.
Pryce, Huw. "British or Welsh? National Identity in Twelfth-Century Wales." *English Historical Review* 116.468 (2001), 775–801.
Ramsay, Nigel. *St Dunstan: His Life, Times, and Cult*. Woodbridge: Boydell Press, 1992.
Reaney, Percy Hide. *The Place-Names of Cambridgeshire and the Isle of Ely*. English Place-Name Society 19. Cambridge: Cambridge University Press, 1943.
Rees, William. *An Historical Atlas of Wales, from Early to Modern Times*. London: Faber and Faber, 1959. [Rpt. many times.]
*Rerum Anglicarum scriptorum veterum*. Ed. William Fulman and Thomas Gale. 3 vols. Oxford: Sheldon Theatre, 1684.
Rhygyfarch. "Rhygyfarch's 'Life' of St. David." Ed. and trans. Richard Sharpe and John Reuben Davies. In Evans and Wooding, 2007. Pp. 107–55.
Riall, Nicholas. "The New Castles of Henry de Blois as Bishop of Winchester: The Case Against Farnham, Surrey." *Medieval Archaeology* 47 (2003), 115–29.
Richard of Cirencester. *Speculum historiale de gestis regum Angliæ*. Ed. John E. B. Mayor. 2 vols. Rolls Series 30. London: Longman, Green, Longman, Roberts, and Green, 1863–69.
Richards, Melville. "Early Welsh Territorial Suffixes." *Journal of the Royal Society of the Antiquaries of Ireland* 95 (1965), 205–12.
Richmond, Velma Bourgeois. *The Popularity of Middle English Romance*. Bowling Green, OH: Bowling Green University Popular Press, 1975.
———. *The Legend of Guy of Warwick*. New York: Garland, 1996.
Rigg, A. G. "Henry of Huntingdon's Metrical Experiments." *Journal of Medieval Latin* 1 (1991), 60–72.

*Riming Chronicle*. In "Two Manuscripts of the Middle English Anonymous *Riming Chronicle*." Ed. Marion Crane Carroll and Rosemond Tuve. *PMLA* 46 (1931), 115–54.

Robert of Gloucester. *Metrical Chronicle of Robert of Gloucester*. Ed. William Aldis Wright. 2 vols. Rolls Series 86. London: Eyre and Spottiswoode, 1887. [Rpt. many times.]

Roberts, Brynley F. "Where Were the Four Branches of the Mabinogi Written?" In *The Individual in Celtic Literatures: CSANA Yearbook 1*. Ed. Joseph Falaky Nagy. Dublin: Four Courts Press, 2001. Pp. 61–73.

Robinson, Fred C. "Old English Literature in its Most Immediate Context." In *Old English Literature in Context*. Ed. John D. Niles. Cambridge: D. S. Brewer, 1980. Pp. 11–29.

Robinson, Fred C., and E. G. Stanley, eds. *Old English Verse Texts from Many Sources*. Early English Manuscripts in Facsimile 23. Copenhagen: Rosenkilde and Bagger, 1991.

Robinson, J. A. *The Times of St Dunstan*. Oxford: Clarendon Press, 1923.

Roffe, David. "The Historia Croylandensis: A Plea for Reassessment." *EHR* 110 (1995), 93–108.

Roger of Howden. *Chronica Magistri Rogeri de Houedene*. Ed. William Stubbs. 4 vols. Rolls Series 51. London: Longman, 1868–71.

Roger Wendover. *Rogeri de Wendover, Chronica sive Flores Historiarum*. Ed. Henry Coxe. 4 vols. London: Sumptibus Societatis, 1841–42.

Rollason, David. *Saints and Relics in Anglo-Saxon England*. Oxford: Blackwell, 1989.

———, ed. *Symeon of Durham: Historian of Durham and the North*. Stamford: Shaun Tyas, 1998.

*The Romance of Guy of Warwick: The Second or Fifteenth-Century Version*. Ed. Julius Zupitza. 2 vols. EETS e.s. 25–26. London: Trübner, 1875–76.

Rouse, Robert Allen. *The Idea of Anglo-Saxon England in Middle English Romance*. Cambridge: D. S. Brewer, 2005.

———. "The Peace of the Roads: Authority and *auctoritas* in Medieval Romance." In *Boundaries in Medieval Romance*. Ed. Neil Cartlidge. Woodbridge: D. S. Brewer, 2008. Pp. 115–28.

Rowe, Elizabeth Ashman. "The Female Body Politic and the Miscarriage of Justice in *Athelston*." *Studies in the Age of Chaucer* 17 (1995), 79–98.

Rumble, Alexander R., and A. D. Mills, eds. *Names, Places and People: An Onomastic Miscellany for John McNeal Dodgson*. Stamford: Paul Watkins, 1997.

Rygh, Oluf. *Norske Gaardnavne: Forord og Indledning*. Oslo: W. C. Fabritius, 1898.

*Sagas of the Icelanders*. Ed. Örnólfur Thorsson. New York: Viking, 2001.

Salvador-Bello, Mercedes. "The Edgar Panegyrics in the *Anglo-Saxon Chronicle*." In *Edgar, King of the English 959–975: New Interpretations*. Ed. Donald Scragg. Woodbridge: Boydell Press, 2008. Pp. 252–72.

Sandred, Karl Inge, and Bengt Lindstrom. *Place-Names of Norfolk*. 3 vols. English Place-Name Society 61, 72, 79. Nottingham: English Place-Name Society, 1989–2002.

Savile, Henry, ed. *Rerum Anglicarum Scriptores Post Bedam Praecipui ex vetustissimis codicibus manuscriptis nunc primum in lucem editi*. London: [n.p.], 1596.

Sawyer, P. H. *Anglo-Saxon Charters: An Annotated List and Bibliography*. Royal Historical Society Guides and Handbooks 8. London: Royal Historical Society, 1968. [S.]

Scragg, Donald. "A Reading of *Brunanburh*." In *Unlocking the Wordhord: Anglo-Saxon Studies in Memory of Edward B. Irving, Jr*. Ed. Mark C. Amodio and Katherine O'Brien O'Keeffe. Toronto: University of Toronto Press, 2003. Pp. 109–22.

Scragg, Donald, and Carole Weinberg, eds. *Literary Appropriations of the Anglo-Saxons from the Thirteenth to the Twentieth Century*. Cambridge: Cambridge University Press, 2000.

Searle, William George. *Onomasticon Anglo-Saxonicum*. Cambridge: Cambridge University Press, 1897.

Seaton, Ethel. "Robert Mannyng of Brunne in Lincoln." *Medium Aevum* 12 (1943), 77.

Sedgefield, Walter John, ed. *The Battle of Maldon and Short Poems from the Saxon Chronicle*. Boston: D. C. Heath, 1904.

Selkirk, Elizabeth O. *Phonology and Syntax: The Relation between Sound and Structure*. Cambridge, MA: The MIT Press, 1984.

Sharpe, Richard. *A Handlist of the Latin Writers of Great Britain and Ireland before 1540*. Publications of the Journal of Medieval Latin 1. Turnhout: Brepols, 1997. [Sharpe.]

Short, Ian. "Gaimar's Epilogue and Geoffrey of Monmouth's *Liber vetustissimus*." *Speculum* 69 (1994), 323–43.

Sievers, Eduard. "Zur Rhythmik des germanischen Alliterationsverses." *Beiträge zur Geschichte der deutschen Sprache und Literatur* 10 (1885), 209–314 and 451–545.

Simmons, Clare A. *Reversing the Conquest: History and Myth in Nineteenth-century British Literature*. New Brunswick, NJ: Rutgers University Press, 1990.

Simpson, James. "Ageism: Leland, Bale, and the Laborious Start of English Literary History, 1350–1550." In *New Medieval Literatures* 1. Ed. Wendy Scase, Rita Copeland, and David Lawton. Oxford: Clarendon Press, 1997. Pp. 213–35.

*Sir Gawain and the Green Knight*. Ed. J. R. R. Tolkien and E. V. Gordon. Second ed. by N. Davis. Oxford: Oxford University Press, 1967.

Sisam, Kenneth, ed. *Fourteenth Century Verse and Prose*. Revised ed. Oxford: Clarendon Press, 1985.

Skene, William Forbes. *Celtic Scotland: A History of Ancient Alban*. Edinburgh: Edmonston and Douglas, 1876.

Smith, A. Hugh. "The Site of the Battle of *Brunanburh*." *London Mediæval Studies* 1 (1937), 56–59.

———. *English Place-Name Elements*. 2 vols. English Place-Name Society 25 and 26. Cambridge: Cambridge University Press, 1956.

Smyth, Alfred P. *Warlords and Holy Men: Scotland AD 80–1000*. London: Edward Arnold, 1984.

———. *Scandinavian York and Dublin: The History and Archaeology of Two Related Viking Kingdoms*. 2 vols. Rpt. Dublin: Irish Academic Press, 1987.

*Stanzaic Guy of Warwick*. Ed. Alison Wiggins. Kalamazoo, MI: Medieval Institute Publications, 2004.

Stenton, Frank M. *Anglo-Saxon England*. Third ed. Oxford: Oxford University Press, 1971.

Stevenson, W. H. "A Latin Poem Addressed to King Athelstan." *English Historical Review* 26 (1911), 482–87.

St. John, James Augustus. *History of the Four Conquests of England*. London: Smith Elder and Co., 1862.

Stockwell, Robert P., and Donka Minkova. "Prosody." In *A Beowulf Handbook*. Ed. Robert E. Bjork and John D. Niles. Lincoln: University of Nebraska Press, 1997. Pp. 55–83.

Sulley, Phillip. *The Hundred of Wirral*. Birkenhead: B. Haram, 1889.

Symeon of Durham. *Symeonis Monachi Opera Omnia*. Ed. Thomas Arnold. 2 vols. Rolls Series 75. London: Longman, 1882–85.

———. *Libellus de exordio atque procursu istius, hoc est Dunhelmensis, ecclesie: Tract on the Origins and Progress of this the Church of Durham*. Ed. and trans. David Rollason. Oxford Medieval Texts. Oxford: Clarendon Press, 2000.

Taylor, John. *The Universal Chronicle of Ranulf Higden*. Oxford: Clarendon Press, 1966.

———. *English Historical Literature in the Fourteenth Century*. Oxford: Clarendon Press, 1987.

Tennyson, Alfred, Lord. *Ballads and Other Poems*. London: Kegan Paul, 1880.

———. *The Poems of Tennyson*. Ed. Christopher Ricks. London: Longman, 1969.

Tennyson, Hallam. *A Memoir, by His Son*. 2 vols. London: Macmillan, 1879.

*The Text of the Bruts from the Red Book of Hergest*. Ed. John Rhys and J. Gwenogvryn Evans. Oxford: Clarendon Press, 1890.

Thompson, Stith, ed. *Motif-index of Folk-literature*. Rev. ed. 6 vols. Copenhagen: Rosenkilde and Bagger, 1955–58.

Thomson, Rodney M. *William of Malmesbury*. Rev. ed. Rpt. Woodbridge, Boydell Press, 2003.

Thormann, Janet. "The *Anglo-Saxon Chronicle* Poems and the Making of the English Nation." In *Anglo-Saxonism and the Construction of Social Identity*. Ed. Allen Frantzen and John D. Niles. Gainesville: University of Florida Press, 1997. Pp. 60–85.

Thornton, David E. "Edgar and the Eight Kings, AD 973: *textus et dramatis personae*." *Early Medieval Europe* 10 (2001), 49–79.

Thurneysen, Rudolf. *A Grammar of Old Irish*. Rev. ed. Dublin: Institute for Advanced Studies, 1980.

Todd, Charles Spilman."The Battle of Brunanburh: Its Cause, History and Site. A Lecture Delivered by Charles Spilman Todd, Esq., F. S. A., Town Clerk of Hull, Before the Hull Literary and Philosophy Society, 14th December, 1875." Hull: Plaxton, Foster and Co., 1875.

Townend, Matthew. *English Place-Names in Skaldic Verse*. Nottingham: English Place-Name Society, 1998.

———. "Pre-Cnut Praise-Poetry in Viking Age England." *Review of English Studies* 51 (2000), 349–70.

Townsend, Julie. "The Metre of the *Chronicle*-verse." *Studia Neophilologica* 68 (1996), 143–76.

Trilling, Renée. *The Aesthetics of Nostalgia: Historical Representation in Old English Verse*. Toronto: University of Toronto Press, 2009.

*Trioedd Ynys Prydein: The Welsh Triads*. Ed. and trans. Rachel Bromwich. Cardiff: University of Wales Press, 2006.

Tudsbery, Francis W. T. *Brunanburh A. D. 937*. London: Oxford University Press, 1907.

Turner, Sharon. *The History of the Anglo-Saxons*. London: Cadell and Davies, 1799. [Rpt. many times.]

Turville-Petre, Thorlac. *England the Nation: Language, Literature, and National Identity, 1290–1340*. Oxford: Clarendon, 1996.

Vaughan, Richard. *Matthew Paris*. Cambridge: Cambridge University Press, 1958.

*The Vercelli Homilies and Related Texts*. Ed. Donald Scragg. EETS o.s. 300. Oxford: Oxford University Press, 1992.

Vipond, Prudence. "*Harrow* Fields in Heswall-cum-Oldfield." *Journal of the English Place-Name Society* 25 (1992/93), 9–10.

*Vita Griffini filii Conani*. Ed. Paul Russell. Cardiff: University of Wales Press, 2005.

Wainwright, Frederick T. "North-West Mercia AD 871–924." *Transactions of the Historical Society of Lancashire and Cheshire* 94 (1942), 3–55. [Excerpt in Cavill, Harding, and Jesch, 2000. Pp. 19–42.]

———. "Field-names." *Antiquity* 17 (1943), 57–66. [Excerpt in Cavill, Harding, and Jesch, 2000. Pp. 98–99.]

———. "The Scandinavians in Lancashire." *Transactions of the Lancashire and Cheshire Antiquarian Society* 58 (1945/46), 71–116. [Rpt. Finberg, 1975. Pp. 181–227.]

———. "Ingimund's Invasion." *English Historical Review* 63 (1948), 147–69. [Rpt. many times.]

Wardhaugh, Ronald. *Languages in Competition*. Oxford: Blackwell, 1987.

Warton, Thomas. *The History of English Poetry from the Twelfth to the Close of the Sixteenth Century*. London: Dodsley, 1774. [Preface by Henry Sweet.]

*Waverley Annals*. In *Annales Monastici*. 2.127–411.

Wawn, Andrew. "Vikings and Victorians." In Cavill, Harding, and Jesch, 2000. Pp. 100–07.

———. *Vikings and Victorians: Inventing the Old North in Nineteenth-Century Britain*. Cambridge: Brewer, 2000.

Whistler, Charles W. *Dragon Osmund: A Story of Athelstan and of Brunanburh*. London: Thomas Nelson and Sons, 1914.

White, Edmund H. *Athelstan: A Tragedy*. London: W. Strange, 1847.

White, Roger H. "Viking Period Sculpture at Neston, Chester." *Journal of the Chester Archaeological Society* 69 (1986), 45–58.

White, Roger H., Stephen E. Harding, and Martin I. Cooper. "The Neston Cross: An Exercise in Community Engagement." Third Symposium of the Vikings Identity Network. Birmingham, 17–18 December 2007.

Whitelock, Dorothy, ed. *English Historical Documents 1: 500–1042*. Second ed. London: Eyre Methuen, 1979.

Wiggins, Alison, and Rosalind Field, eds. *Guy of Warwick: Icon and Ancestor*. Cambridge: D. S. Brewer, 2007.

William of Malmesbury. *The Chronicle of the Kings of England*. Trans. J. A. Giles. London: George Bell and Sons, 1904.

———. *Gesta pontificum Anglorum: The History of the English Bishops*. Ed. and trans. Michael Winterbottom. Oxford Medieval Texts. Oxford: Clarendon Press, 2007. [*GP*.]

———. *Gesta regum Anglorum: The History of the English Kings*. Ed. and trans. R. A. B. Mynors, R. H. Thomson, and Michael Winterbottom. 2 vols. Oxford Medieval Texts. Oxford: Clarendon Press, 1998–99. [*GR*.]

Williams, Ifor. *Lectures on Early Welsh Poetry*. Dublin: Dublin Institute for Advanced Studies, 1944.

———. *Chwedl Taliesin* (1955–56 O'Donnell Lecture). Cardiff: University of Wales Press, 1957.

———. "Taliesin." In *Welsh Biography Online*. National Library of Wales, 2007. <http://wbo.llgc.org.uk/> Accessed 24 June 2010.

Wilson, David. "A Note on OE *hearg* and *wēoh* as Place-Name Elements Representing Different Types of Pagan Saxon Worship Sites." *Anglo-Saxon Studies in Archaeology and History* 4 (1985), 179–83.

Wilson, Edward. "*Sir Gawain and the Green Knight* and the Stanley Family of Stanley, Storeton, and Hooton." *Review of English Studies* 30 (1979), 308–16.

Winterbottom, Michael. "The Style of Æthelweard." *Medium Ævum* 36 (1967), 109–18.

———. "The *Gesta regum* of William of Malmesbury." *Journal of Medieval Latin* 5 (1995), 158–73.

Wood, Michael. "Brunanburh Revisited." *Saga-Book of the Viking Society* 20 (1980), 200–17.

———. "The Making of King Æthelstan's Empire: An English Charlemagne?" In Wormald, Bullough, and Collins, 1983. Pp. 250–72.

———. *In Search of England: Journeys into the English Past*. London: Penguin, 2000.

Woolf, Alex. "Dún Nechtáin, Fortriu and the Geography of the Picts." *Scottish Historical Review* 85 (2006): 182–201.

———. *From Pictland to Alba, 789–1070*. New Edinburgh History of Scotland, vol. 2. Edinburgh: Edinburgh University Press, 2008.

Wormald, Patrick. "The Making of England." *History Today* 45.2 (February 1995), 26–32.

———. *The Making of English Law: King Alfred to the Twelfth Century*. Oxford: Blackwell, 1999.

Wormald, Patrick, Donald Bullough, and Roger Collins, eds. *Ideal and Reality in Frankish and Anglo-Saxon Society*. Oxford: Blackwell, 1983.

Worth, Richard Nicholls. *A History of Devonshire*. London: Elliot Stock, 1895.

Wulfstan of Winchester. *The Life of St Æthelwold*. Ed. Michael Lapidge and Michael Winterbottom. Oxford Medieval Texts. Oxford: Clarendon Press, 1991.

*Ystoria Taliesin*. Ed. Patrick K. Ford. Cardiff: University of Wales Press, 1992.

Zacher, Samantha. "Multilingualism at the Court of King Æthelstan: Latin Praise Poetry and *The Battle of Brunanburh*." In *Conceptualizing Multilingualism in England, 800–1250*. Ed. Elizabeth M. Tyler. Turnholt: Brepols, 2010. Forthcoming.

## JOHN K. BOLLARD
## INDEX TO THE VOLUME

Boldface numerals represent instances in one of the texts or translations. A reference that occurs on a page only in a footnote is so marked (e.g., 308n). Variant forms of a name are listed in square brackets.